ibrary of Congress Cataloging-in Publication Data

uBrin, Andrew J.
Applying psychology : individual and organizational effectiveness / Andrew J. DuBrin.—
th ed.
p. cm.
ncludes bibliographical references and index.
ISBN 0-13-097115-4
1. Psychology, Industrial. 2. Interpersonal relations. 3. Communication in management.
Title.
HF5548.8 .D775 2004
650.1'3—dc21 2003042992

ublisher: Stephen Helba
xecutive Editor: Elizabeth Sugg
roduction Liaison: Brian Hyland
roduction Editor: Lori Dalberg, Carlisle Publishers Services
irector of Manufacturing and Production: Bruce Johnson
lanaging Editor: Mary Carnis
larketing Manager: Leigh Ann Sims
lanufacturing Buyer: Ilene Sanford
esign Director: Cheryl Asherman
enior Design Coordinator: Miguel Ortiz
over Designer: Marianne Frasco
nterior Design: Carlisle Communications, Ltd.
omposition: Carlisle Communications, Ltd.
rinting and Binding: Courier Westford

---

earson Education LTD.
earson Education Australia PTY, Limited
earson Education Singapore, Pte. Ltd.
earson Education North Asia Ltd.
earson Education Canada, Ltd.
earson Educación de Mexico, S.A. de C.V.
earson Education—Japan
earson Education Malaysia, Pte. Ltd.

10 9 8 7 6 5 4 3 2 1
ISBN 0-13-097115-4

SIXTH EDITION

Applying Psychology
Individual and Organizational Effectiveness

Andrew J. DuBrin
College of Business
Rochester Institute of Technology

Upper Saddle River, New Jersey 07458

To Douglas, Gizella, and Camila

CONTENTS

Chapter 9 BUILDING WORKPLACE RELATIONSHIPS 210

Chapter 10 COPING WITH A VARIETY OF PERSONALITIES 232

Chapter 11 COMMUNICATING WITH PEOPLE 254

Chapter 12 GROUPS AND GROUP DECISION MAKING 287

Chapter 13 ADAPTING TO THE ORGANIZATION 310

Chapter 14 LEADING AND INFLUENCING OTHERS 331

Chapter 15 ACHIEVING PERSONAL PRODUCTIVITY 356

PREFACE

Welcome to the sixth edition of *Applying Psychology: Individual and Organizational Effectiveness*. This new edition updates and consolidates the previous editions. *Applying Psychology* was written to fill the need for a basic, career-oriented text with a variety of suggestions for personal improvement and effectiveness. The text is designed to meet the curriculum needs of courses in *applied psychology* and *business psychology* and *human relations* offered in many settings.

Applying Psychology is often used as a follow-up course to an introductory psychology course. Nevertheless, because some readers of this text will not have taken an introduction to psychology course, the book includes a concise overview of the psychology of individuals. The same material serves as a review for those students who have taken a previous course in psychology. This edition remains a work-oriented psychology book with ample information about fundamentals of psychology. Relevant aspects of psychology are also introduced throughout the text.

The framework of this text provides an overview of major psychological concepts and techniques that are relevant to the individual worker in attaining both good performance and personal satisfaction. Concise summaries of major concepts of psychology are presented, including learning, perception, personality, conflict, and motivation. The major classical theories of human behavior at work are summarized. Modern developments stemming from these theories, such as empowerment and working in teams, are treated at greater length. Current topics in applied psychology such as wellness, cross-cultural relations, and 360-degree feedback are also included. The information in the text is based on journal articles, scholarly books, trade books, professional journals, magazines, and the business press.

CHANGES IN THE SIXTH EDITION

Two substantial changes are found in this edition. First, **more information from psychology,** particularly industrial and organizational psychology, is included in chapters throughout the text. We include **more research findings** to support various conclusions presented throughout the text. Chapters 1 through 8 are already closely tied to psychology, so the proportion of psychological content has not increased. A second change is a consolidation, with the information on **goal setting now included in the motivation chapter.** Each chapter now contains a **Web Corner**, pointing to Internet resources for the chapter. More than one-half the cases are new. Several minor features from the previous edition, such as part openers and the job tasks sections have been deleted to further streamline the text. Some of the specific additions to the new edition are as follows:

Chapter 1: Fuller explanation of the contribution of cognitive psychology

Chapter 2: More information about e-learning or computer-based learning; analysis of contrasting values of Baby Boomers and Generation X and Generation Y; ethical guidelines for using the Internet

Chapter 3: More information about the contribution of heredity versus environment to intelligence; updating on the Five-Factor Model of personality; updating on the need for risk taking and thrill seeking

Chapter 4: Description of the self-awareness trap; description of the challenge of positive illusions

Chapter 5: Role of emotional intelligence in problem solving; new analysis of conditions necessary for creativity

Chapter 6: Job crafting as a motivational method

Chapter 7: How adverse environmental conditions contribute to work stress

Chapter 8: Developing empathy through shadowing to resolve conflict; the confront-contain-and-connect method of dealing with another person's anger

Chapter 9: Giving your manager positive reinforcement and recognition

Chapter 10: Information about dealing with uncivil coworkers

Chapter 11: Use of meta-communication to overcome communication barriers

Chapter 12: Description of virtual teams

Chapter 13: New section on fitting in with the organizational culture, including the importance of a good person–organization fit

Chapter 14: A description of servant leadership

Chapter 15: Playing the *inner game of work* to achieve higher productivity

Chapter 16: Successful résumé characteristics as revealed by an experiment with hiring managers; contribution of passion about work to career success; core behaviors of successful employees; description of the proactive personality

How this Book Will Benefit the Reader

A person who studies the information in this book and incorporates its suggestions into his or her way of doing things should derive the four benefits that follow. However, knowledge itself is not a guarantee of success. Individuals vary so widely in learning ability, personality, and life circumstances that some people will be able to attain some objectives and not others. As a case in point, you might be so naturally effective at dealing with coworkers that the chapter on this topic will not add much value from the perspective of personal development. Or you might not yet have enough self-confidence to apply the confrontation techniques described for resolving conflict. Instead, you could benefit more from applying the techniques for developing self-confidence described in Chapter 4, about understanding yourself.

The major benefits this book provides are:

1. **Awareness of relevant information.** Part of feeling comfortable and making a positive impression in any place of work is being familiar with relevant general knowledge about the world of work. By reading this book you will become familiar with many of the buzzwords used on the job such as empowered teams, networking, and 360-degree feedback.
2. **Development of skills in dealing with people.** Anybody who aspires toward higher-level jobs needs to develop proficiency in such interpersonal skills as motivating people, resolving conflict, and overcoming communication barriers. Skill-development sections at the end of most chapters are also aimed at improving skills in dealing with people.
3. **Coping with job problems.** Almost everybody who holds a job involving working with people inevitably runs into human problems. Reading about these problems and prescriptions for coping with them could save you considerable inner turmoil. Among the job survival skills you will learn about in the following chapters are managing job stress and dealing with people who are not easy to get along with. Be alert also to the feature in every chapter, "Guidelines for Personal Effectiveness."
4. **Capitalizing on opportunities.** Many readers of this book will spend part of their working time taking advantage of opportunities rather than resolving daily problems. Every ambitious person needs a few breakthrough experiences to make his or her career more rewarding. Toward this end, we devote attention to the subjects of creative thinking and methods of career advancement.

Material throughout the book familiarizes the student with topics relevant to their work experience:

Attitude, Working in Groups, Communication and its Barriers, Conflict, Leadership, Motivation, and Stress.

Instructor's Manual and TestGen Access

The instructor's web site for this text contains over 750 test questions, chapter outline and lecture notes, answers to discussion questions and case problems, and comments about the exercises. In addition, the manual includes step-by-step instructions for the use of computer-assisted scenario analysis (CASA).

CASA is a user-friendly way of using any word-processing program to assist in analyzing cases. The student enters an existing case into the computer and then analyzes it by answering the case questions in the text. Next, the student makes up a new scenario or twist to the case and **enters this scenario in boldface into the case.** The case questions are reanalyzed in light of this new scenario. Any changes in the answers are **printed in bold.** CASA gives the student experience in a creative application of word processing. Equally important, it helps students develop a "what-if" or contingency point of view in solving business psychology problems.

TestGen is a test generator program that lets instructors view and edit testbank questions, transfer them to tests, and print in a variety of formats. TestGen offers options for organizing and displaying testbanks and tests. An algorithmic number and text generator lets you create numerous iterations of test questions and answers.

Acknowledgments

My primary thanks go to those experts who contributed their expertise and encouragement: Andrea Meld, DeVry University, Washington; Adelia H. Williams, Ph.D., DeVry University, Crystal City; and Christina Halawa, DeVry Institute, Tinley Park, Illinois. More thanks on this project are extended to the editorial, production, and marketing staffs at Prentice Hall Career & Technology. Elizabeth Sugg and Anita Rhodes played key roles in launching the sixth edition. Lori Dalberg at Carlisle Publishers Services also made a major contribution in producing the book. Thanks also to the instructors in the United States, Canada, and overseas who adopted the first five editions of the book, thereby creating a demand for the sixth edition. Many of the changes in this new edition are based on the suggestions offered by our adopters.

My family members give me an additional reason for writing, so I extend my appreciation to Drew, Douglas, Melanie, Gizella, Rosie, Clare, and Camila.

Andrew J. DuBrin
Rochester, New York

CHAPTER 1

Foundations of Business Psychology

Learning Objectives

After reading and studying this chapter and doing the exercises, you should be able to

1. Define the term *business psychology* and explain what it means.
2. Describe several of the major fields within psychology.
3. Describe several of the major schools of thought within psychology.
4. Explain how business psychology fits into the human relations movement.
5. Present an overview of how business psychology makes use of the scientific method.

WHAT IS BUSINESS PSYCHOLOGY?

The study of psychology as applied to the workplace can help you resolve a wide range of human problems encountered in any job. It can also help you prepare for your career. An understanding of the basic principles of applied psychology can help explain why people act as they do in certain situations and suggest what you can sometimes do to change their behavior.

In the chapters that follow there are no foolproof methods for being highly effective with others in the workplace or making worthwhile things happen. However, there are useful guidelines that have proved to be true most of the time in the past. You can rely on these guidelines to help you in your relations with other people in the future. **Business psychology** refers to the application of organized knowledge about human behavior to improve personal satisfaction and productivity on the job. (Business psychology is but one aspect of the broader term, applied psychology.) Business psychology can thus be used in any work setting, such as a company, government agency, community agency, hospital, hotel, restaurant, or school.

Psychology deals with the systematic study of behavior. Defined precisely, **psychology** is the study of behavior and mental processes. Psychology has two major purposes. One is to understand why organisms behave, feel, and think as they do; another is to apply that knowledge to improve human functioning.[1] (Although psychologists also study animal behavior and mental processes, this book deals with human organisms.) Almost any human activity might thus be the subject of study by a psychologist. Yet, in practice, psychology deals more with the mind than the body.

The meaning of psychology becomes clearer when you recognize that the field is both a science and a profession (as already implied in describing the purposes of psychology). Science refers to the fact that many people engaged in psychology primarily conduct research about behavior. The term *profession* means that many people engaged in psychology primarily provide services to (or help) people.

The term *psychology* has gained wide acceptance as the field associated with the scientific study of people and animals. It is important to recognize, however, that fields such as organizational behavior, sociology, anthropology, and economics also are concerned with the study of human behavior. Many of the findings presented in this book stem from the work of researchers in the fields just cited, as well as the work of psychologists.

Before proceeding with the study of business psychology, it will be useful to examine psychology from two perspectives. First, we will describe what psychologists do by examining several fields within psychology. Second, we will describe the major schools of thought within psychology. A school of thought is a major explanation or theoretical position.

WHAT PSYCHOLOGISTS DO

Psychology touches our lives in thousands of ways. Among the best-known contributions of psychology have been mental tests, motivational techniques, and developing more accurate ways of measuring job performance. An example of the last mentioned is evaluating a manager's performance by obtaining feedback from coworkers and group members to supplement evaluation by superiors. Many specialists who are not psychologists nevertheless engage in work that applies psychological knowledge to improve life. Among these professionals are human resource specialists, career counselors, business coaches, and marriage counselors.

One way of understanding the diverse work activities and interests of psychologists is to scan Table 1–1, which lists 55 groups within the American Psychological Association. Recognize however, that these groups overlap. For example, an industrial and organizational psychologist (Division 14) might also be a member of Division 35 (psychology of women) because she deals with women's issues in the workplace. The American Psychological Association has approximately 86,000 members. A similar group, the American Psychological Society, has approximately 15,000 members.

To help you understand the type of work psychologists do, and how they contribute to society, we will describe five key fields of psychology and a small field that nevertheless generates considerable general interest: (1) industrial and organizational, (2) clinical and counseling, (3) developmental, (4) experimental, (5) health, and (6) exercise and sport.

TABLE 1–1
DIVISIONS, SOCIETIES, AND INTEREST GROUPS WITHIN THE AMERICAN PSYCHOLOGICAL ASSOCIATION

Division 1, *General Psychology,* seeks to create coherence among psychology's diverse specialties.

Division 2, *Teaching of Psychology,* promotes teaching excellence, research on teaching, and professional identity and development.

Division 3, *Experimental Psychology,* promotes scientific inquiry through teaching and research, and members conduct research in various fields within psychology.

Division 5, *Evaluation, Measurement, and Statistics,* is concerned with promoting high standards in psychological assessment, evaluation, measurement, and statistics.

Division 6, *Behavioral Neuroscience and Comparative Psychology,* studies the biological bases for behavior in animals, including humans.

Division 7, *Developmental Psychology,* emphasizes research and advocacy to foster the optimal development of infants, children, and adults.

Division 8, *Personality and Social Psychology,* is concerned with how individuals affect and are affected by other people and by their social and physical environment.

Division 9, *Psychological Study of Social Issues,* focuses attention on social problems and issues involving the public welfare.

Division 10, *Psychology and the Arts,* seeks to advance an understanding of the relationship between psychology and the arts.

Division 12, *Clinical Psychology,* represents the science and profession of clinical psychology and has six sections of its own, such as clinical child psychology.

Division 13, *Consulting Psychology,* serves as a forum for psychologists acting as consultants to organizations.

Division 14, *Industrial and Organizational Psychology,* promotes human welfare through various applications of psychology in organizations.

Division 15, *Educational Psychology,* has the mission of creating scientific knowledge relevant to education and psychology.

Division 16, *School Psychology,* is composed of psychologists whose major professional interests lie with children, families, and the schooling process.

Division 17, *Counseling Psychology,* brings together psychologists who specialize in counseling to enhance education, training, scientific investigation, and practice.

Division 18, *Psychologists in Public Service,* responds to the needs of the public in areas such as psychological practice, research, and policy formulation.

Division 19, *Military Psychology,* encourages psychological research, application to military problems, and helping people in military communities.

Division 20, *Adult Developing and Aging,* strives to advance the study of psychological development and change throughout the adult years.

Division 21, *Applied Experimental and Engineering Psychology,* promotes research and application of psychology to the characteristics, design, and use of environment and systems within which people work and live. (The field is also known as ergonomics.)

Division 22, *Rehabilitation Psychology,* seeks to develop high standards and practices for psychologists who help people rehabilitate and overcome disabilities.

Division 23, *Consumer Psychology,* concentrates on those aspects of individual and social psychology demonstrated by people as consumers of goods and services.

Division 24, *Theoretical and Philosophical Psychology,* promotes an interest in theories in psychology and links with modern philosophy.

Division 25, *Behavior Analysis,* is committed to the scientific understanding of behavior.

Division 26, *History of Psychology,* encourages original research in the history of psychology and in its teaching.

Division 27, *Community Research and Action: Community Psychology,* encourages the development of theory, research, and practice to improve the well-being of people in their communities.

Division 28, *Psychopharmacology and Substance Abuse,* advances knowledge on the behavioral effects of drugs that affect the mind, including drugs of abuse.

Division 29, *Psychotherapy,* is committed to education, training, research, and practice in psychotherapy.

Division 30, *Psychological Hypnosis,* is devoted to the exchange of scientific information on hypnosis and developing high standards for using the technique.

(continued)

TABLE 1–1 (CONTINUED)

DIVISIONS, SOCIETIES, AND INTEREST GROUPS WITHIN THE AMERICAN PSYCHOLOGICAL ASSOCIATION

Division 31, *State Psychological Association Affairs,* promotes the interests of state and provincial psychological associations.

Division 32, *Humanistic Psychology,* recognizes the full richness of the human experience and is committed to humanistic values.

Division 33, *Mental Retardation and Developmental Disabilities,* endeavors to advance knowledge and practice in the treatment of mental retardation and developmental disabilities.

Division 34, *Population and Environmental Psychology,* is concerned with conducting research and advancing theory to improve population problems and environmental issues.

Division 35, *Psychology of Women,* provides a forum for the development of a comprehensive feminist and multicultural approach to improving the lives of girls and women.

Division 36, *Psychology of Religion,* seeks to encourage research and knowledge building in the psychology of religion, spirituality, and related ideas.

Division 37, *Child, Youth, and Family Services,* deals with professional and scientific issues related to psychological services for children and youth.

Division 38, *Health Psychology,* seeks to advance contributions of psychology to the understanding of health and illness through research, education, and service activities.

Division 39, *Psychoanalysis,* advances psychoanalytic theory, research, and clinical practice.

Division 40, *Clinical Neuropsychology,* enhances the understanding of brain behavior relationships and the application of such knowledge to human problems.

Division 41, *The American Psychology-Law Society,* promotes the contributions of psychology to understanding of law and legal matters.

Division 42, *Psychologists in Independent Practice,* is devoted to the preservation and promotion of independent practice by psychologists.

Division 43, *Family Psychology,* provides a forum for psychologists interested in families in their many forms.

Division 44, *Psychological Study of Lesbian, Gay, and Bisexual Issues,* advances research to help understand lesbian, gay, and bisexual issues.

Division 45, *Psychological Study of Ethnic Minority Issues,* encourages research on ethnic minority issues and the application of psychological knowledge to these issues.

Division 46, *Media Psychology,* focuses on the roles psychologists play in various aspects of the media, including radio, television, film, print, and newer technologies.

Division 47, *Exercise and Sport Psychology,* brings together individuals with research, teaching, and application interests in exercise and sport psychology.

Division 48, *Peace Psychology,* works to promote peace by encouraging research and teaching on issues concerning peace, nonviolent conflict resolution, and the prevention of destructive conflict.

Division 49, *Group Psychology and Group Psychotherapy,* represents the interests of psychologists interested in group psychology and group psychotherapy.

Division 50, *Addictions,* promotes advances in research, training, and clinical practice for a broad range of addictive behaviors.

Division 51, *Psychological Study of Men and Masculinity,* advances knowledge in the new psychology of men, including improved clinical services for men.

Division 52, *International Psychology,* encourages research into different cultures including understanding psychological problems that predominate in a given region of the world.

Division 53, *Clinical Child Psychology,* represents psychologists who are active in teaching, research, clinical services (treatment), administration, and advocacy in clinical child psychology.

Division 54, *Pediatric Psychology,* is dedicated to research and practice concerning the relationship between children's physical, cognitive, social, and emotional functioning and their physical well-being.

Division 55, *Advancement of Pharmacotherapy,* seeks to enhance psychological treatments combined with psychopharmacological (drugs for emotional distress). The group also encourages the collaborative practice of psychological and pharmacological treatments with other health professions.

Source: American Psychological Association, 2003.

Note: The American Psychological Association does not have a Division 4 or 11.

Industrial and Organizational Psychology

Much of this book deals with the ideas and methods of **industrial and organizational psychology,** the field of psychology that studies behavior in a work environment. Business psychology applies many of the findings of industrial and organizational psychology in a personal way, and thus is not really a different field. Industrial and organizational psychology was one of the first fields of applied psychology. The first text applying psychological principles to problems and business was published in 1903, and the field has grown steadily ever since.[2] Among the major activities of specialists in this field is the design of employee selection methods (such as tests and interviews) and methods for training and developing employees at all job levels. Industrial and organizational psychologists have developed a number of methods for improving teamwork and cooperation in organizations. Among these techniques are self-managing work teams that are given substantial authority to make a product on their own, working as a team, rather than in an assembly-line fashion.

Research in industrial and organizational psychology can solve practical problems. A representative example is an experiment about the effectiveness of self-management training for improving job performance. *Self-management* in this experiment referred to an effort by an individual to exert control over his or her decision making and behavior. Self-management includes being self-motivated and engaging in positive behaviors that lead to good job performance.

Thirty insurance salespeople from a North American life insurance company were assigned to an experimental group that received self-management training. The training taught people how to assess problems and set specific, demanding goals in relation to those problems. Instruction was also given in how to monitor the ways the environment helps or hinders reaching performance goals, and how to reward or punish yourself for working toward or not working toward the goal. A specific example of training content was self-monitoring, or maintaining a record of your progress toward goal attainment. Thirty other insurance salespeople were assigned to a control group, and told that they would receive training later. All 60 participants had not achieved company performance standards the previous year.

A key set of the experimental results related directly to job performance. In comparison to the control group, the salespersons who went through self-management training (1) made more sales calls, (2) sold more new policies, (3) attained higher sales revenue, and (4) received better performance appraisals.[3]

Employers can use this information by sponsoring training in self-management for salespersons, and perhaps for other workers who have production quotas. (However, it could be that self-management training works best for those who are not already average or above-average performers.) You can use this same information now by recognizing that if you have effective self-management skills, you are more likely to achieve work goals.

Clinical and Counseling Psychology

About half of all practicing psychologists work within the fields of clinical and counseling psychology. These psychologists work with individuals or small groups to help them overcome personal problems and cope better with stress. Many clinical psychologists use biofeedback devices to help clients learn how to reduce tension.

These devices give people feedback on stress signals such as rapid heartbeat and muscle tightness. Clinical psychologists also play an important role in diagnosing mental illness. Counseling psychologists tend to work with people with fewer major adjustment problems than clinical psychologists. Yet there is often very little distinction between the work of these two types of psychologists.

We often confuse the work of psychiatrists, psychoanalysts, clinical psychologists, and psychotherapists. **Psychiatry** is a medical specialty that deals with the diagnosis and treatment of emotional problems and mental illness. Psychiatrists can legally treat people with drugs, electroshock, psychosurgery, or psychotherapy. Psychiatrists, however, rarely have a formal degree in psychology.

Psychoanalysis is a specialized type of psychotherapy in which the patient may spend up to three or four years, several times a week, working on personal problems. Psychoanalysts believe that psychoanalysis is the only valid way of getting to the root of emotional problems and reconstructing an individual's personality. To be certified as a psychoanalyst, the therapist must attend a specialized training program beyond regular medical or psychological training. Although the vast majority of psychoanalysts are psychiatrists, a few are clinical psychologists or psychiatric social workers.

Clinical psychologists have formal degrees in psychology, generally a doctor of philosophy (Ph.D.), and sometimes a doctor of education (Ed.D.) or doctor of professional psychology (Psy.D.). In virtually all states and provinces, a certificate or license is required to call oneself a psychologist. Clinical psychologists work in hospitals, health maintenance organizations (HMOs), group practice with psychiatrists, and individual private practice. A growing number of clinical psychologists work with other mental health professionals in clinics that specialize in treating workers whose personal problems adversely affect their job performance. In the days following the terrorist attacks in September 2001, clinical psychologists along with other mental health professionals were called into companies to counsel worried and distraught employees. The mental health professionals were staff members of firms hired by many companies to help workers deal with personal problems (employee assistance programs).

To confuse matters just a bit further, a **psychotherapist** is any mental health professional who helps people with emotional problems through conversation with them. All of the specialties we have described above include psychotherapy. Clinical psychologists play an important role in occupational health. A primary reason is that stress-related conditions are among the most important health problems for people at work. Clinical psychologists can also help people cope with some of the problems surrounding information technology. The accompanying box presents suggestions for helping people deal with a growing addiction.

Developmental Psychology Including Child Psychology

Developmental psychologists study human mental and physical growth throughout the life span: prenatal period, childhood, adolescence, adulthood, and old age. Developmental psychologists study universal patterns of development as well as cultural and individual variations.[4] Developmental psychology began with anecdotal observations of children in the late 19th century, such as an observer jotting down notes while watching children draw.

Child psychology remains the focus of most developmental psychologists, and is better known because so many child psychologists offer services to the pub-

APPLYING PSYCHOLOGY

Is Your Computer Use Out of Control?

For students who are lured to certain academic and social doom by the Internet, there is hope for winning back control of their lives. Psychiatrist Ivan Goldberg, originator of the online Internet Addiction Support Group, and psychologists who work with Internet-obsessed students say that students can overcome the affliction in four steps:

1. **Recognizing overuse patterns.** First, they need to admit that they spend too much time online, says Goldberg. Missed classes and appointments, forgotten papers and homework assignments, and lost contact with family and friends are all tip-offs that they're losing control. "When you start using the Internet to run away from other parts of your life that you don't want to deal with, that's when you know you have a problem," he said.
2. **Pinpointing underlying problems.** Before they can cure themselves, Internet addicts must figure out what's triggering their urge to escape, said psychologist Kimberly Young. For students, underlying problems often relate to uncertainty about their future, fear of a tight job market, social insecurities, poor performance in a class, or frustration over a romantic relationship.
3. **Tackling the real problems.** Some students use the Internet to relieve stress about their real problems. But avoiding life's stress-inducing problems only intensifies them. Instead, they need to overcome the underlying problem, whether it means finding a tutor to improve school work, securing an internship to improve job prospects, or meeting with their romantic partner to work out differences.
4. **Controlling computer use.** Students needn't go "cold turkey" and stop all use, but they should sensibly limit their online time. For instance, they could list all the activities they need to squeeze into their day, and do them all before logging on.

   Or they could assign an hour or two every day for computer use, and set their alarms to signal when the time is up. They could also stop using the services they are the most addicted to, like chat rooms, and only allow themselves to e-mail friends, family, or other students and professors.

   Most of all they need to draw a distinction between what on the Internet is just online fantasy, and what is truly helpful in their "real" lives, said Young.

Source: Adapted with permission from Bridget Murray, "Is Your Computer Use Out of Control?" *APA Monitor,* June 1996, p. 38.

lic. Child psychologists focus on infants and children. Research in child psychology sometimes sheds light on work behavior. For example, one study showed that the victims of childhood abuse and neglect may suffer long-term consequences. Among them are lower IQs and reading ability, more suicide attempts, and more unemployment and low-paying jobs.[5]

Adolescent psychologists focus on the teenage years, and how puberty, changes in relationships with friends and family, and the search for identity can create conflicts for adolescents. *Life-span psychologists* specialize in the adult years and how these people adjust to partnership and parenting, middle age, retirement and the prospects of the end of life. Many people today have become interested in the study of adult phases of human development. The work of life-span psychologists has led to widespread interest in the problems of the middle years, such as the midlife crisis. A job-related problem is why many successful people suddenly discover that the career goals they have been pursuing are no longer meaningful (a symptom of the midlife crisis).

Experimental Psychology

Experimental psychologists can be considered the most "scientific" of all psychologists. Their laboratories often rival those of biologists and medical scientists. Colleges, universities, and research laboratories employ most of the experimental psychologists. These psychologists developed many of the principles of human behavior discussed in this book (such as those associated with learning, thinking, and perception). A major contribution of experimental psychology is the development of methods for conducting experiments about behavior. The best known of these methods is described later in the section about the scientific method. Experimental psychologists also help to design certain parts of computer software, such as commands, to make it easier for users to process information.

An example of how experimental psychology can contribute to work behavior took place in the Cornell Human Factors Laboratory. The purpose of the study was to investigate whether open-office noise creates stress. Forty female clerical workers were assigned to a control condition (no extra noise) or to a three-hour exposure to low-intensity noise of the type typically found in an office. The experimental task was to type into the computer a manuscript of unfamiliar content (aviation safety).

The taped-in, simulated, low-intensity open-office noise produced several negative effects on the subjects. Epinephrine levels in the urine were elevated. (Epinephrine is a hormone released by the adrenal gland in response to stress.) The typists decreased their attempts at unsolvable puzzles assigned to them during the experiment, suggesting depressed motivation. The participants also made less use of work-furniture features designed to provide opportunities to adjust posture during work.

Experimenters Gary W. Evans and Dana Johnson concluded that their study reinforces the finding that low-intensity noise can produce physiological and motivational indicators of stress. Also, experienced clerical workers performing realistic office tasks under low-level noise are 50 percent less likely to use workstation features that allow the opportunity to adjust posture while working.[6]

Health Psychology

Recognition of the key role human behavior plays in preventing and curing disease has created a demand for health psychologists. Health psychology is the study and practice of how human behavior can be modified to prevent and treat illness. When practiced by physicians, the same field is referred to as behavioral medicine. Health psychology is concerned primarily with aspects of health and health care outside the area of mental health. However, emotional problems often must be dealt with to improve physical health. This brief case history illustrates how health psychologists can contribute to improved health care:

> Over the course of a year, Linda G. made repeated visits to her HMO. One problem she complained of was a nagging cough, which she thought might be attributed to her cigarette smoking. When told by the physician to stop smoking, Linda said, "I can't, it's one of my few pleasures in life." She was also treated several times for skin infections traced to overexposure to sunlight. When told to stay out of the sun by a nurse, Linda replied, "I would rather take the medicine you give me; lying in the sun makes the summer worthwhile." A month later she was treated for a head wound she received as a passenger in a minor car accident. Asked by the physician if she was wearing a seat belt, Linda replied, "No, it's a violation of my personal freedom."

The physician finally referred Linda to the mental health unit, where the health psychologist attempted to help Linda overcome her self-destructive behaviors. Without changing her behavior in regard to smoking, sunning, and the use of seat belts, Linda would inevitably return to be treated for physical problems. Health psychologists enhance workplace physical well-being in another important way. Many of them contribute to corporate fitness and wellness programs in such ways as teaching relaxation techniques to overcome work stress. In addition, health psychologists help employees overcome self-defeating behavior, such as food disorders, alcohol abuse, and tobacco use.

Despite the strong logic of health psychology and behavioral medicine, it is not easy to get people to change behaviors that may lead to health and safety problems. One intriguing reason is found in the concept of *risk homeostasis*. According to Gerald J. S. Wilde, people accept what they perceive to be a certain level of risk to their health, safety, and other things of value in exchange for the benefits they hope to receive.[7] For example, some people ski where avalanches are known to occur because of the "incredible thrill of skiing in the wilds." In other words, they risk death to get an occasional emotional high. Can you furnish an example of risk homeostasis?

Exercise and Sport Psychology

A fast-growing field is exercise and sport psychology, in which psychologists develop concepts and provide direct assistance to enhance the performance of athletes. The focus of **exercise and sport psychology** is to assist athletes who are already performing well rather than to help them with mental health problems. Many psychologists who enter this field have some sports background themselves. Sport psychologists devote much of their effort to helping athletes set goals and engage in mental imagery (i.e., visualizing the outcome one would like to achieve). An example is a basketball player creating a mental image of the ball going through the hoop just before he or she takes the shot.

A representative technique of exercise and sport psychology is to train athletes how to focus intently on the task at hand. In this way the athlete learns to not think about consequences such as winning or losing or attend to potential distractions such as people walking by the playing field. Similar techniques are also applied in the workplace. Sport psychologists sometimes help executives and their staffs achieve maximum performance through more intense concentration and ridding themselves of distractions. The sport psychologist is the most likely to apply these high-performance techniques to sales representatives. The reason is that high motivation and self-confidence are vital to success in selling.

SCHOOLS OF THOUGHT IN PSYCHOLOGY

To help explain the field of psychology, we have just described some of the major activities of psychologists. An equally important way of understanding psychology is to review the major schools of thought, or theoretical positions. These schools of thought help to influence which method a given psychologist will use to help solve a particular problem. For example, the cognitive school of psychology holds that people make rational decisions and are often driven by thoughts of self-fulfillment.

TABLE 1–2
SCHOOLS OF THOUGHT IN PSYCHOLOGY

1. Structuralism and Functionalism: study the structure and the functions of the mind
2. Behaviorism: studies overt behavior
3. Psychoanalysis: studies inner motives and the unconscious part of personality
4. Cognitive Psychology: focuses on intellectual or mental aspects of behavior
5. Humanistic Psychology: emphasizes dignity and worth of people

An industrial and organizational psychologist who believes in the cognitive school would recommend an employee motivation program that gives employees a chance to have a choice in making decisions about their own work.

Here we will briefly describe five schools of thought in psychology: structuralism and functionalism, behaviorism, psychoanalysis, cognitive psychology, and humanistic psychology.[8] Business psychology today is influenced much more by behaviorism, cognitive psychology, and humanistic psychology than by the other two schools. Table 1–2 outlines the schools of thought in psychology.

Structuralism and Functionalism

Many historians believe that scientific psychology began in 1879 when Wilhelm Wundt established a laboratory in Leipzig, Germany, to study human consciousness. Wundt aimed to discover the mind by analyzing conscious experiences of the senses and by reducing the mind to its basic elements. His intent was to describe the basic structures or units of human consciousness. **Structuralism** is the school of psychology that emphasized the basic units of experience, and the combinations in which they take place. Wundt's most important contention was that you could take some object in the physical world, present it to a trained subject, and have that subject describe the fundamental elements of his or her conscious experience.

For example, if you presented a watermelon to the subject, that subject might say, "I see an elliptical shape, I see green and white, and I feel a heavy weight." By binding together the inward observations of thousands of people, structuralism hoped to develop a science of conscious experience.

Although historically important, structuralism lost momentum as a useful method of understanding human behavior. William James, an American student of Wundt's, extended the narrow limits of structuralism to the study of many topics that are still of current interest, including learning, motivation, and emotions. James was also concerned with the struggle of people to reach their goals or become reconciled to failure. His school of thought became known as **functionalism** because he tried to understand the functions of the mind. Of note, Wundt observed that mental associations allow us to benefit from previous experiences. For example, if faced with a difficult problem, you might associate that with applying the problem-solving method, rather than starting from scratch.

Behaviorism

Structuralism and functionalism soon came under fire because they focused too much on unscientific, subjective experiences. In their place, John B. Watson proposed **behaviorism,** a school of thought based on the assumption that psychologists should study overt behavior, rather than mental states or other unobservable aspects of living things. He contended that mental life was something that cannot be seen or measured and thus cannot be studied scientifically. To Watson and to all subsequent behaviorists, the key to understanding human beings is their actual behavior, not their inner states. Given that behaviorism is based on observable facts it is referred to as an objective field of study rather than a subjective field based on interpretations of thoughts and feelings.

Watson believed that everything we do is determined by our past experiences, and not by an ability to control our own destiny. In his thinking, all human behavior is a series of events in which a stimulus produces a response. According to behaviorists, almost any kind of stimulus can be made to produce any kind of response. Watson excited the imagination of millions of parents when he proclaimed, "I can take any dozen babies at birth and, by conditioning them in various ways, turn them into anything I wish—doctor, lawyer, beggar, or thief."[9] More will be said about conditioning in Chapter 2.

The next prominent leader of behaviorism was the experimental psychologist B. F. Skinner. His work led to improved methods of learning and motivation in schools, psychiatric wards, prisons, and industry. Skinner's name is closely associated with the terms *positive reinforcement* and *behavior modification.* Skinner held that freedom is an illusion; the behavior of humans and animals is shaped by environmental influences, not internal ones. He championed the **law of effect.** According to this law, rewarded behavior tends to be repeated, whereas behavior that is ignored or punished tends not to be repeated. Feelings and other mental processes are simply the by-products of an endless cycle of pairings between stimuli and responses. Skinner believed strongly that a scientific analysis of human activity excludes the individual as the initiator of behavior. Chapter 6 describes the use of behavior modification for motivating yourself and others.

Psychoanalysis

Another major approach to understanding human behavior is psychoanalysis, founded by Sigmund Freud and his key associate, Carl Jung. Psychoanalytic theory views men and women as constantly torn between internal unconscious forces and external social forces. People are born with powerful biological appetites and passions that demand constant satisfaction, despite the needs of others or themselves. Thus an employee with an urge toward self-punishment may insult his or her boss even though it will anger the boss and possibly cost the employee a job. Our major job in life is to direct these irrational motives and emotions into socially acceptable behaviors. A key point of psychoanalytic theory is that we must learn to control our inborn desires and achieve their fulfillment in ways that are harmonious with others.

The best-known part of Freudian theory deals with the structure of the human **personality** (an individual's characteristic way of behaving, feeling, and thinking). It consists of three major forces interacting with each other:

1. *Id,* unconscious instincts such as sex and aggression.
2. *Ego,* the conscious, rational self, or intellect.
3. *Superego,* the social rules and values of society that govern our behavior.

The ego, or conscious self, is under constant pressure to fight off the pleasure-seeking desires of the id. At the same time, the ego is pressured by the reality forces of the environment and the moral dictates of one's upbringing—the superego. The healthy personality has an ego that does an effective job of coping with the urges of the id and the restrictions of the superego. Thus, the well-adjusted employee refrains from punching his boss, but at the same time is able to challenge authority in an acceptable way.

The psychoanalytic school has had a major impact on understanding human behavior, particularly in regard to analyzing mental health problems. Its impact has been declining for many years, and psychoanalytic theory has been criticized sharply. One criticism is that many of the ideas on which psychoanalysis is based (such as the existence of repressed childhood memories) are difficult to prove with quantitative evidence.[10]

Very little of business psychology deals directly with psychoanalytic theory. There are times, however, when a psychoanalytic interpretation of an executive's personality traits can help explain how the executive shapes the organization. A case in point is the executive who is very methodical and highly concerned with neatness and order is likely to implement a large number of small rules and regulations.[11] Another application of psychoanalysis to organizations is that the concept of the unconscious can be helpful in resolving a work problem. One example is when people procrastinate on an important task because they have an unconscious desire to fail. If the person is made aware of the self-defeating behavior, he or she can sometimes make a positive change.

Cognitive Psychology

Another major movement in psychology explains the behavior of humans in terms of their intellectual, rational selves instead of focusing only on observable behavior. (You will recall that behaviorism focuses on the observable, and psychoanalysis on the unobservable.) A cognitive process is the means by which an individual becomes aware of objects and situations. It includes learning, reasoning, and problem solving. According to the cognitive school of thought, the mind processes information by producing new thoughts, making comparisons, and making decisions. The concept of cognitive processes was a prominent part of the 19th-century philosophical psychology, and represented various faculties of the human mind (as described under structuralism).

Cognitive psychology is the study of mental process such as thinking, feeling, learning, remembering, making decisions and judgments. A key focus of cognitive psychology is the way our perception of events influences our actions. Thus, if an employee perceives it to be true that hard work will lead to a bonus, he or she will put forth extra effort.

Cognitive psychology has had such an important impact on the study of human behavior, that it has been referred to as the cognitive revolution. By studying both observable behavior as well as the inner thought processes, cognitive psychology offers a well-rounded picture of people. The cognitive revolution has been helped along by the widespread acceptance and understanding of computers. Like computers, people accept input, make sense of the input in their central processing unit (the brain!), and retrieve the information from memory when needed. Cognitive psychology has become the most prominent school in contemporary scientific psychology.[12] Many of the topics in this text, such as several motivation theories, perception, and creativity include elements of cognitive psychology.

Humanistic and Positive Psychology

Another important influence on the development of cognitive psychology is a movement within psychology that emphasizes feelings and yearnings, and the positive side of people. **Humanistic psychology** emphasizes the dignity and worth of people, along with many other positive but intangible or "soft" attributes. The field emphasizes both self-help and responsibility for the welfare of others, including achieving peace and understanding among nations. The formal movement of humanistic psychology began about 25 years ago. Its official role was defined in terms that still apply today:

> Humanistic psychology is primarily an orientation toward the whole psychology rather than a distinct area or school. It stands for the respect and worth of persons, respect for differences of approach, open-mindedness as to acceptable methods, and interests in exploration of new aspects of human behavior. As a new force in contemporary psychology it is concerned with topics having little place in existing theories and systems. Among them are love, creativity, self, growth, basic need gratification, self-actualization, higher values, being, becoming, spontaneity, play, humor, affection, naturalness, warmth, ego-experience, peak experience, courage, and related concepts.[13]

Today *positive psychology* refers to about the same field of study as humanistic psychology. A major thrust of positive psychology is to focus on what is right with people rather than what is wrong. According to Martin E. P. Seligman, the overall goal of positive psychology is to enhance our experiences of love, work, and play. For example, a researcher might study optimism so pessimistic people can learn to be more optimistic and happier.[14]

Humanistic psychology has had a substantial impact on business psychology and human relations, in terms of both theories and techniques. Abraham Maslow, who developed the need hierarchy, was also a founder of humanistic psychology. Among the humanistic ideas to be described in this book are the enhancement of self-esteem and developing good workplace relationships. In many ways, business psychology is a blend of behaviorism, humanistic psychology, and cognitive psychology.

Closely related in philosophy to humanistic psychology is another influence on business psychology, the human relations movement.

THE HUMAN RELATIONS MOVEMENT

The **human relations movement** began as a concentrated effort by some managers and their advisors to become more sensitive to the needs of employees or to treat them in a more humanistic manner. In other words, employees were to be treated as human beings rather than as parts of the productive process. The human relations movement was supported by three different historic influences: the Hawthorne studies, the threat of unionization, and industrial humanism (see Figure 1–1).

The Hawthorne Studies

The human relations school of management is generally said to have begun in 1927 with a group of studies conducted at the Hawthorne plant of an AT&T subsidiary. These studies were prompted by an experiment carried out by the company's

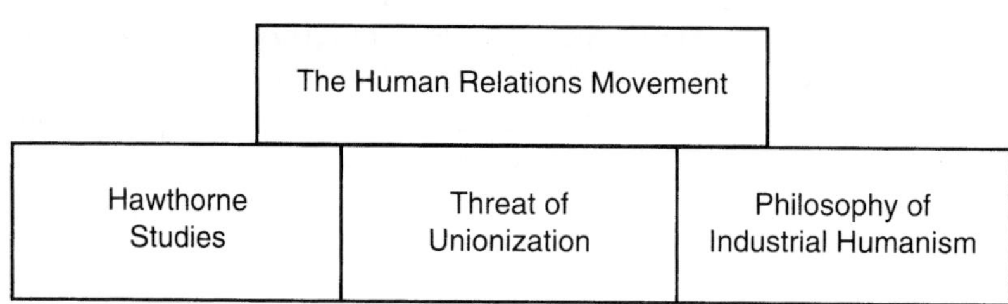

FIGURE 1–1 Influences Supporting the Human Relations Movement

engineers between 1924 and 1927. Following the tradition of scientific management, these engineers were applying research methods to investigate problems of employee productivity.

Two groups were studied to determine the effects of different levels of illumination on worker performance. As prescribed by the scientific method, one group received increased illumination, while the other did not. A preliminary finding was that when illumination was increased, the level of performance also increased. Surprisingly to the engineers, productivity also increased when the level of illumination was decreased almost to moonlight levels. One interpretation of these findings was that the workers involved in the experiment enjoyed being the center of attention. In other words, they reacted positively because management cared about them. Such a phenomenon taking place in any work or research setting is now called the **Hawthorne effect.**[15]

As a result of these preliminary investigations, a team of researchers headed by Harvard professors Elton Mayo and Fritz J. Roethlisberger conducted a series of experiments extending over a six-year period. The conclusions they reached served as the foundations for later developments in the human relations approach to management. Business psychology has been equally influenced by these conclusions:

- Economic incentives are less important than generally believed in influencing workers to achieve high levels of output.
- Leadership practices and work-group pressures profoundly influence employee satisfaction and performance.
- Any factor influencing employee behavior is embedded in a social system. For example, to understand the impact of pay on performance, you have to understand the atmosphere that exists in the work group and how the leader approaches his or her job.

A major implication of the Hawthorne studies was that the old concept of an economic person motivated primarily by money had to be replaced by a more valid idea. The replacement concept was a social person, motivated by social needs, desiring rewarding on-the-job relationships, and more responsive to pressures from coworkers than to control by the boss.[16] Do you believe that workers are more concerned with social relationships than with money?

The Threat of Unionization

Labor union officials and their advocates contend that the benefits of unionization extend to many workers who themselves do not belong to unions. Management in nonunion firms will often pay employees union wages in order to offset the potential advantages of unionization. A similar set of circumstances contributed to the growth of the human relations movement. Labor unions began to grow rapidly in the United States during the late 1930s. Many employers feared that the presence of a labor union would have negative consequences for their companies. Consequently, management looked aggressively for ways to stem the tide of unionization such as using human relations techniques to satisfy workers.[17]

The Philosophy of Industrial Humanism

Partly as a by-product of the Hawthorne studies, a new philosophy arose of human relations in the workplace. Elton Mayo was one of the two key figures in developing this philosophy of industrial humanism. He cautioned managers that emotional factors (such as a desire for recognition) were a more important contributor to productivity than physical and logical factors. Mayo argued vigorously that work should lead to personal satisfaction for employees.

Mary Parker Follett was another key figure in advancing the cause of industrial humanism. Her experience as a management consultant led her to believe that the key to increased productivity was to motivate employees, rather than simply ordering better job performance. The keys to both productivity and democracy, according to Follett, were cooperation, a spirit of unity, and a coordination of effort.[18]

Theory X and Theory Y of Douglas McGregor

The importance of managing people through more effective methods of human relations was advanced by the writings of social psychologist Douglas McGregor. His famous position was that managers should challenge their assumptions about the nature of people. McGregor believed that too many managers assumed that people were lazy and indifferent toward work. He urged managers to be open to the possibility that under the right circumstances people are eager to perform well. If a supervisor accepts one of these extreme sets of beliefs about people, the supervisor will act differently toward them than if he or she believes the opposite. These famous assumptions that propelled the human relations movement forward are summarized as follows:

Theory X assumptions

1. The average person dislikes work and therefore will avoid it if he or she can.
2. Because of this dislike of work, most people must be coerced, controlled, directed, or threatened with punishment to get them to put forth enough effort to achieve organizational goals.
3. The average employee prefers to be directed, wishes to shirk responsibility, has relatively little ambition, and highly values job security.

Theory Y assumptions

1. The expenditure of physical and mental effort in work is as natural as play or rest.
2. External control and the threat of punishment are not the only means for bringing about effort toward reaching company objectives. Employees

will exercise self-direction and self-control in the service of objectives to which they attach high valence.

3. Commitment to objectives is related to the rewards associated with their achievement.
4. The average person learns, under proper conditions, not only to accept but to seek responsibility.
5. Many employees have the capacity to exercise a high degree of imagination, ingenuity, and creativity in the solution of organizational problems.
6. Under the present conditions of industrial life, the intellectual potentialities of the average person are only partially utilized.[19]

The distinction between Theory X and Theory Y has often been misinterpreted. McGregor was humanistic, but he did not mean to imply that being directive and demanding with workers is always the wrong tactic. Some people are undermotivated and dislike work. In these situations, the manager has to behave sternly toward group members to motivate them. If you are a Theory Y manager, you size up your group members to understand their attitudes toward work.

BUSINESS PSYCHOLOGY AND THE SCIENTIFIC METHOD

Much of the knowledge of business psychology is based on research following the scientific method. Experiments are conducted both in the laboratory (particularly with students) and in the field, or actual working conditions. Two experiments have already been described in this chapter. A **field experiment** is an attempt to apply experimental methods to real-life situations, such as the experiment about self-management training for salespeople. Variables, or factors, can be controlled more readily in the laboratory. However, information obtained under actual working conditions is often more relevant.

Suppose an industrial and organizational psychologist were interested in studying the influence of employee empowerment on productivity. **Empowerment** refers to giving workers more power by granting them more authority to make decisions. Examples of empowerment include giving workers more say in resolving customer problems and making suggestions for work improvement. One experimental method to investigate the impact of empowerment on productivity would be to measure the number of claims processed by empowered workers. A representative research design, or scientific method, to study this problem is shown in Table 1–3.

The experimenter would make statistical comparisons of the productivity of the experiment and control groups. Productivity might be measured in claims processed per week. Productivity is referred to as the **dependent variable** because it is measured to see how it is changed by the manipulation of the major variable under study. The experimental group receives the *treatment,* or method under investigation. The treatment is commonly referred to as the **independent variable,** or the variable that is manipulated to test its effects on the dependent variable.

Here the experimental group is given more latitude in settling cases (a form of empowerment). The control group is used as a comparison, therefore not being empowered to make bigger decisions about settling customer claims on their own.

TABLE 1–3
A RESEARCH DESIGN BASED ON THE SCIENTIFIC METHOD

Procedures and Steps	*Experimental Group*	*Control Group 1*	*Control Group 2*
Assign adjusters randomly to groups	Yes	Yes	Yes
Record current productivity level	Yes	Yes	Yes
Empower workers by granting more latitude	Yes	No	No
Administer pamphlet on efficiency	No	No	Yes
Measure productivity after 3 months	Yes	Yes	Yes
Measure productivity after one year	Yes	Yes	Yes

Two control groups are sometimes used to provide more convincing evidence that the changes in productivity are really due to the treatment being investigated.

Assume that the claims adjusters who were empowered processed many more claims than comparable groups of adjusters who were not empowered. Assume also that, in addition, the empowered adjusters performed better than a comparable group who were asked to study a pamphlet about processing claims more efficiently. The tentative conclusion would be that empowerment led to higher productivity than (a) no empowerment or (b) reading a pamphlet about more efficient claims processing. Using the second control group helps rule out the possibility that studying about efficiency improvement enhances productivity of claims adjusters as much as empowerment does.

BUSINESS PSYCHOLOGY AND COMMON SENSE

A student with several years of work experience commented after having attended the first few sessions of a class in business psychology, "Why should I study this field, since it is just common sense? You can't learn how to deal with people by reading a book." The attitudes expressed by this student are shared by many other people who study business psychology or human relations. However logical such an opinion might sound, common sense is not a fully adequate substitute for formal knowledge about business psychology for two major reasons.

COMMON SENSE IS UNCOMMON. A small minority of people are truly effective in dealing with people or organizational forces. If **common sense** (meaning natural wisdom not requiring formal knowledge) were widely held, there would be fewer people problems on the job. The truth is that most organizations, even those that seem highly efficient to outsiders, are plagued with problems involving people. Five high-ranking executives from a telecommunications company resigned within a one-year period. If common sense were so widespread, might not top management have prevented this chaotic situation?

Since few people have a high degree of common sense in matters dealing with people, a knowledge of business psychology (or a similar field such as human relations) is necessary to improve on the chaos found in many business and nonprofit organizations.

Business Psychology Sharpens and Refines Common Sense. People with an adequate degree of common sense often benefit more from a study of business psychology than do people who do not yet possess a well-developed degree of common sense. People who already have some experience tend to derive the most from specialized knowledge in most fields. They tend to build on strengths, which in general has a bigger payoff than overcoming weaknesses. A person with good common sense may already be making good use of his or her potential. With a few refinements, his or her ability to make good use of personal talents may multiply. A team leader is a case in point.

> Recently promoted to team leader, Garth was having difficulty getting the team to pull together. The six members of the team were acting more like a group of individuals rather than a smooth-running team. Garth decided to attempt one of the teamwork techniques he had learned in an applied psychology course. He asked the group to work together to build a mission statement (a brief explanation of its purpose). The group spent three hours one afternoon developing a 25-word statement of who they were and where they were headed. After that afternoon of hard mental effort, the group pulled together and functioned much more like a team. Garth thus strengthened his performance as a team leader, and felt more confident about his future as a leader.

SUMMARY OF KEY POINTS

- Business psychology refers to the application of organized knowledge about human behavior to improve personal satisfaction and productivity on the job. The field is therefore one aspect of applied psychology. Psychology is the science of human and animal behavior, experience, and mental processes. The field of psychology is both a science and a profession.
- Psychology has many different specialty fields, yet there is considerable overlap among these fields. The major specialties or subfields of psychology include (1) industrial and organizational, (2) clinical and counseling, (3) developmental, (4) experimental, and (5) health. Exercise and sport psychology is an example of a small but fast-growing field of psychology.
- Another way of understanding psychology is to understand its major schools of thought or theoretical positions. Structuralism and functionalism are older schools that attempted to understand the workings of the mind. Behaviorism holds that behavior is shaped by its consequences (or the rewards and punishments we receive for our actions). Psychoanalysis views people as constantly torn between internal unconscious forces and external social forces. Cognitive psychology emphasizes the decision-making capabilities and perceptions of people. Humanistic psychology focuses on the desirable qualities of people, such as love and creativity.
- The human relations movement was a concentrated effort to become more sensitive to the needs of employees, or to treat them in a more humanistic manner. The movement was supported by three different historic influences: the Hawthorne studies, the threat of unionization, and the philosophy of industrial humanism. One important conclusion reached by the Hawthorne studies was that showing concern for workers can increase their level of performance as much as or more than improving physical working conditions. The Theory X and Theory Y assumptions of McGregor were an important force propelling the human relations movement forward.

GUIDELINES FOR PERSONAL EFFECTIVENESS

1. Should you be faced with the challenge of attempting to evaluate which work procedure or method is the most effective, conduct an experiment. Even if you do not have the resources to apply a complete experimental design, you can at least use part of the experimental method. Suppose you want to determine which is the best time for telemarketers to telephone people at home to make an appointment with a home-improvement specialist from your company. Keep a carefully documented log of which times yielded the highest number of appointments. Remember to make a random list of the people to contact at the various times, so as not to bias your results. Do not bias your results by getting in touch with the best prospects at what you considered to be prime time for telemarketing.
2. An important supplement to common sense and intuition in dealing with people is to use knowledge provided by business psychology. Specifically, you are likely to increase your personal effectiveness if you learn to use many of the concepts and techniques presented in this text.

- Many findings of business psychology are based on scientific methods, including experiments under actual working conditions. Business psychology is not simply common sense for two reasons: (1) common sense is uncommon, and (2) business psychology sharpens and refines common sense.

DISCUSSION QUESTIONS AND ACTIVITIES

1. Why might the study of applied psychology, and business psychology in particular, still be important in the age of information technology?
2. What is the justification for classifying psychology as a *science*?
3. How might business psychology be used to actually help a business firm increase its profits?
4. After the terrorist attacks against the United States in September 2001, teams of mental health professionals (such as clinical psychologists and psychiatric social workers) were called into business firms. In what ways do you think these mental health professionals helped employees who were not working in the area of the attacks?
5. Identify three of the 55 divisions of psychology that you think offer the most promise of being useful to society. Explain your reasoning.
6. Why might the information studied by cognitive psychologists be particularly relevant to the job activities of higher-level workers?
7. Identify a technique of psychology that you are already using.
8. Why is conducting an experiment generally considered to produce more useful results than information obtained from a survey?
9. Give an example from physical science (such as physics or chemistry) in which common sense is likely to be wrong.
10. How might managers make use of the Hawthorne effect?

A BUSINESS PSYCHOLOGY CASE PROBLEM

How Do We Know If Our Website Is Paying Off?

Robert D. Hof, a business reporter, asked Target Corp. Vice-Chairman Gerald L. Storch whether the chain's online site would turn a profit at some point. The vice chairman assured the reporter that the online site would turn a profit if you include the benefits from developing a strong brand, prompting buyers to visit stores, and cementing closer relationships with customers.

The reporter was skeptical, so he wasn't too surprised when Target announced that it was turning over some of its Web operations to Amazon.com Inc., a move that suggested to Hof that Target was phasing out its Web operations. The opposite was true. Target has not only retained its own site, run partly by Amazon, but it receives massive exposure on Amazon's site because about 50 million people visit it per month.

Storch expects the online visibility to boost the intangible benefits such as building the Target brand, and prompting buyers to visit their stores. Ken Cassar, an analyst from the market research firm Jupiter, supports Storch's thinking. Cassar estimates that about two-thirds of the return on investment on an online site stems from building the brand and physical-store purchases. If they measure only online sales and profits, he says, "There's a real risk that brick-and-mortar retailers may substantially scale back their online investments, which could put them at a big competitive disadvantage."

A Jupiter report found that 50 percent of consumers use a retailer's Website for research before purchasing a product in a physical store. Knowledgeable retailers are not concerned about site visitors failing to click on the "order" button. In contrast, they go with the flow by encouraging shoppers to explore online and pick up or purchase the item in the traditional store. Surveys conducted by Sears, Roebuck & Co., for example, indicate that customers researching online first influenced about $500 million worth of in-store appliance sales. So it doesn't matter if they do not buy a washer and dryer online.

According to reporter Hof, the results of promoting the brand and reinforcing ties with customers are quite difficult to measure. However, that is exactly what some retailers, such as Target, see as the main value of their Websites. Storch says the biggest benefit of Target's online initiatives is deepening relationships with its customers, which he thinks will keep them coming back in physical stores and online. "Can we prove sales in the store? No," he says. "But is the Website valuable? Sure."

Despite the optimism of Storch, some people affiliated with Target would like more evidence that their expensive Website is actually contributing revenue to the company.

1. What kind of evidence should Target Corp. seek to evaluate whether or not its Website is actually boosting sales?
2. Design an experiment that would demonstrate if the Target Website is actually improving sales.

Source: Many of the facts in this case are from Robert D. Hof, "Don't Cut Back Now: Brick-and-Mortar Retailers are Finding that Online Visits Boost In-store Sales," *Business Week e.biz* October 1, 2001, p. EB 34.

REFERENCES

1. Dodge Fernald, *Psychology* (Upper Saddle River, NJ: Prentice Hall, 1997), p. 5.
2. Frank J. Landy, "Early Influences on the Development of Industrial and Organizational Psychology," *Journal of Applied Psychology,* August 1997, p. 467.
3. Collette A. Frayne and Michael Geringer, "Self-Management Training for Improving Job Performance: A Field Experiment Involving Salespeople," *Journal of Applied Psychology,* June 2000, pp. 361–372.

A BUSINESS PSYCHOLOGY CASE PROBLEM

Optimal Performance at Pacifica Fashions

Maureen Blackwell, the CEO of Pacifica Fashions Inc., takes her golf game as seriously as she does running her upscale clothing company. In hopes of improving her golf game, Blackwell attended a workshop given by exercise and sport psychologist Tony Rodin. Among the many pointers Blackwell took away from the seminar was to concentrate totally on the golf ball just before and during her swing.

Rodin's advice worked wonders. During her next three golf outings, Blackwell improved her score by four strokes, three strokes, and five strokes. Blackwell thought to herself, "I'm really on to something. After 15 years of playing golf, I'm moving toward optimal performance." She then remembered how Rodin emphasized that the principles of exercise and sport psychology apply to work and the rest of life as well as athletics. Another thought Blackwell had was, "Rodin is really good. If he helped my golf game so much, I'm pretty sure that his ideas could also improve my skills as a manager. I could learn how to work up to my potential on the golf course and in the office. In fact, Rodin could help improve the performance of all the managers and sales representatives in the company. We all have to concentrate and stay focused."

Blackwell arranged an appointment to meet next Friday with Tony Rodin to discuss his consulting with her company. During the meeting Rodin talked enthusiastically about working with all the company managers to help them work toward optimal performance. He would conduct two seminars with the entire staff and then meet with all of them individually for at least two 30-minute coaching sessions. Maureen Blackwell was excited about the prospects of applying sport psychology to improve the performance of the key people in her company. Based on her enthusiasm, she said she would sign a consulting contract after she first discussed the arrangements with her key people.

Blackwell devoted the first part of her next staff meeting to describing her plans to help the management and sales team work toward optimal performance. To Blackwell's surprise, her plan met with mixed reaction. Five of the people present shared Blackwell's enthusiasm, three were willing to go along with the idea, and two thought the idea was a waste of time. Ricardo Lewis, the head of merchandising, said, "Let's be candid. I've been successful in fashion merchandising for 20 years. No psychologist who has been working with jocks for a few years is going to tell me how to do my job better. I'm not trying to hit a ball into a hole, I'm trying to be supercreative almost every day."

The company head of finance and accounting, Sue Ellen Byrnes, also voiced criticism. "I'm not doubting that your consultant might do somebody some good. I admit that I could benefit from becoming more focused. Yet what about the return on investment? Would we get enough improvement in performance to justify paying Rodin's fees? And what about all the managerial and sales time tied up in these seminars and coaching sessions? That has a cost also."

Blackwell said to the group, "It looks like we have some excellent support for applying sport psychology to improve our performance. At the same time we have a couple of negative reactions. By next week I will make a decision as to how we should proceed."

The group nodded in agreement, and Blackwell proceeded to discuss the new program to develop a stronger presence with Sears, JCPenney, and Dayton Hudson.

1. What is your opinion about the value of applying sport psychology to improving the performance of high-level managers and sales representatives?
2. Describe an experimental design that would help the company determine whether the sport psychology seminars and coaching sessions are a good return on investment. (Is the sport psychology program really effective?)
3. If you were Maureen Blackwell, what would you do after receiving the mixed reaction from the group?

A BUSINESS PSYCHOLOGY EXERCISE

Applying Health Psychology to the Job

Working individually or within groups, develop a list of the top 10 behaviors employees should avoid so they can work more productively and avoid accidents and disease. An illustrative example would be, "Airline pilots should get adequate sleep so they do not feel drowsy or fall asleep at the controls." Compare your list with those of other class members.

4. Several components of this section are from Charles G. Morris and Albert A. Maisto, *Psychology: An Introduction,* 11th ed. (Upper Saddle River, NJ: Prentice Hall, 2002), p. 5.
5. Peter Frieberg, "More Long-term Problems Seen for Abused Kids," *APA Monitor,* June 1991, p. 18.
6. Gary W. Evans and Dana Johnson, "Stress and Open-Office Noise," *Journal of Applied Psychology,* October 2000, pp. 779–783.
7. Gerald J. S. Wilde, *Target Risk: Dealing with the Danger of Death, Disease and Damage in Everyday Decisions* (Toronto, Canada: PDE, 1994), p. 5.
8. Special Issue: The History of American Psychology, *American Psychologist,* February 1992; Thomas Hardy Leahy, *A History of Psychology: Main Currents in Psychological Thought,* 2nd ed. (Upper Saddle River, NJ: Prentice Hall, 1987).
9. Quoted in Jerome Kagan and Ernest Haveman, *Psychology: An Introduction,* 4th ed. (New York: Harcourt Brace Jovanovich, 1980), p. 30.
10. Robert F. Bornstein and Joseph Masling (eds.), *Empirical Perspectives on the Psychoanalytic Unconscious* (Washington, DC: American Psychological Association, 1998); Richard W. Robins, Samuel D. Gosling, and Kenneth H. Craik, "An Empirical Analysis of Trends in Psychology," *American Psychologist,* February 1999, p. 124.
11. Yiannis Gabriel, *Organizations in Depth: The Psychoanalysis of Organizations* (London: Sage, 1999).
12. Morris and Maisto, *Psychology,* p. 19.
13. From the Articles of Association of Humanistic Psychology, 1980. For an update and reinforcement on these ideas see, Arthur C. Bohart and Thomas Greening, "Humanistic Psychology and Positive Psychology," *American Psychologist,* January 2001, pp. 81–82.
14. Robert Kreitner, *Management,* 5th ed. (Boston: Houghton Mifflin, 1992), pp. 51–52.
15. Elton Mayo, *The Human Problems of Industrial Civilization* (New York: Viking Press, 1960).
16. James A. F. Stoner and R. Edward Freeman, *Management,* 4th ed. (Upper Saddle River, NJ: Prentice Hall, 1989), p. 49.
17. Kreitner, *Management,* p. 50.
18. Kreitner, *Management,* p. 52.
19. Douglas McGregor, *The Human Side of Enterprise* (New York: McGraw-Hill, 1960), pp. 33–48.

SUGGESTED READING

Astrid, Stec M., and Bernstein, Douglas A. (eds.). *Psychology: Fields of Application.* Boston: Houghton Mifflin, 1999.

Bevan, William. "Contemporary Psychology: A Tour Inside the Onion." *American Psychologist,* May 1991, pp. 475–483.

Blau, Theodore H. *The Psychologist as Expert Witness,* 2nd ed. New York: Wiley, 1998.

Kahneman, Daniel, Diener, Edward, and Schwarz, Norbert (eds.). *Well-Being: The Foundations of Hedonic Psychology.* New York: Russell Sage Foundation, 2001.

Lowman, Rodney L. (ed.). *The Ethical Practice of Psychology in Organizations.* Washington, DC: American Psychological Association, 1998.

Milton, Joyce. *The Road to Malpsychia: Humanistic Psychology and Our Discontents.* New York: Encounter, 2002.

Richards, Graham. *Putting Psychology in Its Place: An Introduction from a Critical Historical Perspective.* London: Routledge, 1996.

Schwartz, Joseph. *Cassandra's Daughter: A History of Psychoanalysis.* New York: Penguin, 2000.

Todd, James T., and Morris, Edward K. (eds.). *Modern Perspectives on John B. Watson and Classical Behaviorism.* Westport, CT: Greenwood Press/Greenwood, 1994.

Uttal, William R. *Toward a New Behaviorism: The Case Against Perceptual Reductionism.* Mahwah, NJ: Erlbaum, 1998.

WEB CORNER

www.apa.org (The Website of the American Psychological Association. See particularly the section, "Students.")

www.appliedpsychology.com (A firm that offers psychological services to industry.)

www.businesspsychologist.com (A firm that specializes in business travel behavior, such as assessing the dangers of a particular hotel or location.)

CHAPTER 2

PERCEPTION, LEARNING, VALUES, AND ETHICS

Learning Objectives

After reading and studying this chapter and doing the exercises, you should be able to

1. Describe the nature of perception and how it influences job behavior.
2. Explain why our perceptions are often inaccurate.
3. Present an overview of how people learn both simple skills and more complex activities.
4. Explain how values influence job behavior.
5. Apply an ethical test to decisions that present an ethical dilemma.

An important aspect of applying psychology on the job is to gain some basic knowledge about how people function. This chapter focuses on four aspects of behavior that influence the way people behave on the job:

1. How they interpret what takes place outside themselves.
2. How they learn job-related information.
3. The values influencing their behavior.
4. Their ethics.

A tentative interpretation of this information is that it deals with general principles of human behavior. The implication is that most people perceive, learn, and develop values and ethical codes in the same manner. Some generalizations about human behavior can be made, yet you must always be aware of individual differences. (The emphasis in Chapter 3 is on how people differ from one another.) For example, most people—but not everybody—engage in denial when faced with information that attacks their self-esteem or basic beliefs.

PERCEPTION: HOW PEOPLE INTERPRET THE WORLD

Most of us interpret what is going on in the world outside us as we perceive it—not as it really is. You do not usually experience a mass of colors, you experience a color photograph. You do not experience a thousand different vibrations in the air, you hear a favorite compact disc. When we answer a question, we answer in terms of our interpretation of what we hear.

An everyday happening, such as a change in air temperature, helps to illustrate the nature of human perception. Assume that you live in Vermont. A temperature of 52°F (11.1°C) would seem warm in January. The same temperature would seem cold in July. Our perception of temperature depends on many things going on inside our mind and body.

A standard psychology diagram is helpful in illustrating that "truth" depends on what we see as the "facts." An anonymous artist drew Figure 2–1 to be intentionally ambiguous. Upon looking at this line drawing, many people will see an old woman with her chin tucked down, wearing a scarf around her head. Look at the drawing long enough, and you will see a young woman glancing away from you. Another curiosity about human perception is that the figure and the background switch back and forth in such a drawing.

The standard diagram in question illustrates a fundamental problem of visual perception: the visual image of the eye has many possible interpretations.[1] Driving on a highway on a warm, sunny day one person might see a multicolored reflection of sun against the residue of oil from vehicles. Another person might perceive a rainbow down the road. (Have you ever perceived either one of these phenomena?)

Perceptions on the job are very important. Many studies, for example, have investigated the consequences of employee job perceptions. The results show that employees who perceive their job to be challenging and interesting have high job satisfaction and motivation. In addition, these favorable perceptions lead to better job performance.[2]

FIGURE 2–1 An Old Woman Or A Young Woman? Look Again

In summary, **perception** deals with the various ways in which people interpret things in the external world and how they act on the basis of these perceptions. The aspects of perception described here are (1) why perceptual problems exist, (2) agreement about perceived events, and (3) how people perceive the causes of behavior. Our discussion focuses on the social rather than the physical aspects of perception, such as taste, sound, and touch.

Why Perceptual Problems Exist

Under ideal circumstances, people perceive information as it is intended to be communicated or as it exists in reality. Suppose a company promotes a specialist to a team leader position because he or she is thought to have good potential for advancement. The manager offering the promotion hopes the specialist does not see the promotion as a plot to have the person work extra hours without being paid overtime. (Team leaders usually do not receive overtime pay.) Both characteristics of the stimulus (the idea or thing to be perceived) and the mental process of people can lead to distorted perceptions.

Characteristics of the Stimulus. Perceptual problems are most likely to be encountered when the stimulus or cue to be perceived has an emotional meaning. Assume that Brian, an office supervisor, announces to his staff, "I would like you to meet Brenda. She's a temporary worker here to help us out this week." Announcing the presence of an office temporary could trigger several different perceptions. The specific perceptions would depend on many motives, needs, and the knowledge of department employees. Among the possible interpretations are these:

> "An office temporary? I wonder if this means the company is going to cut down the regular workforce and use temporaries to help us through peak loads."
>
> "This seems to be a sure sign that business has picked up. The front office would never authorize extra help unless business were booming. Things look good for getting a decent raise this year."
>
> "I wonder if Brian has brought in a temporary worker to show us we had better get hustling or we could be replaced. I've heard a lot of these so-called temporaries usually wind up with a full-time job if they like the temporary assignment."

To help reduce misperceptions, Brian should provide more complete information on why Brenda is being hired, such as pointing to a surge in orders. Reducing ambiguity helps minimize perceptual errors.

Mental Processes of People. The devices people use to deal with sensory information play a major role in creating perceptual problems. Several of these can also be classified as defensive behavior.

Selective Attention. The major contributor to perceptual distortions is the tendency for us to attend to the stimuli that are most relevant to our needs. Giving exclusive attention to something at the expense of other aspects of the environment is referred to as **selective attention.** If a stimulus fits our needs, desires, or interests we are likely to give it our attention. At the same time, we are likely to pay only minor attention to the surrounding stimuli. Thus, the person who listens with excitement to a presentation about the world of possibilities of being online may not pay attention to an important fact. While online, the person cannot send or receive telephone messages unless he or she purchases a telephone line dedicated to the online service. Later on, when the Internet connection is installed, it dawns on the person that he or she cannot use the telephone for other purposes when online. Because of selective attention, the person did not attend to information about the telephone tie-up.

Denial. If the sensory information is particularly painful to us—for example, hurting our self-esteem—we tend to go one step beyond selective attention. **Denial** is the process of excluding from awareness an important aspect of reality. This mental process is often found in the workplace, especially when people face such threats as job loss. As part of a downsizing, a woman was told by her manager that she would be terminated in 30 days unless somehow she could find another position in the company. That evening she informed her husband, "Our company is going through a downsizing, so it looks like I will be transferred to a different department in 30 days." By denying the reality of the message, the woman failed to search actively for another job within the company. She finally perceived the message correctly when she was handed her severance check.

Stereotyping. A common method of simplifying perception is to evaluate an individual or thing based on our perception of the group or class to which the person or object belongs. A perceptual disadvantage of stereotyping is that you do not look for the way in which somebody or something might be different from others in the same group. For example, a job seeker might say, "I won't look for a job in the retail field, because retailing jobs have such low pay." Such stereotyping might result in the person's neglecting to investigate high-paying opportunities within the retail field, based on the rapid promotions possible. Stereotypes can be positive as well as negative. For example, you might have the stereotype that all accountants are thorough and accurate. As a result, you fail to carefully review the tax return prepared by your accountant.

Halo Effect. We have a tendency to color everything that we know about a person because of one recognizable favorable or unfavorable trait. When a company does not insist on the use of objective measures of performance, it is not uncommon for a supervisor to give a favorable performance rating to people who dress well or smile frequently. The fine appearance or warm smile of these people has created a halo around them. Employees often create a negative halo about a supervisor simply because he or she is gruff or stern in manner or speech.

Projection. Another shortcut in the perceptual process is to project our own faults onto others instead of making an objective appraisal of the situation. Our feelings and thoughts are unacceptable to us, so we attribute them to another person. In this way we feel less anxious about ourselves. A manager who has a self-discipline problem himself might respond negatively to an employee's request to work at home one day per week. The manager might say, "Sorry, can't let you work at home. You would probably goof off half the day before you got down to work."

Perceptual Congruence

The discussion of perception so far has focused on perceptual errors. At times, most people in the organization perceive an event in the same way. **Perceptual congruence** refers to the degree to which people perceive things the same way.[3] High congruence generally implies valid perception, but people can also agree on a distorted perception. For example, four members of a work team might have the authority to choose a fifth team member. All four might share the same inaccurate perception that a particular candidate is a good fit. After one month, they learn that the individual is a loner who functions poorly in a team environment.

Despite the reservation cited, high congruence generally leads to more positive consequences for the organization than low congruence. A case in point is that it is beneficial for managers and group members to perceive the group members' tasks in the same manner.

Attribution Theory: How We Perceive the Causes of Behavior

An important aspect of perception is our explanation for the causes of behavior. Stated differently, to what do we *attribute* a given behavior? **Attribution theory** is the study of the process by which people ascribe causes to the behavior they perceive. A major finding of attribution theory is that most people give relatively little weight to the circumstances in making judgments about a person's behavior. We are more likely to attribute a person's actions or results to personal characteristics than to outside forces. A supervisor who presses us to finish a project is more likely to be perceived as impatient than as caught up in a highly competitive environment.

Another finding of attribution theory is that people have a general tendency to attribute their achievements to good inner qualities, whereas they attribute failure to adverse factors within the environment. A manager would thus attribute increased productivity to his or her leadership skills but blame low productivity on poor support from the organization.

To dig one step further into attribution theory, people attribute causes after gathering information about three dimensions of behavior: consensus, distinctiveness, and consistency.[4] Imagine that Maria, a real estate agent, sold the highest dollar volume of real estate last year of any agent in the company nationwide. *Consensus* concerns whether other people behave similarly. If other people do not behave in the same way, we tend to attribute the cause to the person's characteristics. Because no other agent performed nearly as well, we are inclined to attribute Maria's success to her characteristics. *Distinctiveness* concerns whether the behavior in question occurred in other situations. If we had no evidence that Maria had been an outstanding performer in other situations, we might attribute her success to external factors such as luck. *Consistency* concerns the regularity of the behavior. If Maria had been a high-performing real estate agent in previous years, we would be more likely to attribute her success to personal characteristics such as high motivation and self-discipline.

The combination of all three factors helps us arrive at a final verdict of attribution. We attribute behavior to personal factors when we perceive low consensus, low distinctiveness, and high consistency. (Others aren't doing it, the person has done it in other situations, and the person acts this way consistently.) We attribute behavior to external causes when we perceive high consensus, high distinctiveness, and low consistency. (Others are doing it, the person rarely performs this way, and the person does not perform this way consistently.)

HOW PEOPLE LEARN

Much learning takes place on the job simply because people spend such a large proportion of their lives at work. Furthermore, workers at all levels are expected to learn new job skills and technology continuously. **Learning** is generally considered to be a lasting change in behavior based on practice and experience. Yet it is possible to learn something and store it in your mind without changing your behavior.[5] For example, you read that if you press "F12" in Windows 2000 you open the "Save As" function. You keep it in your mind, but do not use the command yet. The new knowledge is stored in your upper brain, but is not yet put into action.

A person does not learn how to grow physically, hear sounds, see light, or smell freshly cut grass. These are innate, inborn capabilities. But a person does learn how to use a digital camera, conduct an interview, resolve conflict, cut hair, or access a bank account online.

Here we will describe several different methods of learning, beginning with classical conditioning, the simplest type. Then we will describe learning of intermediate complexity, operant conditioning, followed by two ways in which more complicated skills are learned: modeling and informal learning. We conclude with e-learning because of its widespread use in delivering content for learning. Although we describe different methods of learning, most learning is dependent on several methods of learning. For example, in learning to operate a new vehicle you might need to develop simple reflexes to adjust to getting into the car. You would also use higher-level learning to understand how to use the computerized map.

Classical Conditioning: Learning Simple Habits and Reflexes

In the late 1890s a Russian physiologist, Ivan Pavlov, conducted a long series of experiments about digestion. While studying a dog, he noticed that the dog salivated not only to the presence of food in the mouth, but at the sight of the food, the sound of the food trays, and even the footsteps of the experimenter. The principles of **classical conditioning** stemming from his experiments help us to understand the most elementary type of learning—how people acquire uncomplicated habits and reflexes. Since most of work behavior involves more than reflexes and simple habits, classical conditioning itself is not of major consequence to the supervisor or individual worker. Yet its basic principles and concepts are included in more complicated forms of learning.

Classical conditioning works in this manner. Kurt takes an entry-level, unskilled job in a factory. His first day on the job a bell rings in his department at 11:34 A.M. Suddenly, every other worker stops working and opens a lunch box or heads out to the company cafeteria. Kurt says to himself, "The bell must mean it's time for lunch." By the third day on the job, Kurt develops stomach pangs and begins to salivate as soon as the bell rings. Prior to this job, Kurt was in the habit of eating lunch at 1 P.M. and did not begin to have stomach pangs until that time.

Looking at the essentials of classical conditioning, here is what happened to Kurt. Because the food naturally and automatically elicits (brings forth) stomach pangs and salivation, it is referred to as the *unconditioned stimulus* (UCS). Salivating to the food in Kurt's lunch box or in the cafeteria occurs automatically, without any learning. It is therefore called the *unconditioned response* (UCR). The sound of the department bell was originally neutral with respect to the salivary or hunger pang response, since it did not naturally elicit the UCR. Conditioning has taken place when the previously neutral stimulus (the department bell in Kurt's case) acquires the capacity to bring forth hunger pangs and salivation. The previously neutral stimulus is now called the *conditioned stimulus* (CS), and the hunger pangs and salivation to the sound of the bell are known as *conditioned response* (CR).

Two other conditioning concepts are also of major importance. If the department bell rings frequently when it is not time for lunch, Kurt's hunger pangs and salivation responses will gradually cease or extinguish upon hearing a bell. (An important exception is that time alone or the empty feeling in his stomach can also serve as a stimulus to Kurt.) As he goes through life, Kurt will learn not to salivate or experience hunger pangs to every bell that sounds like the one used in his department. At first he may generalize his learning by salivating to many different bells and experiencing hunger pangs in response to a variety of bells. After a while, he will discriminate and only make such responses to the bell in his department (or any other bell that signals food time).

Classical conditioning helps to explain such elementary job behaviors as how people learn to avoid being conked on the head by cranes and low hanging pipes. By classical conditioning, people also learn how to avoid being burned twice by a hot pipe or shocked twice by inserting a screwdriver into an electric outlet.

Operant Conditioning: Learning through the Consequences of Our Behavior

Operant conditioning is learning that takes place as a consequence of behavior. In other words, a person's actions are instrumental in determining whether or not learning takes place. Operant conditioning is the cornerstone of behaviorism, as reflected first in the work of John B. Watson and then later by B. F. Skinner. The process by which a person learns the maximum temperature for safe operation of a personal computer illustrates operant conditioning. (The person in question lacked air conditioning.) Several times on warm days disturbing things begin to happen, such as files disappearing and unusual symbols appearing on screen. In desperation one day, the person shuts off the computer and returns late at night when the room temperature is much cooler. Because the computer now operates correctly, from that time on the person operates the computer only when the temperature is 90°F (32°C) or lower. In this case the operant is waiting for the temperature to drop or turning a fan in the direction of the computer. The person adopted checking the temperature on warm days because that person received reinforcement for the initial effort—the computer performed properly when the room temperature was lowered.

Learning versus Motivation. Motivation and learning are separate but closely related processes. You cannot motivate people to perform a task they do not know how to perform. Yet you can motivate a person to want to learn how to perform that task. Managers are frequently faced with the problems of (1) helping group members to learn, and (2) motivating them to repeat the learned behaviors.

Reinforcement Strategies. The term *reinforcement* in general refers to the means by which behaviors are selected and retained. It gets at the idea that a response, such as shifting your weight on a snowboard to make a turn, is strengthened. The four reinforcement strategies are positive reinforcement, negative reinforcement (avoidance learning or motivation), punishment, and extinction.

Positive Reinforcement and Negative Reinforcement. The distinction between positive and negative reinforcement is very important. Positive reinforcement adds something rewarding to a situation, such as praise or a gift certificate. **Positive reinforcement** is thus receiving a reward for making a desired response. **Negative reinforcement** is effective because it takes away something unpleasant from a situation. It is a form of avoidance learning or motivation. Negative reinforcement is thus being rewarded by being relieved of discomfort. The personal computer incident described earlier included negative reinforcement. Adjusting the room temperature took away the unpleasant situation of the computer malfunctioning.

Note carefully that negative reinforcement is not the same thing as punishment. Negative reinforcement is pleasant and therefore a reward. Punishment, by definition, is something unpleasant, unless the person involved likes to be punished. With masochists, the reward is to be punished!

Punishment. Being punished for your mistakes can be an important part of learning. **Punishment** is the introduction of an unpleasant stimulus as a consequence of the learner having done something wrong (in the eyes of the person in control of the situation). Or the threat of punishment can be used instead of actually punishing people for the wrong response in a learning or motivational situation. Punishment assists the operant conditioning process because it weakens the particular response. You tend not to repeat a response because of its negative consequences.

Extinction. The purpose of punishment is to eliminate a response. The same result can often be achieved through the reinforcement strategy of **extinction.** It refers to the weakening or decreasing of the frequency of undesirable behavior by removing the reward for such behavior. It is the absence of reinforcement. One way to stop the office clown from acting up is for coworkers to ignore that person's antics. The clown's behavior is said to be *extinguished.*

Primary and Secondary Reinforcers. Another important distinction in operant conditioning is between primary reinforcers and secondary reinforcers. A **primary reinforcer** is one that is rewarding by itself, without any association with other reinforcers. Food, water, air, and sex are primary reinforcers. A **secondary reinforcer** is one whose value must be learned through association with other reinforcers. It is referred to as secondary not because it is less important, but because it is learned. Money is a secondary reinforcer. Although it is made of paper or metal, through its association with food, clothing, shelter, and other primary reinforcers, money becomes a powerful reward.

Schedules of Reinforcement. An important issue in operant conditioning (and in motivation) is how frequently to reward people when they make the correct response. So much experimentation has been conducted on this topic that some accurate guidelines are available. Two broad types of schedules of reinforcement are in use, continuous and intermittent.

Under a *continuous schedule*, behavior is reinforced each time it occurs, such as saying "good job" every time a bank teller comes out even at the end of the day. Continuous schedules usually result in the fastest learning, but the desired behavior quickly diminishes when the reinforcement stops. Under an *intermittent schedule* the learner receives a reward after some instances of engaging in the desired behavior, but not after each instance. Intermittent reinforcement is particularly effective in sustaining behavior, because the learner stays mentally alert and interested. At any point in time, the behavior might lead to the desired reward. Slot machines in gambling casinos operate on this principle.

Shaping of Behavior. Instrumental learning can also be used to help people learn a skill one step at a time. **Shaping** is the process of learning through approximations until the total skill is learned. Animals such as dolphins and security dogs learn their complex maneuvers through shaping. Behavior is shaped by the reinforcement of a series of steps that build up to the final or desired behavior. At each successful step of the way, the learner receives some positive reinforcement (such as the dolphin's being served a fresh fish for jumping through the lowest hoop). Unless the learner receives positive reinforcement at each step of the way, that person will probably not acquire the total skill.

As the learner improves in the ability to perform the task, more skill is required to receive the reward. A woman might be shaped into an automobile technician through a series of small skills beginning with changing tires. She receives a series of rewards as she moves along the path from a garage helper to an automotive technician who can diagnose an engine malfunction and repair the problem. Among the forms of positive reinforcement she received along the way were approval for acquired skills, pay increments, and the feeling of pride as new component skills were learned. The negative reinforcement, or avoidance learning, she received was fewer scraped knuckles. When this series of small skills has been put together through a complicated pattern of responses, the woman has been transformed from a fledgling garage assistant to a full-fledged automotive technician. Even if the woman studied automotive technology at school, some shaping of behavior would be helpful on the job.

Modeling and Informal Learning: Learning Complicated Skills

Classical and operant conditioning provide only a partial explanation of how people learn on the job. When you acquire a complicated skill such as speaking in front of a group, preparing a budget, or designing a store display, you learn much more than just a single stimulus—response relationship. You learn a large number of these relationships, and you also learn how to put them together in a cohesive, smooth-flowing pattern. Two important processes that help in learning complicated skills are modeling and informal learning. Both are based on processes that are inferred to take place in the brain.

Complicated learning is called a *cognitive process* because it requires the learner to make a number of judgments and observations, or demanding mental activities. It is possible that cognitive process will someday be observed in such form as electrical charges in nerves. For now, however, scientists can only infer that these cognitive processes take place.

Modeling occurs when you learn a skill by observing another person perform the skill. Modeling is considered a form of social learning, because it is learned in the presence of others. The process is classified as cognitive learning because it is a complex intellectual activity. Modeling, or imitation, often brings forth behaviors people did not previously seem to have in their repertoire. Many apprentices learn part of their trade by modeling an experienced craftsperson who practices the trade. Modeling is widely used in teaching sports through videotapes that give the viewer an opportunity to observe the skill being performed correctly. Although modeling is an effective way of learning, the learner must also have the proper capabilities and motivation.

Informal learning is another way of learning complex skills in the workplace. It is planned or unplanned learning that occurs without a formal classroom, lesson plan, instructor, or examination. The central premise of such learning is that employees acquire important information outside of a formal learning situation. The learning can be spontaneous, such as getting a tip on computer utilization while waiting in line at the cafeteria. Or, the company might organize the work area to encourage such informal learning. The employees capitalize upon a learning situation in an unstructured situation where the rewards stemming from the learning are not explicit.

Informal learning can be regarded as a variation of **implicit learning,** or learning that takes place unconsciously and without an intention to learn.[6] Perhaps, you have not been attempting to learn the Spanish word for danger, but after seeing the word *peligro* adjacent to the English word *danger* many times (such as near electric wires), you learn the Spanish word.

E-Learning: A Method of Delivering Content for Learning

An important innovation in learning in both schools and industry is distance learning, technology-based learning, or e-learning. The learner studies independently outside of a classroom setting, and interacts with a computer in addition to studying course material. An e-learning course usually is carefully structured, with specific lessons plans for the student. E-learning is more of a method of delivering content than a method of learning, yet the process helps us understand more about learning.

Although e-learning is different from more traditional forms of learning, it still is based on the methods of learning described so far. An example is that the learner will often need reinforcement to keep going. Trainers at GE Capital found that whether employees completed the course was dependent on whether managers gave reinforcement on attendance, how important employees were made to feel, and whether progress in the course was tracked.[7]

Another relevant aspect of e-learning here is that its success depends upon cognitive processes of the learner, particularly self-motivation and self-discipline. Self-motivation is important because being assigned to take an e-learning course by the company is often not motivational enough to work independently. Self-discipline is necessary to create a regular time for performing class work, and not being distracted by work or home activities. In educational settings also, successful distance learning requires high motivation. A problem noted is that some students may not take e-learning seriously. Corporate e-learning programs have a high dropout rate, one reason being that most students need the structure of a face-to-face instructor, a classroom, and other students to keep them focused on the course.[8]

The most successful e-learning experiences combine features of technology-based learning with the emotional support possible in a classroom. At the Penn State World Campus, the distance education division of Pennsylvania State University, a recent online course completion rate was 95 percent. The director of the program says that students benefit from frequent interaction with faculty and each other. Bulletin-board discussion and e-mail messages are used extensively. The instructor monitors participation and sends e-mails to students who are not participating or falling behind.[9]

HOW VALUES AND BELIEFS INFLUENCE JOB BEHAVIOR

Another group of factors influencing how a person behaves on the job is that person's values and beliefs. A **value** refers to the importance a person attaches to something. Values are also tied in with enduring beliefs that one's mode of conduct is better than an opposite mode of conduct. If you believe that good interpersonal relations are the most important part of your life, your humanistic values are very strong. Similarly, you may think that people who are not highly concerned about interpersonal relations have poor values.

Understanding values has become a popular topic, as exemplified by the belief that Generation X and Generation Y people have values that sharply contrast with those of Baby Boomers. Table 2–1 summarizes these stereotypes with the understanding that massive group stereotypes like this are only partially accurate because there are literally millions of exceptions. For example, many Baby Boomers are fascinated with technology, and many members of Generation Y like hierarchy.

Here we study four aspects of values: how they are learned, values clarification, how stable they are, and the mesh between individual and organizational values.

How Values are Learned

People are not born with a particular set of values. Rather, values are learned in the process of growing up—many by age 4. One important way we acquire values is through modeling. It is often found that a person who takes considerable pride in his/her work was reared around people who had a strong work ethic. Models can be parents, teachers, friends, siblings, and even public figures. If we identify with a particular person, the probability is high that we will develop some of his or her major values.

Communication of attitudes is another major way in which values are learned. The attitudes we hear expressed directly or indirectly help shape our values. Assume that using credit to purchase goods and services was talked about as an undesirable practice among your family and friends. You might therefore hold negative values about installment purchases.

Unstated, but implied, attitudes may also shape values. If key people in your life showed no enthusiasm when you talked about work accomplishment, you might not place a high value on achieving outstanding results. In contrast, if your family and friends centered their lives about their careers, you might develop similar values. (Or you might rebel against such a value because it interfered with a relaxed lifestyle.)

TABLE 2–1
VALUE STEREOTYPES FOR SEVERAL GENERATIONS OF WORKERS

Baby Boomers (1946–1964)	*Generation X (1965–1977)*	*Generation Y (1978–1984)*
Uses technology as necessary tool	Techno-savy	Techno-savy
Tolerates teams but values independent work	Teamwork very important	Teamwork very important Culturally diverse
Appreciates hierarchy	Dislikes hierarchy	Dislikes hierarchy
Strong career orientation	Strives for work/life balance but will work long hours for now	Strives for work/family balance but will work long hours for now
More loyalty to organization	Loyalty to own career and profession	Belief in informality Wants to strike it rich quickly Highly regards start-up companies
Favors diplomacy	Candid in conversation	Candid in conversation
Favors old economy	Appreciates old and new economy	Prefers the new economy
Expects a bonus based on performance	Would appreciate a signing bonus	Expects a signing bonus

Source: Several of the ideas in this table are from Robert McGarvey, "The Coming of Gen X Bosses," *Entrepreneur,* November 1999, pp. 60–64; Joanne M. Glenn, "Teaching the Net Generation," *Business Education Forum,* February 2000, pp. 6–14; Charlene Marmer Solomon, "Ready or Not: Here Come the Kids," *Workforce,* February 2000, pp. 62–68; Chris Penttila, "Generational Gyrations," *Entrepreneur,* April 2001, pp. 102–103.

Many key values are also learned through religion and thus become the basis for society's morals. A basic example is that all religions emphasize treating other people fairly and kindly.

Clarifying Your Values

The values you develop early in life are directly related to the kind of person you are now and will be and the quality of relationships that you form.[10] Recognizing this fact has led to exercises designed to help people clarify and understand some of their own values. Value-clarification exercises ask you to compare the relative importance you attach to different objects and activities. Self-Assessment Exercise 2–1 gives you an opportunity to clarify your values.

The Stability of Values

Personal values are an important aspect of behavior to the extent that they remain stable for long periods of time. In contrast, if our values change weekly, monthly, or yearly they are not likely to guide our activities. An example of how values guide behavior is that values create needs that can best be satisfied by establishing certain goals. People who value recognition will also have needs for recognition, and they

SELF-ASSESSMENT EXERCISE 2–1

Clarifying Your Values

Directions: Rank from 1 to 20 the importance of the following values to you as a person. The most important value on the list receives a rank of 1; the least important a rank of 20. Use the space next to the two "Other" blanks to include important values of yours that are not on the list.

_____ Having my own place to live
_____ Performing high-quality work
_____ Having one or more children
_____ Having an interesting job and career
_____ Owning a house, condominium, or apartment
_____ Having good relationships with coworkers
_____ Having good health
_____ Watching my favorite television programming
_____ Participating in sports or other pastimes
_____ Being neat, clean, and orderly
_____ Staying current with technology in my field
_____ Being a religious person
_____ Helping people less fortunate than myself
_____ Loving and being loved by another person
_____ Having physical intimacy with another person
_____ Earning a high income
_____ Being in good physical condition
_____ Being a knowledgeable, informed person
_____ Other
_____ Other

1. Discuss and compare your ranking of these values with the person next to you.
2. Perhaps your class, assisted by your instructor, can arrive at a class average on each of these values. How does your ranking compare with the class ranking?
3. Any surprises in the class ranking? Which values did you think would be the highest and lowest?
4. How do you think average ranks for these values would be influenced by a person's culture?

are likely to develop plans and set goals that lead to recognition. For example, a person who values recognition might seek recognition by attempting to win contests.

A person's life stage and circumstances influence which values are dominant at the time. We can expect, for example, that people are likely to value money more at times in their life when they are in greater need of money. Once they earn enough money to meet their needs, people are likely to place more emphasis on other values, such as an appreciation of art and music. Despite the influence of life stage and circumstances on values, the balance of the evidence shows that values tend to be stable, much like personality traits.

One of several studies of the stability of values compared the values of the same people when they were ages 13 and 33. The participants were 94 male and 109 female students who were identified as intellectually gifted (top 1 percent of students). Participants first took a test called "The Study of Values" when they were participating in special educational opportunities for the gifted. Twenty years later they repeated the test, which was mailed to their home. Six dimensions are included in "The Study of Values":

1. Theoretical (dominant value is the discovery of truth).
2. Economic (dominant value is usefulness).

3. Political (dominant value is power and a tendency to desire personal power).
4. Aesthetic (dominant values are form and harmony).
5. Social (dominant value is the altruistic love of others).
6. Religious (dominant value is unity and a tendency to seek to comprehend the cosmos as a whole).

In general, a moderate relationship was found between people's values at ages 13 and 33. A specific finding was that theoretical, economic, aesthetic, and religious values are much more likely to be dominant during adulthood if they were dominant during adolescence. Political and social values were found to be less stable.[11] What about you? How similar to the present do you think your values will be 20 years from today?

The Mesh between Individual and Job Values

Under the best of circumstances, the values of employees mesh with those required on the job. When this state of congruence exists, job performance is likely to be higher. An obvious example would be a person with high integrity working for a company that valued integrity. The values stated by Eastman Kodak Company are representative of the type of values many business firms express in written documents:

- Respect for individual dignity
- Uncompromising integrity
- Trust
- Credibility
- Continuous improvement and personal renewal

Not every business firm claiming to have such values carries them out in practice. As a result, problems are created for some employees. When the demands made by the organization or a manager conflict with the basic values of the individual, the person suffers from **person-role conflict.** The person wants to obey orders but does not want to perform an act that seems inconsistent with his or her values. The situation of one company purchasing another and then consolidating the two firms creates person-role conflict for many workers. Such conflict often occurs when a worker from the acquiring company is told to learn the job of a worker from the acquired company. The first worker knows that after he or she learns the job, the other employee will be terminated. Colin, a purchasing agent, explained this dilemma in these terms:

> I can't recall ever having felt so rotten in my life. I worked at the Texas division of our company. We bought a smaller company in Arkansas. The company asked me to visit the new company and learn the purchasing procedures from Louise, a woman who had been with the company for 20 years. I got to know her. She was a single mom putting two children through school. After I learned her job, she would be fired. She knew the situation too. Here she was teaching me her job so she could be fired. We became friends, and I helped her find a new job by searching on the Internet. One week after the company fired her, she had a new job. I felt like a human being again.

A clash in values between a person and a company also can occur when the company believes that the individual's values fall below the company's standards. For example, a purchasing agent might be dismissed from a company for accepting lavish gifts from a vendor, thereby showing low integrity.

ETHICS AND JOB BEHAVIOR

Values are closely tied in with **ethics,** the study of moral obligations or separating right from wrong. Ethics can also be regarded as the vehicle that converts values into action. You might value a clean environment, and the corresponding ethical behavior is not to place a television set or personal computer in a landfill. Here we approach ethics and job behavior from three perspectives: the extent of ethical problems, causes of ethical problems, and a guide to ethical decision making.

The Extent of Ethical Problems

Ethical problems exist in the workplace, even if the majority of managers and other workers are ethical. According to an analysis by Linda K. Treviño, and Katherine A. Nelson, common ethical problems include lying to customers, job discrimination, sexual harassment, offering or accepting bribes and kickbacks, overstatement of the capability of a product or service, and the use of corporate resources for personal gain.[12] Another ethical problem is reliance on low-paid foreign or domestic labor in order to produce goods at low cost. Low-paid domestic labor usually involves illegal aliens working at well below the minimum wage in factories referred to as sweatshops.

Well-known firms have been accused of profiting from slave labor. For example, the Chun Si Enterprise Handbag Factory in southern China produced Kathy Lee Gifford handbags sold by Wal-Mart stores as well as other handbags sold by Payless ShoeSource Inc. Chun Si was accused of charging workers $15 a month for food and lodging in a crowded dorm, yet paying the workers about $22 per month.[13] Both Wal-Mart and Payless now monitor their suppliers more closely.

Additional data about ethical problems comes from a survey of 2,390 working adults by KPMG, a consulting and advisory group. Among the study highlights were as follows:

- Seventy-six percent of workers say they have witnessed unethical or illegal behavior by coworkers in the past year. The misconduct included theft, harassment and discrimination, lying, mishandling of confidential information, and cutting corners.
- Of those who saw misconduct, 49 percent considered it serious enough to damage public trust in their company if it ever became public knowledge.
- Sixty-one percent suspected that higher-ups caught doing something unethical or illegal would be disciplined less severely than would lower-ranking workers.
- Fifty-three percent of the employees surveyed believed their managers would not protect them from retaliation if they turned in an ethical violator.[14]

Although these findings might suggest that unethical and illegal behavior is on the increase, another explanation is possible. Workers today might be more observant of ethical problems, and more willing to note them on a survey.

Causes of Ethical Problems

To understand ethics in the workplace, it is helpful to analyze the reasons why ethical problems exist. To simplify hundreds of pages of philosophical thought and analysis, ethical problems are created by four possible influences: (1) characteristics of people, (2) characteristics of the environment, (3) the combined influence of people and the environment, and (4) the strength of the relationships between people.[15] (See Figure 2–2.)

Characteristics of People. The bad apple explanation of unethical behavior suggests that people behave unethically primarily because of negative personal characteristics. A person who is dishonest, untrustworthy, and lacking in other virtues therefore will most likely behave unethically when an opportunity presents itself. Such an individual does not have to be placed under pressure by the company to engage in acts such as hiring an incompetent friend or conducting a side business during working hours. People who believe in the bad apple theory would also believe that if people are taught virtues early in life, they will become ethical adults.

Characteristics of the Environment. The bad barrel explanation of unethical behavior suggests that people behave unethically primarily because of negative environmental influences. Both the organization and society exert influences on

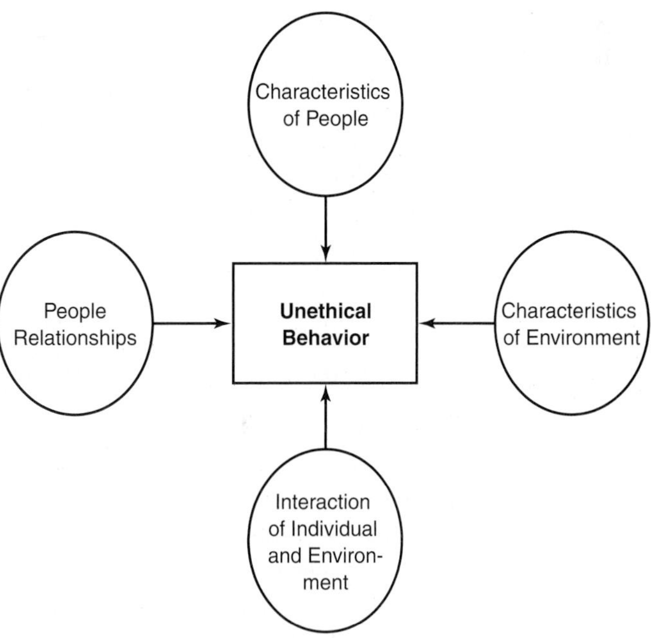

FIGURE 2–2 Causes of Unethical Behavior

the individual to behave unethically. In practice, the bad barrel theory would work this way:

> Top management insists that the company increase sales revenues by 10 percent for the year. Toward the end of the year, the company is falling short of the 10 percent target. The sales manager orders the sales representatives to "book more sales any way you can." To meet her target, an otherwise highly ethical sales representative says to a customer, "Please sign an order for more merchandise than you can use this season. Whatever you have not sold, just ship back to us in January at no cost to you." The sales rep has exceeded her quota, but in an unethical manner that will probably damage the company reputation in the long run.

The bad barrel explanation of unethical behavior is akin to the argument that criminal behavior stems from being raised in an environment with many negative influences. A related argument is that people are driven to criminal behavior out of necessity, such as not having job skills or employment opportunities.

Interaction of Individuals and the Environment. Another explanation of unethical behavior is that it stems from the interaction (combined influence) of the individual and the environment. Neither the undersocialized perspective of individuals acting in isolation nor the view of people being totally obedient to norms and culture is adequate to explain ethical behavior.[16] Instead, the person behaves unethically depending on the circumstances that could trigger certain unethical tendencies. A person with a mild tendency toward being unethical might go for years without behaving unethically. The person is then placed in an environment that encourages unethical treatment of employees and customers. In these circumstances the person might behave unethically—for example, a car rental agent insisting that a customer purchase unnecessary liability insurance.

The Strength of Relationships Between People. A new explanation of the causes of unethical behavior emphasizes the strength of relationships among people as a major factor.[17] Assume that two people have close ties to each other, such as having worked together for a long time or knowing each other both on and off the job. As a consequence they are likely to behave ethically toward each other on the job. In contrast, if a weak relationship exists between two people, either party is more likely to engage in an unethical relationship. The owner of an auto service center is more likely to behave unethically toward a stranger passing through town than toward a long-time customer. The opportunity for unethical behavior between strangers is often minimized because individuals typically do not trust strangers with sensitive information or valuables.

A Guide to Ethical Decision Making

A practical way of improving your ethical decision making is to run contemplated decisions through an ethics test when any doubt exists. A representative test of this nature is the one developed by the Center for Business Ethics at Bentley College as part of corporate training programs. To use this test when faced with an ethical dilemma, ask yourself the following six questions:

1. *Is it right?* This question is based on the theory of ethics that there are certain universally accepted guiding principles of rightness and wrongness, such as "Thou shall not steal."

2. *Is it fair?* This question is based on the theory of justice, implying that certain actions are inherently just and others unjust. For example, it is unjust to fire a high-performing employee to make room for a less competent person who is a personal friend.
3. *Who gets hurt?* This question is based on the notion of attempting to do the greatest good for the greatest number of people.
4. *Would you be comfortable if the details of your decision were reported on the front page of your local newspaper, on television, or on your company's e-mail system?* This question is based on the principle of disclosure.
5. *Would you tell your child (or young family member or relative) to do it?* This question is based on the principle of reversibility, referring to reversing who carries out the decision.
6. *How does it smell?* This question is based on a person's intuition and common sense. For example, bad-mouthing the competition would "smell" bad to a moral person.[18]

A decision that was obviously ethical, such as giving discounts to senior citizens, would not need to be run through the six-question test. Neither would be a blatantly illegal act such as not sending a final paycheck to an employee who quit. But the test is useful for decisions that are neither obviously ethical nor obviously unethical. Among such gray areas would be charging customers based on their ability to pay and developing a clone of a successful competitive product.

The model just presented is a general guide to ethics. Guides also exist for dealing with special situations such as relationships with suppliers, customers, clients, and patients. Table 2–2 presents suggestions for the ethical use of the Internet, including e-mail.

TABLE 2–2
NETIQUETTE TIPS

- Observe the Golden Rule in cyberspace: Treat others as you would like to be treated.
- Act responsibly when sending e-mail or posting messages to a discussion group. Don't use language or photographs that are racist, sexist, or offensive. Be careful when using humor or sarcasm, as they can be misunderstood.
- Respect the privacy of others. Don't read other individuals' e-mail or access their personal files without permission.
- Help maintain the security of your local system and the Internet by taking precautions when downloading files to avoid introducing a virus. Don't engage in hacking. Protect your account number, password, and access codes.
- Respect intellectual property rights. Don't use or copy software you have not paid for. Give proper credit for other people's work—don't plagiarize work from the Net.
- Observe the rules of your school or employer. Most schools have Acceptable Use Policies that outline responsible behavior on the Net.
- Conserve resources. Don't add to network congestion by downloading huge files, sending long-winded e-mail messages, or engaging in spamming.
- Protect your personal safety. Never give personal information, such as your phone number or address, to strangers on the Internet. Report any concerns to a network administrator.

Source: Adapted from "Netiquette Tips," *Keying In,* November 2000, p. 4.

SUMMARY OF KEY POINTS

- Perception, the organization of sensory information into meaningful experiences, influences job behavior. Perceptual problems stem from both a stimulus with an emotional meaning and the mental processes of people. These mental processes, or shortcuts, include selective attention, denial, stereotyping, the halo effect, and projection.
- Perceptual congruence refers to the degree to which people perceive things the same way. High congruence generally leads to more positive consequences for the organization than does low congruence.
- Attribution theory explains how people attribute the causes of behavior. People have a general tendency to attribute their achievements to good inner qualities, whereas they attribute failure to adverse factors within the environment. People attribute causes after gathering information about consensus (comparison among people), distinctiveness (comparison across tasks), and consistency (task stability over time). We attribute behavior to personal factors when we perceive low consensus, low distinctiveness, and high consistency.
- Classical conditioning is the most elementary form of learning. It occurs when a previously neutral stimulus is associated with a natural (unconditioned) stimulus. Eventually, the neutral stimulus brings forth the unconditioned response. For example, a factory whistle blown just prior to the lunch break induces employees to salivate and experience hunger pangs.
- Operant conditioning (or instrumental learning) occurs when a person's spontaneous actions are rewarded or punished, which results in an increase or a decrease in the behavior. Much of human learning occurs through operant conditioning. The four reinforcement strategies involved in such conditioning are positive reinforcement, negative reinforcement, punishment, and extinction.
- A primary reinforcer is rewarding by itself, while the value of a secondary reinforcer must be learned through association with other reinforcers. A continuous reinforcement schedule rewards behavior each time it occurs, whereas an intermittent schedule delivers a reward periodically.
- Instrumental learning, in the form of shaping, helps people learn a skill one step at a time. At each successful step of the way, the learner receives some positive reinforcement. As the learner improves in the ability to perform the task, more skill is required to receive the reward.
- Two important processes that help in learning complicated skills are modeling and informal learning. Modeling occurs when you learn a skill by observing another person perform that skill. Informal learning is unplanned and occurs in a setting without a formal classroom, lesson plan, instructor, or examination. Informal learning can be spontaneous, or the company might organize the work area to encourage such learning.
- Values are learned in the process of growing up by such methods as modeling. Ranking, or clarifying, your values helps you understand them. A person's life stage and circumstances influence which values are dominant at the time, yet the general trend is for values to be stable over time. Job performance is better

GUIDELINES FOR PERSONAL EFFECTIVENESS

1. After your first attempt at interpreting an object or message, ask yourself, "How accurate is my perception? Which perceptual errors might have made my interpretation inaccurate?" If possible, ask another person for feedback to clarify whether your perception is accurate.
2. A generally effective way of helping people to learn complicated skills is for you to serve as an effective model. At the same time, make sure the learner has the opportunity to observe you. Give positive reinforcement such as encouragement as the person progresses, thereby using both modeling and operant conditioning.
3. Throughout your career you are likely to encounter ethical dilemmas—situations in the gray zone in which it is not clear what course of action is ethically sound. One of many examples would be whether to classify as an actual sale a handshake agreement by a customer to buy your product. When in the gray zone, run your decision through an ethical screening such as the one presented in this chapter.

when the values of employees mesh with those of the organization. When the demands made by the organization conflict with the values of the individual, the person suffers from person-role conflict.

- Ethics are strongly determined by values. Many ethical problems exist in the workplace, with one study suggesting that about one-half of all employees engage in unethical or illegal acts. Ethical problems are created by (1) characteristics of people, (2) characteristics of the environment, (3) the combination of individuals and the environment, and (4) the strength of the relationships between people. When faced with an ethical dilemma, you are advised to put the contemplated decision through an ethics test.

DISCUSSION QUESTIONS AND ACTIVITIES

1. Give an example of where it *is* true that "perception is more important than reality."

2. Give an example of where it is *not* true that "perception is more important than reality."

3. Provide an example of knowledge or skill that you have learned *implicitly,* or without a conscious intention to learn.

4. What steps can a company take to encourage *informal learning* among employees?

5. How do the following statements by students illustrate a key finding of attribution theory? "I earned an A in my information systems course." "The instructor gave me a D in my applied psychology course."

6. Give an example from your own life in which a value of yours led to the formation of a goal.

7. Why might it be true that people with strong work values live longer than people with weaker work values?

8. According to several studies, business firms that practice high ethics are generally more profitable than those with low ethics. What explanation can you offer for this finding?

9. A dominant trend in industry since the late 1980s has been to lay off workers during business downturns in order to decrease costs and improve profits (known as downsizing). What is your opinion of the ethics of downsizing?

10. Ask an experienced supervisor, team leader, or manager how he or she trains workers. Relate the answer to learning theory.

REFERENCES

1. Donald D. Hoffman, *Visual Intelligence: How We Create What We See* (New York: Norton, 1998), p. 25.
2. Ricky W. Griffin, "Effects of Work Redesign on Employee Perceptions, Attitudes, and Behaviors: A Long-term Investigation," *Academy of Management Journal,* June 1991, p. 42.
3. John B. Miner, *Organizational Behavior: Performance and Productivity* (New York: Random House, 1988), p. 101.
4. Harold H. Kelley, "The Process of Causal Attribution," *American Psychologist,* February 1973, pp. 107–128.
5. John W. Donahoe and David C. Palmer, *Learning and Complex Behavior* (Boston: Allyn & Bacon, 1994), p. 2.
6. Michael A. Stadler and Peter A. Frensch (eds.), *Handbook of Implicit Learning* (Thousand Oaks, CA: Sage, 1998).
7. Karen Frankola, "Why Online Learners Drop Out," *Workforce,* October 2001, p. 54.
8. "Assessing Online Learning: Defining the Efficacy of Online Learning," *Keying In,* March 2001, p. 3.
9. Frankola, "Why Online Learners Drop Out," p. 54.
10. David C. McClelland, "How Motives, Skills, and Values Determine What People Do," *American Psychologist,* July 1985, p. 815.
11. David Lubinski, David B. Schmidt, and Camilla Persson Benbow, "A 20-Year Stability Analysis of the Study of Values for Intellectually Gifted Individuals from Adolescence to Adulthood," *Journal of Applied Psychology,* August 1996, pp. 443–451.
12. Linda K. Treviño and Katherine A. Nelson, *Managing Business Ethics: Straight Talk and How to Do It Right* (New York: Wiley, 1995), pp. 71–75.
13. Dexter Roberts and Aaron Bernstein, "A Life of Fines and Beatings," *Business Week,* October 2, 2000, p. 122.
14. Brian Sharp, "Reports of Unethical Behavior on the Increase," Gannett News Service, June 12, 2000.
15. Daniel J. Brass, Kenneth D. Butterfield, and Bruce C. Skaggs, "Relationships and Unethical Behavior: A Social Network Perspective," *Academy of Management Review,* January 1998, pp. 14–31.
16. Brass, Butterfield, and Skaggs, "Relationships and Unethical Behavior," p. 14.
17. Brass, Butterfield, and Skaggs, "Relationships and Unethical Behavior," p. 17.
18. James L. Bowditch and Anthony F. Buono, *A Primer on Organizational Behavior,* 5th ed. (New York: Wiley, 2001), p. 4.

AN APPLIED PSYCHOLOGY CASE PROBLEM

The Stunning Plaque

Paul Anderson, a human resources director, was asked by a magazine reporter his opinion of Generation X managers. Anderson explained that based on his observations, most Gen X managers emphasized a team style of management. The journalist thanked Anderson for his comments. About six months later, the journalist's article containing a one-line quote from Anderson appeared in *Entrepreneur* magazine. Anderson was pleased to be quoted in a national magazine, and appreciated the courtesy of *Entrepreneur* sending him a copy of the magazine in which he was quoted. About 30 days after the article appeared, Anderson received the following letter on high-quality stationery at his office:

Date
State License Documentation
22817 Ventura Blvd. Section 858
Woodland Hills, CA 91364

Dear Mr. Anderson,

Congratulations! Your write-up in *Entrepreneur Magazine* is most impressive. You are among a select few that have had the privilege of being published in a major publication. Accomplishments like yours should be displayed proudly.

At State License Documentation we do exactly that. We professionally mount your article in a museum quality plaque preserving your feature for a lifetime. It can then be displayed in your home, office, or conference room. However, your plaque is more than a decoration . . . it connotes respect and credibility.

State License Documentation has earned a reputation of producing the highest quality plaques in the industry today. Our plaques have been made for Fortune 500 companies, government dignitaries, celebrities, most medical and law universities, and numerous corporate executives.

Enclosed please find information on how you can receive a free graphic rendering of your own custom plaque. The rendering allows you to preview your plaque before you order. Order risk free. All plaques are sold on a 100% satisfaction guarantee basis. We look forward to hearing from you and preparing your free custom layout.

Warmest Regards,

R W
Robert B. West
Executive Vice President

The accompanying sheet to the letter includes the following information:

YES!!!

Send me my FREE complimentary graphic layout of what my article/write-up would look like plaqued in a museum quality wall display.

Please provide us with the information requested so we can FAX or mail your custom layout to you. The layout includes a graphic rendering with the plaque's dimensions, color trim combinations, pricing, shipping, and ordering information.

SLD is not affiliated nor endorsed by any newspaper, journal, magazine, or any other publication.

1. What ethical issues do you perceive in this firm calling itself "State License Documentation"?
2. What might be a more accurate name to give the firm selling the plaques?
3. What perceptions are most people likely to have when they receive an envelope in the mail addressed "State License Documentation"?
4. What is the true nature of the business of SLD? (What business are they really in?)

AN APPLIED PSYCHOLOGY CASE PROBLEM

The Socially Conscious Restaurant

You work as a management trainee for a large chain of family restaurants. The vast majority of your customer base are family people seeking to dine at restaurants where servers deliver the food, yet who are not willing to pay for luxury dining. Your restaurants serve breakfast, lunch, and dinner. Some of the restaurants in your chain are company owned, and many others are franchise operations. A home-office executive says to you one day, "Let's do something good for society. We'll find 25 people recently released from prison, or on parole, who are likely to have a difficult time finding employment. We'll put them to work in one of our company-owned restaurants. You'll be the manager in this new restaurant. Your only employees will be these ex-convicts."

You ask, "Which ex-cons shall we hire?" The executive answers, "The first 25 to show up for the job. First come, first hired. I don't care about appearance, schooling, intelligence, literacy, work experience, reasons for conviction, or length of imprisonment. Just put them on the payroll, train them, and run a first-class, profitable restaurant."

You then ask, "Hold on. If I cannot carefully choose the kitchen staff and the dining staff, how can I be held accountable for profits? You would be stacking the deck against me."

The executive responds, "I have carefully selected you to carry out an experiment that shows the strong social consciousness of our firm. I know you can figure out how to run a restaurant without relying on conventional employees. Please don't start making excuses in advance."

1. What will be your biggest challenge in this assignment?
2. What cautions should you exercise in using general learning principles in training your employees?
3. How might the values and ethics of your staff have a negative impact on the operations of the restaurant, and how can you handle this problem?

A BUSINESS PSYCHOLOGY ROLE PLAY

Pondering an Ethical Dilemma

Five class members assume the role of the top-level management team for a major manufacturer of sports apparel, located in the United States. One member of the team has a proposal in hand from a manufacturing broker in Asia. The broker says that he has found a clothing factory in Pakistan that can produce your line of ski apparel and bathing suits at a substantial cost savings. His proposal explains that the wage rates for child labor in his factory are the equivalent of about 26 cents per hour. Furthermore, the children are not paid overtime, and they are willing to work about 60 hours per week. Next, the five members of the team discuss the ethics of this possible alliance with the Pakistani firm. By the end of the discussion, arrive at a tentative decision as to what to do next about the proposal.

SUGGESTED READING

Badaracco, Joseph L. Jr. "The Discipline of Building Character." *Harvard Business Review,* March–April 1998, pp. 114–124.

Blanchard, Ken, and O'Connor, Michael. *Managing by Values.* San Francisco: Berrett-Koehler Publishers, 1997.

Boyle, Matther. "The Prying Game." *Fortune,* September 17, 2001, p. 235.

Parker, Martin (ed.). *Ethics & Organizations.* Thousand Oaks, CA: Sage, 1998.

Petrick, Joseph A., and Quinn, John F. *Management Ethics: Integrity at Work.* Thousand Oaks, CA: Sage, 1997.

Steiner, Gerhand. *Learning: Nineteen Scenarios from Everyday Life.* Cambridge, England: Cambridge University Press, 1999.

Tyler, Kathryn. "E-Learning: Not Just for E-Normous Companies Anymore." *HR Magazine,* May 2001, pp. 82–88.

WEB CORNER

www.bubl.ac.uk/link/p/perception.htm (Extensive information about human perception.)

www.depaul.edu/ethics1.html (The Online Journal of Ethics.)

www.dii.org (Defense Industry Initiative on Business Ethics and Conduct.)

www.infed.org/biblio/inf-lrn.htm (Information about various types of informal learning.)

CHAPTER 3

MAJOR SOURCES OF INDIVIDUAL DIFFERENCES

Learning Objectives

After reading and studying this chapter and doing the exercises, you should be able to

1. Understand how individual differences affect job performance.
2. Describe the nature of intelligence, including practical intelligence, multiple intelligences, and emotional intelligence.
3. Describe how to make effective use of your mental ability.
4. List some skills that account for individual differences in job performance.
5. Identify major personality factors and traits and describe how they relate to job performance.
6. Explain how cultural factors can lead to individual differences in job performance.

Applied psychology began with the awareness that how people perform on the job is influenced by **individual differences**—variations in response to the same situation based on personal characteristics. A study of individual differences is as vital today as it was at the turn of the last century. A person's basic traits and characteristics have a profound influence on a person's job behavior. The situation in which the person works is also important, but the person often influences the situation. Job behavior is always the combined influence of the person and the situation or setting.

The equation expressing the relationship just mentioned reads $B = f(P \times E)$. B stands for behavior, P stands for the person, and E represents the environment.[1] A key implication of this equation is that behavior is determined by the effects of the individual and the environment on each other. For example, a person's tendencies toward impatience might be triggered by working with beginners who have a difficult time understanding the new work procedures. The person is likely to be more patient when working with more experienced or brighter workers. Have you ever noticed that some work environments, and some people, bring out your best traits? Your worst traits?

In this chapter we examine some aspects of human nature that have a direct bearing on how well people perform in their jobs and careers. Among the topics discussed will be mental ability and intelligence, enhancing your ability to learn, skills and job performance, individual differences and personality, sex roles and individual differences, and culturally based individual differences. First, however, we look at the general idea of how individual differences affect work behavior.

IMPLICATIONS OF INDIVIDUAL DIFFERENCES ON THE JOB

It is widely recognized that individual differences exist and that organizations must pay attention to these differences to stay competitive. A well-managed organization would capitalize upon differences among employees by assigning them to work they can perform at their best. Seven illustrative ways in which individual differences have important implications for working with people are noted here.

1. *People differ in productivity.* A general observation about individual differences in productivity is that a small percentage of the workforce contributes most of the results in some types of work. It is often noted, for example, that 20 percent of the sales force produces 80 percent of the sales. (This is an example of the 80–20 principle, which states that 80 percent of the results are produced by 20 percent of activities.)

   A comprehensive analysis of individual differences illustrates the magnitude of human variation in job performance. The researchers synthesized studies involving over 10,000 workers. They found that as jobs become more complex, individual differences have a bigger impact on work output.[2] An outstanding sales representative might produce 100 times as much as a mediocre representative. It contrast, an outstanding sales-order-entry technician might produce only twice as much as a mediocre one. (An industrial sales job is more complex than the work of a sales-order-entry technician.)

2. *People differ in ability and talent.* Factors such as motivation, self-confidence, a favorable appearance, and being politically astute are not sufficient for getting the job done. People also need the right abilities and talents to perform any job well. Ability is a major source of individual differences that influences job performance. A major reason for these differences is that people's brains are not identical. Genetic variations make differences inevitable. Brains are also influenced significantly by cultural opportunities and environmental demands individuals experience in the course of their lives.[3]

3. *People vary in their propensity for achieving high-quality work.* Some people take naturally to striving for high quality because they are conscientious, have a good capacity for being precise, and take pride in their work. Workers who are less conscientious, less precise, and have little pride will have more difficulty for performing work of high quality.

4. *People differ in how much they want to be empowered and involved.* The modern workplace often grants workers authority to make decisions by themselves and to involve them in suggesting improvements. Many workers welcome such empowerment and involvement because they seek self-fulfillment on the job. However, many other workers are not looking for

responsibility and job involvement. Most of their satisfaction derives from family and personal life. As a consequence these individuals prefer jobs that require a minimum of mental involvement and responsibility.

5. *People differ in the style of leadership they prefer and need.* Many individuals prefer as much freedom as possible on the job and can function well under such leadership. Other individuals want to be supervised closely by their manager or team leader. People also vary with respect to the amount of leadership they require. In general, less-competent, less-motivated, and less-experienced workers need more supervision.
6. *People differ in their need for contact with other people.* As a by-product of their personality traits and occupational interest, people vary widely in how much people contact they need on the job to keep them satisfied. Some people can work alone—and even from home—all day and remain highly productive. Others become restless unless they are engaged in business or social conversation with another employee. Sometimes a business luncheon is scheduled more out of a manager's need for social contact than out of a need for discussing job problems.
7. *People differ in their degree of commitment and loyalty to the firm.* Many employees are so committed to their employers that they act as if they were part owners of the firm. As a consequence, committed and loyal employees are very concerned about producing quality goods and services. And they maintain very good records of attendance and punctuality, which helps reduce the cost of doing business. At the other extreme, some employees feel very little commitment or loyalty toward their employer. They feel no pangs of guilt when they produce scrap or when they miss work for trivial reasons.

MENTAL ABILITY AND INTELLIGENCE

Mental ability, or intelligence, is one of the major differences among people that affects job performance. **Intelligence** is traditionally regarded as the capacity to acquire and apply knowledge, including solving problems. Recent approaches to understanding intelligence emphasize the person's ability to adapt to the environment. According to noted authority Robert J. Sternberg, intelligence comprises the mental abilities necessary for adapting to and modifying one's environment.[4] Based on this definition, a person who achieved excellent grades in school would be intelligent, but so would a successful street vendor.

Understanding how intelligence affects job performance has become more complicated because of the growing recognition that people have different types of intelligence. The concept of overall intelligence that helps us solve problems is still important. Recent theories, however, suggest that the different types of intelligence we possess help us solve different types of problems. Here we describe three key approaches to understanding mental ability: the components of traditional intelligence, the triarchic theory of intelligence, and multiple intelligences.

Components of Traditional Intelligence

Intelligence has always been regarded as a complex characteristic. The preponderance of evidence suggests that it consists of a ***g* (general) factor** along with ***s* (special) factors** that contribute to problem-solving ability. The *g* factor represents a person's ability to perform complex mental work, such as abstract reasoning and making analogies. The consensus view of general intelligence (g) is that it sits at the top of a hierarchy of intellectual competencies and processes that support a variety of abilities. (An example of a competency here would be abstract reasoning; a process would include drawing inferences about relationships.) At the next level are groups of verbal and nonverbal abilities (such as working well with numbers) that can be further subdivided into more special abilities such as arithmetic and geometry.[5]

Scores on tests of almost any type (such as math, reading skills, or aptitude for electronic repair) are influenced by g. Furthermore, g correlates more closely with job performance than does any s factor of intelligence, and it also accurately predicts how well workers will do in job training.[6] In addition to representing general intelligence, g is also thought to be an aspect of a healthy nervous system that underlies its readiness to interact with the environment. The nervous system develops this quality during a person's infancy.[7] With a high degree of g the person adapts better to the environment and behaves more intelligently.

Various researchers have identified different s factors contributing to overall mental ability. Table 3–1 lists and defines seven factors that have been consistently noted since the early days of intelligence testing. These seven primary mental abilities include the familiar numerical and verbal. Being strong in any mental aptitude often leads to enjoyment of work associated with that aptitude. Conversely, enjoyment of an activity might lead to the development of an aptitude for that activity.

More intelligent people typically have more diverse sets of specific abilities. People who score in the lower ranges of mental ability tests have not developed those abilities and must use their g for test taking. According to this theory, less intelligent people have relatively more of the g factor—their mental makeup is less diverse.[8]

Mental ability tests have proven useful in predicting academic success and job performance and in understanding the nature of intelligence. (Note that although an IQ test is the best known of mental ability tests, it is but one of many measures of intelligence.) Nevertheless, these tests have received considerable

TABLE 3–1
SPECIAL FACTORS CONTRIBUTING TO OVERALL MENTAL APTITUDE

Verbal comprehension: The ability to understand the meaning of words and their relationship to each other and to comprehend written and spoken information.

Word fluency: The ability to use words quickly and easily, without an emphasis on verbal comprehension.

Numerical: The ability to handle numbers, engage in mathematical analysis, and do arithmetic calculations.

Spatial: The ability to visualize forms in space and manipulate objects mentally, particularly in three dimensions.

Memory: Having a good rote memory for symbols, words, and lists of numbers, along with other associations.

Perceptual speed: The ability to perceive visual details, to pick out similarities and differences, and to perform tasks requiring visual perception.

Inductive reasoning: The ability to discover a rule or principle and apply it in solving a problem and to make judgments that are logically sound.

Source: These seven factors are from the pioneering work of L. L. Thurstone, *Primary Mental Abilities,* Psychological Monographs, 1, 1938.

criticism. Many people believe that mental ability tests are biased against people with limited opportunity for good education. Another criticism is that people whose cultural values are opposed to learning will perform poorly on these tests.

A striking occurrence in mental ability testing of the traditional type is the steady worldwide rise in test scores. Mean (average) IQ scores have increased more than 15 points in the last 50 years, and the gain appears to be increasing. The gains in test scores apply to a wide range of cultural groups. A major factor contributing to the gains in mental ability might be improved nutrition. It has been found, for example, that children who are malnourished or infected with parasites score lower on standard tests of cognitive ability. Such children lack the energy to engage in the strenuous mental activity required in mental ability testing. Gains in mental ability might also be attributed to experience and comfort with testing and improved child-rearing practices.[9]

Triarchic Theory of Intelligence

Many people, including psychologists, are concerned that the traditional way of understanding intelligence inadequately describes mental ability. An unfortunate implication of intelligence testing is that intelligence is largely the ability to perform tasks related to scholastic work. Thus, a person who scored very high on an intelligence test could follow a software manual but might not be "street smart."

To overcome the limited idea that intelligence involves mostly the ability to solve abstract problems, the **triarchic theory of intelligence** has been proposed. The theory holds that intelligence is composed of three different subtypes: analytical, creative, and practical as shown in Figure 3–1. The analytical subtype is the traditional type of intelligence needed for solving difficult problems and engaging in abstract reasoning. Analytical intelligence is required to perform well in most school subjects. The creative subtype is the type of intelligence required for imagination and combining things in novel ways. The practical subtype is the type of intelligence required for adapting your environment to suit your needs.[10]

The idea of practical intelligence helps explain why a person who has a difficult time getting through school can still be a successful businessperson, politician, or athlete. Practical intelligence incorporates the ideas of common sense, wisdom,

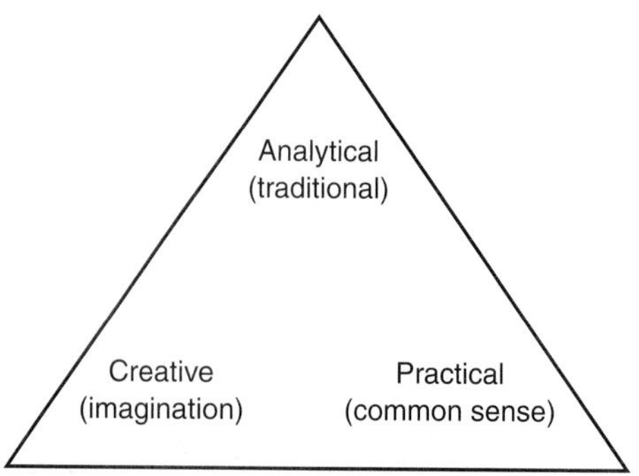

FIGURE 3–1 The Triarchic Theory of Intelligence
A person with effective intelligence would have a combination of analytical, practical, and creative intelligence, and know when to emphasize each type.

and street smarts. The concept of practical intelligence also helps explain why some brilliant people commit foolish acts, as suggested by the following anecdote:

> An 18-year-old high school dropout in New Rochelle was charged with computer tampering for allegedly hacking into the internal computers of America Online and altering programs. Jay Satiro was arrested and his computer confiscated after AOL officials contacted authorities. A complaint filed against Satiro said the teenager altered AOL data and programs that would cost about $50,000 to repair.
>
> "Jay's a genius, but his common sense is a little low," said his 15-year-old brother, Bobby. First-degree computer tampering carries a maximum sentence of five to 15 years in prison.[11]

One reservation about practical intelligence is the implication that people who are highly intelligent in the analytical sense are not practical thinkers. In truth, most executives and other high-level workers score quite well on tests of mental ability.[12]

An important implication for research about practical intelligence centers on problem-solving ability and age. Academic problem-solving ability (analytical intelligence) may decline from early to late adulthood. However, the ability to solve problems of a practical nature is maintained or even increased through late adulthood. As people become older, they compensate for declining raw mental energy by focusing on things they can do well.

Multiple Intelligences

Another approach to understanding the diverse nature of mental ability is the **theory of multiple intelligences,** developed by Howard Gardner. He regards intelligence as a capacity for processing information of a particular type. At the same time, intelligence is much broader than the behaviors evaluated in a typical mental test. According to Gardner's theory, people know and understand the world in distinctively different ways, or look at it through different lenses. Individuals possess the following eight intelligences, or faculties, in varying degrees:

1. *Linguistic:* Enables people to communicate through language, including reading, writing, and speaking.
2. *Logical-mathematical:* Enables individuals to see relationships between objects and solve problems, as in calculus and statistics.
3. *Musical:* Gives people the capacity to create and understand meanings made out of sounds and to enjoy different types of music.
4. *Spatial:* Enables people to perceive and manipulate images in the brain and to re-create them from memory, as is required in making graphic designs.
5. *Bodily/kinesthetic:* Enables people to use their body and perceptual and motor systems in skilled ways such as dancing, playing sports, and expressing emotion through facial expressions.
6. *Intrapersonal:* Enables people to distinguish among their own feelings and acquire accurate self-knowledge.
7. *Interpersonal:* Makes it possible for individuals to recognize and make distinctions among the feelings, motives, and intentions of others, as in managing and parenting.
8. *Naturalist:* Enables a person to be sensitive to similarities and differences between nonhuman living things, and, more generally, to deal with the biological world.

Your profile of intelligences influences how you will best learn and to which types of jobs you are best suited. Gardner believes that it is possible to develop these separate intelligences through concentrated effort. However, any of the intelligences will fade if not used.[13] These separate types of intelligence might also be perceived as different talents or abilities. Having high general problem-solving ability would contribute to high standing on each of the eight intelligences.

Emotional Intelligence

Brain research has combined personality factors with practical intelligence, indicating that how effectively people use their emotions has a major impact on their success. The topmost layers of the brain govern analytical intelligence, such as used in developing a marketing plan. The innermost areas of the brain govern emotion, such as dealing with anger when frustrated by a bureaucratic regulation.

Emotional intelligence refers to qualities such as understanding one's own feelings, empathy for others, and the regulation of emotion to enhance living. This type of intelligence has to do with the ability to connect with people and understand their emotions, as well as responding to nonverbal signals such as voice tone. Workers with high emotional intelligence would be able to engage in such behaviors as sizing up people, pleasing others, and influencing them. Emotional intelligence covers many different aspects of behavior, and has been studied from several perspectives. Five key factors included in emotional intelligence are as follows:[14]

1. *Self-awareness:* The ability to understand your moods, emotions, and needs as well as your impact on others. Self-awareness also includes using intuition to make decisions you can live with happily. (A key objective of Chapter 4 is to help the reader become more self-aware.)
2. *Self-regulation:* The ability to control impulsiveness, calm down anxiety, and react with appropriate anger to situations. The right degree of self-regulation helps prevent a person from throwing temper tantrums when activities do not go as planned. Being low on self-regulation is a quick path to failure in most jobs.
3. *Motivation:* A passion to work for reasons in addition to money or status, such as finding joy in the task itself. Motivation in this context also involves resilience, or drive, persistence, and optimism when faced with setbacks.
4. *Empathy:* The ability to respond to the unspoken feelings of others. Also, the skill to respond to people according to their emotional reactions. Empathy is important because so many interactions on the job involve dealing with the emotional responses of others.
5. *Social skill:* Competency in managing relationships and building networks of support, and having positive relationships with people.

Many training programs are designed to improve emotional intelligence, but the earlier that people develop skills in handling emotional reactions the better. This is true because the key to emotional intelligence lies in the way the brain is programmed in childhood. People learn most of their emotional habits when they are young, but can still learn to improve inappropriate responses later in life.[15]

Emotional intelligence emphasizes the importance of being practical minded and having effective interpersonal skills to succeed in the workplace. The message is an old one: both analytical skills and interpersonal skills are required for success!

Heredity versus Environment in Determining Intelligence

An intense political and scientific debate over the years has been whether traditional intelligence is attributable mostly to genetics (nature) or the environment (nurture). The conservative political position is that genetics play a major role, and therefore special programs to enhance intelligence are mostly ineffective. The liberal position is that environment plays a major role in determining intelligence, and that people with low intelligence are the product of an impoverished environment. Enriched experiences would therefore help people gain in analytical intelligence. (Debates about nature versus nurture and emotional intelligence would relate more to the role of genetic factors in the development of personality.)

A major argument for the inheritability of intelligence is that when monozygotic (identical) twins are reared together or apart they tend to have similar intelligence test scores. In contrast, when dizygotic (fraternal) twins are reared together or apart they differ more in intelligence than do monozygotic twins. Futhermore, adoptive parents and their adopted children differ more in intelligence than do biological parents and their biological children. The counterargument is that when either type of twins lives together, they are closer in intelligence than twins reared apart. One of many arguments that intelligence is influenced substantially by environment is that staying in school tends to elevate a person's IQ. Each year of school completed leads to an average gain of 3.5 IQ points.[16]

Based on hundreds of studies it appears that heredity and environment contribute about equally to intelligence.[17] This finding does not mean that a person with very limited mental capacity can be made superintelligent through specialized training. Nor does it mean that a naturally brilliant person does not need a mentally stimulating environment.

ENHANCING YOUR ABILITY TO LEARN

In Chapter 2 we explained how people learn. Here we look at principles of learning that will help you make good use of your intelligence in school and on the job. In addition, we look at the closely related topics of how people keep their memories sharp over a lifetime, and learning styles.

Principles of Learning

The principles of learning described in the following paragraphs are based on hundreds of experiments and are widely used in school systems and training programs and by serious students.

1. *Concentrate.* Not much learning takes place unless you concentrate carefully on what you are learning. Concentration is basically thinking. Many failures in school are due more to poor concentration than to low mental ability. Concentration improves your ability to do both mental and physical tasks.
2. *Use motivated interest.* You learn best when you are interested in the problem facing you. If your answer is "This subject bores me" or "So far I don't know what interests me," this principle still applies. In any situation, you will probably be able to find something of interest to you. Look for some

relationship between the information at hand and your personal welfare. For instance, as you read this chapter you might say to yourself, "Where do I fit in? What is my mental makeup?", and so on.

3. *Use selectivity.* William James, the famous philosopher and psychologist, said, "The essence of genius is to know what to overlook." You cannot learn everything brought to your attention in school or on the job. Be selective. Try to determine which is the most important. Your course instructor will often alert you to the most important information in a course. Your boss will often alert you to the most important parts of your job.
4. *Intend to remember.* We often do not remember something because we did not intend to commit it to memory. Many executives are particularly effective at remembering names of employees and customers. When one executive was asked how she could commit so many names to memory, she replied, "I look at the person, listen to the name, and try hard to remember." The next time you travel by car to a sporting event or concert at a large stadium, try hard to remember where the car is parked, such as saying to yourself, "We parked in section H2." Your chances of finding your car will increase substantially.
5. *Practice and rehearse the new material.* Those of you who have studied a foreign language or used new software are well aware of how important practice is for learning. Very little learning takes place unless you practice the new skill or rehearse the new knowledge. If you want to retain the information for just a minute or two, the most effective device is rote rehearsal. You recite the information to yourself silently or out loud, several times. By using rote rehearsal constantly, you ensure that information is stored in short-term memory almost indefinitely, providing you intend to learn.

   For longer-term retention, it is usually necessary to use elaborative rehearsal—relating something to information we already know. Suppose you encounter the term *intranet* in relation to information systems. You decide to store the word in long-term memory because it seems important. (*Intranet* refers to an information system within an organization, as opposed to the worldwide *Internet.*) You therefore make the association of an internal network because *intra* reminds you of *intravenous* feeding, which involves putting a needle inside the vein.
6. *Use meaningful organization.* When you have to learn large batches of information, the best method is to organize it into chunks that make sense to you. For instance, in studying portions of this book, you might make such arbitrary groupings as "Ideas I can use for self-development" versus "Ideas that can help me deal with other people."
7. *Acquire the right background.* The more you know about a subject, the easier it is to acquire new information. Knowledge gives you certain "hooks" on which to hang new information. If your hobby is studying antique automobiles, it will be easy for you to learn the names and identifying information about the next generation of automobiles.
8. *Reflect on what you have learned.* Current research indicates that if you think carefully about what you have learned, your retention of the information increases. The idea is to step back from the experience to ponder carefully and persistently its meaning to you.[18] After participating in a team development exercise involving white-water rafting, a person might reflect,

"What did I really learn about being a better team player? How was I perceived by my teammates in the rubber raft? Did they even notice my contribution? Or did they think I was an important part of the team success?"

9. *Get feedback on your progress.* A fundamental principle of learning is that people acquire knowledge better when they receive feedback on their progress. As soon as possible after learning a new skill, try it out. Feedback is thus closely linked to practice and rehearsal. Assume that you read, or are told, how to download a file from the Internet to the hard drive on your computer. If you attempt the skill immediately thereafter—and it works—your learning will be enhanced. Feedback also provides motivation, so you will be energized to look for more Internet files to download.

Keeping Your Memory Sharp

Almost everyone experiences some memory loss with aging, and this slight impairment in memory can begin as early as the 30s. Typically, the decrease in memory efficiency begins in the mid-40s or early 50s. A major contributor to memory loss is a decrease in the efficiency of brain cells. In normal aging, people suffer from a "tip-of-the-tongue" loss, such as not being able to remember the name of the movie they saw four months ago. Such a decrease in efficiency is not the same as Alzheimer's disease, in which people lose names of common objects such as "brick" or "ballpoint pen," or of family members.

Another major contributor to memory loss once human beings reach age 50 is the shrinking of the hippocampus, the portion of the brain responsible for creating, storing, and accessing new information. As a result, the brain's ability to process information slows, leading to common mistakes such as missing keys, wallets, and handbags.[19]

Short-term memory is likely to be much more affected by aging than is long-term memory. This explains why some people in their 70s might be able to provide details of their childhood but cannot recall a news story they watched on television three hours ago. A major contributor to short-term memory loss is that so much brain power is consumed in multitasking, or coping with so many responsibilities at once. Many people in their 40s, for example, hold a full-time job, have family responsibilities, are attending school part-time, and are constantly adapting to new technology.[20]

The reasons surrounding memory loss are complex, and some memory loss with aging is almost inevitable. Therefore, it is not realistic to think that a handful of techniques can entirely reverse memory loss. Nevertheless, certain steps to combat memory loss are backed by extensive research. Consider the following concepts and techniques to preserve your memory:[21]

- **Use it or lose it.** People who continue to stretch their minds with new learning suffer much less memory loss than people who minimize intellectual challenge. Many famous scientists, professors, financiers, politicians, movie producers, and athletic coaches are people in their 70s.
- **Be well organized.** People who carefully organize their work areas and personal items can compensate for short-term memory loss. For example, if you have one place for leaving your keys, wallet, or handbag, you are less likely to misplace such items. Concentrating on one activity at a time not only facilitates learning, it also helps ward off memory loss.

- **Exercise regularly.** Physical exercise builds both the body and the mind simultaneously. An extensive study showed that women who walk regularly are less likely to experience the memory loss and other declines in mental functioning associated with age. Researchers tracked 5,925 women age 65 and older, and then studied them again six to eight years later. About 25 percent of the women who walked the least had a significant decline in mental ability test scores, compared with only 17 percent of the most active groups. Burning calories in other ways, such as tennis or golf, also had a positive effect on cognitive abilities.
- **Practice memory improvement techniques.** Memorization techniques such as making visual associations between new ideas and familiar objects and immediately rehearsing new material help combat memory loss. So does writing down important dates, and to-do lists. The techniques found in books and courses about memory improvement work well if you remember to use them!
- **Take food supplements associated with memory preservation.** Many food supplements are available that are backed by claims of preserving the brain and improving memory. Antioxidants, particularly vitamin E, are a leading protective agent against neuron damage. (An antioxidant combats the harmful effects of oxidation on human tissue.) Impressive claims have also been made for ginkgo biloba, a brain pill for aging memories, concentration, absentmindedness, confusion, dizziness, and Alzheimer's disease.

In addition to the techniques and food supplements just listed, drugs and hormones have been developed that show promise of slowing down mental deterioration associated with age. An example is that a number of anti-inflammatory drugs, including arthritis drugs, are being tested to see if they reduce brain inflammation, another cause of neuron damage and death. No matter how successful these drugs, it will still be important to combat memory loss through the application of techniques of learning.

Learning Styles

Another strategy for making the best use of your mental ability is to recognize your **learning style,** or the way that you learn the best. Some people, for example, acquire new material best through passive learning. Such people quickly acquire information through studying texts, manuals, and magazine articles. They can juggle images in their minds as they read about abstract concepts such as the law of gravity, cultural diversity, or customer service. Others learn better by doing rather than studying, such as those who learn best about customer service by dealing with customers in many situations.

Another key dimension of learning styles is whether you learn best working alone or cooperatively, such as in study groups. Learning by yourself allows for more intense concentration, and you can proceed at your own pace. Learning in groups and through classroom discussion allows you to exchange viewpoints and perspectives. Another advantage of cooperative learning is that it is more likely to lead to changes in behavior. Assume your instructor holds group discussions about individual differences based on culture. You are more likely to respond to such differences on the job than if you only studied these differences by yourself.

Another aspect of learning style is an individual's **cognitive style,** or the characteristic mode of functioning individuals show in their perceptual and intellectual activities. If you understand your cognitive style, you can learn better by emphasizing your preferred style when learning. A large number of cognitive styles have been identified, but most of them center around the basic dimension of **reflectivity-impulsivity,** or the tempo a person uses in approaching a problem.[22]

Reflectivity is the tendency to ponder and reflect on the various alternatives to a problem or the various explanations for an event taking place. People who are reflective stop and think before beginning a task or making a decision. Reflective people also invest time in evaluating their options. Assume that a reflective person is faced with a task of learning how to operate a digital camera. He or she would first read the manual carefully before attempting to use the camera. *Impulsivity* is the tendency to respond impulsively without pausing to think. Impulsive people offer solutions to problems without carefully evaluating options. The impulsive person would most likely grab the new digital camera and start pressing all the buttons. The manual would be consulted only if the person were stuck.

The link between reflectivity-impulsivity and learning style is that reflective people absorb information carefully and deliberately. In contrast, the impulsive person looks for a quick, overall grasp of the information to be learned. Later on he or she fills in the details. Are you reflective or impulsive?

Cognitive style can improve job performance when a person's cognitive style matches the demands of the job. Also, when there is a mismatch between style and the task, performance may not be as good. A study with 396 real estate salespeople investigated which cognitive style would best fit adaptive selling, defined as follows: "The altering of sales behaviors during a customer interaction or across customer interactions based on perceived information about the nature of the selling situation."[23]

The salespersons were classified as *intuitors* versus *sensors.* An intuitor is more the impulsive type because he or she tends to perceive holistic realities, or the overall view. Sensors are more the reflective type because they tend to learn from data and hard facts. It was found that intuitors were more likely to engage in adaptive selling. Adaptive selling led in turn to more of a customer orientation and better self-perceived selling performance. According to the researchers, the intuitive, or impulsive, approach brings insight and originality into the sales situation that is based on deductive logic and customer problem solving. Another aspect of cognitive style investigated was whether the salespersons were *feelers* (emphasis on human factors) versus *thinkers* (emphasis on conventional logic). The feelers were also better at adaptive selling.[24]

SKILLS AND JOB PERFORMANCE

Mental ability can be considered a general skill that contributes to individual differences in performance. Many other skills are also important for accomplishing work. Skills are also the basis for a career. The greater the number of useful skills a person possesses, the greater the chance of securing employment and job advancement. Skills are also another major source of individual differences on the job. People vary widely in such skills as mathematics, keyboarding, selling, and providing customer service.

Figure 3–2 presents a useful way of categorizing skills developed by Julie Griffin Levitt.[25] As you study these skill areas and specific skills, take the opportunity to note your areas of strength. Making these notations may help you appreciate your capabilities and identify areas where training is needed.

Directions: Review the following skill areas and specific skills. In the space provided, write down each one you believe is a strong skill for you. You can also add a specific skill that was not included in the skill area listed at the left.

Skill Area	*Specific Skills*	*A Strong Skill for Me*
Communication	Writing, speaking, knowledge of foreign language, telephone skills, persuasiveness, listening	________
Creative	Originating ideas, thinking up novel solutions	________
Information technology and office	Keyboarding, filing, doing business math, bookkeeping, using spreadsheets, word processing, using database management, Website construction	________
Interpersonal relations	Getting along well with others, being a team player, diplomacy, conflict resolution, understanding others	________
Management	Leading, organizing, planning, motivating others, making decisions, managing time	________
Manual and mechanical	Being mechanically inclined, building, operating, repairing, assembling, installing, driving vehicles	________
Mathematics	Performing math skills, analyzing data, budgeting, using statistical techniques	________
Sales	Persuading others, negotiating, promoting, dressing fashionably	________
Scientific	Investigating, researching, compiling, systematizing, diagnosing, evaluating	________
Service of customers	Serving customers, handling complaints, dealing with difficult people	________
Service of patients	Nurturing, diagnosing, treating, guiding, counseling, consoling, dealing with emergencies	________
Other skill area: ________	____________________	________

FIGURE 3–2 Skills Profile

Source: Abridged and adapted from *Your Career: How to Make it Happen, 2nd edition,* by Julie Griffin Levitt, ©1990. Reprinted with permission of South-Western College Publishing, a division of Thomson Learning. Fax 800 730-2215.

INDIVIDUAL DIFFERENCES AND PERSONALITY

Most job successes and failures are attributed not only to intelligence and technical skills, but also to personality characteristics. Many studies have shown that personality characteristics are related to job performance. The relationship is strongest when a personality trait is related to a person's job description.[26] For example, the trait of extraversion (the technical spelling of extroversion) is a reliable predictor of success in sales.

In the popular sense, the concept of personality is used to evaluate an individual's manner of relating to people. An effective way to insult another person is to say, "Don't ask me to work with him. He has a horrible personality." A psychologist uses the term personality not to make value judgments, but to describe those persistent and enduring behavior patterns of an individual that tend to be expressed in a wide variety of situations. Your personality is what makes you unique as an individual. Your walk, your talk, your appearance, your speech, and your inner values and conflicts all contribute to your personality.

Our discussion of personality emphasizes how individual differences in personality influence job performance and behavior. Toward this end we will describe the five-factor model of personality, along with other key personality traits.

The Five-Factor Model of Personality

Repeated studies have demonstrated that the basic structure of the human personality is represented by five broad factors, or groups of related traits. As described by the **five-factor model of personality,** these factors are neuroticism, extraversion, openness, agreeableness, and conscientiousness.

People develop these factors partially from inborn tendencies and partially from being raised in a particular environment. For example, a person might have a natural tendency to be agreeable. Growing up in an environment in which agreeableness was encouraged would help the person become even more agreeable.

The five-factor model is important for applied psychology because all factors influence job performance. Also, understanding these five factors can help you pinpoint areas for personal development. Although these broad factors are partially genetic, most people can improve their standing on them through self-awareness and self-discipline. The five factors are described in the following list and shown in Figure 3–3.[27]

Many psychologists believe that an individual's personality can be described accurately by his or her standing (high versus low) on the five factors mentioned above.

1. *Neuroticism* reflects emotional instability and identifies people prone to psychological distress and coping with problems in unproductive ways. Traits associated with this personality factor include being anxious, insecure, angry, embarrassed, emotional, and worried. A person of low neuroticism—or high emotional stability—is calm and confident, and usually in control.
2. *Extraversion* reflects the quantity or intensity of social interactions, the need for social stimulation, self-confidence, and competition. Traits associated with extraversion include being sociable, gregarious, assertive,

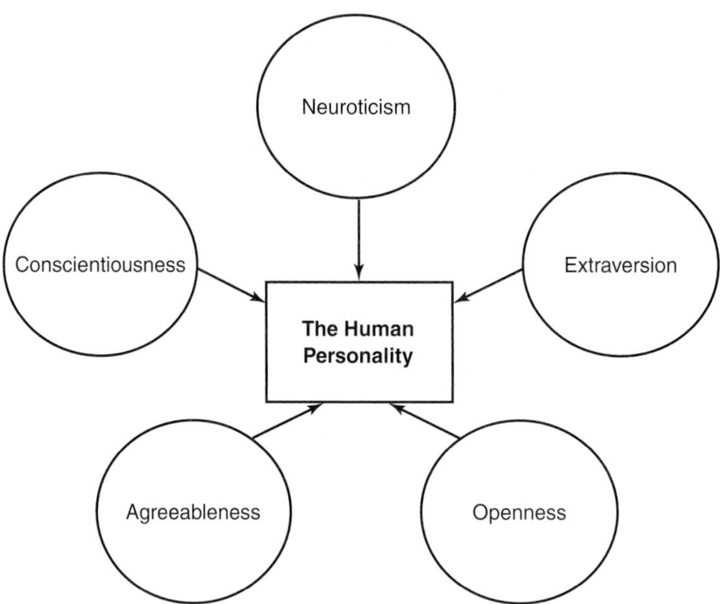

FIGURE 3–3 The Five-Factor Model of Personality

talkative, and active. An outgoing person is often described as extraverted, whereas introverted persons are described as reserved, timid, and quiet. (Note that *extraversion* in everyday language is spelled *extroversion*.)

3. *Openness* reflects the proactive seeking of experience for its own sake. Traits associated with openness include being creative, cultured, intellectually curious, broad-minded, and artistically sensitive. People low on this personality factor are practical, with narrow interests.
4. *Agreeableness* reflects the quality of one's interpersonal orientation. Traits associated with the agreeableness factor include being courteous, flexible, trusting, good-natured, cooperative, forgiving, softhearted, and tolerant. At the other end of the continuum are people who are disagreeable, cold, and antagonistic.
5. *Conscientiousness* reflects organization, self-restraint, persistence, and motivation toward attaining goals. Traits associated with conscientiousness include being hardworking, dependable, well-organized, and thorough. The person low in conscientiousness is lazy, disorganized, and unreliable.

Evidence for the relevance of the five-factor model of personality in understanding human behavior comes from a cross-cultural study involving 7,134 individuals. The five-factor structure of the American personality was also found to hold true for German, Portuguese, Hebrew, Chinese, Korean, and Japanese samples when the personality test questions were translated into each of these languages. Based on this extensive study, it was concluded that personality structure is universal,[28] much like the structure of the brain or the body.

Depending on the job, any one of these personality factors can be important for job success. In fact, conscientiousness is so important it is considered the *g* factor of personality in terms of its ability to predict performance in a wide variety of jobs. According to some researchers, conscientiousness is considered generic to success. Murray R. Barrick and Michael K. Mount reviewed more than 117 studies of personality and job performance. Being conscientious was associated with good performance for all jobs from managerial and sales positions to skilled and semiskilled work. In all cases, workers who were seen as conscientious by themselves and/or by others in the workplace were the more effective employees.

Other personality factors are associated with success in some jobs. For example, extraversion was associated with success in sales and managerial positions.[29] Yet conscientiousness is related to success in all jobs. The small exception is that conscientiousness is less important for jobs requiring considerable innovation and spontaneity.[30] An overly conscientious person might follow rules and regulations so carefully that he or she might fail to be innovative by, for example, deviation from policy to solve an unusual problem.

Although conscientiousness and intelligence are related to job success, they indicate potential and do not guarantee success.[31] Also, being conscientious and intelligent is not sufficient for high job performance in all positions. For most higher-level jobs, specific training, education, and skills are essential for success.

Other Key Personality Traits

The five-factor model of personality is comprehensive, yet many other personality traits that relate to job performance have been studied extensively. Among these are adapting one's behavior to circumstances, or self-monitoring; beliefs about fate being under one's control, or locus of control; degree of honesty; and risk taking and thrill seeking.

Self-Monitoring of Behavior. The **self-monitoring** trait refers to the process of observing and controlling how we appear to others.[32] High self-monitors are pragmatic, and even chameleon-like actors in social groups. They often say what others want to hear. An example would be telling a coworker, "I like that stripe and plaid combination you are wearing" when you think he or she looks dreadful. Very high self-monitoring can lead to an appearance of phoniness. Low self-monitors avoid situations that require them to adopt different outer images. In this way their outer behavior adheres to their inner values. Low self-monitoring often can lead to inflexibility and insensitivity toward others.

Locus of Control. Some people believe they are responsible for the rewards and punishments they receive, while others blame what happens to them on luck and fate. People with an **internal locus of control** are those who believe that fate is pretty much under their control. People with an **external locus of control** believe that external forces control their fate.

In general, internals perform better in technical, professional, and managerial jobs. For instance, a sales representative with an internal locus of control would feel personally responsible for making a quota even if general business conditions were poor. Externals tend to perform better when the work requires compliance and conformity and when pay is not tied to performance. This is true because the person with an external locus of control expects an outside force to control how many rewards he or she receives.[33]

Locus of control is another cross-cultural personality characteristic, suggesting that it is an important part of human nature. A personality questionnaire, including a measure of locus of control, was administered to groups of U.S. men and women, and Indian men and women. The test scores were approximately equivalent for the four groups indicating that locus of control is a relevant personality dimension for Americans and Indians.[34]

Honesty and Dishonesty. An important personality dimension for many jobs is degree of honesty. Dishonest employees engage in such behaviors as stealing merchandise and cash, selling trade secrets, trading stocks on inside information, cheating on time cards, sneaking off from work during regular working hours, falsifying production records, and blaming others for their mistakes. Employee dishonesty is such a problem that several industries—particularly banking, securities, and retailing—use honesty testing. Such testing can take the form of a paper and pencil test or a polygraph (lie detector) test. Federal legislation limits the use of honesty tests to screening employees in highly sensitive occupations such as those dealing with money, legal drugs, and national security.

The trait of honesty, similar to most personality traits, has been shown by research to relate to the five-factor model. Above all, honesty is closely linked to conscientiousness. Honesty also shows a positive relationship to emotional stability and agreeableness. Dishonest people have tendencies toward being undependable, unstable, and disagreeable.[35]

Risk Taking and Thrill Seeking. Some people crave constant excitement on the job and are willing to risk their lives to achieve thrills. The willingness to take risks and pursue thrills is a personality trait that has grown in importance in the high-technology era. According to Marvin Zuckerman, people with this personality trait are sensation-seekers who pursue novel, intense, and complex sensations, and they are willing to take risks for the sake of such experiences.[36] Many people work for employers, start businesses, and purchase stocks with uncertain futures. Both the search of giant payoffs and daily thrills motivate these individuals. A strong craving for thrills may have some positive consequences for the organization, including willingness to perform such dangerous feats as setting explosives, capping an oil well, controlling a radiation leak, and introducing a product in a highly competitive environment. However, extreme risk takers and thrill seekers can create such problems as being involved in a disproportionate number of vehicular accidents, and making imprudent investments.

The study of entrepreneurs provides useful insights on the relevance of risk taking for careers. In general, entrepreneurs score higher on tests of risk taking than do managers within corporations. Furthermore, entrepreneurs with aspirations for growth had a higher propensity to take risks than entrepreneurs who were primarily interested in earning a living.[37]

Do the quiz in Self-Assessment Exercise 3–1 to measure your tendency toward risk taking.

SELF-ASSESSMENT EXERCISE 3-1

The Risk-Taking Scale

Can you look at a person and tell whether he or she is a risk taker? "I've never been able to do it, and I've studied them for more than 30 years," says Frank Farley, a psychologist at Temple University. "You have to scratch the surface and get to know them." Still, there are many clues when you meet them: some risk takers have high energy levels and display impulsiveness. How can you size up your capacity for risk? Here's an informal quiz. Although some of the questions seem obvious, your final score reflects the range of risk that you are comfortable with, not just whether you like taking risks or not. Answer true or false:

	True	*False*
1. I don't like my opinions being challenged.	❑	❑
2. I would rather be an accountant than a TV anchor.	❑	❑
3. I believe that I can control my destiny.	❑	❑
4. I am a highly creative person.	❑	❑
5. I like a lot of varied romantic partners.	❑	❑
6. I don't like trying exotic foods.	❑	❑
7. I would choose bonds over growth stocks.	❑	❑
8. Friends would call me a thrill seeker.	❑	❑
9. I like to challenge authority.	❑	❑
10. I prefer familiar things to new things.	❑	❑
11. I'm known for my curiosity.	❑	❑
12. I would not like to be an entrepreneur.	❑	❑
13. I'd rather not travel abroad.	❑	❑
14. I am easily bored.	❑	❑
15. I wouldn't like to be a stand-up comedian.	❑	❑
16. I've never gotten speeding tickets.	❑	❑
17. I am extremely adventurous.	❑	❑
18. I need a lot of stimulation in my life.	❑	❑
19. I would rather work for a salary than a commission.	❑	❑
20. Making my own decisions is very important to me.	❑	❑

Give yourself 1 point each time your answer agrees with the key. If you score 16–20, you are probably a high risk taker. 10–15: You're a moderate risk taker. 5–9: 0–4: You're a very low risk taker.

1) F	6) F	11) T	16) F
2) F	7) F	12) F	17) T
3) T	8) T	13) F	18) T
4) T	9) T	14) T	19) F
5) T	10) F	15) F	20) T

Source: The lead-in comments are quoted from "We Dare You to Take this Quiz," *Time,* September 6, 1999, p. 36. The quiz is © 1999 by Frank Farley, Ph.D., all rights reserved.

CULTURALLY BASED INDIVIDUAL DIFFERENCES

The culture in which a person is reared influences his or her work behavior.[38] Although culture may be regarded as a group rather than an individual factor, it functions as a source of individual differences. People from different cultural backgrounds may respond quite differently to the same stimulus. For example, workers from large urban areas tend to be more skeptical than people from rural areas.

TABLE 3–2
CULTURAL MISTAKES TO AVOID IN SELECTED REGIONS AND COUNTRIES

EUROPE	
Great Britain	◈ Asking personal questions. The British protect their privacy. ◈ Thinking that a businessperson from England is unenthusiastic when he or she says, "Not bad at all." English people understate positive emotion. ◈ Gossiping about royalty.
France	◈ Expecting to complete work during the French two-hour lunch. ◈ Attempting to conduct significant business during August—les vacances (vacation time). ◈ Greeting a French person for the first time and not using a title such as sir or madam (or monsieur, madame, or mademoiselle).
Italy	◈ Eating too much pasta, as it is not the main course. ◈ Handing out business cards freely. Italians use them infrequently.
Spain	◈ Expecting punctuality. Your appointments will usually arrive 2 to 30 minutes late. ◈ Making the American sign for "okay" with your thumb and forefinger. In Spain (and many other countries) this is vulgar.
Scandinavia (Denmark, Sweden, Norway)	◈ Being overly rank conscious in these countries. Scandinavians pay relatively little attention to a person's place in the hierarchy.
ASIA	
All Asian countries	◈ Pressuring an Asian job applicant or employee to brag about his or her accomplishments. Asians feel self-conscious when boasting about individual accomplishments; they prefer to let the record speak for itself. In addition, they prefer to talk about group rather than individual accomplishment.
Japan	◈ Shaking hands or hugging Japanese (as well as other Asians) in public. Japanese consider these practices to be offensive. ◈ Not interpreting "We'll consider it" as a "no" when spoken by a Japanese businessperson. Japanese negotiators mean "no" when they say, "We'll consider it." ◈ Not giving small gifts to Japanese when conducting business. Japanese are offended by not receiving these gifts.
China	◈ Using black borders on stationery and business cards, because black is associated with death. ◈ Giving small gifts to Chinese when conducting business. Chinese are offended by these gifts.
Korea	◈ Saying "no." Koreans feel it is important to have visitors leave with good feelings.
India	◈ Telling Indians you prefer not to eat with your hands. If the Indians are not using cutlery when eating they expect you to do likewise.
MEXICO AND LATIN AMERICA	
Mexico	◈ Flying into a Mexican city in the morning and expecting to close a deal by lunch. Mexicans build business relationships slowly.
Brazil	◈ Attempting to impress Brazilians by speaking a few words of Spanish. Portuguese is the official language of Brazil.
Most Latin American countries	◈ Wearing elegant and expensive jewelry during a business meeting. Most Latin Americans think people should appear more conservative during a business meeting.

Note: A cultural mistake for Americans to avoid when conducting business in most countries outside the United States and Canada is to insist on getting down to business too quickly. North Americans in small towns also like to build a relationship before getting down to business.

This is one reason that programs designed to offer employees more responsible work tend to fare better in nonurban areas. The internationalization of workplaces has made an awareness of culturally based individual differences more important than ever. For example, a substantial number of sales associate positions in New York City and Los Angeles are held by people from the Far East and Middle East. A retail store manager raised in the United States, who worked in New York City, would therefore have to be sensitive to cultural differences. For example, a sales associate from India might regard the manager as abdicating responsibility if the manager asked the associate for his or her opinion about how to handle a customer problem.

Another major cultural difference in job behavior occurs between Americans and Canadians and Asians. Americans and Canadians are predisposed by culture to welcome confrontation and conflict in the workplace, while Asians tend to avoid confrontation and conflict. This cultural difference helps to explain why Asians often smile even when they strongly disagree with the other person's position on a work issue.

The general principle for handling cultural differences is to be sensitive to their existence. Be aware that culturally based differences in work behavior exist, and be ready to make some adjustments to these differences. A specific example: An employee raised in Taiwan will be more predisposed to accept a manager's authority than an employee from Sweden. Table 3–2 illustrates mistakes, or cultural bloopers, to avoid should you be on assignment in various countries. Some of the same ideas would apply if you were dealing with people from a foreign land in your native land. We will return to the topic of the internationalization of the workplace and cultural diversity at several places in the text.

To practice dealing with individual differences, do Skill-Building Exercise 3–1.

SKILL-BUILDING EXERCISE 3–1

Dealing with Individual Differences

The purpose of this role play is to develop skill in relating to different types of people in a job setting. In each scenario one student assumes the role of the supervisor who needs to achieve high productivity in the department. Another student assumes the role of the group member. Class members not participating in the role play will provide feedback after each scenario is completed.

Scenario 1: Indifferent Worker: The supervisor is having lunch with a group member who lacks enthusiasm for the job. The worker appears to work hard enough to barely meet minimum requirements and frequently asks for direction on even the simplest matters. The supervisor wants to use the lunch together to help figure out the best way to help the worker become a higher performer. In contrast, the worker seems content to use this opportunity to discuss matters unrelated to the job. Conduct a dialogue for about seven minutes.

Scenario 2: Highly Energetic and Productive Worker: The supervisor is having lunch with a group member who is excited about work and takes great pride in being a high producer. The supervisor wants to use the lunch together to help figure out the best approach to sustaining the worker's high performance. Another purpose is to determine whether his or her approach to supervision suits the high performer's preferences. Conduct a dialogue for about seven minutes.

SUMMARY OF KEY POINTS

- Business psychology began with the awareness that individual differences in personal characteristics influence how people perform on the job. Yet job behavior is always the combined influence of the person and the situation, as indicated in the equation $B = f(P \times E)$. (Behavior is a function of the person interacting with the environment or situation.) A study of individual differences is still of major importance today. This chapter concentrates on dimensions of human behavior that have a big impact on job performance, except for the discussion of sex roles.
- The implications of individual differences on the job include the fact that people differ in these ways: (1) how productive they are, (2) their ability and talent, (3) their propensity for high-quality work, (4) their desire for empowerment and involvement, (5) style of leadership they need and prefer, (6) their need for contact with other people, and (7) their degree of commitment and loyalty.
- Mental ability, or intelligence, is one of the major differences among people that affects job performance. From the traditional standpoint, intelligence is composed of a *g* (general) factor along with *s* (special) factors that contribute to problem-solving ability. The best-known special factors are numerical and verbal. In recent years the average IQ scores have been increasing, perhaps related to better nutrition and a variety of cultural factors.
- To overcome the limited idea that intelligence involves mostly the ability to solve abstract problems, the triarchic theory of intelligence has been proposed. The theory holds that intelligence is composed of three different types: analytical, creative, and practical. Practical intelligence incorporates the ideas of common sense, wisdom, and street smarts.
- Mental ability can also be understood in terms of multiple intelligences, which means that people know and understand the world in distinctly different ways. The different intelligences are as follows: linguistic, logical-mathematical, musical, spatial, bodily/kinesthetic, intrapersonal, interpersonal, and naturalist. Your profile of intelligences influences how you will best learn and to which types of jobs you are best suited.
- The concept of emotional intelligence helps explain how emotions and personality factors contribute to success. A worker with high emotional intelligence would be able to engage in such behaviors as sizing up people, pleasing others, and influencing them. Emotional intelligence includes such diverse behaviors as self-awareness, management of feelings, being resilient, and social skill.
- Whether traditional intelligence is mostly attributable to heredity or environment is debated both politically and scientifically. Based on hundreds of studies it appears that heredity and environment contribute about equally to intelligence.
- One way of making good use of your mental abilities is to practice good habits of learning and remembering. Among these habits are (1) concentrate, (2) use motivated interest, (3) use selectivity, (4) intend to remember, (5) practice and rehearse the new material, (6) use meaningful organization, (7) acquire the right background, (8) reflect on what you have learned, and (9) get feedback on your progress.
- Certain concepts and techniques are useful for combating memory loss. These include the following: use it or lose it, be well organized, exercise regularly, prac-

tice memory improvement techniques, and take food supplements associated with memory preservation. Another strategy for making the best use of your mental ability is to recognize your learning style, such as whether you learn best by reading or doing or by studying with others. Knowing your cognitive style such as being reflective versus impulsive, also contributes to effective learning.

- Many other skills, in addition to mental ability, are important for job performance and career building. Among these important skills are communication, creative, interpersonal relations, mathematics, information technology and office, sales, scientific, and customer service.
- Individual differences in personality influence job performance and behavior. Repeated studies have shown that the basic study of personality is represented by five broad factors: neuroticism, extraversion, openness, agreeableness, and conscientiousness. The five-factor model applies in many cultures, suggesting that personality structure is universal. Conscientiousness is related to success in the vast majority of positions. Other key traits related to job performance are self-monitoring of behavior, locus of control, honesty and dishonesty, and risk taking and thrill seeking.
- The culture in which a person is reared influences work behavior. Although culture is a group rather than individual factor, it functions as a source of individual differences. People from different cultures respond quite differently to the same stimulus.

DISCUSSION QUESTIONS AND ACTIVITIES

1. Assume that an organization pays extra careful attention to individual differences in ability. How might this make the organization less democratic?
2. What have you noticed as a major source of individual differences among workers in any positions you have held?
3. Give an example of any person you know who probably has a very high IQ (mental ability) yet a very low EQ (emotional intelligence).
4. If the theory of multiple intelliences is accurate, how might an employer use the theory in selecting workers for positions?
5. At Microsoft Corporation, the software giant, more emphasis is placed on intelligence than on experience when hiring for professional positions. Why might that practice be effective for Microsoft?
6. Identify three jobs for which scoring high on agreeableness would be a major advantage.
7. Identify a job for which scoring high on neuroticism (or low on emotional instability) would not be a particular disadvantage.
8. Draw your own profile as to whether you are high or low on each of the factors in the five-factor model. Ask a family member or friend for his or her assistance in rating you.
9. Why should you have to adjust to cultural differences from another person who is working in your country? Why shouldn't he or she be making the adjustments?
10. Ask an experienced manager his or her opinion about the usefulness of practical intelligence for performing well on the job.

GUIDELINES FOR PERSONAL EFFECTIVENESS

1. If you are an exceptionally good problem solver, it should help you to perform well in most high-level jobs. Remember, however, there are different types of intelligence, such as having good practical intelligence. This is important because most problems in business call for concrete solutions rather than abstract discussions.
2. Dimensions of personality may have as big an impact on your job performance as your skills. It is therefore important to attempt to modify your traits to match job requirements. For example, if you rely too much on external circumstances to control your performance, you might have to develop a stronger take-charge attitude.
3. Your main concern with your basic intelligence should be in making the best use of your capability. The suggestions in this chapter about improving your retention of information should be helpful in this regard. Information presented in other chapters in this book should also help you to make the best use of your intelligence (particularly information about communication skills and work habits).
4. As the workforce continues to become more internationalized, it will help your career to become more sensitive to cultural differences. Sensitivity to such differences will help you to develop good working relationships with people from different cultures. Significant differences in culture can be found from one country to another and within a large country such as the United States.

REFERENCES

1. Kurt Lewin, *A Dynamic Theory of Personality* (New York: McGraw-Hill, 1935).
2. John E. Hunter, Frank L. Schmidt, and Michael K. Judiesch, "Individual Differences in Output Variability as a Function of Job Complexity," *Journal of Applied Psychology,* February 1990, pp. 28–42.
3. Colin Cooper, *Intelligence and Abilities* (New York: Routledge, 1999).
4. Robert J. Sternberg, "The Concept of Intelligence and Its Role in Lifelong Learning," *American Psychologist,* October 1997, p. 1030.
5. Mike Anderson (ed.), *The Development of Intelligence* (Hove, England: Psychology Press, 1999).
6. Malcom James Ree, James A. Earles, and Mark S. Teachout, "Predicting Job Performance: Not Much More than *g*," *Journal of Applied Psychology,* August 1994, pp. 518–524; Orlando Behling, "Employee Selection: Will Intelligence and Conscientiousness Do the Job?" *The Academy of Management Executive,* February 1998, p. 79.
7. Review of Arthur R. Jensen, *The* g *Factor: The Science of Mental Ability* (Westport, CT: Praeger, 1998). *Contemporary Psychology,* April 1999, p. 132.
8. Review of Arthur R. Jensen, p. 132.
9. Uric Nesser, et al. "Intelligence: Knowns and Unknowns," *American Psychologist,* February 1996, p. 96; Jensen, *The* g *Factor,* p. 330.
10. Robert J. Sternberg, *Beyond IQ: A Triarchic Theory of Human Intelligence* (New York: Cambridge University Press, 1985); Bridget Murray, "Sparking Interest in Psychology Class," *APA Monitor,* October 1995, p. 51.
11. "Brother Says Hacker Lacked Common Sense," Rochester, New York, *Democrat and Chronicle,* March 20, 1999, p. 11D.

AN APPLIED PSYCHOLOGY CASE PROBLEM

The Experienced Touch at Heritage Christian Home

Walk into Heritage Christian Home on Yorktown Road in Penfield, New York, and something seems a little older. It's not that the facilities are out of date, or the methods of dealing with the developmentally disabled residents are antiquated, but these days there is a more mature feeling about the staff.

Faced with a tight labor market, homes such as Heritage that serve the developmentally disabled are finding themselves employing an older workforce. A staff job that five years ago might have gone to a recent college graduate might be filled today by a retiree embarking on a second career.

David Loughborough, 65, started working for Heritage at the Penfield home last month. "When you turn 65, there aren't a whole lot of people looking for you," Loughborough said. "But I just wasn't ready to retire."

Bonnie Senkala, 54, spent 30 years at Eastman Kodak Co. before going to work part time for Heritage, a place she "never even heard of" until a friend told her they were hiring. Employed since September, she says she feels right at home. "I feel like the residents relate to me, maybe because I'm the age of their parents," Senkala said.

Loughborough and Senkala work as resident counselors. They help residents with everything from cooking to laundry, cleaning to personal finance. Loughborough and Senkala say they never imagined working in a home for the developmentally disabled. A year ago Heritage wouldn't have expected to hire them.

"Typically three-quarters of our applicants were female, age 22 to 28," said Marisa Geitner, who oversees organizational development at Heritage's 32 homes in the area. Today, 140 of Heritage's 735 employees are over age 40. "A year ago, the company employed only about half as many 40-somethings," said Rod Christian, Heritage's director of development. "The tight labor market in the service industry is only part of the reason," Christian said.

In the late 1990s, state officials launched New York State Cares, a campaign to whittle down the state's 10,000-person waiting list for admission to group homes. In response, many organizations have expanded rapidly, opening more than five homes a year. "There are just more people to hire," said Barbara Wale, chief operating officer for Arc of Monroe County. Wale says her organization is seeing increases in older applicants.

The staffing crunch is forcing service providers to buy more advertising. "We used to just put a classified ad in the paper and we'd get plenty of applications," Wale said. "Now we have to branch out." For the first time, Heritage has spent money on TV and radio ads. The company produced a 10-minute recruiting video shown on local cable access. Arc has gone to the airwaves, also. And Arc and Heritage have started conducting walk-in interviews in their offices.

Officials at Heritage Christian House are not distraught by the graying of their workforce. Christian, the director of development, calls it a plus. "A more mature workforce brings stability and skills with it," he said. "Many older workers also bring parenting skills, for which there are no substitutes," Christian said.

Loughborough thinks his experience rubs off on his often younger bosses. "I feel like I bridge a gap and can serve as an example for some of the people I'm working for," he said.

1. Is the administration at Heritage Christian Home practicing age discrimination by relying heavily on older people to fill their staffing requirements?
2. What does the story about Heritage Home illustrate about differences in job behavior related to demographic differences?
3. What hiring standards should Heritage Home and similar organizations establish when the general unemployment rate increases?
4. What recommendations can you make to homes for the developmentally disabled to improve their recruitment of resident counselors?

Source: David Tyler, "Mature Workers Find New Home: Providers of Care for the Developmentally Disabled Find Older People Fill Staff Needs," (Rochester, New York) *Democrat and Chronicle,* March 7, 2000, p. 1D; www.heritagechristianhome.org/.

AN APPLIED PSYCHOLOGY CASE PROBLEM

Multiple Intelligences in the Office

Liz Russo is the general manager of the Student Loan Division of a major bank. She prides herself on being a modern manager who searches continuously for new ways to manage the student loan business and to manage people. Recently she attended a talk by Harvard university psychologist Howard Gardner given to the management group at the bank. Russo and the other managers listened intently as Gardner explained his theories of intelligence.

The psychologist emphasized that managers must discard the notion that there is only one kind of intelligence. Most of the managers nodded in agreement. Gardner explained that he wants people in charge of managing human resources to recognize that there are at least eight different kinds of intelligence. People with linguistic intelligence are really good at communicating with words. If you have logical-mathematical intelligence, you can deal with abstract relationships like formulating new ideas for products. People with musical intelligence can do wonders with sounds. Those who have spatial intelligence can work well with images and designs.

People who have bodily/kinesthetic intelligence can move their bodies easily, like dancers and athletes. Individuals gifted with intrapersonal intelligence can understand their own feelings well. People with interpersonal intelligence can read other people well. And finally, people with naturalist intelligence can understand and make good use of the environment.

During a lunch following the talk, Russo said to one of the other managers, "What a liberating bunch of thoughts. The way I interpret Dr. Gardner's theories, people who are talented athletes or dancers are just as intelligent as computer whizzes. It's just that they have a different kind of intelligence."

"Why stop there?" responded the other manager. "One of my kids is a great banjo player, but we're wondering if he'll ever make it through high school. His mom and I used to think he was mentally challenged. Now we know his intelligence is the musical type, not the logical type."

Gardner's ideas kept spinning through Russo's mind. She bought a copy of one of his books for each of her managers and asked them all to study the book carefully. Later she scheduled a half-day meeting in a hotel to discuss how to apply the idea of eight human intelligences to the Student Loan Division. Russo said to her management team, "You all seem to agree with the idea that there are eight human intelligences. Now I want us to figure out how to apply Dr. Gardner's theories to make us a more productive business."

Molly Gerbrach, the head of information systems, said with a smirk on her face, "I have a suggestion. If I hire a programmer who proves to be poor at programming, I'll just ask him or her to be the department's official musician!"

"I appreciate the humor, Molly," said Russo, "but now let's get down to business. Let's figure out how to implement these great ideas about different human intelligences."

1. Is Liz Russo being realistic about applying the concept of eight human intelligences to the office setting?
2. Suggest at least two ways in which the theory of eight human intelligences could be applied to improving productivity in the office.

12. Behling, "Employee Selection," p. 79.
13. Howard Gardner, *Intelligence Reframed: Multiple Intelligence in the 21st Century* (New York: Basic Books, 1999); Gardner, *Leading Minds: An Anatomy of Leadership* (New York: Basic Books, 1993).
14. Daniel Goleman, *Working with Emotional Intelligence* (New York: Bantam, 1998); Seymour Epstein, *Constructive Thinking: The Key to Emotional Intelligence* (Westport, CT: Praeger, 1998).

15. Patrick A. McGuire, "Teach Your Children Well—and Early, Goleman Says," *APA Monitor,* October 1998, p. 15.

16. Stephen Ceci, "IQ Intelligence: The Surprising Truth," *Psychology Today,* July/August 2001, p. 50.

17. Saul Kassin, *Psychology,* 3rd ed. (Upper Saddle River, NJ: Prentice Hall, 2001), p. 467; Hans J. Eysenck, *Intelligence: A New Look* (New Brunswick, NJ: Transaction, 1998).

18. Kent W. Seibert, "Reflection-in-Action: Tools for Cultivating On-the-Job Learning Conditions," *Organizational Dynamics,* Winter 1999, p. 55.

19. Catherine Arnst, "How to Keep Your Memory Intact," *Business Week,* October 15, 2001, p. 128E4.

20. Monika Guttman, "Are You Losing Your Mind?" *USA Weekend,* May 16–18, pp. 4–6; Dharma Singh Khalsa and Cameron Stauth, *Brain Longevity* (New York: Warner Books, 1998).

21. Guttman, "Are You Losing Your Mind?", p. 5; Arnst, "How to Keep Your Memory Intact," pp. 128E4–128E6; "Walking Can Keep Female Minds Sharp," *Gannett News Service,* May 20, 2001.

22. Robert J. Sternberg and Elena J. Grigorenko, "Are Cognitive Styles Still in Style?" *American Psychologist,* July 1997, p. 703.

23. Quoted in Roger P. McIntyre, et al., "Cognitive Style as an Antecedent to Adaptiveness, Customer Orientation, and Self-Perceived Selling Performance," *Journal of Business and Psychology,* Winter 2000, p. 180.

24. McIntyre, "Cognitive Style as an Antecedent," p. 190.

25. Julie Griffin Levitt, *Your Career: How to Make it Happen,* 2nd ed. (Mason, OH: South-Western/Thomson Learning, 1990), pp. 11–21.

26. Robert P. Tett, Douglas N. Jackson, and Mitchell Rothstein, "Personality Measures as Predictors of Job Performance: A Meta-Analytic Review," *Personnel Psychology,* Winter 1991, p. 703; Leonard D. Goodstein and Richard I. Lanyon, "Applications of Personality Assessment to the Workplace: A Review," *Journal of Business and Psychology,* Spring 1999, pp. 295, 317.

27. A current description of the meaning of these factors is presented in D. Brent Smith, Paul J. Hanges, and Marcus W. Dickson, "Personnel Selection and the Five-Factor Model: Reexamining the Effects of Applicant's Frame of Reference," *Journal of Applied Psychology,* April 2001, p. 305.

28. Robert R. McRae and Paul T. Costa, Jr., "Personality Trait Structure as a Human Universal," *American Psychologist,* May 1997, pp. 509–516.

29. Murray R. Barrick and Michael K. Mount, "The Big Five Personality Dimensions and Job Performance: A Meta-Analysis," *Personnel Psychology,* Spring 1991, pp. 1–26. Some of these studies are reanalyzed in Goodstein and Lanyon, "Applications of Personality Assessment," p. 295.

30. Beth Azar, "Which Traits Predict Job Performance," *APA Monitor,* July 1995, pp. 30–31.

31. Behling, "Employee Selection: Will Intelligence and Conscientiousness Do the Job?" p. 82.

32. Bernard Asbell, *What They Know About You* (New York: Random House, 1993).

33. John B. Miner, *Organizational Behavior: Performance and Productivity* (New York: Random House, 1988), p. 83.

34. Jai Ghorpade, Keith Hattrup, and James R. Lackritz, "The Use of Personality Measures in Cross-Cultural Research: A Test of Three Personality Scales Across Two Countries," *Journal of Applied Psychology,* October 1999, pp. 670–679.

35. Paul R. Sackett and James E. Wanke, "New Developments in the Use of Measures of Honesty, Integrity, Conscientiousness, Dependability, Trustworthiness, and Reliability for Personnel Selection," *Personnel Psychology,* Winter 1996, p. 822.

36. Marvin Zuckerman, "Are You a Risk Taker?" *Psychology Today,* November/December 2000, p. 53.

37. Wayne H. Stewart, Jr., and Philip L. Roth, "Risk Propensity Differences Between Entrepreneurs and Managers: A Meta-Analytic Review," *Journal of Applied Psychology,* February 2001, pp. 144–153.

38. Harry C. Triandis, *Culture and Social Behavior* (New York: McGraw-Hill, 1994), pp. 1–27.

SUGGESTED READING

Bennett, Milton J. (ed.). *Basic Concepts of Intercultural Communication.* Yarmouth, ME: Intercultural Press, 1998.

Cherniss, Cary, and Goleman, Daniel. *The Emotionally Intelligent Workplace: How to Select for, Measure, and Improve Emotional Intelligence.* San Francisco: Jossey-Bass, 2001.

Ciarrochi, Joseph (ed.). *Emotional Intelligence in Everyday Life.* New York: Routledge, 2001.

Delatt, Jacqueline. *Gender in the Workplace: A Case Study Approach.* Thousand Oaks, CA: Sage, 1999.

Howe, Michael J. *History and the Psychology of Genius.* New York: Cambridge University Press, 1999.

Koss-Feder, Laura. "Able to Work." *Time,* January 25, 1999, pp. 93–99.

Leach, Joy. *A Practical Guide to Working with Diversity.* New York: AMACOM, 2000.

Powell, Gary N. (ed.). *Handbook of Gender and Work.* Thousand Oaks, CA: Sage, 1999.

Scarborough, Jack. *The Origins of Cultural Differences and Their Impact on Management.* Westport, CT: Quorum Books, 2000.

Sterrett, Emil A. *The Manager's Pocket Guide to Emotional Intelligence.* Amherst, MA: HRD Press, 2000.

Wagner, William F. "All Skill, No Finesse." *Workforce,* June 2000, pp. 108–116.

WEB CORNER

www.DiversityInc.com. (Information about cultural diversity.)

www.onlinepsych.com. (Tests and quizzes related to cognitive factors and personality.)

www.queendom.com. (More tests and quizzes related to cognitive factors and personality.)

CHAPTER 4

UNDERSTANDING YOURSELF

Learning Objectives After reading and studying this chapter and doing the exercises, you should be able to

1. Identify and describe ways of learning about yourself.
2. Explain the nature of the self-concept.
3. Describe the nature of self-esteem and how it affects the behavior of people.
4. Develop plans for enhancing your self-esteem.
5. Develop plans for enhancing your self-confidence.

The process of self-examination is an important starting point in applying knowledge in general to yourself. Suppose that instead of a book about business psychology, this were a book all about presentation skills. It would be valuable to read about what other people making presentations do right and wrong. But reading about principles of presentations would be of greater benefit to you if you first took a candid look at your own presentation style. Videotaping several of your presentations would be useful. You might also want to receive comments and suggestions from others about your oral presentations.

Self-understanding is also important because before you can understand other people well, you must first understand yourself. For example, if you had insight into your own level of conscientiousness, it would be easier for you to observe this characteristic in others.

In achieving self-understanding, it is helpful to recognize that the **self** is a complicated idea. It generally refers to a person's total being or individuality. In 1890, pioneering psychologist William James wrote that "a man's self is the sum total of what he can call his."[1] Assuming that James was not referring also to physical possessions, the self has meant about the same thing for at least 115 years.

A distinction is sometimes made between the self a person projects to the outside world and the inner self. The **public self** is what the person is communicating about himself or herself and what others perceive about the person. The **private self** is the actual person that one may be.[2] To avoid making continuous distinctions between these two selves throughout this book, we will use the term self to refer to an accurate representation of the individual.

The fact that this entire chapter is devoted to the self does not imply that other chapters in the book do not deal with the self. Much of this book is geared toward applying psychology for self-development and self-improvement.

DEVELOPING SELF-AWARENESS

To achieve self-understanding, you need to gather accurate information about yourself. An additional benefit of self-understanding is that it appears to be related to high performance. In one study, the self-reports of managers were compared to evaluations of their behavior by group members. High-performing managers showed more congruence between their self-assessments and those made by group members than did average-performing managers. In other words, the high-performing managers had greater self-awareness than did average-performing managers. The more effective managers were able to assess their own behaviors in the workplace more accurately.[3]

Here we describe four methods of gathering information for self-understanding and developing self-awareness: (1) acquiring general information about human behavior, (2) feedback from self-assessment devices, (3) feedback from people on and off the job, and (4) insights gathered in career counseling and psychotherapy.

General Information about Human Behavior

As you read about or listen to facts and systematic observations about people in general, you should also be gaining knowledge about yourself. This book and all other books about human behavior discuss many things that have relevance to you as an individual. At times, the author will explain how this information applies to you. At other times, it is your responsibility to relate the general information to your particular case.

Among the many general topics discussed in Chapter 2 is perception. To improve your self-understanding with respect to perception, you will have to relate that information to yourself. For example, one aspect of perception is selective perception, a tendency to see things according to our need at the time. In reading about selective perception, you might arrive at a self-insight such as, "Maybe that is why I didn't listen when people said I was too inexperienced to start my own business. If I had listened, I wouldn't have the financial problems I do today."

Feedback from Self-Assessment Devices

Psychological testing for learning about one's aptitudes, personality, and interests is standard practice at career centers in schools and large business firms. However, test results can be inaccurate and misleading. You might be functioning as a confident and outgoing individual. If you take a personality test and discover that you rate low on both extraversion and agreeableness, you should not be concerned about the results. In your particular case, the results are misleading. The most effective way to gain self-understanding from psychological tests is to have the results interpreted to you by a professional in the field of mental measurement. Self-Assessment Exercise 4–1 will help you get in the self-analysis mode.

In addition to receiving feedback from standardized tests, you might derive self-understanding from other self-assessment instruments, such as the self-knowledge questionnaire presented near the end of this chapter (Self-Assessment Exercise 4–3). A standardized test or questionnaire has the advantage of having been constructed on the basis of scientific principles. Other self-examination instruments offer less certain results, but they are still valuable for purposes of introspection. A number of such self-examination instruments are presented in this book to help you understand yourself better. Extremely high or low scores on these questionnaires may provide useful clues to self-understanding.

Feedback from People On and Off the Job

A valuable source of information for self-awareness is to find out what people who regularly interact with you think of you. Feedback of this nature sometimes hurts or makes you feel uncomfortable. Yet when it is consistent, it gives you an accurate picture of how you are perceived by others. Virtually all employers provide employees with feedback as part of a performance appraisal system. During a performance appraisal your manager, supervisor, or team leader will convey to you what he or she thinks you are doing well and not so well. Another source of feedback from

SELF-ASSESSMENT EXERCISE 4–1

The Written Self-Portrait

A good starting point in acquiring serious self-knowledge is to prepare a written self-portrait in the major life spheres (or aspects). In each of the spheres listed below, describe yourself in about 25 to 50 words. For example, under the social and interpersonal sphere, a person might write: "I'm a little timid on the surface. But people who get to know me well understand that I'm filled with enthusiasm and joy. My relationships with people last a long time. I'm on excellent terms with all members of my family. And my significant other and I have been together for five years. We are very close emotionally and should be together for a lifetime."

A. Occupational and School:

B. Social and Interpersonal:

C. Beliefs, Values, and Attitudes:

D. Physical Description (body type, appearance, grooming)

superiors is comments made about your performance and behavior on spontaneous occasions. For example, a manager might say, "Why did you turn in a report with so many errors yesterday?" You might then reflect on your level of conscientiousness.

Coworkers are another source of potentially useful feedback, both in their spontaneous comments and in more formal ways. A growing practice in organizations is **peer evaluation,** a system in which coworkers contribute to an evaluation of a worker's job performance. Although coworkers under this system do not have total responsibility for evaluating each other, their input is taken seriously. Salary increases can be affected by peer judgments about performance.

Figure 4–1 shows a portion of a peer rating system. A group of coworkers indicates whether a particular aspect of job performance or behavior is a strength or a **developmental opportunity,** a specific area in which a person needs to improve. The initials under "Peer Evaluations" refer to coworkers doing the evaluation. The person being evaluated then knows who to thank or blame for the feedback. In addition to indicating whether a job factor is a strength or an opportunity, raters can supply comments and developmental suggestions. The results of the peer ratings might then be supplemented by the manager's ratings to achieve a total appraisal.

People who know you in personal life can also be a source of feedback for self-understanding. An informal approach to obtaining such feedback would be to

Person Evaluated: Chris Gupta

Skill Categories and Expected Behaviors	***Peer Evaluations for Each Category and Behavior***					
	TR	***JP***	***CK***	***JT***	***CJ***	***ML***
CUSTOMER CARE						
Takes ownership for customer problems	O	S	O	S	O	S
Follows through on customer commitments	S	S	S	S	S	S
TECHNICAL KNOWLEDGE AND SKILL						
Engages in continuous learning to update technical skills	O	O	S	O	O	O
Corrects problems on the first visit	O	O	S	S	S	S
WORK GROUP SUPPORT						
Actively participates in work group meetings	O	S	S	O	S	O
Backs up other work group members by taking calls in other areas	S	O	O	S	S	S
Minimal absence	S	O	S	S	O	S
FINANCE MANAGEMENT						
Adheres to work group parts expense process	S	S	S	O	S	S
Passes truck audits	S	S	S	O	S	S

FIGURE 4–1 Peer Evaluation of Customer Service Technician

Note: S refers to a strength; O refers to a developmental opportunity.

listen carefully to spontaneous comments made about you by friends and acquaintances. Suppose you have a dinner appointment with a friend, and upon your arrival at the restaurant she says, "I knew you would be on time. You always are." If you hear a similar comment from at least one other person, you can be confident that you are perceived as dependable.

Feedback from people who know you socially can also be obtained more systematically. You might say to a few people, "I'm trying to increase my self-understanding so I can do better in my career. You know me well. What are my strong points? How can I improve?"

When this method of obtaining feedback is mentioned, a few skeptics will argue that friends will not give you a true picture of yourself. Instead, they will say flattering things about you because they value your friendship. Experience has shown, however, that if you impress others with the importance of their opinions they will generally give you some constructive suggestions. Not everybody will give you helpful feedback. You therefore may have to sample a wide range of opinions.

Insights Gathered in Career Counseling and Psychotherapy

An advanced method of achieving self-understanding is to obtain feedback from a career counselor or psychotherapist. Counseling centers located in schools often provide career counseling. The counselors obtain their information from interviews, tests, and questionnaires. A valuable service they provide is to collect information that you have revealed about yourself and gather it into a meaningful whole. Some career counselors provide the counselee with written suggestions. A 27-year-old woman who entered into career counseling received a report with the following conclusion:

> Based on our interview and test findings, it appears you show aptitude for and an interest in managerial work. You have excellent problem-solving ability and organizing ability, and you are interested in working closely with people. You combine these characteristics with above-average needs for getting things accomplished and holding a powerful position.
>
> We recommend that you stay in your present field and take any opportunities offered for supervisory experience. Obtaining a degree or certificate in management would enhance your chances for becoming a manager.

In addition to career counseling, many people seek self-understanding through discussions with a psychotherapist. Most people enter into psychotherapy with the intention of coping better with personal problems. However, many people choose psychotherapy for the purpose of gaining insight into themselves. A representative area of insight would be for the therapist to help the client detect patterns of self-defeating behavior. For example, some people unconsciously do something to ruin a personal relationship or perform poorly on a job when things are going really well. The therapist might point out this self-defeating pattern of behavior. Self-insight of this kind often, but not always, leads to useful changes in behavior.

The Self-Awareness Trap

The theme of this section of the chapter is that self-awareness is a positive force in our lives. Yet, self-awareness also has a negative side or trap. Focusing on the self can highlight shortcomings the way staring into a mirror can dramatize every blemish and wrinkle on our face. Certain situations predictably force us to engage in self-reflection and become the object of our own attention. When we talk about ourselves, answer self-quizzes, stand before an audience or camera, or watch ourselves on videotape, we become more self-aware and make comparisons to some arbitrary standard of behavior. The comparison often results in a negative evaluation in comparison to the standard, and a decrease in self-esteem as we discover that we fall short of standards.[4] Keeping the self-awareness trap in mind will help you minimize needless underevaluation, thereby benefiting from gathering feedback about yourself.

YOUR SELF-CONCEPT: WHAT YOU THINK OF YOU

Another aspect of self-understanding is your **self-concept,** or what you think of you and who you think you are. A successful person, one who is achieving his or her goals, usually has a positive self-concept. In contrast, an unsuccessful person often has a negative self-concept. Such differences in self-concept can have a profound influence on your career. If you do not see yourself as a successful person, you will find ways not to be particularly successful. Three aspects of the self-concept are described here: how it relates to self-confidence, group identification, and the challenge of positive illusions.

The Self-Concept and Self-Confidence

A strong self-concept leads to self-confidence, which in turn is an important requirement for being successful as a leader. Why some people develop strong self-concepts, while others have average or weak self-concepts, is not entirely known. One important contributing factor is the lifelong feedback you receive from other people. If at 2 years old your parents, other children in your family, and playmates consistently told you that you were great, it would probably lead to strong self-concept. A 4-year-old may occasionally look in the mirror and utter statements such as "I like me," "I'm cute," or "I'm a good girl." It appears that in later life she will have a strong self-concept.

In summary, much of what we call the self-concept is a reflection of what others have said about us. If enough people tell you that you are "terrific," after a while you will have the self-concept of a terrific person. When enough people tell you that you are not a worthwhile person, after a while your self-concept will become that of a not worthwhile person. People who say "I'm OK" are expressing a positive self-concept. People who say "I'm not OK" have a negative self-concept. These statements reflect the contrast between high and low self-confidence.

Group Identification and the Self-Concept

Another important source of the self-concept is the groups people join. According to research by social psychologist Marilynn Brewer, people join small groups to achieve some degree of individuality and identity. People develop much of their self-concept by comparing their own group to others. The group you identify with becomes part of your psychological self. Joining the group satisfies two conflicting needs. A person wants to retain some individuality, so being a member of a mega-group such as students or General Motors employees does not quite do the job. Yet people also yearn to have some group affiliation.[5]

So joining a small group that is distinctive from others is a happy compromise. The smaller group the person joins becomes part of the self-image and self-concept for many people. A sampling of the groups that could become part of a person's self-concept include athletic teams, church groups, street gangs, motorcycle gangs, a musical band, and an Internet chat room. What group membership do you have that has become part of your self-concept?

The Challenge of Positive Illusions

We described earlier the problem of making unfavorable self-comparisons in the process of developing self-awareness. An opposite type of discrepancy takes place frequently when we compare ourselves to others. The challenge is that the vast majority of people overevaluate their capabilities in comparison to others. As such, they have an inflated self-concept. A leading example is that the vast majority of workers believe they have superior interpersonal skills. Also of note, participants in studies see positive traits as more descriptive than negative ones, and they rate themselves more highly than they rate others. Furthermore, they rate themselves more highly than others rate them, and they overestimate their contribution to team efforts.[6] Positive illusions do not appear to stem from a conscious attempt to flatter ourselves but from a natural reflex to rate ourselves highly.

The antidote to the challenge of positive illusions is to obtain feedback on your traits and capabilities—without becoming a victim of the self-awareness trap!

THE NATURE AND CONSEQUENCES OF SELF-ESTEEM

Although the various approaches to discussing the self may seem confusing and overlapping, all of them strongly influence your life. A particularly important role is played by **self-esteem.** It refers to appreciating self-worth and importance, being accountable for your own behaviors, and acting responsibly toward others.[7] People with positive self-esteem have a deep-down, inside-the-self feeling of their own worth. Consequently they develop a positive self-concept. Before reading further, you are invited to measure your current level of self-esteem by doing Self-Assessment Exercise 4–2. We look next at the nature of self-esteem and many of its consequences.

The Nature of Self-Esteem

The definition just presented tells a lot about self-esteem, yet there is much more to know about its nature. According to Nathaniel Brandon, self-esteem has two interrelated components: self-efficacy and self-respect.[8] **Self-efficacy** is confidence in your ability to carry out a specific task in contrast to generalized self-confidence. When your self-efficacy is high, you believe you have the ability to

SELF-ASSESSMENT EXERCISE 4–2

The Self-Esteem Checklist

Indicate whether each of the following statements is Mostly True or Mostly False, as it applies to you.

	Mostly True	*Mostly False*
1. I am excited about starting each day.	______	______
2. Most of any progress I have made in my work or my school work can be attributed to luck.	______	______
3. I often ask myself, "Why can't I be more successful?"	______	______
4. When I'm given a challenging assignment by my manager or teacher, I usually dive in with confidence.	______	______
5. I believe that I am working up to my potential.	______	______
6. I am able to set limits to what I will do for others without feeling anxious.	______	______
7. I regularly make excuses for my mistakes.	______	______
8. Someone else's bad mood will affect my good mood.	______	______
9. I care very much how much money other people earn, especially when they are working in my field.	______	______
10. I feel like a failure when I do not achieve my goals.	______	______
11. Hard work gives me an emotional lift.	______	______
12. When others compliment me, I doubt their sincerity.	______	______
13. Complimenting others makes me feel uncomfortable.	______	______
14. I find it comfortable to say "I'm sorry."	______	______
15. It is difficult for me to face up to my mistakes.	______	______
16. My coworkers think I should not be promoted.	______	______
17. People who would want to become my friend usually would not have much to offer.	______	______
18. If my manager praised me, I would have a difficult time believing it was deserved.	______	______
19. I'm just an ordinary person.	______	______
20. Having to face change really disturbs me.	______	______

Score ____________

Scoring and Interpretation:

The answers in the high self-esteem direction are as follows:

1.	Mostly True	11.	Mostly True
2.	Mostly False	12.	Mostly False
3.	Mostly False	13.	Mostly False
4.	Mostly True	14.	Mostly True
5.	Mostly True	15.	Mostly False
6.	Mostly True	16.	Mostly False
7.	Mostly False	17.	Mostly False
8.	Mostly False	18.	Mostly False
9.	Mostly False	19.	Mostly False
10.	Mostly False	20.	Mostly False

17–20 points	You have a very high self-esteem. Yet if your score is 20, it could be that you are denying any self-doubts.
11–16 points	Your self-esteem is in the average range. It would probably be worthwhile for you to implement strategies to boost your self-esteem (described in this chapter) so you can develop a greater feeling of well-being.
0–10 points	Your self-esteem needs bolstering. Talk over your feelings about yourself with a trusted friend or with a mental health professional. At the same time attempt to implement several of the tactics for boosting self-esteem described in this chapter.

do what is necessary to complete a task successfully. Being confident that you can perform a particular task well contributes to self-esteem.

Self-efficacy contributes to job performance in important ways including increasing motivation, focus on the task, and effort, along with decreasing anxiety and self-defeating negative thinking. A study conducted with salespeople from large companies provides evidence of yet another contribution of self-efficacy. The salespeople who scored higher on a test of self-efficacy did a better job of seeking, integrating, and using information to clarify what they were supposed to be doing, and to improve performance. Salespeople with lower self-efficacy did not make such constructive use of information. The types of information under consideration included job expectations, how well they were performing, and technical aspects of the job.[9]

Self-respect, the second component of self-esteem, refers to how you think and feel about yourself. People with self-respect like themselves because of who they are and not because of what they can do or not do. To have self-respect is to like yourself without worrying about comparisons to others.[10] Self-respect fits the everyday meaning of self-esteem. Many street beggars are intelligent and able-bodied and have a good physical appearance. One could argue that it is their low self-esteem that enables them to beg. Also, people with low self-respect and self-esteem allow themselves to stay in relationships in which they are frequently verbally and physically abused. These abused people have such low self-worth that they think they deserve punishment.

Part of understanding the nature of self-esteem is knowing how it develops. As with the self-concept, self-esteem comes about from a variety of early-life experiences. People who were encouraged to feel good about themselves and their accomplishments by family members, friends, and teachers are more likely to enjoy high self-esteem. A widespread explanation of self-esteem development is that compliments, praise, and hugs alone build self-esteem. Yet many developmental psychologists seriously question this perspective. Instead, they believe that self-esteem results from accomplishing worthwhile activities and then feeling proud of these accomplishments. Receiving encouragement, however, can help the person accomplish activities that build self-esteem.

Psychologist Martin Seligman argues that self-esteem is caused by a variety of successes and failures. To develop self-esteem people need to improve their skills for dealing with the world.[11] Self-esteem therefore comes about by genuine accomplishments, followed by praise and recognition. Heaping undeserved praise and recognition on people may lead to a temporary high, but it does not produce genuine self-esteem. The child develops self-esteem not from being told he or she can score a goal in soccer, but from scoring that goal.

The Consequences of Self-Esteem

One of the major consequences of high self-esteem is good mental health. People with high self-esteem feel good about themselves and have a positive outlook on life. One of the links between good mental health and self-esteem is that high self-esteem helps prevent many situations from being stressful. Few negative comments from others are likely to bother you when your self-esteem is high. A person with low self-esteem might crumble if somebody else insulted his or her appearance. A person with high self-esteem might shrug off the insult as simply being the other person's point of view. If faced with an everyday setback such as losing keys, the person with high self-esteem might think, "I have so much going for me, why fall apart over this incident?"

Although people with high self-esteem can readily shrug off undeserved insults, they still profit well from negative feedback. Because they are secure, they can take advantage of the developmental opportunities suggested by negative feedback.

Workers with high self-esteem develop and maintain favorable work attitudes and perform at a high level. These positive consequences take place because such attitudes and behavior are consistent with their personal belief that they are competent individuals. An analysis of 139 studies indicated that people with high self-esteem had higher job satisfaction and performance. The study indicated similarly that a person's level of self-esteem is a good predictor of his or her job satisfaction and performance.[12]

A team of economists conducted a nationwide study of the relationships between productivity and self-esteem (as measured by a personality test). It was found that productivity (as reflected in relative wages) was more sensitive to changes in self-esteem than to changes in schooling, basic skills, and work experience. A specific finding was that a 10 percent rise in self-esteem boosted wages more than a 10 percent increase in education or work experience.[13]

A useful way of summarizing both the nature and consequences of self-esteem is the self-esteem cycle, shown in Figure 4–2. High self-esteem feeds on itself, leading to positive expectations, high effort, success, giving credit to oneself, and more self-esteem.[14]

Enhancing Self-Esteem

Improving self-esteem is a lifelong process because self-esteem is related to the success of your activities and interactions with people. Following are five approaches to enhancing self-esteem that relate to how self-esteem develops.

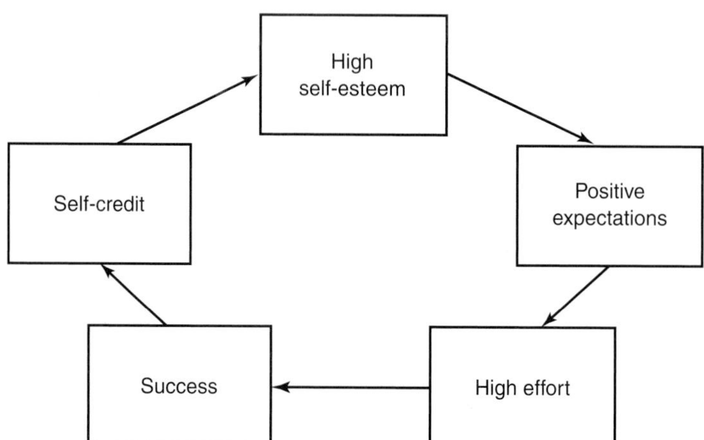

FIGURE 4–2 The Self-Esteem Cycle
High self-esteem is accompanied by positive expectations, which motivate behavior, improve performance, and reinforce the high self-esteem.

Source: Saul Kassin, *Psychology,* 3rd ed., p. 714. Reprinted by permission of Pearson Education, Inc., Upper Saddle River, NJ.

Accomplishing Worthwhile Activities. To emphasize again, accomplishing worthwhile activities is a major contributor to self-esteem in both children and adults. Giving people large trophies for mundane accomplishments is unlikely to raise self-esteem. More likely, the person will see through the transparent attempt to build his or her self-esteem and develop negative feelings about the self. What about you? Would your self-esteem receive a bigger boost by (a) receiving an A in a course in which 10 percent of the class received an A or (b) receiving an A in a class in which everybody received the same grade?

Engaging in Self-Disclosure. One method of increasing your self-esteem is to engage in the right amount of **self-disclosure,** the process of revealing your inner self to others. A person with a high degree of self-disclosure is open, while a person with a low degree of self-disclosure is closed. Self-disclosure aids in self-acceptance because revealing more of oneself allows more for others to accept. As acceptance by others increases, so does self-esteem, because self-esteem is based heavily on how we are perceived by others. Conversely, if you keep yourself hidden from others there is little opportunity to be accepted by them. Keep this sequence of activities in mind: self-disclosure → self-acceptance → self-esteem.

Nevertheless, you must be careful of excessive self-disclosure. Many people feel uneasy if another person is too self-revealing. The overly candid person thus risks rejection. For instance, if you communicate all your negative feelings and doubts to another person, that person may become annoyed and pull away from you.

Developing Awareness of Strengths. Another method of improving your self-esteem is to develop an appreciation of your strengths and accomplishments. Research with more than 60 executives has shown that their self-concept becomes more positive after one month of practicing this exercise for a few minutes every day.[15] A good starting point is to list your strengths and accomplishments on paper. The list is likely to be more impressive than you expected. The list of strengths and accomplishments requested in the Self-Knowledge Questionnaire presented at the end of the chapter can be used for building self-esteem.

A group exercise has been developed to help you build self-esteem through knowledge of your strengths. After group members have compiled their lists of strengths, each person discusses his or her list with the other group members. Each person then comments on the list. Group members sometimes add to your list of strengths or reinforce what you have to say. Sometimes you may find some disagreement. One man told the group, "I'm handsome, intelligent, reliable, athletic, self-confident, very moral, and I have a good sense of humor." A woman in the group retorted, "And I might add that you're unbearably conceited."

Minimizing Situations That Detract from Your Feelings of Competence. Most of us have personal and work situations that make us feel less than our best. If you can minimize exposure to those situations, you will have fewer feelings of incompetence. The problem with feeling incompetent is that it lowers self-esteem. Yet avoiding all situations in which you feel less than competent might prevent you from acquiring needed skills. Also, it boosts your self-esteem and self-confidence to become comfortable in a previously uncomfortable situation.

Dealing with People Who Boost Your Self-Esteem. Psychologist Barbara Ilardie says that the people who can raise your self-esteem are usually those with high self-esteem themselves. They are the people who give honest feedback because they respect others and themselves. Such high-esteem individuals should not be confused with yes-people who agree with others just to be liked. The point is that you typically receive more from strong people than weak ones. Weak people will flatter you but will not give you the honest feedback you need to build self-esteem.[16]

BUILDING YOUR SELF-CONFIDENCE

Enhancing your self-esteem is also likely to boost your self-confidence, because having self-respect and feelings of self-efficacy also boost feeling positive about yourself in general. The self-esteem builders described in the previous section will therefore boost self-confidence. Here we describe some additional strategies and tactics that can lead to a strengthening of self-confidence. As you read them, look for techniques that you think will make sense in terms of your personality and life circumstances.

1. *Score a few easy victories.* Self-confidence builds as a direct result of success. The more little victories you achieve in life, the more likely your self-confidence will be strong. A little victory could include such things as learning to operate a new electronic instrument, receiving a favorable grade on a term paper, or running a mile 10 seconds faster than you did last month. The easy victory is based on the **success cycle.** Each little success builds up your self-confidence, which leads to a bigger success, which leads to more self-confidence, and so on.
2. *Use positive self-talk.* To appear and be self-confident, it is necessary to replace negative statements about oneself with **positive self-talk**—saying positive things about oneself to oneself. It is particularly important to make these positive self-affirmations in front of others. Examples include, "I know I can do it." "Give me a chance, and you will be pleased with the outcome." "My success ratio is very high."
3. *Use positive visual imagery.* To use **positive visual imagery,** imagine yourself performing well in an upcoming situation that represents a challenge. For example, if you will be asking for a loan, visualize yourself making a convincing argument about your creditworthiness. Think of the loan officer smiling agreeably and getting the papers ready for your signature. Positive visual imagery helps you appear self-confident because your mental rehearsal has helped you prepare for the challenge.
4. *Become self-directing.* If you develop an internal locus of control, your self-confidence will increase. When you take responsibility for events around you, others regard you as being self-confident and in control.
5. *Talk with optimism.* Optimistic people, almost by definition, project an image of self-confidence. It will not be necessary to overhaul your personality if you are naturally pessimistic. Nevertheless, you can learn to keep

some of your pessimistic thoughts to yourself and search for optimistic comments to fit the situation. When you have struggled through a rough assignment and finally completed it, talk about how you have benefited from the experience and will do even better next time.

6. *Dress and act professionally.* If you are proud of your clothing and mannerisms, you will project more self-confidence than if you are self-conscious about how you are dressed and act. Dress in a manner that makes you feel good about yourself to achieve a boost in self-confidence. Review your general behavior and mannerisms to decide which facets make you feel the most professional.
7. *Develop a solid knowledge base.* A bedrock for projecting self-confidence is to develop a base of knowledge that enables you to provide sensible alternative solutions to problems. Intuition is important, but working from a base of facts helps you project a confident image. Both formal education and day-by-day absorption of information related to your career are necessary for increasing your knowledge base.
8. *Develop and publicize new skills.* Most people realize it takes courage and confidence to learn a complex new skill. Learning new skills and letting others know about it will therefore project self-confidence and make you feel confident.
9. *Show intense pride in your work.* The saying "Every piece of work you complete (or service you provide) is a self-portrait" is truer than ever. A by-product of being proud is that you project self-confidence. Feeling proud creates a warm inner glow that leads to facial expressions and posture that project self-confidence.
10. *Take risks.* Risk taking is associated with self-confidence. The risk taker consequently projects an image of self-confidence. Taking sensible risks, such as offering an offbeat solution to a problem, will make you appear self-confident.
11. *Be flexible and adaptable.* Self-confident people can adapt to change quickly for the good of the organization. In contrast, people with low self-confidence want to preserve the status quo. If you show a willingness to accept change readily, you will project an image of self-confidence. Of greater significance, adapting to change will enhance your self-confidence.
12. *Overcome shyness by focusing on other people.* Low self-confidence is sometimes a by-product of being shy and therefore not being able to connect with people as often as desired. Shyness is a complex subject within itself. However, the general thrust of advice offered by Bernardo Carducci, the director of a shyness research institute, is worth mentioning here. According to Carducci, the successfully shy get involved in the lives of others. They start small, assuring that they have daily contact with people. For example, when they make a store purchase they don't simply put their money on the counter. Instead, they focus on the salesperson, thanking him or her for the service. The act of thanking creates a social environment favorable to positive interactions.[17] As these positive interactions accumulate, the person becomes less shy and more self-confident.

SUMMARY OF KEY POINTS

- Methods of developing self-awareness included (1) acquiring general information about human behavior, (2) feedback from self-assessment devices, (3) feedback from people on and off the job, and (4) insight gathered in career counseling and psychotherapy. A potential negative side to self-awareness is that focusing on the self can highlight shortcomings.
- An important aspect of self-understanding is the self-concept, or the way a person thinks about himself or herself in an overall sense. The self-concept is based largely on what others have said about us. A strong self-concept leads to self-confidence, which is a basic requirement for success in leadership or sales. The small groups to which a person belongs, such as a team or club, are another contributor to the self-concept. The challenge of positive illusions is that the vast majority of people overrate themselves in comparison to others.
- Self-esteem refers to appreciating self-worth and importance, being accountable for your own behaviors, and acting responsibly toward others. People with high self-esteem develop a positive self-concept. Self-esteem has two interrelated components: self-efficacy (a task-related feeling of competence) and self-respect. Self-efficacy is positively related to job performance and satisfaction. People with self-respect like themselves because of who they are and not because of what they can do or not do.
- Self-esteem develops from a variety of early-life experiences. People who were encouraged to feel good about themselves and their accomplishments by key people in their lives are more likely to enjoy high self-esteem. Of major significance, self-esteem also results from accomplishing worthwhile activities and then feeling proud of these accomplishments. Praise and recognition for accomplishments also help develop self-esteem.
- Good mental health is one of the major consequences of high self-esteem. One of the links between good mental health and self-esteem is that high self-esteem helps prevent many situations from being stressful. Workers with high self-esteem develop and maintain favorable work attitudes and perform at a high level. High self-esteem also appears to be associated with receiving higher wages.
- According to the self-esteem cycle, high self-esteem feeds on itself, leading to positive expectations, more effort, more success, and more self-esteem.
- Self-esteem can be enhanced in many ways. Accomplishing worthwhile activities is a major contributor to self-esteem in both children and adults. The right amount of self-disclosure enhances self-esteem because it may lead to self-acceptance. Developing an appreciation of your strengths and accomplishments is another self-esteem builder. It is also important to minimize settings and interactions that detract from your feelings of competence. In addition, talk and socialize frequently with people who boost your self-esteem.
- Knowledge about the self can be used to strengthen one's self-confidence. Among the tactics for accomplishing this end are (1) score a few easy victories, (2) use positive self-talk, (3) become self-directing, (4) develop a solid knowledge base, (5) develop and publicize new skills, (6) be proud of your work, and (7) take risks.

DISCUSSION QUESTIONS AND ACTIVITIES

1. How can gathering the type of feedback described in this chapter help you become more effective in your career?
2. Describe your self-concept in 25 words or less.
3. How can your self-concept affect your career?
4. How can a worker have high self-efficacy but not be generally self-confident?
5. Explain why high self-esteem among workers can actually help a company become more productive.
6. If you were responsible for hiring a few new workers, how would you evaluate a given applicant's level of self-esteem?
7. What can you do this week to increase your self-esteem?
8. What might a manager do to boost the self-esteem of a worker who appeared to be suffering from low self-esteem?
9. What kind of behavior on the part of a manager might actually lower the self-esteem of a given worker?
10. Ask an experienced manager (or parent) what he or she has found successful in boosting the self-confidence of workers (or child, or children).

GUIDELINES FOR PERSONAL EFFECTIVENESS

1. A major step you can take toward improving your effectiveness as an individual is to strengthen your self-concept. A series of successes, however small, will improve your self-concept and help you to feel more self-confident.
2. A major task in life is to increase one's self-esteem. The best path to enhanced self-esteem is to achieve worthwhile mental and physical tasks and then receive positive feedback about these accomplishments. Your self-confidence will increase at the same time.

AN APPLIED PSYCHOLOGY CASE PROBLEM

Can the President of Microsoft Be Helped?

In 1998 Microsoft Corp. Chairman and Chief Executive Officer Bill Gates promoted Steven A. Ballmer as president of the software giant. Ballmer, who had been executive vice president of sales and support, filled a position that had been vacant for eight years.

A major purpose of the move was to enable Gates to focus on Microsoft's long-term vision and product strategy. Gates said in an interview, "I decided I wanted to spend more time with our product groups and drive the breakthroughs. Think of Steve as the business leader and customer champion. His formal role is to be in charge of sales and product development."

Ballmer has been a self-appointed cheerleader for Microsoft. During a company sales meeting several years ago, he vaulted on stage and shouted at

continued on next page

AN APPLIED PSYCHOLOGY CASE PROBLEM (cont'd)

the top of his lungs: "I love this company! I love this company! I love this company!" The 6,000-member sales team responded with a five-minute standing ovation. Shouting to cheer on employees, discipline them, and express disapproval is characteristic of Ballmer. Another motivational stunt he pulled at one time was to swim across a chilly Microsoft pond on a dare in front of dozens of company employees.

Ballmer, a college chum of Gates, has been co-pilot of Microsoft since 1980. Gates is thought of as the biggest brain in the company, whereas Ballmer is regarded as the biggest heart and inspiring sales leader. Another contrast is that Gates is seen as the company's technology visionary, and Ballmer its top business strategist.

Ballmer's physical presence is imposing. He is six feet tall, and built like a football linebacker. His shiny head is disproportionately large, and he has a booming voice. He is intensely devoted to his company and his family. His intensity, however, is often perceived negatively. He can become infuriated when facing conflict. He has been known to bawl out employees so violently that his voice can be heard through the air vents in company headquarters.

Ballmer has become well known for being outspoken with both company insiders and outsiders. During a discussion of the Justice Department's investigation into Microsoft's business tactics, Ballmer blurted out, "To heck with Janet Reno." Later, however, Ballmer said he regretted making the comment. "That's the way I am," he said. "I have to work on being a better version of myself."

Gates, who can be undiplomatic himself, is not much concerned about Ballmer's roughness with people. "He's my best friend," says Gates. "We love working together on very hard problems. We trust each other and understand how the other thinks." Ballmer has equally warm comments about Gates. "Our friendship has grown much stronger as a result of working together. It's like a marriage," says Ballmer. (Both Gates and Ballmer are married with children.)

The Microsoft board deliberated six months before appointing Ballmer president. One concern was his fiery personality. A board member pointed out that "Steve's greatest strength can also be seen as a weakness." Ballmer shouts when he gets excited or angry (as mentioned previously). His voice rises so suddenly that it shocks and intimidates many people. Most likely attributed to his shouting, Ballmer lost his voice during a business trip to Japan in the early 1980s, and required vocal chord surgery to regain his speech.

Some of Ballmer's motivational techniques appear heavy-handed to employees. When he directed the Microsoft Window's product group, he created fear in engineers by bellowing at them and pounding a baseball bat into his hand. In the last few years, Ballmer has made progress in becoming calmer in demanding business situations.

Gates cleared the way for Ballmer to be promoted, by ensuring that each of the executives who would report to him was satisfied with the arrangement. Gates also convinced the board that he could modify Ballmer's behavior.

Despite his rough edges, Ballmer has many supporters. Many people who know Ballmer find him joyful and refreshing and a good sport. He is willing to engage in publicity stunts such as participating in videos that mock the competition. Several years into his CEO position, Ballmer was proud of his accomplishments in helping launch Windows XP, Microsoft's new PC operating system.

1. What needs for interpersonal skill development does Steven Ballmer appear to have?
2. To what extent do you believe that Bill Gates can modify Ballmer's behavior?
3. What positive interpersonal skills does Ballmer appear to have?
4. If it were your decision, would you have approved Steve Ballmer's appointment as president of Microsoft Corp?

Source: "Remaking Microsoft," *Business Week,* May 17, 1999, pp. 106–116; Steve Hamm, "Bill's Co-pilot," *Business Week,* September 14, 1998, pp. 76–90; "Microsoft Names President," http://cnnfn.com/digitaljam/9807/21/ballmer/; David Kirkpatrick, "Can XP Save the Economy? No Way," *Fortune,* November 12, 2001, p. 106.

AN APPLIED PSYCHOLOGY CASE PROBLEM

Self-Esteem Building at Pyramid Remanufacturing

Pyramid Remanufacturing opened for business 10 years ago in a cinder-block building with four employees. Today Pyramid is housed in an old factory building in a low-rent district. The company has 100 full-time employees and about 50 part-timers. The nature of the company's business is to salvage parts from used or broken equipment sent to them by other companies. One of Pyramid's remanufacturing projects is to salvage the workable parts from single-use cameras and recycle the balance of the plastic parts. Another large company contract is to salvage parts from children's toys that are returned to retailers because they do not function properly. Both contracts also call for making new single-use cameras and toys, incorporating the salvaged parts.

The basic remanufacturing jobs can be learned in several hours. The work is not complex, but it is tedious. For example, a remanufacturing technician would be expected to tear down, salvage, and assemble about 100 single-use cameras per day. The jobs pay about twice the minimum wage, and full-time workers receive standard benefits.

Derrick Lockett, the president and founder of Pyramid, believes that his company plays an important role in society. As he explains, "First of all, note that we are remanufacturers. We are helping save the planet. Think of the thousands and thousands of single-use cameras that do not wind up in landfills because of our recycling efforts. The same goes for plastic toys. Consider also that we hire a lot of people who would not be working if it were not for Pyramid. A lot of our employees would be on welfare if they were not working here. We hire many people from the welfare roles. We also hire a lot of troubled teenagers, and seniors who can't find employment elsewhere.

"Some of our other employees have a variety of disabilities, which makes job-finding difficult for them. Two of our highest producers are blind. They have a wonderful sense of touch, and they can visualize the parts that have to be separated and assembled. Another source of good employees for us is recently released prisoners."

Lockett was asked whether all Pyramid manufacturing employees were performing up to standard. He explained that about one-fourth of the workforce were either working so slowly or doing such sloppy work that they were a poor investment for the company. "Face it," said Lockett, "some of our employees are dragging us down. After a while we have to weed out the workers who just don't earn their salary."

Next, Lockett gave his analysis of why some remanufacturing technicians are unable to perform properly. "Lots of reasons," said Lockett. "Some can't read; some have a poor work ethic; some have attention deficit disorders. But the big problem is that many of the poor performers have such rotten self-esteem. They don't believe in themselves. They think nobody wants them—that they are incapable of being valuable employees."

Lucy Winters, the director of human resources and administration, explained what Pyramid was attempting to do about the self-esteem problem. "You have to realize," she said, "that it's not easy for a company to build the self-esteem of entry-level employees. Derrick and I would both like to save the world, but we can't do everything. But we are taking a few initiatives to build the self-esteem of our employees.

"One approach is that our supervisors give out brightly colored badges imprinted with the words 'I'm a real remanufacturer.' The supervisors are supposed to give out the badges when a technician appears to be down in the dumps. We also have a newsletter that features stories about our remanufacturing technicians. Each month we choose somebody to be the Remanufacturer of the Month. Usually it's an employee whose self-esteem appears to be hurting.

"Another approach is more informal. We ask our supervisors to remember to be cheerleaders. They're supposed to lift the spirits of employees who don't think much of themselves by saying things like 'I know you can do it,' or 'I believe in you.'"

When asked how the self-esteem building program was working, Winters and Lockett both said it

continued on next page

AN APPLIED PSYCHOLOGY CASE PROBLEM (cont'd)

was too early to tell with certainty. Winters did comment, however, "I see a few bright smiles out there among our technicians. And the turnover rate is down about 5 percent. So the program might be working."

1. What is your evaluation of Lockett's analysis that low self-esteem could hurt the work performance of entry-level remanufacturing technicians?
2. What is your evaluation of the self-esteem-building program at Pyramid?
3. What other suggestions can you offer for building the self-esteem of the Pyramid employees who appear to be having a self-esteem problem?

SELF-ASSESSMENT EXERCISE 4–3

The Self-Knowledge Questionnaire

Directions: Complete the following questionnaire for your personal use. You might wish to create a computer file for this document, enabling you to readily edit and update your answers. The answers to these questions will serve as a source document for such purposes as self-understanding, career planning, and résumé preparation.

I. Education

1. How far have I gone in school?
2. What is my major field of interest?
3. Which are, or have been, my best subjects?
4. Which are, or have been, my poorest subjects?
5. Which extracurricular activities have I participated in?
6. Which ones did I enjoy? Why?

II. Work and Career

7. What jobs have I held since age 16?
8. What aspects of these jobs did I enjoy? Why?
9. What aspects of these jobs did I dislike? Why?
10. What have been my three biggest job accomplishments?
11. What compliments did I receive from managers, coworkers, or customers?
12. What criticisms or suggestions did I receive?
13. What would be an ideal job for me? (Give the job title and major responsibilities.)

III. Attitudes Toward People

14. What kind of people do I get along with best?
15. What kind of people do I get along with the least?
16. How much time do I prefer to be in contact with people versus working alone?
17. What are my arguments with people mostly about?
18. What characteristics of a boss would be best for me?

IV. Attitudes Toward and Perceptions about Myself

19. What are my strengths and good points?
20. What are my areas for improvement, or developmental opportunities?
21. What is my biggest problem?
22. What aspects of my life do I enjoy the most?
23. What aspect of my life do I enjoy the least?

24. What has been the happiest period of my life? What made it so happy?
25. What are my key values (the things most important to me)?
26. What do I do to defeat my own purposes?

V. How People Outside of Work See Me

27. What is the best compliment a loved-one has paid me?
28. In what ways would any of my loved-ones want me to change?
29. What do my friends like the most about me?
30. What do my friends like the least about me?

VI. Hobbies, Interests, Sports

31. What hobbies, interests, sports, or other pastimes do I pursue?
32. Which of these do I really get excited about, and why?

VII. My Future

33. What are my plans for further education and training?
34. What positions would I like to hold, or type of work would I like to perform, in the future?
35. What type of work would I like to be doing at the peak of my career?
36. What hobbies, interests, and sports would I like to pursue in the future?
37. What goals and plans do I have relating to friends, family, and marriage or partnership?

Additional Thoughts

1. What topics not covered in this questionnaire would contribute to my self-understanding?
2. To what uses can I put all this information, aside from those mentioned in the directions?
3. How did answering these questions contribute to my self-understanding?

REFERENCES

1. William James, *The Principles of Psychology* (New York: Holt, 1890), p. 291.
2. C. R. Snyder, "So Many Selves," *Contemporary Psychology,* January 1988, p. 77.
3. Allan H. Church, "Managerial Self-Awareness in High-Performing Individuals in Organizations," *Journal of Applied Psychology,* April 1997, pp. 281–292.
4. Saul Kassin, *Psychology,* 3rd ed. (Upper Saddle River, NJ: Prentice Hall, 2001), p. 714.
5. Cited in Scott Sleek, "People Craft Their Self-Image from Groups," *APA Monitor,* November 1993, p. 22.
6. S. E. Taylor, *Positive Illusions: Creative Self-Deception and the Healthy Mind* (New York: Basic Books, 1989), as cited in Kassin, *Psychology,* p. 715.
7. California State Department of Education, *Toward a State of Esteem* (Sacramento: Department of Education, January 1990), p. 19.
8. Cited in Wayne Weiten and Margaret Lloyd, *Psychology Applied to Modern Life* (Pacific Grove, CA: Brooks/Cole Publishing, 1994), p. 51.
9. Steven P. Brown, Shankar Ganesan, and Goutam Challagalla, "Self-Efficacy as a Moderator of Information-Seeking Effectiveness," *Journal of Applied Psychology,* October 2001, pp. 1043–1051. The conclusions about the impact of self-efficacy are also from this source.

10. Ellen Lager, "Self-esteem vs. Self-respect: The Power Lies in the Difference," *Psychology Today*, November/December 1999, p. 32.
11. Cited in Randall Edwards, "Is Self-Esteem Really All That Important?" *APA Monitor*, May 1995, p. 43.
12. Timothy A. Judge and Joyce E. Bono, "Relationship of Core Self-Evaluation Traits—Self-Esteem, Generalized Self-Efficacy, Locus of Control, and Emotional Stability—With Job Satisfaction and Performance," *Journal of Applied Psychology*, February 2001, pp. 80–92.
13. "The Vital Role of Self-Esteem: It Boosts Productivity and Earnings," *Business Week*, February 2, 1998, p. 26.
14. Kassin, *Psychology*, p. 714.
15. Daniel L. Aroz, "The Manager's Self-Concept," *Human Resources Forum*, July 1989, p. 4.
16. "Self-Esteem: You'll Need It to Succeed," *Executive Strategies*, September 1993, p. 12.
17. Bernardo Carducci, "Shyness: The New Solution," *Psychology Today*, February 2000, pp. 45, 78.

SUGGESTED READING

Branden, Nathaniel. *A Woman's Self-Esteem: Struggles and Triumphs in the Search for Identity.* San Francisco: Jossey-Bass, 2000.

Gallagher, Shaun, and Shear, Jonathan (eds.). *Models of the Self.* Exeter, England: Imprint Academic, 1999.

Gini, Al. *My Job, My Self: Work and the Creation of the Modern Individual.* New York: Routledge, 2000.

Hoyle, Rick H., et al. *Selfhood: Identity, Esteem, Regulation.* Boulder, CO: Westview Press, 1999.

McKay, Matthew, and Fanning, Patrick. *Self-Esteem,* 3rd ed. Oakland, CA: New Harbinger, 2000.

McKay, Matthew, et al. *The Self-Esteem Companion.* Oakland, CA: New Harbinger, 1999.

Palladino, Connie. *Developing Self-Esteem.* Los Altos, CA: Crisp Publications, 1996.

Pitino, Rick. *Success Is a Choice.* New York: Broadway Books/Bantam Doubleday Dell, 1997.

Zampelli, Sheri. *From Sabotage to Success: How to Overcome Self-Defeating Behavior and Reach Your True Potential.* Oakland, CA: New Harbinger, 2000.

WEB CORNER

http://www.foryoumagazine.com/summer02/selfrespect.html (Information about self-respect.)

www.utexas.edu/student/lsc/handouts/1914.html (Information about building self-esteem.)

www.utexas.edu/student/cmhc/selfest.html (Information about the consequences of low self-esteem.)

CHAPTER 5

PROBLEM SOLVING AND CREATIVITY

Learning Objectives

After reading and studying this chapter and doing the exercises, you should be able to

1. Solve problems and make decisions more systematically.
2. Pinpoint key factors that influence the quality of problem solving and decision making.
3. Explain the contribution of creativity to problem solving and decision making.
4. Increase your creative problem-solving ability.
5. Explain several approaches organizations take to enhance creativity.

Solving problems and making decisions is an important part of all but the most routine jobs. The higher the job level, the greater the problem-solving and decision-making skill required. Executives, for example, are expected to make decisions that affect the entire organization and have long-term consequences. A good decision can move the organization forward, while a bad decision can destroy the organization. Decisions made at lower levels in the organization, however, also have important consequences. Choosing the wrong supplier for a small component, for example, could result in a failed product.

Our study of problem solving and creativity includes the following: problem-solving stages; influences on the quality of problem solving and decision making; and nature and development of creativity. Creativity is emphasized because of its impact on the success of an organization and the individual.

PROBLEM-SOLVING STAGES

We begin our study of problem solving and decision making with a situation facing Raul. He has worked many years in a large company and saved a substantial sum of money in order to go into business for himself. Raul is faced with a **problem,** a gap between an existing and a desired situation. His career is proceeding satisfactorily, but not with quite the challenge and excitement he thinks might be present in self-employment. To solve this problem, Raul has a heavy decision to make. A **decision** is a choice between two or more alternatives. A person who contemplates self-employment faces many alternatives.

Your decision-making effectiveness increases when you use a systematic approach to solving problems and making decisions, such as the one presented in Figure 5–1. It summarizes the explanation of solving problems and making decisions presented here.[1] The diagram implies that decision making should take place in an orderly flow. However, there will be times when even good decision makers deviate from this step-by-step sequence. The decision faced by Raul will be used to illustrate the process of solving problems and making decisions.

Be Aware of the Problem

Problem solving and decision making begin with an awareness that a problem exists. Raul is aware that although he enjoys his work as an office manager, he would like to attempt self-employment. Solving a major problem such as this simultaneously involves solving a series of other problems. For example, Raul might have to borrow money to start a business.

In most instances of decision making, problems are given or assigned. Somebody hands us a problem for which a decision has to be made. For example, your manager might ask you to decide whether the company should convert from telephone answering machines to voice mail.

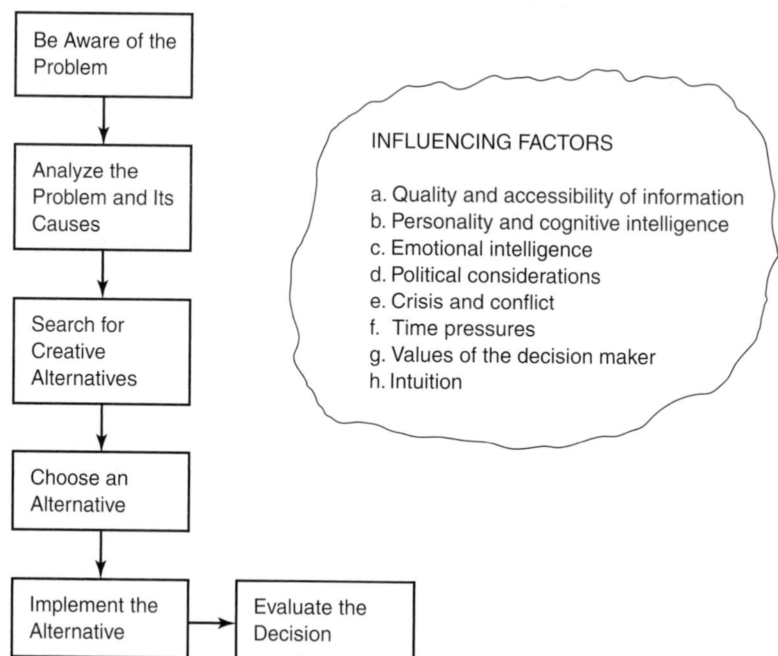

FIGURE 5–1 Problem-Solving Stages and Influencing Factors
Problem solving and decision making should ordinarily follow an orderly process. The quality of problem solving and decision making is influenced by a variety of factors such as those shown in the drawing at the right.

Analyze the Problem and Its Causes

The second step in problem solving and decision making is to analyze the problem and its causes. Raul must ask himself why he wants to be self-employed. He should ask such questions as, "What seems to be so attractive about self-employment? What is the real reason I want to leave corporate life? Am I looking for more money? Am I searching for more satisfaction? Is it that I just don't like my boss?"

Part of good problem solving is to identify the true cause of the problem. Many decisions prove to be poor decisions because the underlying or true problem was not resolved. For example, management might observe that company morale is low. The antidote they choose to boost morale is to build a company fitness center. After completion of the project, morale might decrease. The underlying cause of low morale might be that the employees have so little voice in the affairs of the company. Constructing a fitness center without consulting the employees has simply aggravated the problem.

When faced with a problem, a typical behavior is to use scripts to help deal with the situation. In this context, a **script** is a program in the brain that orients a person in a particular direction toward solving a problem. Scripts both enable individuals to understand situations and guide behavior appropriate to these situations.[2] The individual may have multiple scripts in his or her brain that pave the way toward coping with a problem. For example, Raul may have one or two scripts in his brain that will help guide him toward alleviating his discontent.

Search for Creative Alternatives

The essence of creativity and effective problem solving is found in this step: Search for and generate a number of sensible alternatives to the problem at hand. A sound decision is more likely when the decision maker chooses among a number of plausible alternatives. Conversely, many people make poor decisions simply because they did not search long enough for a good alternative. Bob Moog, 43, chairman and CEO of AreYouGame.com, explains the importance of searching for alternatives, as follows:

> Suspending judgment is something that I learned in a creativity class that I use in business today. We live in a world where things are changing so fast that if you rely on what you knew five years ago, you're not going to come up with the best answer today. Instead of doing what they normally do, which is always trying to be fast and efficient, I tell people to slow down. Never go with the first answer. Suspend your judgment: Listen to the whole idea and try to figure out how to make it an even better solution, instead of going back to something that you did previously in a similar situation—because new ideas are better than recycled solutions.[3]

In Raul's case, he might explore such alternatives to self-employment as establishing a brand new business, purchasing an existing business, becoming a franchise operator, or running his own business part time.

Choose an Alternative

In this stage the pros and cons of each alternative are weighed, and one of them is chosen. In facing a major decision, each alternative would have to be given serious consideration. Raul is facing a major career decision and thus must weigh each alternative carefully. A useful mechanical aid for weighing alternatives is to list each on a separate piece of paper. The sheet is then divided into two columns. Advantages are listed on the left side and disadvantages on the right.

An alternative that has many more advantages than disadvantages would usually be considered a favorable alternative. Once in a while a disadvantage could be so striking that it would outweigh the larger number of advantages. For example, purchasing a McDonald's franchise for $500,000 would be out of the question for many people, however good the prospects. After an analysis of the pros and cons of each alternative is made, one is chosen. The alternatives always include taking no action. Raul, for example, may finally decide to stay with his corporate job.

Implement the Alternative

Implementing an alternative is a logical extension of the previous step. Implementation can also be regarded as converting a decision into action, such as exploring the purchase of a franchise and then speaking to a lawyer. Implementing a solution requires time, effort, and money. In large organizations, many more possible solutions to problems are generated than are ever implemented. As noted by Brian Dorval, of the Center for Studies in Creativity, "Brainstorming will generate a lot of novelty, but what do you do with all those tons of flip-chart papers filled with ideas? How do you get them implemented and accepted by others?"[4]

Evaluate the Decision

The final stage of problem solving and decision making involves evaluating the quality of the decision made. Answering the deceptively simple question "How effective is the decision I made?" is complex. If the decision clearly achieves what it was supposed to, evaluating it is easy. Assume that Raul wanted self-employment to feel more independent. If self-employment does bring him a feeling of independence, Raul has made a good decision.

Evaluating the outcome of a decision is important for another basic reason. Feedback of this type can improve decision-making skills. One might say, for example, "This time around I chose an alternative without giving careful thought to how difficult it would be to implement."

To begin developing your skills in making major decisions, do Skill-Building Exercise 5–1.

FACTORS INFLUENCING PROBLEM SOLVING AND DECISION MAKING

Many factors can influence a person's problem-solving ability and ability to make decisions, as depicted by the "cloud" diagram in Figure 5–1. For example, an individual's ability to be aware of a problem is related to many traits and characteristics, such as cognitive intelligence and intuition. These same factors are closely related to a person's ability to make decisions. In combination, these influencing

SKILL BUILDING EXERCISE 5–1

Using the Problem-Solving Process

Imagine that you have just received $500,000 in cash with the gift or income taxes already paid. The only stipulation is that you will have to use the money to establish some sort of enterprise, either a business or a charitable foundation. Solve this problem using the worksheet provided below. Describe what thoughts you have or what actions you will take for each stage of decision making.

I. *Be aware of the problem:* Have you found your own problem or was it given to you?

____

____

____

II. *Analyze the problem and its causes:* What is the true decision that you are facing? What is the underlying problem (or cause of the problem)?

____

____

____

III. *Search for creative alternatives:* Think of the many alternatives facing you. Let your imagination flow and be creative.

____

____

____

IV. *Choose an alternative:* Weigh the pros and cons of each of your sensible alternatives.

	Alternatives	***Advantages***	***Disadvantages***
1.	________	________	________
2.	________	________	________
3.	________	________	________
4.	________	________	________
5.	________	________	________

V. *Implement the alternative:* Outline your action plan for converting your chosen alternative into action.

____

____

____

VI. *Evaluate your decision:* Do the best you can here by speculating how you will know if the decision you reached was a good one.

____

____

____

____

factors help to account for individual and situational differences in decision-making ability. Some people are much better at making decisions than others and because of this achieve a higher quality of work and personal life. Here we explore a number of important factors that influence problem solving and decisions.

Quality and Accessibility of Information

Having ready access to high-quality (current and relevant) information places you in a good position to identify problems and make decisions. In Raul's situation, his decision would probably be of higher quality if he consulted a source such as the Small Business Council of the local Chamber of Commerce or the Small Business Administration. Communicating with a variety of self-employed people in person or over the Internet might also yield information to help Raul make an informed decision.

Personality and Cognitive Intelligence

The personality and cognitive intelligence of the decision maker influence his or her ability to find effective solutions. One key personality dimension is cautiousness and conservatism. A cautious, conservative person typically opts for a low-risk solution. If a person is extremely cautious, he or she may procrastinate important decisions for fear of being wrong, and thereby be indecisive. Cautiousness and conservatism can be in opposition to self-confidence. Confident people are willing to take reasonable risks because they have faith in the quality of their decisions. Perfectionism has a notable impact on decision making. People who seek the perfect solution to a problem are usually indecisive because they are hesitant to accept the fact that a particular alternative is good enough. Self-Assessment Exercise 5–1 provides an opportunity to examine your own degree of decisiveness.

Rigid people have difficulty identifying problems and gathering alternative solutions. People who are mentally flexible perform well in these areas. Optimism versus pessimism is another relevant personality dimension. Optimists are more likely to find solutions than pessimists are. Pessimists are likely to give up searching because they perceive situations as hopeless.

Cognitive intelligence has a profound influence on the effectiveness of decision making. In general, intelligent and well-educated people are more likely to identify and diagnose problems and make sound decisions than are those who have less intelligence and education. A notable exception applies, however. Some intelligent, well-educated people have such a fondness for collecting facts and analyzing them that they suffer from *analysis paralysis.*

Emotional Intelligence

Emotional intelligence is important for decision making because how effective you are in managing your feelings and reading other people can affect the quality of your decisions. For example, if you cannot control your anger, you are likely to make decisions that are motivated by retaliation, hostility, and revenge. An example would be shouting and swearing at your team leader because of an assignment you received.

Your emotional intelligence could also influence your career decision making. If you understand your own feelings, you are more likely to enter an occupation, or accept a position, that matches your true feelings. For example, if you feel that the most important type of work is to create things of lasting value, you might find satisfaction in the construction industry.

Political Considerations

Under ideal circumstances, business decisions are made on the basis of the objective merits of competing alternatives. In reality, many decisions are based on political considerations, such as favoritism, alliances with friends, or the desire of the decision maker to stay in favor with people who wield power. Political factors sometimes influence which information is given serious consideration in evaluating alternatives. The decision maker may select data that support the position of an influential person. For instance, one manufacturing analyst was asked to investigate the effectiveness of having a key product manufactured by another firm (outsourced). The analyst believed that the executive who presented the problem

SELF-ASSESSMENT EXERCISE 5–1

Test Your Decisiveness

Answer the following questions by placing a check in the appropriate space:
N = never; R = rarely; Oc = occasionally; Of = often.

	N	*R*	*Oc*	*Of*
1. Do you let the opinions of others influence your decisions?	___	___	___	___
2. Do you procrastinate when it's time to make a decision?				
3. Do you let others make your decisions for you?	___	___	___	___
4. Have you missed out on an opportunity because you couldn't make a decision?	___	___	___	___
5. After reaching a decision do you have second thoughts?	___	___	___	___
6. Did you hesitate while answering these questions?	___	___	___	___

Scoring and Interpretation: Score 1 point for each "often" response, 2 points for each "occasionally," 3 points for each "rarely," and 4 points for each "never."

20–24 points	You are very decisive and probably have no problem assuming responsibility for the choices you make.
15–19 points	Decision making is difficult for you. You need to work at being decisive.
14 points or below	You are going to have a big problem unless you learn to overcome your timidity. When a decision has to be made, face up to it and do it!

Source: Adapted from Roger Fritz, "A Systematic Approach to Problem Solving and Decision Making," *Supervisory Management,* March 1993, p. 4. Reprinted with permission of the American Management Association.

was in favor of outsourcing. So the analyst gave considerable weight to the "facts" supplied by a possible subcontractor. This allowed the analyst to make a positive recommendation for outsourcing.

A person with professional integrity arrives at what he or she thinks is the best decision and then makes a diligent attempt to convince management of the merits of that solution.

Crisis and Conflict

In a crisis, many decision makers panic. They become less rational and more emotional than they would in a calm environment. Decision makers who are adversely affected by crisis perceive it to be a stressful event. As a consequence, they concentrate poorly, use poor judgment, and think impulsively. Under crisis, some managers do not bother dealing with differences of opinion because they are under so much pressure. A smaller number of managers perceive a crisis as an exciting challenge that energizes them toward their best level of problem solving and decision making. After the terrorist attacks on the World Trade Center, a handful of managers whose workplaces were destroyed had their firms up and running in temporary headquarters within two days. Although grieving for the dead and missing, these managers made rapid decisions under crisis that enabled their firms to stay in business.

Time Pressures

The quality of decisions may suffer when the decision making is hurried. An exception is that some people make their best decisions when faced with a tight deadline. For most people, tight time pressures make it difficult to identify enough alternatives to make a good decision. A laboratory study of business students forced the subjects to make decisions under varying degrees of pressure and distraction. Under heavy time pressure and many distractions, the students placed much more weight on negative than positive evidence in arriving at decisions. The particular decision that they faced was something of interest to most people about to graduate from business school: making an automobile purchase.[5]

Making quick decisions about such matters as introducing a new product often gives companies a competitive advantage. Thinking quickly can also help you in your career by helping you to get more work done and by impressing superiors.

Values of the Decision Maker

Values influence decision making at every step. Ultimately all decisions are based on values. A manager who places a high value on the personal welfare of employees tries to avoid alternatives that create hardship for workers and implements decisions that lessen turmoil. Another value that significantly influences decision making is the pursuit of excellence. A worker who embraces the pursuit of excellence (and is therefore conscientious) will search for the high-quality solution.

Attempting to preserve the status quo is a value held by many workers. Clinging to the status quo is perceived as a hidden trap in decision making that can prevent making optimum decisions. People tend to cling to the status quo because by not taking action they can prevent making a bad decision.[6] If you value the status quo too highly, you may fail to make a decision that could bring about major improvements. For example, you might fail to recommend a software upgrade simply because you are comfortable with an older, but less useful software.

Intuition

Intuition is a key personal characteristic that influences decision making. Effective decision makers do not rely on analytical and methodological techniques alone. Instead, they use hunches and intuition. **Intuition** is an experience-based way of knowing or reasoning in which weighing and balancing evidence are done automatically. When relying on intuition, the decision maker arrives at a conclusion without using the step-by-step logical process. Intuition must be cultivated over many years of experience and training. One cognitive psychologist who has studied people who make do-or-die decisions such as firefighters and intensive-care nurses, advises people to trust their instincts and forget analysis paralysis. As one courageous firefighter said, "Nothing is written down about what to do during a fire. You just learn through experience."[7]

To use intuition to your advantage, you have to know when to rely on facts and figures and when to rely on intuitive skills. Intuition is often required when the facts and figures in a situation still leave you with uncertainty. One way of honing your intuition is to keep an idea journal. Whenever an insight comes to you, record it on paper. If you notice that you shut off these insights without carefully processing them, you will know that you must learn to give them more careful thought.[8]

The focus of our attention about influences on decision making has been factors somewhat under control of the individual. The corporate environment also exerts an influence on the quality of decisions. A key example is that the inability to take decisive action is rooted in a company's culture or atmosphere. According to Ram Charan, workers become more decisive under three conditions. First, employees must be encouraged to be intellectually honest with each other, thereby expressing their true opinions about each other's work. Second, people must have candid and honest dialogue with each other in the presence of others. *Honest dialogue* would include a manager expressing reservations about a proposal made during a meeting. Third, feedback should be used to reward high achievers and coach people who are struggling. Feedback should also be used to discourage workers who are blocking the company's progress.[9] The discouragement might take the form of suggesting that the employee had a limited future in the company.

CREATIVITY IN PROBLEM SOLVING AND DECISION MAKING

Creativity is helpful at any stage of decision making, but is essential for identifying problems, analyzing them and detecting their causes, and searching for alternative solutions. In its current meaning, **creativity** refers to the ability to produce work that is novel and useful. Novel means that the work or an idea is original or unexpected. Useful means that the idea or work adds value,[10] such as developing a system that reduces scrap. A survey of 500 CEOs included the question, "What must one do to survive in the 21st century?" The most frequent answer was "Practice creativity and innovation," yet only 6 percent thought that their organizations were doing a "great job of it."[11] An important implication is that employers need creative problem solvers. Being creative is important for your career because employees in complex jobs are expected to contribute original ideas for improving efficiency or earnings.

Our discussion of creativity will encompass characteristics of creative workers, how to improve your creativity, and what organizations are doing to foster creativity. A useful starting point in studying creativity is to gain a tentative awareness of your creative potential. Toward this end, you are invited to do Self-Assessment Exercises 5–2 and 5–3.

Characteristics of Creative Workers

Creative workers tend to have intellectual and personality characteristics different from their less creative counterparts. Considerable evidence and opinion point toward one distinguishing overall characteristic that blends both cognitive and personality factors. Creative people are more mentally flexible than others, which allows them to overcome the traditional way of looking at problems. The

SELF-ASSESSMENT EXERCISE 5–2

Word Hints to Creativity

The object of this exercise is to find a fourth word that is related to all three words listed below. For example, what word is related to these?

cookies sixteen heart ________

The answer is "sweet." Cookies are sweet; sweet is part of the word "sweetheart" and part of the phrase "sweet sixteen."

What word is related to these words?

poke go molasses ________

Answer: slow.

Now try these words:

1.	surprise	holiday	birthday	________
2.	base	snow	dance	________
3.	rat	blue	cottage	________
4.	nap	rig	call	________
5.	golf	foot	country	________
6.	house	weary	ape	________
7.	tiger	plate	news	________
8.	painting	bowl	nail	________
9.	proof	sea	priest	________
10.	maple	beet	loaf	________
11.	oak	show	plan	________
12.	light	village	golf	________
13.	merry	out	up	________
14.	cheese	courage	oven	________
15.	bulb	house	lamp	________

If you were able to think of the "correct" fourth word for ten or more of these combinations of words, your score compares favorably to that of creative individuals. A very low score (about one, two, or three correct answers) suggests that performing such remote associations is not yet a strength of yours. Here are the answers:

1) party	5) club	9) high	13) make
2) ball	6) dog	10) sugar	14) Dutch
3) cheese	7) paper	11) floor	15) light
4) cat	8) finger	12) green	

Source: This test, developed by Eugene Raudsepp, is from "Ideas: Test Your Creativity," *Nation's Business,* June 1965, p. 80. The version presented here is updated. Reprinted with permission.

SELF-ASSESSMENT EXERCISE 5–3

Creativity Personality Test

Answer each of the following statements as "mostly true" or "mostly false." We are looking for general trends, so do not be concerned that under certain circumstances your answer might be different in response to a particular statement.

		Mostly True	*Mostly False*
1.	I think novels are a waste of time, so I am more likely to read a nonfiction book.	____	____
2.	You have to admit, some crooks are ingenious.	____	____
3.	I pretty much wear the same style and colors of clothing regularly.	____	____
4.	To me most issues have a clear-cut right side or wrong side.	____	____
5.	I enjoy it when my boss hands me vague instructions.	____	____
6.	When I'm surfing the Internet, I sometimes investigate topics I know very little about.	____	____

	Mostly True	Mostly False
7. Business before leisure activities is a hard and fast rule in my life.	_____	_____
8. Taking a different route to work is fun, even if it takes longer.	_____	_____
9. From time to time I have made friends with people whose sex, race, religion, or ethnic background is different from my own.	_____	_____
10. Rules and regulations should be respected, but deviating from them once in a while is acceptable.	_____	_____
11. People who know me have said that I have an excellent sense of humor.	_____	_____
12. I have been known to play practical jokes or pranks on people.	_____	_____
13. Writers should avoid using unusual words and word combinations.	_____	_____
14. Detective work would have some appeal to me.	_____	_____
15. I am much more likely to tell a rehearsed joke than make a witty comment.	_____	_____
16. Almost all national advertising on television bores me.	_____	_____
17. Why write letters to friends when there are so many clever greeting cards already available in the stores and on the Net?	_____	_____
18. For most important problems in life, there is one best solution available.	_____	_____
19. Pleasing myself means more to me than pleasing others.	_____	_____
20. I'm enjoying taking this test.	_____	_____

Score: ___________

Scoring: Give yourself a plus 1 for each answer scored in the creative direction as follows:

1. Mostly False	11. Mostly True
2. Mostly True	12. Mostly True
3. Mostly False	13. Mostly False
4. Mostly False	14. Mostly True
5. Mostly True	15. Mostly False
6. Mostly True	16. Mostly False
7. Mostly False	17. Mostly False
8. Mostly True	18. Mostly False
9. Mostly True	19. Mostly True
10. Mostly True	20. Mostly True

Interpretation: A score of 15 or more suggests that your personality and attitudes are similar to those of a creative person. A score of between 9 and 14 suggests an average similarity with the personality and attitudes of a creative person. A score of 8 or less suggests that your personality is dissimilar to that of a creative person. You are probably more of a conformist and not highly open-minded in your thinking at this point in your life. To become more creative you may need to develop more flexibility in your thinking and a high degree of open-mindedness.

story behind the invention of Teflon that took place over 65 years ago, illustrates how flexible thinking contributes to creativity:

> Roy Plunkett was a 27-year-old chemist working for DuPont. He was conducting an experiment on a possible new refrigerant. Plunkett recalls looking disappointedly at a glob of white waxy material inside a laboratory cylinder. He thought the experiment was a failure, when he decided to test the material for properties other than refrigeration. He discovered that the new substance was

> resistant to heat and chemically inert. Of even greater interest, the mysterious new substance had very low surface friction, so it would not stick to anything.
>
> Plunkett recognized almost at once that the material was different and that it had potential. Teflon, the trade name for the new resin, became a household name in cooking pans. Three-quarters of the pots and pans sold in the United States are now coated with either Teflon or a related chemical compound.[12]

A person who was not as mentally flexible as Plunkett might have said, "Too bad. I was hoping to find a new refrigerant, and all I produced was a useless glob that won't stick to anything." Next, we look more specifically at three areas in which creative workers have special characteristics: knowledge, intellectual abilities, and personality.[13]

KNOWLEDGE. Creative thinking requires a broad background of information including facts and observations. Knowledge is the storehouse of building blocks for generating and combining ideas. This is particularly true because creativity usually boils down to combining two or more existing things or ideas in a new and different way. For example, a sports utility vehicle (SUV) is a combination of a truck, station wagon, and sedan. Expert knowledge is often necessary to achieve creative results. Some research has shown that 10 years are usually required to reach expert status. A contradiction to this research, however, is that many adolescents become experts within a few years of working with computers.

INTELLECTUAL ABILITIES. The cognitive aspects of creativity have been studied extensively. In general, creative workers tend to be bright rather than brilliant. Extraordinarily high intelligence is not required to be creative, but creative people are good at generating alternative solutions to problems in a short period of time. According to Robert Sternberg, the key to creative intelligence is **insight,** an ability to know what information is relevant, find connections between the old and the new, combine facts that are unrelated, and see the "big picture."[14] Following this definition, creative people combine words and concepts in unique ways. The term *couch potato* could be considered the product of creative thinking.

Creative people also maintain a youthful curiosity throughout their lives. And the curiosity is not centered just on their own field of expertise. Instead, their range of interests encompasses many areas of knowledge, and they generate enthusiasm toward almost any puzzling problem. It has also been observed that creative people are open and responsive to feelings and emotions and the world around them.

Creative people are able to think divergently. They can expand the number of alternatives to a problem, thus moving away from a single solution. Yet the creative thinker also knows when it is time to think convergently, narrowing the number of useful solutions. For example, the divergent thinker might think of 27 different names for a Web site to sell term life insurance. Yet at some point he or she will have to converge toward choosing the best domain name, such as www.termlife.com.

Creativity can stem from both *fluid intelligence* and *crystallized intelligence*. Fluid intelligence depends on raw processing ability, or how quickly and accurately you learn information and solve problems. Like raw athletic ability, fluid intelligence begins to decline by age 30, partly because our nerve conduction slows. Crystallized intelligence is accumulated knowledge that increases with age and experience.[15] A creative group should therefore be staffed with workers of varying age. Generation Y members of the group might have the wildest, most unique ideas. However, the Baby Boomers might have better intuition into what will work (and still contribute some creative ideas of their own).

Personality Factors. Personality and emotional traits play a major role in determining whether or not a person will be a creative worker. Some of the more frequently observed personality factors found among creative people are as follows:

- Creative workers have an intense preoccupation with a field of creative expression or discovery. As a consequence they can pursue their creative interests for long stretches of time without becoming bored or restless.
- Creative people are frequently nonconformists who place a high value on their own independence and originality. They do not have a strong need to gain approval from the group.
- Creative people have a well-developed sense of humor, often manifesting itself in witty comments, practical jokes, and other forms of playfulness. (Many training programs in creativity get people to laugh, so as to release imagination.)
- Creative people tend to have a positive self-image. They feel good about themselves but are not blindly self-confident. Because they are reasonably self-confident, creative people are able to cope with criticism of their ideas.
- Creative people have the ability to tolerate isolation. Isolation is useful because it helps put a person into a receptive mood for ideas. Working alone also helps creative people avoid the distraction of talking to others. Creativity, however, is often facilitated by interaction with others.
- Creative people often have a pronounced personality trait of risk taking and thrill seeking. Their thrill-seeking tendencies often lead to outstanding creativity because finding imaginative solutions to problems is thrilling.
- Creative people are persistent. Persistence is important because finding creative solutions to problems is hard work and requires intense concentration.
- Creative people are resistant to frustration in the sense that they have a high tolerance for ambiguity and chaos.

Synthesizing these lists leads to a general picture of the creative person. He or she is more flexible than rigid, open than closed, playful than always serious, adventuresome than safety-seeking. Several of these characteristics support the popular stereotype of the creative person as somewhat of a maverick, both intellectually and socially. Later we will present some suggestions for helping you to develop into a more creative person.

The Conditions Necessary for Creativity

Creativity is not just a random occurrence. Creativity researcher Teresa M. Amabile has summarized 22 years of research about the conditions necessary for creativity in organizations. Creativity takes place when three components join together: expertise, creative-thinking skills, and the right type of motivation.[16] Expertise refers to the necessary knowledge to put facts together. The more facts floating around in your head, the more likely you are to combine them in some useful way. The salesman who invented a convenient way of serving TV dinners about 50 years ago linked together knowledge about food serving and the promising technology of television. (Notice that the conditions for creativity are closely linked to characteristics of creative people.)

Creative thinking refers to how individuals flexibly and imaginatively approach problems. If you know how to keep digging for alternatives, and to avoid getting stuck in the status quo, your chances of being creative multiply. Perseverance, or sticking with a problem to a conclusion, is essential for finding creative solutions. A few rest breaks to gain a fresh perspective may be helpful, but the creative person keeps coming back until a solution emerges. The right type of motivation is the third essential ingredient for creative thought. A fascination with, or passion for, the task is more important than searching for external rewards. (Emotional intelligence also contains this type of motivation.) People will be the most creative when they are motivated primarily by the satisfaction and challenge of the work itself. Creativity guru Michael Ray recommends that to become a creative thinker, you should first do what you really want with your life.[17] Although Jeff Bezos ultimately became wealthy from building Amazon.com, he was primarily motivated by the challenge of finding a way to capitalize upon the potential of the Internet as a marketing vehicle.

Passion for the task and high intrinsic motivation contribute to a total absorption in the work and intense concentration, the **experience of flow.** It is an experience so engrossing and enjoyable that the task becomes worth doing for its own sake regardless of the external consequences.[18] Perhaps you have had this experience when completely absorbed in a hobby or being at your best in a sport or dance. (Flow also means *being in the zone.*) A highly creative businessperson, such as an entrepreneur developing a plan for worldwide distribution of a product, will often achieve the experience of flow.

In addition to the internal conditions that foster creativity, three factors outside the person play a key role. An environmental need must stimulate the setting of a goal. This is another way of saying, "Necessity is the mother of invention." For example, a manager of materials management might be told, "We've got too much inventory in the warehouse. Reduce it by 75 percent, but do not lose money for us." No standard solution is available. The manager sets the goal of reducing the inventory, including working with the marketing department to accomplish the feat.

Another condition that fosters creativity is enough conflict and tension to put people on edge. Robert Sutton advises managers to goad happy people into fighting among themselves to stimulate creativity. The fights should be about ideas, not personality conflicts and name-calling. For example, a group member should be given time to defend his or her work, and then the ideas should be sharply critiqued by the other group members.[19]

Another form of tension, job dissatisfaction, can also lead to creativity under certain conditions. A study with office employees measured creativity by supervisory ratings of behaviors such as, "Suggests new ways to achieve goals or objectives," and "Comes up with creative solutions to problems." Job satisfaction/dissatisfaction was measured by self-ratings. The study found that dissatisfied employees are creative when (a) they wanted to remain with the firm, (b) they received useful feedback from coworkers about improving their work performance, and (c) the organization was perceived to support creativity.[20]

An irritant on the premises may stimulate creativity. Nevertheless, another external factor in creativity is encouragement, including a permissive atmosphere that welcomes new ideas. A manager who encourages imaginative and original thinking and does not punish people for making honest mistakes is likely to receive creative ideas from employees.

Improving Your Creativity

Because of the importance of becoming a creative problem solver, many techniques have been developed to improve creativity. Some people, however, wonder if creativity can be improved. The teachings of Michael Ray indicate strongly that creativity can be developed. His conviction is that creativity exists within everyone. It is a question of learning how to bring forth the inner creativity. When your creativity is dormant, says Ray, it is being suppressed by the voice of judgment—that self-esteem destroyer, heavily influenced by society and parents that says, "you can't, you shouldn't, and you're going to look stupid if you try."[21]

Here we describe both specific techniques and general strategies for becoming more creative. The goal of these experiences is to think like a creative problem solver. Such a person lets his or her imagination wander. In addition, he or she makes deliberate jumps in thinking and welcomes chance ideas whenever they come along. The creative problem solver ventures beyond the constraints that limit most people.

Brainwriting. In its usual format, brainstorming involves group problem solving that contributes multiple solutions to a problem. **Brainwriting,** or solo brainstorming, is arriving at creative ideas by jotting them down. After you have exhausted your list of ideas, they can be refined and edited. It is often best to edit the ideas a few hours or even a day later. An important requirement of brainwriting is that you set aside a definite time for generating ideas. The ideas discovered in the process of routine activities can be counted as bonus time. Even five minutes a day is much more than most people are accustomed to investing in creative problem solving. Give yourself a quota with a time deadline. A good way to get started with brainwriting is to use the method for your next work, school, or personal problem that requires an imaginative solution.

Forced-Association Technique. A widely used method of releasing creativity is to make forced associations between the properties of two objects in order to solve a problem. The method works in this way. You select a word at random from a dictionary. Next you list all the properties and attributes of this word. You then force-fit these properties and attributes to the problem you are trying to solve. The properties of the random object are related to the properties of the object involved in your problem. Listing the properties of a time bomb supposedly led to the development of a new way of delivering medicine. One key property was "slow release," leading to medicine that goes to work several hours after it is taken—a time capsule.[22]

Develop a Synergy between Both Sides of the Brain. Neurological and psychological studies of the brain have shed light on creativity. Researchers have been able to demonstrate that the left side of the brain is the source of most analytical, logical, and rational thought. It performs the tasks necessary for well-reasoned arguments. The right side of the brain grasps the work in a more intuitive, overall manner. It is the source of impressionistic, creative thought. People with dominant right brains thrive on disorder and ambiguity—both characteristics of a creative person.

The findings just mentioned often lead to the erroneous impression that logical people are "left brained" and creative people are "right brained." The left hemisphere tends to be analytical and logical and concerned with words. The right hemisphere is more holistic and intuitive and concerned with spatial relations. Because of this, creativity involves contributions from the integrated activity of both hemispheres. A brain part called the corpus callosum joins the hemispheres so they can work simultaneously. The message for creativity improvement is that both logical and intuitive thinking are required. The creative person needs a fund of accessible facts in order to combine them to solve problems. He or she also needs to rely on hunches and intuition to achieve flashes of insight.

The highly creative person achieves a synergy between the two sides of the brain. **Synergy** is a combination of things with an output greater than the sum of the parts. The unique capabilities of both sides of the brain are required. Robert Gundlach, a leading inventor into his seventies (and a person who endorses brainwriting), explains it this way:[23]

> Being creative means developing a synergy between the left half of the brain—the analytical half—and the right half of the brain—the creative half. I learned that at home during my childhood. My mother was an artist, a painter of landscapes. My father was a chemist, and inventor of Wildroot hair oil. Both my parents influenced me equally well.

Twelve Useful Exercises and Principles. Eugene Raudsepp has developed a set of 12 exercises and principles as a guide to creative growth. Many of his suggestions have been incorporated into current creativity training programs. Based on Raudsepp's research and supplemented by new developments, the principles are as follows:[24]

1. *Keep track of your ideas at all times.* Keeping an idea notebook at hand will help you to capture a permanent record of flashes of insights and good ideas borrowed from others.
2. *Pose new questions every day.* If your mind is questioning and inquiring, it will be creatively active. It is also a mind that constantly enlarges the circumference of its awareness. Have fun, and enjoy your creative probings and experiences.
3. *Maintain competence in your field.* The information explosion makes knowledge become obsolete quickly. Having current facts in mind gives you the raw material to form creative links from one bit of information to another.
4. *Read widely in fields that are not directly related to your field of interest.* Look for the relationship between what you read and what you already know. Once you learn how to cross-index the pieces of information you gather, you will be able to cross-fertilize seemingly unrelated ideas.
5. *Avoid rigid patterns of doing things.* Strive to overcome fixed ideas and look for new viewpoints. Experiment and always generate several alternative solutions to your problems. Develop the ability to let go of one idea in favor of another.
6. *Be open and receptive to your own as well as to others' ideas.* Seize on tentative, half-formed ideas and hunches. A new idea seldom arrives in finished form. Entertain and generate your own far-fetched or silly ideas. If you are receptive to the ideas of others, you will learn new things that can help you behave creatively.

7. *Be alert in observation.* Search for the similarities, differences, and unique features of things and ideas. The greater the number of new associations and relationships you form, the greater your chances of arriving at creative and original combinations and solutions.
8. *Engage in creative hobbies.* Develop hobbies that allow you to produce something with your hands. You can also keep your brain tuned up by playing games and doing puzzles and exercises. Creative growth is possible only through constant and active use of your mind.
9. *Improve your sense of humor and laugh easily.* Humor helps to relieve tension, and most people are more productively creative when they are relaxed. Also, humor is an everyday expression of creativity.
10. *Adopt a risk-taking attitude.* The fear of failure suppresses creativity, so be willing to fail on occasion.
11. *Have courage and self-confidence.* Move ahead on the assumption that you can solve your problems or achieve your goals. Many people surrender just when they are on the brink of a solution, so persist when you are seeking a creative solution to a problem.
12. *Learn to know and understand yourself.* Creativity is an expression of one's uniqueness. To be creative, then, is to be oneself. (Review Chapter 4 for ideas about self-understanding.)

A message underlying these suggestions is that self-discipline is required to develop more creative behavior. The advice offered also assumes that you have sufficient control over emotions and intellect to develop new habits and break old ones. Assuming you have such control, following these suggestions over time would most likely help you to become a more creative person.

Be an Explorer, Artist, Judge, and Lawyer. A method for improving creativity has been proposed that incorporates many of the suggestions already made. The method calls for you to adopt four roles in your thinking.[25] *First,* be an explorer. Speak to people in different fields and get ideas that you can use. For example, if you are a telecommunications specialist, speak to salespeople and manufacturing specialists.

Second, be an artist by stretching your imagination. Strive to spend about 5 percent of your day asking "what if" questions. For example, a sales manager at a fresh-fish distributor might ask, "What if some new research suggests that eating fish causes intestinal cancer in humans?" Also, remember to challenge the commonly perceived rules in your field. An example is that a bank manager challenged why customers needed their canceled checks returned each month. This questioning led to some banks not returning canceled checks unless the customer paid an additional fee for the service.

Third, know when to be a judge. After developing some wild ideas, at some point you have to evaluate these ideas. Do not be so critical that you discourage your own imaginative thinking. However, be critical enough to prevent attempting to implement weak ideas.

Fourth, achieve results with your creative thinking by playing the role of a lawyer. Negotiate and find ways to implement your ideas within your field or place of work. The explorer, artist, and judge stages of creative thought might take only a short time to develop a creative idea. Yet you may spend months or even years getting your brainstorm implemented. For example, it took a long time for the developer of the electronic pager to finally get the product manufactured and distributed on a large scale.

What Organizations Are Doing to Foster Creativity

To achieve creative solutions to problems and think of new opportunities, an organization needs more than creative people. Creativity is the combined influence of people with creative potential working in an environment that encourages creativity. Here we look at three related ways in which organizations contribute to creativity: establishing a climate favorable for creativity, conducting creativity training programs, and creating a "kitchen for the mind."

A Favorable Climate for Creativity. You will recall that one of the conditions necessary for creativity is the right climate or atmosphere. Organizations that are able to capitalize on much of the creative potential of their members have a general characteristic in common. Employees are given encouragement and emotional support for attempts at creativity. Encouragement also involves top-level managers' supporting innovation and imagination. At the same time, workers must receive positive feedback and an occasional tangible reward for making innovative suggestions. Of considerable importance, employees are not penalized for taking sensible risks and trying new ideas.

Another approach to developing a climate favorable to creativity is to attain a state of positive turbulence in the workplace. Part of the idea is to shake up the status quo. Positive turbulence at the individual level includes foreign assignments, membership in groups that cut across departments, and dealing with crises. At the organizational level, sources for positive turbulence include developing cross-functional (interdepartmental) teams, and inviting outside experts to speak to employees on matters of interest. Each year Hallmark brings into its headquarters 50 or more speakers who management believes have fresh ideas. The purpose of these speakers is to provide intellectual stimulation to the world's largest creative staff that generates more than 15,000 original designs for cards and related products each year.[26]

Another aspect of creating a physical climate for creativity is to restructure space to fire up creativity, harness energy, and enhance the flow of knowledge and ideas. The general point is that any configuration of the physical environment that decreases barriers to the free flow of ideas is likely to stimulate creative thinking. Among the specifics are that creative thinking is more likely to be enhanced by cubicles rather than corner offices, by elevators rather than escalators, and by atriums rather than hallways. In short, creating the opportunity for physical interaction facilitates the flow of ideas, which in turn facilitates creative thinking.[27]

Getting Workers into a Playful Spirit. As a specific method of developing a climate for creativity, many companies deliberately develop a playful spirit among employees. A consultant might be called in to administer a training program that places employees on a playful track, including having them color outside the lines in a coloring book, ride tricycles, shoot water pistols at each other, and toss around oversized beach balls. A marketing agency named Play (located in Richmond, Virginia) is an extreme example of encouraging playfulness of the mind. According to the people at Play, "You can't sit in a boring meeting, in a boring conference room and expect to generate much beyond boring ideas."[28] All 31 employees are expected to contribute to the creative process.

The playful features of Play include the following:

- The 20 or so staff members in the corner office called the "playroom" are instructed to invent their own superheroes or superheroines, create costumes for them, identify their superpowers, and develop alter egos for each character. Participants are given 10 minutes to complete the exercise.
- On any given afternoon you might find that a UPS guy has been pulled into a brainstorming session, or that a visitor has been asked to join a role-playing exercise.
- The group invents its own job titles. The cofounder calls himself "in charge of what's next." Other unusual titles include "what if," "Houston, we've got a problem," and "1.21 jigawatts." (One purpose of these titles is to avoid dividing positions into "creative" versus "noncreative" in the agency.)

Play has many leading companies as clients, and about 30 percent of the agency's business comes from teaching companies to be more creative themselves using the methods developed by Play. Also, the Center for Creative Leadership rates the company as the most creative in its entire database.[29]

Equipping a Kitchen for the Mind. According to Mike Vance, the former dean of Disney University (the training program for The Walt Disney Company), every business needs a kitchen for the mind, a space designed to nurture creativity. The supplies can be ordinary items, such as a chalkboard, flip charts, a coffeepot, a refrigerator, a pencil sharpener, and a personal computer with graphics software. Creativity rooms are also sometimes supplied with children's toys, such as dart guns, Frisbees, Nerf balls, and stuffed animals. The purpose of the toys is to help workers loosen up intellectually and emotionally, thus stimulating creative thinking. Many large corporations, including General Electric and Motorola, have established creative kitchens, often supplying them with VCRs and multimedia computers.

More important than the equipment within the kitchen for the mind is the existence of a common meeting place where people can get together and think creatively. Vance contends that even when people's resources are limited, they can still use their ingenuity to produce creative ideas.[30]

SUMMARY OF KEY POINTS

- A problem is a gap between an existing and a desired situation. A decision is a choice among two or more alternatives to solve that problem. Decision making consists of six continuous and somewhat overlapping stages: being aware of the problem, analyzing the problem and its causes, searching for creative alternatives, choosing an alternative, implementing the alternative, and evaluating the decision.

- At any stage of problem solving and decision making, certain factors influence our thinking and therefore the quality of the ultimate decision. These factors include quality and accessibility of available information, personality and cognitive intelligence, emotional intelligence, political considerations, crisis and conflict, time pressures, values of the decision maker, and intuition.
- Creativity refers to the ability to produce work that is novel and useful. Creative potential can sometimes be measured through questionnaires. Creative workers tend to have intellectual and personality characteristics that are different from those of their less creative counterparts. In general, they are more mentally flexible than others, thus allowing them to overcome traditional ways of looking at problems. Creative people also tend to be intellectually playful and adventuresome.
- Creativity takes place when three components join together: expertise, creative thinking skills, and the right type of motivation. Expertise refers to the necessary knowledge to put facts together. Creative thinking refers to how individuals flexibly and imaginatively approach problems. Passion for the task and high intrinsic motivation lead to the experience of flow. An environmental need must be present to stimulate the setting of a creativity goal. Some conflict and tension may be useful in stimulating creativity, yet supportive supervision facilitates creative problem solving.
- People can improve their creativity by engaging in a variety of activities. Among them are brainwriting, using the forced-association technique, developing a synergy between both halves of the brain, and engaging in the twelve exercises and principles cited here. Another useful approach to creativity improvement is to be an "explorer, artist, judge, and lawyer."
- Because creativity is so important, organizations support creativity in many ways. Among them are setting up a climate favorable to creativity (including the right physical climate), getting workers into a playful spirit, and equipping a kitchen for the mind.

GUIDELINES FOR PERSONAL EFFECTIVENESS

1. Use a deliberate, systematic approach, such as following the stages in the decision-making process, when making major decisions in business and personal life. An impulsive, hasty decision will often neglect some important information that should have been included before you reached your decision.
2. Although a systematic approach to decision making is highly recommended, it does not mean that you should avoid using your insight and intuition. Intuition is particularly helpful in finding a problem to work on and in selecting from among the available alternatives. Top-level decision makers still rely heavily on intuition.
3. Improving you creativity can improve your chances for success in your career. When faced with a problem or decision, discipline yourself to search for several alternatives, since this is the essence of creative behavior.

DISCUSSION QUESTIONS AND ACTIVITIES

1. Give three examples of problems for which it would be helpful to go through the problem-solving stages presented in Figure 5–1.
2. Faced with declining sales, many companies react by lowering the price of their products. What wrong assumptions might the companies be making about the cause of their problem?
3. What standards should a person use to determine whether or not a decision he or she made was a good one?
4. How might being a perfectionist create performance problems for an industrial sales representative? For a paralegal? For a Web designer?
5. A man who escaped a fire in a skyscraper told a newspaper reporter, "I survived because I used the information about making decisions I learned in business school." What do you think he learned about decision making that saved his life?
6. The firm Play described in this chapter is a marketing agency with 30 employees. How useful would their idea of using unusual job titles (like "1.21 jigawatts") be to a company like GE or IBM?
7. Think of the most creative person you know. How well does he or she fit the characteristics of a creative worker summarized in this chapter?
8. Why is studying a foreign language often helpful in developing an individual's creative problem-solving ability?
9. Some managers are concerned that a "kitchen for the mind" might simply become a refuge for employees who want to goof off for awhile. What is your opinion about this risk?
10. Search the Internet using the keywords creativity training or creativity in business. Based on your search, what type of creativity training appears to be in vogue these days?

SKILL-BUILDING EXERCISE 5–2

Brainwriting

A problem for which many useful alternative solutions are sought is the water crisis faced by industry. Water is becoming scarcer in supply and more costly. To help solve this problem, each class member will write down five water-saving suggestions for business and industry. After devoting about 10 minutes to this task, each class member makes a two-minute presentation of his or her suggestions to the rest of the class. By listening to the other class members' suggestions, students can gauge their originality.

Although somebody else may have already presented a suggestion identical to yours, present it anyway. It gives others a chance to learn which ideas are more obvious.

AN APPLIED PSYCHOLOGY CASE PROBLEM

The Thinking Expedition

"This is *NOT* a meeting. This is *NOT* a training session. This is *NOT* an exercise," shouts Rolf Smith, who is standing before the Face 2005 Team—22 chemical engineers, biologists, and project leaders from Procter & Gamble Co. Smith says, "This is an expedition. And there will be no whining. No sniveling. No excuses. Please take off your watches, and place them in this basket. We will give them back to you in five days." A former U.S. Air Force officer, 59-year-old Smith was known throughout the ranks as "Colonel Innovation."

The Challenge and Rationale for the Expedition

The 22 P&G employees from Hunt Valley, Maryland, are part of a company effort to double the company's revenue by 2005. The team's mandate is to develop new products that will redefine the future of cosmetics. Cathy Pagliaro, 34, an associate director of product development, is responsible for launching this expedition. She says, "Our CEO has declared that Organization 2005 is about three things: stretch, innovation, and speed. The challenge for our small group is to help make those words a reality. My department has a charter to do new and different things to help fulfill our revenue goal. The only way we can change is if we start to think differently."

Rolf Smith's job is to help the team to begin to think differently—and to turn what can feel at times like a crushing burden into a thrilling intellectual adventure. A Thinking Expedition combines creative problem solving with challenging outdoor experiential learning. According to Smith, "The days are intense, full, and demanding. There are no scheduled meals, and no scheduled breaks. We deliberately design the expedition to push people out of their 'stupid zone'—a place of mental and physical normalcy—so that they can start to think differently, explore what they don't know, and discover answers to mission critical problems."

Smith believes that breakthrough ideas come from the edge—that uncomfortable point at which levels of stress, tension, and exhaustion are pushed beyond the comfort zone. "People like to complain that they don't think well when they're tired or hungry. I take those people aside and tell them, 'That's the whole point. We don't want you to think well. We want you to think differently.'"

The Expedition Itself

"You are not who you were yesterday," Smith tells the members of the P&G team, who are now outfitted in safari vests. The first day of the expedition, which ended at 11:30 P.M., is now behind them. Team members have been briefed on the mission, the found rules, and their roles. The main objective is not to solve the specific product-development challenges that the team faces—no one is going to invent a new mascara or face cream in the next five days. Rather it is to define and refine the challenge itself ("the mess") that the team faces as it tries to invent new products.

Smith and the P&G team began working on the mess long before they arrived here. Each participant filled out an Expedition Visa, a detailed questionnaire with open-ended and fill-in-the-blank questions. The answers to the questions help to give Smith and his team leaders insight into designing the expedition. Cathy Pagliaro didn't tell anyone what they were doing, where they were going, or what to expect. All she told them was to block off several days to go off-site. A lot of the people couldn't handle not knowing, but the idea is to knock them out of the comfort zone.

To capture ideas, Smith uses blue slips—a piece of light blue paper measuring two and three-quarter inches by four and one-quarter inches (deliberately not three-by-five) that expedition members carry with them at all times. The key to capturing an idea, emphasizes Smith, is to write it down. The hundreds of blue-slip ideas that the Face 2005 Team will generate over its five days are gathered into the "Trail Ahead Travel Log." The log is divided into sections that list the team's discoveries, results, vision, and concepts of operation, and how to keep the sense of expedition alive upon the return to the office. During the expedition Smith maintains a barrage of questions. Some are intentionally vague, and seemingly silly, such as "What's a thought that you've never thought before?"

One hot, humid, and overcast day the agenda is rock climbing. Harnessed, helmeted, and with all the appropriate legal waivers signed, the Face 2005 Team starts hiking down a narrow path in Virginia's Great Falls Park toward the Potomac River—and toward a sheer rock face at the water's edge.

It's dark as the team hikes back up the steep trail after hours of climbing. Some made it to the top of the cliff, others did not, and some fell off trying, avoiding serious injury or death via the safety ropes. Still, everyone is pumped. Despite groans from a blue-slip-fatigued group, Smith prompts the usual flurry with his pointed questions. One woman shares her insight: "We're conditioned to think that small steps aren't good enough. But I realize that small steps are just what you need to get to the top."

The trip back down the mountain, called the "long trek home," represents the work required to turn the big ideas that were generated at the summit into useful action items that can be implemented when the team returns. During descent, team members are tired, they want to get home, and worse, they stop thinking. The danger is that they return to their organization with the "high" of climbing but without the "how" of getting things done differently.

The P&G team experienced several breakthroughs but also breakdowns. A 50-year-old research psychologist on the team wound up in the emergency room with severe rope burns on her hands. She tried a rope swing at 2 A.M. when she lacked the strength to hold on. At 11 P.M. on the second night, one of the teams within the overall team, acted so arrogant about its capabilities, that tensions exploded. There was crying, pouting, yelling, finger-pointing, and some door slamming.

Cathy Pagliaro thought that the blowout was one of her biggest take-aways. "The 'troublemakers' had no idea how they were being perceived," she says. "And the rest of the group was ____ off because they felt undervalued, cut off, and unappreciated. This stuff happens all the time in the real world of work. For me, there was no clearer way to demonstrate the power of differences among teams. And once you understand that power, you can leverage it when forming teams or tackling a problem."

Discussion Questions

1. What creativity principles does the Thinking Expedition illustrate?
2. How can a company justify a creativity-improvement program that results in physical injury to even one member, and the potential injury to many others?
3. How do you think going on a Thinking Expedition would benefit you?

Source: Adapted from Anna Muio, "Idea Summit," *Fast Company,* January/February 2000, pp. 150–164.

REFERENCES

1. The problem-solving and decision-making process presented here follows the logic of the approach used at such diverse places as the Center for Creative Leadership and Nissan Motors.
2. J. C. Wofford and Vicki L. Goodwin, "Effects of Feedback on Cognitive Processing and Choice of Decision Style," *Journal of Applied Psychology,* December 1990, p. 603.
3. Curtis Sittenfeld, "The Most Creative Man in Silicon Valley," *Fast Company,* June 2000, p. 276.
4. Quoted in James Bragham "Eureka!" *Machine Design,* February 6, 1992, p. 36.
5. William Q. Judge and Alex Miller, "Antecedents and Outcomes of Decision Speed in Different Environmental Contexts," *Academy of Management Journal,* June 1991, p. 449.
6. John S. Hammond, Ralph L. Keeney, and Howard Rafia, "The Hidden Traps in Decision Making," *Academy of Management Executive,* November 1999, pp. 91–95.

AN APPLIED PSYCHOLOGY CASE PROBLEM

The Really Cool Toaster

Robin Southgate needed a good idea for a final project at Brunel University in Britain. After months of heavy thought and individual brainstorming, he sketched out an idea for a toaster that would give the user a brief weather report in the form of a symbol. The device Southgate developed was a toaster equipped with a modem and a Java-run microprocessor that hooks to the Web and browns bread with a symbol—a sun, cloud, or a cloud with rain—indicating the local weather. "We wanted to do something that would be a benefit to mankind, and this really fit our view of the world," Southgate says.

The market for toast in the United States has been rapidly declining since the 1950s, when bacon and eggs were at the height of their popularity. Although toast is still the number two breakfast food, only 14.5 percent of breakfasts eaten at home include toast. In 1985, 26 percent of breakfasts included toast.

Harry Balzer, who helps prepare the *Annual Report on Eating Patterns in America* for the market research firm, the NPD group, blames the decline on handheld foods. These include the portable McMuffin-type meals and the bagel (which he refers to as the Nasdaq of the breakfast market because its consumption mysteriously follows the highs and lows of the Nasdaq stock index).

"I never eat toast for breakfast," says Southgate who does not make mention of the connection between his breakfast preferences and the larger problem in the marketplace. "The thing about toast is, 'Who really supports it?'" Balzer says. "There are no major brands." When the senior Vice President for Marketing at the toaster company was asked by a *Fortune* reporter why Wonderbread is not considered a brand of toast, the VP said he had not thought that one through.

Although Southgate dislikes toast for breakfast, or at any other meal, he still sees potential in his creation of a toaster that imprints a symbol for a weather report on the toast. Southgate explains that "You have a screen on the piece of bread. You have the output device (the toaster). It costs less than a PC. So the toast is wasted space for anything except, maybe, eating."

Part of Balzer's reasoning is that as homes become more and more computerized, a toaster that prints a weather report on the toast will be regarded as an important addition to the household.

1. Based on the definition of creativity presented in this chapter, is the weather toaster a creative idea?
2. What problem is the weather toaster solving? (Or, what unmet consumer need might be satisfied by the device?)
3. How much passion does Robin Southgate appear to have for his product?
4. What effect might importing the weather toaster have on toast consumption in the United States?

Source: Based on and expanded from Grainger David, "Cool 2001," *Fortune,* June 25, 2001, p. 143.

7. Bill Breen, "What's Your Intuition?" *Fast Company,* September 2000, p. 294.
8. "When to Go with Your Intuition," *WorkingSmart,* May 27, 1991, pp. 1–2.
9. Ram Charan, "Conquering a Culture of Indecision," *Harvard Business Review,* April 2001, pp. 74–82.
10. Robert J. Sternberg and Todd I. Lubart, "Investing in Creativity," *American Psychologist,* July 1996, p. 677; John Kao, *Jamming: The Art and Discipline of Business Creativity* (New York: HarperCollins, 1996), p. i.
11. Stanley S. Gryskiewicz, "Cashing In On Creativity at Work," *Psychology Today,* October 2000, p. 63.

12. "Roy Plunkett: Invented Teflon," Associated Press obituary, May 15, 1994.
13. Thomas R. Ward, Ronald A. Finke, and Steven M. Smith, *Creativity and the Mind: Discovering the Genius Within* (New York: Plenum Press, 1995); John A. Gover, Royce Ronning, and Cecil R. Reynolds (eds.), *Handbook of Creativity* (New York: Plenum Press, 1989), p. 10; Robert J. Sternberg (ed.), *Handbook of Creativity* (New York: Cambridge University Press, 1999).
14. Sternberg, *Handbook of Creativity.*
15. "Why Kids Beat Adults at Video Games: The Two Types of Intelligence," *USA Weekend,* January 1–3, 1999, p. 5.
16. Teresa M. Amabile, "How to Kill Creativity," *Harvard Business Review,* September–October 1998, pp. 78–79.
17. Sittenfeld, "The Most Creative Man," p. 282.
18. Mihaly Czikzentmihalyi, "If We Are So Rich, Why Aren't We Happy?" *American Psychologist,* October 1999, p. 824.
19. Robert I. Sutton, "The Weird Rules of Creativity," *Harvard Business Review,* September 2001, p. 101.
20. Jing Zhou and Jennifer M. George, "When Job Dissatisfaction Leads to Creativity: Encouraging the Expression of Voice," *The Academy of Management Journal,* August 2001, pp. 682–696.
21. Sittenfeld, "The Most Creative Man," p. 284.
22. Edward Glassman, "Creative Problem Solving: New Techniques," *Supervisory Management,* March 1989, p. 16.
23. Phil Ebersole, "Xerox's Gundlach Retires to Work on Inventions After 42 Years and 149 Patents," Rochester (N.Y.) *Democrat and Chronicle,* February 20, 1995, pp. 1–4.
24. Eugene Raudsepp, "Exercise for Creative Growth," *Success,* February 1981, pp. 46–47; Mark Hendricks, "Good Thinking: Knock Down the Barriers to Creativity—and Discover a Whole World of Ideas," *Entrepreneur,* May 1996, p. 158.
25. "Be a Creative Problem Solver," *Executive Strategies,* June 6, 1989, pp. 1–2.
26. Gryskiewicz, "Cashing In On Creativity at Work," p. 64.
27. Dorothy Leonard and Walter Swap, "Igniting Creativity," *Workforce,* October 1999, pp. 87–89.
28. Cheryle Dahle, "Mind Games," *Fast Company,* January/February 2000, p. 169.
29. Dahle, "Mind Games," p. 170.
30. Robert McGarvey, "Turn It On: Creativity Is Crucial to Your Business's Success," *Entrepreneur,* November 1996, p. 156.

SUGGESTED READING

Amabile, Teresa, and Conti, Regina. "Changes in the Work Environment for Creativity during Downsizing." *Academy of Management Journal,* December 1999, pp. 630–640.

Green, Heather. "Innovation Drought." *Business Week e.biz,* July 9, 2001, pp. EB 14–22.

Grossman, Robert J. "Behavior at Work." *HR Magazine,* March 2001, pp. 50–54.

Hammonds, Keith H. "Grassroots Leadership: Ford Motor Co." *Fast Company,* April 2000, pp. 286–307.

Mitroff, Ian. *Smart Thinking for Crazy Times: The Art of Solving the Right Problems.* San Francisco: Berrett-Koehler, 1998.

Perry, Susan K. *Writing in Flow: Keys to Enhanced Creativity.* Cincinnati, OH: Writer's Digest Books, 1999.

Rosenfeld, Jill. "Here's an Idea!" *Fast Company,* April 2000, pp. 97–130.

Simon, Julian L. *Developing Decision-Making Skills for Business.* Armonk, NY: M. E. Sharpe, 2000.

WEB CORNER

www.intuition.org (Presents in-depth information about intuition.)

www.jamming.com (Offers fresh approaches to creativity for business.)

www.thinksmart.com (Learn more about problem solving.)

CHAPTER 6

MOTIVATING OTHERS AND YOURSELF

Learning Objectives

After reading and studying this chapter and doing the exercises, you should be able to

1. Describe the key elements of Maslow's need hierarchy and the expectancy theory of motivation.
2. Explain how goal theory is used to motivate workers.
3. Point out how behavior modification is applied to motivate employees.
4. Pinpoint the conditions under which financial incentives are effective motivators.
5. Describe how to motivate people through the work itself.
6. Explain how employee empowerment contributes to motivation.
7. Develop a strategy for enhancing your own motivation.

Motivation is concerned with the "why" of behavior, the reason people do things. Many psychologists believe that all behavior is motivated; there is a reason for doing everything you do. If you are late for work regularly it could mean that you find many of your tasks boring; or perhaps you are trying to get fired so you can take a break from work. In its technical meaning, **motivation** is an energizing force that stimulates arousal, direction, and persistence of behavior. Or more simply stated, to motivate is to *move*. To understand an individual's motivation to work, you would need to understand:

- The amount of effort the individual intends to expend on the job (arousal).
- The nature of the job-related tasks the individual will choose to engage in (direction).
- How long these behaviors will last (duration).[1]

Motivation is both a force within an individual and a process used to get others to expend effort. You might be motivated to succeed in your career, and you might also engage in activities to get others to work hard toward some important goal. Self-interest plays a key role in motivation. People ask "What's in it for me?" or "WIIFM" (pronounced wiff'em) before engaging in any form of behavior. In one way or another, people act in a way that serves their self-interest. Even when people act in a way that helps others, they are doing so because helping others helps them. For example, a person may give money to poor people because this act of kindness makes him or her feel wanted and powerful.

Our approach to studying work motivation is first to explain two foundation theories of motivation. We then present a variety of approaches used to motivate employees, followed by a discussion of self-motivation. The "what's in it for me" principle is embedded in all the approaches to motivating others except for the manager raising expectations.

TWO KEY EXPLANATIONS OF MOTIVATION

Motivation is such an important part of human behavior that many different explanations of motivation have been proposed. In this section we describe two cognitive explanations of human motivation: (1) the classical theory of Abraham Maslow and (2) a more recent, widely quoted explanation called expectancy theory.

Maslow's Need Hierarchy

Based on his work as a clinical psychologist, Abraham M. Maslow developed a comprehensive view of individual motivation.[2] **Maslow's need hierarchy** arranges needs into a pyramid-shaped model with basic physiological needs at the bottom and self-actualization needs at the top. According to this theory, people have an internal need pushing them toward self-actualization and personal superiority. However, before higher-level needs are activated, physiological needs must be satisfied. When a person is generally satisfied at one level, he or she looks for satisfaction at a higher level. As Maslow describes it, a person is a perpetually wanting animal. Very few people are totally satisfied with their lot in life, not even the rich and famous.

Maslow arranged the five sets of human needs into a five-rung hierarchy, as shown in Figure 6–1. Each of the rungs refers to a group of needs, not one need per rung. The need for self-actualization, however, is sometimes considered a solitary need. Higher-order needs are concerned with personal development and reaching one's potential. Lower-order needs are concerned more with taking care of deficits and more basic concerns. The following list describes the hierarchy of needs in ascending order.

1. *Physiological needs* are bodily needs, such as the requirements for food, water, shelter, and sleep. In general, most jobs provide ample opportunity to satisfy physiological needs. Nevertheless, some people go to work hungry or in need of sleep. Until such a person gets a satisfying meal or takes a nap, he or she will not be concerned about finding an outlet on the job for creative impulses.

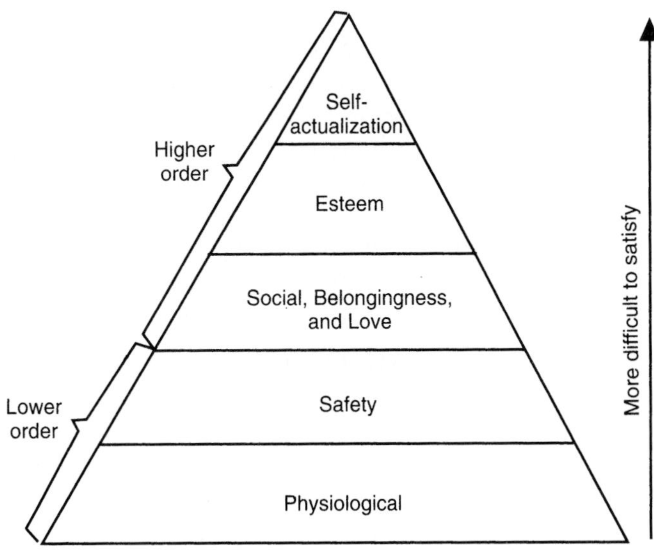

FIGURE 6–1 Maslow's Need Hierarchy

2. *Safety needs* include actual physical safety, as well as a feeling of being safe from both physical and emotional injury. Many jobs frustrate a person's need for safety (e.g., police officer, taxicab driver). Therefore, many people would be motivated by the prospects of a safe environment. The threat of job loss so prevalent in recent years can frustrate safety needs. People who do very unsafe things for a living (such as race-car drivers and tightrope walkers) find thrills and recognition more important than safety. Many people are exceptions to Maslow's need hierarchy.
3. *Social needs* are essentially love or belonging needs. Unlike the first two levels of needs, they center on a person's interaction with other people. Many people have a strong urge to be part of a group and to be accepted by that group. Peer acceptance is important in school and on the job. Many people are unhappy with their job unless they have the opportunity to work in close contact with others.
4. *Esteem needs* represent an individual's demands to be seen by others—and to appear to himself or herself—as a person of worth. Esteem needs are also called ego needs, pointing to the fact that people want to be seen as competent and capable. A job that is seen by oneself and others as being worthwhile provides a good opportunity to satisfy esteem needs.
5. *Self-actualization needs* are the highest level of needs and include the needs of self-fulfillment and personal development. True **self-actualization** is an ideal to strive for, rather than something that automatically stems from occupying a challenging position. A self-actualized person is somebody who has become what he or she is capable of becoming. Few of us reach all our potential, even when we are so motivated.

Not everybody can have as much need satisfaction as he or she wishes. There are substantial individual differences in the amount of need satisfaction. Some construction jobs, for example, frustrate both physiological and safety needs. Ordinarily, there is much more opportunity for approaching self-actualization when a person occupies a prominent position, such as a top executive or famous athlete. However, a person with low potential could approach self-actualization by occupying a lesser position.

Maslow's need hierarchy is a convenient way of classifying needs and has spurred thousands of people to take the subject of human motivation more seriously. Its primary value has been the fact that it highlights the importance of human needs in a work setting. A practical application of the need hierarchy is that when a manager wants to motivate a group member, he or she must offer the individual a reward that will satisfy an important need.

The Expectancy Theory of Motivation

How much effort you expend to accomplish something depends on how much you expect to receive in return, according to **expectancy theory.** The theory assumes that people are rational decision makers. Based on mental calculations, they choose from among the alternatives facing them the one that appears to have the biggest personal payoff at the time. Expectancy theory as applied to work has recently been recast as a theory called *motivation management.* As with expectancy theory, the basis idea is that employees are motivated by what they expect are going to be the consequences of their efforts. At the same time, they must be confident they can perform the task. Here we will examine the basic aspects of expectancy theory.[3]

Basic Components. The expectancy theory of motivation has three major components: expectancy, instrumentality, and valence. A summary of expectancy theory is presented in Figure 6–2.

Expectancy is the probability assigned by the individual that effort will lead to performing the task correctly. An important question rational people ask themselves before putting forth effort to accomplish a task is this: "If I put in all this work, will I really get the job done properly?" Each behavior is associated in the individual's mind with a certain expectancy of or hunch about the probability of success. Expectancies range from 0 (no chance at all) to 1.0 (guaranteed success).

Expectancies thus influence whether you will even attempt to earn a reward. Self-confident people have high expectancies, and being well trained will increase your subjective hunch that you can perform the task. Self-efficacy also contributes to expectancies. If you have high self-efficacy about the task, your motivation will be high. Low self-efficacy leads to low motivation.[4] Some people are poorly motivated to sky dive because they doubt they will be able to pull the rip cord while free-falling at 120 mph.

Instrumentality is the probability assigned by the individual that performance will lead to certain outcomes or rewards. When people engage in a particular behavior, they do so with the intention of achieving a desired outcome or

Person will be motivated under these conditions	A. Expectancy is high: person believes he or she can perform the task. B. Instrumentality is high: person believes that performance will lead to certain outcomes. C. Valence is high: person highly values the outcomes.

FIGURE 6–2 A Basic Version of Expectancy Theory

reward. Instrumentalities also range from 0 to 1.0. If you believe there is no chance of receiving the reward, the assigned probability is 0. If you believe the reward is certain to follow from performing correctly, the assigned probability is 1.0. For example, "I know for sure that if I show up for work every day this two-week period I will receive my paycheck."

Valence is the attractiveness of an outcome. In each work situation there are multiple outcomes, each with a valence of its own. For instance, if you make a substantial cost-saving suggestion for your employer, potential outcomes include cash award, good performance evaluation, promotion, recognition, and status. Most work situations include outcomes with both positive and negative valences. For instance, a promotion may have many positive outcomes, such as more pay and responsibility. Yet it may also have the negative outcomes of less time for family and friends and being envied by some people.

In the version of expectancy theory presented here, valences range from −100 to +100. A valence of −100 means that you strongly desire an outcome. A valence of + 100 means that you are strongly motivated to avoid an outcome, such as being fired from a job. A valence of 0 means that you are indifferent toward an outcome. An outcome with a 0 valence is therefore of no use as a motivator.

A seeming contradiction in expectancy theory requires explanation. Some people will engage in behaviors with low expectancies, such as trying to invent a successful new product or becoming a top executive at a major corporation. The compensating factor is the large valences attached to the second-level outcomes associated with these accomplishments. The payoffs from introducing a successful new product (or service) or becoming a CEO are so great that people are willing to take a long shot.

How Motivation and Ability Are Linked to Performance. Another important contribution of expectancy theory is that it helps to explain how motivation and ability are linked to job performance. As depicted in Figure 6–3, to achieve performance (actual job results), both motivation and ability must be present. If one is absent, no performance will be possible. It is important to recognize the contribution of ability in bringing about performance, because our culture tends to overdramatize the contribution of motivation to performance. Too many people uncritically accept the statement "You can achieve anything you want if you try hard enough." In reality, a person also needs the proper education, ability, tools, and technology.

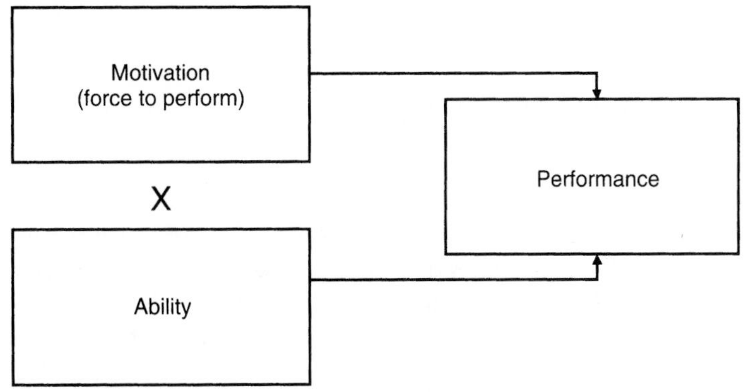

FIGURE 6–3 How Motivation and Ability Influence Performance

SKILL-BUILDING EXERCISE 6–1

Uncovering Valences

The class divides into pairs of students. In each pair, one student plays the role of a team leader who is developing a plan to highly motivate the team member being interviewed. The other student plays the role of the team member being interviewed. The twist to this role play is that the team member reflects on his or her actual motivators (rewards that he or she would like to attain).

The team leader might ask several questions while conducting an interview for approximately 15 minutes. In addition, when the team member reveals an important piece of information, the team leader will dig for more details. Suggested interview questions are as follows:

1. Why are you working on this team?
2. What can the company do to make you really happy?
3. What would be a fair reward for performing up to your capacity? On a 1-to-10 scale, how badly do you want this reward?
4. What would be an outstanding reward for you for performing up to your capacity?
5. What would be a fantasy reward for you for performing up to your capacity? On a 1-to-10 scale, how badly do you want this reward?
6. What do you hope to get out of this job?

A brief class discussion might follow the completion of the interviews. A key issue to address in the discussion is the extent to which each interview appeared helpful in motivating the team member. For example, were the interviews an effective method of uncovering the valences the team members attached to specific rewards?

Motivation is often the key to attaining good results. Yet at other times, factors other than motivation come into play. For example, as a member of a work group you might want to be a high producer, but group pressures may keep you from producing much more work than the group standard.

One way to use the information presented about motivation is to diagnose why you (or another person) are not well motivated in a given situation. Ask questions such as these: (1) Is there an opportunity to satisfy an important need? (2) Are the expectancies high enough? Do you believe you can accomplish the task? (3) Are the instrumentalities high enough? Do you believe that hard work will lead to a reward? (4) Is the reward meaningful to you?

Skill-Building Exercise 6–1 gives you an opportunity to practice applying an important aspect of expectancy theory to motivate others.

MOTIVATION THROUGH THE APPLICATION OF GOAL THEORY

Goal setting is a basic process that is directly or indirectly part of all major theories of work motivation. Goals are also widely used in the workplace as a means to improve and sustain work performance. To help you better understand how goals operate, here we describe three topics: the conditions under which goals are likely to be effective, how they affect your brains, and two opposing orientations toward goal setting.

Goal Theory

Hundreds of studies have been conducted about the relationship between goal setting and work performance. There is enough consistency in the findings of these studies to provide guidelines for motivating people.[5] A **goal** is what a person is trying to accomplish. The basic premise underlying goal theory is that behavior is regulated by values and goals. Our values create within us a desire to behave consistently with them. For example, if an executive values honesty, he or she will establish a goal of trying to hire only honest employees and will therefore make extensive use of background checks and honesty testing. The following best-established facts in goal theory are outlined in Figure 6–4.

- **Specific goals lead to higher performance than do generalized goals.** Telling someone to "do your best" is a generalized goal. A specific goal would be, "Process an average of four more cases per day." (Here is an example of where common sense can be wrong. Many people believe that telling others to "do your best" is an excellent motivator.)
- **Performance generally increases in direct proportion to goal difficulty.** The more difficult your goal, the more you accomplish. An important exception is that when goals are too difficult, they may lower performance. Difficulty in reaching the goal leads to frustration, which in turn leads to lowered performance.
- **For goals to improve performance, the worker must accept or be committed to them.** If you reject a goal, you will not incorporate it into planning. This is why it is often helpful for managers to discuss goals with group members, rather than imposing goals on them. Participating in setting goals has no major effect on job performance except when it improves goal acceptance. Yet participation is valuable because it can lead to higher satisfaction with the goal-setting process. Being committed to a goal is a stronger attitude than merely accepting a goal. Goal commitment indicates that the person will struggle mightily to attain the goal. Commitment to a goal is a necessary condition for difficult goals to result in higher task performance. Without commitment, it is easy to become frustrated with pursuing a highly difficult goal.
- **Goals are more effective when they are used to evaluate performance.** When workers know that their performance will be evaluated in terms of how well they attained their goals, the impact of goals increases.

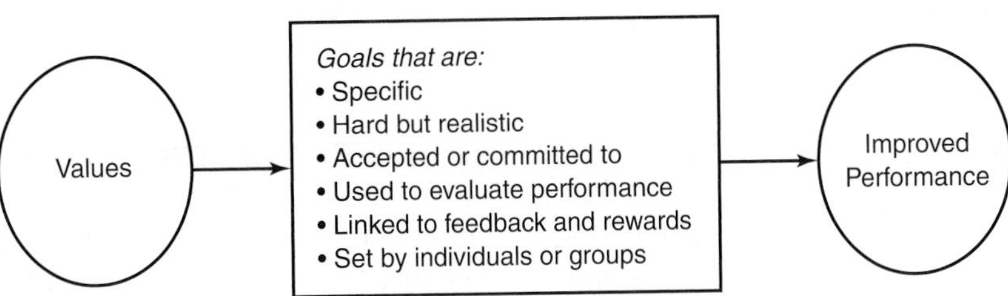

FIGURE 6–4 The Basics of Goal Theory

- **Goals should be linked to feedback and rewards.** Workers should receive feedback on their progress toward goals and be rewarded for reaching them. Rewarding people for reaching goals is perhaps the most widely accepted principle of management.
- **Group goal setting is as important as individual goal setting.** Having employees work as teams with a specific team goal, rather than as individuals with only individual goals, increases productivity. Furthermore, the combination of compatible group and individual goals is more effective than either individual or group goals alone.

Cognitive and Neurological Reasons Why Goals Are Effective

To fully understand the contribution of goals to motivation, it is important to uncover the cognitive and neurological reasons for their effectiveness. One cognitive explanation of the effectiveness of goals states that they are not motivational by themselves. Rather, the discrepancy between what individuals have and what they aspire to achieve creates dissatisfaction. The self-dissatisfaction serves as an incentive, and people respond to reduce the discrepancy. A positive self-evaluation results from achieving the goal.[6]

An example will help clarify this cognitive explanation. Jeff might be working as a telemarketer. He sets a goal of being promoted to an outside sales position where he can call on customers and earn a bigger commission. Having set this goal, he is dissatisfied with the discrepancy between his present job and being an outside sales representative. Jeff's dissatisfaction prompts him to work extra hard to perform well as a telemarketer. Because of this, his manager might offer him a promotion.

The motivational effects of goal setting also have a neurological (nervous system) explanation. A building block for this explanation is that many of our actions are influenced by an arousal mechanism. The strength of the arousal moves along a continuum from a low point during sleep to a high point of frantic effort or excitement. (Have you ever observed a sports fan watch his or her team win the "big game" at the final buzzer?) The state of being aroused is associated with activity in the sympathetic nervous system. The sympathetic nervous system readies the body for action. It also governs the amount of energy available for performing a task.[7]

Assume that on Monday paralegal Carla establishes the goal of preparing the paperwork for 15 house closings. The goal is a stretch for Carla, but not impossible. Her nervous system will be activated to gear up for the task. By having extra energy to meet these demands, Carla will be well motivated. A problem, however, is that if the task is too demanding, the goal may produce overarousal. As a result, the person may be too "hyper" to perform well and will back away from getting the task accomplished.

The Learning and Performance Orientations Toward Goals

Another useful perspective on understanding how goals influence motivation is that goals can be aimed at either learning or performing.[8] A learning-goal orientation means that an individual is focused on acquiring new skills and mastering new situations. For example, you might establish the goal of developing skill in videotaping shoppers. You say to yourself, "My goal is to learn how to make interesting, high-quality videotapes."

A performance-goal orientation is different. It means that you want to demonstrate and validate the adequacy of your competence by seeking favorable judgments. At the same time, you want to avoid seeking negative judgments about your competence. For example, your goal might be to prepare videotapes that will highly impress whoever watches them. Your focus is on looking good and avoiding negative evaluations of your videotaped productions.

A study with 167 medical supplies sales representatives indicated that a learning-goal orientation was associated with higher sales performance. The data for the study were collected during a quarterly product promotion, and the two types of learning orientation were measured with a questionnaire. Sales performance was measured as the number of units sold during the promotion. The study also found that sales reps with a learning-goal orientation were more likely to set higher goals.[9]

A person's goal orientation usually affects his or her desire for feedback. People with a learning-goal orientation are more likely to seek feedback on how well they are performing. In contrast, people with a performance-goal orientation are less likely to seek feedback. If you focus too much on setting performance goals, you might have a tendency to overlook the value of feedback. Yet the feedback could help you improve your performance in the long run. It is also important to recognize that if you, the goal setter, seek feedback, you will create a good impression.

MOTIVATION THROUGH BEHAVIOR MODIFICATION

A widely used technique of work motivation is **behavior modification**—changing behavior by rewarding the right responses and/or punishing or ignoring the wrong responses. Behavior modification is therefore a form of operant conditioning.

The application of behavior modification is concerned with the actual job behavior of an employee (such as making a sale) and the consequences of that behavior (such as getting a commission for making the sale). The emphasis on behavior and its consequences is based on the *law of effect.* According to this law, behavior that leads to a positive consequence for the individual tends to be repeated, whereas behavior that leads to a negative consequence tends not to be repeated. Here we describe how managers, team leaders, and supervisors can use behavior modification in the form of positive reinforcement. In addition, we summarize the evidence for the effectiveness of company programs of behavior modification.

Rules for Using Behavior Modification

Behavior modification (or behavior mod) programs in organizations generally emphasize positive reinforcement rather than negative reinforcement, punishment, or extinction. Furthermore, managers are more likely to use positive reinforcement than other behavior mod strategies when motivating group members. Despite this emphasis on the positive, punishment is used occasionally to motivate employees. The information about operant conditioning presented in Chapter 2 applies to motivation as well as to learning. To use positive reinforcement effectively on the job, certain rules or procedures must be followed. The best results will be achieved if these rules are combined with a genuine interest in the welfare of workers. The following rules are presented from the standpoint of the manager.

1. *State clearly what behavior will lead to a reward.* The nature of good performance, or the goals, must be agreed upon by manager and team member. Clarification might take this form: "We need delivered units that are returned by no more than 1 percent of our customers because of complaints about quality." It is also important to reward specifically the behavior you want reinforced. If good customer service is the goal, customer service reps should be rewarded for solving customer problems, and not for processing a large number of customers.
2. *Choose an appropriate reward or punishment.* An appropriate reward or punishment is both effective in motivating a group member or group and feasible from the company standpoint. Rewards should have a high positive valence and punishments a high negative valence. If one reward does not work, another should be tried. A list of feasible rewards is presented in Table 6–1. When rewards do not work, it may be necessary to use punishment. It is generally best to use the mildest form of punishment that will motivate the person, such as expressing disappointment.
3. *Supply ample feedback.* Behavior modification tactics cannot work well without frequent feedback to individuals. Feedback can take the form of simply telling people they have done something right or wrong. Brief handwritten notes or e-mail messages are another form of feedback. Be aware, however, that many workers resent seeing a message with negative feedback on their computer monitor.
4. *Vary the size of the reward with the size of the accomplishment.* Big accomplishments deserve big rewards; small accomplishments deserve small rewards. Rewards of the wrong magnitude lose some of their motivational power. An important corollary of this principle is that people become embarrassed when praise is overlavish. If an employee reloads a jammed printer, he or she should not be told, "Incredible job! This should boost department productivity immensely." A more realistic compliment would be, "Thanks for helping us out of a jam."
5. *Schedule rewards intermittently.* Rewards should not be given on every occasion for good performance. Intermittent rewards sustain desired behavior longer and slow the process of behavior fading away when it is not rewarded. A reward that is given continuously may lose its impact. A practical value of intermittent reinforcement is that it saves time. Few managers have enough time to dispense rewards for every appropriate response forthcoming from group members.
6. *Make sure that rewards and punishments follow the deserved behavior closely in time.* For maximum effectiveness, workers should be rewarded shortly after doing something right and punished shortly after doing something wrong. A built-in feedback system, such as software working or not working, capitalizes on this principle. If you are administering rewards and punishments, strive to administer them the same day they are earned.

TABLE 6–1
REWARDS SUITABLE FOR USE IN POSITIVE REINFORCEMENT

A large number of potential rewards can be used to motivate individuals and teams, and many of them are low cost or no cost. An important condition for something being rewarding is that the person being motivated thinks it is valuable. The viewpoint of the reward giver alone about the value of a reward is not sufficient.

MONETARY
Salary increases or bonuses
Company-paid vacation trip
Bonus or profit sharing
Company stock ownership
Stock options
Bonus or profit sharing
Paid personal holiday (such as birthday)
Movie, concert, or athletic event tickets
Free or discount airline tickets
Discounts on company products or services
Gift selection from catalog
Race-car driving camp

JOB AND CAREER RELATED
Challenging work assignment
Empowerment of employee
Change of job status from temporary to permanent
Promise of job security
Assignment to high-prestige team or project
Favorable performance appraisal
Freedom to choose own work activity
Promotion
Build fun into work
More of preferred task
Role as boss's stand-in when he or she is away
Contribute to presentations to top management
Job rotation
Encourage learning and continuous improvement
Allow employees to set own goals

FOOD AND DINING
Business luncheon paid by company
Company picnics
Department parties or special banquet
Holiday turkeys and fruit baskets

RECOGNITION AND PRIDE RELATED
Thanking orally or in writing
Encouragement
Comradeship with boss
Access to confidential information
Pat on back or handshake
Public expression of appreciation
Meeting of appreciation with executive
Flattering letter from customer distributed over e-mail
Compliment
Open note of thanks distributed over e-mail
Employee-of-the-month award
Wall plaque indicating accomplishment
Special commendation
Company recognition program
Team uniforms, hats, T-shirts, or mugs

STATUS SYMBOLS
Bigger desk
Bigger office or cubicle
Private office
Freedom to personalize work area
Frequent business travel

Time Off
Three-day weekend
Company time bank with deposits made for unusual effort or success
Personal leave days for events chosen by employee

Source: A few of the rewards above are suggested from Dot Yandle, "Rewarding Good Work: What Do Your Employees Want? *Success Workshop* (A supplement to *Managers Edge*) May 1999, pp. 1–4; Bob Nelson, "Does One Reward Fit All?" *Workforce,* February 1997, p. 70; Jennifer J. Laabs, "Targeted Rewards Jump-start Motivation," *Workforce,* February 1998, pp. 88–93.

7. *Make the rewards visible.* Another important characteristic of an effective reward is the extent to which it is visible, or noticeable, to other employees. When other workers notice the reward, its impact multiplies because the other people observe what kind of behavior is rewarded.[10] Assume that you are being informed about a coworker having received an exciting assignment because of high performance. You might strive to accomplish the same level of performance.
8. *Reward groups as well as individuals.* Given that so much work is accomplished through groups, it is important to reward groups as well as individuals.[11] An example is throwing a banquet as a reward for a high-performing team. Another approach is to base bonus pay on a combination of individual and group performance.
9. *Change rewards periodically.* Rewards grow stale quickly, making it necessary to change them periodically. A related problem is that a repetitive reward can become an annoyance. How many times can a person be motivated by the phrase "Fabulous job"? How many recognition plaques can a person wish to receive for making quota? Financial rewards, however, are less likely to grow stale because they can be used for so many purposes that lead to need satisfaction.

Employee Recognition Programs as Behavior Modification

The workplace provides a natural opportunity to satisfy the **recognition need,** the desire to be acknowledged for one's contributions and efforts and to feel important. Table 6–1 lists several types of recognition rewards. A manager can thus motivate many employees by making them feel important. Employee needs for recognition can be satisfied both through informal recognition and by formal recognition programs. If the recognition prize is made contingent upon achievement, the recognition program functions like behavior modification. (For examples of dozens of recognition awards, see www.awards.com.)

Praising workers for good performance is closely related to informal recognition. An effective form of praise describes the worker's performance rather than merely making an evaluation. Describing good performance might take this form: "You turned an angry customer into an ally who referred new business to us." A more general evaluation would be "You are great with angry customers."

Although praise costs no money and requires only a few minutes of time, many workers rarely receive praise. One researcher found that out of 1,500 workers surveyed, more than 50 percent said they seldom or never receive spoken or written thanks for their efforts.[12] Managers and team leaders therefore have a good opportunity to increase motivation by the simple act of praising good deeds. Other informal approaches to recognizing good performance include taking an employee to lunch, a handshake from the manager or team leader, and putting flowers on an employee's desk.

Formal recognition programs are more popular than ever as companies attempt to retain the right employees, and keep workers productive who worry about losing their jobs or having no private work area. Company recognition programs include awarding watches and jewelry for good service, plaques for good performance, and on-the-spot cash awards (around $25 to $50) for good performance. For example, Federal Express managers are authorized to make awards on the spot by giving employees a set of flags symbolizing a job well done, and a check for $50 to $100. Because so many workers are not in face-to-face contact with their managers, managers often deliver verbal recognition by e-mail or telephone. Furthermore, some recognition programs are administered through Web sites in which the employee can choose from among a list of possible awards.[13]

Evidence about the Effectiveness of Behavior Modification

Behavior modification has a long history of improving productivity on the job. Fred Luthans and Alexander D. Stajkovic reviewed all the quantitative research findings conducted with OB Mod over a 20-year period, involving 2,818 workers. In general, behavior mod programs increased various measures of task performance by 17 percent. The overall improvement in manufacturing settings was 33 percent, and 13 percent in service settings. For manufacturing groups, nonfinancial incentives such as recognition and praise were as effective as financial incentives. However, in service organizations financial reinforcers seemed to improve performance more than nonfinancial incentives. Yet for both manufacturing and service organizations, nonfinancial incentives were useful in boosting performance.[14]

FINANCIAL INCENTIVES AND MOTIVATION

A controversy has raged for decades about the effectiveness of financial incentives as motivators of performance. At one extreme are those who point to studies showing that employees rank compensation low in importance in comparison to such job factors as challenging work, opportunities for advancement, and recognition. (Compensation includes money and other financial incentives such as medical insurance and retirement plans.) At the other extreme are those who argue that people are still primarily motivated by money, and therefore that money is still an excellent motivator.

Less controversy seems to exist over the contribution of financial incentives to attracting and retaining employees. Companies known to pay huge bonuses attract large numbers of unsolicited résumés. It has also become common practice for companies to pay signing bonuses to attract high-caliber personnel. In addition, companies pay bonuses to retain employees, particularly when one company is being merged with another. For example, workers whose expertise is needed during a merger often are paid bonuses to stay put.

A challenge in understanding the role of money and other forms of compensation is that they are not pure concepts. High pay is also closely associated with other outcomes such as status and recognition. Thus, a person may work hard to earn more money as a way of achieving more status and recognition. Here we describe programs making pay partially contingent upon performance, individual factors that influence the effectiveness of financial incentives, and problems with financial incentives.

Linking Compensation to Performance

Many employers make a systematic effort to link some portion of pay to performance to make pay more motivational. Such practices are based on reinforcement theory. Good performance leads to the reward of a salary increase, while poor performance leads to punishment or no increase.

To relate pay to performance, many companies use variable pay as a method of motivating people with money. **Variable pay** is an incentive plan that intentionally pays good performers more money than poor performers. Employees receive more money by excelling on performance measures such as number of sales or number of computer programs completed. Variable pay is also referred to as *merit pay.* Whatever the specific plan, employees receive a base level of pay along with a bonus related to performance. The better your performance as measured by your employer, the higher your pay. Recent evidence specifies several conditions under which pay for performance actually increases productivity and satisfaction with compensation.[15]

- **Pay for performance should be measurable and objective.** The pay-for-performance plan is more likely to increase productivity and be accepted by employees when the basis for receiving merit pay appears tangible. Performance in professional jobs is typically measured by supervisory evaluations. At MetLife, for example, employees are compared with one another on a 1-to-5 scale. The company then classifies employees into the top, middle, and bottom. Employees at the top receive about 65 percent more in bonuses than those in the middle. Performance in jobs that lead to tangible output, such as processing claims or sales, can be measured by counting output, rather than by relying on performance evaluations.
- **The entire organization should be included in pay for performance.** A program of merit pay is more likely to be accepted when all workers, including management, receive merit pay. During times of very small profits, even token rewards of 1 percent of salary should be distributed.
- **Performance expectations are clear.** Along with pay for performance being measurable and objective, it is also essential for workers to know what tasks are expected of them. When workers meet or surpass expectations, they know they will be eligible for variable pay. Making expectations known helps create an environment where top performers can thrive.
- **The organization is committed to training and administrative support.** Many workers will need training to be skilled enough to earn merit pay. The workers will also need administrative support such as being supplied with the right equipment and sufficient budget to perform well.

One reason many pay-for-performance programs do not raise motivation and productivity as much as expected is that programs are not administered systematically according to the principles of behavior modification. Two OB Mod researchers conducted a field experiment comparing the effects of a routine pay-for-performance program versus one that closely followed the principles of behavior modification. Routine pay for performance was defined as the group receiving supplemental pay for increased performance. The principles of behavior modification were much the same as those described earlier in this chapter.

Comparisons were made among employees performing similar work in two facilities of the same company. The work involved processing and mailing credit-card bills for several hundred commercial customers, such as banks and retail stores. Routine pay for performance increased performance over its baseline (pre-experimental) level 11 percent. Financial incentives administered through the systematic procedures of OB Mod increased performance by 31.7 percent.[16]

Another approach to relating pay to performance is to link bonuses to results obtained by the work group or the entire company. Three such approaches are bonuses based on company profits, employee stock ownership, and stock options. A company-wide bonus plan ties individual merit pay to overall company or division performance, such as a year-end bonus based on company profits. These plans are sometimes referred to as *winsharing* because the "wins" or gains are shared with employees. The financial results on which the bonuses are determined can be measured at the division, group, business-unit, or company level. Sometimes the bonus is based on a combination of the levels just mentioned.[17]

Employee stock ownership plans encourage employees to purchase company stock, often at a discount. In this way the employees are part owners of the company, so they should be motivated to work hard and minimize waste. If the company prospers, the stock is likely to elevate in price, earning the employees a profit. W. Jack Duncan, among others, believes that ownership for all employees is an important key to high-performing individuals and companies. A stock that rises in values reinforces employee behaviors such as giving good customer service and cutting costs.[18] A stock ownership plan can lead to employee discouragement if the stock declines in value, and employees believe that they have made a poor investment.

Stock options are another form of giving employees the opportunity to own part of the firm. However, they are more complicated than straightforward stock ownership. Stock options give employees the right to purchase a company stock at a specified price at some point in the future. The option price is usually the market price on the day the option is granted. If the stock rises in value, you can purchase it at a discount. If the stock sinks below your designated purchase price, your option is worthless (referred to as being *under water*). Many workers in a variety of fields have become wealthy because of stock options. One of these success stories is as follows:

> When Jessica Gleeson began work a decade ago making lattes and cappuccinos at a Starbucks café, her goal was to save enough money to buy a house when she was 30. She beat that, signing the papers for a Victorian home in Seattle on her 28th birthday. New Year's Eve, 2000, to celebrate the millennium, she and friends flew to Paris to watch the fireworks light up the Eiffel Tower.
>
> All this was possible because Gleeson, like all other employees of Starbuck Corp., gets stock options that have grown in value as the company has prospered. "It's not so much about the things I can get with them, but that they provide me with choices," said Gleeson, 33, who now works as a leader for international learning and development at the Seattle coffee company. "I have additional resources I can invest in things that are important to me."[19]

Personal Factors Influencing the Power of Financial Incentives

Individual differences profoundly influence the motivational power of financial incentives. Workers who attach a high valence to financial incentives will be more motivated by money than those who attach a low valence. Here we look at two of many possible individual factors. A major influencing factor is that money is a good motivator when you need it badly enough. Money has a motivational pull for most people who perceive themselves to have a strong need for money. Once people have enough money to pay for all those things they think are important in life, money may lose its effectiveness. There are tremendous individual differences in what people classify as necessities. If, for example, somebody thinks owning three cars and having two residences is a necessity, that person will be motivated by money for a long time. The following example sheds some insight on the use of financial rewards with a person of modest tastes:

> A supervisor was busily signing up people to work overtime hours for the holiday season. A 23-year-old woman said to not include her on the list. In disbelief, the supervisor said to her, "How can anybody turn down overtime work during the holidays?" She replied, "Money is no big hassle for me. I lead a simple life. I make the presents for all my friends and relatives. I'd rather spend holiday time with my loved ones than work overtime in a store hustling a few extra dollars."

Another practical consideration is that a financial incentive tends to be an effective motivator when it can change your lifestyle. Many people will work hard to earn enough money to change the way they live, whether that change involves the purchase of a yacht or a used car. A surveyor took on a part-time job installing window coverings in addition to his regular job. Asked why he was willing to tie up so many nights and weekends for relatively modest pay, he replied, "My part-time job enables my family and me to live in a much larger house than if I only brought home money from one job."

Problems Created by Financial Incentives

Despite their effectiveness as motivators, financial incentives also create problems. One problem is that after people receive several increases based on performance, merit pay comes to be perceived as a right or entitlement. A person who does not receive a merit increase one quarter often feels that he or she has been punished. Another problem with cash awards is that they sometimes interfere with teamwork as employees concentrate on individual financial rewards. Business professor Marc Holzer observes, "Pay-for-performance programs do more harm than good. They set up competition between people. They emphasize the individual rather than the team. Virtually all innovations are group efforts. Yes, the exceptional person should be rewarded. But that exceptional person is dependent on others, on support services, which is often ignored."[20]

Financial rewards can lead a person to focus on rewards rather than the joy built into exciting work. (See the discussion of intrinsic motivation that follows.) Furthermore, it may be difficult to motivate a worker day by day through the prospects of stock rising in price at an uncertain future date.

MOTIVATING OTHERS THROUGH THE WORK ITSELF (INTRINSIC MOTIVATION)

Many management experts contend that if you make jobs more interesting, there may be less need for motivating people with external rewards. Also, attempting to motivate people by external rewards may not be sufficient. Motivating people through interesting work is based on the principle of **intrinsic motivation.** It refers to a person's beliefs about the extent to which an activity can satisfy his or her needs for competence and self-determination. Instead of looking to somebody else for rewards, a person is motivated by the intrinsic or internal aspects of the task. Here we describe the rationale behind intrinsic motivation and two of its applications: job enrichment and the flow experience.

The Rationale behind Intrinsic Motivation Theory

Intrinsic motivation and self-management go hand in hand. According to the theory of intrinsic motivation, individuals are active agents rather than passive recipients of environmental forces. Two factors can affect perceptions of intrinsic motivation. Certain characteristics of the task (such as challenge, autonomy, and feedback) can promote intrinsic motivation because they allow for satisfaction of needs for competence and self-management. Intrinsically motivated workers are passionate and energetic about their work. As a result, they are typically committed to their work, as if it were an important cause they were pursuing.[21] For example, an intrinsically motivated structural engineering technician might believe that he or she is on a mission to help erect buildings that will offer safety and beauty to the world.

An individual's perceptions of why he or she performs a task can also affect intrinsic motivation. Specifically, intrinsic motivation may increase when people perceive that they perform tasks for themselves rather than for an external reward. This is true because such perceptions provide individuals with the opportunity to satisfy their needs for self-determination (or self-management).

In contrast, when an individual performs a task to achieve an external reward (such as money or recognition), the perceived cause of behavior shifts from within the individual to the external reward. Money or recognition is literally controlling the person's actions. In this instance, the individual no longer perceives that he or she is self-managing and, as a result, intrinsic motivation may decrease. An attitude of self-management is especially important because many experts perceive self-management as the most effective method of managing workers.[22]

Job Enrichment and Job Crafting

Job enrichment refers to making a job more motivating and satisfying by adding variety and responsibility. Job crafting, a new variation on job enrichment, allows workers to personalize their jobs. A job is considered enriched to the extent that it demands more of an individual's talents and capabilities. As the job becomes more meaningful to you, you become better motivated and it is hoped more productive. Unless you want an enriched job, these positive results may not be forthcoming. An angry worker had this comment to make about a job-enrichment program in his department:

> My job is more exciting, but it's also more taxing. I'm doing more things now, which means I have to learn more skills. I'm more tired at the end of the day. What really gripes me, though, is that my paycheck hasn't gotten any bigger. If management enriches the job, let them also enrich the paycheck. I don't want to be taken advantage of.

General Characteristics of an Enriched Job. Substantial research and practical experience has gone into enriching jobs. Industrial psychologist Frederick Herzberg, for example, has supervised programs for enriching the jobs of over 100,000 employees in both the military and private industry. His classic work shows that an enriched job has eight important characteristics:[23]

1. *Direct feedback.* A worker should get immediate knowledge of the results he or she is achieving. This evaluation of performance can be built into the job (such as a highway patrol officer catching a speeder) or provided by a supervisor.
2. *Client relationships.* An employee with an enriched job has a client or customer to serve, whether that client is inside or outside the organization. In this regard, both a customer service representative and a hairstylist have enriched jobs.
3. *New learning.* An enriched job allows its incumbent to feel that he or she is growing psychologically. In contrast, an impoverished job allows for no new learning.
4. *Scheduling.* In an enriched job, employees have the freedom to schedule some part of their own work, such as deciding when to tackle which assignment.
5. *Unique experience.* An enriched job has some unique qualities or features, such as custodial assistants having the opportunity to report on building damage to management.
6. *Control over resources.* In enriched jobs groups of workers might have their own minibudgets and be responsible for their own costs. Or individual workers might be authorized to order as many supplies as needed to get the job done.
7. *Direct communication authority.* An enriched job allows the worker to communicate directly with other people who use his or her output, such as a quality-control technician handling customer complaints about quality.
8. *Personal accountability.* A good job makes workers accountable for their results. In this way they can accept congratulations for a job well done and blame for a job done poorly.

A superenriched job would have all eight of these characteristics, whereas an impoverished job would have none. The more of these characteristics present, the more enriched the job. High-level managers usually have enriched jobs. At times their jobs are too enriched: they have too much responsibility and too many different tasks to perform. Production workers are generally thought to have unenriched jobs. Today, however, many production workers are encouraged to make suggestions about quality improvement. In addition, a dominant trend is to organize workers into teams in which they have more responsibility. These work teams are described later and can be considered a form of group job enrichment.

Job Crafting as Job Enrichment. The traditional view of a job is that a competent worker carefully follows a job description, and good performance means that the person accomplishes what is specified in the job description. A contemporary view is that a job description is only a guideline: the competent worker is not confined by the constraints of a job description. He or she takes on many constructive activities not mentioned in the job description. By taking on these activities, the jobholder enriches his or her own job and enhances intrinsic motivation.

According to the research of Amy Wrzesniewski and Jane E. Dutton, employees craft their jobs by changing the tasks they perform and their contacts with others to make their jobs more meaningful.[24] To add variety to the job, for example, a team leader might make nutritional recommendations to team members. The team leader has altered his or her task of coaching about strictly work-related issues to also coaching about personal health. The team leader has also broadened his or her role in terms of impact on the lives of work associates.

Job crafting refers to the physical and mental changes made in the task or relationship aspects of a worker's job. Three common types of job crafting are changing (1) the number and types of job tasks, (2) the interactions with others on the job, and (3) one's view of the job. The most frequent purpose of crafting is to make the job more meaningful or enriched. A cook, for example, might add flair to a meal that was not required, just to inject a little personal creativity. Table 6–2 illustrates these three forms of job crafting, including how crafting affects the meaning of work. After studying the exhibit think through whether you have ever engaged in job crafting.

The Flow Experience. The ultimate form of job enrichment is a task so intriguing to the jobholder that it is capable of totally absorbing the individual's attention. The **flow experience** is the phenomenon of total absorption in one's work. It is akin to "being in the zone" in athletics. When you are in the zone, you are achieving peak performance largely because your concentration is so complete. (You will recall that flow is involved in creative thinking.) When flow occurs, things go just right. You feel alive and fully attentive to what you are doing. In flow, there is a sense of being lost in the action.

TABLE 6–2
Forms of Job Crafting

Form	*Example*	*Effect on Meaning of Work*
Changing number, scope, and type of job tasks	Design engineers engage in changing the quality or amount of interactions with people, thereby moving a project to completion	Work is completed in a more timely fashion; engineers change the meaning of their jobs to be guardians or movers of projects
Changing quality and/or amount of interaction with others encountered in the job	Hospital cleaners actively caring for patients and families, integrating themselves into the work flow of their floor units	Cleaners change the meaning of their jobs to be helpers of the sick; see the work of the floor unit as an integrated whole of which they are a vital part
Changing the view of the job	Nurses taking responsibility for all information and "insignificant" tasks that may help them to care more appropriately for a patient	Nurses change the way they see the work to be more about patient advocacy, as well as high-quality technical care

Source: Adapted from Amy Wrzesniewski and Jane E. Dutton, "Crafting a Job: Revisioning Employees As Active Crafters of Their Work," *Academy of Management Review,* April 2001, p. 185.

The common features of flow experience are high challenge, clear goals, a focus of psychic energy and attention, and continuous feedback. There is also a loss of self-consciousness. People experiencing flow are not concerned with themselves. A person who experiences flow is well motivated, whether or not status, prestige, or large amounts of money are associated with the job. Achieving flow is also a major contributor to happiness.[25]

Flow is found frequently in musical activities and athletics. Fortunately, for purposes of job motivation, people in other types of work can experience flow. An office worker can experience flow in the process of putting together a computer graphic portraying recent financial developments in the company. The feedback a person receives from doing a task correctly serves as a signal that things are going well. As the tennis player hits the ball squarely in the middle of the racket, there is a delightful thud indicating that things are going well. As the truck driver maneuvers properly around a curve, he or she receives a road-hugging feeling up through the wheels, indicating that the turn has been executed properly.

Despite the importance of control and feedback, when you are experiencing flow you don't stop to think what is happening. It is as if you are an onlooker and the precise actions are taking place automatically. Your body is performing pleasing actions without much conscious control on your part. When you are totally absorbed in reading a book, you do not realize you are turning the pages—your fingers take over for you.

MOTIVATION THROUGH EMPOWERMENT

A comprehensive strategy for employee motivation is to grant workers more power by allowing them to participate in decisions affecting themselves and their work. Empowerment basically involves passing decision-making authority and responsibility from managers to employees. Workers experience a greater sense of self-efficacy and ownership of their jobs when they share power. According to this logic, empowerment is the process by which a manager shares power with team members, thereby enhancing their feelings of self-efficacy.[26] Because the worker feels more effective, empowerment contributes to intrinsic motivation. Sharing power with team members enables them to feel better about themselves and perform at a higher level. Here we look at the psychological dimensions of empowerment and work teams as a form of empowerment.

The Psychological Dimensions of Empowerment

Empowerment is more complicated than it appears on the surface. An analysis by Gretchen M. Spreitzer of several studies indicates that psychological empowerment involves four cognitions, or mental dimensions, that contribute to higher intrinsic motivation:

1. *Meaning:* the value of a work goal or purpose judged in relation to an individual's own ideals or standards. Work that has meaning shows a good match between job requirements and a person's beliefs, values, and behaviors.
2. *Competence:* self-efficacy, or a person's belief in his or her capability to perform activities with skill.

3. *Self-determination:* an individual's sense of having a choice in initiating and regulating actions (as described in relation to intrinsic motivation theory).
4. *Impact:* the degree to which an individual can influence a variety of important outcomes at work.[27]

Taken together, these four dimensions reflect an active, rather than a passive, orientation to a work role. The worker feels in control by wanting and being able to shape his or her work role to a large extent. Viewed from this perspective, empowerment is not a management technique. Instead, it is a mind-set the workers have about their role in the organization.

Employee empowerment is commonplace in the service industry in companies such as Marriott and Federal Express. It takes the form of giving customer-contact employees more freedom in making decisions. At the same time, the employees are encouraged to exercise initiative and imagination (such as figuring how to satisfy an unusual customer demand), and they are rewarded for doing so. Package carrier UPS empowers its managers to deal with crises at the local level so they can respond quickly. Immediately following the September 11, 2001, terrorist attacks, UPS in lower Manhattan was left with thousands of undeliverable packages to World Trade Center addresses. The UPS managers decided on their own to first sort out all those packages containing medical and pharmaceutical supplies, so the supplies would be available immediately to treat the wounded. Decisions were made later about what to do with packages addressed to demolished addresses.

Although employees are empowered, they are still given overall direction and limits to the extent of their authority. For example, a customer-service worker cannot overturn a company rule, thereby creating a health or safety hazard. At a New York City hotel, a young woman wanted to check in with a boa constrictor draped around her shoulders. The snake lover insisted that her boa did not fit the ordinary pet category such as a dog, cat, or bird. The hotel associate replied firmly, "Sorry, I'm not empowered to allow boa constrictors into our hotel."

Work Teams and Empowerment

A widespread vehicle for empowerment is to give work groups more authority to manage themselves. A work team is a small group of workers with total responsibility for a task that manages itself to a large extent. Members of the team perform a variety of tasks, in contrast to the high specialization of an assembly line. Worker teams are empowered to perform many traditional management functions, including assigning tasks; solving quality problems; and selecting, training, and counseling team members. The shift away from traditional departments and toward work teams has been the most dramatic change in organizations in the past 20 years.

Among the positive results of these work teams have been higher productivity, better use of the intellectual and creative capacity of employees, less turnover, and improvement in both product quality and the quality of work life for employees.[28] All these benefits stem in part from the high motivation associated with being part of a work team. Success factors associated with work teams will be pinpointed in Chapter 14.

A mammoth example of work team empowerment is the global electricity giant AES Corporation. The employee-run company organizes its 40,000 workers into small teams that are responsible for operations and maintenance. Every plant manager oversees about 5 to 20 teams. Teams are empowered to make decisions outside their normal responsibilities. In one extreme example, a maintenance crew was given the responsibility to invest $13 million in cash surplus at the plant. The crew had volunteered to learn how to invest money, and did a credible job.

AES has eliminated the hierarchy found in most large corporations, as well as traditional corporate departments such as marketing or human resources. Every employee has multiple skills, and total responsibility for many decisions. Managers at company headquarters do not make major decisions for the company. Instead, they act as advisers and encouragers.[29]

TECHNIQUES FOR SELF-MOTIVATION

Many practicing managers and students of applied psychology interpret theories and techniques of motivation as a way to motivate other people. Equally important, a study of motivation should help you energize yourself to accomplish worthwhile tasks. In general, applying the techniques discussed in this chapter to yourself should help you understand the conditions under which you are likely to work and study hard consistently. Described next and shown in Figure 6–5 are seven techniques for motivating yourself, all based on theory and research about human behavior.

Set Goals for Yourself

Goals are fundamental to human motivation. Set yearly, monthly, weekly, daily, and sometimes even morning or afternoon goals for yourself. For example, "By noontime I will have responded to all my e-mail messages and made one suggestion to improve safety practices in our shop." Longer-range, or life, goals can also be helpful in gathering momentum in spurring yourself on toward higher levels of achievement. However, these have to be buttressed by a series of short-range goals. You might have the long-range goal of becoming a bank vice president, but first it would be helpful to earn an A in a business law course. The contribution of goal setting to your career is explained again in Chapter 17.

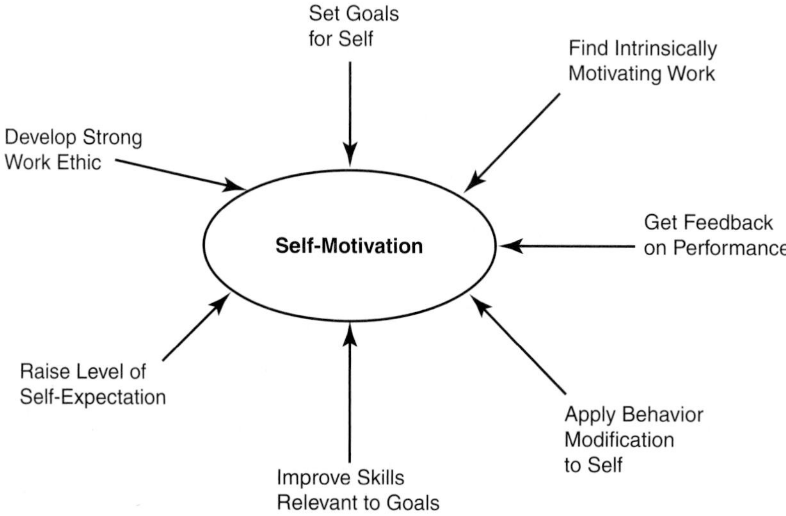

FIGURE 6–5 Self-Motivation Techniques

Find Intrinsically Motivating Work

Having read this chapter, combined with some serious introspection, you should be able to identify work you perceive to be intrinsically motivating. Next, find a job that offers you motivators in ample supply. For example, you might have good evidence from your past experience that the opportunity for close contact with people is a personal motivator. Find a job that involves working in a small, friendly department or team.

Owing to circumstances, you may have to take whatever job you can find, or you may not be in a position to change jobs. In such a situation, try to arrange your work so you have more opportunity to experience the reward(s) that you are seeking. Assume that solving difficult problems excites you, but your job is 85 percent routine. Develop better work habits so that you can take care of the routine aspects of your job more quickly. This will give you more time to enjoy the creative aspects of your work.

Get Feedback on Your Performance

Few people can sustain a high level of drive without getting an objective or subjective opinion on how well they are doing. Even if you find your work exciting, you will need feedback. Packaging design specialists may be emotionally involved with the core aspects of their work, yet these designers enjoy having their work displayed. A display delivers the message "Your work is good enough to show to other people."

If your boss or company does not recognize the importance of feedback (or simply forgets to tell people how they are doing), don't hesitate to ask an occasional question such as:

"Is my work satisfactory so far?"

"How well am I doing in meeting the expectations of my job?"

"I haven't heard anything good or bad about my performance. Should I be worried?"

Apply Behavior Modification to Yourself

To boost your own motivation through behavior modification, you will first have to decide which specific motivated actions you want to increase (such as working two hours on Saturday morning). Second, you will have to decide on a suitable set of rewards and punishments. You may choose to use rewards only, because rewards are generally better motivators than punishments.

Improve Skills Relevant to Your Goals

A practical way of using expectancy theory is to increase the subjective probability that your effort will lead to good performance on a given task. One way to increase your expectancy is to increase your level of skill with respect to a task for which you want to be highly motivated. In this way you are simultaneously increasing your self-efficacy. If a person has the necessary skills to perform a particular task, that person will usually elevate his or her subjective hunch about the chances of getting the task accomplished. Increasing your self-confidence, as described in Chapter 4, can help you increase your expectancies in a wide variety of situations. The result will be increased motivation.

Raise Your Level of Self-Expectation

Another strategy for increasing your motivation level is to simply expect more of you. If you raise your level of self-expectation, you are likely to achieve more. Because you expect to succeed, you do succeed. The net effect is the same as if you had increased your level of self-motivation. The technical term for improving your performance through raising your own expectations is the **Galatea effect.** In one experiment, the self-expectations of subjects were raised in brief interviews with an organizational psychologist. The psychologist told the subjects they had high potential to succeed in a problem-solving task they were about to begin. The subjects who received the positive information about their potential did better than those who did not receive such encouragement.[30]

High self-expectations and a positive mental attitude take a long time to develop. However, they are critically important to becoming a well-motivated person in a variety of situations.

Develop a Strong Work Ethic

A highly effective strategy for self-motivation is to develop a strong work ethic. If you are committed to the idea that most work is valuable and that it is joyful to work hard, you will automatically become strongly motivated. A person with a weak work ethic cannot readily develop a strong one, because the change requires a profound value shift. Yet if a person gives a lot of serious thought to the importance of work and follows the right role models, a work ethic can be strengthened. The shift to a strong work ethic is much like the shift of a person who has a casual attitude toward doing fine work to becoming quality conscious.

Self-Assessment Exercise 6–1 provides some research-based ideas about the conditions under which workers are self-motivated as well as motivated by the company.

SUMMARY OF KEY POINTS

- Motivation is an energizing force that stimulates arousal, direction, and persistence of behavior. It can also be regarded as both a force within an individual and a process used to get others to expend effort. Self-interest plays a key role in motivation.
- Maslow's need hierarchy is widely used to explain work motivation. It contends that people have an internal need pushing them on toward self-actualization. However, needs are arranged into a five-step ladder. Before higher-level needs are activated, certain lower-level needs must be satisfied. In ascending order, the group of needs are physiological, safety, social, esteem, and self-actualization.
- The expectancy theory of motivation assumes that people are decision makers who choose among alternatives by selecting the one that has the biggest personal payoff at the time. The expectancy model has three major compo-

SELF-ASSESSMENT EXERCISE 6–1

The Motivation and Satisfaction Quiz

The following questions have been shown to predict how employees will perform in the workplace. Each question is answered on a 1-to-5 scale, with 1 signifying "Strongly Disagree"; 2, "Disagree"; 3, "Neutral"; 4, "Agree"; and 5, "Strongly Agree." If possible, relate these questions to a job you hold now, or have held in the past. Otherwise, just relate these questions to what you imagine would be an outstanding place to work.

	SD (1)	D (2)	N (3)	A (4)	SA (5)
1. I know what is expected of me at work.	❑	❑	❑	❑	❑
2. I have the materials and equipment I need to do my work right.	❑	❑	❑	❑	❑
3. At work, I have the opportunity to do what I do best every day.	❑	❑	❑	❑	❑
4. In the last seven days, I have received recognition or praise for doing good work.	❑	❑	❑	❑	❑
5. My supervisor, or someone else at work, seems to care about me as a person.	❑	❑	❑	❑	❑
6. Someone at work encourages my development.	❑	❑	❑	❑	❑
7. My opinions seem to count at work.	❑	❑	❑	❑	❑
8. The mission/purpose of my company makes me feel my job is important.	❑	❑	❑	❑	❑
9. My coworkers are committed to doing quality work.	❑	❑	❑	❑	❑
10. I have a best friend at work.	❑	❑	❑	❑	❑
11. In the last six months, someone at work has talked to me about my progress.	❑	❑	❑	❑	❑
12. This last year, I have had opportunities at work to learn and grow.	❑	❑	❑	❑	❑

Scoring and Interpretation: According to extensive research, employees who answered "Strongly Agree" to the 12 questions were 50% more likely to work in business units with lower employee turnover, 38% more likely to work in more productive business units, and 56% more likely to work in business units with high customer loyalty.

Source: Adapted from Marcus Buckingham and Curt Coffman, *First, Break All the Rules: What the World's Greatest Managers Do Differently* (New York: Simon & Schuster, 1999).

nents: expectancies (Can I do the job?), instrumentality (Will getting the job done lead to a reward?), and valence (How valuable is the reward?). Expectancy theory also points out that both motivation and ability are necessary for performance.

- According to goal theory, behavior is regulated by values and goals. Specific and difficult goals improve performance. The goals should be accepted or committed to by the person, used to evaluate performance, and linked to feedback and rewards. Group goals are also important. Goals create a discrepancy between what individuals have and what they aspire to achieve. Self-dissatisfaction with this discrepancy serves as an incentive to achieve. Goals also create a state of arousal, which readies people for accomplishment. Goals can be aimed at either learning or performing. A learning-goal orientation means that an individual is focused on acquiring new skills and mastering new situations. A performance-goal orientation is aimed at wanting to demonstrate and validate the adequacy of your competence by seeking favorable judgments of performance.

- Behavior modification, particularly in the form of positive reinforcement, is a standard motivation program in the workplace. Nine rules are presented here for applying behavior modification. They are (1) state what behavior will lead to a reward, (2) choose an appropriate reward or punishment, (3) supply ample feedback, (4) match the reward to the accomplishment, (5) schedule rewards intermittently, (6) make sure that rewards and punishments quickly follow the behavior, (7) make the rewards visible, (8) reward groups and individuals, and (9) change rewards periodically.
- The workplace provides a natural opportunity to satisfy the recognition need. Making workers feel important helps motivate them, as does praise because few workers receive enough praise. Recognition programs can be used as a type of behavior modification.
- Although the subject is controversial, financial incentives are effective in increasing motivation. Many employers make a systematic effort to link some portion of pay to performance to make pay more motivational. Pay for performance will work best when the plan is measurable and objective, everyone is included, performance expectations are clear, and training and support are given. Building OB Mod into a pay-for-performance program can increase its effectiveness. Employee stock ownership plans and stock options are widely used financial incentives. Personal factors such as the need for money influence the motivational value of financial incentives. Financial incentives create problems, such as focusing people's attention on the reward instead of the work.
- Another major motivational strategy is motivating people through the work itself, or intrinsic motivation. The theory of intrinsic motivation, or self-management, emphasizes that people are active agents, rather than recipients of environmental forces. Intrinsic motivation is tied in with needs for competence and self-determination.
- Job enrichment capitalizes on intrinsic motivation by adding variety and responsibility to the job. Dimensions of an enriched job include direct feedback, client relationships, control over resources, and person accountability. Another way of enriching jobs is to encourage employees to craft, or personalize, their jobs. Three types of job crafting are changing the number and types of tasks, interactions with people, and one's view of the job.
- An ultimate state of job enrichment is when the jobholder experiences flow, a feeling of total absorption in the job at hand. It is characterized by intense concentration and effortlessness in performing the job.
- A comprehensive strategy for employee motivation is to grant workers more power by allowing them to participate in making important decisions. Empowerment basically involves passing decision-making authority and responsibility from managers to group members. Power sharing leads to a sense of self-efficacy and ownership. Psychological empowerment involves four cognitions: meaning, competence (self-efficacy), self-determination, and impact on work outcomes.
- A widespread vehicle for empowerment is to give work groups more authority to manage themselves by forming work teams. Such teams have a variety of positive outcomes, including increased productivity and creativity, all deriving from enhanced employee motivation.

GUIDELINES FOR PERSONAL EFFECTIVENESS

1. One critical factor related to success in all occupations is motivation—the expenditure of effort toward goals. To increase or sustain your level of motivation, it is recommended that you pick and choose from the techniques described in the chapter.
2. A major improvement that you can probably make in your career or personal life is to set realistic goals. In addition, you must develop action plans for attaining these goals. (An action plan is a specific step toward a goal such as studying a foreign language to help you attain your goal of working in international business.)
3. A well-documented and highly recommended approach to motivating others is to apply positive reinforcement systematically. The same reinforcement can be helpful in self-motivation.
4. Your level of satisfaction and motivation will increase substantially if you find a job activity so interesting that you experience flow—total absorption in what you are doing.
5. A general strategy for motivating others is to find ways to empower them through participation in decision making. If you are a team member and you want to demonstrate that you are motivated, ask to be empowered.

- Techniques of self-motivation include the following: (1) set goals for yourself, (2) find intrinsically motivating work, (3) get feedback on your performance, (4) apply behavior modification to yourself, (5) improve skills relevant to your goals, (6) raise your level of self-expectation (referred to as the Galatea effect), and (7) develop a strong work ethic.

DISCUSSION QUESTIONS AND ACTIVITIES

1. Give an example from your own life of how Maslow's need hierarchy is a valid explanation of motivation.
2. Give an example of a person you think is self-actualized. Explain your reasoning.
3. Identify two rewards that have a very strong positive valence for most people getting started in their careers.
4. To what extent do you think that behavior modification would be effective with higher-levels jobs such as a department manager or top-level executive?
5. How effective would it be to decrease an employee's pay to motivate a poor performer to improve performance?
6. Identify three occupations or professions in which much of the work is intrinsically motivating.
7. Identify several characteristics of workers that might influence the effectiveness of empowerment as a motivational tactic.
8. What kind of work would give you the flow experience? Would you take a lower-paying job to get that flow?
9. Describe the approaches you think the instructor in this course uses to enhance student motivation.
10. Ask two managers or supervisors what they think is the most effective technique of employee motivation. Be prepared to discuss your findings in class.

AN APPLIED PSYCHOLOGY CASE PROBLEM

Exciting Work at Fresh Cut Mowing

Fresh Cut Mowing, owned and operated by Tom Ellis, has been in the landscaping and lawn service business for seven years. Fresh Cut employs seven people and provides lawn service for more than 100 residential and commercial accounts. Tom oversees his two crew chiefs who are responsible for two employees each. Typically the crews are sent out to either mow or landscape, a service that includes cutting or trimming bushes and trees. Tom says, "When I send my guys out I expect them to do a good job, as good a job as I would do. If they don't perform that well, then we have a problem."

Crew chief Jesus Vega says, "We try to make a customer's yard as nice as we can. It feels good when Tommy or the customer compliments us. You have to take pride in this work. If you don't you shouldn't be in this business."

When finished with landscaping jobs, Jesus and the other crew chief, Scott Beck, receive immediate evaluations of their work. Both Ellis and the customer evaluate the quality of the work. Landscaper John Sackeli said, "You never have to wonder whether you did a job well. The customer always tells us if they like it or not. If they don't like it, they tell us what we could do differently. We then make the adjustments on the spot, or the next week when we visit the customer again."

Landscapers will hear complaints directly from the customer if that person is not satisfied with the design or appearance. By the time the landscapers have finished a job, the customer, Tom Ellis, and the crew chief are satisfied. As Ellis notes, "As soon as the guys are done with a job, I go look at it because if it's not nice, it must be fixed immediately."

One of the most important aspects of a crew chief's job is his relationship with customers. In the business model at Fresh Cut, the crew chiefs work for the owner and the customers. The crew chiefs interact with the customers regularly, whether it is over a problem, just casual conversation, or talking with prospective customers. The company is looking to expand, so prospecting for new business is essential.

Angela Balonek, a customer who had over $2,000 worth of landscaping done recently, stated, "I talked to Jesus and Scott more than I did to Tom. If I needed something done, or had a question, I asked one of the crew chiefs. Jesus and Scott provide customer service."

Ellis emphasizes customer satisfaction, so it is therefore valuable for the landscapers to appease the customer. Ellis has found that pleasing customers leads to repeat contracts, and to references for new work.

Entry-level workers at Fresh Cut typically have limited knowledge of the business but learn quickly through experience. To be profitable, the company needs to get workers productive quickly. Many commercial accounts take about two hours to mow initially, but with search for more effective work methods, the time can be reduced by 30 minutes. Tom noted, "When Jesus started working here a few years ago, he didn't even know how to put down mulch, so I had to visit customers with him. This cost me money and time. Now he is skilled, so it saves time and money."

John Sackeli said, "Before I started working here, I didn't know anything about landscaping or lawn cutting. Now I know how to fix most problems on a mower, install a retaining wall, lay down mulch, use a chain saw properly, among other useful skills. When I own a home some day, I will be able to tackle a lot of outside jobs."

The crew chief and the workers are entrusted with over $50,000 worth of equipment, including the truck, trailer, mowers, weed trimmers, blowers, and any other special equipment needed. Jesus said, "As a crew chief I think managing the equipment is our biggest responsibility. That stuff costs so much money, and when we go out we are in charge because Tommy isn't with us. If the equipment doesn't come back like it left the shop, we are blamed."

Tom said that one of his biggest concerns is sending guys out with such valuable equipment. He thinks to himself at the start of the workday, "There goes my life savings. But I trust the guys that work for me because they have shown that they are responsible and careful. If I couldn't trust them, I wouldn't have a business."

Fresh Cut offers its employees flexible scheduling. Two of the workers attend colleges outside the region, so they can only work from mid-May until the end of August. Tom said, "We have a low turnover rate every year. I think one of the reasons is that I employ mostly college students. They know they have some freedom in choosing their hours while working here. If they need a day off here and there, they are granted the time off, or can find a coworker to fill in."

1. In what ways are Fresh Cut employees experiencing elements of job enrichment?
2. What suggestions can you offer the owner of Fresh Cut for motivating employees?
3. What is your analysis of the reason why Fresh Cut employees have low turnover (or are motivated to stay with the firm)?

Source: Case researched by Scott Beck, Rochester Institute of Technology, November 2001.

AN APPLIED PSYCHOLOGY CASE PROBLEM

Rewards and Recognition at Tel-Service

Tel-Service is a fast-growing customer-service and fulfillment firm based in New Jersey. The company's core business is responding to customer questions, complaints, and comments that arrive via an 800-telephone number. Companies such as Sony, Tetley, and PR Newswire outsource much of their customer-service activities to Tel-Service. Any time a customer of the client companies calls the 800-number listed on the packaging and literature, they are actually reaching Tel-Service.

At Tel-Service headquarters, 300 employees respond to customer phone calls. In order to maintain high levels of both customer phone calls and end-customer satisfaction, Tel-Service employees are closely monitored. Workers are evaluated based on criteria such as courteousness, thoroughness, and calls answered per hour. A particular challenge is meeting performance standards when dealing with very annoyed customers.

Up until one year ago, employee turnover at Tel-Service was unacceptably high. Employees stayed at the job for an average of only eight months. Considering that each new employee received two months of training, the eight-month average stay was particularly troublesome to management. Nathan Samuels, the Director of Operations at Tel-Service, knew that the high turnover had to be reduced. An increasing amount of money was invested in training staff, and less skilled customer service representatives (CSRs) were responding to customer inquiries. If the CSRs were doing a poor job, customers might complain, which could lead to Tel-Service losing a client. Samuels recognized that skilled customer service representatives were critical to the success of the firm.

Samuels decided that the first step in fixing the high turnover problem was to determine what was wrong in the first place. He decided to interview a sample of customer service representatives. Samuels thought that a good perspective on the problem could be reached by interviewing experienced employees and those less experienced. The sample consisted of those who had been working for the company for three years, and others who were barely out of training.

The interview questions focused mostly on the working atmosphere. Among the questions were "What do you enjoy about your work?" and "What could make your work time better?" Interviewees were encouraged to be frank, and it was made clear that there would be no repercussions from making negative comments. Based on the interviews, Samuels observed several themes:

- The more experienced employees remained because they needed the job. Most of these employees were not thrilled with the work, but they stayed with it to pay for necessities. Samuels reasoned that the motivation of this group of employees was not high enough to result in superior performance.

continued on next page

AN APPLIED PSYCHOLOGY CASE PROBLEM (cont'd)

- The new employees were excited about the work but nervous about the horror stories told by their peers.
- Customer service representatives felt overworked and underappreciated by the rude and degrading customers they dealt with daily.

Based on these interview findings, Samuels believed he had a good grasp of the problems facing the customer service representatives. After reading a few leadership trade journals, Samuels decided that a rewards and recognition program might be enough to motivate the reps and make them feel appreciated. He decided to give some sort of reward for those employees who maintain a superior level of customer service. The reward would serve a dual function. First, it would motivate the CSRs to work harder to achieve their reward. Second, it would help the CSRs feel better appreciated by management to help compensate for the lack of appreciation by customers.

The plan was to hold an office party during the presentation of rewards. In this way, other employees in addition to the winner would receive something of value. After receiving approval from the CEO, Samuels decided that every three months one employee would win a vacation to Disney World. Tel-Service would pay for the accommodations and airfare. Samuels and the CEO thought that a reward of this magnitude would be very motivational.

The customer service representatives were elated when they heard about the new program. Average performance based on the standards in use jumped 39 percent, including the number of telephone calls handled per hour. For the next three months not a single CSR left without giving notice. Several clients sent letters or e-mail messages explaining how satisfied their customers were with the telephone support. During this same period, two large new accounts joined Tel-Service through recommendations from other firms.

When the first three months were completed, it was time to reward the winner and throw the party. Since not all representatives could leave the phones at the same time, coffee and cake were placed at a central location where the reps could serve themselves at breaks. During lunch hour, when a large number of reps were off the phone, the winner was announced—Kristine Santora. Albeit the competition was fierce, all employees were very proud of Santora. Samuels made sure to remind them that the start of the next contest was immediate, and everyone else had a chance to win. The fervor and motivation created three months prior was now fueled with new life.

After giving the reward of the Disney trip three times, Samuels phased down the program and replaced it with smaller, more personalized rewards like watches and sporting equipment. The office parties to celebrate the rewards were retained.

One year after the start of the program, CSR turnover at Tel-Service is approximately 15 percent, and the representatives appear happier in their jobs. According to Samuels, "I doubt we would have ever gotten the customer service rep problem under control without having implemented the reward and recognition program."

DISCUSSION QUESTIONS

1. Identify the motivational techniques used by Samuels to enhance performance of the customer service reps.
2. What can Samuels do to keep the customer service staff motivated in the future?
3. Use expectancy theory to analyze why the reward and recognition program is working.

REFERENCES

1. Susan M. Keaveney, "Working Smarter: The Effects of Motivation Orientations on Purchasing Task Selection and Retail Buyer Performance," *Journal of Business and Psychology*, Spring 1995, p. 253; Terrence R. Mitchell, "Motivation: New Directions for Theory, Research, and Practice," *Academy of Management Review*, January 1982, pp. 80–88.

2. Abraham Maslow, *Motivation and Personality,* 3rd ed. (New York: Harper & Row, 1987).
3. Donald A. Nadler and Edward Lawler, "Motivation: A Diagnostic Approach." In John R. Hackman, Edward E. Lawler, and Lyman W. Porter (eds.), *Perspectives on Behavior in Organizations* (New York: McGraw Hill, 1977), pp. 26–34; Wendelien Van Eerde and Hank Thierry, "Vroom's Expectancy Models and Work-Related Criteria: A Meta-Analysis," *Journal of Applied Psychology,* October 1996, pp. 548–556; Thad Green, *Motivation Management: Fueling Performance by Discovering What People Believe About Themselves and Their Organizations* (Palo Alto, CA: Davies-Black Publishing, 2000).
4. Alexander D. Stajkovik and Fred Luthans, "Social Cognitive Theory and Self-Efficacy: Going Beyond Traditional Motivational and Behavioral Approaches," *Organizational Dynamics,* Spring 1998, p. 66.
5. Edwin A. Locke and Gary P. Latham, *A Theory of Goal Setting and Task Performance* (Upper Saddle River, NJ: Prentice Hall, 1990); Howard J. Klein, et al., "Goal Commitment and the Goal-Setting Process: Conceptual Clarification and Empirical Synthesis," *Journal of Applied Psychology,* December 1999, p. 893.
6. P. Christopher Earley and Teri R. Lituchy, "Delineating Goals and Efficacy: A Test of Three Models," *Journal of Applied Psychology,* February 1991, pp. 81–82.
7. Ian R. Gellatly and John P. Meyer, "The Effects of Goal Difficulty on Physiological Arousal, Cognition, and Task Performance," *Journal of Applied Psychology,* October 1992, p. 695.
8. Don VandeWalle and Larry L. Cummings, "A Test of the Influence of Goal Orientation on the Feedback-Seeking Process," *Journal of Applied Psychology,* June 1997, pp. 390–400.
9. Don VandeWalle, et al., "The Influence of Goal Orientation and Self-Regulation Tactics on Sales Performance: A Longitudinal Field Test," *Journal of Applied Psychology,* April 1999, pp. 249–259.
10. Steven Kerr, "Organizational Rewards: Practical, Cost-Neutral Alternatives That You May Know, But Don't Practice," *Organizational Dynamics,* Summer 1999, p. 65.
11. Bob Nelson, "Does One Reward Fit All?" *Workforce,* February 1997, p. 70.
12. Research by Gerald Graham reported in "Motivating Entry-level Workers," *WorkingSMART,* October 1998, p. 2.
13. Bob Nelson, "Long-Distance Recognition," *Workforce,* August 2000, pp. 50–52.
14. Fred Luthans and Alexander D. Stajkovic, "Reinforce for Performance: The Need to Go Beyond Pay and Even Rewards," *Academy of Management Executive,* May 1999, pp. 52–54.
15. Janet Wiscombe, "Can Pay for Performance Really Work?" *Workforce,* August 2001, pp. 28–34.
16. Alexander D. Stajkovic and Fred Luthans, "Differential Effects of Incentive Motivators on Work Performance," *Academy of Management Journal,* June 2001, pp. 580–590.
17. Patricia K. Zingheim and Jay R. Schuster, "Value Is the Goal," *Workforce,* February 2000, p. 57.
18. W. Jack Duncan, "Stock Ownership and Work Motivation," *Organizational Dynamics,* Summer 2001, pp. 1–11.
19. "Options Become Common Currency," The Associated Press, November 19, 2000.
20. Quoted in Wiscombe, "Can Pay for Performance Really Work?" August 2001, p. 32.
21. Kenneth W. Thomas, *Intrinsic Motivation at Work: Building Energy and Commitment* (San Francisco: Berrett-Koehler, 2000).
22. Thomas, *Intrinsic Motivation;* Edward L. Deci, James P. Connell, and Richard M. Ryan, "Self-Determination in a Work Organization," *Journal of Applied Psychology,* August 1989, p. 580.

23. Frederick Herzberg, "The Wise Old Turk," *Harvard Business Review,* September–October 1974, pp. 70–80.
24. Amy Wrzesniewski and Jane E. Dutton, "Crafting a Job: Revisioning Employees As Active Crafters of Their Work," *Academy of Management Review,* April 2001, pp. 179–201.
25. Mihalyi Czikzentmihalyi, *Flow: The Psychology of Optimal Experience* (New York: Harper & Row, 1990); Czikzentmihalyi, *Finding Flow* (New York: Basic Books/HarperCollins, 1997).
26. Robert C. Ford, "Empowerment: A Matter of Degree," *Academy of Management Executive,* August 1995, p. 21.
27. Gretchen M. Spreitzer, "Psychological Empowerment in the Workplace: Dimensions, Measurement, and Validation," *Academy of Management Journal,* October 1995, pp. 1443–1444.
28. Ruth Wageman, "Critical Success Factors for Creating Superb Self-Managing Teams," *Organizational Dynamics,* Summer 1997, p. 49; Bradley L. Kirkman and Benson Rosen, "Beyond Self-Management: Antecedents and Consequences of Team Empowerment," *Academy of Management Journal,* February 1999, pp. 58–74.
29. Suzy Wetlaufer, "Organizing for Empowerment: An Interview with AES's Roger Sant and Dennis Bakke, *Harvard Business Review,* January–February 1999, pp. 110–123.
30. Taly Dvir, Dov Eden, and Michal Lang Banjo, "Self-Fulfilling Prophecy and Gender: Can Women Be Pygmalion and Galatea?" *Journal of Applied Psychology,* April 1995, p. 268.

SUGGESTED READING

Covey, Stephen R., with Pofeldt, Elaine. "Why Is This Man Smiling?" *Success,* January 2000, pp. 38–43.

Forrester, Russ. "Empowerment: Rejuvenating a Potent Idea." *Academy of Management Executive,* August 2000, pp. 67–90.

Hay Group. "What Qualities Make an Incentive Pay Plan Succeed? *HRFocus,* December 2001, p. 13.

Katzenback, Jon R., and Santamaria, Jason A. "Firing Up the Front Line." *Harvard Business Review,* May–June 1999, pp. 107–117.

Kirkman, Bradley L., and Rosen, Benson. "Powering Up Teams." *Organizational Dynamics,* Winter 2000, pp. 48–66.

Laabs, Jennifer. "Demand Performance for Benefits." *Workforce,* January 2000, pp. 42–46.

Randolf, W. Alan. "Re-Thinking Empowerment: Why Is It So Difficult to Achieve? *Organizational Dynamics,* Fall 2000, pp. 94–107.

Zenger, Todd R., and Marshall, C. R. "Determinants of Incentive Intensity in Group-Based Rewards." *Academy of Management Journal,* April 2000, pp. 149–163.

WEB CORNER

www.awards.com (One-stop supersite for rewards and recognition.)

www.betterbricks.com (Information about healthy workplaces.)

www.keepersinc.com (Information on how to implement job enrichment.)

CHAPTER 7

ACHIEVING WELLNESS AND MANAGING STRESS

Learning Objectives

After reading and studying this chapter and doing the exercises, you should be able to

1. Describe and implement strategies for achieving wellness.
2. Explain the symptoms and consequences of stress, including its relationship to job behavior and performance.
3. Explain the general adaptation syndrome model of job stress.
4. Describe how personality factors contribute to job stress.
5. Identify the major sources of stress on the job.
6. Develop a program for managing your own stress.
7. Give examples of what employers can do to help employees manage stress.

A subject of major interest to career people of all types has been to stay well and manage stress effectively. The problem of work stress is so pervasive that stress-related illnesses are rapidly becoming the leading reason for worker disability claims, reports the National Institute for Occupational Safety and Health.[1] In this chapter we study wellness and stress, including the nature of stress, and what individuals and organizations can do to effectively manage stress.

STRATEGIES FOR ACHIEVING WELLNESS

Health psychology and behavioral medicine have had a major impact on organizations. In particular, a major thrust in human resource management today is helping employees stay healthy and achieve **wellness,** a state of mental and physical well-being that makes it possible to function at one's highest potential. Achieving wellness is a desirable lifestyle to work toward. It helps you to become physically and mentally healthy and develop a positive self-image. Achieving wellness also helps you ward off harmful amounts of stress. Self-Assessment Exercise 7–1 will help you achieve insight into your current level of wellness. Here we describe four strategies and tactics that make a major contribution to achieving wellness:

1. Get appropriate exercise and rest.
2. Maintain a healthy diet.
3. Develop resilience.
4. Minimize obvious risks to health and safety.

Appropriate Exercise and Rest

Exercising properly and obtaining sufficient rest are cornerstones for achieving wellness. The right amount and type of physical exercise contribute substantially to wellness. To achieve wellness it is important to select an exercise program that is physically challenging but does not lead to overexertion and muscle injury. Competitive sports, if taken too seriously, can actually increase stress. The most beneficial exercises are aerobic exercises, because they make you breathe faster and raise your heart rate. Yoga as a form of physical exercise and approach to managing stress continues to gain popularity, with an estimated 15 million Americans including Yoga in their fitness regimen. Yoga goes far beyond being physical exercise because it is based on an Eastern, mystical view of human nature.[2]

Most of a person's physical exercise requirements can be met through everyday techniques such as walking or running upstairs, vigorous housework, yard work, or walking several miles per day. However, many people need the structure of a health club or Yoga class to keep them focused on physical exercise.

The physical benefits of exercise include increased respiratory capacity, increased muscle tone, improved circulation, increased energy, increased metabolism rate, reduced body weight and improved fat metabolism, and slowed aging process. Of enormous importance, physical activity strengthens the heart, and reduces harmful cholesterol (LDL) while increasing the level of beneficial cholesterol (HDL).

The mental benefits of physical exercise are also plentiful. A major mental and emotional benefit stems from *endorphins,* morphine-like chemicals produced in a portion of the brain called the thalamus. The endorphins are also associated with a state of euphoria referred to as a "runner's high." Other mental benefits of exercise include increased self-confidence; improved body image and self-esteem; improved mental functioning, alertness, and efficiency; release of accumulated tensions; and relief from mild depression.[3]

Rest offers similar benefits to exercise, such as improved concentration, stress reduction, and improved energy. Achieving proper rest is closely linked to proper exercise. Exercise makes it easier to rest, and being well rested makes it easier to exercise. The current interest in adult napping reflects the awareness that proper rest enhances productivity and that improper rest may impair concentration and efficiency. According to one estimate, if someone loses an hour of sleep a night for a week, that person's productivity drops 25 percent.[4] Several firms now have a napping facility for workers, and many workers nap at their desks or in their

SELF-ASSESSMENT EXERCISE 7–1

The Wellness Inventory

Answer Yes or No to each question.

1. I rarely have trouble sleeping. Yes No
2. My energy level is high when I get up in the morning, and it stays high until bedtime. Yes No
3. In the past year, I've been incapacitated by illness less than five days. Yes No
4. I am generally optimistic about my chances of staying well. Yes No
5. I do not smoke or drink alcoholic beverages habitually. Yes No
6. I am pain free except for minor ailments, which heal quickly. Yes No
7. I am generally considered to be slim, not fat. Yes No
8. I am careful about my diet. I restrict my intake of alcohol, sugar, salt, caffeine, and fats. Yes No
9. I am moderate in food and drink, and I choose fresh, whole foods over processed ones. Yes No
10. I exercise strenuously at least three times a week for at least 20 minutes. Yes No
11. I do not need any medicine (prescribed or self-prescribed) every day or most days in order to function. Yes No
12. My blood pressure is 120/80 or lower. Yes No
13. I am concerned about the future, but no one fear runs through my mind constantly. Yes No
14. My relationships with those around me are usually easy and pleasant. Yes No
15. I have a clear idea of my personal goals and choices. Yes No
16. Disappointments and failures might slow me down a bit, but I try to turn them to my advantage. Yes No
17. Taking care of myself is a high priority for me. Yes No
18. I spend at least 20 minutes a day by myself, for myself. Yes No
19. I know how much sleep I require, and I get it. Yes No
20. I accept the fact that daily life can be stressful, and I am confident I can handle most problems as they arise. Yes No
21. I have at least one hobby or form of creative expression (e.g., music, art, gardening) that is a passion for me. Yes No
22. I can share my feelings with others and allow them to share their feelings with me. Yes No
23. I enjoy and respect my connection to nature and the environment. Yes No
24. I am aware of what my body feels like when I am relaxed and when I am experiencing stress. Yes No
25. I find meaning in life and generally anticipate death with minor fear. Yes No

Score:__________

Scoring: Give yourself four points for each Yes answer.

88–100 points	Excellent health/wellness awareness. You are probably well adapted to handle stress.
76–88 points	Good awareness, but there are areas where improvement is needed. Look at your No answers again.
Less than 76 points	You need to evaluate your health and lifestyle habits to improve the quality of your life and your ability to handle stressful situations.

Source: Anita Schambach, Mercy Regional Health System, Cincinnati, OH.

parked vehicles during lunch breaks. Power Naps of about 15 minutes duration taken during the workday are used as both energizers and stress reducers.

Maintaining a Healthy Diet

Eating nutritious foods is valuable for mental as well as physical health. For example, many nutritionists and physicians believe that eating fatty foods, such as red meat, contributes to colon cancer. Improper diet, such as consuming fewer than 1,300 calories per day, can weaken you physically. In turn, you become more susceptible to stress.

Advice abounds on what to eat and what not to eat. Some of this information is confusing and contradictory, partly because not enough is known about nutrition to identify an ideal diet for each individual. For example, many people can point to an 85-year-old relative who has been eating the wrong food (and perhaps consuming considerable alcohol) most of his or her life. The implication is that if this person has violated sensible habits of nutrition and lived so long, how important can good diet be?

The food requirements for wellness differ depending on age, sex, body size, physical activity, and other conditions such as pregnancy and illness. A workable dietary strategy is to follow the guidelines for choosing and preparing food developed by the U.S. Department of Agriculture,[5] as shown in Figure 7–1. At each successive layer of the pyramid, a food group should be eaten less frequently. Note the emphasis on eating a particular food group less frequently, rather than eliminating the group. A good example is that fat provides the body with energy and is also the source of vitamins A, D, E, and K. Fat also helps keep hair and nails healthy. Another fact favoring fat is that fish contain omega-3 fatty acids that seem to promote cardiovascular health.[6]

The U.S. Department of Agriculture guidelines are for people who are already healthy and do not require special diets because of disease or conditions that interfere with normal nutritional requirements. No guidelines can guarantee health and well-being. Health depends on many things, including heredity, lifestyle, personality traits, mental health, attitudes, and environment, in addition to diet. However, good eating habits based on moderation and variety can keep you healthy and even improve your health.

Developing Resilience

The ability to overcome setbacks is an important characteristic of successful people. It therefore follows that **resilience,** the ability to withstand pressure and emerge stronger for it, is a strategy for achieving wellness.[7] Most people at one time in their lives experience threats to their wellness. Among these threats are the death of a loved one, having a fire in one's home, a family breakup, or a job loss. Recovering from such major problems helps a person retain wellness and become even more well in the long term.

Resilience also deals with being challenged and not breaking down. The ability to bounce back from a setback, or being resilient, is another aspect of emotional intelligence. In the context of emotional intelligence, resilience refers to being persistent and optimistic when faced with setbacks.[8] Being resilient is also closely associated with self-confidence, as described in Chapter 4, and with managing stress as described later in this chapter.

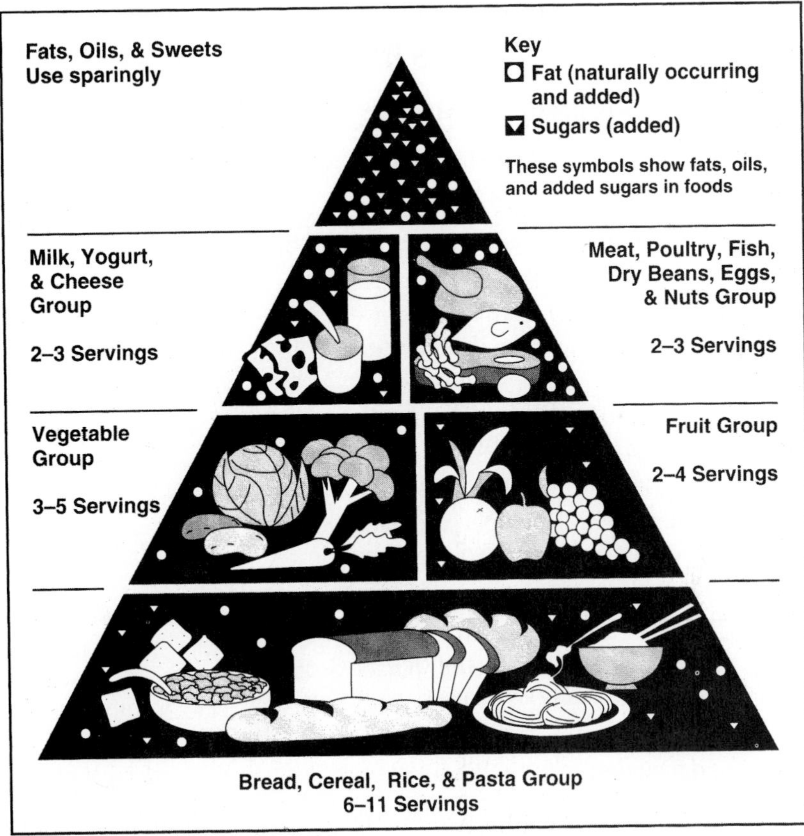

FIGURE 7–1 The Food Guide Pyramid (A Guide to Daily Food Choices)

Source: U.S. Department of Agriculture, 1992, 1996, 2000.

Self-Assessment Exercise 7–2 gives you an opportunity to examine your tendencies toward being resilient.

Minimize Obvious Risks to Health and Safety

To achieve and maintain wellness, it is important to minimize a variety of habits and behaviors that bring on personal defeat, disease, injury, and death. We use the term minimize with careful thought. Many people who make occasional use of alcohol or periodically binge on unhealthy foods still lead productive, happy, and healthy lives. Wellness is more likely to be blocked by **addictive behavior,** a compulsion to use substances or engage in activities that lead to psychological dependence and withdrawal symptoms when use is discontinued.

Research about brain chemistry and behavior helps explain why addictions to substances are so widespread. The moment a person ingests a substance such as tobacco, alcohol, marijuana, or chocolate, trillions of strong molecules surge through the bloodstream and into the brain. The molecules trigger a flood of chemical and electrical events that result in a temporary state of pleasure and euphoria. The common thread to all these mood-altering drugs is their ability to elevate levels of **dopamine.** Dopamine is a chemical substance in the brain and a neurotransmitter that is associated with pleasure and elation. (A neurotransmitter is a molecule

SELF-ASSESSMENT EXERCISE 7–2

Find Out How Resilient You Are

From 1 to 5, rate how much each of the following applies to you (1 = very little, 5 = very much).

1 2 3 4 5 You are curious, ask questions, want to know how things work, experiment.

1 2 3 4 5 You constantly learn from your experience and the experience of others.

1 2 3 4 5 You need and expect to have things work well for yourself and others. You take good care of yourself.

1 2 3 4 5 You play with new developments, find the humor, laugh at yourself, chuckle.

1 2 3 4 5 You adapt quickly to change, and are highly flexible.

1 2 3 4 5 You feel comfortable with paradoxical qualities.

1 2 3 4 5 You anticipate problems and avoid difficulties.

1 2 3 4 5 You develop better self-esteem and self-confidence every year. You develop a conscious self-concept of professionalism.

1 2 3 4 5 You listen well and read others, including difficult people, with empathy.

1 2 3 4 5 You think up creative solutions to challenges, invent ways to solve problems, and trust intuition and hunches.

1 2 3 4 5 You manage the emotional side of recovery. You grieve, honor, and let go of the past.

1 2 3 4 5 You expect tough situations to work out well, and you keep on going. You help others and bring stability to times of uncertainty and turmoil.

1 2 3 4 5 You find the gift in accidents and bad experiences.

1 2 3 4 5 You convert misfortune into good fortune.

Add Numbers to Get Your Total:

If you scored 60–70, you're highly resilient. 50–59: You're better than most. 40–49: Adequate. 30–39: Struggling. Under 30: Seek help! NOTE: To improve your resilience, practice more of the traits above.

Source: Adapted from Al Siebert, *The Survivor Personality* (Encinitas, CA: Perigree/Berkeley Books, 1999).

in the brain that transports messages from one common neuron in the brain to another. It moves across the connectors among brain cells called synapses.) Dopamine is so effective that some scientists regard it as the master molecule of addiction.[9]

Many other counterproductive behaviors can prevent wellness. Common forms include physical exercise to the point of injury and illness, sleep deprivation, excessive sleeping, unprotected casual sex, and driving at excessive speeds. Certain sports can interfere with wellness, including skydiving, bungee jumping, and high-risk mountain climbing. However, proponents of these sports contend that with proper supervision they are relatively safe.

Table 7–1 specifies several behaviors already mentioned in our analysis of achieving wellness. Use the information in the table as a checklist for living longer and better. Part of staying well is staying alive. An encouraging note is that it is often possible to reverse the damage done by many unhealthy behaviors. Scientists have accumulated a wealth of data in recent years about what happens when people engaged in unhealthy behaviors like eating poorly and using alcohol and to-

TABLE 7–1
A SURVEY OF UNHEALTHY BEHAVIOR

Unhealthy behavior accounts for nearly half of the deaths in the USA. Here are the percentages of American adults who choose to engage in specific risky behaviors.	
Don't use sunscreen	71%
Don't eat enough fruits, vegetables	59%
Don't see dentist regularly	39%
Don't take steps to control stress	35%
Don't always wear seat belt	34%
Are overweight	29%
Get no leisure-time physical activity	29%
Smoke cigarettes	22%
Get less than 6 hours of sleep per night	20%
Are chronic drinkers (at least 60 drinks a month)	3%

Sources: Centers for Disease Control and Prevention, U.S. Department of Agriculture, Rodale Press, U.S. Department of Transportation, as gathered by *USA Weekend,* March 6–8, 1998, p. 5.

bacco to excess decide to turn their lives around. The conclusion reached is that the body has the capacity to heal itself, providing the underlying damage is not too great. Jeffrey Koplan, director of the Centers for Disease Control, notes:[10]

> At any time you decide to improve your behavior and make lifestyle changes, they make a difference from that point on. Maybe not right away. It's like slamming on the brakes. You do need a certain skid distance.

An example of the body's ability to rebound included in the above research is that the day a person quits smoking, the carbon monoxide levels in the blood drop dramatically. Within a week the blood becomes less sticky, and the risk of dying from a heart attack starts to decline.

SYMPTOMS AND CONSEQUENCES OF STRESS

A major challenge in achieving wellness is to understand and manage stress. In its technical meaning, **stress** is the mental and physical condition that results from a perceived threat or demand that cannot be dealt with readily. If you perceive something to be dangerous or challenging, you will experience the bodily response known as stress. A **stressor** is the external or internal force that brings about the stress. The fact that something is dangerous or challenging makes it a stressor.

To add just one more complexity, stress is also tied in with **burnout,** a state of exhaustion stemming from long-term stress. Burnout is a set of behaviors that result from long-term stress. Keep this relationship in mind to sort out the key terms mentioned so far: Stressor → Stress → Burnout.

The symptoms and consequences of job stress are organized into four categories: physiological, psychological, behavioral, and job performance. Changes in job performance accompanying stress are a by-product of the three other sets of symptoms and consequences.

Physiological Symptoms

The body's physiological and chemical battle against the stressor is the **fight-or-flight response.** The person either tries to cope with the adversity in a head-on battle or tries to flee the scene. The physiological changes within the body are virtually identical for different stressors. All types of stressors produce the release of hormones such as adrenaline, norepinephrine, and cortisol into the bloodstream, which in turn produces certain short-term physiological changes.

Recent studies suggest the possibility that women, along with females of other species, react differently to major stressors. Instead of the fight-or-flight response typical of males, they *tend and befriend.* When stress levels mount, women are more likely to protect and nurture their children (tend) and turn to social networks of supportive females (befriend). The researchers speculate that the tend-and-befriend behavior became prevalent over the centuries because women who tended and befriended were more likely to have their offspring survive and pass on their mother's traits. The tend-and-befriend response can be traced to a hormone, oxytocin, produced in the brain. Although this research may not be politically correct, it has stimulated the interests of many scientists.[11]

Among the most familiar reactions to a stressor are an increase in heart rate, blood pressure, blood glucose, and blood clotting. To help you recognize these symptoms, try to recall your internal bodily sensations the last time you were almost in an automobile accident or heard some wonderful news. Less familiar changes are a redirection of the blood flow toward the brain and large muscle groups and a release of stored fuels from places throughout the body into the bloodstream.

If stress is continuous and accompanied by these short-term physiological changes, certain annoying or life-threatening conditions can occur. Among them are heart attacks, strokes, hypertension, increased bad cholesterol level, migraine headaches, skin rashes, ulcers, allergies, and colitis. Prolonged stress can also lead to a weakening of the body's immune system, which makes recuperation from illness difficult. The reason is that when too much adaptive energy is required of a person in a given period of time, his or her immune system breaks down. As a result, disease is likely to happen. People experiencing emotional stress may have difficulty shaking a common cold or recovering from a sexually transmitted disease. In general, any disorder classified as psychosomatic is precipitated by emotional stress.

Psychological Symptoms

The psychological or emotional symptoms of stress cover a wide range. The major positive psychological consequence is a heightened sense of alertness, perception, and awareness. Among the more frequent negative psychological consequences are tension, anxiety, discouragement, boredom, complaints about bodily problems, prolonged fatigue, feelings of hopelessness, and various kinds of defensive thinking and behavior. The defensive behaviors for dealing with sensory information, described in Chapter 2, are also psychological symptoms of stress. People may also experience disturbed inner states as a result of intense or prolonged stress.

Behavioral Symptoms and Consequences

Psychological symptoms of stress indicate how people think and feel when faced with job or personal pressures. These symptoms often lead to actual behavior that is of particular concern to the student of applied psychology. Among the more frequently observed behavioral consequences of stress are the following:

- Agitation, restlessness, and other overt signs of tension, including moving legs back and forth while seated at a meeting.
- Drastic changes in eating habits, including decreased or increased food consumption. Under heavy stressors, some people become junk food addicts.
- Increased cigarette smoking, coffee drinking, alcohol consumption, and use of illegal drugs.
- Increased use of prescription drugs such as tranquilizers and amphetamines, including diet pills.
- Errors in concentration and judgment.
- Panic-type behavior, such as making impulsive decisions.

A general behavioral symptom of intense stress is for people to exaggerate their weakest tendencies. For instance, a person with a strong temper who usually keeps cool under pressure may throw a tantrum under pressure.

Burnout is an extreme behavioral reaction to stress, consisting of emotional, mental, and physical exhaustion, along with cynicism toward work in response to long-term job stressors. Burnout is a complex phenomenon, but it often occurs when people feel out of control. Other critical factors that contribute to burnout are insufficient reward, a lack of emotional support in the workplace, or an absence of fairness. According to Christina Maslach, the key feature of burnout is the distancing that occurs in response to work overload. Burnout sufferers shift into a mode of doing the minimum as a way of protecting themselves. They start leaving work early and dehumanizing their clients, patients, or customers. People experiencing burnout may do their jobs, but their heart is not in it anymore.[12]

The symptoms a burnout victim experiences depend somewhat on his or her perception of the causes of work exhaustion. Lower commitment to the organization and higher cynicism are more likely to accompany burnout when the individual perceives the cause to be external, and controllable by others in the organization (such as the absence of appreciation). Lower self-esteem on the job is more likely to accompany burnout when the cause is perceived to be internal (such as setting unrealistic expectations of what he or she can accomplish).[13]

Job Performance Consequences of Stress

Few people can escape work stress. This is fortunate, because escaping all forms of stress would be undesirable. An optimum amount of stress exists for most people and most tasks. Figure 7–2 depicts this relationship. In most situations, job performance tends to be best under low to moderate amounts of ordinary stress. Too much stress makes people temporarily ineffective because they may become distracted or choke up. Too little stress tends to make people lethargic and inattentive. Have you experienced being under such low stress that your performance suffered?

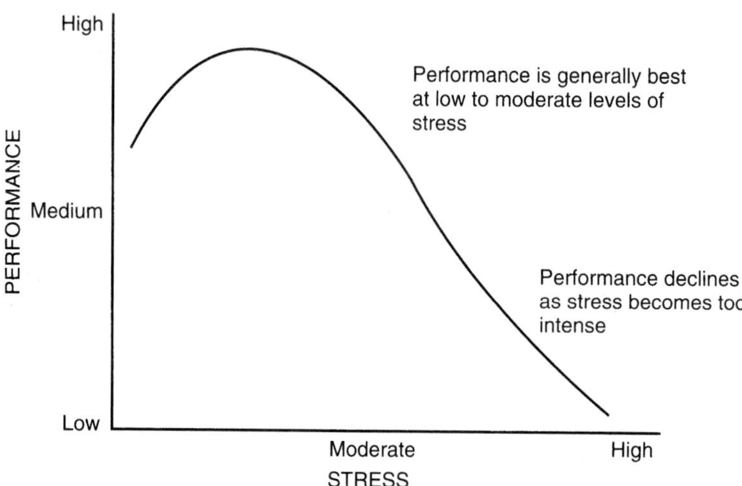

FIGURE 7–2 The Short-Term Relationship Between Stress and Job Performance

An analysis of stress studies by Steve M. Jex concludes that certain factors influence the extent to which stress decreases job performance. A drop off in performance is less likely to take place when employees clearly understand what to expect in their jobs. Other key factors that help ward off decreases in performance are when workers have high self-esteem, a strong commitment to the organization, and low levels of Type A behavior (impatience and hostility).[14] Another conclusion to consider is that for most people, challenge and excitement improve job performance. Irritation and threatening events, such as an intimidating boss, generally lower performance.

The General Adaptation Syndrome Model of Stress

A model of stress developed by the famous physician Hans Selye ties together the consequences of job stress.[15] According to the **general adaptation syndrome,** the body's response to stress occurs in three stages: alarm, resistance, and exhaustion (see Figure 7–3). In the *alarm* stage, the person identifies the threat or stressor. The threat can be physical (such as the presence of a mugger) or psychological (such as a layoff notice). Physiological changes take place such as those described under the fight-or-flight and tend-and-befriend responses.

In the *resistance* stage, the person becomes resistant to the pressures created by the stressor. The symptoms that occurred in the alarm stage disappear, even though the stressor is still present. Increased levels of hormones secreted by the pituitary gland and the adrenal cortex mount this resistance.

If exposure to the stressor persists over a long period of time, the person reaches the *exhaustion* stage, in which the resistance fails. The pituitary gland and adrenal cortex no longer provide sufficient hormones to combat the stressor. As a result, the physiological symptoms that took place in the first stage reappear. Severe psychosomatic disorders, such as a heart attack, occur in the exhaustion phase. Burnout is also a distinct possibility.

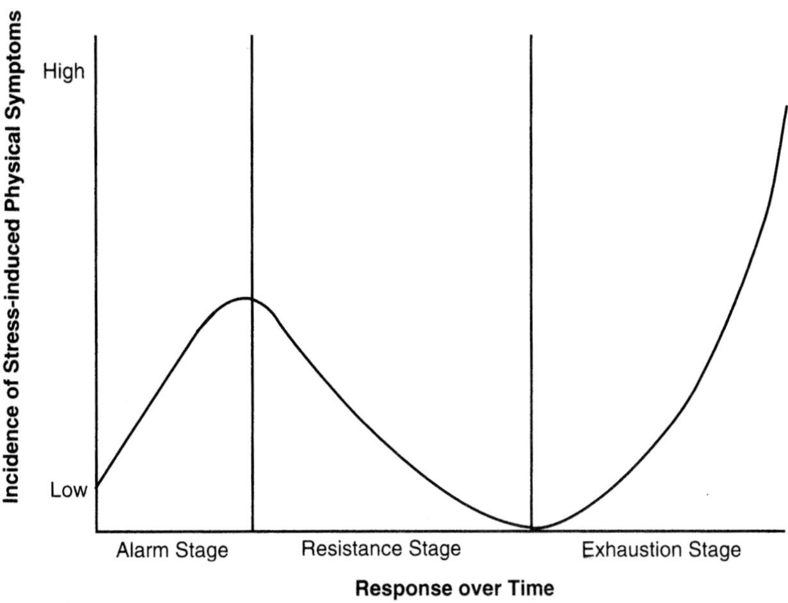

FIGURE 7–3 The General Adaptation Syndrome

PERSONALITY FACTORS CONTRIBUTING TO JOB STRESS

Workers vary considerably in their susceptibility to job stress based on their personality traits and characteristics. Four characteristics that predispose people to job stress are Type A behavior, negative affectivity, low perceived control, and low self-efficacy.

Type A Behavior

A person who exhibits **Type A behavior** is demanding, impatient, and overstriving, and is therefore prone to distress. Type A behavior has two main components. One is a tendency to try to accomplish too many things in too little time. This leads the Type A individual to be impatient and demanding. The other component is free-floating hostility. Because of this sense of urgency and hostility, people with Type A behavior are irritated by trivial things. On the job, these people are aggressive and hardworking. Off the job, they keep themselves preoccupied with all kinds of errands to run and things to do. As students, they often take on an unrealistically heavy workload.

Type A personalities frequently have cardiac diseases, such as heart attacks and strokes, at an early age. Be aware, however, that only certain features of the Type A personality pattern may be related to coronary heart disease. The heart attack triggers are hostility, anger, cynicism, and suspiciousness, as contrasted to impatience, ambition, and being work driven. Hard chargers who like what they are doing, including many executives, professionals, and technicians, are remarkably healthy and outlive less competitive people.[16] A study with mental health workers suggests other factors also influence the susceptibility of Type A people to cardiac disease. Healthy Type A workers combined high achievement striving with high optimism. Furthermore, people with high achievement striving tended to have lower blood pressure—therefore being less resistant to heart disease.[17]

Negative Affectivity

A major contributor to being stress prone is **negative affectivity,** a tendency to experience aversive emotional states. In more detail, negative affectivity is a pervasive disposition to experience emotional stress that includes feelings of nervousness, tension, and worry. The same disposition also includes such emotional states as anger, scorn, revulsion, guilt, self-dissatisfaction, and sadness.[18] Such negative personalities seem to search for important discrepancies between what they would like and what exists. People with negative affectivity are often distressed even when working under conditions that coworkers perceive as interesting and challenging. In one company, a contest was announced that encouraged company departments to compete against each other in terms of improving quality. An employee with a history of negative affectivity said:

> Management is doing it to us again. We're being asked to push ourselves to the limit when we are already overworked. No extra pay, just extra work. The stress level is getting intolerable in this place.

A more recent study about job stress indicated that negative affectivity is a less stable personality characteristic than suggested by previous research. An explanation offered is that negative affectivity is somewhat subject to the circumstances a person faces. Nevertheless, if you have considerable negative affectivity during a brief time in your life you would still be more susceptible to the adverse affects of stress.[19]

Low Perceived Control

As described in Chapter 3, locus of control refers to whether an individual believes internal or external forces control his or her fate. A special case of locus of control is **perceived control,** the belief that an individual has at his or her disposal a response that can control the aversiveness of an event. A survey of over 100 studies indicated that people with a high level of perceived control had low levels of physical and psychological symptoms of stress. (The same people also had relatively high job satisfaction and performance.)[20] Conversely, people with low perceived control are more likely to experience stress.

The link between perceived control and job stress works in this manner: If people believe they can control potential adverse forces on the job, they are less prone to the stressor of worrying about them. At the same time, the person who believes that he or she can respond effectively to potential stressors experiences a higher level of job satisfaction. Work is more satisfying and less stressful when you perceive that you can make the right response should a discrepancy arise between the real and the ideal.

Self-Efficacy

Self-efficacy, like perceived control, is another personal factor that influences susceptibility to stress. (Note that because self-efficacy is tied to a specific situation it is not strictly a personality trait.) When workers have both low perceived control and low self-efficacy the stress consequences may be much worse. However, having high self-efficacy (being confident in one's abilities) softens the stress consequences of demanding jobs.[21]

Two studies with about 2,300 U.S. Army soldiers each showed that respondents with strong self-efficacy were less stressed out mentally and physically by long work hours and work overload. Psychological strain was measured with a mental health questionnaire. Physical strain was measured by self-reports on health symptoms thought to be at least partially stress-related. Examples included headaches, back problems, and stomach intestinal upset. A key conclusion of the studies is that high levels of self-efficacy may help employees cope more effectively with job stressors. Also of note, soldiers with high self-efficacy who also used active coping methods to overcome or eliminate the stressor experienced even less negative stress.[22] To illustrate, an active coping method would be to reorganize an overwhelming workload so it can be performed more efficiently.

SOURCES OF JOB STRESS

Almost any job situation can act as a stressor for some employees, but not necessarily for others. As just described, personal characteristics can influence job stress. Also, life stress can influence job stress because stress is additive. If a person already has a high stress level from grappling with financial problems, minor job problems may be perceived as insurmountable. For example, a study of 100 professionals showed that stress symptoms thought to originate in the workplace may actually originate in personal life.[23] Here we describe five frequently encountered job stressors, as shown in Figure 7–4. We also describe the infrequent stressor of workplace catastrophes.

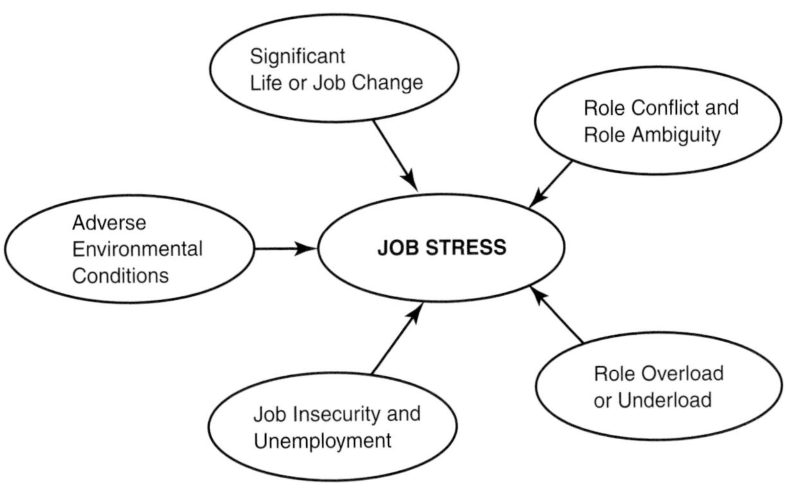

FIGURE 7–4 Frequently Observed Job Stressors

Significant Life Change or Job Change

A general stressor that encompasses both work and personal life is having to cope with significant change such as finding new employment. Thomas Holmes and Richard Rahe conducted a pioneering series of studies over a period of 25 years dealing with stressful life events. Their research and updated studies showed repeatedly that being compelled to change one's life pattern created stress. The more significant the change you have to cope with in a short period of time, the greater the probability that you will experience a stress disorder.[24]

As shown in Table 7–2, the maximum negative change is the death of a spouse. Twenty-four other stressors created by change are listed in the table in decreasing order of impact. Individual differences are important in understanding the stressful impact of life changes. The rank orders presented in Table 7–2 are averages and do not hold true for everybody. For example, a person who could fall back into working for a family business might not find being fired from the job (number 8) to be so stressful.

Role Conflict and Role Ambiguity

A major job stressor is **role conflict,** having to choose between competing demands or expectations. If you comply with one aspect of a role (or set of expectations), compliance with the other is difficult. Role conflict has been divided into four types:[25]

- **Intrasender** conflict occurs when one person asks you to accomplish two objectives that are in apparent conflict. If your boss asked you to hurry up and finish your work but also decrease your mistakes, you would experience this type of conflict.

TABLE 7–2
THE TOP 25 STRESSORS AS MEASURED BY LIFE-CHANGE UNITS

1. Death of a spouse
2. Divorce
3. Marital separation
4. Jail term/imprisonment
5. Death of a family member
6. Personal injury or illness
7. Marriage
8. Fired from the job
9. Marital reconciliation
10. Retirement
11. Change in health of family member
12. Pregnancy
13. Sexual difficulties
14. Change in financial status
15. Number of arguments with spouse
16. Major mortgage
17. Foreclosure of a loan
18. Change in responsibilities at work
19. Son or daughter leaves home
20. Trouble with in-laws
21. Outstanding personal achievement
22. Spouse begins or stops work
23. Begin or end school
24. Change in living conditions
25. Revision of personal habits

Source: These stressors continue to change over time. This version is from Thomas H. Holmes and Richard H. Rahe, "The Social Adjustment Rating Scale," *Journal of Psychosomatic Research,* 15, 1971, pp. 210–223, with permission from Elsevier Science; with an interview updating from Sue MacDonald, "Battling Stress," *The Cincinnati Enquirer,* October 23, 1995, p. C4.

- **Intersender** conflict occurs when two or more senders give you incompatible directions. Your immediate superior may want you to complete a crash project on time, but company policy temporarily prohibits authorizing overtime payments to support staff.
- **Interrole conflict** results when two different roles that you occupy are in conflict. Your employer may expect you to travel 50 percent of the time, while your spouse threatens a divorce if you travel over 25 percent of the time.
- **Person–role conflict** occurs when the role(s) your employer expects you to occupy is in conflict with your basic values. You might be asked to fire substandard performers, but this could be in conflict with your humanistic values.

Role ambiguity is a condition in which the jobholder receives confusing or poorly defined expectations. Workers in all kinds of organizations are placed in a situation where jobholders are uncertain of their true responsibilities. Many people become anxious and tense when faced with role ambiguity. A contributing reason is that being out of control is a stressor. If you lack a clear picture of what you should be doing, it is difficult to get your job under control.

Role Overload or Underload

Having too much or too little to do can create job stress. **Role overload,** having too much work to do, can create negative stress for a person in two ways. First, the person may become fatigued and thus be less able to tolerate annoyances and irritations. Think of how much easier it is to become provoked over a minor incident when you lack proper rest. Second, a person subject to unreasonable work demands may feel perpetually behind schedule, a situation that in itself is a powerful stressor. The widespread problem of role overload was suggested by a Harris Research study of 5,300 adults in 16 countries. Fifty-four percent of the respondents indicated that the leading cause of stress was overwork.[26] Since the time of the study, the trend toward understaffing in companies has intensified the problem.

A disruptive amount of distress can also occur when people experience **role underload,** or too little work to do. People find role underload frustrating because it is a normal human desire to want to work toward self-fulfillment. Also, making a contribution on the job is one way of gaining self-respect. However, there are exceptions. Some people find it relaxing not to have much to do on the job. One direct benefit is that it preserves their energy for personal life. Role underload has become less frequent because so many organizations today are thinly staffed.

A study conducted with over 400 employees in a variety of companies supports the belief that too much or too little work leads to stress. Specifically, the researchers found that jobs with limited or excessive scope (the number of activities performed) created stress. However, a very small scope was more stressful than a very large scope.[27]

Job Insecurity and Unemployment

People have traditionally worried about losing their jobs because of budget cuts and automation. Two current sources of job insecurity, even during prosperity, are layoffs caused by mergers and acquisitions and corporate restructuring or downsizing. Layoffs occur for two primary reasons when one firm acquires or merges with another: (1) The merged organization will have duplicate positions, such as two vice presidents of marketing, and (2) the organization may have to trim the payroll in order to save money. Major expenses involved in purchasing another firm include stock purchases and legal fees. Restructuring or downsizing is a planned method of reducing the number of layers of management, thus laying off many managers and their assistants. Whatever the specific reason for the layoff, worrying about losing one's job is a potential stressor.

Many workers who survive a layoff experience elevated stress. The workplace often becomes more political and cutthroat than before the downsizing, leaving family members with even less time for family activities. Another stressor surrounding a downsizing is that many workers receive pay cuts resulting in worries about finances.[28]

Unemployment itself generates more stress than job insecurity. Unemployed people have much higher rates of depression, suicide, homicide, child abuse, and partner abuse. The dramatic increase in workplace violence, such as killing company officials, is related to unemployment stress.

Adverse Environmental Conditions

A variety of adverse organizational conditions are stressors, as identified by the National Institute of Occupational Safety and Health (NIOSH). Among these adverse organizational conditions are unpleasant or dangerous physical conditions, such as crowding, noise, air pollutions, or ergonomic problems. Enough polluted air within an office building can create a *sick building* in which a diverse range of airborne particles, vapors, molds, and gases pollute the indoor environment. The result can be headaches, nausea, and respiratory infections as well as the stress created by being physically ill.

Ergonomic problems refer to a poor fit between the physical and human requirements of a job. Working at a computer monitor for prolonged periods of time can lead to adverse physical and psychological reactions. The symptoms include headaches and fatigue, along with eye problems. Common visual problems are dry eyes and blurred or double vision. An estimated one out of five visits to vision-care professionals is for computer-related problems. Another vision-related problem is that people lean forward to scan the monitor, leading to physical problems such as back strain.

A repetitive-motion disorder most frequently associated with keyboarding and the use of optical scanners is **carpal tunnel syndrome.** The syndrome occurs when repetitive flexing and extension of the wrist causes the tendons to swell, thus trapping and pinching the median nerve. Carpal tunnel syndrome creates stress because of the pain and misery. The thoughts of having to permanently leave a job requiring keyboarding is another potential stressor. If ergonomic principles, such as erect posture, are incorporated into computer usage, these stress symptoms diminish.

Workplace Catastrophes

Workplace catastrophes, such as homicides, deadly accidents, radiation leaks, and bombings occur infrequently yet can be overwhelming stressors. If the event is highly intense, such as seeing a coworker shot to death, the worker may suffer from the battlefield-like stress reaction called **post-traumatic disorder.** The symptoms include recurring anxiety, sleeplessness, nightmares, vivid flashbacks, disturbing thoughts, difficulties in concentration, and withdrawing from people.

The attacks on the World Trade Center and the Pentagon on September 11, 2001, were perhaps the most intense job stressors ever. People who worked in or close to the destroyed or damaged buildings, and those who lost family members and friends were the most frequent sufferers of post-traumatic disorder. However, thousands of workers who were not even near the attack suffered stress symptoms similar to post-traumatic disorder. Because the attacks struck office buildings, many employees began to associate work with terror.[29] Many employers offered professional counseling services to help employees cope with the problem. Many managers themselves helped workers deal with the disaster by providing emotional support, and encouraging people to talk about the trauma in groups before concentrating on their work. (A return to productive activity after a trauma helps reduce stress.)

INDIVIDUAL METHODS OF STRESS MANAGEMENT

Unless stress is managed properly, it may lead to harmful long-term consequences, including disabling physical illnesses and career retardation. Managing stress refers to controlling stress by making it become a constructive force in your life. Managing thus refers to both preventing and reducing stress. However, the distinction between methods of preventing and reducing stress is not clear-cut. For example, physical exercise not only reduces stress, it also contributes to a relaxed lifestyle that helps you prevent stress. Methods of stress management under your control vary from highly specific techniques, such as the relaxation response, to general strategies that reflect a lifestyle. Included in the latter would be maintaining a diet geared toward wellness, as described earlier. Here we describe five do-it-yourself techniques of stress management. However, should your stress be so overwhelming that self-remedies will not work, seek professional help.

Identify Your Own Stress Signals

An effective program of stress management begins with self-awareness. Learn to identify your own particular reactions to stress. Take note of their intensity as well as the time of the day when the symptoms occur. Often the mere act of keeping a record of stress symptoms lessens their incidence and severity. More than likely, this phenomenon is related to the realization that you are starting to take charge of your health.

Once you have learned to pick up warning signs, the next step is to identify what and how you were thinking and feeling prior to the onset of the symptoms. For example, if your team leader tells you that your report is needed in a hurry, you may begin to fret. What usually triggers stress is your own stream of negative thoughts, such as "I will be criticized if this report isn't finished on time."

It is crucial to learn how to terminate unproductive, worrisome thoughts. A recommended technique is that of thought stopping, or canceling. It works this way: Choose either the term "stop" or "cancel" and quietly but emphatically repeat it whenever you catch yourself engaging in anxiety-provoking thoughts. At first, this may be as many as 50 to 100 times per day.

Eliminate or Modify the Stressor

The most potent method of managing stress is to eliminate or modify the stressor giving you trouble. One value of tranquilizing medication is that it calms down a person enough that he or she can deal constructively with the source of stress. A helpful way to attack the cause of a stressor is to follow the steps in problem solving and decision making. You clarify the problem, identify the alternatives, weigh the alternatives, select one alternative, and so forth. One difficulty, however, is that your evaluation of the real problem could be inaccurate. There is always a limit to self-analysis.

Suppose a worker experiences job stress because of small problems on the job, such as a few cross words from a coworker or the team leader. He or she carefully analyzes the problem and decides that his or her preoccupation with financial problems is creating so much stress that small annoyances are insufferable. The worker then tackles the major stressor by (a) reducing expenses, and (b) increasing income through supplemental employment. As his or her stress from the major problem subsides, the worker is better able to deal with minor annoyances.

Build a Support Network

A **support network** is a group of people who can listen to your problems and provide emotional support. These people, or even one person, can help you through difficult episodes. Members of your network can provide you with a sense of closeness, warmth, and acceptance that will reduce your stress. Also, the simple expedient of putting your feelings into words can be a healing experience. The way to develop this support network is to become a good listener so that the other person will reciprocate.

Practice Everyday Methods of Stress Reduction

The simple expedient of learning how to relax is an important method of reducing the tension and anxiety brought about by both positive and negative stress. A sample of everyday suggestions for relaxation and other methods of stress reduction is presented in Table 7–3. If you can accomplish these you are less likely to need tranquilizing medication to keep you calm and in control. In addition to scanning this list, do Skill-Building Exercise 7–1.

Practice the Relaxation Response

The **relaxation response (RR)** is a bodily reaction in which you experience a slower respiration rate and heart rate, lowered blood pressure, and lowered metabolism. The response can be brought about in several ways, including meditation, exercise, or prayer. By practicing the RR, you can counteract the fight-or-flight response associated with stress.

Cardiologist Herbert Benson explains that four things are necessary to practice the relaxation response: a quiet environment, an object to focus on, a passive attitude, and a comfortable position. The RR is practiced 10 to 20 minutes, twice a day. To evoke the relaxation response, "Close your eyes. Relax. Concentrate on one word or prayer. If other thoughts come to mind, be passive, and return to the repetition."[30]

TABLE 7–3
STRESS BUSTERS

- Take a nap when facing heavy pressures. Napping is regarded as one of the most effective techniques for reducing and preventing stress.
- Give in to your emotions. If you are angry, disgusted, or confused, admit your feelings. Suppressing your emotions adds to stress.
- Take a brief break from the stressful situation and do something small and constructive like washing your car, emptying a wastebasket, or getting a haircut.
- Get a massage, because it can loosen tight muscles, improve your blood circulation, and calm you down.
- Get help with your stressful task from a coworker, boss, or friend.
- Concentrate intensely on reading, surfing the Internet, a sport, or a hobby. Contrary to common sense, concentration is at the heart of stress reduction.
- Have a quiet place at home and have a brief idle period there every day.
- Take a leisurely day off from your routine.
- Finish something you have started, however small. Accomplishing almost anything reduces some stress.
- Stop to smell the flowers, make friends with a young child or elderly person, or play with a kitten or puppy.
- Strive to do a good job, but not a perfect job.
- Work with your hands, doing a pleasant task.
- Hug somebody you like, and who you think will hug you back.
- Find something to laugh at—a cartoon, a movie, a television show, a Web site for jokes, even yourself.
- Minimize drinking caffeinated or alcoholic beverages, and drink fruit juice or water instead. Grab a piece of fruit rather than a can of beer.

SKILL-BUILDING EXERCISE 7–1

The Stress-Buster Survey

Each class member thinks through carefully which techniques he or she uses to reduce work or personal stress. Class members then come to the front of the room individually to briefly present their most effective stress-reduction techniques. After the presentations are completed, class members analyze and interpret what they heard. Among the issues to explore are:

1. Which are the most popular stress-reduction techniques?
2. Did you hear about a stress-reduction technique that you are not using now but appears like it might be helpful?
3. How do the stress-reduction techniques used by the class compare with those recommended by experts?
4. Which techniques did you hear about that might be good for eliminating or modifying the stressor?

The sampling of stress-management techniques described here should be integrated with proper diet and exercise to achieve the best results. The president of a sports conditioning center supports this idea: "Rigorous dieting and exercising alone don't improve a person's health as effectively as moderate diet and exercise along with a consistent stress-management regimen."[31]

ORGANIZATIONAL METHODS OF STRESS MANAGEMENT

Negative stress is disruptive to both productivity and employee well-being. As a consequence, organizations are actively involved in stress management. Next we describe three important ways in which organizations help to prevent and treat job stress: improved job design, emotional support to employees, and establishing a corporate culture of wellness.

Improved Job Design

A major strategy for decreasing job dissatisfaction and stress is to design low-stress jobs. Four key factors that determine satisfaction and stress are task complexity, physical strain, task meaningfulness, and control. In general, a low-stress job would be moderately complex, carry moderate physical strain, be very meaningful, and allow the jobholder control,[32] as shown in Figure 7–5.

Task complexity refers to how many different operations there are in a job and how difficult the operations are to learn. Many workers are bored by jobs too low

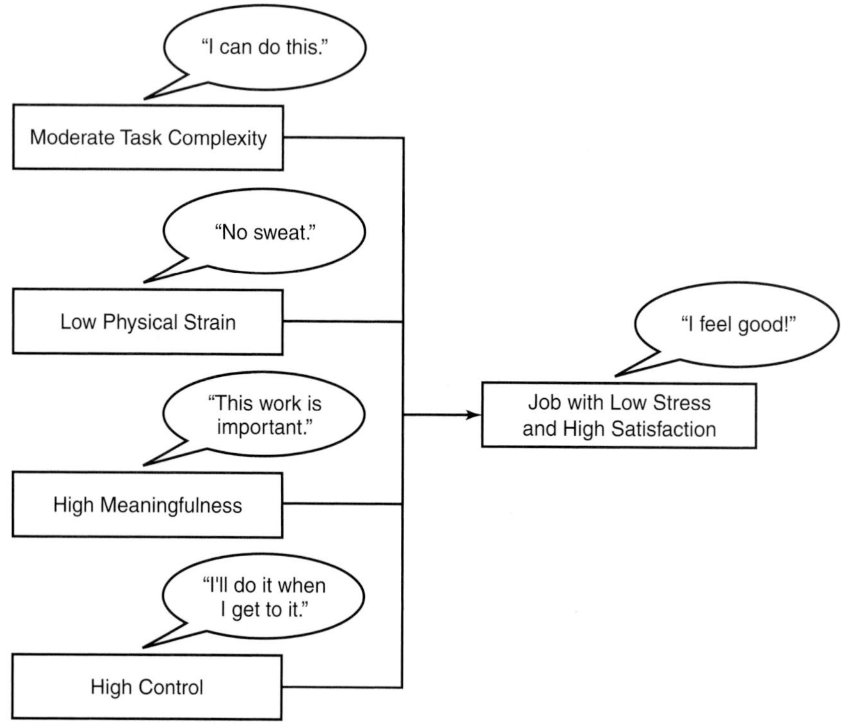

FIGURE 7–5 The Design of a Low-Stress Job

in complexity, but frustrated by those too high in complexity. The complexity of a job is somewhat influenced by an individual's perceptions and abilities. A person with low practical intelligence might find selling real estate to be too complex; a person with high practical intelligence might find the complexity to be just right.

Physical strain is related to how much physical exertion the job requires. In an era of high technology, jobs can still make high physical demands. For example, the job of supermarket cashier carries with it considerable strain despite the presence of optical scanners. Cashiers sometimes suffer from back pain and repetitive-motion disorders because the new technology pushes them toward working so rapidly. Can you think of any other job where high tech has actually increased the amount of physical strain?

Meaningful jobs are those that workers think have value, such as making a direct contribution to society. Many employees of the Fisher-Price Company, for example, think their jobs are meaningful because the company produces toys of recreational and educational value. Managers can help to build meaningfulness into a job by explaining to an employee why the job's output is important to society. A telephone-manufacturing technician might be told, for example, that he or she is helping keep families together.

Control refers to how much responsibility the jobholder has for sequencing activities and establishing priorities. In terms of job enrichment, control means the same thing as scheduling in which the worker can decide when to tackle each assignment. Being in control generally reduces stress. Empowerment can also reduce stress, because having more power leads to more control. A customer service representative explained his empowerment experience in these terms: "I used to absorb a lot of heat from customers because I was powerless to solve some of their stickiest problems. I had to get approval for any resolution of significance. Now that I have much more authority, I have better control over the problem. As a result, I have much less conflict."

Emotional Support

Managers can play an active role in preventing and reducing stress by emotionally supporting employees and empowering them. Several studies have found that social support may reduce stress. For example, a good relationship with your manager may make work situations less stressful. It is also possible that workers experiencing stress may solicit social support from their managers.[33] One study compared the illness rate between two groups of employees who faced comparable heavy stressors. Employees who felt they had their managers' support suffered only half as much illness in 12 months as those who felt they lacked such support. The most helpful manager asks himself or herself this question: "How can I make the group members feel as effective as I do?" Supportive behaviors that help employees feel more effective include the following:

- **Keep communication channels open.** Managers can help ward off major stressors by encouraging group members to talk about real or imagined problems.
- **Provide the right kind of backup.** Different workers may require different kinds of help, such as a day off to recover from stress, or additional training.
- **Act as a catalyst.** Helping the employee solve the problem improves the employee's effectiveness more than solving the problem for the employee.

- **Hold back on disseminating stressful information.** Although being open with group members is usually beneficial, burdening the already stressed employee with additional stressful information may be overwhelming.[34]

A Corporate Culture of Wellness

A comprehensive approach to keeping employees well and managing stress effectively is to develop a culture that encourages a healthy lifestyle. In such an organization, top-level managers talk about being healthy and managing stress and are good models of physical and mental fitness. At the core of a corporate culture of wellness is a **wellness program,** an organization-sponsored activity to help employees stay well and avoid illness. The types of physical-fitness and stress-management techniques described in this chapter are included in most wellness programs. Workshops, seminars, activities, and medical procedures offered in wellness programs include the following:[35]

- Medical examination comprised of lifestyle questionnaire, blood analysis, flexibility testing, hearing and vision exams, skin inspection, body-fat measurement, blood-pressure screening, and mammograms (screening for breast cancer)
- Stress management
- Weight control (for both overweight and underweight)
- Smoking cessation programs
- Alcohol and illegal drug control
- Substance abuse counseling and referral
- Preventive health care
- Safety on the job and at home
- Hypertension (high blood pressure) control
- Healthy lifestyle and self-care

In addition, many companies offer employee assistance programs where employees who are experiencing stress because of personal or job problems can find professional help. The employee assistance counselor typically offers one session of help and then refers the employee for further assistance, such as debt counseling or drug counseling. The assistance program frequently takes responsibility for dealing with the more acute problems that might otherwise be dealt with in the wellness program. All these interventions relate to wellness, or stress management, or both. The directors of these programs are enthusiastic about the contribution of wellness programs to preventing stress-related disorders and reducing medical claims.

Although various individual and organizational approaches to stress management have been described in positive terms, a disclaimer is in order. It is not always certain that a particular environmental factor, such as low control, leads to stress. Also, the various approaches to stress management are not effective for everybody.[36] Furthermore, an approach to stress management that works well for one problem may not always be effective for another. Managing stress effectively involves some trial and error.

SUMMARY OF KEY POINTS

- A major thrust in human resource management today is helping employees stay healthy and achieve wellness. Four strategies and tactics for achieving wellness are (1) get appropriate exercise and rest, (2) maintain a healthy diet, (3) develop resilience, and (4) minimize addictive and physically dangerous behaviors.
- Stress has a variety of physiological, psychological, and behavioral symptoms or consequences. The physiological symptoms are tied in with the fight-or-flight and tend-and-befriend responses when faced with a stressor. Psychological symptoms include fear, anxiety, emotional disorder, and defensive attitudes and behavior. Burnout is a long-term consequence of stress that often occurs when people feel out of control.
- Changes in job performance are another important consequence of stress. Performance tends to be best under a moderate amount of stress. Stressors that represent challenge and excitement improve job performance. Irritation and threatening events generally lower performance.
- According to the general adaptation syndrome, the body's response to stress occurs in three stages: alarm, resistance, and exhaustion. During the last stage, the physiological symptoms that took place in the first stage reappear, and severe stress disorders take place.
- Some people are more susceptible to stressors than others because of personal factors. Four such factors predisposing workers to stress are Type A behavior (impatience and hostility), negative affectivity (a "nasty disposition"), low perceived control over an aversive event, and low self-efficacy.
- Job stress has many sources, including life stress that has a spillover to the job. Significant life changes create both job stress and personal stress. Specific

GUIDELINES FOR PERSONAL EFFECTIVENESS

1. A major life goal that would benefit anyone would be to achieve wellness. A state of wellness is much more uplifting than merely being free from disease.
2. Discover through trial and error what is the optimum amount of job stress for you. If you avoid virtually all stress, you might become lethargic and complacent. Yet, too much stress over a prolonged period of time can have detrimental consequences to your physical and mental health. Your job performance might also suffer.
3. To be successful in today's competitive world, you are strongly urged to maintain an active program of stress management. At a minimum, it is important to eliminate or modify key stressors and to practice relaxation techniques.
4. No one best technique exists for reducing job stress. If you feel tense owing to work or school pressures, experiment with different methods of stress reduction and prevention. Repeat the technique that feels best.

sources of job stress studied here are role conflict and role ambiguity, role overload or underload, job insecurity and unemployment, adverse environmental conditions including repetitive-motion disorder, and workplace catastrophes.

- Methods of stress management under an individual's control vary from highly specific techniques to strategies that reflect a lifestyle. The individual methods of stress management described here are (1) identify your own stress signals, (2) eliminate or modify the stressor, (3) build a support network, (4) practice everyday methods of stress reduction, and (5) practice the relaxation response.
- Organizational methods of reducing and preventing stress include improved job design with an emphasis on moderate task complexity, low physical strain, high meaningfulness, and high control. Other techniques described here are giving workers emotional support and empowering them, and establishing a corporate culture of wellness including a wellness program and an employee assistance program.

DISCUSSION QUESTIONS AND ACTIVITIES

1. If exercise contributes so much to wellness, why are so many athletes stressed out?
2. What is the relationship between wellness and self-actualization?
3. Does a "well" person ever eat such foods as pizza, hamburgers, and hot dogs and drink milk shakes and beer? Explain.
4. Identify several specific ways in which being well might enhance your career.
5. Some researchers have suggested that the term *challenge* be substituted for the term *stress.* What do you think of the merit of their suggestion?
6. Suppose you believed that your work performance would improve if only you were experiencing more stress. What could you do to increase your level of stress?
7. A student told his instructor, "You have to give me a deadline for my paper. Otherwise, I can't handle it." What does this statement tell you about (a) the stressor he was facing, and (b) how pressure influences his work performance?
8. You have probably met workers or students who claim to be burned out. Which specific symptoms or problems were they referring to?
9. In some wellness programs, employees are paid a bonus for losing weight or stopping smoking. What is your opinion of the ethics of this practice?
10. Interview a person in a high-pressure job in any field. Find out whether the person experiences significant stress and what method he or she uses to cope with it.

AN APPLIED PSYCHOLOGY CASE PROBLEM

The New Marketing Assistant

One year ago Jennie DaSilva returned enthusiastically to the workforce after 12 years of being a full-time homemaker and a part-time direct sales representative for beauty products. Jennie's major motive for finding a full-time professional job was to work toward her career goal as a marketing manager in a medium-size or large company. To help prepare for this career, DaSilva completed a business degree over a five-year period.

Another compelling reason for returning to full-time employment was financial need. DaSilva's husband owned and operated an appliance and electronics store that was becoming less profitable each year. Several large appliance stores had moved into the area, resulting in fewer customers for Northside Appliances (the name of the family business). DaSilva and her husband Fred concluded that the family could not cover its bills unless Jennie earned the equivalent of a full-time income.

After three months of searching for full-time employment, Jennie responded to a newspaper ad for a marketing assistant position. The ad described the position as part of a management training program with an excellent future. Ten days after submitting her cover letter and résumé, Jennie was invited for an interview. The company proved to be a national provider of long-distance telephone service. The human resources interviewer and the hiring manager both explained that Jennie's initial assignment would be as a telemarketer. Both people advised Jennie that large numbers of people were applying for these telemarketing positions.

Jennie would be required to telephone individual consumers and small-business owners, and make a sales pitch for them to transfer their long-distance telephone service to her company. The company supplied a computerized list with an almost inexhaustible list of names and telephone numbers across the country. In this way Jennie could take advantage of time-zone differences to telephone people during their dinnertime, as well as at other times. Jennie would receive a small commission for each customer who made the switch to her company. Her major responsibility in addition to telephone soliciting would be to enter the results of her conversations into a computer, as well as prepare summaries.

One week after the interview, Jennie was extended a job offer. She accepted the offer despite some concern that the position was a little too far removed from the professional marketing position she sought. Jennie was assigned to a small cubicle in a large room with about 25 other telemarketers. She found the training program exciting, particularly with respect to techniques for overcoming customer resistance. Jennie reasoned that this experience, combined with her direct selling of beauty products, would give her excellent insights into how consumers think and behave. For the first two weeks Jennie found the calls to be uplifting. She experienced a surge of excitement when a customer agreed to switch to her company. As was the custom in the office, she shouted "Yes" after concluding each customer conversion to her company.

As the weeks moved slowly on, Jennie became increasingly restless and concerned about the job. Her success ratio was falling below the company standard of a 3 percent success rate on the cold calls. A thought kept running through Jennie's mind, "Even if I'm doing well at this job, 97 percent of people I call will practically hang up on me. And I can't stand keyboarding all these worthless reports explaining what happened as a result of my calls. It's a horrible waste of time."

Jennie soon found it difficult to sleep peacefully, often pacing the apartment after Fred had fallen asleep. She also noticed that she was arguing much more with Fred and the two children. Jennie's stomach churned so much that she found eating uncomfortable. She often poked at her food, but drank coffee and diet soft drinks much more than previously. After six months of working at the long-distance carrier, her weight plunged from 135 pounds to 123 pounds. Jennie's left thumb and wrists were constantly sore. One night when Fred asked her why she was rubbing the region below her thumb, Jennie said, "I keep pushing the mouse around so much during the day that my thumb feels like it's falling off."

continued on next page

AN APPLIED PSYCHOLOGY CASE PROBLEM (cont'd)

During the next several months, Jennie spoke with her supervisor twice about her future in the company. Both times the supervisor explained that the best telemarketers become eligible for supervisory positions, providing they have proved themselves for at least three years. The supervisor also cautioned Jennie that her performance was adequate, but not exceptional. Jennie thought to herself, "I'm banging my head against the wall, and I'm considered just average."

As Jennie approached a full year in her position, she and Fred reviewed the family finances. He said, "Sales at the store are getting worse and worse. I predict that this year your salary will be higher than profits from the store. It's great that we can count on at least one stable salary in the family. The kids and I really appreciate it."

Jennie thought to herself, "Now is the worst time to tell Fred how I really feel about my job. I'm falling apart inside, and the family needs my salary. What a mess."

1. Which aspects of work stress are revealed in this case?
2. What suggestions can you make to the company for decreasing the stressors in the position of telemarketer?
3. What advice can you offer Jennie to help her achieve wellness?

AN APPLIED PSYCHOLOGY CASE PROBLEM

Dark Days at Dell

The e-mail looked harmless enough. Be at the Renaissance Austin Hotel, 20 minutes from the office, in about an hour. Just another senseless meeting, no doubt. But by the time Dell IT specialist Chuck Peterson walked into a room filled with 75 of his coworkers and a few managers he had never seen before, he knew what was up. "None of them would look at us," he says. "They had their backs to us, or they were looking at their feet."

The bosses stuck to their script. The economy is bad. We can't afford to keep you. So we're not. Hand in your badges on the way out. There were no individual explanations for why these workers—out of a workforce of 40,000—had been picked. The members of the firing squad never even introduced themselves. It was over in eight minutes. Peterson, 40, is one of 1,700 full-time workers who lost their jobs in the first few months of 2001, in an economy that had been shedding 100,000 workers a month since the beginning of the year.

Dell isn't a Rust Belt dinosaur or a business plan-and-a-prayer dotcom. Its workers helped write one of the great business success stories of modern times. Dell was founded in 1984 to sell computers without a middleman (Direct from Dell, the ads said). Its hyperefficient model helped it pass Compaq to become North America's largest PC manufacturer. Nor is Dell's good news all behind it. Its earnings were on track in 2001, and the previous year the company earned $2.3 billion on sales of $32 billion.

Many of the fired workers and their supporters are attacking the cuts as unnecessary and poorly handled—and antithetical to the company Michael Dell created. The Dell culture is fiercely meritocratic, with workers expected to do whatever it takes to make the company succeed. The reward was rich option packages that turned many tech workers in their thirties into millionaires.

Dell said it did not undertake the cuts lightly. "It's one of the hardest most gut-wrenching decisions you can make as a leader," Michael Dell told *Time*. He admits that the layoffs are "an admission that we messed up by overhiring." If there's a lesson, he says, it's that "when things heat up quite a bit, we should take some pause."

Not everyone got the bad news as impersonally as Peterson. When senior recruiter Kathleen Sullivan, 47, was let go, her boss led her from her cubicle into a "team room" where they could have some privacy. He apologized profusely and said he hoped that they would stay in touch. "Then a tear started rolling down his cheek," she says. "I'm getting laid off, and I'm asking him if he needed a Kleenex."

But the pain was mostly hers. Sullivan had initially resisted going to Dell. But when it recruited her, she was enticed by the high pay, the 401(k), the stock options, and the heady work environment. During the boom, she says, she once hired 600 people in five weeks. Dell hired 16,000 workers in the past two years alone. With money tight, there was pressure to cut back on departments that didn't generate revenue—administration, marketing, and recruiting. Dell was also pushing to have in-house managers do more of their own job interviewing, leaving less work for Sullivan.

Gary Davidson's firing was mercifully brief. Davidson, 39, a network administrator in a factory that makes laptops, got to work at 7:30 A.M., and his boss called him into the human resources building. He was told that he was history and was asked to hand over his badge, cell phone, and corporate cards. "They gave me the option of coming back later to clean out my desk," he says. "By 7:45 A.M., I was out."

The news didn't come as a complete shock. When Davidson started out, money ran freely. But in the spring of 2000 when the dotcom bubble burst, everything changed. It was harder to get anything more than a bare-bones computer to work on, and training was halted for several months. "You could practically hear the screws being tightened," says Davidson.

By early 2001, rumors were rampant that job cuts were coming. But Dell traditionally kept a 10 percent to 30 percent buffer of temps and contractors, who normally got the boot during slow times. The company usually lays off an additional 10 percent of full-time staff after annual evaluations in February. The regular staff had hoped that those traditional purges were all that were needed.

Many of the fired workers object to the way they were let go. Just days before D-day, as February 15 is now known at Dell, management was denying planned job cuts. On D-day, officers from the Texas Department of Public Safety showed up at the Dell campus to escort the doomed to their cars. Workers were encouraged to sign "the bribe," an agreement not to discuss their package or sue Dell, in exchange for up to four extra weeks of severance.

One of the biggest complaints among redundant Dell workers is that the company did not explain how it chose whom to fire. Dell rigorously evaluates its employees, ranking each on a descending 1-to-5 scale; fives get fired first. But performance didn't seem to matter this time. "The first guy in my department to go was the second highest rated on the team," says Davidson. "It was more like a shotgun blast, or a lottery."

Some of the workers let go accuse Dell of targeting older, more highly paid workers. "The people left are not the ones who built the company," says Peterson. "We did all the sweat, and now they're getting our stock options." Dell counters that "older workers who say they were singled out are just expressing sour grapes or don't understand where they fit in the process."

According to observers, the fired Dell workers should land on their feet. Most have highly marketable skills, and unemployment in the area stood at 2 percent during the time of the layoffs. Every day they troop to a career center in northwest Austin. They check out Web sites like computerjob.com and a bulletin board that boasts 30 "success stories"—only limited consolation given that companies where they might naturally land have also been trimming workers. Doug Hutter, 41, with two kids at home, lost his job as an IT specialist. Two months later he said he was starting to get scared. "I'm wondering where the next house payment is coming from."

1. Why is being downsized so stressful for some of the Dell employees?
2. How much of a stressor is Dell's annual practice of laying off the bottom 10 percent of its workforce?
3. What steps should Dell take to reduce the stress associated with downsizing?

Source: Adapted from Adam Cohen, with Cathy Booth Thomas, "Inside a Layoff: An Up-Close Look at How One Company Handles the Delicate Task of Downsizing," *Time,* April 16, 2001, pp. 38–40.

REFERENCES

1. William Atkinson, "When Stress Won't Go Away," *HR Magazine,* December 2000, p. 106.
2. Richard Corliss, "The Power of Yoga," *Time,* April 23, 2001, pp. 54–62.
3. Philip L. Rice, *Stress and Health: Principles and Practices for Coping and Wellness* (Monterey, CA: Brooks/College Publishing Company, 1987), pp. 353–354.
4. Research cited in Maggie Jackson, "New Skill for Today's Workplace: Sleeping on the Job," Associated Press, May 19, 1997.
5. *Dietary Guidelines for Americans,* 3rd ed. (Washington, DC: U.S. Department of Agriculture, 1990); updated with Food Guide Pyramid, May 2000.
6. Christine Gorman, "We Love Fish," *Time,* October 30, 2000, p. 76.
7. Emory L. Cowen, "In Pursuit of Wellness," *American Psychologist,* April 1991, p. 406.
8. Daniel Goleman, "Leadership that Gets Results," *Harvard Business Review,* March–April 2000, p. 80.
9. J. Madeleine Nash, "Addicted," *Time,* May 5, 1997, pp. 69–76.
10. Quoted in Christine Gorman, "Repairing Damage," *Time,* February 5, 2001, p. 54.
11. Shelley E. Taylor, et al., "Biobehavioral Responses to Stress in Females: Tend-and-Befriend, not Fight-or-Flight," *Psychological Review,* 107, 2000, pp. 411–429.
12. Christina Maslach, *The Truth About Burnout* (San Francisco: Jossey-Bass, 1997).
13. Jo Ellen Moore, "Why Is This Happening? A Causal Attribution Approach to Work Exhaustion Consequences," *Academy of Management Review,* April 2000, p. 345.
14. Steve M. Jex, *Stress and Job Performance: Theory, Research, and Implications for Managerial Practice* (Thousand Oaks, CA: Sage, 1998).
15. Hans Selye, *The Stress of Life,* 2nd ed. (New York: McGraw-Hill, 1976).
16. Jeffrey R. Edwards and A. J. Baglioni, Jr., "Relationships Between Type A Behavior Pattern and Mental and Physical Symptoms: A Comparison of Global and Component Measures," *Journal of Applied Psychology,* April 1991, p. 276.
17. Thomas M. Begley, Cynthia Lee, and Joseph M. Czajka, "The Relationship of Type A Behavior and Optimism with Job Performance and Blood Pressure," *Journal of Business and Psychology,* Winter 2000, p. 224.
18. Peter Y. Chen and Paul E. Spector, "Negative Affectivity as the Underlying Cause of Correlations between Stressors and Strains," *Journal of Applied Psychology,* June 1991, p. 398.
19. Paul E. Spector, Peter Y. Chen, and Brian J. O'Connell, "A Longitudinal Study of Relations Between Job Stressors and Job Strains While Controlling for Prior Negative Affectivity and Strains," *Journal of Applied Psychology,* April 2000, pp. 211–218.
20. Cynthia Lee, Susan J. Ashford, and Philip Bobko, "Interactive Effects of 'Type A' Behavior and Perceived Control on Worker Performance and Satisfaction," *Academy of Management Journal,* December 1990, p. 870.
21. John Schaubroeck and Deryl E. Merrit, "Divergent Effects of Job Control on Coping with Work Stressors: The Key Role of Self-Efficacy," *Academy of Management Journal,* June 1997, p. 750.
22. Steve M. Jex and Paul D. Bliese, "Efficacy Beliefs as a Moderator of the Impact of Work-Related Stressors: A Multilevel Study," *Journal of Applied Psychology,* June 1999, pp. 349–361; Jex, Bliese, Sheri Buzell, and Jessica Primeau, "The Impact of Self-Efficacy on Stressor-Strain Relations: Coping Style as an Explanatory Mechanism," *Journal of Applied Psychology,* June 2001, pp. 401–409.

23. Debra L. Nelson and Charlotte Sutton, "Chronic Work Stress and Coping: A Longitudinal Study and Suggested New Directions," *Academy of Management Journal,* December 1990, p. 865.
24. Rabi S. Bhagat, "Effects of Stressful Life Events on Individual Performance and Work Adjustment Processes within Organizational Settings: A Research Model," *Academy of Management Review,* October 1983, pp. 660–671.
25. Daniel Katz and Robert L. Kahn, *The Social Psychology of Organizations* (New York: Wiley, 1966).
26. "Too Much Work Causes Stress," *Management Review,* March 1995, p. 6.
27. Jia Lin Xie and Gary Johns, "Job Scope and Stress: Can Job Scope Be Too High?" *Academy of Management Journal,* October 1995, pp. 1288–1309.
28. Michelle Conlin, "Savaged by the Slowdown," *Business Week,* September 17, 2001, p. 75.
29. Andrea C. Poe, "Aftershocks of the 11th," *HR Magazine,* December 2001, p. 48.
30. Herbert Benson (with William Proctor), *Beyond the Relaxation Response* (New York: Berkeley Books, 1985), pp. 96–97.
31. Kevin Lamb, "Workout Warriors: Try Kicking Back," Cox News Service, August 31, 2001.
32. Barry Gearhart, "How Important Are Dispositional Factors as Determinants of Job Satisfaction? Implications for Job Design and Other Personnel Programs," *Journal of Applied Psychology,* August 1987, pp. 366–373; Deborah J. Dwyer and Marilyn L. Fox, "The Moderating Role of Hostility in the Relationship Between Enriched Jobs and Health," *Academy of Management Journal,* December 2000, pp. 1086–1096.
33. M. Afzalur Rahim, "Relationships of Stress, Locus of Control, and Social Support to Psychiatric Symptoms and Propensity to Leave a Job: A Field Study with Managers, *Journal of Business and Psychology,* Winter 1997, p. 163.
34. Sandra L. Kirmeyer and Thomas W. Dougherty, "Work Load, Tension, and Coping: Moderating Effects of Supervisor Support," *Personnel Psychology,* Spring 1998, pp. 125–139.
35. Gillian Flynn, "Companies that Make Wellness Work," *Personnel Journal,* February 1995, pp. 63–66; Charlene Marmer Solomon, "Stressed to the Limit," *Workforce,* September 1999, p. 52.
36. Lawrence R. Murphy, et al. (eds.), *Job Stress Interventions* (Washington, DC: American Psychological Association, 1995), p. 323.

SUGGESTED READING

Atkinson, William. "When Stress Won't Go Away." *HR Magazine,* December 2000, pp. 104–110.

Brooks Waltman, Alicia, with Chatterjee, Camille. "A Guide to Health." Special Section, *Psychology Today,* March/April 2000, pp. 37–52.

Carey, John. "Is Your Office Killing You?" *Business Week,* June 5, 2000, pp. 114–128.

Davis, Martha, Robbins Eshelman, Elizabeth, and McKay, Matthew. *The Relaxation & Stress Reduction Handbook,* 5th ed. Oakland, CA: New Harbinger, 2000.

Epstein, Robert. "Stress Busters: 11 Quick, Fun Games to Tame the Beast." *Psychology Today,* March/April 2000, pp. 30–36.

Matheny, Kenneth B., and McCarthy, Christopher J. *Write Your Own Prescription for Stress.* Oakland, CA: New Harbinger, 2000.

McCauley, Lucy (ed.). "Don't Burn Out! Keep the Fires Burning." *Fast Company,* May 2000, pp. 101–132.

Miley, William M. *The Psychology of Well Being.* Westport, CT: Praeger/Greenwood Publishing Group, 1999.

Weeks, Holly. "Taking the Stress Out of Stressful Conversations." *Harvard Business Review,* July–August 2001, pp. 112–119.

WEB CORNER

www.betterbricks.com/healthy.asp (Describes some of the characteristics of a healthy workplace.)

www.fastcompany.com/keyword/goodwork53 (Offers advice on combating the potential stress caused by a disaster.)

www.pressanykey.com/stresstest.html (Evaluation of resistance to stress.)

www.stress.org (Institute for Stress Management)

CHAPTER 8

MANAGING CONFLICT AND ANGER

Learning Objectives After reading and studying this chapter and doing the exercises, you should be able to

1. Understand how conflict, frustration, and anger relate to each other.
2. Identify the major sources of job conflict.
3. Summarize the negative and positive consequences of job conflict.
4. Pinpoint the major conflict management styles.
5. Describe several key techniques for resolving conflicts with others, including negotiation.
6. Obtain insight into managing anger.

A substantial challenge for those whose work involves interaction with people is to deal effectively with conflict. To help you understand and better manage conflict, we first examine how conflict, frustration, anger, and stress are related. Other key topics in this chapter include sources of job conflict, the constructive and destructive sides of conflict, how to resolve conflict, and how to deal with anger.

THE INTERRELATIONSHIP OF CONFLICT, FRUSTRATION, ANGER, AND STRESS

A **conflict** is the simultaneous arousal of two or more incompatible motives or demands. Conflict acts as a stressor and is usually accompanied by unpleasant emotions and feelings such as frustration and anger. It helps to understand conflict if you also regard it as a process in which one or both sides intentionally interferes in the efforts of the other side to achieve an objective. Because one side attempts to prevent the other from attaining an objective, the conflict leads to a hostile relationship between individuals or groups.

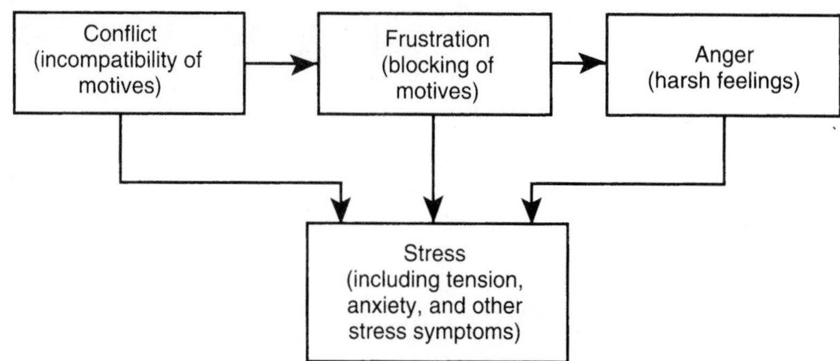

FIGURE 8–1 The Relationship Among Conflict, Frustration, Anger, and Stress

Conflict typically leads to **frustration,** a blocking of need or motive satisfaction by some kind of obstacle. You experience a sense of frustration when something stands between you and the goal you want to achieve. It is usually your perception of an event, situation, or thing that determines whether or not it is an obstacle. For example, if you want to borrow money from a bank to start a business, you will be required to develop a business plan. Some people will regard the business plan as a bureaucratic obstacle making it difficult to borrow money. Others will regard the plan as a sensible way of communicating the success potential of their business.

Anger is a feeling of extreme hostility, indignation, or exasperation. The feeling of anger creates stress, including the physiological changes described in Chapter 7. One noticeable physical indicator of anger is that eye pupils may enlarge, causing the wide-eyed look of people in a rage. Blood may rush to the face, as indicated by reddening in light-skinned people.

Conflict, frustration, anger, and stress are interrelated. Conflict leads to frustration, which leads to anger, and all three lead to stress. Figure 8–1 summarizes these relationships.

SOURCES OF JOB CONFLICT

There are a number of reasons why conflicts arise in organizational life. We will describe six important sources of conflict here. All these reasons for, or sources of, conflict stem from the same underlying theme of two incompatible motives, demands, or events. You and another person or your department and another department cannot both have what you both want at the same time, and you cannot be in two places at the same time.

Competition for Limited Resources

A fundamental reason that you might experience conflict with another person is that not everybody can get all the money, material, and human help he or she wants. You might have an important idea you want to present to your boss before he leaves for vacation. When you ask to see the boss before he leaves, he says, "I'm sorry, but I have already agreed to meet with Debbie and Mike. Why don't you catch me first thing after vacation?"

At that moment you will probably feel frustrated because your goal of presenting your idea to the boss is blocked. You might also be in conflict with Debbie and Mike, who have monopolized your boss's time for the balance of the day. The limited resource in this situation is the boss's time.

Differences in Goals and Objectives

When two individuals or two groups have major differences in objectives, the potential for conflict is high. Although one might argue that everybody working for the same organization should have the same ultimate goal—the success of the organization—this does not always happen in practice. Frequently, individuals and departments have different aspirations than management.

Conflict between instructors and students sometimes reflects a difference between goals and objectives. An instructor might look on his or her course as a valuable contribution to each student's career. The instructor's goal is for students to maximize their effort in study and classroom participation. Some of the students may have the goal of receiving the maximum grade for the minimum amount of study and participation. When an examination question is posed based on a minor point made in supplementary reading, conflict occurs. If the students shared the goal of maximizing learning, they would not object to the question. If the instructor shared the goal of maximum grade for minimum effort, he or she might not have asked the obscure question.

The Generation Gap and Personality Clashes

Various personality and cultural differences among people contribute to workplace conflict. Differences in age, or the generation gap, can lead to conflict because members of one generation may not accept the values of another. As described in Chapter 2, members of different generations often have different values, and these differences can lead to workplace conflict. Another potential area of conflict is that according to the stereotype, the older generation sees the younger generation as disrespectful of rules, not willing to pay their dues, and being disloyal to employers. Members of the younger generation see the older generation as worshiping hierarchy (layers of authority), being overcautious, and wanting to preserve the status quo. Both groups, of course, see themselves in a more favorable light. Members of Generation X and Generation Y believe that employers have been disloyal to them, and Baby Boomers believe the search for job security is highly sensible.

Members of older generations, such as the Baby Boomers, often place more value on seniority and traditional departments. In contrast members of younger generations, such as Generation X and Generation Y, may place more value on merit and teamwork. However, according to one analysis, many Baby Boomers have also embraced a team-based approach to leadership because they are eager to shed the command-and-control style of their predecessor generation.[1]

The generation gap, as well as other forms of cultural diversity in the workforce, has increased the potential for conflict. William L. Ury, a negotiation expert, says, "Conflict resolution is perhaps the key skill needed in a diverse workforce."[2] When conflicts are properly resolved, diversity lends strength to the organization because the various viewpoints make an important contribution to solving a problem. A manager from Boston in his mid-40s offers insight into dealing effectively with the generation gap.[3]

> First, managing young people is part of workplace diversity. Generations are at least as different from one another—maybe even more so—as are races or sexes, yet few corporations bother to point this out with their managers or to suggest ways of dealing with the gap in communication that so often results. We are trained to accept, understand, and to make positive use of the differences that come from someone's being of a different race, nationality, or gender. We don't know how to do the same if the person in question is 20 years our junior.

Somewhat related to generational differences in values, many disagreements on the job arise because some people simply dislike each other. A **personality clash** is thus an antagonistic relationship between two people based on differences in personal attributes, preferences, interests, values, and styles. People involved in a personality clash often have difficulty specifying why they dislike each other. The end result, however, is that they cannot maintain an amiable work relationship. A strange fact about personality clashes is that people who get along well may begin to clash after working together for a number of years. Many business partnerships fold because the two partners eventually clash.

Gender Differences

Another type of conflict between cultures can stem from differences in gender, or the culturally based roles carried out by men and women. One explanation for gender conflicts is that many women want more power and many men are reluctant to share power. Conflict between men and women may also take place for other reasons. Men more typically want rewards to be handed out equitably, or based on contribution. Women are more likely to want rewards to be handed out more equally, so that nobody in the group suffers from receiving too few rewards. Pay differences between men and women performing similar work is another contributor to gender conflict. Many men perceive having to attend sexual harassment workshops as an insult to their manners and behavior.

Competing Work and Family Demands

Balancing the demands of career and family life has become a major challenge facing today's workforce. The challenge is particularly intense for employees who are part of a two-wage-earner family. **Work–family conflict** occurs when an individual has to perform multiple roles: worker, spouse, and, often, parent.[4] This type of conflict is frequent because the multiple roles are often incompatible. Imagine having planned to attend your child's solo recital and then being ordered at the last minute to attend an after-hours meeting.

Work–family conflict can be a major stressor, and can lead to emotional disorders as revealed by a study of 2,700 employed adults. Two types of work–family conflict were studied: family life creating problems at work, and work creating problems at home. Emotional problems were measured by diagnostic interviews. Both types of conflict were associated with having mood disorders, disturbing levels of anxiety, and substance abuse. Also, employees who reported work–family conflict were much more likely to have a clinically significant mental health problem.[5]

The conflict over work versus family demands intensifies when the person is serious about both work and family responsibilities. The average professional employee works about 55 hours per week, including five hours on weekends. Adhering to such a schedule almost inevitably results in some incompatible demands from work versus those from family members and friends. Conflict arises because the person wants to work sufficient hours to succeed on the job, yet still have enough time for personal life. In Chapter 14, we describe various approaches to resolving work versus family demands.

Sexual Harassment

Many employees face conflict because they are sexually harassed by a supervisor, coworker, or customer. **Sexual harassment** is generally defined as unwanted sexually oriented behavior in the workplace that results in discomfort and/or interference with the job. It can include an action as violent as rape or as subdued as telling a sexually oriented joke. The prevailing opinion about sexual harassment is that it is about power and the need to dominate, not uncontrollable physical attraction. At the same time, sexual harassment is an aggressive act designed to achieve the aggressor's goals.[6] Carrying the power analysis of sexual attraction to the extreme, when a lower-ranking male harasses a higher-ranking female, he is attempting to momentarily gain power for himself.

Sexual harassment creates conflict because the harassed person has to make a choice between two incompatible motives. One motive is to get ahead, keep the job, or have an unthreatening work environment. But to satisfy this motive, the person is forced to sacrifice the motive of holding on to his or her moral values or preferences. For example, a person might say, "I want to be liked by my coworkers and not be considered a prude. Yet to do this must I listen to their gross jokes about the human anatomy?" Of even greater conflict, "I want a raise, but to do this must I submit to being fondled by my boss?" Here we focus on the types and frequency of sexual harassment, research evidence about its effects, and guidelines for dealing with the problem.

Types and Frequency of Harassment. Two types of sexual harassment are legally recognized. Both are violations of the Civil Rights Acts of 1964 and 1991, and are therefore a violation of your rights when working in the United States. Canada also has human rights legislation prohibiting sexual harassment. In quid pro quo sexual harassment, the individual suffers loss (or threatened loss) of a job benefit as a result of his or her response to a request for sexual favors. The demands of a harasser can be blatant or implied. An implied form of quid pro quo harassment might take this form: A manager casually comments to one of his or her employees, "I've noticed that workers who become very close to me outside of the office get recommended for bigger raises."

The other form of sexual harassment is hostile-environment harassment. Another person in the workplace creates an intimidating, hostile, or offensive working environment. No tangible loss has to be suffered under this form of sexual harassment. According to a 1993 U.S. Supreme Court ruling, the person does not have to suffer severe psychological injury for an act to be classified as harassing. So long as a "reasonable person" would be offended by the behavior in question, the act could be considered harassment. Sexual harassment of both types is widespread in the workplace even though the vast majority of these complaints are related to a hostile environment. In one of the biggest federal sexual-harassment lawsuits in history, 29 women filed a class action suit against Mitsubishi Motor Manufacturing of America Inc. Female employees at the Normal, Illinois, plant complained of sexual misbehavior on the factory floor, including obnoxious comments, the display of sexually oriented drawings, and forced sex play. Part of the lawsuit contended that the Japanese managers were complacent about charges.

According to one compilation of figures, at least half of all women have been harassed at some point in their career. Furthermore, at least 10 percent have quit a job because of sexual harassment.[7] A study conducted in a business firm and among female faculty and staff of a large Midwestern university measured the frequency of both hostile-environment and quid pro quo sexual harassment. Of the business firm employees studied, 68 percent indicated that they had experienced at least one sexually harassing behavior on the job during the previous 24 months; 63 percent of the university employees reported such an experience.[8] One reason sexual harassment is so frequent is that it can take place between manager and group member; between coworkers; and between employees and customers, clients, or patients. Furthermore, sexual harassment can take place between members of the same sex. According to a 1998 U.S. Supreme Court ruling, workers can sue for sexual harassment under federal civil rights law even if the alleged harassers are the same sex as the victim.

In addition to legal definitions of harassment, workers' perceptions of what constitutes harassment are important in understanding the problem. A review of studies on the subject found that women perceive a broader range of social-sexual behaviors as constituting hostile-environment harassment. Although the differences were small, women were more likely to perceive the following behaviors as harassing:

- Obscene gestures, not directed at target
- Sex-stereotyped jokes
- Obscene phone calls
- Belittling the target's competence
- Repeated requests to go out after work or school
- Proposition for an affair
- Embracing the target
- Congratulatory hug

Men and women, however, had little disagreement that various types of sexual coercion, such as encounters that are made a condition of promotion, can be classified as quid pro quo harassment.[9]

Research Evidence about the Effects of Sexual Harassment. Aside from being unethical, immoral, and illegal, sexual harassment is widely thought to have adverse consequences. The harassed person may experience job stress, lowered morale, severe conflict, and lowered productivity. The study with business and university workers documented some of the problems associated with sexual harassment. It was found that even at low levels of frequency, harassment exerts a significant impact on women's psychological well-being, job attitudes, and work behaviors. For both business and university workers, women who had experienced high levels of harassment reported the worst job-related and psychological effects. The study also found that women who had experienced only a moderate level of harassment also suffered from negative outcomes.[10]

Another study with women university employees indicated that the negative effects of sexual harassment were not related to personality factors within the person being harassed. Independent of any personality factors studied, women who were sexually harassed experienced decreases in life satisfaction and psychological well-being. (The study was conducted at two points in time, making it possible to study changes in satisfaction and well-being after being harassed.) The sample included many women in nontraditional occupations such as working in maintenance departments or female professors in physics or engineering, because women in such roles are frequently harassed.[11]

Guidelines for Preventing and Dealing with Sexual Harassment. A starting point in dealing with sexual harassment is to develop an awareness of the types of behaviors that are considered sexual harassment. Often the difference is subtle. Suppose, for example, you placed copies of two nudes painted by a famous painter on a coworker's desk. Your coworker might call that harassment. Yet if you took that coworker to a museum to see the originals of the same nude paintings, your behavior usually would not be classified as harassment. Education about the meaning of sexual harassment is therefore a basic part of any company program to prevent sexual harassment. Following is a sampling of the behaviors that will often be interpreted as environmental sexual harassment.[12]

- *Inappropriate remarks and sexual implications.* Coworkers, subordinates, customers, and suppliers should not be referred to as sexual beings, and their appearance should not be referred to in a sexual manner. Telling a coworker she has gorgeous legs, or he has fabulous biceps, is out of place at work.
- *Terms of endearment.* Refrain from calling others in the workplace by names such as "cutie," "sweetheart," "honey," "dear," or "hunk." Even if these terms are not directly sexually suggestive, they might be interpreted as demeaning.
- *Suggestive compliments.* It is acceptable to tell another person he or she looks nice, but avoid sexually tinged comments such as mentioning that the person's clothing shows off his or her body to advantage.
- *Physical touching.* To avoid any appearance of sexual harassment it is best to restrict physical touching to handshakes and an occasional sideways hug. Some people consider the "corporate A-frame" hug, whereby the two people's bodies only touch at the top, to be acceptable. When a work associate is a longtime friend, the rules for hugging are more liberal.
- *Work-related kissing.* It is best to avoid all kissing in a work context, except perhaps a light kiss at an office party. It is much more professional to greet a work associate with a warm, sincere handshake.

The easiest way to deal with sexual harassment is to speak up before it becomes serious. The first time it happens, respond with a statement such as "I won't tolerate that kind of talk," "I dislike sexually oriented jokes," or "Keep your hands off me." Write the harasser a stern letter shortly after the first incident. Confronting the person in writing dramatizes your seriousness of purpose in not wanting to be sexually harassed. If the problem persists, say something to this effect: "You're practicing sexual harassment. If you don't stop, I'm going to exercise my right to report you to management."

THE CONSTRUCTIVE AND DESTRUCTIVE SIDES OF CONFLICT

Although conflict sparks images of negative behavior, it has both positive and negative consequences. We approach the constructive and destructive sides of conflict from two perspectives: the functional and dysfunctional sides of conflict, and stimulating the right type of conflict within teams.

Functional and Dysfunctional Conflict

As shown in Figure 8–2, conflict in the right amount improves performance, whereas too little or too much conflict can decrease performance. **Functional conflict** occurs when the interests of the organization are served as a result of a dispute or disagreement. **Dysfunctional conflict** occurs when a dispute or disagreement harms the organization.

Functional conflict fosters high levels of performance through such means as arousing motivation, problem-solving ability, creativity, and constructive change. Given that conflict creates some stress, the people in conflict become mentally energized so they work harder and think harder. An example is two workers in conflict over the best approach to attracting talented workers to the firm. Because of

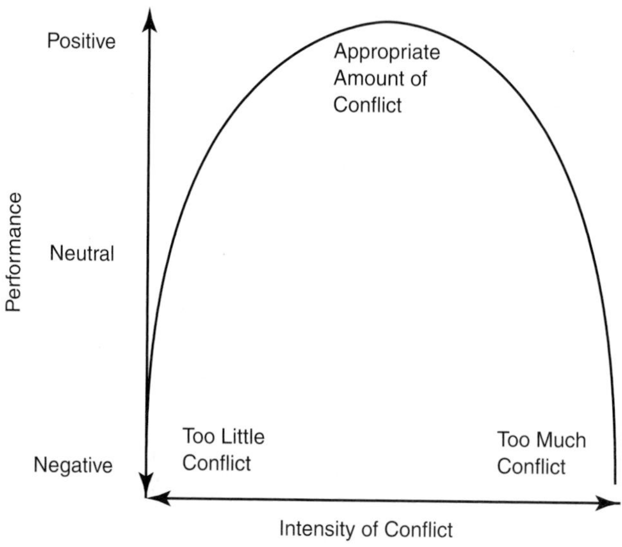

FIGURE 8–2 The Relationship Between Conflict Intensity and Performance

their conflict they both offer innovative solutions to the problem, and their manager decides to try both. The recruiting tactics both work well, and the company attracts the talent it needs.

Michael Eisner, the CEO and Chairman of Walt Disney Company, presents an anecdote of how conflict helped his company save production costs in a particular film. The film script included a scene in which the main character asks her parents for money to attend ballet school. Because the film was over budget, management wanted to cut the scene. The writer did not want the scene cut, and there was conflict over how to reduce the budget, and whether or not to cut the scene. From these conversations, an idea emerged that the scene could be played with the actress making her request into the intercom in front of her parents' apartment building. No sets or additional actors were needed. The actress is basically begging them through a phone buzzer in an already-built exterior set. And when she's done, you see a check floating down into the scene.

The revised scene cost virtually nothing to make, and it was funnier and better than the original idea because somebody had a different point of view of how the scene could be enacted. Eisner said, "There was a nice resolution of conflict that made sense in terms of creativity and cost."[13]

Dysfunctional conflict is disruptive in many ways, including wasting time and placing personal welfare above the interests of the firm. Conflict can divert time and energy away from reaching important goals. It is not uncommon for two managers in conflict to spend time sending e-mail messages proving each other wrong in a dispute. Another dysfunctional consequence of conflict is that it may result in one party retaliating for the perceived wrongdoing of another party. An example would be a worker and his manager in angry dispute over a disciplinary suspension. As a result, the worker sabotages valuable computer files.

Workplace violence is a dysfunctional conflict of enormous concern. Violence has become so widespread that homicide is the second leading cause of workplace deaths, with about 1,000 workers murdered each year.[14] Most of these deaths result from a robbery or commercial crime. Many other killings are perpetrated by disgruntled workers who are typically former employees harboring unresolved conflicts. Workplace violence is sometimes referred to as *desk-rage,* and includes such diverse behavior as distracting rudeness, attacks on trashcans, keyboards, and even coworkers. A tentative profile of the violence-prone employee drawn by the Federal Bureau of Investigation and industry experts is as follows:

- obsession with weapons
- repeated direct or veiled threats
- relatively young, single male loner
- obsessive involvement with the job
- paranoid, aggressive behavior
- unwanted romantic interest in a coworker
- overreaction to company policies
- refusal to accept criticism
- interest in recently published violent events
- increased mood swings
- damage or destruction of company property

- poor workplace relationships
- decreased productivity or inconsistent work performance[15]

The violent-prone employee would most likely exhibit several of these symptoms, and no one should be classified as potentially violent because of one symptom. For example, many peaceful workaholics have an obsessive involvement with the job. (See the case, "A Concern about Violence" at the end of this chapter.) Keep in mind also, that the violence-prone employee will act out the violence primarily when triggered by intense conflict.

Stimulating the Right Type of Conflict

While the right amount of conflict can enhance performance, a group of case history analyses in organizations suggests that stimulating the right type of conflict is perhaps more important. A team of researchers classified the conflict found in teams and other work groups into two types.[16] **C-type conflict** focuses on substantive (having substance), issue-related differences. The C stands for cognitive, indicating that the conflict relates to tangible, concrete issues that can be dealt with more intellectually than emotionally. **A-type conflict** focuses on personalized, individually oriented issues (such as personality clashes). The A stands for affective, indicating that the conflict relates to subjective issues that are dealt with more emotionally than intellectually.

C-type conflict is functional because it requires teams to engage in activities that foster team effectiveness. Team members engaged in C-type conflict would critically examine alternative solutions and incorporate different points of view into their team goals. Because frank communication and different points of view are encouraged, C-type conflict encourages innovative thinking. C-type conflict is also more likely to make use of the talents of all team members. In contrast, A-type conflict undermines group effectiveness by blocking constructive activities and processes. By such means as directing anger toward individuals and blaming each other for mistakes, A-type conflict leads to cynicism and distrust. Teams engaged in A-type conflict are less likely to involve all members in problem solving.

A recent study provides more support for the idea that conflict about tasks leads to higher productivity than conflict about relationships within the group. The study involved 51 three-person groups of business students, all of whom also held full-time jobs. The groups worked as consulting teams for companies, such as helping a coffee shop develop a marketing plan to compete with national chains. Teams performing well were characterized by low levels of relationship conflict that rose near project deadlines. The same teams had low but increasing levels of conflict about processes (or methods), and moderate levels of task conflict.[17]

CONFLICT MANAGEMENT STYLES

Before describing specific methods of resolving conflict, it is useful to understand five general styles, or orientations, of handling conflict. As shown in Figure 8–3, Kenneth Thomas identified five major styles of conflict management: competitive, accommodative, sharing, collaborative, and avoidant. Each style is based on a combination of satisfying one's own concerns (assertiveness) and satisfying the concerns of others (cooperativeness).[18]

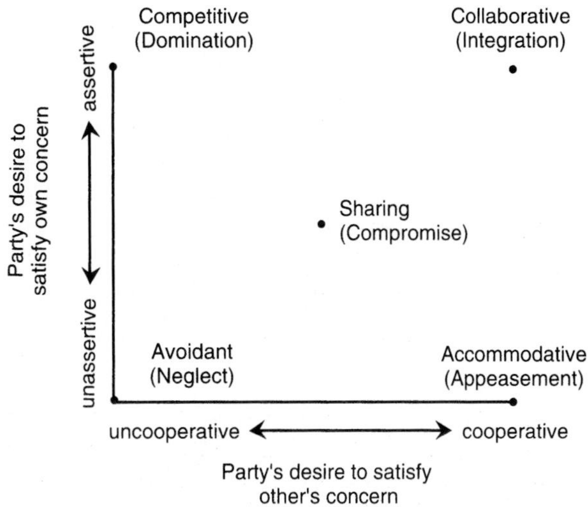

FIGURE 8–3 Conflict-Handling Styles According to Degree of Cooperation and Assertiveness

Source: Kenneth W. Thomas, "Organizational Conflict," in Steven Kerr, ed., *Organizational Behavior* (Columbus, Ohio: Grid Publishing, 1979), p. 156.

Competitive. The competitive style is a desire to win one's own concerns at the expense of the other party, or to dominate. A person with a competitive orientation is likely to engage in win–lose power struggles.

Accommodative. The accommodative style favors appeasement, or satisfying the other's concerns without taking care of one's own. People with this orientation may be generous or self-sacrificing just to maintain a relationship. An irate customer might be accommodated with a full refund "just to shut him (or her) up." The intent of such accommodation might also be to retain the customer's loyalty.

Sharing. The sharing style is halfway between domination and appeasement. Sharers prefer moderate but incomplete satisfaction for both parties, which results in a compromise. The term "splitting the difference" reflects this orientation and is commonly used in such activities as purchasing a house or car.

Collaborative. In contrast to the other styles, the collaborative style reflects a desire to fully satisfy the desires of both parties. It is based on an underlying philosophy of **win–win,** the belief that after conflict has been resolved both sides should gain something of value. The user of win–win approaches is genuinely concerned about arriving at a settlement that meets the needs of both parties, or at least does not badly damage the welfare of the other side. When a collaborative approach to resolving conflict is used, the relationship between the parties is built on and improved. Here is an example of a win–win approach to resolving conflict.[19]

> During a management meeting in Detroit several years ago, Dieter Zetsche, CEO of DaimlerChrysler, told Chrysler dealers that the company planned to take away subsidies worth $300 to $500 per vehicle. Taking away these subsidies would save Chrysler as much as $1 billion per year. When dealers refused, Zetsche agreed to consider alternatives that would bring the same result. He

finally accepted a proposal that would allow dealers to compensate for the lost money with bonuses for beating new sales targets.

Avoidant. The avoider is a combination of uncooperative and unassertive. He or she is indifferent to the concerns of either party. The person may actually be withdrawing from the conflict or be relying on fate. A manager who stays out of a conflict between two team members who are left to resolve their own differences sometimes uses the avoidant style.

In the following description of specific techniques for resolving conflict, you should be able to relate most of them to these five key styles. For example, you will see that the confrontation and problem-solving technique reflects the collaborative style.

TECHNIQUES FOR RESOLVING CONFLICTS WITH OTHERS

Because of the inevitability of job conflict, a career-minded person must learn effective ways of resolving conflict. Here we concentrate on methods of conflict resolution that you can use on your own. Most of them emphasize a win–win philosophy. Several of the negotiating and bargaining tactics to be described may be close to the competitive orientation.

Confrontation and Problem Solving

The most highly recommended way of resolving conflict is **confrontation and problem solving,** a method of identifying the true source of conflict and resolving it systematically. The confrontation in this approach is gentle and tactful rather than combative and abusive. Reasonableness is important because the person who takes the initiative in resolving the conflict wants to maintain a harmonious working relationship with the other party. Confronting and problem solving a conflict involves six steps:

Step 1: *Awareness.* Party A recognizes that a conflict exists between himself or herself and party B.

Step 2: *The decision to confront.* Party A decides the conflict is important enough to warrant a confrontation with party B and that such a confrontation is preferable to avoiding the conflict.

Step 3: *The confrontation.* Party A decides to work cooperatively and confronts party B. At this point, party B may indicate a willingness to accept the confrontation or may decide to gloss over its seriousness. Often the conflict is resolved at this step, particularly if it is not of a serious and complicated nature.

Step 4: *Determining the cause of the conflict.* The two parties discuss their own opinions, attitudes, and feelings in relation to the conflict and attempt to identify the real issue. For example, the real cause of conflict between two people might be that they have a different concept of what constitutes a fair day's work.

Step 5: *Determining the outcome and further steps.* In this step the parties attempt to develop specific means of reducing or eliminating the cause of the conflict. If the cause cannot be changed (such as changing one's opinion of a fair day's work), a way of working around the cause is devised. If both parties agree on a solution, then the confrontation has been successful.

Step 6: *Follow-through.* After the solution has been implemented, both parties should check periodically to ensure that their agreements are being kept.[20]

When the other party has a power advantage over you, it is particularly important to express the confrontation in a tactful manner that does not hint at retaliation. Suppose that you find out that a coworker is being paid $300 more per month than you, yet he is doing the same job and has the same amount of experience and education. Confronting the issue gently, you would tactfully discuss this problem with your boss and ask if the inequity could be resolved. One statement you might make would be, "I wonder if there has been a mistake in setting my salary. The fellow I work with is being paid $300 more per month than another person doing the same job."

Negotiating and Bargaining

Conflicts can be considered situations calling for **negotiating and bargaining,** conferring with another person in order to resolve a problem. When you are trying to negotiate a fair salary for yourself, you are simultaneously trying to resolve a conflict. At first the demands of both parties may seem incompatible, but through mutual gains negotiation, a salary may emerge that satisfies both parties. The term *mutual gains* refers to the idea that both parties win.

COMPROMISE. In compromise, one party agrees to do one thing if the other party agrees to do something else. "I'll get my reports to you on time if you agree to get them back to me with your suggestions within 10 days." Compromise is a realistic approach to resolving conflict and is almost inescapable in our culture. People enter into negotiation and bargaining sessions expecting a compromise solution. Assume, for example, that a company has agreed to have a custom-designed machine built for a certain price. The buyer does not expect to get all the features desired at that price, while the seller anticipates throwing in more features than he or she first offered.

The major problem with compromise is that the two parties may wind up with a solution that pacifies both but does not solve the problem. One example would be buying two department heads half the equipment that each requests. As a result, neither department really shows the productivity gain that would have been possible if the full request had been granted to either side.

ALLOW ROOM FOR NEGOTIATION, BUT BE PLAUSIBLE. The basic tactic of compromise is to begin with a demand that allows you room for compromise and concession. Anyone who has ever negotiated for the price of an automobile or house recognizes this basic approach. If you think your 10-speed bicycle is worth $400 you might put it on sale for $500. A potential buyer makes an initial offer of $300. After negotiation you wind up with an offer of $400, precisely what you wanted. However, be prepared to go beyond common sense. Most people believe that allowing room for negotiation includes beginning with an extreme demand or offer. (An example would be the seller asking $850 for the bicycle, or the potential buyer offering $150.) The final compromise will therefore be closer to your true demand or offer than if you opened negotiations more realistically. But a plausible demand is better because it shows you are bargaining in good faith. Also, if a third party has to resolve the conflict, a plausible demand or offer will receive more sympathy than an implausible one.

Focus on Interests, Not Positions. Rather than clinging to specific negotiating points, keep your overall interests in mind and try to satisfy them. Remember that the true object of negotiation is to satisfy the underlying interests of both sides. Here is how this strategy works:

> While job hunting, you are made an offer for a position you really want. You have a certain starting salary in mind, which is $3000 more per year than the job offer. Your real interests are probably to be able to live a particular lifestyle with your salary, whereas your position is to attain a particular starting salary. Your interests are best served by examining the total compensation package including employee benefits, along with the cost of living in the area. Your true interests might be served by agreeing to a starting salary lower than you had planned.

A key benefit of focusing on interests rather than positions is that it helps place the emphasis away from winning and toward what you really want to achieve. If you focus on mutual interests your intent will be to solve a problem rather than outmaneuver the other side. For example, if a customer makes an unrealistic demand, your best interest is to somehow satisfy that demand without losing money and retain the customer.

Make Small Concessions Gradually. Making steady concessions leads to more satisfactory agreements in most situations. Gradually, you concede little things to the other side, such as throwing in an air pump and a backpack if the person agrees to move up the offer for the 10-speed bike. The small-concession tactic is described as a soft approach to bargaining. The hard-line approach is to make your total concession early in the negotiation and grant no further concessions. In our example, "My bike is for sale at $400 including an air pump and a backpack. I will keep the bike rather than let it go for less."

Use Deadlines. Giving the other side a deadline is often helpful in winning a negotiation or resolving a conflict. Deadlines often force people into action because they require some type of external control or motivation. Here are two examples of how you might be able to use deadlines to gain advantage in your negotiation:

- "Will I be receiving a promotion to restaurant manager by December 31? If not, I will be forced to accept employment at another restaurant that has offered me such a promotion."
- "I am willing to paint your house for $6,000 if you agree to sign the contract by July 15. After that date my price will go up to $6,500."

Ask the Other Side, "What Do You Want Me to Do?" An effective tactic for both negotiation and other forms of conflict resolution is to ask the other side what he or she would like you to do in order to reach an agreement. If you do what the other side wants, you will often have reached an agreement. The underlying psychology is that having suggested the solution, the other side will feel committed. Here is an example:

> Your teammates and you are dividing up the work for a large task. It appears that several of your teammates do not think you are making an equitable contribution. After negotiating your contribution for about 30 minutes, you find that negotiations are stalled. You then ask, "What would you people like me to do?" Because you are so cooperative, the other team members will probably not make an outrageous demand. Also, they will probably regard your contribution as equitable because they formulated it.

MAKE A LAST AND FINAL OFFER. In many instances, presenting a final offer will break a deadlock. You might frame your message something like this: "I am willing to set up your Web page for $450. Call me when you are willing to pay that much for this specialized piece of work." Sometimes the tactic will be countered by a last and final offer from the other side. "Thanks for your interest in helping me set up a Web page. But the maximum price I am willing to pay is $250. Call me or send me an e-mail if that price is acceptable to you." One of you will probably give in and accept the other person's last and final offer.

After having studied negotiating and bargaining tactics, along with other techniques of conflict resolution, now do Skill-Building Exercise 8–1. It deals with the most important goal of negotiation.

Disarm the Opposition

In many instances of interpersonal conflict, the other side has a legitimate complaint about specific aspects of your behavior. If you deny the reality of the complaint, the person will continue to harp on that point and the issue will remain unresolved. A good alternative is to use **disarm the opposition,** a technique of

SKILL-BUILDING EXERCISE 8–1

Mutual Gains Bargaining

The class is organized into groups of six, with each group divided into negotiating teams of three each. The members of the negotiating teams would like to find integrative (win–win) solutions to the issue separating them. The team members are free to invent their own pressing issue or choose one from among the following:

- Management wants to control costs by not giving cost-of-living adjustments in the upcoming year. The employee group believes that a cost-of-living adjustment is absolutely necessary for its welfare.
- The marketing team claims it could sell 250,000 units of a toaster wide enough to toast bagels if the toasters could be produced at $13 per unit. The manufacturing group says it would not be feasible to get the manufacturing cost below $18 per unit.
- Blockbuster Video would like to build in a new location, adjacent to a historic district in one of the oldest cities in North America. The members of the town planning board would like the tax revenue and jobs that the Blockbuster store would bring, but they still say they do not want a Blockbuster store adjacent to the historic district.

After the teams have arrived at their solutions through high-level negotiating techniques, the creative solutions can be shared with teammates.

conflict resolution in which one person disarms another by agreeing with his or her criticism. By agreeing with the criticism, you may set the stage for a true resolution of the problem. Disarm the opposition can also be described as psychological judo, because you can disarm an attacker by agreeing with the criticism. Such agreement is the last thing he or she expects.[21]

Disarming the opposition has widespread application. It works more effectively than launching a counterattack against the person with whom you are in conflict. Assume that your boss is angry with you because your sales are 25 percent below target. You recognize that your boss might even be angry enough to threaten you with an ultimatum—improve sales or leave the company. Your worst strategy would be to marshal an immediate counterattack during a meeting with your boss. Do not try to dazzle him or her with a long list of reasons why sales have been below forecast. Instead, disarm your boss with a statement such as, "You are probably upset because my sales are 25 percent below target. I agree that I should not be proud of my performance. Maybe you can help me develop a plan of attack to improve my sales situation."

Exchange Images with Your Antagonist

The essential point to this advanced method of resolving conflict is that you and your antagonist make it clear that you understand the other person's point of view. Empathy of this kind may then lead to a useful and productive compromise. A convenient application of this method is for you to list on a sheet of paper (1) your side of the argument and (2) what you think is the other person's side of the argument. Next, he or she does the same for you. Table 8–1 is an example of how images might be exchanged. Each person makes up his or her image sheet without consulting the other person. After the images are exchanged, discussion (and sometimes fireworks) begins.

TABLE 8–1

An Image-Exchange List Between You and Your Supervisor Based on a Conflict About Punctuality

You:	
My Side of the Story	***What I Think Is Your Side of the Story***
a. I'm usually on time for work.	a. I'm not very dependable.
b. I live on the other side of town.	b. I live too far from the office.
c. Public transportation is unreliable in this city.	c. I take the last possible bus.
Your Supervisor:	
My Side of the Story	***What I Think Is Your Side of the Story***
a. You are late too often.	a. I'm as punctual as most people in the office.
b. If you cared more about your job, you would consider moving closer to the office.	b. I think you don't take my transportation problems seriously.
c. If you got out of bed earlier, you could take an earlier bus.	c. I try hard to get here on time. It's not my fault that I'm late sometimes.

Cognitive Restructuring

An indirect way of resolving conflict between people is to lessen the conflicting elements in a situation by viewing them more positively. According to the technique of **cognitive restructuring,** you mentally convert negative aspects into positive ones by looking for the positive elements in a situation.[22] How you frame or choose your thoughts can determine the outcome of a conflict situation. Your thoughts can influence your actions. If you search for the beneficial elements in a situation, there will be less area for dispute. Although this technique might sound like a mind game to you, it can work effectively.

Imagine that a coworker of yours, Nick, has been asking you repeated questions about how to carry out a work procedure. You are about ready to tell Nick, "Go bother somebody else. I'm not paid to be a trainer." Instead, you look for the positive elements in the situation. You say to yourself, "Nick has been asking me a lot of questions. This does take time, but answering these questions is valuable experience. If I want to become a manager, I will have to help group members with problems."

After having completed this cognitive restructuring, you can then deal with the conflict more positively. You might say to Nick, "I welcome the opportunity to help you, but we need to find a mutually convenient time. In that way, I can better concentrate on my own work."

Make an Upward Appeal

At times you may be placed in a conflict situation where the other party holds the major share of the power. Perhaps you have tried techniques such as confrontation and problem solving or disarming the opposition, yet he or she still won't budge. In these situations you may have to enlist the help of a third party with power—more power than you or your adversary has. Among such third parties are union stewards, human resource managers, a highly placed relative in the organization, or your boss's boss (when you are convinced that you have been done an injustice).

In some situations, just implying that you will bring in that powerful third party to help resolve the conflict is sufficient for you to gain advantage. One woman believed she was repeatedly passed over for promotion because she was over age 50. She hinted that if she were not given fairer consideration she would speak to the state fair employment practices commission. She was appointed to assistant department manager shortly thereafter.

Develop Empathy through Shadowing

A standard approach to resolving conflict is to develop empathy for the situation facing the other side. A powerful approach to developing empathy is to observe first hand the problems and challenges the other side faces, such as taking over his or her job for a day. A recent approach to developing empathy in this way is referred to as **shadowing.** The process involves closely observing the work activities of a coworker by following him or her around for a prescribed period of time. Suppose you as a marketing specialist were in conflict with a customer service representative about handling customer complaints. To understand the legitimacy of your complaints, you might sit next to that person at the call desk for a day.

AN APPLIED PSYCHOLOGY CONCEPT IN ACTION

Shadowing to Show What the Other Side Is Like

"Fifteen years ago, I remember being completely annoyed about some infighting between office and warehouse staff," said Cathy Filgas, cofounder of Anthro Corp., Technology Furniture of Tualatin, Oregon. The company is a manufacturer and e-tailer of computer furniture. "I thought if they could see how the other half lives." Thus started the company's "shadow program."

Every month, four of Anthro's employees shadow four others in different departments, walking in a coworker's shoes for a full day. "The result is that our employees communicate better," she said. "There is mutual respect because they've been there, done that. The shadow and the shadowee get a chance to know each other as people, rather than just as fellow employees."

Anthro recommends two steps for developing a shadow program:

- Be committed. Sure you lose some production time during shadowing visits, but keep with the program. You gain some far-reaching benefits: better information-sharing, and employees who have a "big picture" view.
- Start small. Even companies with a handful of employees can benefit from shadowing. Maybe more than larger firms, since communication is so important.

Source: "Shadowing Can Show What Other Side Is Like," Rochester, New York, *Democrat and Chronicle,* September 11, 2000, p. 14D.

A major theme running through the various approaches to conflict resolution, including negotiating and bargaining, is that cooperating with the other side is usually preferable to competing. A study with 61 self-managing teams with 489 employees supports this idea of the superiority of cooperation over competition in successful conflict resolution. The style of conflict resolution was measured through questionnaires. For example, a question geared toward cooperative behavior was "We seek a solution that will be good for the whole team." Conflict efficacy was measured by a questionnaire indicating that the extent to which team members believed that they could successfully measure different conflict situations. Group effectiveness was measured by the ratings of supervisor and team leaders on productivity, quality, and cost savings—central reasons why self-directed teams are formed.

The study found that the cooperative approach to conflict was positively related to conflict efficacy. In contrast, the competitive approach to conflict was negatively related to conflict efficacy. Equally important from the perspective of applied psychology, conflict efficacy was strongly associated with supervisory and team leader ratings of team effectiveness.[23]

MANAGING ANGER

Limited ability to manage anger damages the careers and personal lives of many people. Anger creates stress, as described at the outset of this chapter. Workplace violence, such as a former employee shooting a manager who fired the employee, is an extreme in expressing anger. What angry behavior have you observed on the job?

The ability to manage your anger, and the anger of others, is an important interpersonal skill now considered to be part of emotional intelligence. A person who cannot manage anger well cannot take good advantage of his or her intellectual intelligence. As an extreme example, a genius who swears at the manager regularly will probably lose his or her job despite being so talented. Our concern here is with several tactics for managing your own anger and that of others effectively.

Managing Your Own Anger

A starting point in dealing with your anger is to recognize that at its best, *anger can be an energizing force.* Instead of letting it be destructive, channel your anger into exceptional performance. If you are angry because you did not get the raise you thought you deserved, get even by performing so well that there will be no question you deserve a raise next time. Develop the habit of expressing your anger before it reaches a high intensity. Tell your coworker that you do not appreciate his or her using a cell phone while you are having dinner together the first time the act of rudeness occurs. If you wait too long, you may wind up grabbing the cell phone and slamming it to the floor.

As you are about to express anger, *slow down.* (The old technique of counting to 10 is still effective.) Slowing down gives you the opportunity to express your anger in a way that does not damage your relationship with the other person. Following your first impulse, you might say to the other person, "You're a stupid fool." If you slow down, this might translate into "You need training on this task."

Closely related to slowing down is a technique taught in anger-management programs: think about the consequences of what you do when you are worked up.[24] Say to yourself as soon as you feel angry, "Oops, I'm in the anger mode now. I had better calm down before I say something or do something that I will regret later." To gauge how effectively you are expressing your anger, ask for feedback. Ask a friend, coworker, or manager, "Am I coming on too strong when I express my negative opinion?"[25]

Managing Anger in Other People

A variation of confrontation and problem solving has developed specifically to resolve conflict with angry people: confront, contain, and connect. *Confront* in this context means that you jump right in and get agitated workers talking to prevent future blowups. The confrontation, however, is not aimed at arguing with the angry person. If the other person yells, you talk more softly. *Contain* refers to moving an angry worker out of sight and out of earshot. At the same time you remain impartial. The supervisor is advised not to choose sides or appear to be a friend.

You *connect* by asking open-ended questions such as "What would you like us to do about your concern?" to get at the real reasons behind an outburst. Using this approach, one worker revealed he was upset because a female coworker got to leave early to pick up her daughter at daycare. The man also needed to leave early one day a week for personal reasons but felt awkward making the request. So instead of being assertive (explicit and direct) about his demands, he flared up.

An important feature of the confront, contain, and connect technique is that it provides angry workers a place where they can vent their frustrations, and report the outbursts of others. Mediator Nina Meierding says that "Workers need a safe outlet to talk through anger and not feel they will be minimized or put their job in jeopardy."[26]

Skill-Building Exercise 8–2 will give you an opportunity to develop your anger-management skills. The exercise will require some work outside of class.

SKILL-BUILDING EXERCISE 8–2

Learning to Manage Anger

The next few times you are really angry with somebody or something, use one or more of the good mental health statements described below. Each statement is designed to remind you that you are in charge, not your anger. To begin, visualize something that has made you angry recently. Practice making the statements below in relation to that angry episode.

- I'm in charge here, not my emotional outbursts.
- I'll breathe deeply a few times and then deal with this.
- I feel _____ when you _____.
- I can handle this.
- I'm going to take time out to cool down before I deal with this.
- Yes, I'm angry and I'll just watch what I say or do.

Now describe the effect that making these statements had on your anger.

Source: Based on Lynne Namka, "A Primer on Anger: Getting a Handle on Your Mads," http://members. aol.com/AngriesOut/grown2.htm, p. 4 (April 21, 1998).

Choosing a Tactic for Resolving a Conflict or Managing Anger

How does a person know which of the tactics or strategies presented in this chapter will work best for a given problem? The best answer is to consider both your personality and the situation. With respect to your personality, or personal style, pick a tactic for resolving conflict that you would feel comfortable using. One person might say, "I would like the tactic of using deadlines because I like to control situations." Another person might say, "I prefer confrontation because I'm an open and up-front type of person." Still another person might say, "I'll avoid disarming the opposition for now. I don't have enough finesse yet to carry out this technique."

In fitting the strategy to the situation, it is important to assess the gravity of the topic for negotiation or the conflict between people. A woman might say to herself, "My boss has committed such a blatant act of sexual harassment that I had best take this up with a higher authority immediately." Sizing up your opponent can also help you choose the best strategy. If she or he appears reasonably flexible, you might try to compromise. Or if your adversary is especially upset, give that person a chance to simmer down before trying to solve the problem.

SUMMARY OF KEY POINTS

- A conflict is the simultaneous arousal of two or more incompatible motives or demands and is usually accompanied by frustration and anger. Frustration is the blocking of need or motive satisfaction by some obstacle.
- Job conflict is almost inevitable because so many different factors breed conflict. Six important reasons for, or sources of, job conflict are (1) competition for limited resources, (2) differences in goals and objectives, (3) the generation gap and personality clashes, (4) gender differences, (5) competing work and family demands, and (6) sexual harassment.

- Sexual harassment usually involves an attempt by one person to exercise power over another. The two legally recognized types of harassment are (1) quid pro quo and (2) the creation of a hostile environment. Most complaints of sexual harassment fall into the latter category. About 50 percent of working women have experienced at least one incident of sexual harassment. Research shows that harassment exerts a significant impact on women's psychological well-being, job attitudes, and work behaviors.
- A starting point in dealing with harassment is to understand the types of behaviors that are considered harassment. The easiest way to deal with sexual harassment is to speak up before it becomes serious. A caution about combating sexual harassment is that some people may be accused of sexual harassment for minor mistakes in judgment.
- Functional conflict occurs when the interests of the organization are served as a result of a dispute or disagreement. Dysfunctional conflict occurs when a dispute or disagreement harms the organization. Workplace violence is a major negative consequence of conflict. Team performance is enhanced by stimulating C-type conflict, which deals with substantive, work-related issues. A-type conflict, which deals with personal issues and emotions, generally lowers team performance.
- Five major styles of conflict management have been identified: competitive, accommodative, sharing, collaborative, and avoidant. Each style is based on a combination of satisfying one's own concerns (assertiveness) and satisfying the concerns of others (cooperativeness).
- The techniques for resolving conflicts with others described in this chapter are:
    1. Confrontation and problem solving (deal with the real issue).
    2. Negotiation and bargaining (use compromise; allow room for negotiation but be plausible; focus on interests, not positions; make small concessions gradually; use deadlines; ask the other side "What do you want me to do?"; and make a last and final offer).
    3. Disarming the opposition (agree to the criticism made of you, and ask for assistance).
    4. Exchanging images with your antagonist (each side states its and the other side's point of view).
    5. Cognitive restructuring (you reframe the conflict with a positive spin).
    6. Making an upward appeal (take your problem to a higher authority if gentle approaches do not work).
    7. Developing empathy through shadowing.
- Limited ability to manage anger damages the careers and personal lives of many people. The ability to manage anger is part of emotional intelligence. In managing your own anger, remember that anger can be an energizing force. Express your anger before it reaches a high intensity. As you are about to express your anger, slow down. Ask for feedback on how you deal with anger. In dealing with the anger of others, use confront, contain (move the angry worker out of sight), and connect (ask open-ended questions to get at the real reason behind the outburst).
- In choosing a tactic for resolving conflict, consider both your personality or style and the nature of the situation facing you. The situation includes such factors as the gravity of the conflict and the type of person you are facing.

GUIDELINES FOR PERSONAL EFFECTIVENESS

1. If your job involves dealing with people, it is almost inevitable that you will experience person-to-person or group-to-group conflict from time to time. Rather than suppress or ignore conflict, it is to your advantage to learn effective techniques to cope or deal with conflict.
2. Underlying most techniques of resolving conflict is being able to face up to (confront) the real issues. Thus, to resolve conflict, you must face your opponent and candidly discuss the problem between the two of you.
3. A general plan for using techniques of conflict resolution is to begin with a tactful, low-key approach and see if that works. If not, try an approach with more power and force. To illustrate, it might be worth your while to begin with a tactful confrontation. If that does not work, appeal to a more powerful third party. As with any strategy for dealing with people, you have to use techniques that you feel fit both your personality and the circumstances.

DISCUSSION QUESTIONS AND ACTIVITIES

1. Some conflicts between countries have lasted for over 50 years despite periodic peace talks. Why is it so difficult to resolve conflicts between countries?
2. A new trend in programs for understanding cultural diversity is to train people in getting along better with people from different generations. What type of conflicts might this training help prevent or resolve?
3. Give an example from your own life of how competition for limited resources can breed conflict.
4. Give an example from your own life in which conflict had beneficial effects.
5. Search the newspapers or the Internet for a recent example of worker violence. Identify the conflict that the worker involved may have been experiencing before the act of violence.
6. A policy in some companies is that male managers who confer with a female employee in their offices must leave the door open to minimize the chances of being charged with sexual harassment. Does this policy reflect good judgment, or are the companies being overly cautious?
7. Give an example of a conflict in which a compromise solution would probably be ineffective.
8. How might a person use cognitive restructuring to help deal with the conflict of having received a below-average raise after expecting an above-average one?
9. Assume that a man addresses women coworkers and customers by such terms as "sweetheart," "honey," "cutie," and "babe." In response to complaints, the man's manager accuses him of sexual harassment. Explain how the man can use the disarm the opposition technique to deal with the complaint and profit from the experience.
10. Ask a successful person how much conflict he or she experiences in balancing the demands of work and personal life. Be prepared to report your findings in class.

AN APPLIED PSYCHOLOGY CASE PROBLEM

A Concern about Violence

Vernon Bigsby is the CEO and owner of a large soft-drink bottling company in Fort Wayne, Indiana. The company periodically invests money in training to help the management and supervisory staff remain abreast of important new trends in technology and managing human resources. Bigsby recently became concerned about workplace violence. Although the company had not yet experienced an outbreak of violence, Bigsby was intent on preventing violence in the future. To accomplish this goal, Bigsby hired a human resources consultant, Sara Toomey, to conduct a seminar on preventing workplace violence.

The seminar was given twice, with one-half the managers and supervisors attending each session. Chad Ditmar, a night-shift supervisor, made the first wisecrack during the seminar. He said, "What are we here for? To prevent workers from squirting 'pop' at each other?" Toomey responded, "My job would be easy if I were here only to prevent horseplay. Unfortunately the reality is that there are thousands of lethal weapons going past your workers every day. Just think how much damage one angry worker could do to an innocent victim with one slash of a broken bottle." The laughter in the room quickly subsided.

About one hour into the seminar, Sara Toomey projected an overhead transparency outlining characteristics of a worker with potential for violence. She said, "Recognize that not every person who has many of these characteristics will become violent. However, they do constitute early warning signals. I would watch out for any worker with a large number of these traits and behaviors." (See Exhibit 1 for the overhead in question.)

Ditmar supervises 45 workers directly involved in the bottling of three company brands of soft drinks. The workers in his department range in age from 18 to 57. The job can usually be learned within three days, so the workers are classified as semi-skilled. After his initial wisecrack, Ditmar took the seminar quite seriously. He made extensive notes on what the consultant said, and took back to his office a printed copy of the overhead transparency.

Exhibit 1. Profile of the Violent Employee

- Socially isolated (a loner) white male, between the ages of 30 and 40.
- Fascination with the military and weapons.
- Interest in recently published violent events.
- Temper control problem with history of threats.
- Alcohol and/or drug abuser.
- Increased mood swings.
- Makes unwanted sexual advances toward other employees.
- Accepts criticism poorly and holds a grudge against the criticizer.
- Shows paranoid thinking and believes that management is out to get him (or her).
- Blames others for his or her problems.
- Makes violent statements such as spoken threats about beating up other employees.
- Threatens damage or destruction of company property.
- Decreased productivity or inconsistent work performance.

The morning following the seminar, Chad sent an e-mail to Gary Bia, the vice president of operations. Chad said, "I must see you today. I'm worried about a potentially explosive personnel problem." Bia made arrangements to see Ditmar at 5:45 in the afternoon, before Ditmar's shift began.

"What's up, Chad?" asked Bia.

"Here's what's up," said Ditmar. "After attending the seminar on violence, I think I've found our suspect. As you know, you do get some strange types working the night shift. Some of them don't have a normal life. I've got this one guy, Freddie Watkins. He's a loner. He wears his hair weird, with pink-colored spikes. He's got a tattoo and a huge gun collection that he brags about. I doubt the guy has any friends. He talks a lot about how he plays violent video games. Freddie told about how he once choked to death a dog that bit him.

continued on next page

AN APPLIED PSYCHOLOGY CASE PROBLEM (cont'd)

What really worries me is that Freddie once said he would punch out the next person who made a smart ______ comment about his hair.

Do you agree or not that we might have a candidate for workplace violence right here in my department? I'm talking to you first, Gary, but maybe I should be speaking to the antiviolence consultant or to our security officer. What should we do next?"

Bia said, "I'm happy that you are bringing this potential problem to my attention, but I need some more facts. First of all, have you had any discipline problems yet with Freddie?"

Chad responded, "Not yet Gary, but we're talking about a potential killer right here on my shift. I think we have to do something."

Bia said, "Chad, I'm taking your concerns seriously, but I don't want to jump too fast. Let me think over your problem for at least a day."

1. What actions, if any, should Gary Bia take?
2. What type of conflict is Chad Ditmar facing?
3. What career advice can you offer Freddie Watkins?

Source: Several items on the profile of the violent employee are from Gillian Flynn, "Employers Can't Look Away from Workplace Violence," *Workforce,* July 2000, p. 69.

REFERENCES

1. Katharine Mieszkowski, "Generation *# #@**# #@!!" *Fast Company,* October 1999, pp. 106–108.
2. Quoted in Sybil Evans, "Conflict Can Be Positive," *HR Magazine,* May 1992, p. 50.
3. Anne Fisher, "Readers Sound Off: Are Generation Xers Arrogant or Just Misunderstood?" *Fortune,* February 17, 1997, p. 139.
4. Linda Elizabeth Duxbury and Christopher Alan Higgins, "Gender Differences in Work–Family Conflict," *Journal of Applied Psychology,* February 1991, p. 64.
5. Michael R. Frone, "Work–Family Conflict and Employee Psychiatric Disorders: The National Comorbidity Survey," *Journal of Applied Psychology,* December 2000, pp. 888–895.
6. William O'Donohue (ed.), *Sexual Harassment: Theory, Research, and Treatment* (Boston: Allyn & Bacon, 1997); Anne M. O'Leary-Kelly, Ramona L. Paetzold, and Ricky W. Griffin, "Sexual Harassment as Aggressive Behavior: An Actor-Based Perspective," *Academy of Management Review,* April 2000, pp. 372–388.
7. O'Donohue, *Sexual Harassment.*
8. Kimberly T. Schneider, Suzanne Swan, and Louise F. Fitzgerald, "Job-Related and Psychological Effects of Sexual Harassment in the Workplace: Empirical Evidence from Two Organizations," *Journal of Applied Psychology,* June 1997, p. 406.
9. Maria Rotundo, Dung-Hanh Nyguyen, and Paul R. Sackett, "A Meta-Analytic Review of Gender Differences in Perceptions of Sexual Harassment," *Journal of Applied Psychology,* October 2001, p. 916.
10. Schneider, Swan, and Fitzgerald, "Job-Related and Psychological Effects," pp. 412–413.
11. Liberty J. Munson, Charles Hulin, and Fritz Drasgow, "Longitudinal Analysis of Dispositional Influences and Sexual Harassment: Effects on Job and Psychological Outcomes," *Personnel Psychology,* Spring 2000, pp. 21–46.
12. Kathleen Neville, *Corporate Attractions: An Inside Account of Sexual Harassment with the New Sexual Roles for Men and Women on the Job* (Reston, VA: Acropolis Books, 1992).

AN APPLIED PSYCHOLOGY PROBLEM

Caught In a Squeeze

Heather Lee is a product development specialist at a telecommunications company. For the last seven months she has worked as a member of a product development team composed of people from five different departments within the company. Heather previously worked full-time in the marketing department. Her primary responsibilities were to research the market potential of an idea for a new product. The product development team is now working on a product that will integrate a company's printers and copiers.

Heather's previous position in the marketing department was a satisfactory fit for her lifestyle. Heather thought that she was able to take care of her family responsibilities and her job without sacrificing one for the other. As Heather explains, "I worked about 45 predictable hours in my other job. My hours were essentially 8:30 A.M. to 4:30 P.M. with a little work at night and on Saturdays. But I could do the work at night and on Saturdays at home.

"Brad, my husband, and I had a smooth-working arrangement for sharing the responsibility for getting our son Christopher off to school, and picking him up from the after school childcare center. Brad is a devoted accountant, so he understands the importance of giving high priority to a career yet still being a good family person."

In her new position as a member of the product development team, Heather is encountering some unanticipated demands. Three weeks ago, at 3 P.M. on a Tuesday, Tyler Watson, Heather's team leader, announced an emergency meeting to discuss a budget problem with the new product. The meeting would start at 4, and probably end at about 6:30. "Don't worry folks," said the team leader, "if it looks like we are going past 6:30 we will order in some Chinese food."

With a look of panic on her face, Heather responded to Tyler, "I can't make the meeting. Christopher will be expecting me at about 5 at the childcare center. My husband is out of town, and the center closes at 6 sharp. So count me out of today's meeting."

Tyler said, "I said that this is an emergency meeting, and that we need input from all the members. You need to organize your personal life better to be a contributing member to this team. But do what you have to do, at least this once."

Heather chose to leave the office at 4:30 so she could pick up Christopher. The next day, Tyler did not comment on her absence. However, he gave her a copy of the minutes and asked for her input. The budget problem surfaced again one week later. Top-level management asked the group to reduce the cost of the new product and its initial marketing costs by 15 percent.

Tyler said to the team on a Friday morning, "We have until Monday morning to arrive at a reduced cost structure on our product development. I am dividing up the project into segments. If we meet as a team Saturday morning at 8, we should get the job done by 6 at night. Get a good night's rest, so we can start fresh tomorrow morning. Breakfast and lunch will be on the company."

Heather could feel stress overwhelming her body, as she thought to herself. "Christopher is playing in the finals of his little league soccer match tomorrow morning at 10. Brad has made dinner reservations for 6, so we can make it to *Phantom of the Opera* at 8 P.M. Should I tell Tyler he is being unreasonable? Should I quit? Should I tell Christopher and Brad that our special occasions together are less important than a Saturday business meeting?"

1. What type of conflict is Heather facing?
2. What should Heather do to resolve her conflicts with respect to family and work responsibilities?
3. What should the company do to help deal with the type of conflict Heather is facing? Or, should the company not consider Heather's dilemma to be their problem?

SKILL-BUILDING EXERCISE 8–3

Conflict Resolution

Imagine that Heather, in the case just presented, decides that her job is taking too big a toll on her personal life. However, she still values her job and does not want to quit. She decides to discuss her problem with her team leader Tyler. From Tyler's point of view, a professional person must stand ready to meet unusual job demands, and cannot expect an entirely predictable work schedule. One person plays the role of Heather, another the role of Tyler, as they attempt to resolve this incident of work–family conflict.

13. Suzy Wetlaufer, "Common Sense and Conflict," *Harvard Business Review,* January–February 2000, p. 118.
14. Gillian Flynn, "Employers Can't Look Away from Workplace Violence," *Workforce,* July 2000, p. 68.
15. Flynn, "Employers Can't Look Away," p. 69.
16. Allen S. Amson, Wayne A. Hockwarter, Kenneth R. Thompson, and Allison W. Harrison, "Conflict: An Important Dimension in Successful Management Teams," *Organizational Dynamics,* Autumn 1995, pp. 20–33.
17. Karen A. Jehn and Elizabeth A. Mannix, "The Dynamic Nature of Conflict: A Longitudinal Study of Intragroup Conflict and Group Performance," *Academy of Management Journal,* April 2001, pp. 238–251.
18. Kenneth W. Thomas, "Conflict and Conflict Management," in Marvin D. Dunnette (ed.), *Handbook of Industrial and Organizational Psychology* (Chicago: Rand-McNally College Publishing, 1976), pp. 900–902.
19. Joann Muller, "Can This Man Save Chrysler?" *Business Week,* September 17, 2001, p. 92.
20. D. H. Stamatis, "Conflict: You've Got to Accentuate the Positive," *Personnel,* December 1987, pp. 48–49.
21. "Is Your Boss Showing Stress? Can You Profit from It?" *Executive Strategies,* February 1995, p. 8.
22. Kenneth Kaye, *Workplace Wars and How to End Them: Turning Personal Conflicts into Productive Teamwork* (New York: AMACOM, 1994).
23. Steve Alper, Dean Tjosvold, and Kenneth S. Law, "Conflict Management, Efficacy, and Performance in Organizational Teams," *Personnel Psychology,* Autumn 2000, pp. 625–642.
24. John Cloud, "Classroom for Hotheads," *Time,* April 10, 2000, p. 54.
25. Fred Pryor, "Is Anger Really Healthy?" *The Pryor Management Newsletter,* February 1996, p. 3.
26. Cited in Lisa Lee Freeman (ed.), *Working Woman,* April 2000, p. 71.

SUGGESTED READING

Braverman, Mark. *Preventing Workplace Violence: A Guide for Employers and Practitioners.* Thousand Oaks, CA: Sage, 1999.

Cloke, Kenneth H., and Goldsmith, Joan. *Resolving Personal and Organizational Conflict.* San Francisco: Jossey-Bass, 2000.

Deutsch, Morton, and Coleman, Peter T. *Handbook of Conflict Resolution: Theory and Practice.* San Francisco: Jossey-Bass, 1999.

Fisher, Roger, Kopelman, Elizabeth, and Schneider, Andrea Kupfer. *Beyond Machiavelli: Tools for Coping with Conflict.* Cambridge, MA: Harvard University Press, 2000.

Janove, Jathan W. "Sexual Harassment and the Three Big Surprises." *HR Magazine,* November 2001, pp. 123–130.

Kruger, Pamela. "Jobs for Life." *Fast Company,* May 2000, pp. 236–252.

Levine, Stuart. *Getting to Resolution: Turning Conflict Into Cooperation.* San Francisco: Berrett-Koehler, 2000.

Mayer, Bernard S. *The Dynamics of Conflict Resolution: A Practitioner's Guide.* San Francisco: Jossey-Bass, 2000.

Poe, Andrea C. "The Daddy Track." *HR Magazine,* July 1999, pp. 82–89.

Winters, Jeffrey. "The Daddy Track: Men Who Take Family Leave May Get Frowned Upon at the Office." *Psychology Today,* October 2001, p. 18.

WEB CORNER

www.fastcompany.com/online/01/disagree.html (Learning to disagree without being disagreeable.)

www.mediate.com (Resolving workplace conflict.)

www.parenting-qa.com/cgi-bin/detailworkfamily/ (Resources for integrating work and family.)

CHAPTER 9

BUILDING WORKPLACE RELATIONSHIPS

Learning Objectives After reading and studying this chapter and doing the exercises, you should be able to

1. Choose several effective approaches for building good relationships with superiors.
2. Choose several effective approaches for building good relationships with coworkers.
3. Choose several effective approaches you might use in building good relationships with customers.
4. Develop an appreciation of cultural diversity in the workplace.

Anyone who wants to achieve career success must have good working relationships with superiors, coworkers, and lower-ranking employees. A survey revealed that 90 percent of firings stem from poor attitude, inappropriate behaviors, and difficulties with interpersonal relationships rather than ineffective technical skills.[1] To receive a sizeable salary increase, be promoted, or receive a favorable transfer, you almost always need the endorsement of your immediate manager. By having good relationships with your coworkers, you will usually receive the kind of cooperation you need to get your job done. Also, with increasing frequency, the opinion of your peers is asked when you are being considered for promotion.

People of lower rank than yourself have about the same impact on your career and your ability to get your job done as peers. We will therefore not have a separate discussion of downward relationships. A separate discussion on building customer relationships is warranted because of the widespread attention now being paid to customer satisfaction.

Keep in mind that the behaviors that contribute to a good working relationship with one group of workers usually work at other levels. For example, being courteous will hold you in good stead with high-level managers, your immediate manager, your coworkers, those of lower rank, and customers.

BUILDING GOOD RELATIONSHIPS WITH SUPERIORS

In attempting to build relationships with superiors, as with coworkers and customers, your strategy should be to build satisfying partnerships. The term *partnership* connotes a cooperative relationship in which you and the other person are pursuing compatible goals, such as getting work accomplished or earning a profit.

Good performance refers not only to being able to do your job but also to being well motivated and displaying initiative—looking for problems to work on and getting started without being told to do so. The 11 strategies and techniques described next must rest on a bedrock of solid job performance. Otherwise, they may backfire by bringing attention to the fact that the individual is more show than substance. Several of the ideas presented will help you to achieve good job performance and assist you in impressing your manager or team leader through merit.

Perceive Things from Your Manager's Perspective. An excellent starting point in building a relationship with your manager is to view the work situation from his or her perspective. Part of understanding the work situation from your manager's perspective is to understand that person's **style,** or typical way of doing things. For example, does your manager like to throw out ideas on a trial basis before reaching a decision? If this is true, the manager might appear to be asking your opinion on an issue, but in reality he or she is mostly thinking out loud. You should not be discouraged if your reaction to the trial idea is not incorporated into the final decision.

Often a manager and a group member will have a different perspective because the manager has information the group member lacks. A manager might know that a major cost-cutting effort is forthcoming, but the information is still confidential. The group member asks to visit a trade show at company expense, and the manager has to decline the request without much explanation. Even without a careful explanation, the group member might say to himself or herself, "Too bad about the trip, but my manager might be turning me down for a good reason that cannot be revealed now."

Clarify Expectations. Some people perform poorly on the job simply because they have an incomplete understanding of what their supervisor expects of them. At times, the individual has to take the initiative to find out what is expected because the boss neglects to do so. One highly regarded manager explains how he clarifies expectations:

> Whenever I get a new boss, I sit down with that person and ask that his or her expectations be made explicit. We try to list not my job activities but the main purposes of my job. To do that, we continue each statement of activity with "In order to . . . ," and try to complete the sentence. By recording my job purposes, we get a clear picture of what I should be accomplishing; and that's what counts—results.[2]

Using this tactic, one office assistant found out that she was supposed to take care of her manager's work first. Once her manager's work was done, she would be free to do work for other professionals in the department. Before the assistant in question asked for clarification, she was trying to give everyone's work equal attention. (Your reaction might be, "The manager should have told her that at the outset." Unfortunately, not all managers are aware of the importance of clarifying work expectations.)

Establish a Relationship of Trust. A fundamental way of impressing superiors is to behave in a trustworthy manner. Trust is established over the long range through such behaviors as meeting deadlines, following through on promises, having good attendance and punctuality, and not passing along confidential information to the wrong people. Five conditions are necessary for trust to develop:[3]

1. *Accessibility.* An accessible group member is a person who takes in ideas freely and gives them out freely. A subordinate who does not respect the boss's ideas will not be trusted and will not receive help in developing his or her own ideas.
2. *Availability.* The trusted group member is attentive and available physically, mentally, and emotionally when the manager or team leader is under pressure and needs support.
3. *Predictability.* This refers to being a predictably good performer and to being dependable about getting things done on time. A group member who does not get things done on time loses the trust of his or her supervisor quickly.
4. *Personal loyalty.* An important way of showing loyalty is to support your manager's ideas. For example, your manager may want to purchase an industrial robot. You could display loyalty by investigating on your own the advantages of robots in factories and then talking about those advantages to others. Loyalty can also mean not misusing inside information given to you by the boss. In short, loyalty breeds trust.
5. *Honesty about problems.* Be frank about bringing problems to your manager's attention. (As described later, also bring forth good news.) However, if your manager is already burdened with an overload of problems, soften the impact of the problem without lying. As a sales representative told the sales manager, "One of our biggest accounts has left us, but the news isn't all bad. Our contact said that if the other firm's service proves to be worse than ours, we'll get the account back."

Respect Your Manager's Authority. A frequent complaint about modern society is that respect for authority is decreasing. You can capitalize on this problem to help to develop a good relationship with your boss. By showing appropriate respect for your manager's authority, you can enhance your relationship with that person. Here are two statements that might appeal to a boss's sense of authority without making you appear unduly status conscious:

- "Yes, that sounds like a good idea."
- "As the leader of this team, what do you think we should do about this?"

Bring Forth Solutions as Well as Problems. An advanced tactic for developing a good working relationship with your manager or team leader is to bring solutions to his or her attention, not just problems. Too often group members ask to see their bosses only when they have problems requiring help. A boss under pressure may thus anticipate additional pressure when a group member asks for an appointment. The group member who comes forth with a solved problem is thus regarded as a welcome relief. In short, you ease your manager's suffering by walking into his or her office and saying "Here's what I did about that mess that was plaguing us yesterday. Everything is under control now."

EXPRESS CONSTRUCTIVE DISAGREEMENT. At one time the office politician thought an effective way of pleasing the boss was to be a "yes person." Whatever the supervisor thought was right, the yes person agreed with. A more intelligent tactic in the modern business world is to be ready to disagree in a constructive manner when you sincerely believe the boss is wrong. In the long run you will probably earn more respect than if you agree with the boss just to please that person. Constructive disagreement is based on a careful analysis of the situation and is also tactful.

The right way to disagree means not putting your manager in a corner or embarrassing your manager by confronting him or her loudly or in public.[4] If you disagree with your boss, use carefully worded, inoffensive statements. In this way you minimize the chances of a confrontation or hostile reaction. Walter St. John suggests statements of this type:

- "I'm able to agree with you on most things, but on this matter I wonder if you would be willing to reconsider for these reasons."
- "I like your basic idea and wonder if I could make a suggestion that I think would make it work even better."

The reason constructive disagreement helps you build a good relationship with most managers is that the boss comes to respect your job knowledge and your integrity. However, if you are working with a very insecure boss, he or she may be taken aback by disagreement. In that case, you have to be extra tactful in expressing disagreement.

GIVE YOUR MANAGER POSITIVE REINFORCEMENT AND RECOGNITION. An effective manager is supposed to praise group members for good performance and behavior. Reversing the process can help build a sound relationship with your manager, particularly because your manager may not be receiving positive reinforcement from his or her boss. Recognition and appreciation can take such forms as saying thanks when the boss grants you a special favor, or showing your boss what you have been able to achieve because of the new equipment he or she authorized.

TALK BIG, SHUN TRIVIA. Small talk can keep you placed in a small job. If you have a predilection for talking about the weather, television sitcoms, or the food in the company cafeteria, save these comments for the right occasion. The right occasion is when you are spending time with people who enjoy small talk. The wrong occasion is when you are trying to impress higher-ups (including your manager). When you have a chance to talk to an influential person, some trivia may be necessary for an initial warm-up. But quickly shift the topic to "big" talk.

Here is an example of the difference between making small talk and making big talk over the same issue when meeting a high-ranking official from your organization. The person talking is the manager of a branch motor vehicle department. The visitor is the state commissioner of motor vehicles.

MANAGER (USING SMALL TALK): Look at that rain outside. It's been like this for three days. This sure is the rainiest place I've ever lived. I guess it's fine if you're a farmer or a plant.

COMMISSIONER: Did you say something?

MANAGER (USING BIG TALK): This rain creates an interesting problem for the Motor Vehicle Department at the branch level. Common sense would suggest that our workload would decrease when it rains. My calculations and those of my staff indicate that we are extra busy on rainy days. I think a good number of people wait for a rainy day to take care of their routine business with us. I wonder if this is a national trend?

COMMISSIONER: You have raised an important issue about our workload. I think the problem warrants further study.

USE DISCRETION IN SOCIALIZING WITH YOUR MANAGER. A constant dilemma facing employees is how much and what type of socializing with the manager is appropriate. Advocates of socializing contend that off-the-job friendships with the boss lead to more natural work relationships. Opponents of socializing with the manager say that it leads to **role confusion**—being uncertain about what role you are carrying out. For example, how can your manager make an objective decision about your salary increase on Monday morning when he or she had dinner with you on Sunday? To avoid charges of favoritism, your manager might recommend you for a below-average increase.

One guideline to consider is to have cordial social relationships with the boss of the kind shared by most employees. "Cordial" socializing includes activities such as company-sponsored parties, group invitations to the boss's home, and business lunches. Individual social activities such as camping with the boss, double-dating, and so forth, are more likely to lead to role confusion.

Socializing with the boss should be kept at a professional level if your boss might possibly have a romantic inclination toward you. The more relaxed the setting, the greater the opportunity for misinterpretation of language and behavior. Workers who suspect that their boss's intentions may be romantic or sexual are advised to mention their spouses or significant others, if the conversation takes such a turn.[5]

In summary, there are no absolute principles about the influence of socializing with the boss on your relationship with that person. A tentative guideline is that you must carefully evaluate the pros and cons of anything more than ceremonial socializing (office parties, company picnics, and so forth) with the boss. It leads to a conflict of roles that can work to your disadvantage. However, many marriages stem from a relationship between the manager and a group member.

CAREFULLY SELL YOUR IDEAS TO YOUR MANAGER. An important part of maintaining an effective relationship with the manager is to sell your ideas to him or her without becoming an annoyance. It is important not to waste the manager's time with every idea you have. Wait until you have an idea of considerable merit, yet also be ready to list the potential disadvantages of your plan. Write several electronic or print messages on the same proposal, and mention that you will be in touch in the future. State the benefits of your proposal in the front of your message, and be specific. An example: "If we ship all our products in boxes with a trim size one inch smaller, we can save $150,000 in shipping costs next year." Involve your manager by asking him or her to contribute input to the idea. Check the progress on the acceptance of your idea, tactfully and constructively.[6]

Engage in Favorable Interactions with Your Manager. The many techniques just described support the goal of engaging in favorable interactions with your manager. A series of studies were conducted of interactions between employees in banks and nonacademic jobs in universities and their supervisors. It was shown that purposely trying to create a positive impression on the supervisor led to better performance ratings. Employees who tried to please their supervisors were perceived by the supervisors as being more like them. Employees who were demographically similar to the supervisors also received higher ratings. (Examples of demographic similarity would include race, age, and sex.) Whether through impression management or demographic likeness, being perceived as similar to the supervisor improved performance ratings. Self-Assessment Exercise 9–1 lists the behaviors used by employees in the studies to create positive interactions with their supervisors.

Many readers may be concerned that some of the tactics for impressing the manager might be interpreted as going overboard to win favor. One way to circumvent this problem is to engage only in relationship-building tactics that you perceive to be honest and sincere. For example, give the manager recognition only when you think praise is warranted. Career advisor Marilyn Moats Kennedy offers another suggestion for applying these tactics effectively. She notes that the balancing act between enthusiasm and obsequiousness is one we all have to learn and practice throughout our careers.[7]

SELF-ASSESSMENT EXERCISE 9–1

The Supervisor Interaction Checklist

Use the following behaviors as a checklist for achieving favorable interactions with your present manager or a future one. The more of these actions you are engaged in, the higher the probability that you are building a favorable relationship with your manager.

____ 1. Agree with your supervisor's major opinions outwardly even when you disagree inwardly.

____ 2. Take an immediate interest in your supervisor's personal life.

____ 3. Praise your supervisor on his or her accomplishments.

____ 4. Do personal favors for your supervisor.

____ 5. Do something as a personal favor for your supervisor even though you are not required to do it.

____ 6. Volunteer to help your supervisor on a task.

____ 7. Compliment your supervisor on his or her dress or appearance.

____ 8. Present yourself to your supervisor as being a friendly person.

____ 9. Agree with your supervisor's major ideas.

____10. Present yourself to your supervisor as being a polite person.

Source: Adapted from Sandy J. Wayne and Gerald R. Ferris, "Influence Tactics, Affect, and Exchange Quality in Supervisor–Subordinate Interactions: A Laboratory Experiment and Field Study," *Journal of Applied Psychology,* October 1990, p. 494. Copyright © 1990 by the American Psychological Association. Adapted with permission.

BUILDING GOOD RELATIONSHIPS WITH COWORKERS

Good relationships with coworkers are important for several reasons. No matter what your job level, there comes a time when you need the cooperation of people over whom you have no formal authority. By developing these relationships and practicing good human relations, you can get them working in concert with you. Ignore these relationships, and you may fail to get many of your projects completed. Mutual cooperation must also exist for a work group to be productive.

A study with 174 workers in an electric utility points to another important reason for building good coworker relationships. It was found that friendship opportunities are associated with increases in job satisfaction and job involvement. Workers who had developed friendships on the job also perceived themselves as more committed to the organization and therefore less likely to quit. The researchers summarized their results with this model: friendship opportunities → job involvement → job satisfaction → organizational commitment → lowered intention to turnover.[8]

In this section of the chapter, we describe methods designed to help you gain favor or avoid disfavor with peers. Although several follow common sense, many people violate them. Many people think they are such experts at human relations that they neglect to think systematically about their behavior in relation to others. Before studying the strategies and tactics described in this section, do Self-Assessment Exercise 9–2.

ADHERE TO GROUP NORMS. The basic principle to follow in getting along with coworkers is to pay heed to **group norms.** These refer to the unwritten set of expectations or standards of conduct that tell group members what they ought to do. Norms become a standard of what each person should do within the group. Employees learn about norms through simple observation and direct instruction from other group members. If you do not deviate too far from these norms, the group will accept much of your behavior. If you deviate too far, you will be subject to much rejection. Here is one example of how group norms influence work output:

> Kathy worked as a receptionist-assistant for the county government. She was one of five women occupying a similar job in the same division of the county. The women had developed the procedure whereby if one receptionist-assistant was overloaded with work, she would ask one of the other women to help her. This was accomplished by calling each of the other receptionist-assistants in turn to see if one of them had some slack time. It became apparent that Kathy frequently asked for help, but never assisted any of the other women. During a coffee break one day, two of the other receptionist-assistants confronted Kathy. They told her that if she didn't soon do her share of overload work she would be criticized to her boss. In addition, they would refuse to have coffee or lunch with her. Within a few days, Kathy was volunteering to help the other women.

Group norms also influence the social aspects of behavior in work settings. Many of these norms relate to such things as the people to have lunch with, getting together with other employees for an after-hours drink on Friday, joining a department team, and the type of clothing you wear to work.

SELF-ASSESSMENT EXERCISE 9–2

The Coworker Relationships Quiz

Answer the following questions based on any work experience you have had. If your work experience is very limited, base your answer on how you imagine you would react toward coworkers. Use the following scale: 0 = never or rarely; 1 = occasionally or sometimes; 2 = usually; 3 = always.

1.	I am ready, willing, and able to share information, supplies, and equipment with others.	0 1 2 3
2.	I offer ideas and advice without appearing to be dominating or controlling.	0 1 2 3
3.	I compliment my coworkers on their work and accomplishments.	0 1 2 3
4.	When I feel I must criticize, I do so in private.	0 1 2 3
5.	I remain even-tempered, even in frustrating situations.	0 1 2 3
6.	People trust me.	0 1 2 3
7.	I'm honest, fair, and consistent in my actions and comments.	0 1 2 3
8.	When I speak about the boss, I speak about his or her actions, not his or her personality.	0 1 2 3
9.	I look for ways to make the workplace more harmonious.	0 1 2 3
10.	I accept new employees and try to make them feel at home.	0 1 2 3
11.	Although I am efficient, I make others feel welcome when they stop to chat.	0 1 2 3
12.	Whenever I see the opportunity, I do simple favors for coworkers.	0 1 2 3
13.	I am interested in the needs of coworkers without appearing to interfere with their lives.	0 1 2 3
14.	Even when I dislike an individual, I remain cordial.	0 1 2 3
15.	I'm willing to help coworkers do a better job and look good without taking credit for my help.	0 1 2 3
16.	I express gratitude to others when they help me.	0 1 2 3
17.	When somebody wants to express an opinion, I'm a good listener.	0 1 2 3
18.	I make a sincere effort to understand, and follow, workplace policies.	0 1 2 3
19.	When I observe that a coworker is overloaded with work, I offer assistance.	0 1 2 3
20.	People who work with me would say that I'm a good team player.	0 1 2 3

Scoring and Interpretation:

50–60 points	You have excellent coworker relationship skills.
40–49 points	Your coworker relationship skills are in the average range. Look for ways to enhance your relationships with coworkers.
0–39 points	Your coworker relationships are not strong enough for you to be regarded by others as a friendly and cooperative group member. You are advised to put considerable effort into developing your skills as a group member. Get some ideas from this chapter, and the section on teamwork in Chapter 13.

Source: Adapted and expanded from "The Happy Coworker Quiz!" http://royalneighbors.com/coworkquiz.htm.

If you deviate too far from work or social norms, you run the risk of being ostracized from the group. In some instances you might even be subjected to physical abuse if you make the other employees look bad. The risk of conforming too closely to group norms is that you lose your individuality. You become viewed by your superiors as "one of the guys or gals," rather than as a person who aspires to move up in the organization. Getting along too well with peers has its price as well.

Make Others Feel Important. A fundamental principle of fostering good relationships with coworkers and others is to make them feel important. Visualize that everyone in the workplace is wearing a small sign around the neck that says, "Please make me feel important."[9] Although the leader has the primary responsibility for satisfying this recognition need, coworkers also play a key role. One approach to making a coworker feel important would be to bring a notable accomplishment of his or hers to the attention of the group. Investing a small amount of time in recognizing a coworker can pay large dividends in terms of cultivating an ally.

Be a Good Listener. The simplest technique of getting along with coworkers within and outside your department is to be a good listener. The topics that you should be willing to listen to during working hours include job problems and miscellaneous complaints. Lunch breaks, rest breaks, and after hours are better suited to listening to people talk about their personal lives, current events, sports, and the like. Becoming an effective listener takes practice. As you practice your listening skills, try the suggestions offered in Chapter 11. The payoff is that listening builds constructive relationships.

Maintain Honest and Open Relationships. Humanistic psychology attaches considerable importance to maintaining honest and open relationships with other people. Giving coworkers frank but tactful answers to their requests for your opinion is one useful way of developing open relationships. Assume that a coworker asks your opinion about an e-mail message the coworker intends to send to his or her team leader. As you read it, you find it somewhat incoherent and filled with word misuse and grammatical errors. An honest response to this e-mail might be: "I think your idea is good. But I think your e-mail needs more work before that idea comes across clearly."

Display a Helpful, Cooperative, and Courteous Attitude. Many jobs require teamwork. If you display a willingness to help others and work cooperatively with them, you will be regarded as a good team player. Organizations are designed with cooperation in mind. If people do not cooperate with each other, the total system breaks down. Not all your coworkers are concerned about the smooth functioning of the total organization, but they do want cooperation from you.

When evaluating your work performance, many companies include a rating of your cooperativeness. Both management and peers value cooperative behavior on your part. The questions on page 219 are reproduced from a rating form used by many companies.

Keep a Large Balance in the Favor Bank. To maintain good relationships with others, you need to make deposits in the Favor Bank says Robert Dilenschnei-

COOPERATION AND CONTACTS

Goal: Rating ability to work for and with others.
Criteria: Willing to follow directions? Accept suggestions? Does he or she consider others' viewpoints? Adapt to changing situations? What is his or her attitude toward others? Does he or she respect them and earn their respect? Successful in dealing with others?

- ❑ Best; upper 10%
- ❑ Next 20%
- ❑ Average; 40% of group
- ❑ Next 20%
- ❑ Bottom 10%

der, a public relations executive.[10] The strategy is based on the idea that if you make deposits in the Favor Bank other people owe you favors. Ways of making deposits include building good will and looking for favors you can do. You should also take credit discreetly for your favors. For example, if you handled a customer complaint for a coworker who was on break, let him or her know, but do not inform the manager.

Phrase Demands as a Request for Help. When you need the assistance of a coworker, express your demand as a request for help rather than a demand. Assume, for example, that you need a coworker's help in interpreting a spreadsheet. A recommended approach is to say, "I have a problem that I wonder if you could help me with. . . ."[11] This approach is likely to be more effective than saying, "You have to help me interpret this spreadsheet, or I won't get my work done." Requesting help is effective because most people enjoy giving advice and assistance. However, most workers resent being given demands or orders from coworkers.

Be a Nurturing, Positive Person. A comprehensive strategy for building good coworker relationships is to be a positive person. A **nurturing person** is one who promotes the growth of others. Nurturing people are positive and supportive, and they typically look for the good qualities in others. A **toxic person** stands in contrast to a nurturing person because he or she dwells on the negative.[12] Visualize the following scenario to appreciate the difference between a nurturing person and a toxic one:

> Randy, a purchasing specialist, enters the office where two coworkers are talking. One is a nurturing person, the other is toxic. With a look of panic, Randy says, "I'm sorry to barge in like this, but can anybody help me? I've been working for three hours preparing a file on the computer, and it seems to have vanished. Maybe one of you can help me retrieve it."
>
> Margot, the nurturing person, says, "I'm no computer expert, but since I'm not the one who lost the file, I can be calm enough to help. Let's go right now." Ralph, the toxic person, whispers to Margot: "Tell Randy to use his computer manual. If you help him now, you'll only find him on your doorstep every time he needs help."

If you listen to toxic people long enough, you are likely to feel listless, depressed, and drained. Nourishing people, in contrast, are positive, enthusiastic, and supportive. The guideline for enhancing coworker relationships is to engage in thoughts and actions every day that will be interpreted by others as nourishing.

BUILDING GOOD RELATIONSHIPS WITH CUSTOMERS

Another important requirement for success is to build good relationships with both external and internal customers. External customers fit the traditional definition of customer that includes clients and guests. External customers can be classified as retail or industrial. The latter represents one company buying from another, such as purchasing machinery or a fleet of cars. Internal customers are the people you serve within the organization, or those who use the output from your job. For example, if you are a payroll supervisor, your customers include the people whose payroll you process and your manager.

Good customer service is good for business, especially because satisfied customers usually result in repeat business. Loyal customers contribute substantially to profits. The Bain Consulting Group provide data indicating that a mere 5 percent increase in customer retention can increase profits as much as 25 percent to 100 percent depending on the industry. For example, in the insurance industry a 5 percent increase in customer retention results in \$60 more in profits.[13] Another study documenting the importance of good customer service was conducted in the automobile service field. As shown in Figure 9–1, profits jumped considerably as the customer was retained over time.[14] And good service is the primary factor that keeps customers coming back.

The previous two chapter sections dealt with internal relationships. In this section, we emphasize techniques for pleasing the external customer. (Yet some of the techniques described here could also fit elsewhere in the chapter, and vice versa.) Eight representative techniques for building constructive customer relationships are presented next.[15]

1. *Establish customer satisfaction goals.* Decide jointly with your manager how much you intend to help customers. Find answers to questions such as the following: Is your company attempting to satisfy every customer within 10 minutes of his or her request? Are you striving to provide the finest customer service in your field? Is your goal zero customer defections to competitors? Your goals will dictate how much and the type of effort you put into pleasing customers. It is also possible that your company intends to provide better service to bigger customers, and provide more limited service to smaller customers.

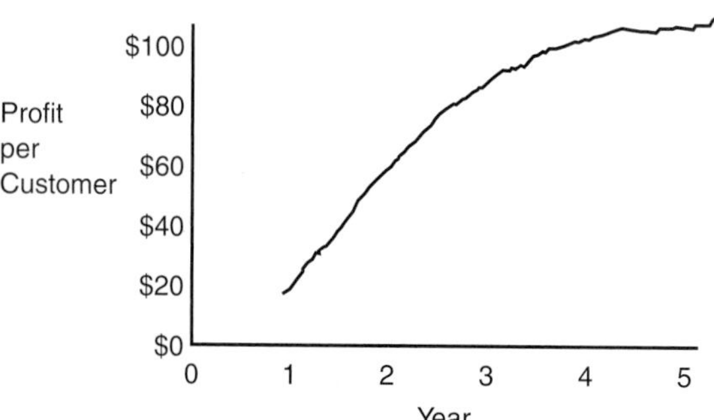

FIGURE 9–1 Profits Over Time per Auto Servicing Customer

2. *Understand your customer's needs.* The most basic principle of selling is to identify and satisfy customer needs. Many customers may not be able to express their needs clearly. Also, they may not be certain of their needs. To help identify customer needs, you may have to probe for information. For example, the associate in a camera and video store might ask, "What uses do you have in mind for your video camera?" Knowing such information will help the store associate identify which camcorder will satisfy the customer's needs.
3. *Put customer needs first.* After you have identified customer needs, focus on satisfying them rather than doing what is convenient for you or your firm. Assume, for example, the customer says, "I would like to purchase 10 jars of rubber cement." The sales associate should not respond, "Sorry, the rubber cement comes in boxes of 12, so it is not convenient to sell you 10 jars." The associate might, however, offer a discount for a purchase of 12 jars if such action fits company policy.
4. *Show care and concern.* During contacts with your customer, show concern for his or her welfare. Ask questions such as the following: How have you enjoyed the video camera you bought here a while back? How are you feeling today? After asking the question, project a genuine interest in the answer.
5. *Communicate a positive attitude.* A positive attitude is signaled by such factors as appearance, friendly gestures, a warm voice tone, and good telephone communication skills. If a customer seems apologetic about making a heavy demand, respond, "No need to apologize. My job is to please you. Without you we wouldn't be in business." Another aspect of being positive is to smile at every customer. Smiling is a natural relationship builder and can help you bond with your customer. Smile several times during each customer contact, even if your customer is angry about your product or service. In Chapter 10, we offer suggestions for dealing with abrasive customers who make smiling difficult even for the most patient salesperson.
6. *Take problems away from customers.* Never hesitate to fix a customer's problem even if the problem is not entirely your fault. For example, if your company installed equipment that is not working well because the customer is misusing the equipment, show the customer how to use the equipment properly.
7. *Follow up on requests.* The simple act of following up to see if your service is satisfactory is a powerful principle of good customer service. A simple telephone call to the requestor of your service is usually sufficient follow-up. A follow-up is effective because it completes the loop in communication between two people.
8. *Resolve conflict constructively.* When conflict arises between you and a customer, seek to achieve mutual gains, as described in Chapter 8. In addition, keep two other approaches in mind: Allow the customer to "climb Mount Anger" and enlist the customer as a partner. Mount Anger refers to the peak of anger customers must be allowed to climb before they can calm down and become reasonable. If angry people are interrupted before they have finished yelling and screaming, they will fall back to the

bottom of the mountain and have to start climbing again. Most angry people, like hockey players in a fight, get to the top in about two minutes. When you hear a sigh, you will know the angry customer has simmered down. He or she is now ready to climb down the other side of the mountain and begin resolving the problem.

Enlisting the customer as a partner refers to working jointly to solve the problem, such as a customer being upset about an order that will not be ready on time. Phrases designed to bring about collaborative action include: "Let's work together to see how we can resolve this" and "Will you work with me so that we can develop a solution that's good for both of us?"

The importance of satisfying customers is so well known that many service firms solicit customer feedback about service. You have probably seen these cards at hotels and retail stores. Figure 9–2 presents a customer feedback card from a popular diner.

APPRECIATING CULTURAL DIVERSITY

The workforce in the United States and Canada has become more diverse. One out of 10 Americans is foreign born, leading to further diversity in the workplace. The majority of new workers are women, African Americans, Hispanics (or Latinos), and immigrants. Only one-third of the 145-million-person workforce are native-born White males. The fastest-growing segments of the workforce are women and people of color.

Succeeding in a diverse environment requires more than avoiding discriminatory behavior. Instead, success is facilitated by working comfortably with people of different sexes, races, religions, ethnic backgrounds, values, sexual orientations, and physical capabilities. One viewpoint in appreciating cultural diversity is that White males should be included in the diversity web. Many White males feel that they are being omitted from concerns about appreciating diversity. The group, White Men as Full Diversity Partners, attempts to get White males actively contributing to achieving diversity in the workplace. If White men are engaged in the process, they will have more responsibility to further diversity and cultural understanding in organizations. Members of the same group believe they are excluded from some job opportunities because of their sex and race.[16]

Various groups that have been discriminated against in the past are demanding more equal treatment and greater acceptance. The current theme in diversity efforts is *inclusion,* meaning that all types of differences are included when appreciating diversity. Many gay and lesbian employees, for example, have stepped forward to request the same employee benefits offered to married heterosexuals. In response to these demands, some employers, such as U.S. West, Inc., have conducted workshops to address discrimination against gays and lesbians and the expansion of benefits to these same groups.

The information already presented for dealing with managers, coworkers, and customers can be applied toward building relationships with diverse groups. In addition, it is important to develop an appreciation of cultural diversity in the workplace. Toward this end, we will discuss recognizing diversity on the job and describe a training program for such purposes.

FIGURE 9–2 Customer Satisfaction Card From a Diner

Source: Reprinted with permission of the Silver Diner, Rockville, MD.

____

____

____

(Use Reverse Side For Additional Comments)

Did the Silver Diner experience meet, exceed or fall below your expectations?

	Exceed Expectations 5	4	Meet Expectations 3	2	Below Expectations 1
Food Quality	❑	❑	❑	❑	❑
Service	❑	❑	❑	❑	❑
Cleanliness	❑	❑	❑	❑	❑
Value	❑	❑	❑	❑	❑

DATE TIME NO. IN PARTY SERVER

NAME PHONE

ADDRESS

CITY STATE ZIP

RESTAURANT LOCATION

What time of day is it?

❑ 7am-11am ❑ 11am-4pm ❑ 4pm-11pm ❑ 11pm-close

Including today how often have you eaten at Silver Diner in the past 4 weeks?

❑ First Time Ever ❑ One Time ❑ Two Times
❑ Three Times ❑ Four Times ❑ Five + Times

Please drop this card in the Comment Card Box located at the front door or give it to your server. **Please speak to the store manager for immediate response.** To speak directly with Silver Diner Proprietor, Ype Von Hengst, please call (301) 230-8467 or write us at 11806 Rockville Pike, Rockville, MD 20852.

Thanks for dining with us and helping us to ***be the best we can be.***

Bob Giaimo
Proprietor

Ype Von Hengst
Proprietor

SILVER DINER™
DINE IN DINE OUT

1 2 3 4 5 6 7 8 9 10 11 12 13 14 15

Recognizing Cultural Differences

As described in Chapter 3, cultural diversity can be better understood if it is recognized that many apparent differences in personality actually arise from culture. For example, White and Black North Americans feel that authority should often be challenged. However, Asians and Hispanics tend to respect and obey authority. Another notable difference is that Hispanic culture perceives music, family members, and food as appropriate for the workplace. Americans and Canadians reject these practices and may regard them as unprofessional.

Some forms of discrimination become more explainable, even if still unacceptable, when their culture origins are recognized. For example, in many Asian countries few women hold key positions in industry. It is therefore difficult for some Asian workers employed in North America to accept women as their administrative superiors.

To appreciate cultural diversity, it is also important to fine-tune your perceptions and not lump diverse people under one group. People of one race, as identified by skin color and facial appearance, may have very different ethnic and cultural backgrounds. For example, Blacks who grew up in New York City, Jamaica, and Central Africa have different sets of cultural values.

A good starting point in applying this information is to recognize that everybody has his or her own ethnic background. Similarly, everybody has an "accent." Identifying your own cultural values is a starting point for becoming flexible in dealing with the ethnicity of superiors, coworkers, and customers.

A company approach to recognizing cultural differences is to permit and encourage employees to form **employee network groups.** The network group is composed of employees throughout the company who affiliate on the basis of group characteristics such as race, ethnicity, sex, sexual orientation, or physical ability status. Group members typically have similar interests, and they look to the groups as a way of sharing information about succeeding in the organization. Although some human resource specialists are concerned that network groups can lead to divisiveness, others believe they play a positive role. At 3M Corporation, employee network groups serve as advisors to business units. For example, the 3M product development groups often consult the company's network group for employees with disabilities. Company network groups also help their organizations recruit through such means as providing links to minority group members in the community.[17]

After recognizing cultural differences an important next step is to help diverse workers, including newcomers, fit into the work environment. The real challenge is to create an atmosphere in which people work together harmoniously. Unless the corporate culture emphasizes cooperation and teamwork, efforts to bring about corporate diversity will break down.[18]

Diversity Training Programs

To help employees relate comfortably to people of different cultures and appreciate diversity, many companies conduct **diversity programs.** These programs provide an opportunity for employees to develop the skills necessary to deal effectively with each other and with customers in a diverse environment.

Lewis Griggs, a diversity consultant, describes the conditions necessary for diversity training to achieve its goals. Above all, top management must be committed and provide leadership. All participants in the program must start with

SKILL-BUILDING EXERCISE 9–1

Developing Empathy for Differences

Depending on the size and physical layout of the classroom, choose one of the following exercises. If the seats are movable and the class has 25 members or less, organize the class into a large circle. Each person in turn describes in what way he or she has been perceived as different from others. The difference can include such factors as race, ethnic background, physical characteristics, religious affiliation, disability status, or speaking accent. Any difference can be meaningful. Each person explains his or her feelings about being different, including any thoughts of being discriminated against. Other group members then react to the person's perceptions. Finally, the class members discuss what they have learned from the empathy-circle exercise.

If the class has more than 25 members or the seats are stationary, the exercise just described can be conducted by having students come up in front of the class one at a time.

themselves and recognize that they have a cultural identity that influences their perceptions, values, and style of communication.

The next major step is for workers to realize that they are already making adaptations to different people in different settings. People behave very differently when relating to others at a sporting event, place of worship, or school. After cultural awareness and appreciation have been achieved, the workers are ready for employees to speak about their cultural differences and to perform exercises.[19] Skill-Building Exercise 9–1 gives you an opportunity to engage in a representative cultural diversity exercise.

SUMMARY OF KEY POINTS

- To prosper in your career, it is essential to have good working relationships with managers, coworkers, lower-ranking employees, and customers. The behaviors that contribute to a good working relationship with one group of workers usually work at other levels.
- The starting point in building satisfying partnerships with managers is to perform well in your job. Other important approaches include the following:
  1. Perceive things from your manager's perspective.
  2. Clarify expectations of what you are supposed to be doing.
  3. Establish a relationship of trust.
  4. Respect your manager's authority.
  5. Bring forth solutions as well as problems.
  6. Express constructive disagreement: Disagree with your manager when necessary, but be tactful.
  7. Give your manager positive reinforcement and recognition.
  8. Talk big, shun trivia: Keep small talk to a minimum, and engage in some talk about important organizational outcomes.
  9. Use discretion in socializing with your manager.
  10. Carefully sell your ideas to your manager.
  11. Engage in favorable interactions with your manager.

- The following suggestions are particularly geared toward developing good relationships with coworkers but should also be useful in developing constructive relationships at all levels:
  1. Adhere to group norms (unofficial standards of conduct).
  2. Make others feel important.
  3. Be a good listener.
  4. Maintain honest and open relationships.
  5. Display a helpful, cooperative, and courteous attitude.
  6. Keep a large balance in your Favor Bank. (Make sure people owe you a favor.)
  7. Phrase demands as a request for help.
  8. Be a nurturing, positive person.
- Another important success requirement is to build good relationships with both external and internal customers. Representative techniques for building constructive customer relationships include: (1) establish customer satisfaction goals, (2) understand your customer's needs, (3) put your customer's needs first, (4) show care and concern, (5) communicate a positive attitude, (6) take problems away from customers, (7) follow up on requests, and (8) resolve conflict with customers constructively.
- The North American workforce has become increasingly culturally diverse. Job success is facilitated by working comfortably with people of different sexes, races, religions, ethnicity, values, sexual orientations, and physical capabilities. To work comfortably with diverse groups, it is important to appreciate and enjoy cultural diversity. A starting point is to recognize cultural differences by examining your own cultural background. A company approach to recognizing cultural differences is to permit and encourage employees to form employee network groups. Many companies sponsor diversity training to help employees appreciate cultural diversity.

GUIDELINES FOR PERSONAL EFFECTIVENESS

1. Although job knowledge is indispensable for performing well in your job, it is not sufficient to make you a high performer. Another important set of behaviors necessary to perform well on the job is maintaining constructive relationships with other employees at all levels and with customers. Other important behaviors contributing to job performance (such as high motivation and work habits) are discussed elsewhere in this text.
2. If you ignore the strategies presented in this chapter, you do so at great risk of not gaining a wide base of support in your present or future place of work. An important success strategy is to make a deliberate effort to form constructive working relationships with coworkers.
3. To be successful in today's culturally diverse workforce, it is necessary to work comfortably and effectively with diverse groups of people. If a person feels, for example, "I would not want an Arab man for my boss," he or she must attempt to uncover the root of the problem. Next, the person should attempt to bring about an attitude change toward an appreciation of cultural diversity. An attitude shift may occur as the individual engages in frequent positive interactions with Arab people in positions of authority.

DISCUSSION QUESTIONS AND ACTIVITIES

1. Many workplaces today are supposed to be more democratic, with managers having less power than in the past. Why, then, is it so important to know techniques for getting along with one's manager?
2. How can a person implement the tactic "give your manager positive reinforcement and recognition" without appearing to be "kissing-up" to the boss?
3. How can a person learn the group norms operating in his or her place of work?
4. Give an example of a technique you think would make a coworker feel important.
5. Give an example of excellent customer service you have received recently. What impact did the service have on your intention to return to the store or Web site?
6. Give an example of atrocious customer service you have received recently. What impact did the service have on your intention to *not* return to the store or Web site?
7. A survey of industrial companies revealed that 90 percent of them prefer the sales representatives who call on them to use a soft sell. How does this finding fit the information in this chapter about customer relationships?
8. What might you do to impress to a job interviewer that you have good cultural diversity skills?
9. Suppose your goal is to develop your cultural diversity skills. You are looking for a seat in the company (or school) cafeteria. Sitting at one table are about 10 people from one ethnic or racial group different from yours. Would you ask to sit among these people? Explain your reasoning.
10. Ask an experienced manager to identify the best methods a worker might use to form a constructive relationship with that manager. Be prepared to report your findings to the class.

REFERENCES

1. Survey cited in book review, *Personnel Psychology,* Summer 2000, p. 498.
2. J. B. Ritchie and Paul Thomson, *Organization and People* (St. Paul, MN: West Publishing, 1980), p. 298.
3. Eugene E. Jennings, *The Mobile Manager* (New York: McGraw-Hill, 1967), pp. 47–50; Roger Fritz, "Career Key: How to Influence Your Boss," *Supervisory Management,* August 1980, p. 10.
4. Walter St. John, "Stressful Communications between Supervisors and Employees," *Personnel Journal,* January 1983, p. 76.
5. "Socializing with Your Boss," *Personal Report for the Executive,* January 1, 1998, p. 76.
6. Joseph D. O'Brian quoted in "Selling Your Idea to the Boss," *Communication Briefings* 17, no. 2, 1998, p. 2.
7. Anne Fisher, "Do I Have to Kiss Up? . . . How Do I Gather Skills? . . . And Other Queries," *Fortune,* March 31, 1997, p. 123.

AN APPLIED PSYCHOLOGY CASE PROBLEM

The Unnoticed Group Member

Troy Winston worked as a desktop publishing technician for a large printing firm, Tri-City Graphics. With five years of experience behind him, Troy was looking to be promoted into a supervisory position. His long-range goal was to become a printing company executive. Over the last three years, Troy received average or above-average ratings on his performance evaluation. During his most recent performance evaluation, Troy took the initiative to discuss his prospects for being promoted to team leader in his work group or supervisor in another department. Troy's boss, Penny Jacobin, shrugged her shoulders and said, "I wouldn't rule out your being promoted, but right now I don't see any openings. Bring up the issue again during next year's evaluation."

Troy was so concerned about Penny's lukewarm response to his interest in being promoted that he spoke to his mentor in the company, Sydney Marlin, a veteran production manager. Troy said to Sydney, "I don't seem to be getting anywhere in this company. I like being a desktop publishing specialist, but I also want to combine it with supervision or leadership."

Sydney said, "Your career plan sounds fine, as we've discussed in the past. Yet somehow your boss is kind of neutral about your potential for promotion. What is your explanation of Penny's lack of enthusiasm for your promotability?"

Troy thought for a moment, then answered: "Penny is a good manager and a fair manager. I have no major complaints about her. It's just that she doesn't notice me much. To her I'm just another professional worker who is getting the job done. The only tangible suggestion Penny has offered me is that I should strive to stay current with new technology in the field. You could say that about anybody. In desktop publishing, some new development comes along every month."

Sydney told Troy, "Next time I talk with Penny, I'll ask how you are doing. Since I'm your mentor, that type of question would not be out of line."

Ten days later, Sydney met with Penny for another reason, and asked about how Troy was coming along in his career. Penny commented, "That's right, you are Troy's mentor. He is a competent worker, but he kind of blends into the group. During a busy week, it's easy for me not to give Troy much thought. He's a nice guy, but I don't see anything remarkable about him. I see no reason for me or the other managers to look upon him as being more promotable than lots of other good technical workers in the company."

"Thanks," said Sydney. "What you have told me could be useful in my advising Troy."

QUESTIONS

1. If you were Sydney, what advice would you give Troy?
2. What techniques for getting along with one's manager might Troy be neglecting?
3. Is Penny being fair in her evaluation of Troy?

8. Christine M. Riordan and Rodger W. Griffith, "The Opportunity for Friendship in the Workplace: An Underexplored Construct," *Journal of Business and Psychology,* Winter 1995, pp. 141–154.
9. Shelia Murray Bethel, *Making a Difference* (New York: G. P. Putnam's Sons, 1989).
10. Robert L. Dilenschneider, *Power and Influence: Mastering the Art of Persuasion* (New York: G. P. Putnam's Sons, 1989).
11. Joseph D. O'Brian, "Negotiating with Peers: Consensus, Not Power," *Supervisory Management,* January 1992, p. 4.
12. Jeffrey Keller, "Associate with Positive People," *A Supplement to the Pryor Report,* 1994.
13. Reported in Theodore W. Garrison III, "The Value of Customer Service," in Rick Crandall (ed.), *Celebrate Customer Service* (Corte Madera, CA: Select Press, 2000), p. 7.
14. Frederick F. Reichfeld and Earl Sasser, Jr., "Zero Defections: Quality Comes to Services," *Harvard Business Review,* September–October 1990, p. 106.

AN APPLIED PSYCHOLOGY CASE PROBLEM

Hold on to Our Bilingual Workers

Jaime Ornelas' Spanish-language skills and technology know-how helped him go global. Ornelas, a chemical engineer by training, who has been stationed all over the world, said he's an example of how bilingual skills—and the cultural lessons that come with them—can be a huge plus for tech workers.

"It's important in the sense of making sure there's no miscommunication in terms of anecdotes and idioms," said Ornelas, who now works as a cost and financial planning analyst at Texas Instruments in Dallas. "But more importantly, it's the notion that you have the ability to see things from a different perspective."

Ornelas was born in Mexico City, went to college and graduate school in Texas, and then held chemical engineering jobs in Waco, Mexico City, and San Antonio. While working in San Antonio, he switched to financial planning, becoming an expert in compliance with environmental regulations. At Texas Instruments, he helps the environmental and safety groups meet government standards.

With such a varied background, Ornelas said he has learned a lot about how different cultures interact. "Not only can bilingual tech workers communicate around the world, but they can also help companies understand the cultural backgrounds of their global partners and their employees," he said.

That's exactly the help that Lois Melbourne needs. She's president of Irving, Texas-based TimeVision Inc., a software company that makes organizational charting programs for human resources departments. TimeVision already has customers in Europe and wants to expand in Latin America. But it needs technology-savvy Spanish speakers for customer support and sales help.

"In our job postings, we say 'multilingual preferred.' But because the job market is so tight, we hire quality people regardless of that requirement," she said. "To find somebody with all those skills would be almost too good to be true."

Melbourne said her company is so eager to sell to Latin America that one bilingual employee is teaching Spanish at lunchtime. "Not having the bilingual employees really slows us down," she said.

Other tech companies say they also need bilingual workers to help serve the growing Spanish-speaking market in the United States. Studies indicate that almost half of all Hispanic households are online.

Angelo Ioffreda, a spokesperson for America Online Inc., said that most jobs at tech companies that require Spanish skills are in customer service, sales, and marketing.

Steve Adams, a spokesperson for Dallas-based Internet America Inc., said that his company is actively searching for bilingual tech support experts. "We have trouble holding on to them," he said. "There's such a demand for people with bilingual skills."

Questions

1. What does the information provided by the people in this case tell you about the relationship between cultural diversity within a firm and its ability to compete effectively in international business?
2. What suggestions can you offer the companies mentioned above to attract and retain Spanish-speaking employees?
3. As an executive in one of the above companies, which of the two following strategies would you choose in order to have a larger number of Spanish-speaking employees? (a) Teach Spanish to technology-skilled workers, or (b) teach technology to Spanish-speaking workers. Explain your reasoning.

Source: Adapted from Crayton Harrison, "Tech Companies Hunting for Bilingual Employees," *Knight Ridder,* October 15, 2000.

SKILL-BUILDING EXERCISE 9–2

Developing Your Multicultural Skills through the Net

A useful way of developing skills in a second language and learning more about another culture is to create an Internet "bookmark" or "favorite" written in your target language. In this way, each time you go online, you'll see fresh information in the language you want to develop.

To get started, use a search engine like Yahoo that offers choices in several languages. After choosing your target language, enter a keyword like "newspaper" or "current events" in the search probe. Once you find a suitable choice, enter the edit function for "Favorites" or "Bookmarks" and insert that newspaper or information site as your cover page, or front page. For example, imagine if French were your choice. The Yahoo France search engine might bring you to www.france2.fr. This Web site keeps you abreast of French and international news, sports, and cultural events—written in French. Now every time you access the Internet, you can spend five minutes becoming multicultural. You can save a lot of travel costs and time by using the Internet to help you become multicultural.

15. Jennifer Reingold, "Teacher in Chief," *Fast Company,* September 2001, pp. 66–68; William B. Martin, *Quality Customer Service: A Positive Guide to Superior Service,* rev. ed. (Los Altos, CA: Crisp Publications, Inc. 1989); Raenelle Hanes, "What Business Owners Need to Know about Customer Service," *Business Education Forum,* February 1996, p. 4.
16. William Atkinson, "Bringing Diversity to White Men," *HR Magazine,* September 2001, pp. 76–83; Charlene Marmer Solomon, "Are White Males Being Left Out?" *Personnel Journal,* November 1991, p. 88.
17. Patricia Digh, "Well-Managed Employee Networks Add Business Value," *HR Magazine,* August 1997, pp. 67–72.
18. Annie Finnigan, "Different Strokes," *Working Woman,* April 2001, p. 46.
19. Cited in Bill Leonard, "Ways to Make Diversity Programs Work," *HR Magazine,* April 1991, p. 38.

SUGGESTED READING

Adams, Marc. "Showing Good Faith Toward Muslims." *HR Magazine,* November 2000, pp. 52–64.

"America's 50 Best Companies for Minorities." *Fortune,* July 9, 2001, pp. 122–128.

Bowen, David E., Gilliland, Stephen W., and Folger, Robert. "How Being Fair with Employees Spills Over to Customers." *Organizational Dynamics,* Winter 1999, pp. 310–326.

Brown, Stephen. "Torment Your Customers (They'll Love It)." *Harvard Business Review,* October 2001, pp. 82–88.

Chase, Richard B., and Dasu, Sriram, "Want to Perfect Your Company's Service? Use Behavioral Science," *Harvard Business Review,* June 2001, pp. 78–84.

Cross, Elsie Y. *Managing Diversity: The Courage to Lead.* Westport, CT: Quorum Books, 2000.

Dwyer, Diana. *Interpersonal Relationships.* New York: Routledge, 2000.

Gilbert, Jacqueline A., and Ivancevich, John M. "Valuing Diversity: A Tale of Two Organizations." *The Academy of Management Executive,* February 2000, pp. 93–105.

Leonard, Bill. "Linking Diversity Initiatives: A High-tech Network in Seattle is Causing a Positive Chain Reaction." *HR Magazine,* June 1999, pp. 60–64.

Seybold, Patricia B. "Get Inside the Lives of Your Customers." *Harvard Business Review,* May 2001, pp. 80–89.

WEB CORNER

www.workingwounded.com (Information on the uncivil workplace.)

CHAPTER 10

COPING WITH A VARIETY OF PERSONALITIES

Learning Objectives After reading and studying this chapter and doing the exercises, you should be able to

1. Take problems professionally rather than personally.
2. Acquire insights into how to confront and criticize counterproductive people.
3. Be aware of the importance of interpreting the games of counterproductive people.
4. Use sympathy to help handle the personality quirks of coworkers.
5. Deal with difficult customers.
6. Be ready to handle a variety of personalities by using tact and diplomacy, humor, and recognition and affection.
7. Recognize that some moodiness may be related to the physical status of the brain.

Most jobs would be much easier if one were not forced to deal with a variety of personalities, some of whom can block your attempts to be productive. Workers can be counterproductive or difficult for many reasons besides intelligence or ability. From the standpoint of a manager, a **counterproductive (or difficult) person** can be anybody who turns in substandard performance, yet who could perform well if he or she wanted to. From the standpoint of the individual worker, a peer is classified as counterproductive or difficult if he or she is uncooperative, touchy, defensive, hostile, or even very unfriendly. From the standpoint of any group member, a counterproductive or difficult boss is similarly any boss who is uncooperative, insensitive, touchy or defensive, aggressive, hostile, or very unfriendly.

The behavior of the variety of personalities described in this chapter can lower productivity. A major productivity drain is that difficult people divert us from our goals because of the time spent dealing with their unsettling behavior. For example, after being insulted by a difficult coworker you may need several minutes to concentrate again on your work. At their worst, the behavior of difficult people can be disruptive to the entire work group. In a national poll, 90 percent of respondents indicated that incivility (extreme rudeness) is a serious problem that contributes to violence and erodes moral values. Furthermore, in another national poll 75 percent believed that incivility is getting worse.[1]

In this chapter we explore some of the psychological techniques that a person might use to deal more effectively with people who are counterproductive or difficult, but not necessarily unintelligent or incompetent. We are dealing primarily with the situation in which the difficult person is a coworker rather than a subordinate. However, if you have formal authority over another individual (you're the boss), the same techniques can be used to advantage. Also, if the difficult person is your manager or team leader, several of the techniques can be used, but with considerable sensitivity and tact.

Many different approaches exist for classifying difficult or counterproductive people.[2] A representative classification of difficult behavior patterns is presented in Figure 10–1. Although not scientifically developed, the categories provide some insight into the nature of counterproductive behavior on the job.

SEE IF YOU RECOGNIZE THESE PEOPLE...

The Know-It-Alls:
They're experts on everything. They can be arrogant, and they usually have an opinion on any issue. Yet when they're wrong, they pass the buck or become defensive.

The Passives:
You can spot them with their deadpan faces, their weak handshakes, their blank stares. Avoiding controversy at all costs, these people never offer opinions or ideas and never let you know where you stand

The Dictators:
They bully, cajole and intimidate. They're blunt to the point of being insulting. They're constantly demanding and brutally critical. These folks can cause ulcers.

The Yes-People:
They'll agree to any commitment, promise any deadline, yet they rarely deliver. While they're always sorry (and often charming), you can't trust them to do what they say.

The No-People:
Negative and pessimistic, they're quick to point out why something won't work. Worse, they're inflexible; they resist change. They can throw a wet blanket over an entire organization.

The Complainers:
Is anything ever right with these people? You get the feeling they'd rather complain about things than change them. Even though they're often right, their negativity and nit-picking turn people off.

OF COURSE YOU RECOGNIZE THEM. They're the people you work with, sell to, depend on, live with. Now you can learn to deal with them more effectively, at How To Deal With Difficult People, CareerTrack's one-day seminar.

FIGURE 10–1 Difficult Behavior Patterns

Source: *Source:* Brochure for CareerTrack Seminars, 3085 Center Green Drive, Boulder, CO 80301-5408. Reprinted with permission of CareerTrack. For more information, call 800/334-6780.

TAKING PROBLEMS PROFESSIONALLY, NOT PERSONALLY

A key principle in dealing with a variety of personalities is to take what they do professionally, not personally. Difficult people are not necessarily out to get you. You may just represent an obstacle or a steppingstone for them to get what they want.[3] For example, if a customer insults you because she thinks your prices are too high, she probably has nothing against you personally. She just wants a bargain! Dru Scott, a human relations trainer, provides an example of the type of thinking one needs in order to take problems with difficult people professionally rather than personally:[4]

> One savvy representative explained how he taught himself to take things professionally when dealing with difficult people. He reminded himself at key moments, "I'm being paid to do this job. This means I'm a professional. Those with whom I deal don't have to like me. I don't have to like them, but I make my living by handling people professionally and will learn something everytime I encounter a difficult situation."

As you learn to take insults, slights, and backstabbing professionally rather than personally, you will experience less stress and harassment on the job. Imagine how short the career of a baseball umpire would be if he or she took every tirade from coaches, players, and fans personally.

Before delving further into techniques for coping with a variety of personalities, do Self-Assessment Exercise 10–1. It will give you a quick read on your understanding of how to deal with difficult people.

CONFRONTING THE DIFFICULT PERSON

A good starting point for overcoming problems created by a difficult person is to confront that individual with his or her annoying or counterproductive behavior. In some instances, simply confronting the problem will make it go away. One coworker said to another, "Please stop suggesting that we take two-hour lunch breaks every payday. It makes me tense to have to reject you." The requests for the luncheon sojourns stopped immediately.

A fundamental reason why we resist confronting another person, particularly a subordinate, about a sensitive issue is that we recognize how uncomfortable we feel when confronted by a boss about a sensitive issue. A manager who is about to confront a subordinate about irregularities on an expense account might say to himself, "I know how bad I would feel if I were told by my boss that I had been overcharging the company on trips. Maybe if I let it pass one more time, Jack [the subordinate] will shape up by himself."

Another reason many people are hesitant to confront another person is fear of reprisal or a quarrel. What specific kind of reprisal might be chosen by the confronted person (should the roles be reversed) is usually unknown, which makes the confrontation seem all the more hazardous. One member of a task force was going to confront another with the opinion that the latter was not carrying her fair share, thus increasing the burden for other members of the task force. The would-be confronter backed off, thinking that the woman to be confronted might tell lies about her to their mutual boss.

SELF-ASSESSMENT EXERCISE 10–1

Helping Difficult People

For each of the following scenarios choose the method you think would be the most effective for handling the situation. Make a choice, even though more than one method of handling the situation seems plausible.

1. A coworker in the cubicle next to you is talking loudly on the telephone about the fabulous weekend she and a few friends enjoyed. You are attempting to deal with a challenging work problem. To deal with this situation, you
   a. Get up from your chair, stand close to her and say loudly, "Shut up you jerk. I'm trying to do my work."
   b. Slip her a handwritten note, or send her an instant message that says, "I'm happy that you had a great weekend, but I have problems concentrating on my work when you are talking so loudly. Thanks for your help."
   c. Get the boss on the phone and ask that she please do something about the problem.
   d. Wait until lunch and then say to her, "I'm happy that you had a great weekend, but I have problems concentrating on my work when you are talking so loudly. Thanks for your help."
2. One of your coworkers, Olaf, rarely carries his fair load of the work. He forever has a good reason for not having time to do an assignment. This morning he has approached you to load some new software into his personal computer. You deal with this situation by
   a. Carefully explaining that you will help him, providing he will take over a certain specific task for you.
   b. Telling him that you absolutely refuse to help a person as lazy as he.
   c. Counsel him about fair play and reciprocity.
   d. Review with him a list of five times in which he has asked other people to help him out. You then ask if he thinks this is a good way to treat coworkers.
3. In your role as supervisor, you have noticed that Diane, one of the group members, spends far too much time laughing and joking. You schedule a meeting with her. As the meeting opens, you
   a. Joke and laugh with her to establish rapport.
   b. Explain to Diane that you have called this meeting to discuss her too-frequent laughing and joking.
   c. Talk a few moments about the good things Diane has done for the department, then confront the real issue.
   d. Explain to Diane that she is on the verge of losing her job if she doesn't act more maturely.
4. As a team leader, you have become increasingly annoyed with Jerry's ethnic, racist, and sexist jokes. One day during a team meeting, he tells a joke that you believe is particularly offensive. To deal with the situation, you
   a. Meet privately with the team leader to discuss Jerry's offensive behavior.
   b. Catch up with Jerry later when he is alone, and tell him how uncomfortable his joke made you feel.
   c. Confront Jerry on the spot and say, "Hold on Jerry. I find your joke to be offensive."
   d. Tell the team an even more offensive joke to illustrate how Jerry's behavior can get out of hand.
5. You have been placed on a task force to look for ways to save the company money, including making recommendations for eliminating jobs. You interview a supervisor about the efficiency of her department. She

continued on next page

SELF-ASSESSMENT EXERCISE 10–1(cont'd)

suddenly becomes rude and defensive. In response, you

a. Politely point out how her behavior is coming across to you.
b. Get your revenge by recommending that three jobs be eliminated from her department.
c. Explain that you have used up enough of her time for today and ask for another meeting later in the week.
d. Tell her that unless she becomes more cooperative this interview cannot continue.

Scoring and Interpretation: Use the following key to obtain your score:

1) a. 1
   b. 4
   c. 2
   d. 3
2) a. 4
   b. 1
   c. 3
   d. 2
3) a. 1
   b. 4
   c. 3
   d. 2
4) a. 2
   b. 4
   c. 3
   d. 1
5) a. 4
   b. 1
   c. 2
   d. 3

18–20 points	You have good intuition into helping difficult people.
10–17 points	You have average intuition into helping difficult people.
5–9 points	You need to improve your sensitivity about helping difficult people.

Helpful Confrontation Techniques

Seven suggestions are in order to ease the confrontation process.[5] Since confrontation of some sort is a vital step in attempting to influence the behavior of another individual, the suggestions are worth giving serious thought.

1. *Have a clear perception of what constitutes acceptable behavior.* Confrontation makes more sense when you have specific ideas of the limits to acceptable behavior. The widespread problem of incivility is a case in point. Given that many people are rude you may need flexible standards of what constitutes serious incivility. You might decide, for example, that a person who consistently blocks the doorway while rambling about personal life is being uncivil. Or you might have a clear idea in mind of what type of swearing is acceptable in the office. Company policy can often be consulted to help define what constitutes unacceptable behavior.
2. *Attempt to relax during the confrontation session.* If you appear overly tense, you might communicate the message in body language that you are not confident of the position that you are taking about the individual's negative behavior. Sometimes a rehearsal interview with a friend will be helpful in reducing your tension about the confrontation.

3. *Get to the central purpose of your meeting almost immediately.* Too often when people attempt to confront somebody else about something sensitive, they waste time talking about unrelated topics. Discussions about vacations, professional sports, or business conditions have some value as warm-up material for other kinds of interviews.
4. *Avoid being apologetic or defensive about the need for the meeting.* You have a right to demand constructive relationships with other people in your work environment. For instance, there is no need to say, "Perhaps I may be way off base, but it seems like you slam the door shut every time I can't process your request immediately." Let the door-slamming coworker correct you if your observations are inaccurate.
5. *Confront the other individual in a nonhostile manner.* Confrontations about counterproductive behavior should be conducted with feeling (particularly sincerity), but not with hostility. Confrontations are associated with bitter conflict so frequently that the concept of confrontation connotes hostility. Yet all forms of confrontation need not be conflagrations. Hostility begets hostility. Confrontation mixed with hostility comes across to the person being confronted as an attempt at retribution or punishment.
6. *Confront job-related behavior.* The essential skill to be acquired in constructive confrontation is to translate counterproductive behavior into its job-related consequence. Once the counterproductive or difficult behavior is translated into its consequences in terms of actions, the situation is placed on a problem-solving basis. Instead of confronting a person about feelings, attitudes, or values, discuss their job-related consequences. These consequences are much easier to deal with than internal aspects of people. Two examples follow, designed to illustrate the difference between confrontation related to job behavior and confrontation unrelated to job behavior.

   Manager to Sales Associate: (job-related) I wish you would smile at customers more frequently. They are likely to purchase more goods when they receive a warm smile from the sales associate.

   Same Manager to Sales Associate: (not directly job-related) I wish you would smile at customers more frequently. If your attitude isn't right, you'll never make a good sales associate.

   One Supervisor to Another: (job-related) I can't help but overhear you use all those four-letter words. If you keep that up, you may lose the respect of your employees. Then they won't listen to you when you need something done out of the ordinary.

   One Supervisor to Another: (not job-related) I can't help but overhear you use all those four-letter words. There's nothing worse than a foul-mouthed supervisor.

7. *Show that you care.* Human resource consultant Pamela Cole suggests that you show that you care when you confront. She says, "You have to care enough to confront because it's easier not to confront and to avoid the problem. Caring enough to confront increases the likelihood that the situation will be resolved. When I do not confront a situation, I can be pretty much assured that it will go on the way it is or get worse."[6]

Communicating the fact that you care can sometimes be done by the sincerity in your voice and the concerned way you approach the difficult person. Using the words *care* and *concern* can be helpful. To illustrate, "The reason I'm bringing up this problem is that I care about our working relationship. And I'm concerned that things have been a little rough between us."

THE ART OF CRITICIZING CONSTRUCTIVELY

Confrontation and criticism are closely linked. Confrontation precedes the actual criticism, and both are part of the same process of trying to get other people to change their behavior. It is difficult to criticize productive people in a constructive manner. The challenge multiplies when you try to criticize counterproductive people. One of the problems in criticizing anybody in a job setting is that the person being criticized may have put considerable emotional energy into the job. The person therefore interprets the criticism as an attack on his or her ego.

A second problem is the sense of competitiveness that typically develops among coworkers. If you criticize a peer, your criticism may be interpreted as an attack on his or her work just so your work seems better in comparison. A copywriter in an advertising agency made this comment about the criticisms he was exchanging with a peer:

> Everytime I came up with an idea, Steve managed to find something wrong with it. Of course, we were both playing the same game—every time Steve made a suggestion I found a reason to downgrade and reject it. We were not only competing to see who could come up with the better idea, we were competing to see who could find the most flaws in the other fellow's ideas.[7]

Here are several suggestions for criticizing a difficult person in a constructive manner. Recognize, however, that these suggestions also apply to criticizing anybody on the job.[8] (Several may also be used when making criticisms in personal life.)

Criticize in Private. A primary principle of good human relations is to criticize in private. The counterproductive person will only become more defensive if you confront and criticize him or her in the presence of peers. It also may prove to be less threatening to criticize the person away from the work area. The company cafeteria, parking lot, or vending machine area may prove to be a reasonable place to confront and criticize.

Begin with Mild Criticism. Harsh criticism, however well intended, hurts the criticized person's ego and triggers defensive behavior. It is therefore helpful to begin with mild criticism and strengthen it later if necessary. Harsh criticism is also a problem because it is difficult to retract.

Base the Criticism on Objective Facts. In criticizing anybody, it is important to base your criticism on objective facts, rather than on subjective perceptions. Much criticism is rejected because it is thought to be invalid. When you use facts to aid your case, you have a better chance of getting through to the counterproductive person. Assume that you are dealing with a superagreeable person who has failed to supply you some information that you need to accomplish your job. A criticism based on subjective interpretation would be, "Your unwillingness to cooperate has messed things up for me." An objective—and potentially more effective—criticism would be, "Because I did not get the information you promised me, I was unable to finish my report for our boss."

Express Your Criticism in Terms of a Common Goal. As just implied, if your criticism points toward the accomplishment of a purpose that both of you are trying to achieve, it may get across to the difficult person. Use words that emphasize cooperation rather than competitiveness and blame. For example, "We can get the report done quickly if you'll firm up the statistical data while I edit the text," will be more effective than "Unless you get moving faster on the statistics I won't be able to finish the report on time."

Avoid Playing Boss. Most employees resent a coworker assuming the boss's role while criticizing them. Difficult people will resent it all the more because most of them are defensive. "Playing boss" means that you act as if you have formal authority over the other person, when in reality you are a peer or subordinate. One manifestation of playing boss would be to tell a coworker, "If you don't get that program written for me by this afternoon, you'll have to work overtime to get it done."

When Criticizing Your Boss, Relate It to Your Work Performance. It takes extra tact to do a good job of criticizing your boss, particularly if he or she is a difficult person. An important guideline is to show how your boss's behavior, however well intended, is hampering your job performance. A case in point took place in a retail store chain.

> The loss-prevention managers in each store were supervised by a zone manager, who in many ways behaved in a counterproductive manner. One of his worst practices was to swear at loss-prevention managers (LPMs) when losses were above average at their store. One of the LPMs decided that she could no longer tolerate her boss's tirades. Confronting him after one of his verbal reprimands, she said calmly, "Cliff, when you swear and scream at me, it interferes with my ability to perform my job well. My records show that I make my biggest mistakes in counting inventory soon after you have screamed at me for something that is not even my fault." Cliff did temper his criticism in the future.

INTERPRETING THE GAMES OF COUNTERPRODUCTIVE PEOPLE

A considerable amount of game playing takes place on the job. A **game** is a repeated series of exchanges between people that appears different on the surface from its true underlying motive. A game always has a hidden agenda or purpose. The game player acts in a way that is superficially plausible, but there is a concealed motivation.

With a little practice, you can become sensitive to games that a counterproductive person might be playing. Once you think that you have his or her game pegged, you can confront that person with the game. The game player might then stop the game and deal with you more honestly. Dozen of appealing names have been given to games that people play frequently. Following are five games often observed on the job.

The Back Stab

The game of Back Stab involves a person pretending to be nice, but all the while planning to discredit or remove another person. A frequent form of backstabbing is to initiate a conversation with a rival about the weaknesses of a common boss, encouraging negative commentary and making careful notes of what the person says. When these comments are passed along to the boss, the rival appears disloyal and foolish. In addition to being a game, the back stab is a form of unethical office politics. During periods of downsizing, backstabbing becomes more frequent because some workers want to discredit others so the discredited worker will more than likely be laid off.

E-mail has become a medium for backstabbing. The sender of the message documents a mistake made by another individual and includes key people on the distribution list. A sample message sent by one team member to a rival began as follows: "Hi Alice. I'm sorry you couldn't make our important meeting. I guess you had some other important priorities. But we need your input on the following major agenda items we tackled . . . ." (The game here is that the sender of the e-mail message pretends to have the best interests of the recipient in mind, but is really attempting to damage his or her reputation.) Managers sometimes play Back Stab by praising an employee in his or her presence, yet bad-mouthing the person to others in the organization.[9]

Blemish

Blemish is a simple game to play and is often used by superiors to keep subordinates in line. All that is required is for the boss to find some small flaw in every assignment completed by subordinates. The game-playing boss stays one up with comments such as, "Marty, you did a great job on that report except for your conclusion. It just didn't seem to fit the body of the report."

A tactful rejoinder to this Blemish-playing boss might be, "I notice that you usually find one thing wrong with an otherwise acceptable job of mine. Is it your policy to always find at least one fault? Knowing the answer to this question would be very helpful to me in my work."

If It Weren't for That Other Person

A convenient way of avoiding responsibility for our errors is to find somebody else to blame. The person who habitually plays If It Weren't for That Other Person tries to con someone else into being sympathetic. A group member might say to you, "I'm sorry to let you down by being one hour late for work. If it weren't for that preposterous rush hour traffic, I would have been here before the office even opened."

One way of stopping such a game player (and a counterproductive individual) in his or her tracks is to retort, "You've been traveling the same route as long

The study of psychology can help you come to grips with the wide range of human problems encountered in any job. *Grant LeDuc/Monkmeyer Press*

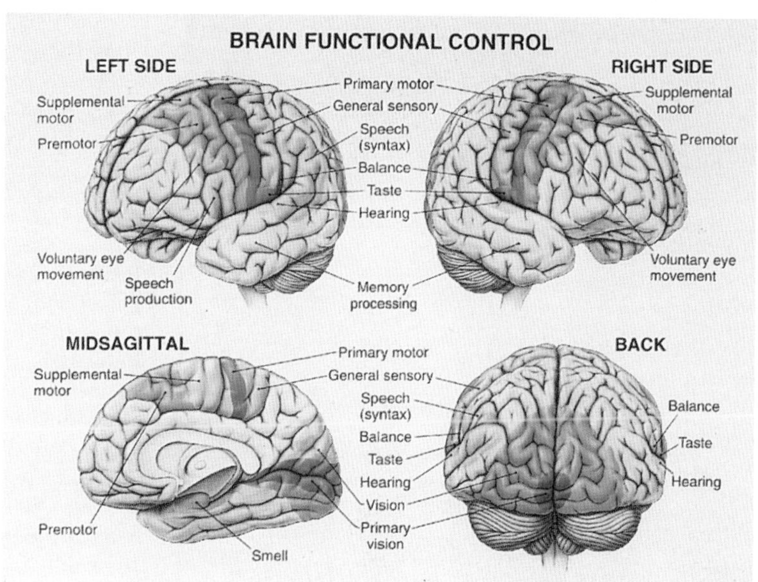

The vast majority of individual difference's among workers can be attributed to factors controlled by the brain, such as intellect and emotion. *MVI/Science Source/Photo Resaerchers*

People attending a meeting may interpret the presentation quite differently depending upon thier motovation, values, and intelligence.
Randy Matusow

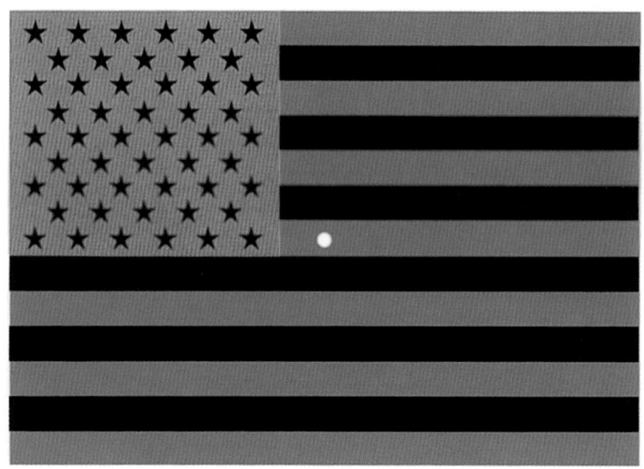

The brain plays an important role in perception. Stare at the dot in the center of the flag for approximately 30 seconds, until the colors begin to shimmer, and then stare at the dot in the center of the white rectangle. You should see a faint image of the U.S. flag as it normally appears - blinking once or twice helps if you do not see it at first. The colors of the afterimage are the complements of the original stimulus colors.

PART II Dealing with Individuals

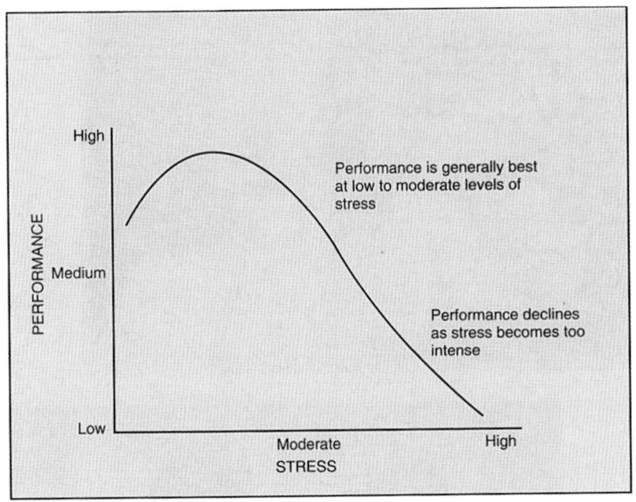

The short-term relationship between stress and job performance.

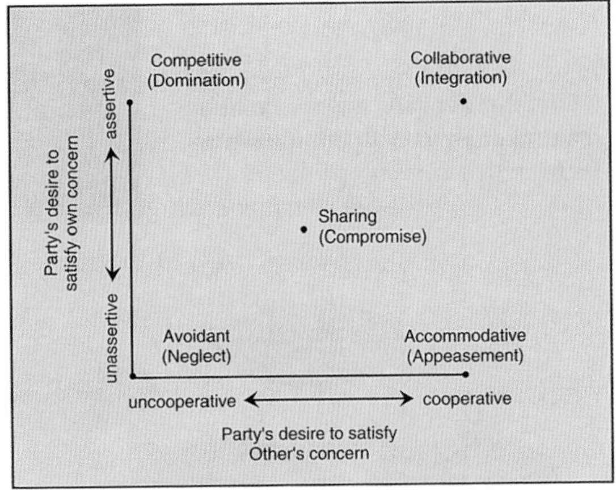

Conflict-handling styles according to degree of cooperation and assertiveness.

Physical fitness is an important part of achieving wellness, including being able to reduce and prevent job stress.
Michael Keller/FPG International

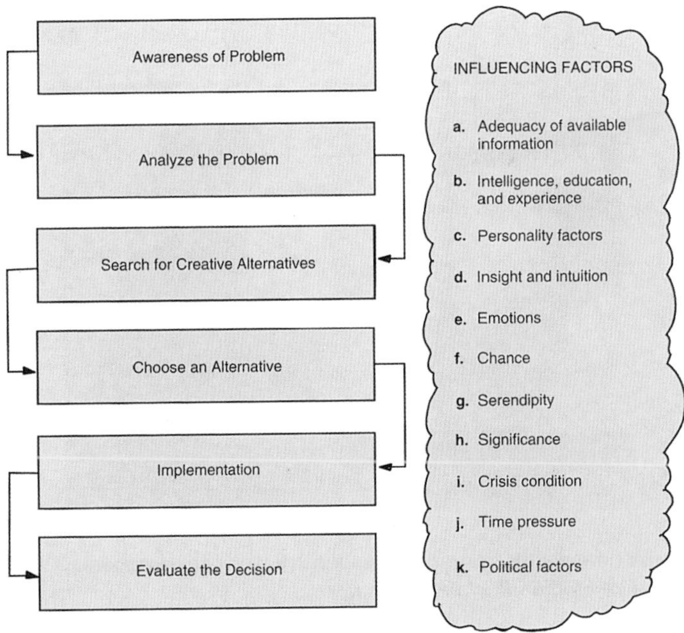

Stages in problem solving and decision making.

Effective decision makers combine careful analysis with intution when faced with a complex problem. *Dick Luria/FPG International*

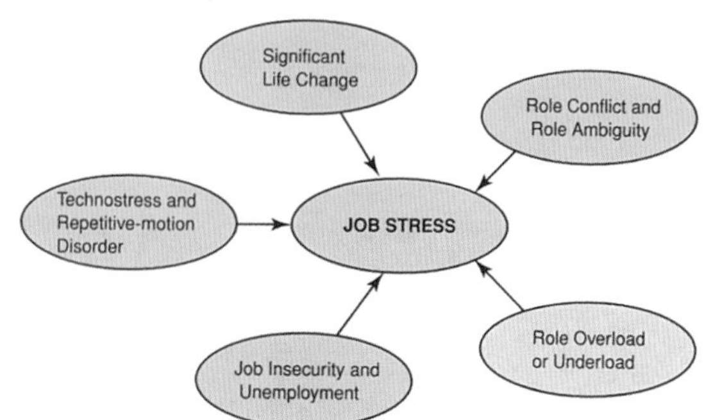

Frequently observed job stressors.

Goal setting is a standard way of increasing work productivity. *Ron Chapple/FPG International*

Conflict inevitably arises in a competitive work environment. *Ed Taylor Studio/FPG International*

People who use a win-win style of conflict resolution believe that both sides should gain something of value. *Ed Taylor Studio/FPG International*

PART III Personal Realationships on the Job

Informal interaction among workers often helps build better relationships that carry over to the job. *L.O.L. Inc./FPG International*

Adhering to the dress code and appearing professional are important parts of adjusting to the organization. *Mike Malyszko/ FPG International*

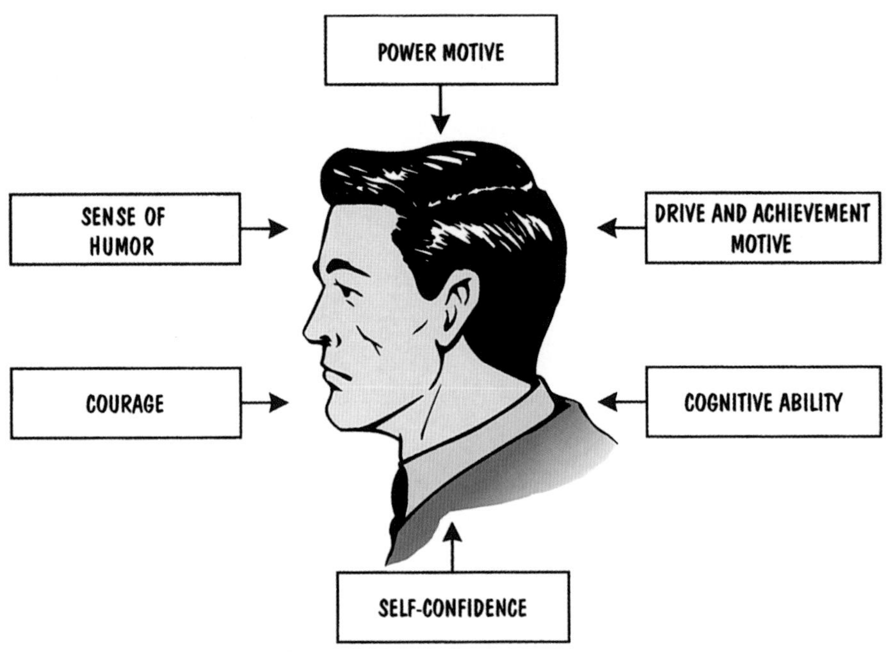

Portrait of a leader.

A charismatic and transformational leader can influence large numbers of people to pursue corporate objectives. *Spencer Grant/ Monkmeyer Press*

The vast majority of key decisions in organizations are group decisions. *Roger Dollarhide/Monkmeyer Press*

Communication barriers are likely to surface when the topic is both complex and emotional. *Blair Seiitz/Photo Researchers.*

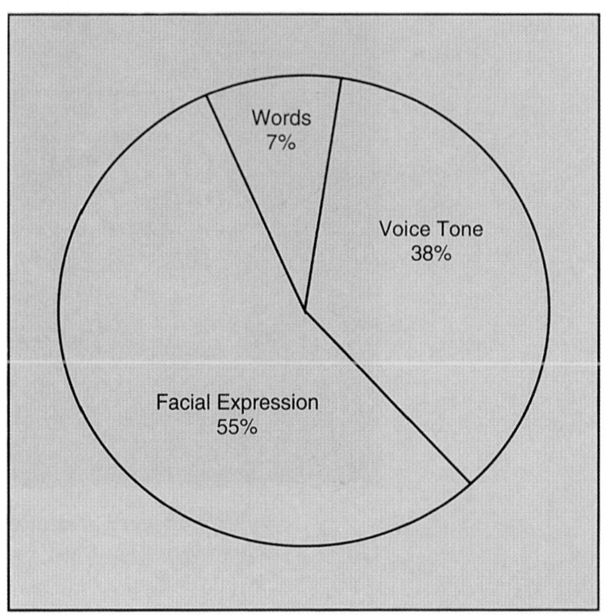

The emotional impact of messsages.

An important strategy for career advancement is to contribute outstanding job performance. *Arthur Tilley/FPG International*

A cluttered work area often lowers productivity, and creates a poor impression. *Telegraph Colour Library/FPG International*

as I've known you. Why don't you leave 30 minutes earlier? If you do arrive at the office early, you can read the paper and have a cup of coffee. Why blame the traffic for your lateness? Blame yourself."

The Setup

A very small minority of bosses like to see you fail. A technique they use is to set goals so unrealistically high for you that you are unlikely to reach them. Frustration and discouragement are the predictable results. Your boss can then criticize you for not reaching your objectives and for having a "poor attitude." Here is a portion of a review session where The Setup is being played:

Boss: I see that you only cut the cost of cleaning our guest rooms by 8 percent during the last six months. Your goal was to cut costs by 12 percent.

You: But with the increase in the state minimum wage, it was impossible to cut costs by 12 percent. I think the housekeepers did an enormous job of improving their productivity. I made all the savings I could find without letting service suffer by laying off staff.

Boss: Nevertheless, you failed to reach your objective. I therefore cannot recommend you for a good salary increase this year.

The best way around this type of game playing is to negotiate any unrealistic goals handed to you by your boss. If you think the goal is unrealistically high, carefully explain your position.

Dr. Jekyll and Mr. (or Ms.) Hyde

The Dr. Jekyll and Mr. (or Ms.) Hyde game refers to managers who have a split personality. When dealing with superiors, customers, or clients, they are pleasant, engaging people—much like Dr. Jekyll. Yet when carrying out the role of a manager they become tyrannical—much like Hyde. Sufferers of this syndrome believe that their need to be liked by group members is inconsistent with satisfying their needs for control and self-esteem in their new role.[10] The Jekyll and Hyde manager therefore works extra hard at gaining control of subordinates, hoping to achieve organizational objectives and therefore self-esteem in the process.

Employees who deviate from Hyde's expectations are publicly reprimanded. The basic strategy of these individuals is never to allow their Hyde side to be seen by superiors or peers. Consequently, higher-level managers and peers tend not to believe a group member who complains that this manager is being tyrannical.

It is difficult for a group member to deal with a Jekyll and Hyde manager because he or she can be vindictive. However, if several group members agree to bring the topic up in a group meeting, the manager might acquire some insight into his or her problem. As a last resort, several group members can agree to discuss the tyrannical behavior with Hyde's boss. Similarly, they might write a letter to the higher-level manager explaining the gravity of the problem.

BEING SYMPATHETIC TOWARD THE PERSONALITY QUIRKS OF COWORKERS

Both on and off the job, many people have personality quirks that make them difficult to deal with. A **personality quirk** is a persistent peculiarity of behavior that annoys or irritates other people. The manager is usually in the best position to help these people control their quirks so that job performance does not suffer. Often a human resources specialist will assist the manager in dealing with quirks.

Your best defense as a coworker is to show sympathy for employees with these quirks without submitting to all their demands. Be understanding even if you do not find all their behavior acceptable. When shown sympathy, the coworker with the quirk may shift to more tolerable behavior. Following are several of the more frequently observed personality quirks.[11]

The Uncivil Person. The uncivil person is insensitive to the point of rudeness and disregard for the rights and needs of others. He or she violates the workplace norms for mutual respect and cooperation. Incivility can take many forms including talking loudly outside a person's work area, sitting on another person's desk, and using foul language. As mentioned in regard to confrontation, the starting point in dealing with an uncivil person is to set expectations of what constitutes civil behavior. (Show a little sympathy, with a statement such as "I recognize you did not intentionally leave your waste paper on top of the copier, but it created a problem for me." At the same time, give specific feedback about what behavior you consider uncivil, and how it adversely affects your work or well-being.)

The Person Who Has a Strong Need to Always Be Correct. Employees with this quirk set up situations so that people who disagree with them are made to look naive or foolish. For example, "All well-educated and intelligent people believe as I do that this is the way we should go on this project. If anybody disagrees, please speak up now." The person with a strong need to be correct may also be a perfectionist, so the character trait is ingrained and difficult to change. (You can sympathize in this manner: "I recognize, Jennifer, that you research everything before reaching an opinion, and that you are usually right. Nevertheless, I want to point out another perspective on this problem.")

The Person Who Has a Strong Need for Attention. Attention seekers may shout louder than others, play the role of the office clown, or tell coworkers all their woes. The attention they seek can be positive as well as negative. To be noticed by others, attention seekers will often brag about even their smallest accomplishments. (You can sympathize in this manner: "We all know, Gus, that you like to occupy center stage. You do deserve our attention, but now it is Amy's turn to speak.")

The Rebel. A rebel resents control, direction, or advice from others. Employees with this quirk are so oversensitive to being controlled that they misinterpret hints as suggestions and orders as direct challenges to their intelligence and self-worth. Rebels complain a lot but infrequently take action to change the conditions that bother them. (You might express sympathy—yet still get through—to a coworker with this quirk by a statement such as this: "Carlos, I know you like to be your own person. I admire you for it, but I have a teeny suggestion that could strengthen the graphics you just put together." Rebels like to get involved in a tug of war, so it helps not to lose your temper when dealing with them.)

The Cynic with a Negative Attitude Toward Management. Workers with this quirk view everything management does as negative and also question every action in an attempt to uncover the true reason behind it. Rebels, also, are anti-management. The same cynics create doubts in other workers similar to the ones they exhibit, thereby contributing to morale problems. (You can sympathize with cynics and perhaps help them achieve insight into their behavior with a comment such as this: "I appreciate your analytical attitude Sarah, but did you ever think that management sometimes does something kind or generous? Is management really always the villain?" As with the rebel, it helps to ask the cynic to suggest a remedy for the problem he or she is complaining about.)

The Jealous Coworker. This person wants what you have and has feelings of ill will toward you. Jealousy can surface when several workers are competing for a promotion, bonus, or recognition from management. Because of his or her emotional turmoil, the jealous worker may attempt to discredit you.[12] (If you spot a jealous coworker, express sympathy toward his or her wanting what you have. Explain that yours is a fair company and good deeds will eventually be rewarded. Also mention that discrediting a coworker hurts the accuser's reputation.)

The Passive-Aggressive Coworker. A **passive-aggressive worker** typically becomes sulky, irritable, or forgetful when asked to do something against his or her will. A passive-aggressive personality expresses anger and hostility by not performing expected tasks. A personality of this type resents authority and craves better treatment. Yet he or she intensely dislikes direct conflict. Since passive-aggressiveness is a true personality disorder, such behavior is difficult to change. (Show some sympathy by explaining to the sulking person that you realize the task at hand is not something he or she relishes. Point out that, nevertheless, the project is a joint one that requires the effort of two people.)

The Chronic Complainer. Nearly every workplace has one or two chronic complainers: people who look for conditions to complain about. (You will recall that complainers can also be classified as a type of difficult person. The same is true for other personality quirks.) Unlike the personality quirk of complaining just about management, these people find fault with many people, policies, working conditions, and so forth. The chronic complainer is often a perfectionist who is rarely satisfied with anything. (You might sympathize with the chronic complainer by saying you, too, agree that everything is not perfect. Ask the complainer, "What would you do if you were in charge?" This might tempt the complainer to search for a constructive solution rather than merely complaining.)

The Joker. Laughter is an important contributor to the workplace, but when one person jokes most of the time, work and serious thought are disrupted. The behavior modification strategy of extinction is useful in dealing with the joker because the person does not get the reaction he or she wants. (You might show sympathy by telling the person you think he or she has a wonderful sense of humor. Also add something to the effect that "You should know that your frequent joke telling and outrageous remarks have become a distraction.")[13]

THE MOODY PERSON. Everyone has bad days, but the moody person has so many lows that he or she can bring other people down. A person with extreme mood swings may need the help of a mental health professional, but that is not your responsibility. What you are concerned about is that the person's poor moods make it difficult to gain his or her cooperation when you need help. (Show sympathy by acknowledging that the person is not having a good day. Make a simple observation such as, "You seem down."[14] Then specify what you need from the moody person even if your timing is not the best. Try a statement like, "I recognize today is not your best day, but we need your figures by 3 this afternoon.")

DEALING WITH DIFFICULT CUSTOMERS

In an era when customer satisfaction is so highly valued, customers are likely to be vocal in their demands because they know they have power. A personal reason for resolving issues with difficult customers is that faking emotion can lead to inner turmoil and stress. Alicia A. Grandey defines **emotional labor** as the process of regulating both feelings and expressions to meet organizational goals. The process involves both surface acting and deep acting. Surface acting means faking expressions such as smiling, whereas deep acting involves controlling feelings such as suppressing anger toward a customer whom you perceive to be uncivil. Sales workers and customer service representatives carry the biggest emotional labor among all workers because so often they have to fake facial expressions and feelings to please customers.[15]

In Chapter 9 we mentioned the importance of allowing an angry customer to "climb Mount Anger." When faced with an angry or difficult customer, you might also use the following techniques recommended by Donna Deeprose.[16]

1. *Acknowledge the customer's point of view.* Make statements such as "I understand," "I agree," and "I'm sorry." Assume, for example, that a customer says, "The bank made a $1,000 error in its favor. I want this fixed right away." You might respond, "I understand how difficult this must be for you. Let's work on the problem right away."
2. *Avoid placing blame.* Suggesting that the customer is responsible for the problem intensifies the conflict. With the overdrawn customer, refrain from saying, "People who keep careful checkbooks never have your problem."
3. *Use six magic words to defuse anger.* I understand [that this is a problem]; I agree [that it needs to be solved]; I'm sorry [that this happened to you].

In dealing with a variety of customer personalities, keep in mind also that any of the other techniques in this chapter might apply.

FOUR MULTIPURPOSE APPROACHES TO A VARIETY OF PERSONALITIES

Overcoming problems with a variety of personalities always involves selecting a plausible tactic and then hoping for the best. If the first attempt does not work, use a backup tactic. Four multipurpose tactics are described next that will improve your human relations effectiveness both with difficult people and those with more pleasant dispositions. The tactics involve the use of tact and diplomacy, humor, recognition and affection, and boosting the difficult person's self-confidence.

Use Tact and Diplomacy in Dealing with Annoying Behavior

Coworkers who irritate you rarely do annoying things on purpose. Tactful actions on your part can sometimes take care of these annoyances without having to confront the problem. Close your door, for example, if noisy coworkers are gathered outside. When subtlety does not work, it may be necessary to proceed to the confrontation tactics described earlier. Tact and diplomacy can also be incorporated into confrontation. In addition to confronting the person, you might also point out an individual's strength. For example, "I realize you are creative and filled with good ideas. However, I wish you would give me an opportunity to express my opinion."

Use Humor in Dealing with Difficult People

Nonhostile humor can often be used to help a difficult person understand how his or her behavior is blocking others. Also, the humor will help you to defuse conflict between you and that person. The humor should point to the person's unacceptable behavior, yet not belittle him or her. Assume that you and a coworker are working jointly on a report. Whenever you turn over a portion of your work for her to review, she finds some fault. You suspect she is playing Blemish. An example of nonhostile humor that might change her behavior here is:

> Judy, I know that you believe in zero defects and doing things right the first time. But aren't you worried about my mental health? I've read that striving for absolute perfection can create loads of stress.

Your humor may help Judy realize that she is placing unrealistic standards on her review of your work. By pointing to your own weaknesses, you are being self-effacing and thus drawing criticism away from her. In addition, self-effacement is a proven humor tactic.

Give Recognition and Affection

Counterproductive (or difficult) people, like misbehaving children, are sometimes crying out for attention. By giving them recognition and affection, their counterproductive behavior will sometimes cease. If their negative behavior is a product of a deeper-rooted problem, recognition and affection alone will not work. Other actions will need to be taken. The most direct strategy is to give the misbehaving individual attention and affection. If the negative behavior stops, you have found the proper antidote. The successful resolution of such a problem took place in a photo studio:

> Rich, one of the commercial photographers, had an annoying habit of interrupting the conversation of other people during staff meetings or with customers. In one instance during negotiations with an important customer, Rich blurted out, "I'm the local expert on nature photographs. If you want anything done along those lines, your best bet would be for me to shoot the job."
>
> Mandy, Rich's boss, then tried spending a few minutes each week telling Rich how great a photographer he was and how much the studio needed him (not a lie because Rich was talented and valuable). In addition, Mandy arranged for Rich to have some of his work put on display at a local photo show.
>
> Rich changed his behavior toward that of a more subdued and contented individual. In the words of one of his colleagues, "I can't understand what happened to Rich. He's become much easier to live with."

Help the Difficult Person Feel More Confident

Many counterproductive employees are simply low in self-confidence and self-efficacy. They use stalling and evasive tactics because they are afraid to fail. Working with your manager or team leader you might be able to arrange a project or task in which you know the difficult person will succeed. With a small dose of self-confidence and self-efficacy, the person may begin to complain less. With additional successes, the person may soon become less difficult.[17] As described in Chapter 4, self-confidence building takes time. However, self-efficacy can build more quickly as the person learns a new skill.

To help integrate some of the many ideas presented about dealing with a variety of personalities, do Skill-Building Exercise 10–1. The conflict-resolution skills you practiced in Chapter 9 should also be helpful in doing the exercise.

BRAIN STRUCTURE AND CHEMISTRY AND UNUSUAL BEHAVIOR

Most counterproductive job behavior is attributable to a combination of personality factors and situational pressures. For example, if an employee has high negative affectivity, he or she will be hostile toward others during a peak workload. It has been speculated that mood swings may also be related to brain structure and brain chemistry. In Chapter 3 we described how the top and bottom halves of the brain govern the intellect and emotions, respectively. In Chapter 5 we described how the two brain halves are related to differences in intellectual functioning. It is also possible that the brain hemispheres are specialized for different emotional experiences.[18] Here we look at four still tentative explanations of how brain structure and chemistry might prompt people toward difficult behavior in the workplace.

Depression and Brain Waves. An example of research attempting to link emotional experiences with brain hemispheres was conducted with college students. The students were given a test measuring emotional depression, and their brain

SKILL-BUILDING EXERCISE 10–1

Dealing with Difficult People

In both of the following scenarios, one student plays the role of a group member whose work and morale suffer because of a difficult person. The other student plays the role of the difficult person, who may lack insight into what he or she is doing wrong. It is important for the suffering person to put emotion into the role.

Scenario 1: The Dictator. A dictator is present at a meeting called to plan a morale-boosting company event. Several students play the role of the group members. One student plays the role of a group member who suggests that the event center around doing a social good such as refurbishing a poor family's house or conducting a neighborhood cleanup. Another student plays the role of a dictator who thinks the idea is a bummer. The group member being intimidated decides to deal effectively with the dictator.

Scenario 2: A No-Person. One student plays the role of a worker with a lot of creative energy whose manager is a no-person. The energetic worker has what he or she thinks is a wonderful way for the company to generate additional revenue—conduct a garage sale of surplus equipment and furnishings. The worker presents these ideas to the no-person manager, played by another student. If the manager acts true to form, the worker will attempt to overcome his or her objections.

waves were measured by EEGs. The more depressed students had more electrical activity in the brain's right frontal region, suggesting that the right hemisphere plays a special role in depressed feelings.

Brain Injury and Emotional Brakes. Another tie-in may exist between the status of the brain and negative emotions. A neuropsychologist has speculated that under normal circumstances, mood fluctuations are consistent with what is happening in our lives. However, anything that jars that neural system, such as brain injury or a severe emotional loss, is likely to release negative emotions. According to this theory, the depressed person lacks the "brakes" to stop the flood of negative emotion. The counterproductive behavior of a worker could then in some instances be attributed to a brain injury caused by physical or emotional trauma.

The Role of Both Hemispheres. Another theory of how the brain is linked to emotion suggests that either hemisphere can be involved in pleasant or unpleasant emotions. Yet each hemisphere has its special linkages. The left hemisphere is involved with emotional states characterized by alert expectation—positive ones such as happy anticipation and negative ones such as anxious worry. In contrast, the right hemisphere is involved with more reflective emotional states—positive ones such as relaxed awareness and negative ones such as depression.

Brain Chemistry (Dopamine and Serotonin). A plausible explanation for some types of negative behavior in the workplace is that people who exhibit such behavior are deficient in key brain chemicals. One such chemical is dopamine, a neurotransmitter that is associated with euphoria, sleeplessness, loss of appetite, and a surge of motivation. (A neurotransmitter is a chemical substance that transmits nerve impulses across the nerve connections called synapses.) In addition to feeling happier, people with high levels of dopamine are also more goal directed and able to concentrate better. Instead of complaining so much, they are more likely to focus on job tasks. As explained in Chapter 5, dopamine is released by exciting experiences, as well as by a variety of drugs and chocolate. If high levels of dopamine were always associated with a pleasant disposition, management could curb difficult behavior by handing out chocolate bars!

Serotonin is a master transmitter associated with tranquillity, reason, and calmness. Antidepressant medication, such as Prozac, works by keeping serotonin levels high. Many grumpy workers (such as the no-person) might be less negative in their outlook if they had higher levels of serotonin in their brains.

Assume that some moodiness among workers can be traced to differences in brain structure and chemistry. Dealing with their behavior becomes more difficult, but it is not impossible. Behavior that is related to brain structure or chemistry can still be modified or controlled, just as people who are left-brain dominant can learn to become more creative.

SUMMARY OF KEY POINTS

- Counterproductive (or difficult) people are found in most places of work and also include customers. Such people include those who are uncooperative, touchy, defensive, hostile, unfriendly, and substandard performers. The difficult employee is not necessarily of low intelligence or ability.
- A key principle for dealing with a variety of personalities is to take what they do professionally, not personally. This is true because for a difficult person you may just represent an obstacle or a steppingstone for them to get what they want.
- A major aspect of dealing with counterproductive people is to confront them with the job-related consequences of their behavior. Confrontation is difficult for most people because it makes them feel uncomfortable. Suggestions for effective confrontation include these: (1) know what constitutes acceptable behavior, (2) attempt to relax during the session, (3) quickly get to the core topic, (4) avoid being apologetic or defensive, (5) be nonhostile in your confrontation, (6) confront job-related behavior, not personal traits, characteristics, and motives, and (7) show that you care.
- Criticism and confrontation are both part of the same process of trying to get other people to change their behavior. Criticizing difficult people is especially challenging because they are usually defensive. Suggestions for constructive criticism include: (1) be sensitive to the setting, (2) begin with mild criticism, (3) base the criticism on objective facts, (4) express criticism in terms of a common goal, (5) avoid playing boss, and (6) when criticizing your boss, show how the behavior is interfering with your work performance.
- Another approach to dealing with counterproductive people is to interpret their games. A game is a repeated series of transactions between people with a concealed motive. The five described here are: The Back Stab (pretending to be nice but discrediting the person to others); Blemish (finding flaws in another's work); If It Weren't for That Other Person (blaming somebody else); The Setup

GUIDELINES FOR PERSONAL EFFECTIVENESS

Corporate training director Donald H. Weiss advises that after you identify the problem with a difficult person, engage the person in a discussion that follows these four steps:

First, set the other person at ease by talking in private. State the meeting's purpose in nonthreatening terms, and show that you want to work with the person on the problem by using "we" rather than "you" statements.

Second, exchange viewpoints by first listening to the other person's proposed solution to the problem.

Third, if you don't agree, state your opinion concisely and clearly. Attempt to resolve the disagreement by exchanging viewpoints again.

Fourth, design an action plan for ending the difficulty. Set deadlines and dates for reviewing progress in overcoming the difficulty the person has created for you.[19]

(setting somebody up to fail); and Jekyll and Hyde (a person who is polite to higher-level managers and coworkers but tyrannical as a team leader).

- Being sympathetic toward the personality quirks of coworkers without submitting to all their demands is another approach to dealing with a variety of personalities. A personality quirk is a persistent peculiarity of behavior that annoys or irritates others, such as resenting control, direction, or advice. Personality quirks include incivility, a need to be correct, a strong need for attention, rebelliousness, cynicism, jealousy, passive-aggressive behavior, chronic complaining, excessive joking, and moodiness.
- Three tactics are suggested for dealing with difficult customers: (1) acknowledge the customer's point of view, (2) avoid placing blame on the customer, and (3) say "I understand," "I agree," and "I'm sorry."
- A multipurpose approach to dealing with difficult people and improving your human relations skills in general is to use tact and diplomacy, humor, recognition and affection, and self-confidence building.
- Most counterproductive behavior is attributable to a combination of personality factors and situational pressures. However, mood swings and other emotional states might also be related to brain structure. Among these speculative findings are the following: (1) The right hemisphere of the brain is linked to depressed feelings. (2) When the brain is physically or psychologically traumatized, it loses its capacity to brake negative emotions. (3) The left hemisphere is involved with emotional states of alert expectation, and the right hemisphere with more reflective emotional states. (4) Workers with negative dispositions might be deficient in the neurotransmitters called dopamine and serotonin.

DISCUSSION QUESTIONS AND ACTIVITIES

1. Identify three or more personality traits described in the previous chapters that could predispose an employee toward being a difficult person.
2. Prepare a memo of 25 words or less informing managers how to deal with difficult people.
3. In what way might the variety of personalities described in this chapter lower productivity?

4. Work individually or in teams to identify 10 examples of uncivil behavior found in the workplace.

5. Suppose a coworker is rude toward you. How can you relate this rudeness to objective facts, rather than a subjective interpretation?

6. How might an employee bring about harm to company property through passive-aggressive behavior?

7. In what way does backstabbing in the workplace qualify as a game?

8. What is the purpose of showing sympathy toward a coworker with a personality quirk?

9. Should difficult employees still be held responsible for their actions, even if their problem might be related to a brain condition?

10. Obtain the opinion of an experienced worker about what he or she perceives to be the most difficult type of person in the workplace. Relate this perception to the categories of difficult people described in this chapter.

REFERENCES

1. Christine M. Pearson, Lynne M. Andersson, and Christine L. Porath, "Assessing and Attacking Workplace Incivility," *Organizational Dynamics,* Fall 2000, p. 123.
2. A representative scheme is presented in Muriel Solomon, *Working with Difficult People* (Upper Saddle River, NJ: Prentice Hall, 1991).
3. "Help! I'm Surrounded by Difficult People," *Working Smart,* March 25, 1991, p. 2.
4. Dru Scott, *Customer Satisfaction: The Other Half of Your Job* (Los Altos, CA: Crisp Publications, 1991), p. 16.
5. Gary G. Whitney, "When the News Is Bad: Leveling with Employees," *Personnel,* January–February 1983, pp. 37–45; Dot Yandle, "Incivility: Has it Gone Too Far to Fix?" *Pryor Report/Success Workshop,* March 1997, p. 1.
6. Quoted in Priscilla Petty, "Shortest Route to Good Communication Is Often a Straight Question," Gannett News Service, October 18, 1983.
7. Hendrie Weisinger and Norma M. Lobsenz, *Nobody's Perfect: How to Give Criticism and Get Results* (New York: Warner Books, 1981), p. 204.
8. Weisinger and Lobsenz, *Nobody's Perfect,* p. 214.
9. Anne Fisher, "Is My Salary Too Low? . . . Do I Whack That Backstabber? . . . And Other Queries," *Fortune,* March 3, 1997, pp. 177–178.
10. Eric Flamholtz, "The Dr. Jekyll and Mr. Hyde Game Managers Play," *Management Solutions,* November 1987, pp. 4–9.
11. Michael E. Cavanagh, "Personalities at Work," *Personnel Journal,* March 1985, pp. 55–64; Pearson, Andersson, and Porath, "Assessing and Attacking Workplace Incivility," p. 133; James Waldroop and Timothy Butler, "Managing Away Bad Habits," *Harvard Business Review,* September–October 2000, pp. 95–96; Jospeh D. O'Brian, "Declawing the Chronic Complainer," *Supervisory Management,* June 1993, pp. 1–2; Timothy D. Schellhardt, "How to Handle Those Nightmare Employees," The *Wall Street Journal,* October 16, 1996, p. B1.
12. Teresa Brady, "When a Jealous Coworker is Giving You a Hard Time," *Supervisory Management,* June 1991, p. 5.
13. "Silencing Compulsive Jokers," *Executive Strategies,* June 1997, p. 2.

AN APPLIED PSYCHOLOGY CASE PROBLEM

Critical Carrie of the Claims Department

Carrie Donahoe is one of five claims examiners in a regional office of a large casualty and property insurance company. The branch is still thriving despite the insurer selling many policies online, and billing conducted by a centralized office. The sales group sells policies and services to already existing business such as consulting with managers and business owners about upgrading their policies. The sales representatives also answer questions about policies, such as questions about whether the policy owner is covered against a terrorist attack.

Carrie works with four other examiners, as well as her supervisor Michelle Pettigrew. The essential job of the claims examiner is to visit the site of a client with a demand for reimbursement for damages such as a fire, flood, or industrial accident. The claims examiner then files a report with a recommendation for payment that is reviewed by the examiner's supervisor. Also, the home office reviews estimated payments beyond $15,000. Carrie has held her position for five years. She has received satisfactory performance evaluations, particularly for the accuracy and promptness of her insurance claim reports.

Carrie has frequent negative interactions with her coworkers who resent many of her suggestions and criticisms. Jim, a senior claims analyst, says his nickname for Carrie is "Ms. Pit Bull," although he has not shared this nickname with her. Asked why he refers to Carrie as a pit bull, he replied, "It's not that Carrie physically attacks people, but it's that she's so negative about so many things. I'll give you two recent examples:

"Carrie asked me to show her a sample claims report for mud damage. I e-mailed her a report. Two days later she sent me back the report, underlining six words or phrases she said were wrong. She didn't even thank me for the report.

"I came back from a two-day trip to inspect a building damaged by a runaway truck. When I returned to the office, Carrie asked me why it took me two days to investigate a simple claim."

Sharon, a junior claims examiner, says that at her best Carrie is a charming coworker. Yet at her worst, she grates on people's nerves. "Here's what I'm talking about. Last week I came to work wearing a blue skirt and a red blouse, on a day the Vice President of Claims was coming to visit our office. Carrie tells me that a person should never wear a red-and-blue combination for a special event. Not only is Carrie critical, her criticisms are sometimes way off base.

"Another time she told me that I should not waste my time studying for advanced certification in claims because it's a waste of time. She said that no manager in the company really cares about certification. Either you can do your job or you can't."

A human resource specialist from the home office asked Michelle Pettigrew how she was handling Carrie's personality clashes with coworkers as well as with her personally. Michelle said that she was mildly concerned about Carrie's personality problems, but that Carrie still gets her work done. Yet Michelle did mention that several clients indicated that Carrie surprised them with some of her criticisms of their operation. She told one tool-and-die shop owner that a well-managed firm never has a serious accident. That was the company's first claim in 50 years being insured by us.

"When she's snippy with me, I just shrug it off unless it gets too personal. Then I tell Carrie that she's gone too far. Like a week ago she told me that I don't do a good job of getting enough resources for our branch. That if I were a strong branch manager, we would have our offices refurbished by now. I told Carrie that our conversation was now over."

The human resources director said to Michelle, "I think you and I should talk about effective ways of dealing with Carrie and her problems."

Questions

1. What do you recommend that Michelle Pettigrew do to improve Carrie's interpersonal relationships in the office?
2. What is your evaluation of Michelle's approach to dealing with Carrie so far?
3. What do you recommend that Carrie's coworkers do to develop more harmonious relationships with her?

 AN APPLIED PSYCHOLOGY CASE PROBLEM

The Nightmare in the Logistics Department

Larry Smits was happy to join the distribution department of his company as a logistics specialist. His position centered around keeping track of shipments to customers and from vendors. A distribution specialist works extensively with computers to track shipments, but part of the job description involves telephone and face-to-face contact with company insiders and outsiders. As Larry enthusiastically explained his new job to his girlfriend, "Here's a great opportunity for me. I'll be using a sophisticated software system, and I'll have lots of contact with a variety of people. I'll be talking to marketing executives, purchasing agents, truckers, package-delivery people, and office assistants. Equally good, I'll be learning about a very important part of the business. If the company doesn't ship goods to customers, we can't collect money. And if we don't receive shipments of supplies that we need, we can't produce anything ourselves."

During the first four months on the job, Larry's enthusiasm continued. The job proved to be as exciting as he anticipated. Larry got along well with all his coworkers and developed his closest friendship with Rudy Bianchi, a senior distribution specialist. Rudy said that since he had several more years of experience than Larry, he would be willing to help him with any job problem he encountered. One day Larry took Rudy up on his offer. Larry was having a little difficulty understanding how to verify the accuracy of tariffs paid to several European countries. Part of Larry's job was to make sure the company was paying its fair share of tariffs, but no more than necessary. Larry sent Rudy an e-mail message asking for clarification on three tariff questions. Rudy answered promptly and provided Larry with useful information.

When Larry next saw Rudy in person during lunch, he thanked him again for the technical assistance. "No problem," said Rudy. "I told you that I'm always willing to help a buddy. By sharing knowledge, we multiply our effectiveness." Larry detected a trace of insincerity in Rudy's message, but later thought he might be overreacting to Rudy's colorful way of expressing himself.

Several days later Larry was reviewing a work assignment with his supervisor, Ellie Wentworth. She said to him, "How are you coming along with the problems you were having understanding how to verify tariffs? That's a key part of your job, you know." Larry explained to Wentworth that he wasn't having any real problems, but that he had asked for clarification on a couple of complicated rates. He also pointed out that he quickly obtained the clarification he needed. Larry thought to himself, "Oh, I guess Ellie must have misinterpreted a comment by Rudy about my clarifying a few tariff rates with him. I doubt Rudy would have told our boss that I was having trouble. Why should I be paranoid?"

One week later Rudy stopped by Larry's cubicle. At the moment, Larry had the classified ad section of the Los Angeles Times on his desk. "Are you job hunting, Larry? You're a rising star in our department. Why look elsewhere?"

"I'm not job hunting," said Larry. "I was just curious to see what kind of demand exists for logistics specialists. It's just part of my interest in the field. It's reassuring to know we're part of a growing profession."

"That's a great answer," said Rudy. "I was just pulling your chain a little anyway."

A week later Ellie was reviewing some work assignments with Larry. As the discussion about the work assignment was completed, Ellie said, "I think highly of how you are progressing in your job Larry, but I want to make sure of one thing. Before we give you another major assignment, I want to know if you are happy in your job. If for any reason, you are planning to leave the company, please let us know now."

"What are you talking about?" said Larry with a puzzled expression. "I intend to be with the company for a long, long time. I can't imagine what gave you the impression that I am not happy here."

As Larry left the office, he was furious. He began to wonder if someone were spreading malicious rumors about him. He muttered silently, "It couldn't be Rudy. He's supposed to be my friend, my mentor. But I have to get to the root of this problem. I feel like I'm being sabotaged."

Questions

1. What devious technique might Rudy, or another coworker, be using against Larry?
2. What motivation might a coworker have for raising questions about Larry's job knowledge and loyalty to the company?
3. How should Larry deal with his suspicions?
4. How effectively has Ellie dealt with her two concerns about Larry?

14. "Handle Moody Employees," *Executive Strategies,* July 2000, p. 6.

15. Alicia A. Grandey, "Emotion Regulation in the Workplace: A New Way to Conceptualize Emotional Labor," *Journal of Occupational Health Psychology* 5, no. 1, 2000, pp. 95–110.

16. Donna Deeprose, "Helping Employees Handle Difficult Customers," *Supervisory Management,* September 1991, p. 6. Point three is quoted from Deeprose, p. 6.

17. "How to Deal with 'Problem' Workers," *Positive Leadership,* sample issue distributed 2001.

18. Laurence Miller, "The Emotional Brain," *Psychology Today,* February 1988, pp. 34–42; Deborah Blum, "The Plunge of Pleasure," *Psychology Today,* September–October 1997, pp. 46–49.

19. Donald H. Weiss, "How to Deal with Unpleasant People Problems," *Supervisory Management,* March 1992, pp. 1–2.

SUGGESTED READING

Bernstein, Albert J., and Rozen, Craft Sydney. *Dinosaur Brains: Dealing with All Those Impossible People at Work.* New York: Wiley, 1989.

Carter, Stephen L. *Civility: Manners, Morals, and the Etiquette of Democracy.* New York: Basic Books, 1998.

Giacalone, Robert, and Greenberg, Jerald. *Antisocial Behavior in Organizations.* Newbury Park, CA: Sage Publications, 1997.

Grensing-Pophal, Lin. "High-Maintenance Employees." *HR Magazine,* February 2001, pp. 86–91.

Grote, Dick. *Discipline without Punishment: The Problem Strategy That Turns Problem Employees into Superior Performers.* New York: AMACOM, 1995.

Oldham, John. *The New Personality Self-Portrait.* New York: Bantam, 2000.

Parrott, Lee. *The Control Freak.* New York: Tyndale, 1999.

Ury, William. *Getting Past No: Negotiating with Difficult People.* New York: Bantam Books, 1991.

Wild, Russell. *Games Bosses Play.* Chicago: Contemporary Books, 1997.

WEB CORNER

www.freemaninstitute.com/openltr.htm ("Dealing with Difficult People Who Drive You Crazy!")

CHAPTER 11

COMMUNICATING WITH PEOPLE

Learning Objectives

After reading and studying this chapter and doing the exercises, you should be able to

1. Describe the steps in the communication process.
2. Explain the difference between formal and informal communication channels.
3. Identify the major types of nonverbal communication.
4. Develop tactics for overcoming communication barriers, including cross-cultural and gender differences.
5. Explain what needs to be done to become a more persuasive communicator.
6. Know how to improve your listening and telephone communication skills.

Changes in the workplace are pressuring workers to become heightened communicators and information managers who are skilled in sorting and setting priorities to messages. Workers must also work with different technologies and communicate directly with people. A study showed that employees at all levels choose among the 16 different communication tools listed in Table 11–1.[1] A thorough understanding of communications in the workplace can prevent problems such as misunderstood directions and improve productivity by helping to reduce wasted time and effort. Understanding how to communicate effectively is also important for obtaining a good job and advancing your career.

STEPS IN THE COMMUNICATION PROCESS

Communication is the sending, receiving, and understanding of messages. It is also the basic process by which managers and professionals accomplish their work. The purpose of communication is to gather, process, and disseminate information.

TABLE 11–1
TOOLS OF COMMUNICATION

◈ Computer	◈ Pager
◈ Post-Its	◈ E-mail and instant messaging
◈ Express mail	◈ Internet
◈ Telephone	◈ Voice mail
◈ Overnight couriers	◈ Fax
◈ Cellular telephones	◈ World Wide Web
◈ Interoffice and intraoffice mail	◈ Message slips
◈ Information-sharing software	◈ Spoken messages

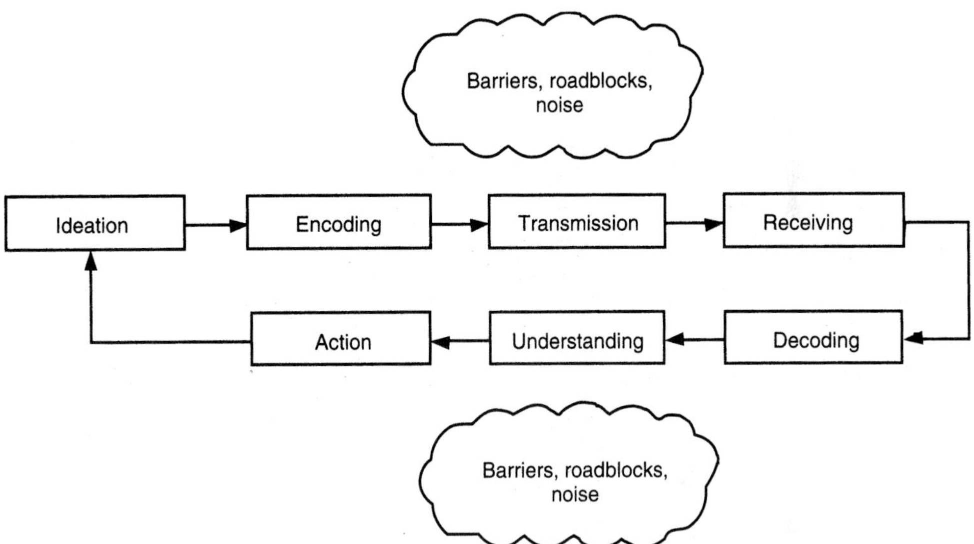

FIGURE 11–1 Steps in the Communication Process

A convenient starting point in understanding how people communicate is to examine the steps involved in the transmission and reception of a message. The process involves the following sequence of events: ideation, encoding, transmission over a medium, receiving, decoding, understanding, and finally taking action. The clouds above and below the diagram in Figure 11–1 symbolize barriers to communication (noise, roadblocks, and so forth) that can take place at any stage in communication. Later in the chapter we will deal with the challenge of overcoming major barriers to communication.

The communication process is cyclical. Upon decoding a message, understanding it, and then taking action, the receiver sends out his or her own message. The cycle is thus repeated at least once. Assume that Conrad wishes to communicate to his manager, Barbara, that he wants a salary increase.

Step 1: *Ideation.* Conrad organizes his thoughts about this sensitive problem. This stage is both the origin and the framing of the idea or message in the sender's mind. Conrad says to himself, "I think I'll ask for a raise."

Step 2: *Encoding.* Here the ideas are organized into a series of symbols such as words, hand gestures, body movements, or drawings. The symbols are designed to communicate to the intended receiver. Conrad says, "Barbara, there is something I would like to talk to you about if you have the time."

Step 3: *Transmission.* The message is transmitted orally, in writing, or non-verbally. In this situation, the sender chose the oral mode.

Step 4: *Receiving.* The other party receives the message. Barbara can receive the message only if she pays attention to Conrad.

Step 5: *Decoding.* The symbols sent by the sender to the receiver are decoded. In this case, decoding is not complete until Barbara hears the whole message. The opening comment, "Barbara, there is something I would like to talk to you about . . . ," is the type of statement often used by employees to broach a sensitive topic, such as discussing a resignation or salary increase. Barbara therefore listens attentively for more information.

Step 6: *Understanding.* Decoding should lead to understanding. Barbara has no trouble understanding that Conrad wants a salary increase. When communication barriers exist, understanding may be limited.

Step 7: *Action and Feedback.* Understanding sometimes leads to action. Barbara understands Conrad's request, but she does not agree. She acts by telling Conrad that he will have to wait three more months until his salary will be reviewed. Action is also a form of feedback, because it results in a message being sent back to the original sender from the receiver.

The action step in communication has an important practical implication. After sending a message, you will often have to follow up to see whether action has been taken. Following up your message measures whether your message has been understood. The follow-up also serves as a prompt or motivator to achieve the action. Effective communication involves much more than delivering a message and waiting for the desired action to take place.

FORMAL AND INFORMAL COMMUNICATION PATHWAYS

Communication between and among people in the workplace travels in several directions. Some messages are sent downward, as from top-level management to workers. Others are sent upward, as from an entry-level worker sending an e-mail message to a vice president. People also communicate horizontally, as from one coworker to another. In addition to traveling in more than one direction, messages are sent over both formal and informal pathways.

Formal Communication Pathways

The official path over which a message is supposed to travel is referred to as the **formal communication pathway.** Assume that an office assistant in a sales office has an idea that she thinks would improve sales—selling over the Internet (or

E-Commerce). The formal pathway for her message might be as follows: office assistant → sales manager → regional marketing manager → vice president of marketing → CEO. If the assistant used formal channels, her message would have to follow the formal chain of command, or the path dictated by the organization structure. In a less traditional organization, the assistant might simply use e-mail to transmit her suggestion to top management. However, even in the modern organization an office assistant in a branch sales office would be unlikely to drop in unannounced to the CEO's office and present her suggestion.

An example of a formal communication pathway used to resolve employee problems is the **open-door policy.** According to this policy, any employee can bring a gripe to higher-level management's attention without checking with his or her immediate manager. The open-door policy is popular as a grievance procedure because it allows problems to be settled quickly. The open-door system works the best when the manager is a good listener, including welcoming the grievant with a smile and maintaining eye contact.[2]

A significant feature of formal communication pathways is that they are sometimes casual and relaxed. An organizational practice of relaxed formal communication is to conduct conversations at the start of the workday. For example, at PQ Systems of Dallas, Texas, all 40 employees meet in the company's training room and sit in a large circle. The gathering lasts anywhere from 10 to 30 minutes, while the employees talk openly about everything from the company's financial condition to new-product development to significant developments in the family lives of employees. The sessions help connect the workers to each other emotionally.[3]

Informal Communication Pathways

The paths by which messages travel from person to person are more numerous than those designated by the organization chart and other formal communication pathways. An **informal communication pathway** is an unofficial network of communications used to supplement a formal pathway. Many of these pathways arise out of necessity. For example, employees may consult with someone outside their department to solve a technical problem. Another important fact about informal pathways is that they account for some of the most baffling communication problems. A good way of gaining insight into these pathways is to study the grapevine, the rumors it carries, gossip (everybody's favorite topic), and chance encounters.

The Grapevine. The **grapevine** is the major informal communication channel in an organization. The term refers to the tangled branches or wires that can distort information. Yet there are times when information transmitted along the grapevine is accurate. The speed with which messages travel along the grapevine is legendary, as indicated by the comments of Allen Zaremba.[4]

> Many messages travel along the grapevine at an extremely rapid pace. This innate speed can pose some serious organizational problems. Rumors spread quickly and inaccurate information can move throughout a large organization in a matter of hours. Incorrect information is tough to stall once it begins to travel. As a British politician once said, "A lie can be half-way around the world before the truth has its boots on."

The grapevine is sometimes used deliberately by management to transmit information that it may not wish to transmit formally. One example would be to feed the grapevine with the news that salary increases will be very small this year. When increases turn out to be average, most employees will be satisfied. A related use of the grapevine is to measure the reaction of employees to an announcement before it is transmitted through formal channels. If the reaction is too bad, management can sometimes modify its plans, such as not going ahead with a program of shortening vacations.

RUMORS. A **rumor** is a message transmitted over the grapevine, although not based on official word. The message can be true or false. An important problem with rumors is that they are capable of disrupting work and lowering morale. A dress company in Brooklyn found itself the victim of an untrue rumor that created morale problems during its peak season. A disgruntled employee started the rumor that the company had formalized plans to subcontract its dressmaking to a company in Pakistan. Consequently, most of the workforce would be laid off after this season. When the owner learned of the problem, he held a companywide meeting to dispel the rumor.

Another problem with rumors is that participating in or not controlling the office grapevine can result in a legal liability. A frequent source of liability is defamation of character, in oral form (slander) or written form (libel). Such liability takes place when one worker communicates something that is not true to a third party without any kind of privilege to do so, such as being an attorney or physician. Even if you are only passing along a rumor told to you by another person, you can still be held liable.[5] An example of a slanderous rumor would be, "I heard from a good source that Bill is facing charges of income tax fraud."

Preventive measures are the most effective strategy for managing rumors. Management should be alert to situations that promote rumors. Among them are when employees are confused about what is happening and information is unclear, incomplete, or lacking, and when there is excessive anxiety and conflict present in the workplace.[6] Despite these preventive measures, there may be times when management or an individual has to combat a potentially harmful rumor. Here are several things that can be done:

- A key strategy is to *structure uncertainty,* or clarify ideas about uncertain events. If rumors are rampant about changes in the organization, state the procedures by which the upcoming changes will be decided. For example, explain that members of senior management will confer with other managers to decide which workers will be offered early retirement.
- Enhance formal communication about changes because employees seek more information during times of intense rumors. Keep open formal channels of communication and encourage employees to use them. ("Call my assistant for an appointment any time you want to see me, about anything you think is important.") In some cases it might be necessary to confirm the rumor, such as admitting that a particular product will soon be manufactured overseas resulting in the loss of some domestic jobs.[7]
- As a countermeasure, feed the grapevine with actual information to get the facts through informal communication channels. At the same time, formal channels of communication should not be neglected. If the rumor is of grave enough consequences, have members of top management meet with small groups of employees to place matters in proper perspective.

- It is sometimes advisable to wait out the rumor because it may run its course before doing too much damage.[8]

Gossip. A special form of rumor is **gossip,** the idle talk or tidbits of information about people that are passed along informal communication channels. We all know that gossip can hurt reputations, cause personal pain, and it wastes time (it is often the raw material for schmoozing). E-mail has facilitated the spread of gossip, including destructive comments about other workers. Negative gossip is the most prevalent in companies where employees compete heavily against each other for promotions and bonuses.[9] Yet gossip also serves a number of useful purposes on the job. It can be a morale booster, a socializing force, a guidebook to group norms, and an expression of employee concerns.

Gossip can improve morale by adding spice and variety to the job. It may even make some highly repetitive jobs bearable. In an increasingly technological and depersonalized workplace, gossip may be an important humanizing factor. Gossip serves as a socializing force because it is a mode of intimate relationship for many employees. People get close to each other through the vehicle of gossip.

Gossip acts as a guidebook because it informs employees of the real customs, values, and ethics of the work environment. For instance, a company might state formally that no employee can accept a gift of over $30 from a supplier. Gossip may reveal, however, that some employees are receiving expensive gifts from suppliers. Furthermore, the company makes no serious attempts to stop the practice.

Gossip is an important barometer of employee concerns. Gossip is an important way for employees to express anger or fear. As one human resources specialist notes, "In the case of organizational changes such as mergers and acquisitions, gossip can dilute the shock factor." Employees mutually support each other and share the experience, thereby reducing some stress.[10]

A new perspective is that being a source of positive gossip brings a person power and credibility. Workmates are eager to communicate with a person who is a source of not-yet-verified developments. Having such inside knowledge enhances your status and makes you a more interesting communicator. Positive gossip would include such tidbits as mentioning that the company will be looking for workers who would want a one-year assignment in Europe, or that more employees will soon be eligible for stock options. In contrast, spreading negative gossip will often erode your attractiveness to people.[11]

Chance Encounters. Another informal channel of significance is chance encounters. Unscheduled informal contact between managers and employees can be an efficient and effective communication channel. John P. Kotter found that effective managers do not confine their communication to formal meetings. Instead, they collect valuable information during chance encounters.[12] Spontaneous communication events may occur in the cafeteria, near the water fountain, in the halls, in the company fitness room, and on the elevator. In just two minutes the manager might obtain the information that would typically be solicited in a 30-minute meeting or through a series of e-mail exchanges. To increase the chances that a spontaneous encounter will be a rich communication event, the manager can simply ask, "How are things going?"

NONVERBAL COMMUNICATION IN THE WORKPLACE

Our discussion so far has emphasized the use of words, or verbal communication. However, a substantial amount of communication between people takes place at the nonverbal level. **Nonverbal communication** refers to the transmission of messages through means other than words. These messages accompany verbal messages and sometimes take place alone. The general purpose of nonverbal communication is to convey the feeling behind a message. For instance, you can say "no" with a clenched fist or with a smile to communicate the intensity of your negative feelings.

A widely quoted study by Albert Mehrabian dramatizes the relevance of nonverbal communication. He calculated the relative weights of three elements of overall communication. The words we choose account for only about 7 percent of the emotional impact on others; our voice tone accounts for 38 percent; our facial expression for 55 percent. Nonverbal communication therefore accounts for 93 percent of the emotional meaning of a message,[13] as shown in Figure 11–2. This famous study should not be interpreted to mean that 93 percent of communication is nonverbal. It deals with the emotional force of your message and does not mean that the content of your message is unimportant.

The three aspects of nonverbal communication covered here are modes of transmission, problems revealed by body language, and cross-cultural differences.

Modes of Transmission of Nonverbal Communication

Nonverbal messages can be transmitted in many modes, as described in the following paragraphs. We will also describe mirroring, because it is an interesting application of nonverbal communication.

ENVIRONMENT. The environment or setting in which you send a message can influence the receiving of that message. Assume that your manager invites you

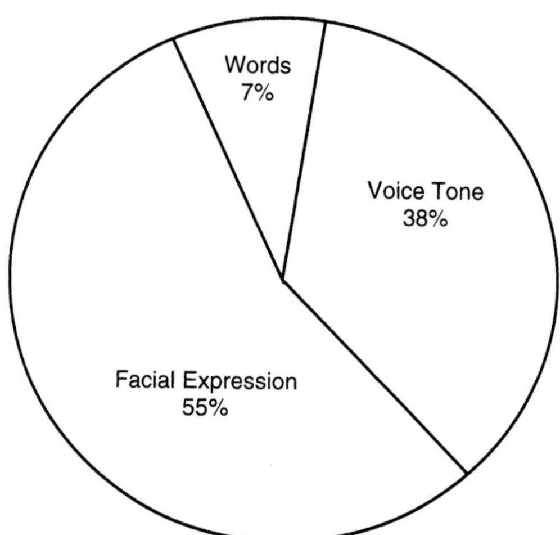

FIGURE 11–2 The Emotional Impact of Messages

out to lunch to discuss a problem. You will think it is a more important topic than if the manager had lunch with you in the company cafeteria. Other important environmental silent messages include room color, temperature, lighting, and furniture arrangement. A person who sits behind a large, uncluttered desk, for example, appears more powerful than a person who sits behind a small, messy desk.

Interpersonal Distance. The placement of one's body in relation to someone else is widely used to transmit messages. In general, getting physically close to another person conveys a positive attitude toward him or her. Putting your arm around someone is generally interpreted as a friendly act. (Some people, however, recoil when touched by someone other than a close friend.) Practical guidelines for judging how close to stand to another person in the United States and Canada, or in a similar culture, are shown in Figure 11–3.

Posture. Your posture communicates a variety of meanings. If you stand erect, it usually conveys the message that you are self-confident and experiencing positive emotion. If you slump, you will appear to be lacking in self-confidence or down in the dumps. Another interpersonal meaning of posture involves the direction of leaning. Leaning toward another individual suggests that you are favorably disposed toward his or her message; leaning backward communicates

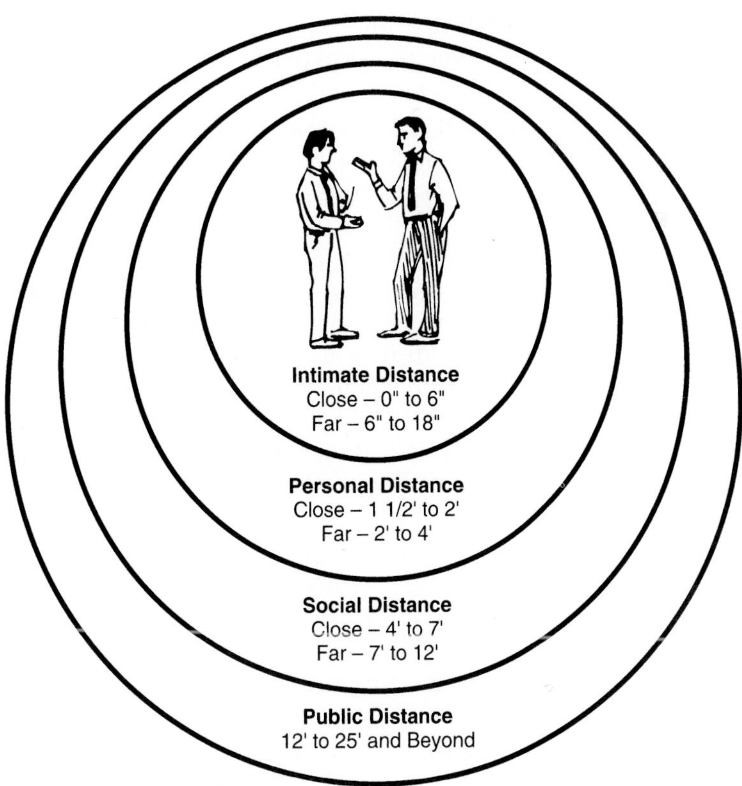

FIGURE 11–3 Four Circles of Intimacy

the opposite. Openness of the arms or legs serves as an indicator of liking or caring. In general, people establish closed postures (arms folded and legs crossed) when speaking to people they dislike.

Can you think of an aspect of your posture that conveys a specific message?

GESTURES. Your hand and body movements convey specific information to others. Positive attitudes toward another person are shown by frequent gesturing. In contrast, dislike or disinterest usually produces few gestures. An important exception here is that some people wave their hands while in an argument, sometimes to the point of making threatening gestures. The type of gesture displayed also communicates a specific message.

Gestures are also said to provide clues to levels of dominance and submission. The gestures of dominant people are typically directed outward toward the other person. Examples include the steady, unwavering gaze and the touching of one's partner. Submissive gestures are usually protective, such as touching oneself or shrugging the shoulders.

FACIAL EXPRESSIONS. Using your head, face, and eyes in combination provides the clearest indications of interpersonal attitudes. Looking at the ceiling—without tilting your head—combined with a serious expression almost always communicates the message "I doubt what you are saying is true." As is well known, maintaining eye contact with another person improves communication with that person. To maintain eye contact, it is usually necessary to move your head and face correspondingly. Moving your head, face, and eyes away from another individual is often interpreted as defensiveness or a lack of self-confidence.

VOICE TONE. The tone of voice deals with aspects such as pitch, volume, quality, and the rate of the spoken word. As with most nonverbal messages, there is a danger of overinterpreting a single voice quality. A team member might speak to you about the status of a project in a high-pitched voice, not out of fear but because of laryngitis. Three emotions frequently experienced on the job—anger, boredom, and joy—can often be interpreted from voice quality.[14]

Anger is best perceived when the source speaks loudly, at a fast rate, in a high pitch, with irregular inflection and clipped enunciation. Boredom is often indicated by moderate volume, pitch, and rate and a monotone inflection. Joy is often indicated by loud volume, high pitch, fast rate, upward inflection, and regular rhythm. Skill-Building Exercise 11–1 will help you recognize the importance of voice tone in communicating a message.

USE OF TIME. A subtle mode of nonverbal communication in organizations is the use of time. High-status individuals, such as executives, send messages about their power by keeping lower-ranking people waiting. It is extremely rare for a low-status worker to keep a high-status worker waiting. Ambitious people attempting to get ahead are seldom late for appointments (in U.S. culture). However, a high-ranking official might be late for a meeting, and that lateness might be perceived as a symbol of importance or being busy. Looking at your watch is usually interpreted as a sign of boredom or restlessness. Yet when a high-status person looks at his or her watch in a two-person meeting, the action

SKILL-BUILDING EXERCISE 11-1

Using Voice Tone to Emphasize the Elements in a Message

Consider the following statement: "The boss is giving Sheila a promotion." By emphasizing a particular word in this message through tone of voice, we can obtain different interpretations of the statement:

The *boss* is giving Sheila a promotion.

THE BOSS is the one giving the promotion, not the president of the company, not the boss's supervisor, but the boss.

The boss is *giving* Sheila a promotion.

The boss is GIVING the promotion, implying that perhaps Sheila is not qualified.

The boss is giving *Sheila* a promotion.

The person getting the promotion is SHEILA, not Art, not Betty, not Ken, but Sheila.

The boss is giving Sheila a *promotion.*

Sheila is receiving a PROMOTION, not a raise, not a demotion, not "the sack."

Source: Lyle Sussman and Paul D. Krivnos, *Communication for Supervisors and Managers* (Sherman Oaks, CA: Alfred Publishing Co., 1979), p. 83.

is likely to be interpreted as meaning, "Hurry up and make your point. You have almost used up the time I can grant you."

PERSONAL APPEARANCE. Your external image plays an important role in communicating messages to others. Job seekers show recognition of this aspect of nonverbal communication when they carefully groom for a job interview. People pay more respect and grant more privileges to people they perceive as being well dressed and attractive. The meaning of being well dressed depends heavily on the situation. In an information technology firm, neatly pressed jeans, a stylish T-shirt, and clean sport shoes might qualify as being well dressed. The same attire worn in a financial service firm would qualify as being poorly dressed. A recent tendency is a return to more formal business attire, to suggest that a person is ambitious and successful. A *New York Times* analysis concluded that formal dress frequently makes a better impression than casual wear on customers and bosses.[15] The best advice for using appearance to communicate nonverbal messages is to size up the environment to figure out what type of appearance and dress connotes the image you want to project. Some research supports the common belief that a favorable personal appearance leads to higher starting salaries and, later, salary increases.[16]

MIRRORING TO ESTABLISH RAPPORT. One form of nonverbal communication used to achieve rapport with another is **mirroring (or posturing).** To mirror someone is to imitate that individual subtly. It is one small aspect of neurolinguistic programming, a method of communication that combines features of hypnosis, linguistics, and nonverbal behavior. "Neuro" refers to the way the human nervous system processes communication. "Linguistic" refers to the way that words, tone, timing, gestures, and inflection can be used in communication. "Programming" refers to using a systematic technique to communicate with others.[17]

The most successful mirroring technique for establishing rapport is to imitate another's breathing pattern. If you adjust your own breathing rate to match someone else's, you will soon establish rapport with that individual. Adjusting your

TABLE 11–2
NONVERBAL SIGNALS OF JOB PROBLEMS

1. *Stress:* A blank expression or phony smile; tight posture, with arms held stiffly at the side; abrupt motion, such as suddenly shifting the eyes, a quick turn of the head, nervous tapping of a leg; sudden mood shifts in speech, from toneless and soft answers to animated and loud ones.
2. *Depression:* Sagging shoulders; sad facial expression; slower than usual speech; decrease in gesturing; slow breathing rate; frequent sighing.
3. *Lack of comprehension:* Knitted brows; a deadpan expression; tentative, weak nodding or smiling; one slightly raised eyebrow; "Yes" or "I see" in a strained voice; "I understand," accompanied by looking away.
4. *Hesitation to speak about a sensitive topic:* A slight raising of the head and eyebrows; licking the lips; deep breathing with eye contact.
5. *Disagreement in the form of hostile submission:* Downward movement of the body or eyes, or both, resembling bowing to authority; closed eyes and a hand put over the nose, as saying, "Oh no!"
6. *Lying, fraud, and deception:* A lying smile reveals itself in subtle ways, particularly eye wrinkles that are more like crow's-feet than laugh lines. (In contrast, an authentic smile is usually characterized by crinkly eyes and a generally relaxed expression.) Fraud and deception are suggested by inappropriate finger or foot tapping; body shifting or some other movement that suddenly appears. Inability to maintain eye contact is a less reliable indicator.
7. *Fatigue and burnout:* Yawning is always rude, even if you cover your mouth. A yawn may also indicate fatigue and possibly low motivation for the task at hand, or burnout.

Source: "Silent Language: 7 Costly Sins of Bad Body Language," *Executive Strategies,* May 1996; "Body Language," *Executive Strategies,* June 5, 1990; "Use Your Body Language," *Executive Strategies,* April 17, 1990; Pauline E. Henderson, "Communicate without Words," *Personnel Journal,* January 1989, p. 27; Frederic Golden, "Lying Faces Unmasked," *Time,* April 5, 1999, p. 52.

speech rate to the person with whom you are attempting to establish rapport is another mirroring technique. If the person speaks rapidly, so do you. If the other person speaks slowly, you decelerate your pace. This technique could get confusing if you attempt to establish rapport simultaneously with two people who speak at substantially different rates.

Problems Revealed by Nonverbal Communication

Nonverbal messages sometimes signal the existence of problems. For example, if a supplier promises you a delivery date while looking away from you and blushing, you might suspect that the date is unrealistic. Table 11–2 describes nonverbal signals that could be indicative of significant problems.

Cross-Cultural Differences in Nonverbal Communication

People from different cultures obviously speak and write different languages. Cultural differences in language can also be found within the same country, such as some groups using "go" to mean "say." A variety of cross-cultural differences are also found with respect to nonverbal communication. Being aware of the existence of these differences in silent messages will alert you to look for them when dealing with people from another culture. A sampling of these differences follows:

- A Japanese person smiling and nodding connotes understanding, not necessarily agreement.
- In many Asian and some Middle Eastern cultures it is considered improper to look a superior in the eye too often. A bowed head is therefore a sign of deference, not an indicator of low self-confidence.
- Japanese, as well as many other Asians, regard handshaking or hugging in public to be offensive.
- Asians may smile to avoid conflict, rather than to show approval.
- British, Scandinavians, and other Northern Europeans prefer plenty of space between themselves and another person. They seldom touch when talking. In contrast, French, Italians, Latin Americans, and Eastern Europeans tend to stand close together, and they touch one another, indicating closeness or agreement.
- A German manager appearing in short sleeves at a business meeting would be displaying substantial indifference, while an American or Canadian would just be behaving informally.
- Americans are eager to get down to business quickly and will therefore spend less time than people from other cultures building a relationship. (The difference in nonverbal communication here refers to differences in the use of time.)
- For Americans, forming a circle with one's thumb and forefinger and extending the remaining three fingers signifies, "OK." To the Japanese the same signal means money, to the French it means zero, in some Arab countries it's viewed as a curse. In Germany, Brazil, and the Commonwealth of Independent States, the American OK gesture is obscene. A Japanese businessperson may interpret the American OK symbol as a gesture that you are asking for a kickback.

A realistic approach to making use of cross-cultural differences in nonverbal communication is to investigate these differences before dealing with people of another culture. The conservative approach is to minimize using nonverbal symbols with people from a different culture until you are confident of how they will be interpreted.

GENDER DIFFERENCES IN COMMUNICATION STYLE

Despite the movement toward equality of the sexes in the workplace, substantial interest has arisen in identifying differences in communication style between men and women. The bestseller *Men Are from Mars, Women Are from Venus* fueled curiosity about this topic.[18] People who are aware of these differences face fewer communication problems between themselves and members of the opposite sex. The basic difference between women and men, according to Deborah Tannen, is that men emphasize and reinforce their status when they talk, whereas women downplay their status. As part of this difference, women are more concerned about building social connections.[19]

As we elaborate on differences in communication style between men and women, we recognize that they are group stereotypes. Individual differences in communication style are usually more important than group differences. An extensive analysis of gender differences and similarities in communication concluded that gender differences are generally so small and so insignificant they do not merit serious attention.[20] Here we will describe the major findings of research on gender differences in communication patterns.[21]

1. *Women prefer to use conversation for rapport building.* For most women, the intent of conversation is to build rapport and connections with people. It has been said that men are driven by transactions, while women are driven by relations. Women are therefore more likely to emphasize similarities, to listen intently, and to be supportive.
2. *Men prefer to use talk primarily as a means to preserve independence and status by displaying knowledge and skill.* When most men talk they want to receive positive evaluation from others and maintain their hierarchical status within the group. Men are therefore more oriented to giving a report, while women are more interested in establishing rapport.
3. *Women want empathy, not solutions.* When women share feelings of being stressed out, they seek empathy and understanding. If they feel they have been listened to carefully, they begin to relax. When listening to a woman, the man may feel blamed for her problems or that he has failed the woman in some way. To feel useful, the man might offer solutions to the woman's problem.
4. *Men prefer to work out their problems by themselves, whereas women prefer to talk out solutions with another person.* Women look upon having and sharing problems as an opportunity to build and deepen relationships. Men are more likely to look upon problems as challenges they must meet on their own. The communication consequence of these differences is that men may become uncommunicative when they have a problem.
5. *Men tend to be more directive and less apologetic in their conversation, while women are more polite and apologetic.* Women are therefore more likely to use the phrases "I'm sorry" and "Thank you" frequently, even when there is no need to express apology or gratitude. Men say they are sorry less frequently for the same reason they rarely ask directions when they are lost while driving: They perceive communication as competition, and they do not want to appear vulnerable.
6. *Women tend to be more conciliatory when facing differences, while men become more intimidating.* Again, women are more interested in building relationships, while men are more concerned about coming out ahead.
7. *Men are more interested than women in calling attention to their accomplishments or hogging recognition.* One consequence of this difference is that men are more likely to dominate discussion during meetings. Another consequence is that women are more likely to help a coworker perform well. In one instance a sales representative who had already made her sales quota for the month turned over an excellent prospect to a coworker. She reasoned, "It's somebody else's turn. I've received more than my fair share of bonuses for the month."

8. *Men and women interrupt others for different reasons.* Men are more likely to interrupt to introduce a new topic or complete a sentence for someone else. Women are more likely to interrupt to clarify the other person's thought or offer support.
9. *During casual conversation, women focus more on other people, whereas men emphasize sports and other leisure activities.* Women enjoy talking about interpersonal relationships to a greater extent than do men. Men are more likely to emphasize talk about sports, automobiles, and outdoor activities. (Although the subject of current research, this represents the oldest, most sexist stereotype about gender differences.)
10. *Women are more likely to use a gentle expletive, while men tend to be harsher.* For example, if a woman locks herself out of the car she is likely to say, "Oh dear." In the same situation a man is likely to say "Oh __________ ." (Do you think this difference really exists?)

How can the information just presented help you overcome communication problems on the job? As a starting point, remember that gender differences often exist. Understanding these differences will help you interpret people's communication behaviors. For example, if a male coworker is not as polite as you would like, remember that he is simply engaging in gender-typical behavior. Do not take it personally.

A woman can remind herself to speak up more in meetings because her natural tendency might be toward holding back. She might say to herself, "I must watch out to avoid gender-typical behavior in this situation." A man might remind himself to be more polite and supportive toward coworkers. The problem is that although such behavior is important, his natural tendency might be to skip saying "Thank you."

A woman should not take it personally when a male coworker or subordinate is tight-lipped when faced with a problem. She should recognize that he needs more encouragement to talk about his problems than would a woman. If a man persists in not wanting to talk about the problem, the woman might say, "It looks like you want to work out this problem on your own. Go ahead. I'm available if you want to talk about the problem."

Men and women should recognize that when women talk over problems, they might not be seeking hard-hitting advice. Instead, they may simply be searching for a sympathetic ear so they can deal with the emotional aspects of the problem.

OVERCOMING BARRIERS TO COMMUNICATION

Communication problems in the workplace are ever-present. Some interference usually takes place between ideation and action, as suggested by the clouds in Figure 11–1. The type of message influences the amount of interference. Routine or neutral messages are the easiest to communicate. Interference is most likely to occur when a message is complex or emotionally arousing or clashes with a receiver's mental set.

An emotionally arousing message deals with such topics as a relationship between two people or money. A message that clashes with a receiver's mental set

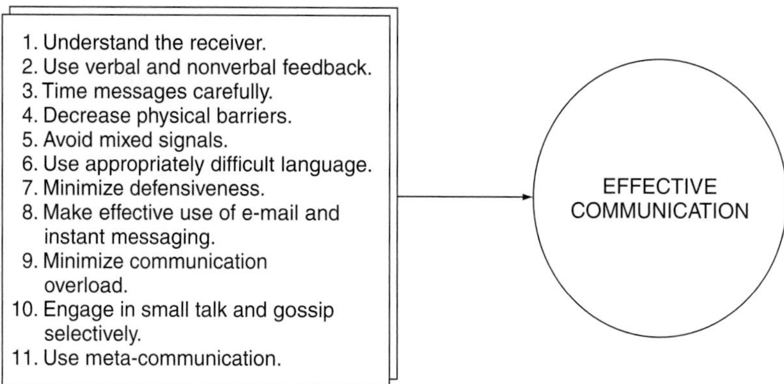

FIGURE 11–4 Overcoming Communication Barriers: Strategies and Tactics

requires the person to change his or her typical pattern of receiving messages. Try this experiment. The next time you visit a restaurant, order dessert first and the entrée second. The waiter or waitress will probably not receive your dessert order, because it deviates from the normal sequence.

Next we describe approaches to overcoming some of the more frequently observed communication problems in organizations, as outlined in Figure 11–4. The following section deals with overcoming cross-cultural communication barriers. We then deal with general approaches to overcoming barriers—being more persuasive and improving listening and telephone skills. The discussion of gender differences also provided ideas for decreasing communication barriers.

Understand the Receiver

Understanding the person who you are trying to reach is a fundamental principle of overcoming communication barriers. The more you know about your receiver, the better able you are to deliver your message in an effective manner. Three important aspects of understanding the receiver are: (1) developing empathy, (2) recognizing that person's motivational state, and (3) understanding the other person's frame of reference.

To develop empathy, you are required to figuratively put yourself in the receiver's shoes. To accomplish this, you have to imagine yourself in the other person's role and assume the viewpoints and emotions of that individual. Assume a 25-year-old customer service representative works at a public utility. She is responsible for helping a group of older employees to understand the importance of becoming customer oriented. The customer service rep must ask herself, "If I had been working in a monopoly for 20 years, how difficult would it be for me to understand that we now have competition? And that we must therefore please the customer?"

The receiver's **motivational state** could include any active needs and interest at the time. People tend to listen attentively to messages that show promise of satisfying an active need. The hungry person who ordinarily does not hear low tones readily hears the whispered message, "How would you like to eat dinner?" And management usually listens attentively to a suggestion framed in terms of cost savings or increased profits.

People perceive words and concepts differently because their vantage points and perspectives differ. Such differences in **frame of reference** create barriers to communication. To reduce this barrier, you have to understand where the receiver "is coming from." The following example of different frames of reference creating a communication barrier took place in a financial services agency:

> Jeb, a second-year agent, showed his sales figures for the month to his boss, Gary. Proud of his good results, Jeb said, "Well, what do you think of this kind of production for a man of my age?" Gary replied, "That's fine if you want to make $40,000 a year for the rest of your life." Jeb responded, "Sounds fine to me."
>
> Gary looked at him quizzically and said, "You mean you'd be happy making $40,000 a year for the rest of your life? I made that comment to shake you up a bit." Jeb answered, "No disrespect, Gary, but where I come from $40,000 is one big lump of money. My parents never came close to that."

Use Verbal and Nonverbal Feedback

To be able to conclude that your message has been received as intended, ask for feedback. A frequent managerial practice is to conclude a conference with a question such as, "Okay, what have we agreed on today?" Unless feedback of this nature is obtained, you will not know whether your message has been received until the receiver later carries out (or fails to carry out) your request. After speaking to a group you are trying to influence, it would be helpful to ask them to state what message they thought you were trying to convey. Nonverbal signals are sometimes more revealing than verbal signals. Here is an example of nonverbal behavior (or body language) that could help you to interpret whether or not your comments are being accepted:

> You ask your boss when you will be eligible for a promotion and he looks out the window, cups his mouth to cover a yawn, and says, "Probably not too far away. I would say your chances aren't too bad." Keep trying. He is not yet sold on the idea of promoting you in the near future.

Soliciting feedback is important also because it is the essence of two-way communication. Face-to-face communication is more effective when it results in an exchange of information between two people. One person may send messages to another to initiate the conversation. However, the second person must react (a form of feedback) to complete the communication loop. Two-way transactions help to clarify meanings because they communicate feelings as well as facts.

Time Messages Carefully

Many messages do not get through to the receiver because they are sent at the wrong time. It is a waste of time to send a message when the receiver is distracted with another issue or is rushing to get somewhere. The best time to deliver a message depends on the particular situation. Many sales representatives and consultants have found that Tuesday morning is a good time to get a message across to a busy manager. On Mondays, many managers are preoccupied with meetings and getting the week started with a burst of productivity. By Tuesday morning, they are more willing to attend to new business. Later in the week, the managers may be absorbed in attempting to complete the goals for the week.

Another aspect of timing is to postpone delivering an important message when the intended receiver is angry or upset. The best time to ask for a major commitment is when your intended receiver is in a good mood. Thinking about good news, such as record profits or a triumph in personal life, can be distracting. Nevertheless, thinking about good news is less distracting than thinking about bad news.

Decrease Physical Barriers

Do you ever try to communicate with somebody while standing in the doorway of his or her office or room? Do you ever try to communicate with somebody with a huge desk separating the two of you? In both situations your communications effectiveness would probably increase if you reduced the barriers. In the first instance, it would be helpful to enter the room and stand closer to the person. In the second situation, it would be preferable to move around the table to a point where you are both seated at adjacent corners of the desk.

In a conference setting, a major way of increasing and improving person-to-person communication is to seat people in a circle without a table separating them. (Student chairs with an arm big enough for note taking are particularly useful in this regard.) Another way of decreasing physical barriers is to provide employees with ample opportunity to chat with each other about work-related topics. Informal interaction of this type is particularly important for employees involved in creative or complex work. "Batting around" ideas with a coworker can help clarify thinking on a challenging problem.

Avoid Mixed Signals

Another reason for communication failure is **mixed signals**—sending different messages about the same topic to different audiences.[22] For example, a company might brag about the high quality of its products in its public statements. Yet on the shop floor and in the office the company tells its employees to cut corners wherever possible to lower costs. Another type of mixed signal occurs when you send one message to a person about desired behavior, yet behave in another way yourself. A mixed signal of this type would occur when an executive preaches the importance of social responsibility, yet practices blatant job discrimination.

Use Appropriately Difficult Language

"From this point forward you folks are going to have to interface with a CAD/CAM robotics configuration in our operations environment," said the production-engineering manager to the manufacturing specialists. Seeing mostly blank stares on the faces of his intended receivers, the manager rephrased his message, "In the future, all of our production work is going to be computerized." At first the manager was falling prey to a common communication barrier, speaking at too high a level of complexity for the intended receiver. The manager recovered by rephrasing his message in a form that was: (1) simpler and (2) less filled with jargon.

It is not always advisable to avoid complexity and jargon. People may feel patronized when you send messages that are too easy to understand. (Do you like this book? See the pictures. Aren't they nice?) In an effort to reduce complexity, some people create communication barriers. One way to alienate your intended receivers is to say, "I'm going to explain this to you in such a way that even a layperson can understand it."

When specialists speak among themselves, jargon is a convenient language shortcut.[23] For example, a credit analyst might say to his manager, "I might need your help. I've got a subprime in my office." (The credit analyst is referring to a customer who has a poor credit rating, and therefore it will be challenging to make the right lending decision.) Jargon can also play an important psychological role, because it communicates the message that the receiver is part of the sender's in-group.

Minimize Defensiveness

An important general communication barrier is **defensive communication,** the tendency to receive messages in such a way that one's self-esteem is protected. Defensive communication is also responsible for people sending messages to make themselves look good. For example, when criticized for achieving below-average sales, a store manager might shift the blame to the sales associates in the store.

Overcoming the barrier of defensive communication requires two steps. First, people have to recognize the existence of defensive communication. Second, they have to try not to be defensive when questioned or criticized. Such behavior is not easy because of the unconscious or semiconscious process of denial, the suppression of information we find uncomfortable. For example, the store manager just cited would find it uncomfortable to think of herself as being responsible for below-average performance.

Another approach to minimizing defensive communication is to decrease terms and statements that are likely to make others defensive. An easy way to make the receiver defensive is to use terms that he or she could interpret as an insult or put-down, such as being sexist or racist. The purpose of politically correct language is to avoid offending anyone, especially with respect to implying that a person or group has inferior status. An extreme example would be to refer to an engineering technician in the group as a "nonengineer."

Make Effective Use of E-mail and Instant Messaging

E-mail has simplified interpersonal communication in the workplace. Nevertheless, e-mail can create many barriers to effective communication. To avoid such barriers, consider the following suggestions for making e-mail a force for improved communications.[24] Above all, *avoid the indiscriminate sending of messages so as not to overwhelm people.* Many people receive about 100 e-mail messages per workday, making it difficult to conduct other work. *Minimize using e-mail for the political purpose of proving to others you are not at fault for a problem that has occurred.* Many people tune out when they read another "hide-protecting" e-mail message.

E-mail and instant messaging should not be used as a *substitute for face-to-face interactions about sensitive issues such as resolving conflict or reprimanding another person.* Do not develop habits of indecisiveness by *requesting e-mail input from many others before making a decision.* Such action lowers your credibility as a sender of messages. Avoid the immature act of using e-mail to *flame (sending harsh, angry, and sometimes vulgar notes to) others.* People who flame are perceived to be poor communicators because they use e-mail as a tool for aggression. "Shouting" with e-mail, or *sending most of your message in all capitals, should be done sparingly.* Routinely sending messages in all capitals may annoy the receiver, thus creating a communication barrier.

On the positive side, *respond to as many e-mail messages as feasible.* By being a rapid responder, you overcome the barrier of appearing to lack interest in the receiver. Yet do not become overwhelmed by responding to all messages you receive that are not specifically directed toward you, such as general announcements. Also, create a professional impression with your e-mail by using complete sentences and being "cute" sparingly. An example of a cute expression is "C U there."Ü

Minimize Communication Overload

A major communication barrier facing higher-level workers today is **communication overload,** with e-mail and instant messaging being a major contributor. So much information comes across the desk and computer monitor that it is often difficult to figure out which information should receive attention and which should be discarded. A study conducted in large companies found that 71 percent of employees felt overwhelmed by the number of messages they received at work each day. Close to 85 percent reported being interrupted by messages three or more times per hour.[25] A flood of information reaching a person acts as a communication barrier because people have a tendency to block out new information when their capacity to absorb information becomes taxed. Literally, their "circuits become overloaded." Being overwhelmed with information may also create a memory dysfunction in which useful retained information fades from memory.

You can decrease the chances of suffering from information overload by such measures as carefully organizing and sorting through information before plunging ahead with reading. Focus on information that you think will help you do your job better, be more successful in your studies, or enjoy life better.

Engage in Small Talk and Constructive Gossip

The terms *small talk* and *gossip* have negative connotations for the career-minded person with a professional attitude. Nevertheless, the effective use of small talk and gossip can help a person melt communication barriers. (The positive aspects of gossip have already been described.) Small talk is important because it contributes to conversational skills, and having good conversational skills enhances interpersonal communication. Trainer Randi Freidig says, "Small talk helps build rapport and eventually trust. It helps people find common ground on which to build conversation."[26] A helpful technique is to collect tidbits of information to use as small talk to facilitate work-related conversations. Keeping abreast of developments in the industry of the stock market is a good conversation opener. After a conversation opens smoothly, communication barriers in regard to the major topic often diminish.

Use Meta-Communication

When confronted with a communication problem, one response is to attempt to work around the barrier, perhaps by using one of the methods already described. A more typical response is to ignore the barrier by making no special effort to deal with the problem—a "take-it-or-leave-it" approach to communication. Another possibility is to **meta-communicate,** or communicate about your communication to help overcome barriers or resolve a problem. If you as a team leader were facing heavy deadline pressures, you might say to a team member, "I might appear brusque today and tomorrow. Please don't take it personally. It's just that I have to make heavy demands on you because our team is facing a gruesome deadline." Or, if you are trying to get through to a coworker with an angry facial expression, you might say, "You look upset about our conversation. Is this a bad time to communicate with you about something important?"

OVERCOMING CROSS-CULTURAL COMMUNICATION BARRIERS

We have already discussed the importance of understanding culturally based differences among people. In Chapter 3, we described how cultural differences might create individual differences. Earlier in this chapter we described how culture might influence nonverbal communication. Understanding how to react to cultural differences is important because the workforce has become more culturally diverse in two major ways. More subgroups from within our own culture have been assimilated into the workforce. In addition, there is increasing interaction with people from other countries.

Because of this diversity, many workers face the challenge of preventing and overcoming communication barriers created by differences in language and customs. The approaches to overcoming communication barriers described earlier should be effective with different cultural groups. Here we describe several approaches particularly relevant for overcoming cross-cultural communication barriers.

Be sensitive to the fact that cross-cultural communication barriers exist. If you are aware of these potential barriers, you will be ready to deal with them. When you are dealing with a person in the workplace with a different cultural background than yours, solicit feedback in order to minimize cross-cultural barriers to communication. Being aware of potential barriers helps you develop **cultural sensitivity,** an awareness of and a willingness to investigate the reasons why people of another culture act as they do.

Show respect for all workers. An effective strategy for overcoming cross-cultural communication barriers is to simply respect all others in the workplace.[27] A key component of respect is to perceive other cultures as being different from but not inferior to your own. Respecting other people's customs can translate into specific attitudes, such as respecting one coworker for wearing a yarmulke on Friday or another for wearing an African costume to celebrate Kwanzaa. Another way of being respectful would be to listen carefully to the opinion of a senior worker who says the company should have converted to marketing through the Internet (even though you disagree).

Use straightforward language and speak slowly and clearly. When working with people who do not speak your language fluently, speak in an easy-to-understand manner. Minimize the use of idioms and analogies specific to your language. An accountant from Taiwan left confused after a performance review with her manager. The manager said, "I will be giving you more assignments because I notice some good chemistry between us." (He was referring to good work rapport.) The woman did not ask for clarification because she did not want to appear uninformed.

Speaking slowly is also important because even people who read and write a second language at an expert level may have difficulty catching the nuances of conversation. Facing the person from another culture directly also improves communication because your facial expressions and lips contribute to comprehension.

Observe cultural differences in etiquette. Violating rules of etiquette without explanation can erect immediate communication barriers. A major rule of etiquette is that in many countries people address higher-ranking people by last name, unless they have worked together for a long time. The more the country respects age and rank, the less likely it is that addressing senior officials by their first name is acceptable. If the senior official suggests that he or she be addressed by the first name, then such informality is acceptable.

Do not be diverted by style, accent, grammar, or personal appearance. Although these superficial factors are all related to business success, they are difficult to interpret when judging a person from another culture. It is therefore better to judge the merits of the statement or behavior.[28] A brilliant individual from another culture may still be learning your language and thus make basic mistakes in speaking your language. He or she also might not yet have developed a sensitivity to dress style in your culture.

Listen for understanding, not agreement. When working with diverse teammates, the differences in viewpoints can lead to conflict. To help overcome such conflict, listen for understanding, not agreement. In this way you gear yourself to consider the viewpoints of others as a first resort. Example: Some older workers may express some intense loyalty to the organization, while their younger teammates may speak in more critical terms. If everyone listens to understand, they can begin to appreciate one another's paradigms and accept differences of opinion.[29]

BECOMING A MORE PERSUASIVE COMMUNICATOR

An elegant tactic for overcoming communication barriers is to communicate so persuasively that obstacles disappear. **Persuasiveness** refers to the sender convincing the receiver to accept his or her message, and thus involves selling ideas to others. Being able to persuade others is especially important in today's workplace. As Jay Conger explains, "Work today gets done in an environment where people don't just ask, 'What should I do?' but, 'Why should I do it?'"[30] Hundreds of articles, books, tape cassettes, and videos have been developed to help people become more persuasive. Following are some representative suggestions for becoming a more persuasive communicator both in speaking and in writing.[31]

1. *Know exactly what you want.* Your chances of selling an idea increase to the extent that you have clarified the idea in your own mind. The clearer and more committed you are at the outset of a selling or negotiating session, the stronger you are as a persuader.
2. *Develop fallback positions.* Keep in mind what you might do if you cannot convince the other side to accept your first proposal. If plan A does not work, shift to plan B, then to plan C.
3. *Never suggest an action without telling its end benefit.* In asking for a raise, you might say, "If I get this raise, I'll be able to afford to stay with this job as long as the company likes."
4. *Phrase your proposition in terms of people's interest.* This basic rule of selling is an extension of the communication strategy "understand the receiver." People are far more likely to accept your idea if it is clear how they will benefit. Almost every receiver wants to know, "What's in it for me?"
5. *Explore the reasons for people's objections.* Assume a potential customer says, "I like this model but I don't want it in my living room." An effective response would be, "What is it that you don't like about it?" Another would be, "What features do you like in this product?"
6. *Say why you are asking whenever you ask a question.* The sales representative above might say, "The reason I asked you about features is that maybe we have another model with similar features."
7. *Get a "yes" response early on.* It is helpful to give the selling session a positive tone by establishing a "yes pattern" at the outset. Assume that an employee wanted to convince his manager to allow the employee to perform some of his work at home during normal working hours. The employee might begin the idea-selling session with the question, "Is it important for the company to obtain maximum productivity from all its employees?"
8. *Use power words.* An expert tactic for being persuasive is to sprinkle your speech with power (meaning powerful) words. Power words stir emotion and bring forth images of exciting events. Examples of the use of power words include decimating the competition, bonding with customers, surpassing previous profits, capturing customer loyalty, and rebounding from a downturn.
9. *Back up conclusions with data.* You will be more persuasive if you support your spoken and written presentations with solid data. You can collect the data yourself or quote from a printed or electronic source. Relying too much on research has a potential disadvantage, however. Being too dependent on data could suggest that you have little faith in your intuition. For example, you might convey a weak impression if, when asked your opinion, you respond, "I can't answer until I collect some data."
10. *Minimize "wimp" phrases.* Persuasive communicators minimize statements that make them appear weak and indecisive. Such phrases convey the

impression that you are not in control of your time or actions. Among such wimp phrases are the following: "It's one of those days." "Things are crazy around here." "I'm not sure about that." "Don't quote me on that." "I'll try my best to get it done." (It is better to commit yourself forcibly by saying, "I'll get it done.")

11. *Minimize common speech flaws.* Flawless grammar and word use is not necessary to communicate persuasively. However, avoiding certain common speech flaws makes you more convincing. Among these common flaws are mumbling, making a whining sound, speaking in a monotone, and using too much *upspeak.* The last flaw refers to making statements sound like questions by raising your voice at the end of the sentence.[32]

Persuasion and negotiation are closely related. Additional suggestions for improving persuasiveness can be obtained by reviewing the negotiating techniques described in Chapter 8.

IMPROVING YOUR LISTENING SKILLS

Persuasion deals primarily with sending messages. Improving one's receiving of messages is another important aspect of developing better communication skills. Although many workers spend more time at computers than they do communicating orally, speaking directly to people and listening are still major aspects of work. Unless you receive messages as they are intended, you cannot perform your job properly or be a good companion. Listening is a particularly important skill for anyone whose job involves troubleshooting, since one needs to gather information to solve problems.

Another reason that improving the listening skills of employees is important is that insufficient listening is extraordinarily costly. Listening mistakes lead to word processing letters a second time, rescheduling appointments, reshipping orders, and recalling defective products. The accompanying box illustrates how listening contributes to business success.

A starting point in being a good listener is to concentrate and avoid distractions. Improved concentration leads to improved listening. If you concentrate intently on the sender, you will receive much more information than if you pay superficial attention. While listening, attempt to leave distracting problems and concerns behind. External distractions and concerns, such as another person in the room, have to be resisted. In short, a good listener fights distraction.

A major component of effective listening is to be an **active listener,** one who listens intently with the goal of empathizing with the speaker. Empathy does not necessarily mean that you sympathize with the other person. For example, you may understand why some people are forced to beg in the streets, but you may have little sympathy for their plight. A useful way of showing empathy is to accept the sender's figure of speech. By so doing, you make the sender feel understood and accepted. Also, if you reject the person's figure of speech by rewording it, the sender may become defensive. Many people use the figure of speech "I'm stuck" when they cannot accomplish a task. You can facilitate smooth communication by a response such as "What can I do to help you get unstuck?" If you respond with something like "What can I do to help you think more clearly?" the person is forced to change mental channels and may become defensive.[33]

THE IMPORTANCE OF LISTENING TO THE TEAM

Judy George is chair and CEO of Boston-based Domain Home Fashions, a company with 250 employees. She learned about the importance of listening to team members the hard way. George, age 60, was fired from her last company—after building revenue from $2 million to $100 million in seven years—because she stepped on everybody's toes. "I treated everybody as if they were all Judy Georges running around. I thought enthusiasm was contagious. After I was fired, I began to realize that not everybody operated the same way I did," she says. After the trauma of being fired settled down, George reflected that she should look for the good in what workers are saying or doing, even if their thoughts and actions were different from hers.

When George founded Domain in 1985, she made certain to hire people who didn't share her personality traits—and she promised herself that she would listen to them. "The change helped the business thrive," she says. When she wanted to launch a Web site for selling furniture several years ago, for instance, her managers persuaded her that the company was not ready to handle returns.

Net shoppers typically take a try-it-and-see approach. If a buyer in Sante Fe didn't like a sofa, Domain would have been saddled with the costs of warehousing it out West or shipping it back to the manufacturer. "This is why, after five years, no major furniture company is making money online," says George. "If we had done what I wanted to do, we would have lost a fortune. But I learned to listen to my team."

Source: Adapted from Margaret Littman, "Best Bosses Tell All," *Working Woman,* October 2000, pp. 51–52; www.domainhomefashions.com.

Another key aspect of active listening is to observe the nonverbal aspects of the message. For example, you can judge the sincerity of a message by the sender's voice tone and whether he or she has a serious facial expression.

To be an active listener, it is also important to **paraphrase,** or repeat in your own words what the sender says, feels, and means. You might feel awkward the first several times you paraphrase. Therefore, try it with a person with whom you feel comfortable. With some practice, it will become a natural part of your communication skill kit. Here is an example of how you might use paraphrasing:

Other Person: I'm getting annoyed at working so hard around here. I wish somebody would pitch in and do a fair day's work.

You: You're saying that you do more than your fair share of the tough work on our team.

Other Person: You bet. Here's what I think we should be doing about it.

A final point here is to offer encouragement to the sender. Good listeners encourage senders by asking questions, giving nods of approval, and finding points of agreement. Skill-Building Exercise 11–2 gives you an opportunity to practice your listening skills.

ENHANCING TELEPHONE AND VOICE-MAIL COMMUNICATION SKILLS

Another approach to being a more effective communicator is to use effective telephone and voice-mail communication skills, because these two communication media often create communication problems. Also, many businesses attract and

SKILL-BUILDING EXERCISE 11–2

Active Listening

Before conducting the following role plays, review the suggestions for active listening in this chapter. The suggestion about paraphrasing the message is particularly relevant, because the role plays involve emotional topics.

The Elated Coworker: One student plays the role of a coworker who has just been offered a promotion to supervisor of another department. She will be receiving 10 percent higher pay and be able to travel overseas twice a year for the company. She is eager to describe the full details of her good fortune to a coworker. Another student plays the role of the coworker to whom the first worker wants to describe her good fortune. The second worker decides to listen intently to the first worker. Other class members will rate the second student on his or her listening ability.

The Discouraged Coworker: One student plays the role of a coworker who has just been placed on probation for poor performance. His boss thinks that his performance is below standard and that his attendance and punctuality are poor. He is afraid that if he tells his girlfriend, she will leave him. He is eager to tell his tale of woe to a coworker. Another student plays the role of the coworker whom the first worker corners to discuss his problems. The second worker decides to listen intently to the first worker's problems but is pressed for time. Other class members will rate the second student on his or her listening ability.

hold on to customers because their representatives interact positively with people through the telephone and voice mail. Many other firms lose money, and nonprofit organizations irritate the public, because their employees have poor telephone and voice-mail communication skills. Speech recognition systems, such as those used to provide information to customers, require people to articulate clearly enough to be understood by voice recognition software.

Furthermore, despite the widespread use of computer networks, a substantial amount of work among employees is still conducted via telephone and voice mail. Most of the previous comments about overcoming communication barriers apply to telephone communications. A number of suggestions related specifically to improving telephone and voice-mail communication are worth considering. The general goal of the suggestions presented in the accompanying box is to help people who communicate by telephone to sound courteous, cheerful, cooperative, and competent.[34]

SUMMARY OF KEY POINTS

- Communication is the transmission of a message from a sender to a receiver. Its purpose is to gather, process, and disseminate information, making it a vital work activity. The seven steps in the communication process are ideation, encoding, transmission, receiving, decoding, understanding, and action. Interference, or barriers to communication, can take place at any of these steps.
- The formal communication pathway is the official path over which a message is supposed to travel. An open-door policy is conducted through formal pathways. Informal pathways are more numerous than formal pathways. The grapevine is the major informal communication network in an organization.

EFFECTIVE TELEPHONE AND VOICE-MAIL COMMUNICATION SKILLS

1. When answering the telephone, give your name and department or team. Also give the company name if the call is not a transfer from a main switching center.
2. When talking to customers or clients, address them by name, but not to the point of irritation. Make sure to address customers and clients by their last name unless specifically directed otherwise by your manager or the caller. If the caller does not identify himself or herself, ask "Who is calling please?" Knowing the caller's name helps give a human touch to the conversation.
3. Speak at a moderate pace of approximately 150 to 160 words per minute. A rapid pace conveys the impression of impatience, while a slow rate might suggest disinterest.
4. Smile while speaking on the phone. Somehow a smile gets transmitted over the telephone wires or optic fibers!
5. Exercise good listening skills, and take notes while listening. Be alert to both verbal statements and nonverbal signals, such as voice hesitancy or sighs of exasperation.
6. Use fast and friendly language that builds cooperation. Certain phrases in response to telephone callers are perceived as friendly and helpful while others come across as irritating and not so helpful. Here are some examples: "I'll try" versus "I will." "Your problem" versus "This situation." "As soon as I can get to it" versus "Before ______ o'clock."
7. Use upbeat, modern language. Given that it is more difficult to make a positive impression over the phone than in person, sprinkle your conversation with modern, hip words. For example, you might say that some of your customers like "modern primitive," which refers to the revival of body modification (mutilation?) processes such as tattooing and piercing. Or you might try, "dead tree edition," referring to the paper version of a newspaper or magazine that also appears in electronic form.
8. Use voice mail to minimize "telephone tag" rather than to increase it. If your greeting specifies when you will return, callers can choose to call again or leave a message. When you leave a message, suggest a good time to return your call. Another way to minimize telephone tag is to assure the person you are calling that you will keep trying. Or, leave your e-mail address!
9. Place an informative and friendly greeting (outgoing message) on your voice mail or answering machine. Used effectively, a voice-mail greeting will minimize the number of people irritated by not talking to a person.
10. When leaving your message, avoid the most common voice-mail error by stating your name and telephone number clearly enough to be understood. Most recipients of a message dislike having to listen to it intensely several times to pick up identifying information.

- A rumor is a message transmitted over the grapevine, although not based on official word. Rumors are capable of disrupting work and lowering morale. Clarifying ideas about uncertain events can help stop rumors, as can enhancing formal communication about rumor topics. Gossip is a special form of rumor that does waste time but also serves a few useful purposes. Gossip can be a morale booster, a socializing force, and a guidebook to group norms. Being a source of positive gossip brings a person power and credibility. Chance encounters are another important informal channel.
- Nonverbal communication refers to the transmission of messages through means other than words. It is used to communicate the feeling behind your

message. Eight common forms of nonverbal communication are the environment or setting of the message, interpersonal distance, posture, gestures, facial expression, voice tone, use of time, and personal appearance. Mirroring is a form of nonverbal communication that involves imitating some aspect of a person, such as breathing pattern, to establish rapport. Nonverbal messages sometimes reveal the existence of problems, such as lack of comprehension or deception. Cross-cultural differences in nonverbal communication are worth observing because, if not observed, they can lead to misunderstanding.

- The basic difference between men and women in communication style is that men emphasize and reinforce their status when they talk, whereas women downplay their status. Women are more concerned about building social connections. Another example of a gender difference is that men prefer to work out their problems by themselves, whereas women prefer to talk out solutions with another person. To the extent that gender differences in communication style really exist, understanding these differences can help you interpret the communication behavior of people.
- Communication problems are ever-present in the workplace. Interference is most likely to occur when a message is complex, is emotionally arousing, or clashes with a receiver's mental set. Specific methods of overcoming communication barriers include: (1) understand the receiver, (2) use verbal and nonverbal feedback, (3) time messages carefully, (4) decrease physical barriers, (5) avoid mixed signals, (6) use appropriately difficult language, (7) minimize defensiveness, (8) make effective use of e-mail and instant messaging, (9) minimize communication overload, (10) engage in small talk and constructive gossip, and (11) use meta-communication.
- To overcome cross-cultural communication barriers, consider the following approaches: Be sensitive to the existence of the barriers, respect all workers, use straightforward language and speak slowly and clearly, observe cultural differences in etiquette, do not be diverted by style, accent, grammar, or personal appearance, and listen for understanding, not agreement.
- Communication problems can also be overcome through persuasive communication. Persuasiveness can be increased through such techniques as knowing exactly what you want, stating the benefits of your proposition, and appealing to the interests of the other party. Improving listening skills can also improve communication. A major improvement in listening can be achieved through better concentration. Improving telephone communication skills should receive special attention.

DISCUSSION QUESTIONS AND ACTIVITIES

1. Employers consistently say that one of the most important attributes they look for in a new hire from a career or business school is good spoken and written communication skills. Why is there so much emphasis on communication skills?
2. Suppose you are supervising or working with a group of people who use poor grammar and incorrect word choices. Should you do the same to establish good rapport with the group?
3. Why do rumors about negative news travel so fast?

GUIDELINES FOR PERSONAL EFFECTIVENESS

1. **Practice two-way rather than one-way communication if you are concerned about getting your message across.** While delivering your message, ask for verbal feedback and be sensitive to nonverbal cues about how your message is getting across.
2. **Becoming a persuasive communicator is an important part of achieving success in a wide range of jobs.** To be persuasive, you need to make an effective presentation and understand the needs and interests of the person you are trying to persuade.
3. **A requirement of the modern workplace is to deal effectively with people from different cultures both within your own country and from other countries.** Learning more about their customs and etiquette is very helpful. In addition, if you want to develop exceptional skills in an international environment, learn to speak, read, and write in another language. In the near future, some of the best jobs for business graduates will be reserved for those who are bilingual.

4. In what way might improving your nonverbal communication skills help you advance in your career?
5. How can you tell from nonverbal communication whether your manager or team leader likes you?
6. A coworker of yours says, "I'm trying to find out on the Internet how many cars and trucks the United States sold to Japan last year. I'm getting nowhere, and I'm frustrated." Respond to your coworker using empathy.
7. In what way might using politically correct speech sometimes create communication barriers?
8. After reading about cross-cultural communication barriers, one manager said, "Enough about Americans always bending over backward. What about foreigners adapting to our way of doing things when they are working in the United States?" How would you respond to this manager?
9. Now that you have studied gender differences in communication, how will this information influence your communications on the job?
10. Ask a few people what they think are the most frequent acts of telephone discourtesy. Report your findings to the class.

REFERENCES

1. Results of a Gallup survey for Pitney Bowes, Inc., reported in Mildred L. Culp, "The Communication Demands of Today's Workplace," WorkWise®, syndicated column, November 23, 1997. Updated with observations from 2002.
2. "4 Tips for Creating a Genuine Open Door Policy," *HRfocus,* December 1999, p. 13.
3. Tom Terez, "Can We Talk?" *Workforce,* July 2000, pp. 46–55.
4. Allen Zaremba, "Working with the Organizational Grapevine," *Personnel Journal,* July 1988, p. 39.
5. Mary-Kathryn Zachary, "The Office Grapevine: A Legal Noose?" *Getting Results,* August 1996, pp. 6–7.

AN APPLIED PSYCHOLOGY CASE PROBLEM

The Scrutinized Team Member Candidate

HRmanager.com is a human resources management firm that provides human resource services such as payroll, benefits administration, affirmative action programs, and technical training to other firms. By signing up with HRmanager, other firms can outsource part or all of their human resources functions. During its seven years of operation, HRmanager.com has grown from 3 to 50 employees, and last year had total revenues of $21 million.

Most of the work of the firm is performed by teams, led by a rotating team leader. Each team member takes an 18-month turn at being a team leader. The four-person new ventures team is regarded by CEO and founder, Jerry Clune, as vital for the future of the company. In addition to developing ideas for new services, the team members are responsible for obtaining clients for any new service they propose that is approved by Clune. The new ventures team thus develops and sells new services. After the service is launched and working well, the sales group is responsible for developing more clients.

As with other teams at HRmanager.com, the team members have a voice as to who is hired to join their team. In conjunction with Clune, the new ventures team decided it should expand to five members. The team posted the job opening for a new member on an Internet recruiting service, ran classified ads in the local newspaper, and also asked present employees for referrals. One of the finalists for the position was Gina Cleveland, a 27-year-old business graduate. In addition to interviewing with Clune and the two company vice presidents, Cleveland spent one-half day with the new ventures team, breakfast and lunch included. About two-and-one-half hours of the time was spent in a team interview in which Gina sat in a conference room with the four team members.

The team members agreed that Cleveland appeared to be a strong candidate on paper. Her education and experience were satisfactory, her résumé was impressive, and she presented herself well during a telephone-screening interview. After Cleveland completed her time with the new ventures team, the team leader, Lauren Nielsen, suggested that the group hold a debriefing session. The purpose of the session would be to share ideas about Cleveland's suitability for joining the team.

Nielsen commented, "It seems like we think that Gina is a strong candidate based on her credentials and what she said. But I'm a big believer in nonverbal communication. Studying Gina's body language can give us a lot of valuable information. Let's each share our observations, about what Gina's body language tells us she is *really* like. I'll go first.

Lauren: I liked the way Gina looked so cool and polished when she joined us for breakfast. She's got all the superficial movements right to project self-confidence. But did anybody else notice how she looked concerned when she had to make a choice from the menu? She finally did choose a ham-and-cheese omelet, but she raised her voice at the end of the sentence when she ordered it. I got the hint that Gina is not very confident.

I also noticed Gina biting her lips a little when we asked her how creative she thought she was. I know that Gina said she was creative, and gave us an example of a creative project she completed. Yet nibbling at her lips like that suggests she's not filled with fire power.

Michael: I didn't make any direct observations about Gina's being self-confident or not, but I did notice something that could be related. I think Gina is on a power trip, and this could indicate high or low self-confidence. Did anybody notice how Gina put her hands on her hips when she was standing up? That's a pure and clear signal of somebody who wants to be in control. Her haircut is almost the same length and style as most women who've made it to the top in Fortune 500 companies. I think she cloned her hairstyle from Carly Fiorina, the HP honcho.

Another hint I get of Gina's power trip is the way she eyed the check in the restaurant at lunch. I could see it in her eyes that she really wanted to pay for the entire team. That could mean a desire to control and show us that she is very important. Do we want someone on the team with such a strong desire to control?

Brenda: I observed a different picture of Gina based on her nonverbal communication. She dressed just right for the occasion; not too conservatively, not too far business casual. This tells me she can fit into our environment. Did you notice how well groomed her shoes were? This tells you she is well organized and good at details. Her attaché case was a soft, inviting leather. If she were really into power and control she would carry a hard vinyl or aluminum attaché case. I see Gina as a confident and assertive person who could blend right into our team.

Larry: I hope that because I'm last, I'm not too influenced by the observations that you three have shared so far. My take is that Gina looks great on paper, but she may have a problem in being a good team player. She's too laid back and distant. Did you notice her handshake? She gave me the impression of wanting to have the least possible physical contact with me. Her handshake was so insincere. I could feel her hand and arm withdrawing from me, as she shook my hand.

I also couldn't help noticing that Gina did not lean much toward us during the roundtable discussion. Do you remember how she would pull her chair back every so slightly when we got into a heavy discussion? I interpreted that as a sign that Gina does not want to be part of a close-knit group.

Lauren: As you have probably noticed, I've been typing as fast as I can with my laptop, taking notes on what you have said. We have some mixed observations here, and I want to summarize and integrate them before we make a decision. I'll send you an e-mail with an attached file of my summary observations by tomorrow morning. Make any changes you see fit and get back to me. After we have finished evaluating Gina carefully, we will be able to make our recommendations to Jerry (Clune).

Questions

1. To what extent are the new ventures team members making an appropriate use of nonverbal communication to size up Gina Cleveland?
2. Which team member do you think made the most realistic interpretation of nonverbal behavior? Why?
3. Should Lauren, the team leader, have told Gina in advance that the team would be scrutinizing her nonverbal behavior? Justify your answer.

6. Walter St. John, "In-house Communication Guidelines," *Personnel Journal,* November 1981, p. 877.
7. Nicholas DiFonzo and Prashant Bordia, "How Top PR Professionals Handle Hearsay: Corporate Rumors, Their Effects, and Strategies to Manage Them," *Public Relations Review,* Summer 2000, p. 179.
8. The last two points are from Donald D. Simmons, "The Nature of the Organizational Grapevine," *Supervisory Management,* November 1985, p. 42.
9. Samuel Greengard, "Gossip Poisons Business: HR Can Stop It," *Workforce,* July 2001, pp. 24–28.
10. "Gossip Can Convey the Awful Truth," *Personal Report for the Executive,* October 1, 1985, p. 5.
11. Nancy B. Kurland and Lisa Hople Pelled, "Passing the Word: Toward a Model of Gossip and Power in the Workplace," *Academy of Management Review,* April 2000, pp. 428–438.
12. John P. Kotter, *The General Manager* (New York: Free Press, 1991).

AN APPLIED PSYCHOLOGY CASE PROBLEM

A Grapevine Turned Sour[35]

Deborah Carvalho was hired as a technician in the photography department of a major automotive manufacturer. She welcomed the challenge of being the youngest worker in the department. Before reporting to work, Deborah was asked to visit the human resources department to complete several forms and participate in a preliminary orientation to the company. She was concerned about the visit taking more than two hours because she was participating in a drug study for a pharmaceutical firm. Her father was an organic chemist at the pharmaceutical firm, and he recruited her for the study. Deborah had been given an experimental drug designed to dilate the bronchial tubes. In time, the drug was to be used in treating asthmatics.

Deborah was informed by the staff physician that she should expect few to no side effects. Nevertheless, she was told that it is usually advisable to stay within close distance to the clinic in case uncomfortable side effects should surface. Since the risk of negative side effects of the drug seemed small, Deborah decided to make the visit to the human resources department. A follow-up visit was scheduled for the next day as part of the experimental procedure.

Deborah completed the paperwork within one hour. As she was about to leave, the photography department notified her that the department was behind schedule, and her help was therefore needed immediately. As Deborah was setting up the equipment to photograph a prototype car model, she felt dizzy and began to regret her decision to start work while under the influence of the experimental drug. She approached the acting manager (the regular supervisor was out of town) with her problem and requested that she be allowed to begin work on the following Monday as originally planned. The acting manager sympathized with Deborah's predicament and encouraged her to go home.

When Deborah started work on Monday morning, her manager informed her that she had a pressing appointment with the human resources director, Ron Kostel. He asked diplomatically whether perhaps she needed to make an appointment with the company medical unit and then be referred to the company-sponsored drug rehabilitation center.

Upset by Kostel's request, Deborah inquired why it was made. Kostel said that he heard from certain sources that Deborah was experimenting with hallucinogens and that it was affecting her ability to perform in her new position. Deborah attempted to explain that her father was an organic chemist at a pharmaceutical company who recruited her to participate in a drug experiment. She emphasized strongly that hallucinogens were not part of her drug protocol.

Kostel was still uneasy about the situation, even after Deborah furnished him with some literature about the clinical procedures and practices and how the side effects of the drug last up to two days maximum. Kostel decided to limit Deborah to work in the studio rather than visit manufacturing sites containing heavy equipment. He expressed concern that Deborah's reaction time might not be fast enough to avoid dangers in working with heavy equipment. Faced with these concerns by the human resources director, Deborah decided to discontinue participating in the drug experiments.

Coworkers continued to talk about Deborah's "drug problem." Every time she dropped a piece of equipment or bumped into someone, Deborah would hear people making wisecracks about what type of drug she might be on that day.

One of Deborah's coworkers took her aside one day to explain why these rumors about her were circulating. Apparently the acting manager thought his position would be threatened by the presence of a formally trained photo technician. So when the manager inquired where Deborah was, the answer was something to this effect: "Oh, Deb? She took some bad drugs, almost passed out, and went home." The statement was overheard by another employee, who shared the information with others.

QUESTIONS

1. What does this case illustrate about organizational rumors?
2. How could the rumor about Deborah's having a drug problem have been prevented?
3. When Deborah first realized others in the company perceived her to have a drug problem, what could she have done to combat this perception?

13. Albert Mehrabian and M. Weiner, "Decoding of Inconsistent Communications," *Journal of Personality and Social Psychology,* 6, 1967, pp. 109–114.

14. John Baird, Jr., and Gretchen Wieting, "Nonverbal Communication Can Be a Valuable Tool," *Personnel Journal,* September 1979, p. 609.

15. Amie Parnes, "Formal Business Dress Coming Back: Dot-com Casual Wears Off," *The New York Times,* syndicated story, June 17, 2001.

16. Irene Hanson Frieze, Josephine E. Olson, and Jane Russell, "Attractiveness and Business Success: Is It Important for Women or Men?" Paper presented at the Academy of Management, Washington, DC, August 1989.

17. Sue Knight, *NLP at Work: Neurolinguistic Programming* (London: Nicholas Brealey Publishing, 1995), p. 1.

18. John Gray, *Men Are from Mars, Women Are from Venus* (New York: HarperCollins, 1992).

19. Deborah Tannen, *Talking from 9 to 5* (New York: Avon, 1995).

20. Daniel J. Canary and Kathryn Dindia, *Sex Differences and Similarities in Communication* (Mahwah, NJ: Erlbaum, 1998).

21. Tannen, *Talking from 9 to 5;* Tannen, *You Just Don't Understand* (New York: Ballentine, 1990); Gray, *Men Are from Mars;* Tannen, "The Power of Talk: Who Gets Heard and Why," *Harvard Business Review,* September–October 1995, pp. 138–148; Canary and Dindia, *Sex Differences and Similarities,* p. 318.

22. Valorie McClelland, "Mixed Signals Breed Distrust," *Personnel Journal,* March 1987, pp. 24–29.

23. L. Marilyn Stinson, "Communication in the Workplace: Implications for Business Teachers," *Business Education Forum,* October 1995, p. 29.

24. Several of the ideas in this section are based on Carrie Patton, "Mind Your Messages, *Working Woman,* May 2000, p. 81; S. C. Gwynne and John F. Dickerson, "Lost in the E-mail," *Time,* April 21, 1997, pp. 88–90; Calvin Sun, "E-mail Etiquette," *Entrepreneur,* September 1997, pp. 132–137.

25. Study cited in Tom McNichol, "Yadda-Yadda @Work," *USA Weekend,* September 5–7, 1997, p. 6; John Yaukey, "E-mail Out of Control for Many, Gannet News Service, May 8, 2001.

26. Cited in Jacquelyn Lynn, "Small Talk, Big Results," *Entrepreneur,* August 1999, p. 30.

27. Jack L. Mendleson and C. Dianne Mendleson, "An Action Plan to Improve Difficult Communication," *HR Magazine,* October 1996, p. 119.

28. David P. Tulin, "Enhance Your Multi-Cultural Communication Skills," *Managing Diversity* 1, 1992, p. 5.

29. "Use Team's Diversity to Best Advantage," *ExecutiveSTRATEGIES,* April 2000, p. 2.

30. Jay A. Conger, "The Necessary Art of Persuasion," *Harvard Business Review,* May–June 1998, pp. 85–86.

31. Jimmy Calano and Jeff Salzman, "Persuasiveness: Make It Your Power Booster," *Working Woman,* October 1988, p. 124; "Innocent Phrases That Can Hurt: Avoid These Wimpy Remarks," *Working Smart,* December 1997, p. 6.

32. Carl Vogel, "You Don't Say: Six Easy Fixes for Common Speech Flaws," *Working Woman,* June 2000, p. 112.

33. Daniel Araoz, "Right-Brain Management (RBM): Part 2," *Human Resources Forum,* September 1989, p. 4.

34. Janice Alessandra and Tony Allessandra, "14 Telephone Tips for Ernestine," *Management Solutions,* July 1988, pp. 35–36; Donna Deeprose, "Making Voice Mail Customer Friendly," *Supervisory Management,* December 1992, pp. 7–8; Steven Daly and Nathaniel Wice, alt.culture (New York: HarperCollins, 1996); Dru Scott, *Time Management and the Telephone: Making It a Tool and Not a Tyrant* (Los Altos, CA: Crisp Publications, 1991).

35. Case researched by Deborah S. Krolls, Rochester Institute of Technology, 1998.

SUGGESTED READING

Balu, Rekha. "Listen Up: It Might Be Your Customer Talking." *Fast Company,* May 2000, pp. 304–314.

Blustain, Sarah. "The New Gender Wars." *Psychology Today,* November–December 2000, pp. 42–49.

Grensing-Pophal, Lin. "Got the Message?" *HR Magazine,* April 2000, pp. 74–79.

Kiger, Patrick J. "Lessons from a Crisis: How Communication Kept a Company Together." *Workforce,* November 2001, pp. 28–36.

McGarvey, Robert. "Get the Word Out . . . and Get Employees Communicating—Faster, Cheaper, and More Effectively." *Entrepreneur,* February 2000, pp. 131–134.

Solomon, Charlene Marmer. *Workforce,* November 1999, pp. 50–56.

Tosca, Elena. *Communication Skills Profile.* San Francisco: Jossey-Bass/Pfeiffer, 2000.

Whalen, D. Joel. *I See What You Mean: Persuasive Business Communication.* Thousand Oaks, CA: Sage, 1996.

WEB CORNER

www.west2k.com/wpdocs/q155.htm (How can we stomp out rumors?)

www. zzyx.ucse.edu/~archer/ (Exploring nonverbal communication.)

CHAPTER 12

Groups and Group Decision Making

Learning Objectives After reading and studying this chapter and doing the exercises, you should be able to

1. Explain the nature of groups and teams, formal and informal groups, and cross-functional teams.
2. Summarize the characteristics of an effective work group.
3. Explain three methods of group problem solving: brainstorming, the nominal group technique, and cause-and-effect diagrams.
4. Conduct yourself more effectively in a meeting.
5. Summarize some of the advantages and disadvantages of group effort, including group decision making.

Groups are vital to the understanding of business psychology because they are the building blocks of the larger organization. The department you are assigned to, the people you share a rest break with, and the special meeting you are asked to attend are among the many groups found within a firm. Because so much of organizational life involves group effort, much of your time on the job will be spent working with a small group of people. Another important reason for studying groups is that most of the achievements of modern organizations are really the product of team effort, rather than the accomplishments of individual superstars.

If you understand the nature of work groups, including teams, you will be able to contribute more effectively to group effort. Also, you will be better able to avoid some of the problems a group might create for you.

Aspects of working effectively within a group, especially teamwork, are studied at various places in this text. For example, Chapter 6 looks at the motivational contribution of team membership. Chapter 13 describes how to be a good team player. In this chapter we describe the major types of groups, characteristics of effective work groups, several approaches to group decision making, how to conduct yourself in a meeting, and the advantages and disadvantages of group effort.

MAJOR TYPES OF GROUPS

A **group** is a collection of people who interact with each other, are aware of each other, are working toward some common purpose, and perceive themselves to be a group. Thus, two state troopers seated in a patrol car, watching for speeders and other violators, would be a group. So would the head of a company copy and print center and his or her staff. In contrast, 12 people in an airport waiting for the same plane would not be a group in the technical sense. Although they might talk to each other, their interaction would not be on a planned or recurring basis. Nor would they be engaged in collective effort, a fundamental justification for forming a group.

An important insight into groups is that people often behave and perform differently as group members than they would individually. A group of people may laugh at a comment that its members individually would not find humorous. A group can accomplish a task, such as building a house, that could not be accomplished by combining the individual contributions of its members. And, unfortunately, a group of people will sometimes commit acts of vandalism and physical violence that the individual members would never do.

To further your understanding of groups we look at the difference between groups and teams and at informal versus formal groups. We also describe the cross-functional work team and a virtual team, two widely used formal work groups.

Groups versus Teams

Some researchers and managers believe that groups and teams function quite differently.[1] A **team** is a special type of group. Keep in mind that all teams are groups, but not all groups are teams. Team members have complementary skills and are committed to a common purpose, a set of performance goals, and a specific approach to the task. An important part of team functioning is **teamwork,** an understanding and commitment to group goals on the part of all team members.

Groups and teams can also be differentiated in other ways. A working group has a strong, clearly focused leader, whereas a team leader shares leadership roles. A group is characterized by individual accountability, whereas a team has both individual and mutual accountability. Another distinction is that the team delivers actual joint work projects—such as creating a new product.

Formal versus Informal Groups

Different schemes have been developed to classify the many types of groups found in work organizations. One particularly useful distinction is that drawn between formal and informal groups. Unless you understand the difference in functioning between formal and informal groups, you will have a difficult time adjusting to almost any place of work.

FORMAL GROUPS. A **formal group** is one deliberately formed by the organization to accomplish specific tasks and achieve objectives. The most common type of formal group is a work unit or department such as accounting, quality control, or young women's apparel. Formal groups can also be committees or task forces (a special-purpose group with a time limit). Formal groups are frequently

TABLE 12–1
A SAMPLING OF FORMAL WORK GROUPS

Because organizations are composed of work groups, many types of work groups are found in an organization. Quite often an employee belongs to both a permanent work group (such as a department) and a temporary work group (such as a committee). The following is a sample of six types of formal work groups.

1. *Department.* A basic unit within the firm that carries out a specific task over an indefinite period of time. For example, it is the job of the maintenance department to keep company equipment running smoothly and to keep the building and grounds in good shape.
2. *Committee.* A group of workers from the same or different parts of the organization who are asked to study a particular problem and then make recommendations to management. Standing committees are permanent, while ad hoc committees are temporary groups set up to study a nonrecurring problem.
3. *Work unit (or staff meeting).* A meeting composed of a department head and key department members (the staff). Its purposes include solving a particular problem and communicating information from the manager to the staff members, or in the opposite direction.
4. *Project team.* A group of people called together by the firm to accomplish a particular purpose or mission (such as building a space station or launching a new product). It involves a temporary group of specialists from diverse disciplines working together under the same project leader.
5. *Cross-functional team.* A work group composed of workers from different specialties, but about the same level in the organization, who come together to accomplish a task. (Described separately in this section.)
6. *Labor–management teams.* Groups composed of management and labor (usually union members) who jointly try to solve production and morale problems. They represent a high level of cooperation between management and labor and are based on a belief in group decision making and employee participation.

designated by the organization chart. At other times they are indicated in office correspondence. For example, "The people listed below are hereby assigned to the safety committee." Several different types of formal groups are defined in Table 12–1.

INFORMAL GROUPS. An organization cannot be understood by studying its formal groups alone. A large number of groups evolve naturally in an organization to take care of the desire for friendship and companionship, and sometimes to accomplish work. Such entities are referred to as **informal groups.** Although these groups are often thought of in relation to production and support workers, informal groups can be formed at any level in the organization. Here are three examples of informal groups.

1. Three assistants from the marketing department meet once a month for lunch to discuss mutual concerns and to seek relief from the tedious aspects of their job.
2. Four computer analysts form a jogging club that meets three days per week at lunch time to run two miles.
3. Three managers from different parts of the company commute to work together every business day when they are all in town. They often discuss current events and the stock market, but they also discuss company business while commuting to work.

As examples 1 and 3 suggest, informal groups are often work related. One function of the informal organization is to fill in the gaps left by the formal organization. Few organizations have a job description written for the "coffee pot tender," yet such a person arises on a rotating basis in many offices. Similarly, when somebody in your department is absent for legitimate reasons, you might take care of his or her emergency work, even though it is not a formal part of your job.

Cross-Functional Teams

The purpose of the cross-functional team is to get workers from different specialties to blend their talents toward a task that requires such a mix. A typical application of a cross-functional team would be to develop a new product such as a Net TV. Among the specialties needed on such a team would be computer science, engineering, manufacturing, industrial design, marketing, and finance. (The finance person would help guide the team toward producing a Net TV that could be sold at a profit.) When members from different specialties work together, they can take each other's perspectives into account when making their contribution. For example, if the manufacturing representative knows that a Net TV must sell for about one-half the price of a personal computer, then he or she will have to build the device inexpensively. In addition to product development, cross-functional teams are used for such purposes as improving quality, reducing costs, and running a company (in the form of a top-level management team).

A major advantage of cross-functional teams is that they enhance communication across groups, thereby saving time. A challenge with these teams, however, is that they often breed conflict because of the different points of view. Also, the members may lack the teamwork skills to bring about collaboration.[2] To perform well on a cross-functional team it is necessary to think in terms of the good of the larger organization, rather than in terms of one's specialty. For example, a manufacturing technician might say, "If I propose using expensive components for the Net TV, will the product cost too much for its intended market?"

Virtual Teams

Some teams conduct most of their work by sending electronic messages to each other. A **virtual team** is a small group of people who conduct almost all of their collaboration by electronic communication rather than face-to-face meetings. In the language of information technology, they engage in "cybercollaboration" by conducting "cybermeetings." E-mail including instant messaging is the usual medium for sharing information and conducting meetings. *Groupware* is another widely used approach to conducting a cybermeeting. Using groupware, several people can edit a document at the same time, or in sequence. Videoconferencing is another technological device that facilitates the virtual team.

Many high-tech companies make some use of virtual team and cybermeetings. Geographically dispersed companies that work with each other, such as in producing a world car, are a natural for virtual teams. It's less expensive for the field technician in Nigeria to hold a cybermeeting with his or her counterparts in South Africa, Portugal, and California than to bring them all together in one physical location.

Virtual teams enable companies to recruit people from many different locations who prefer to stay where they are located. Working at home is also more feasible with virtual teams because the people working from their homes can at least meet electronically. Despite the efficiency of virtual teams, there are times when face-to-face interaction is necessary to deal with complex and emotional issues. Negotiating a new contract between management and a labor union, for example, is not well suited for a cybermeeting. Another problem is that it is difficult to manage people who are supposed to work collaboratively and interactively, yet rarely ever see each other.[3]

CHARACTERISTICS OF EFFECTIVE WORK GROUPS

Groups, like individuals, have characteristics that contribute to their uniqueness and effectiveness. Effectiveness includes such factors as objective measures of production (e.g., units produced), favorable evaluations by the manager, and worker satisfaction. A recent buzzword for an extremely effective and enthusiastic work group is a *hot group*. It is the "contagious single-mindedness and the all-out dedication to doing something important that distinguishes hot groups from all other groups."[4] As shown in Figure 12–1, and based on dozens of different studies, effective work group characteristics can be grouped into the following eight characteristics or factors:[5]

1. *Enriched job design.* Effective work groups generally follow the type of job design associated with job enrichment (described in Chapter 6). For example, the task is perceived to be significant, and the group members work on an entire task. A major theme is self-management, as practiced by self-managing work teams. Frequent feedback on performance also contributes to group effectiveness.
2. *A feeling of empowerment.* An effective work group believes that it has the authority to solve a variety of problems without first obtaining approval from management. Empowered teams share the experiences of empowerment described in Chapter 6 about motivation: meaning, competence (self-efficacy), self-determination, and impact.
3. *Interdependent tasks and rewards.* In effective work groups the members depend on one another in several ways. Such groups show *task interdependence* in that the members interact with and depend on one another to accomplish the work. Task interdependence also contributes to satisfaction because members of a work group enjoy working jointly on tasks. *Interdependence of rewards* refers to the fact that the group members are working toward a common goal and receive at least some of their rewards based on achieving group goals.
4. *Right mix and size.* A variety of factors relating to the mix of group members are associated with effective work groups. A group whose members have diverse experience, knowledge, and education generally has improved problem solving. Cultural diversity tends to enhance creativity because various viewpoints are brought into play. However, only when each team member enjoys high-quality interactions can the full benefits of diversity be realized. The interactions relate to both the task itself (such as talking about improving a lawnmower starter) and social interactions

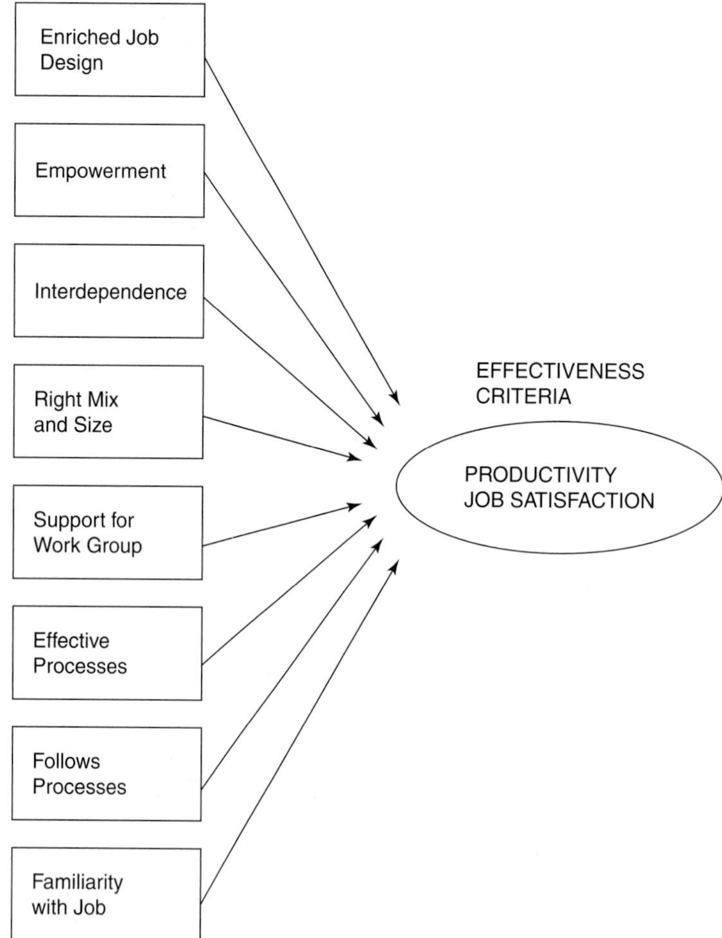

FIGURE 12–1 Work Group Characteristics Related to Effectiveness

Source: Synthesized from Michael A. Campion, Ellen M. Papper, and Gina Medsker, "Relations between Work Team Characteristics and Effectiveness: A Replication and Extension," *Personnel Psychology,* Summer 1996, p. 431; Brian D. Janz, Jason A. Colquitt, and Raymond A. Noe, "Knowledge Worker Team Effectiveness: The Role of Autonomy, Interdependence, Team Development, and Contextual Support Variables, *Personnel Psychology,* Winter 1997, pp. 877–904; Bradley L. Kirkman and Benson Rosen, "Powering Up Teams," *Organizational Dynamics,* Winter 2000, pp. 48–52; Gerben S. Van Der Vegt, et al., "Patterns of Interdependence in Work Teams: A Two-Level Investigation of the Relations with Job and Team Satisfaction," *Personnel Psychology,* Spring 2001, pp. 51–69.

(such as chatting about the stock market during a break).[6] Groups should be large enough to accomplish the work, but when they become too large, confusion and poor coordination may result. Also, larger groups tend to be less cohesive. Committees, work teams, and task forces tend to be most productive with 7 to 10 members.

Another important mix factor is the quality of work group members. A study of 51 work teams found that teams with members higher in mental ability, conscientiousness, extraversion, and emotional stability received higher supervisory ratings for team performance. (Put winners on your team and you are more likely to have a winning team.)[7] The group itself should have high emotional intelligence in the sense of being able to build relationships both inside and outside the team, and make constructive use of its emotion.[8]

5. *Good support for the work group.* One of the most important characteristics of an effective work group is the support it receives from the organization. Key support factors include giving the group the information it needs, coaching group members, providing the right technology, and providing recognition and other rewards. Training quite often facilitates work group effectiveness. The training content typically includes group decision making, interpersonal skills, technical knowledge, and the team philosophy.
6. *Effective processes within the group.* Many processes (activities) take place within the group that influence effectiveness. One is the belief that the group can do the job, reflecting high team spirit. Effectiveness is also enhanced when workers provide social support to each other through such means as helping each other to have positive interactions. Workload sharing is another process characteristic related to effectiveness. Communication and cooperation within the work group also contribute to effectiveness. Collectively, the right amount of these process characteristics contributes to *cohesiveness,* or a group that pulls together. Without cohesiveness, a group will fail to achieve synergy.
7. *Adherence to processes and procedures.* Teams that can be trusted to follow work processes and procedures tend to perform better. Adhering to such processes and procedures is also associated with high-quality output.
8. *Familiarity with jobs and coworkers.* Another factor related to work group effectiveness is familiarity. It refers to the specific knowledge group members have of their jobs, coworkers, and the work environment. Appropriate experience is therefore another factor that helps a group perform better.

To help you pull together loads of information about the characteristics of effective work groups and teams, study the following summary of research conducted with professional-level workers in a financial services firm. The researchers concluded:

> The high-performing teams performed a variety of tasks that members perceived to be significant. They were allowed a high degree of self-management; were interdependent in terms of tasks, goals, and feedback; and functioned as a single team. They tended to have members with complementary skills who were flexible in the tasks they performed. They were not too large for the tasks assigned them. They were well supported by the organization in terms of training, managerial support, and cooperation and communication from other teams. They had confidence in their teams' abilities, and members supported one another, communicated, cooperated, and fairly shared the workload.[9]

In short, if all the factors associated with work group effectiveness are present, the members might become a hot group!

GROUP DECISION MAKING AND PROBLEM SOLVING

Groups rather than individuals make most big decisions in organizations. Even if a group of people does not sit together to thrash out a decision, several people provide their input to any major decision. In general, decision making by groups has proved superior to individual decision making.[10] Yet this generalization is not overwhelmingly true. Many talented and imaginative individuals do not require group discussion to make an effective decision.

Our description of group decision making and problem solving is divided into five parts: (1) group decision-making styles, (2) general problem-solving groups, (3) brainstorming, (4) the nominal group technique, and (5) the cause-and-effect diagram.

Group Decision-Making Styles

The term *group decision making* refers to the fact that the group plays a role in making the decision. The opposite would be individual decision making in which the group leader makes a decision without consulting anybody. Group decision making takes place in different degrees. One extreme is *consultative,* in which the group leader consults with members before making a decision. The other extreme is *democratic decision making,* in which the problem at hand is turned over to the group, and they are delegated the authority to arrive at a decision themselves.

Midway between the two is *consensus decision making,* in which the manager shares the problem with group members. Together they generate and evaluate alternatives and attempt to reach agreement on a solution. Consensus is achieved when every member can say, "I have had an opportunity to express my views fully, and they have been thoughtfully considered by the group. Even though this solution is not the one I believe is optimal, it is acceptable and I will support it. I endorse the validity of the process we have undertaken."[11]

General Problem-Solving Groups

When a group of workers at any level gathers to solve a problem, they typically hold a discussion, rather than rely on a formal method of group decision making. These general problem-solving groups are likely to produce the best results when they follow the decision-making steps outlined in Chapter 5. Equally important, the group members should follow the suggestions for conducting themselves in a meeting, described later in this chapter. Table 12–2 describes recommended steps for conducting group decision making; these are similar to the decision-making steps outlined in Figure 5–1.

Brainstorming

One of the best methods of understanding how a group can contribute to problem solving is to observe group **brainstorming.** This method has become a standard way of generating multiple alternatives for solving a problem. The term

TABLE 12–2
STEPS FOR EFFECTIVE GROUP DECISION MAKING

1. *Identify the problem.* Describe specifically what the problem is and how it manifests itself.
2. *Clarify the problem.* If group members do not perceive the problem the same way, they will offer divergent solutions to their own individual perceptions of the problem.
3. *Analyze the cause.* To convert "what is" into "what we want," the group must understand the causes of the specific problems and find ways to overcome those causes.
4. *Search for alternative solutions.* Remember that multiple alternative solutions can be found to most problems.
5. *Select alternatives.* Identify the criteria that solutions must meet, and then discuss the pros and cons of the proposed alternatives. No solution should be laughed at or scorned.
6. *Plan for implementation.* Decide what actions are necessary to carry out the chosen solution to the problem.
7. *Clarify the contract.* The contract is a restatement of what group members have agreed to do and deadlines for accomplishment.
8. *Develop an action plan.* Specify who does what and when to carry out the contract.
9. *Provide for evaluation and accountability.* After the plan is implemented, reconvene to discuss progress and to hold people accountable for results that have not been achieved.

Source: Derived from Andrew E. Schwartz and Joy Levin, "Better Group Decision Making," *Supervisory Management,* June 1990, p. 4.

brainstorm has become synonymous with a clever idea. It really means to "storm the brain" in order to search for alternatives. Brainstorming is best suited to finding lists of alternatives to problems. Later, the technical details of how to achieve and implement these alternatives can be worked out. Brainstorming was developed for use in creating advertising campaigns. It is now put to such diverse uses as thinking of new products, making recommendations for new employee benefits, finding ways of raising money for a cause, and improving software. Brainstorming is not well suited to arriving at complex solutions to problems or working out the details of a plan (for example, how to arrange the equipment in an office).

RULES FOR BRAINSTORMING. To conduct an effective brainstorming session, keep in mind these straightforward rules:

1. Group size should be about five to seven people. If there are too few people, not enough suggestions are generated. If too many people participate, the session becomes uncontrolled.
2. No criticism is allowed. All suggestions should be welcome, and it is particularly important not to use derisive laughter. As the old saying goes, "They laughed at Thomas Edison."
3. Freewheeling is encouraged. The more outlandish the idea, the better. It's always easier to tame down an idea than to think it up.
4. Quantity and variety are very important. The greater the number of ideas put forth, the greater the likelihood of a breakthrough idea.
5. Combinations and improvements are encouraged. Building on the ideas of others, including combining them, is very productive. "Hitchhiking" is an essential part of brainstorming.

6. Notes must be taken during the sessions either manually or with an electronic recording device. One person serves as a recording secretary.
7. The alternatives generated during the first part of the session should later be edited for duplication and refinement. At some point the best ideas can be set aside for possible implementation.
8. Do not overstructure by following any of the preceding seven rules too rigidly. Brainstorming is a spontaneous small-group process.

A current practice in brainstorming is **electronic brainstorming.** Using this method, group members simultaneously enter their suggestions into a computer, and the ideas are distributed to the screens of other group members. Although the group members do not talk to each other, they are still able to build on each other's ideas and combine ideas. Electronic brainstorming is much like the nominal group technique, to be described shortly. An experiment with electronic brainstorming indicated that with large groups, the method produces more useful ideas than does verbal (the usual type of) brainstorming.[12]

Brainstorming has to be implemented in the right environment (or corporate culture) to produce good results. The discussion in Chapter 5 about the right atmosphere for creativity supports this insight. In an innovative culture, a technique like brainstorming is more likely to yield creative ideas. IDEO, the world's leading industrial design firm makes extensive use of brainstorming. At the same time, innovation is a defining value of their business.[13]

Skill-Building Exercise 12–1 will give you an opportunity to apply brainstorming for one of its original purposes—improving the marketing of an everyday service.

The Nominal Group Technique

At times a leader is faced with a major problem that would benefit from the input of group members. Because of the magnitude of the problem, it would be helpful to know what each member thought of the others' positions on the problem. Brainstorming is not advisable because the problem is still in the exploration phase

SKILL-BUILDING EXERCISE 12–1

1-800-Insight

Using conventional brainstorming, huddle in small groups. Your task is to develop 800, 888, or 900 telephone numbers for firms in various fields. Keep in mind that the best 800 (or 888, or 900) numbers are easy to memorize and have a logical connection to the goods or services provided. After each group makes up its list of telephone numbers (approximately five for each firm on the list), compare results with the other groups. Here is the list of enterprises:

- A nationwide chain of funeral homes
- An air-conditioning firm
- A software problem help line for Microsoft Corporation
- A used-car chain
- A prayer service (a 900 number)
- An introduction (dating) service (a 900 number)

and requires more than a list of alternative solutions. A problem-solving technique developed to fit this situation is the **nominal group technique (NGT).** It calls people together in a structured meeting with limited interaction. The group is called "nominal" because people present their ideas initially without interacting with each other, as they would be in a "real" group. George P. Huber provides a general description that will help you gain insight into the process.[14]

> Imagine a meeting room in which seven to ten individuals are sitting around a table in full view of each other. At the beginning of the meeting they are not speaking to one another. Instead, each individual is writing ideas on their pads of paper. (E-mail or groupware often replaces pads of paper.) At the end of five to ten minutes, a structured sharing of ideas takes place. Each individual, in round-robin fashion, presents one idea from his or her private list. A recorder or leader writes that idea on a flip chart in full view of other members. There is still no discussion at this point of the meeting—only the recording. Round-robin listing continues until all members indicate they have no further ideas to share.

The output from this phase is a list of ideas. For example, a school system faced with a declining student population arrived at these alternatives, using the nominal group technique: "Why not sell three small schools and replace them with one large, central building?" or "I wonder if we should be talking about consolidation until we first obtain more information about population trends in this district?"

Next, a very structured discussion takes place; this is called the interactive phase of the meeting. Questions and comments are solicited for each idea posted on the flip chart. ("What do you folks think about this idea of selling the smaller buildings and constructing one new, large building?") When the process of asking for reactions to the ideas is complete, independent evaluation of the ideas takes place. Each group member, acting alone, indicates his or her preference by ranking the various ideas. Again, these ideas may be alternative solutions to the problem or factors the group should take into consideration in trying to solve the problem. (The total rank is the sum of all the ranks given an idea by the members, such as 10, 9, 8, 9, 7, and so forth.) At this stage, we know the total rank the group has attached to each idea. The idea with the highest total rank becomes the alternative chosen—and therefore the decision made—by the group.

A key feature of the nominal group technique is that it provides all participants with an equal voice. The NGT makes it difficult for one member to control the discussion and dominate the decision-making process.[15]

Cause-and-Effect Diagram

To improve customer satisfaction, many companies turn to **quality-improvement teams,** groups of workers who use problem-solving techniques to enhance customer satisfaction. Because quality is usually defined in terms of meeting customer needs, any change that increases customer satisfaction results in quality improvement. A **cause-and-effect diagram** is a decision-making technique widely used by quality-improvement teams. The diagram is also known as the *fishbone diagram* because of its shape. According to this technique, any manufacturing process can be divided into four major categories or causes, as shown in Figure 12–2. The causes have an impact on a quality characteristic, or effect. The four causes are person, machine, method, and material.

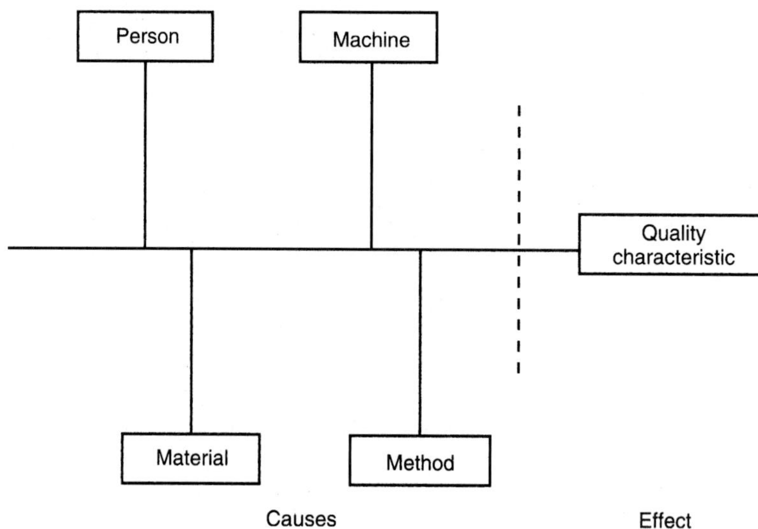

FIGURE 12–2 Basic Cause-and-Effect Diagram

In the cause-and-effect diagram, the four causes are usually subdivided. For example, the person category might be divided into selection of employee, education, training, motivation, and job satisfaction. A quality defect might be traced to the low job satisfaction of employees who are disgruntled about physical working conditions. The job of the quality-improvement team would be to investigate such a possibility.

Many people will have the opportunity to use the four problem-solving techniques just described. We turn next to a small-group activity that virtually every member of this book will experience.

HOW TO CONDUCT YOURSELF IN A FACE-TO-FACE MEETING

A substantial part of work life takes place in meetings. One analysis concluded that managers spend as much as 60 percent of their time in meetings,[16] with many top-level managers spending up to 30 hours in face-to-face meetings. With the increased emphasis on teamwork, professional, technical, and support workers are also required to attend many meetings.

It is fashionable to put down meetings with such statements as "Ugh, not another meeting!" or "I wish I didn't have to attend today's meeting. I'd much prefer to work." Despite these criticisms, collective effort would be very difficult without formal meetings. A constructive viewpoint about meetings is not to try to avoid them, but to learn how to be an effective contributor to them. The task at hand most likely serves some worthwhile purpose. Also of significance, face-to-face meetings represent an exceptional opportunity to be observed by important people in your firm. If you observe the guidelines presented in the following paragraphs, you will most likely perform well in meetings.

Be qualified to serve. People perform the best in meetings when they have the necessary background of knowledge and interest to do a good job. If you know the topic of the meeting in advance, do your homework. Carefully read some relevant information about the topic and/or speak to some knowledgeable people. In this way you will be prepared to make intelligent comments and suggestions.

A major factor in unproductive business meetings is having the wrong people present. Meetings often include people who are "dead weight"—people who are not directly involved in the matter under discussion.[17] Preparing in advance for a meeting and knowing how the meeting applies to you or your work unit can help you to avoid being classified as dead weight.

Resolve small issues ahead of time with e-mail. Meetings can be briefer and less mundane when small issues are resolved ahead of time. E-mail is particularly effective for resolving minor administrative issues, and also for collecting agenda items in advance.

Be punctual and stay to the end. Arriving late at a meeting is taboo unless you are a high-ranking executive who has called the meeting. Leaving early creates an equally negative impression. Why irritate the influential people who might be present at the meeting?

Take notes on key points during the meeting. By so doing you will be able to refer back to useful ideas when you want to formulate a suggestion of your own. The notes can also be used when you are studying the problem at a later time. Taking notes will also serve to impress the meeting chairperson. To be up to date, bring along a laptop computer for note taking.

Do not dominate or contribute too little. An effective attendee at a meeting participates neither too much nor too little. The dominator quickly irritates others and tends to subvert a major purpose of the meeting—gathering ideas from several people. The person who contributes too little may be perceived as uninterested in the meeting or as too shy to become a leader. One of the most destructive forces in a group can be the participant who is trying harder than everybody else.

Stick with the agenda. Other people present at the meeting, including the leader, will become annoyed if you digress to irrelevant topics. If somebody else is going off on a tangent, perhaps you can salvage the situation by asking, "Excuse me, but how do your comments relate to the agenda?"

Ask intelligent questions. If you do not have relevant ideas to contribute to the meeting, you can at least ask intelligent questions. The ability to ask intelligent questions is characteristic of competent people in all fields. An example of a multipurpose intelligent question to ask at most meetings is, "If we followed your suggestion, what would be the impact on other departments in the organization?" When you ask this question, some people will perceive you as a systems thinker—a person who understands how the different parts of the organization are interrelated.

Focus your attention on surmountable problems. Many problem-solving groups make the mistake of spending time discussing who is to blame for the problem or what should have been done to avoid the problem. Rather than try to change the past, an impossible task, it is better to focus on how things can be improved in the future.

Use nonverbal communication to show that you are interested. Use gestures, posture, and facial expressions to communicate an intense interest in the topic under discussion. Smile frequently, sit erect, lean toward a member who makes a useful comment, and so forth. You might even try mirroring the person presenting at the moment to establish stronger rapport.

Display good manners and meeting etiquette. Your manners—good, bad, or mediocre—are always on display in a meeting. It is therefore important to display good manners such as being polite and encouraging others. Bad manners often displayed in meetings include side conversations, reading information other than handouts for the meeting, and eating food during the meeting when it is not served to all participants.

ADVANTAGES AND DISADVANTAGES OF GROUP EFFORT AND GROUP DECISION MAKING

Group effort, including group decision making, is essential for collective activity, but it has many well-known disadvantages. A description of the major advantages and disadvantages is helpful in recognizing when a group approach to problem solving is advisable. The "Guidelines for Personal Effectiveness" box at the end of the chapter provides additional insight into choosing between individual and collective effort.

Advantages of Group Activity

Group effort and group decision making offer several advantages over the same activities carried out individually. First, a key advantage is that groups often accomplish tasks not readily done by individuals such as developing a new product. Second, group decision making is helpful in gaining acceptance and commitment. If you and your friends were planning a vacation together, you would probably have less bickering after the decision was made if it were a joint decision. If one person arbitrarily chose a lakeside cottage, the other members of the group would probably complain heatedly about the mosquitoes. If you all agreed to the lakeside, the mosquitoes would probably be less bothersome. People tend to accept a decision when they have contributed to its making.

Third, groups can help people overcome blocks in their thinking, leading to more creative solutions to problems. Also, groups are less likely than individuals to get into ruts in their thinking. Another group member can step in and help the blocked person pursue another path by gentle prodding.

Fourth, group members evaluate each other's thinking, so major errors are likely to be avoided. The marketing manager of an Internet service provider decided to launch a campaign emphasizing teenagers and young adults. Two team members pointed out that the fastest-growing segment of Internet users are seniors who use e-mail to stay in touch with family members. The campaign was changed to be more inclusive of all age groups, resulting in a substantial number of new subscribers.

Fifth, working in a group enhances the job satisfaction of many members. Being a member of a work group makes it possible to satisfy more needs than if one worked alone. Among these are needs for affiliation, security, self-esteem, and self-fulfillment. For example, many people prefer working in groups to individual effort because of the opportunity the former provides for socializing with others and being part of the office gang. In this way, the need for affiliation can be satisfied.

Sixth, the group is an important socializing force in the organization. New workers learn about the customs, traditions, dos and don'ts, and preferred modes of behavior from work group members. At the same time, the group helps new employees develop commitment to the firm.[18]

Disadvantages of Group Effort

Group activity, including decision making, has some potential disadvantages for individuals and organizations. We will first describe two disadvantages of group activity, followed by three disadvantages of group decision making.

Neglect of the Importance of the Individual. An overemphasis on the contributions of groups to the organization can overlook the importance of the individual. Without talented members, a group would have little to offer. Inspirational leadership is more likely to stem from an individual than a group. (How often do you see a statue of a committee in a park or office-building lobby?) Athletic teams also search for talented individuals who can blend their talents with other group members to achieve superior results.

Social Loafing. Unless assignments are given out carefully to each group member, an undermotivated person can often squeeze by without contributing his or her fair share. **Social loafing** is the psychological term for shirking individual responsibility in a group setting. The larger the group, the greater the tendency toward loafing, because some individuals may think that their contribution is not so important. Another explanation offered for social loafing is that some group members believe that others are likely to withhold effort when working in a group. As a consequence they withhold effort themselves to avoid being played for a sucker.

The social loafer risks being ostracized by the group but may be willing to pay the price rather than work hard. Loafing of this type is sometimes found in groups such as committees and project teams. For example, when the committee leader asks for volunteers to serve on a subcommittee, some people turn their head or look down at the conference table. Have you ever worked on a group project for school in which one or more people were social loafers?

Individual Dominance. A problem frequently encountered in group decision making is **individual dominance**—one individual dominates the group, thus negating the potential benefits of input from all the members. Dominance by one member tends to take place more frequently when people in the group are of unequal rank. An authoritarian manager often dominates the group because people are hesitant to criticize him or her. David Hampton suggests that if you are the head of a group or a high-status participant, you should do four things to circumvent the problem of individual dominance.[19]

- Refrain from announcing your preferred solution while the group is working through the problem.
- Listen carefully to suggestions from every group member.
- Encourage every group member to participate.
- Demonstrate concern for achieving a high-quality solution.

Problems such as individual dominance take place frequently during meetings, because people bring their personal characteristics into a meeting. For example, extraverted individuals will tend to dominate, while introverted individuals will be more laid back.

Group Polarization. During group problem solving, or group discussion in general, members often shift their attitudes. Sometimes the group moves toward taking greater risks; this is called the risky shift. At other times the group moves toward a more conservative position. The general term for moving in either direction is **group polarization,** a situation in which postdiscussion attitudes tend to be more extreme than prediscussion attitudes.[20] For example, as a result of group discussion the members of a production team might make a more conservative forecast of how many units they can produce in a month.

Group discussion facilitates polarization for several reasons. Discovering that others share our opinions may reinforce and strengthen our position. Listening to persuasive arguments may also strengthen our convictions. The devil-made-me-do-it attitude is another contributor to polarization. If responsibility is diffused, a person will feel less responsible—and less guilty—about taking an extreme position.

Groupthink. A potential disadvantage of group decision making is **groupthink,** a deterioration of mental efficiency, reality testing, and moral judgment in the interest of group solidarity. Simply put, groupthink is an extreme form of consensus. The group atmosphere values getting along more than getting things done.[21] The group thinks as a unit, believes it is impervious to outside criticism, and begins to have illusions about its own invincibility. As a consequence, the group loses its powers of critical analysis.

One historically important example of groupthink took place in relation to the explosion of the space shuttle *Challenger.* According to several analyses of the incident, NASA managers were so committed to reaching space program objectives that they ignored safety warnings from people both within and outside the agency. As reported in the internal NASA briefing paper dated July 20, 1986, both astronauts and engineers expressed concern that the agency's management had a groupthink mentality.

Of related significance, the management style of NASA managers is characterized by a tendency not to reverse decisions and not to heed the advice of people outside the management group. The analysis of their styles was conducted by a series of management-style tests administered several years prior to the *Challenger* explosion.[22]

Although groupthink is almost always perceived to be a disadvantage of group decision making, new evidence suggests that groupthink can make a positive contribution to group performance. Jin Nam Choi and Myung Un Kim examined groupthink and team activities in 30 organization teams faced with impending crises such as a fire at a franchise gas station, or a new branch being opened by a competitor. Various symptoms of groupthink studied showed a positive relationship with team performance. These symptoms were the illusion of invulnerability, belief in inherent group morality, and the illusion of unanimity. Attitudes such as feeling invulnerable can promote morale and confidence, which, in turn, elevate motivation.[23]

The negative aspects of groupthink can often be prevented if the team leader, or a member, encourages all team members to express doubts and criticisms of proposed solutions to the problem or suggested courses of action. It is also helpful to periodically invite qualified outsiders to meet with the group and provide suggestions.

To integrate the information about the advantages and disadvantages of groups and group decision making, we specify the conditions under which groups and teams are likely to offer an edge over individual effort. Groups and teams offer the most advantage in the following situations:[24]

- When work is conducted with people from different specialties, and the work has to be integrated
- The task is so complex that different types of skills are required to accomplish the task
- The task is so large that it is beyond the grasp of one person
- When the environment changes rapidly, such as keeping up with high technology.

Since the conditions just stated are so frequently found in organizations, groups, teams, and group decision making are often valuable.

SUMMARY OF KEY POINTS

- Groups are the building blocks of the larger organization. A team is a special type of group in which members have complementary skills and are committed to a common purpose, a set of performance goals, and a specific approach to the task. A team leader is more likely to share leadership tasks than a group leader would be.
- A formal group is one deliberately formed by the organization to accomplish specific tasks and achieve objectives. An informal group is one that evolves naturally in an organization to take care of people's desires for friendship and companionship. The purpose of the cross-functional team is to get workers from different specialties to blend their talents toward a task that requires such a mix. Virtual teams accomplish their work by meeting electronically rather than face-to-face.
- The characteristics of effective work groups are: (1) enriched job design, (2) empowerment, (3) interdependent tasks and rewards, (4) right mix and size, (5) good support for the work group, (6) effective processes within the group, (7) adherence to processes and procedures, and (8) familiarity with jobs and coworkers.
- Most major decisions in organizations are made by groups. Group input into decisions varies from merely being consulted to having full authority for making the decision.
- General problem-solving groups are widely used for decision making. They are likely to produce the best results when they follow the recommended decision-making steps.
- Brainstorming is a method by which a group arrives at a wide range of potential solutions to a problem. Each group member basically contributes as many ideas as his or her imagination will allow. After a while, the ideas are sorted out and refined. Brainstorming works best in an innovative culture.

- The nominal group technique (NGT) is a method of exploring the nature of a problem and generating alternative solutions. It involves a group of 7 to 10 individuals contributing their written thoughts about the problem and then all other members responding to their ideas. Members rank or rate the ideas, and the final group decision is the pooled outcome of the individual votes.
- A cause-and-effect diagram is a decision-making technique widely used by quality-improvement teams. According to this technique, any manufacturing process can be divided into four major categories or causes: person, machine, method, and material. The causes have an impact on a quality characteristic (or effect).
- If you advance in your career, it is almost inevitable that you will be required to attend meetings. A number of suggestions for performing well in them are offered in this chapter. Among the major suggestions are these: (1) be qualified to serve, (2) do not dominate or contribute too little, (3) stick with the agenda, (4) ask intelligent questions, and (5) display good manners.
- Group effort, including group decision making, offers several advantages. Groups often accomplish tasks not readily done by individuals. Acceptance and commitment increase, members help each other overcome blocks in their thinking, major errors are avoided, and job satisfaction may increase.
- Group effort also has some potential disadvantages. The importance of the individual to the organization might be neglected. Social loafing, or shirking individual responsibility, is commonly found. A given individual may dominate the meeting, thus taking away the advantages of a group. Group polarization may take place in which the members shift their attitude toward a more extreme position. Another problem is groupthink, an extreme form of consensus whereby the group loses its power of critical analysis and may make outrageously bad decisions. However, some aspects of groupthink, such as feeling invulnerable, may raise morale and productivity.
- Groups and teams are most advantageous when work is conducted with people from different specialties, the task is complex and large, and the environment changes rapidly.

GUIDELINES FOR PERSONAL EFFECTIVENESS

1. Being able to function well in a group is a requirement for effectiveness, in virtually any organization. However, from the standpoint of long-term career growth, be willing to loosen your ties with your work group. Identifying too closely with a work group narrows your perspective and may lead to overconformity.
2. Group decision making is an important contribution to improving the quality of decisions. However, it is time consuming and is best reserved for major decisions. Group decision making also offers an advantage when group-member commitment is important.
3. When faced with an important problem for which an out of the ordinary solution is required, it could be to your advantage to utilize brainstorming or the nominal group technique. As with other skills, both techniques require practice to make perfect.
4. An important skill for advancing your career is to perform well in meetings. They are good vehicles for making suggestions to the organization. In addition, many judgments are made about you on the basis of your actions in meetings. To improve your skills as a participant in a meeting, follow the suggestions presented in the chapter.

DISCUSSION QUESTIONS AND ACTIVITIES

1. In your own words, what is the alleged difference between a group and a team?
2. Being a member of a work group is a source of job satisfaction for many people. What psychological needs might the group satisfy for these people?
3. Are the company workers who run a company physical fitness center a formal group? Explain your reasoning.
4. Take a group familiar to you such as a study group, work group, or athletic team. Analyze the group from the standpoint of having the characteristics of an effective work group.
5. Why do the vast majority of people enjoy group brainstorming?
6. Identify two problems that you think are well suited to solving through the NGT.
7. How does the cause-and-effect diagram fit in with the general approach to group decision making summarized in Table 12–2?
8. Provide an example of social loafing that you have observed. What actions, if any, did the group take to improve the contribution of the social loafer?
9. High-level managers, such as CEOs, typically spend about 30 hours per week in meetings. How does this fact influence your attitude toward becoming an executive?
10. Find an example of groupthink by searching the Internet, or describe an original example you have observed.

REFERENCES

1. Jon R. Katzenbach and Douglas K. Smith, "The Discipline of Teams," *Harvard Business Review,* March–April 1993, p. 113; Oren Harari, "The Dream Team," *Management Review,* October 1995, pp. 29–31.
2. Avan R. Jassawalla and Hemant C. Sashittal, "Building Collaborative Cross-Functional New Product Teams," *Academy of Management Executive,* August 1999, pp. 50–63.
3. Charlene Marmer Solomon, "Managing Virtual Teams," *Workforce,* June 2001, pp. 60–65.
4. Jean Lipman-Blumen and Harold J. Leavitt, "Hot Groups 'With Attitude': A New Organizational State of Mind," *Organizational Dynamics,* Spring 1999, p. 63.
5. Michael A. Campion, Ellen M. Papper, and Gina Medsker, "Relations between Work Team Characteristics and Effectiveness: A Replication and Extension," *Personnel Psychology,* Summer 1996, p. 431; Brian D. Janz, Jason A. Colquitt, and Raymond A. Noe, "Knowledge Worker Team Effectiveness: The Role of Autonomy, Interdependence, Team Development, and Contextual Support Variables, *Personnel Psychology,* Winter 1997, pp. 877–904; Bradley L. Kirkman and Benson Rosen, "Powering Up Teams," *Organizational Dynamics,* Winter 2000, pp. 48–52; Gerben S. Van Der Vegt, et al., "Patterns of Interdependence in Work Teams: A Two-Level Investigation of the Relations with Job and Team Satisfaction," *Personnel Psychology,* Spring 2001, pp. 51–69.
6. Priscilla M. Ellass and Laura M. Graves, "Demographic Diversity in Decision-Making Groups: The Experience of Women and People of Color," *Academy of Management Review,* October 1997, p. 968.
7. Murray R. Barrick, et al., "Relating Member Ability and Personality to Work-Team Processes and Team Effectiveness," *Journal of Applied Psychology,* June 1998, pp. 377–391.

AN APPLIED PSYCHOLOGY CASE PROBLEM

Struggling to Make a Decision at BMI

Building Maintenance Inc., a firm of 325 full- and part-time employees is engaged in the cleaning and general maintenance of offices and shopping plazas. Bud Nyrod founded BMI as "one man and one van" 10 years ago. The four other members of the executive team also have a financial stake in the business.

BMI is headquartered in an old office building scheduled for demolition. The pending demolition has forced the firm to face a relocation decision. Bud called a 10 A.M. meeting of the executive team to address the problem. As he entered the conference room, Karen, Liz, Marty, and Nick were already seated.

Bud: Good to see the whole team here. I assume that you have already given some thought to our relocation decision. Let me review the alternatives I see. We can either relocate to some decent space in one of the newly refurbished downtown buildings, or we can get some slightly better space in a suburban park. Karen, as our financial officer, you must have some relevant facts and figures.

Karen: As you requested a few weeks ago, Bud, I have looked into a variety of possibilities. We can get some decent downtown space at about $30 per square foot. And, we can get first-rate accommodations in a suburban office park for about $33 per square foot. Relocation costs would be about the same.

Marty: Customers are influenced by image. So long as we have a good image, I think the customer will be satisfied. By the way, we are doing something that is negatively affecting our image. Our customer-service representatives are just too rude over the phone. I think these folks should have proper training before we turn them loose on the customer phone. Lots of other companies have good brooms, vacuum cleaners, and power-cleaning equipment. Our only edge is the good service we offer customers.

Bud: Liz, what is your position on this relocation decision?

Liz: As employment director, I have a lot to say about relocation. I agree with Marty that customer service should receive top weight in any decision we make about relocation. Customer service, of course, is a direct result of having an efficient crew of maintenance employees. A suburban office park may sound glamorous, but it could be a disaster in terms of recruiting staff. Maintenance workers can afford to get downtown. The vast majority of them live in the city, and they are dependent on mass transit to get to work.

You typically need private transportation to get to an office park. The vast majority of our permanent and temporary employees do not own cars or trucks. And many of them who do own vehicles, usually can't afford to keep them in good repair. Many of the temporary help can only put gas in their cars on payday.

So if we relocate to a suburban park, we'll have to rent a small employment office downtown anyway.

Bud: So you're telling us that maybe we should choose both alternatives. We should open an employment office downtown and move the executive office to a suburban office park.

Liz: Now we're introducing a third alternative. We could have two offices downtown: one for the executive and clerical staff and one for hiring maintenance workers.

Bud: Nick, what do you think? Which location would be best for you as director of maintenance operations?

Nick: I'm not in the office too much. I spend most of my time in the field overseeing our supervisors and their crews. Most of our help never see the office after they are hired unless they have a major problem. They report directly to the site. To them their place of work is the building or shopping plaza where they are assigned. Other things are more important than the location of company headquarters.

One of the most important things we should be considering is a big holiday party for this year. I think a year-end party is a real morale builder. It's cost effective in terms of how much turnover it reduces. Some of the maintenance staff will stay on an extra month just to attend the party.

Marty: It looks like you folks have got the major issues out on the table. I really don't care where we locate so long as the needs of our customers come first. I'm eager to know what you people decide. But right now I have to run. I have a luncheon appointment on the other side of town that could mean a big shopping plaza contract for us.

Bud: Good luck with the sales call, Marty. However, I think you could have scheduled that luncheon for another day. This is a pretty important issue. I'd like you to stay for five more minutes.

Nick: It seems that it's premature for us to reach a decision on this important matter today. Maybe we should call in an office location consultant to help us decide what to do. In the meantime, let's talk some more about the office party. I kind of like that idea.

Questions

1. How effective is the BMI team as a problem-solving group?
2. What recommendations can you make to the BMI team to better solve the problem it is facing?
3. How might the team have used the nominal group technique to help solve the problem of office relocation?

AN APPLIED PSYCHOLOGY CASE PROBLEM

The Torpedoed Submarine Rolls

Chad Davis is the sales manager for Guarino's Bakery, a supplier of bread products, cakes, and pastries to local restaurants and stores. He enjoys the challenge of his job and welcomes the opportunity to practice the skills and techniques of a professional manager. Chad has acquired some of these techniques through experience and many others through reading business books and through course work.

During the last three months, five accounts have stopped ordering the Italian bread from Guarino's that they use for submarine sandwiches. The president and owner, Angelo Guarino, told Chad, "Our submarine bread sales are being torpedoed. Our reputation is getting so bad that we'll soon be out of business. Find out by next week what has gone wrong with our line of bread. Max (the head baker) swears the bread hasn't changed."

"Angelo, I've been trying hard to find the answer," responded Chad. "So far, the only clue I have is that our submarine rolls just don't taste right. Something is wrong, but our customers don't know what it is. Several of them have complained that their customers say the bread is just not as good as in the past."

Angelo retorted, "Then go back and investigate some more. We've got to know what's wrong."

Chad said to himself, "Now is the time for action. But I'm not sure which action. Should I take a survey of dissatisfied customers? Should I increase the advertising budget?"

Questions

1. Why is this case included in a chapter about groups and group decision making?
2. Which technique should Chad use to solve the problem of customer resistance to the submarine rolls?
3. What is the underlying, or true, problem facing Guarino's Bakery?

8. Vanessa Urch Druskat and Steven B. Wolff, "Building the Emotional Intelligence of Groups," *Harvard Business Review,* March 2001, pp. 80–90.
9. Campion, Papper, and Medsker, "Relations between Work Team Characteristics and Effectiveness," p. 450.
10. Larry K. Michaelsen, Warren E. Watson, and Robert H. Black, "A Realistic Test of Individual versus Group Decision Making," *Journal of Applied Psychology,* October 1989, pp. 834–839.
11. William B. Eddy, *The Manager and the Working Group* (New York: Praeger, 1985), pp. 150–151.
12. R. Brent Gallupe and Associates, "Electronic Brainstorming and Group Size," *Academy of Management Journal,* June 1992, p. 352.
13. Tom Kelley with Jonathan Littman, *The Art of Innovation: Lessons in Creativity from IDEO, America's Leading Design Firm* (New York: Doubleday/Currency Books, 2001).
14. George P. Huber, *Managerial Decision Making* (Glenview, IL: Scott, Foresman, 1980), p. 199. See also "Nominal Group Technique," http://www.dipoli.hut.fi/org/TechNet/org/eurocinet/tool18.html.
15. Bob Debold, "The Nominal Group Technique," www.deboldgroup.com/TQM/nominal.htm. Copyright 1996.
16. Dave Day, "Making the Most of Meetings," *Personnel Journal,* March 1990, p. 34.
17. Daniel Goleman, "New Research Is Changing Old Concepts of How Groups Function," *New York Times* syndicated story, June 12, 1988.
18. Marlene Turner (ed.), *Groups at Work: Theory and Research* (Mahwah, NJ: Lawrence Erlbaum Associates, 2001).
19. David R. Hampton, *Contemporary Management* (New York: McGraw-Hill 1977), p. 397.
20. Our discussion is based on Gregory Moorhead and Ricky W. Griffin, *Organizational Behavior: Managing People and Organizations,* 4th ed. (Boston: Houghton Mifflin, 1995), pp. 278–279.
21. Irving L. Janis, *Victims of Groupthink: A Psychological Study of Foreign Policy Decisions and Fiascos* (Boston: Houghton Mifflin, 1972), 39–40; Glenn Whyte, "Groupthink Reconsidered," *Academy of Management Review,* January 1989, pp. 40–56.
22. Kenneth A. Kovach and Barry Bender, "NASA Managers and *Challenger:* A Profile of Possible Explanations," *Personnel,* April 1987, p. 40.
23. Jin Nam Choi and Myung Un Kim, "The Organizational Application of Groupthink and Its Limitations in Organizations," *Journal of Applied Psychology,* April 1999, pp. 297–306.
24. Theresa Kline, *Rethinking Teams: The Revolutionary Research-Based Guide That Puts Theory Into Practice* (San Francisco: Jossey-Bass/Pfeiffer, 1999); Russ Forrester and Allan B. Drexler, "A Model for Team-Based Performance," *Academy of Management Executive,* August 1999, p. 47.

SUGGESTED READING

Eisenhardt, Kathleen M., Kahwajy, Jean L., and Bourgeois, L. J. III. "How Management Teams Can Have a Good Fight." *Harvard Business Review,* July–August 1997, pp. 75–85.

Heimbouch, Hollis. "Should This Team Be Saved?" *Harvard Business Review,* July–August 2001, pp. 31–40.

Katz, Nancy. "Sports Teams as a Model for Workplace Teams: Lessons and Liabilities." *Academy of Management Executive,* August 2001, pp. 56–67.

Katzenbach, Jon R. "The Myth of the Top Management Team." *Harvard Business Review,* November–December 1997, pp. 82–92.

Kirkman, Bradley L., Gibson, Cristina B., and Shapiro, Debra L. "'Exporting' Teams: Enhancing the Implementation and Effectiveness of Work Teams in Global Affiliates," *Organizational Dynamics,* Summer 2001, pp. 12–27.

Lipman-Blumen, Jean, and Leavitt, Harold J. *Hot Groups: Seeding Them, Feeding Them,* and *Using Them to Ignite Your Organization.* New York: Oxford University press, 2001.

Parcells, Bill. "The Tough Work of Turning Around a Team." *Harvard Business Review,* November–December 2000, pp. 179–184.

WEB CORNER

www.theabc.org/work.htm (Studies of social loafing.)

www.deboldgroup.com/TQM/nominal.htm (The nominal group technique.)

www.groupthink.ca (Links to information about groupthink.)

CHAPTER 13

ADAPTING TO THE ORGANIZATION

Learning Objectives

After reading and studying this chapter and doing the exercises, you should be able to

1. Recognize the importance of adapting to the informal rules of conduct in the organization.
2. Be familiar with the forms of business etiquette often associated with success in business.
3. Describe the importance of fitting in with the organizational culture.
4. Describe various approaches to balancing the demands of work and personal life.
5. Pinpoint tactics for becoming a team player.

A challenge faced by workers at all career stages and types of work is meeting the various demands other than direct job responsibilities placed on them by their employer. Adapting to the organization includes many activities discussed in this book such as managing job stress, resolving conflict, and getting along with others. In this chapter we highlight four major challenges in adapting to organizational life: (1) following formal and informal rules, including business etiquette, (2) fitting in with the organizational culture, (3) balancing the demands of work and personal life, and (4) being an effective team player.

FORMAL AND INFORMAL RULES IN ORGANIZATIONS

Organizations are governed by both formal and informal rules. Adjusting to the formal rules is often easier than adjusting to the informal ones. Formal rules are part of the **formal organization**—the job descriptions, organization charts, procedures, and other documents that specify how individuals should work with each other. The formal organization is thus the official, sanctioned way of doing things. By consulting the formal organization you can learn who reports to whom (the organization chart). The formal organization also tells you how various problems should be handled (see the policies and procedures manual).

A much more subtle set of rules that govern behavior are part of the **informal organization**—a pattern of work relationships that develops both to satisfy people's social needs and to get work accomplished. The informal organization also includes the customs and traditions that develop in the firm and contribute to the organizational culture. The informal groups described in Chapter 12 are part of the informal organization. Informal rules stem from the informal organization. Examples of informal rules governing behavior include these: (1) An office supervisor should never invite the chief executive officer to lunch. (2) A production employee should never wear a three-piece suit to work. Examining codes of dress and appearance is a good starting point in understanding adjustment to the organization.

Informal rules are learned primarily through **socialization,** the process of coming to understand the values, norms, and customs essential for adapting to the organization. Newcomers to the organization often actively seek out information about the job and selectively choose sources of information they consider to be reliable. The key sources of information for socialization are supervisors, team leaders, coworkers, and other newcomers. An important purpose of seeking the input of others is to make sense of the new environment.[1]

Assume, for example, that you join an organization and you read the following in the handbook for new employees: "All employees are expected to lead a balanced life. We want loyal employees, but we recognize that your role as a worker is but one part of your life. Family and friends are more important." However, you observe that the workers who are treated the best are those who work many nights and weekends. You ask an experienced person for clarification, and she explains, "Top management just pays lip service to a balanced life. They would prefer that you really think the company is the primary focus of your life."

As implied by this example, a major by-product of socialization is judging how hard to work. Stated from a negative perspective, socialization also informs us just how much loafing is tolerated on the job. Loafing, or taking a break from work, can be interpreted as wasting company resources. The same behavior can also be interpreted as a stress reducer that ultimately increases productivity. The newcomer must learn which types of loafing (or work breaks) are tolerated. Many supervisors, for example, will tolerate a worker's leaving the work area to get a cup of coffee or soft drink and returning in 10 minutes. These same supervisors might not tolerate a worker taking a 10-minute break to play solitaire on the computer. Table 13–1 presents some commonly observed forms of loafing (or stress breaks) in the workplace. Your socialization task is to decide which ones are morally acceptable to you and are tolerated by your employer.

BUSINESS ETIQUETTE AND MANNERS

Adapting to an organization includes practicing the type of etiquette considered acceptable to that organization. The type of etiquette considered acceptable by a given organization typically parallels the standards of etiquette considered important in

TABLE 13–1
Common Forms of Loafing (or Work Breaks) on the Job

- Leaving the office early
- Taking coffee breaks
- Calling friends or family members
- Recapping or discussing TV shows
- Surfing non-business-related Web sites such as ESPN.COM
- Ordering concert tickets
- Playing solitaire on the computer
- Staring out the window
- "Schmoozing" (informal chatting with coworkers)
- Taking long lunches
- Sending e-mail messages to friends
- Showing off vacation photos
- Job surfing on the Internet

Source: Sampled from Brenda Paik Sunoo, "This Employee May Be Loafing: Can You Tell? Should You Care?" *Personnel Journal,* December 1996, p. 57.

the society in general. **Business etiquette** is the special code of behavior required in work situations. The term *manners* has an equivalent meaning. Both manners and etiquette refer to behaving in a polite and kind way, with rules of etiquette being more specific about behavior in a particular situation. Business etiquette is usually based on informal rather than formal organizational rules. Displaying good etiquette and manners has important business consequences. A study by the U.S. Office of Consumer Affairs found that 91 percent of all customers will never conduct repeat business with a company that offends them.[2]

Jim Rucker and Jean Anna Sellers explain that business etiquette is much more than knowing how to use the correct utensil or how to dress in a given situation. Businesspeople today must know how to be at ease with strangers and with groups, be able to offer congratulations smoothly, know how to make introductions, and know how to conduct themselves at company social functions.[3] A challenge in understanding etiquette is that standards shift over time. A key example is that up until several years ago it was considered good etiquette in a business situation for a man to open the door for a woman. Today, the lead person opens the door.

Here we introduce business etiquette by highlighting appropriate behavior in nine different categories or situations.[4] Useful information about etiquette can also be learned from observing people who are both successful and polite. Remember that appropriate manners and etiquette are influenced somewhat by the situation. For example, vulgarities are more acceptable on the manufacturing floor than they would be in a legal firm.

General Office Etiquette. Despite the emphasis on informality in most aspects of life, certain standards of professionalism are still part of an office environment. Communicating with frequent use of vulgarities, grossly incorrect grammar, and in sound bites creates a negative impact. Racist, sexist, and ethnic jokes are taboo, as is doing impressions of foreigners speaking. It is important to respect people's senses. Any assault on other people's senses—sight, sound, smell, or touch—should be avoided. Thus, strong cologne and perfume are unwelcome, as are grotesque color combinations in your clothing, pinching coworkers, or making loud noises with chewing gum.

Allowing others to finish what they are saying is a key, general-purpose act of etiquette. Interrupting others is high on the rudeness scale. Waiting for the other person to finish speaking indicates that you are polite and a good listener. Also, you will better understand the message sender.

Relationships between Men and Women and between People of Different Ages. Social etiquette is based on chivalry and the sex of the person, whereas business etiquette is based on generally equal treatment for all. Women should no longer be treated differently when approaching a door, riding in an elevator, or walking in the street. According to the new rules, the person in the lead (no matter the sex or age) should proceed first and hold the door for the others following. However, a man should still follow a woman when using an escalator. When using stairs, a man usually follows a woman going up and precedes her going down. Men no longer have to walk next to the street when walking with one or two women. Correct etiquette now states that men should always walk on either side, but not in the middle of two women. Elders should still be respected, but not in such ways as holding doors open for them, helping them off with their overcoats, or getting coffee for them.

Unless you are good friends who typically hug when meeting, it is best to avoid touching others of the same or opposite sex except for a handshake. Some people believe that nonsexual touching is part of being charming and warm, yet many workers are offended when touched by another worker. The subject is controversial because public figures often drape their arms around others, and physical touching is part of the ritual of offering congratulations in sports.

Introducing People. The basic rule for introductions is to present the lower-ranking person to the higher-ranking person regardless of age or sex. "Ms. Barker (the CEO) I would like you to meet my new coworker, Reggie Taylor." If the two people being introduced are of equal rank, mention the older one first. Providing a little information about the person being introduced is considered good manners. When introducing one person to the group, present the group to the individual. "Sid Foster, this is our information systems team." When being introduced to a person, concentrate on the name and repeat it soon, thus enhancing learning. A fundamental display of good manners is to remember people's names and to pronounce them correctly. When dealing with people senior to you or of higher rank, call them by their last name and title until told otherwise. (Maybe Ms. Barker above, will tell you, "Please call me Kathy.")

It is good manners and good etiquette to remember the names of work associates to whom you are introduced, even if you see them only occasionally. If you forget the name of a person, it is better to admit this than to guess and come up with the wrong name. Just say, "I apologize, but I have forgotten your name. Tell me once more, and I will not forget your name again."

A major change in introducing people is that both men and women are now expected to extend their right hand when being introduced. Give a firm, but not overpowering, handshake, and establish eye contact with the person you are greeting.

Dressing. The basic rule for dressing properly is to make your selections based on what others in your company are wearing, particularly the successful people. Looking professional and well groomed is an eternal rule of etiquette. Dress-down days in the office are an opportunity to wear casual clothing that does not detract from your image, but not such items as a stained sweatshirt or cutoff jeans. When meeting customers or others external to the firm, dress in traditional business attire such as a suit. If instructed to wear "business casual" clothing to a meeting, ask for a definition or example, because casual is interpreted in many ways.

Dining. Hundreds of specific rules have been formulated for proper dining, including such obscure items as rotating the bottle clockwise when serving wine. Among the dining specifics requiring attention are putting a napkin in the lap as soon as you are seated, using the right hand for the fork (in North America), not moving dishes and silverware to another part of the table, not placing used silverware on the table, not pushing food with bread, and not overdoing condiments such as salt or ketchup. The greatest taboo of all is talking with food in your mouth. Also taboo is holding your knife like a dagger and the fork like a cello, and picking or poking your teeth.

An area of considerable confusion about etiquette surrounds business meals and who should pay the check, the man or the woman. The new rule of etiquette is that the person who extends the invitation pays the bills. (Do you think this same rule should be extended to social life?) Another rule of thumb is that the person doing the selling pays for the potential buyer. The selling could involve a product or service, or it could be an attempt to sell you on the idea of working for the other person.

Travel. Rules of etiquette about travel have become more complicated now that men and women coworkers often travel together. Men are no longer obligated to assist women with their luggage or to pay for meals and snacks while traveling together. Men are no longer expected to open a car door for a woman, but the male or female driver should unlock the door for passengers. (Observe that in social situations many men and women still prefer the man to open the car door for the woman.) When men and women travel together on business, it is important not to confuse the business trip with a vacation with an intimate. Acting as if the opposite-sexed person is a date when having dinner together on a business trip is considered poor etiquette.

Using Electronic Devices. Electronic devices, including e-mail, the Internet, copying machines, and cellular telephones, create opportunities for good and poor etiquette. Key examples of poor etiquette surrounding e-mail include flaming, peering at the e-mail messages being sent by others, and overloading coworkers with trivial messages. Etiquette violations surrounding the Internet include retrieving pornographic material on your monitor in the presence of others, surfing the Internet on company time, and asking annoying questions in discussion groups. An annoying question would be to repeat a FAQ (frequently asked question on a Web site). Reproducing other people's work as your own and putting it on your Web site is poor etiquette and also poor ethics.

Key violations of copy-machine etiquette include hogging the machine, jumping in ahead of others, and leaving the machine at a setting only you require. A generally accepted guideline is that if you are using the photocopying machine for a large job and somebody approaches with a small job, let him or her go first. Also, refill paper trays that you have depleted. A major etiquette problem with cellular telephones in the workplace is similar to that in personal life. Cell phone users often speak loudly in an open area, interrupting the concentration and tranquility of others.

International Relations. Etiquette varies considerably across cultures. As a consequence, it is important to learn about local customs before conducting business with people from other cultures. The discussions of cross-cultural differences in Chapters 3 and 11 illustrate many differences in customs across countries. One difference not previously mentioned is that the appropriate handshake (reflecting good etiquette) differs across countries. Germans use a firm grip and one decisive pump. Asians, in contrast, grasp the hand delicately and shake quite briefly. If your handshake differs significantly from what the other person anticipates, you might be perceived as having poor etiquette. Another difference to consider is that Asian people treat elderly people with more respect than do Americans. If you speak in a patronizing manner to an 80-year-old executive in China, for example, you will be considered rude.

Interacting with People with Disabilities. Many able-bodied people are puzzled by what is proper etiquette in working with people with disabilities. The president of the National Easter Seal Society recommends that you be as natural and open as you can. In addition, he offers these guidelines for displaying good manners when dealing with a physical disability:

- Speak directly to a person with a disability, not to the person's companion.
- Don't assume that a person with a disability needs help. If someone is struggling, ask for permission to assist.
- When talking to a person in a wheelchair, place yourself at that person's eye level.
- When speaking to a person with impaired vision, identify yourself and anyone who may be with you.
- To get the attention of a deaf person, tap the person's shoulder or wave your hand.
- Treat a person with a disability as you would anyone else except for the differences noted in this list.[5]

The most general principle to consider in developing business etiquette and manners is to treat others with consideration. Reflect on what you might be doing that would annoy, irritate, or offend a rational person. A person might ask, for example, "I wonder if my chewing gum would annoy anybody at this meeting?"

FITTING IN WITH THE ORGANIZATIONAL CULTURE

The discussion so far in this chapter, and at many other places in the text, has hinted at the importance of adapting to the key values and customs of the firm that contribute to its culture. **Organizational culture** is a system of shared values and beliefs that influence worker behavior. The foundation of any organizational culture is values. A firm's philosophy is expressed though values, and values guide behavior on a daily basis. For example, a study demonstrated that when top management has a lax attitude toward honesty, employee theft increases above the norm of 30 percent.[6] Here we look at a sampling of the values and practices that guide organizations, and the importance of a good fit between you and the organization.

Dimensions of Organizational Culture

As with the human personality, organizational culture can be described by a wide number of characteristics or dimensions. These facets of culture are important to the individual because they point toward the type of performance and behavior that is considered acceptable or desirable by upper management. Among these many dimensions of culture are as follows:

- **Concern for the customer.** Many firms believe that the needs of customers must receive top priority. In such a firm, you can expect to inconvenience yourself to meet customer demands.
- **Concern for employee welfare.** Many firms believe that the needs of employees come first, and that satisfied employees are the most likely to satisfy customer needs. In such a firm, you would be expected to treat coworkers with the highest respect. As a manager, you would emphasize such activities as coaching team members, encouraging them, and dismissing employees only as a last resort.
- **Innovation and risk taking.** Some firms emphasize attempting new ideas and taking risks, whereas other firms downplay innovation and risk taking. An adventuresome firm would expect you to take risks, and not be afraid to fail. A firm low on innovation and risk taking would expect you to value the status quo, and might punish you for suggesting new ideas that failed.
- **Degree of stability.** A fast-paced dynamic firm has a different culture from that of a slow-paced stable one. In a fast-paced firm, you would be expected to work rapidly, think rapidly, and perhaps even talk rapidly. You would face tighter deadlines, and be expected to take very brief lunch breaks or even eat at your desk.
- **A sense of ownership.** The movement toward stock ownership for an increasing number of employees has created an ownership culture in many firms whereby workers are inspired to think and act like owners. In an ownership culture, you would be expected to engage in such behaviors as conserving energy, making gradual improvements, and not tolerating sloppy work by coworkers.[7]

The above five dimensions illustrate the nature of organizational culture. The general point is that an organizational culture has considerable depth and power in terms of controlling behavior and performance.[8] In recognition of this fact, many executives believe that the most important strategy for improving a firm is to change the culture in the right direction, such as being more innovative and taking more risks. Carol Lavin Bernick, the President of Alberto Culver North America (personal care and household products), at one point faced the problem of a company slipping badly. She analyzed the problems in these terms:

> It wasn't our people who were to blame; Culver employees have always been decent and hardworking. It was our culture. We needed people to have a sense of ownership and urgency around the business, to welcome innovation and take risks. But in the existing culture, people dutifully waited for marching orders, and thought of their bosses' needs before their customers'.[9]

After the executive team revamped the culture, Alberto Culver became more successful than ever in terms of sales, profits, and low turnover. One of the many initiatives Bernick took was to make culture visible and elevate it to priority status. She often highlighted desired values and behavior that already existed at isolated places in the company.

The Importance of a Good Person–Organization Fit

Assuming that you have the luxury of selecting among different prospective employers, it is best to work for a company where your personality and style fit the organization culture. A **person–organization fit** is the compatibility of the individual and the organization. The compatibility often centers on the extent to which a person's major work-related values and personality traits fit major elements of the organizational culture. Following this idea, a person who is adventuresome and a risk taker would achieve highest performance and satisfaction in an organization where adventuresome behavior and risk taking are valued. Conversely, a methodical and conservative individual should join a slow-moving bureaucracy.

Job interviews represent a good opportunity for evaluating a person–organization fit for both the applicant and the employer.[10] Person–organization fit can also include superficial aspects of behavior such as physical appearance and dress. For example, a person who dressed like a Wall Street investment banker might not feel comfortable working in a high-tech firm in California where jeans and sandals were standard work attire. As a consequence of not feeling comfortable in your work environment, you might not perform at your best.

A study conducted with 68 companies in the Netherlands supports the idea that finding a good person–organization fit can benefit both the individual and the organization. Two dimensions of organizational culture were measured: concern for people and concern for goal accomplishment. Measurements were made of the organizational culture preferences along the two dimensions for 154 newcomers, 104 peers, and 101 supervisors. The results indicated that when the culture preferences of the newcomers were similar to the preferences of the supervisors, the newcomers felt more committed to their employer—they intended to stay with the firm.[11] For example, if a newcomer had a high concern for goal accomplishment, and so did the supervisors, the newcomer had a stronger desire to stay with his or her employer. A culture-preference fit with peers had no effect on intention to stay with the firm.

4 BALANCING WORK AND PERSONAL LIFE

Balancing the demands of work and personal life is a major challenge facing the workforce. (*Personal life* is used here to encompass family life and not to exclude people who do not live with a family.) A large segment of the workforce seeks a reasonable balance between work and family life, with many people leaving

- Plan ahead for family events.
- Discuss work commitments with your partner or prospective partner.
- Become a downshifter.
- Maintain a buffer between work and home.
- Become a telecommuter.
- Make use of organizational support systems.

FIGURE 13–1 Balancing Work and Personal Life Demands

corporate life early to find such a balance. The challenge of finding a balance is particularly intense for employees who are part of a two-wage-earner family, a group that includes about 50 percent of the workforce in the United States and Canada.

As described in Chapter 7, work–family conflict is a stressor. More specifically, being unable to resolve work–family conflict lowers both job satisfaction and life satisfaction, as demonstrated in a large number of scientific studies.[12] Furthermore, not being able to achieve a balance between work and personal life has a major negative effect on relationships between couples. Conflict over one partner's investing too much time and energy into the career can take a heavy toll on a relationship. Here we describe several of the steps individuals can take, including assistance from the organization, to better balance the demands of work and personal life. Figure 13–1 outlines the steps.

Plan Ahead for Family Events. Advanced personal planning is a way of minimizing conflict between work and important family events. This would involve marking on one's office calendar, at the beginning of each year, important family dates (such as birthdays and anniversaries). In this way an attempt could be made to minimize business travel and late meetings on those dates. Similarly, the family could be advised of times when work demands would be at their peak.[13]

Discuss Work Commitments with Your Partner or Prospective Partner. A substantial amount of conflict over work versus family demands can be prevented if each partner has an accurate perception of the prospective mate's work schedule. For example, some career people are prepared to work 60 hours per week to achieve their career objectives, while others prefer to avoid working over 40 hours. A couple who cannot agree or compromise on how much time is suitable to invest in a career may not be compatible.

Become a Downshifter. Some employers are making it possible for managers and professionals to choose a career track that allows more time for parenting. Investing more time in family and less in career is often referred to as **downshifting.** A person placed on a parent track would avoid positions that interfere heavily with family responsibilities. For instance, if you were on a parent track, you would avoid a position that required frequent overseas travel. The way to get on a parent track would be to first make sure that such an arrangement with your employer is possible. You would then explain to your superiors that you want to perform well, but not be overloaded with career responsibilities at the expense of personal life.

Downshifting can sometimes be accomplished in small steps, and to a small degree. One modest approach would be to devote part of lunch hours to getting in touch with family and friends. Setting more reasonable deadlines can also allow more time for personal life. Declaring your family a priority may help prevent an employer from making unreasonable demands. Cutting back on business travel by making better use of conference calls and virtual meetings can also contribute to a gentle form of downshifting.[14]

Maintain a Buffer Time between Work and Home. Commuting time between work and home plays an important psychological role in helping people get mentally prepared for work in the morning and unwind in the afternoon or early evening. The commute serves as a buffer between work life and personal life. People who live too close to work often complain that they are still thinking about the job when they arrive at home. A simple solution to the problem of a too-short commute is to walk around the block before entering the house. Two researchers suggest a commuting time of about 30 minutes is ideal, because it facilitates "gearing up in the morning and winding down in the evening."[15]

Make Use of Work/Life Programs. Many employers now provide a group of services and programs that support workers in their quest to manage work and family life successfully. Among the most important of these work/life programs are flexible work hours and dependent-care options. Flexible working hours come in different forms. Some employees with flexible working hours may work four 10-hour days, rather than five 8-hour days. Other people with flexible working hours may begin work at 10:00 A.M. and leave at 6:00 P.M. A **dependent-care option** is any company-sponsored program that helps an employee take care of a family member. Child-care programs, including on-site day-care centers, and parental leave (for mothers and fathers) are the most frequently offered. Other company-sponsored programs include eldercare (day care for elderly dependents who cannot take care of themselves entirely) and seminars on work versus family issues.

A modified work schedule specifically designed to help people juggle work and family demands is **job sharing,** an arrangement in which two people share one job by each working half-time. Job sharing has its biggest appeal for workers whose family commitments do not allow for full-time work. Consultant John Lloyd says that "Sharing is a little like having custody of a child—it will take a lot of compromise, maturity, and selflessness to make sure the job doesn't suffer."[16] An advantage of such an arrangement to the employer is that the company gets an output in excess of the equivalent of one full-time person. Two people working half-time will usually produce more than one person working full-time, particularly in creative work.

Become a Telecommuter. A major program for achieving work and family life balance is the opportunity to work from home. For some people, working at home part or all of the workweek can help achieve a better balance between work and personal life. A **telecommuter** is an employee who performs regular job responsibilities from home or another location. (Some telecommuters in the investment-banking field telecommute from yachts and ski chalets.) There are close to 10 million corporate employees in the United States who work at home at least three days per month. (At least another 13 million employees work full-time at home, using computers and related equipment.) Companies sponsor telecommuting because it lowers overhead and often increases productivity for independent jobs such as claims processor or computer programmer.[17]

Telecommuting can help some people achieve a better work and family life balance because they spend less time commuting and are more readily available to take care of urgent family matters, such as retrieving a sick child from school. However, telecommuting can also backfire and create an imbalance. Because the workplace is so readily available, the telecommuter might be prompted to maintain almost no separation between work and family life. For workers who lack strong self-discipline, working at home is difficult because of all the possible distractions. As a result, the telecommuter might work late into the night to make up for the time lost in personal matters during the day.

Many human resource professionals contend that work/life programs increase productivity by reducing absenteeism and turnover and enabling parents to concentrate on their work. A *Business Week* survey found that family-friendly companies enjoy a big return on their investment from their work–family programs. Absenteeism falls, turnover decreases, and productivity and profits rise.[18] A survey at DuPont found that employees who took full advantage of the company's work/life programs were 45 percent more likely to agree that they would "go the extra mile" to see that DuPont succeeds.[19] Table 13–2 provides a representative list of programs that are part of an organizational support system for balancing the demands of work and personal life. During a prolonged business downturn many of these benefits are likely to be eliminated, particularly luxuries such as a concierge service.

Despite the popularity of work/life programs, many employees are hesitant to use them extensively. These employees are concerned that if they ask for concessions such as flexible working hours, it will appear they are not strongly committed to the firm or their careers. A study was conducted with engineers of their perception of the company work–family program. The engineers believed that the work–family program had a negative impact on their careers because of the assumption that there is a direct relationship between quality of work and hours spent in the office.[20]

BECOMING A TEAM PLAYER

A major aspect of adjusting to the organization is learning how to work as part of a team. Team skills have gained in importance as organizations face greater change and complexity. At every level of the organization, it is important to work cooperatively and jointly with others. Organizing people into work teams is a common practice with production workers, support workers, and managers. Also of significance, a survey of 125 companies in 34 industries indicates that top-level managers rate team play as the most desirable workplace trait. Nearly 40 percent of the

TABLE 13–2
A VARIETY OF WORK AND FAMILY LIFE PROGRAMS

- Child-care resource and referral
- Part-time options
- Flexible work schedules
- Compressed workweek
- Telecommuting
- Job sharing among two or more employees
- Eldercare resource and referral
- Eldercare case management and assessment
- Subsidy for emergency care for dependents
- "Family sick days," which permit employees to stay home and care for sick children or relatives
- Arrangements for school counselors to meet with parents on site during regular working hours
- Electric breast pumps for mothers of young children who want to return to work and continue breast-feeding
- Maintenance worker on company payroll whom employees can hire for household tasks, paying only for supplies
- On-site conveniences such as banking services, travel services, and dry cleaners
- Concierge service in which company employee runs a variety of errands for other employees
- Postal service
- Automatic teller machines
- On-site fitness centers

Source: Michelle Neely Martinez, "An Inside Look at Making the Grade," *HR Magazine,* March 1998, p. 61; Jim Harris, *Getting Employees to Fall in Love with Your Company* (New York: AMACOM, 1996); William M. Mercer's Work/Life Diversity Initiatives Benchmarking Survey, 1996 (Louisville Galleria, Louisville, KY 40202); Dayton Fandray, "What Is Work/Life Worth?" *Workforce,* May 2000, pp. 64–71.

managers ranked "team player" as top among desirable work traits. The other traits ranked in the survey were "self-starter," "dependable," "company-focused," "responsible," "adaptable," and "likable."[21]

Our approach to understanding how to become an effective team player is divided into two parts. First, we outline the types of skills, knowledge, and attitudes expected of team members. Second, we describe a handful of major tactics for becoming a strong team player in the workplace. The information about groups and teams presented in Chapter 12 can also provide insights into working well with teammates.

A Ladder of Team Player Skills, Knowledge, and Attitudes

Like many other industrial companies, The Eastman Kodak Company has created teams throughout its operations. Teamwork is so important that Kodak has developed a ladder of team player skills, knowledge, and attitudes to guide newcomers and established employees. Although Kodak designed this ladder to inform and enlighten entry-level workers, it applies to team players at all levels. Starting at the bottom of the ladder are basic team player skills, knowledge, and attitudes. At the top of the

SELF ASSESSMENT EXERCISE 13–1

A Ladder of Skills, Knowledge, and Attitudes for Teamwork

In the right-hand column, circle the letter that indicates whether you have that competence (N) or it is an area for improvement (I). If a given statement does not seem to apply to you in terms of work experiences, relate the statement to your experiences at school.

Skill, Knowledge, or Attitude	***Competency Level***	
1. Attends team meetings regularly	N	I
2. Participates in team brainstorming	N	I
3. Works effectively as a team member by:		
◈ Sharing communication	N	I
◈ Negotiating	N	I
◈ Facilitating	N	I
◈ Participating	N	I
◈ Cooperating	N	I
◈ Trusting	N	I
◈ Working toward and accepting consensus	N	I
◈ Functioning as a teacher and learner	N	I
◈ Valuing and using leadership skills	N	I
◈ Using conflict resolution skills	N	I
4. Makes original contributions to team issues; builds upon others' contributions	N	I
5. Volunteers to handle action items or to participate in new teams	N	I
6. Actively participates in establishing team's purpose, direction, strategy, or goals	N	I
7. Positively questions and challenges others; utilizes conflicting views in a constructive manner	N	I
8. Acts to create and promote team cohesiveness	N	I
9. Offers to relieve a team member's heavy workload	N	I
10. Considers impact on external interfaces when influencing team outcomes	N	I

ladder are teamwork competencies required of outstanding team players. The competitive employee has most of the skills, knowledge, and attitudes indicated at the top of the ladder. Self-Assessment Exercise 13–1 gives you a chance to think through the competencies you need now or in the future to be an outstanding team player.

Tactics for Becoming a Strong Team Player

An important part of adapting to the organization is learning how to work as part of a team. Team skills have gained in importance as organizations face greater change and complexity. At every level of the organization it is important to work cooperatively and jointly with others. Organizing people into work teams is a common practice with production workers, office support workers, and managers. A group of representative tactics for becoming a strong team player is presented next.

Trust Your Teammates. Teamwork is based on trust and cooperation, so to be an effective team player you must trust your teammates. *Trust* can take many forms such as having confidence that teammates will do their share of work, having faith in their skills and judgment, and being able to share confidential information with your teammates. Another manifestation of trust is taking risks with others. You can take a risk by trying out one of their unproved ideas. Working on a team is akin to a small-business partnership. If you do not believe that the other team members have your best interests at heart, it will be difficult for you to share your opinions and ideas. You will fear that others will make negative statements behind your back.

A laboratory experiment with college students suggests that the contribution of trust to group performance may be indirect rather than direct. The experiment involved three-person teams building towers out of wooden blocks, under either high- or low-trust conditions. In the high-trust condition, the students were told that both partners were (a) reliable, and (b) would not take advantage of you. The opposite was true of the low-trust condition. In high-trust groups, motivation was transformed into joint efforts, leading to higher performance. In low-trust groups, motivation was transformed into individual efforts. The effect of trust was therefore to influence how motivation was channeled.[22]

Skill-Building Exercise 13–1 is a widely used trust-building exercise in which the direct contribution of trust can be examined firsthand.

ENGAGE IN ORGANIZATIONAL CITIZENSHIP BEHAVIOR. A good team player works for the good of the organization even without the promise of a specific reward. Such activity is called **organizational citizenship behavior.** The aggregate result of organizational citizenship behavior is that the organization functions more effectively in such ways as improved product quantity and quality.[23] Good citizenship on the job encompasses many specific behaviors, including helping a coworker with a job task and refraining from complaints or petty grievances. A good organizational citizen would carry out such specific acts as picking up litter in the company parking lot. He or she would also bring a reference to the office that could help a coworker solve a job problem. Most of the other team player tactics described here are related to organizational citizenship behavior.

COMMIT WILLINGLY TO TEAM GOALS. The goals of individual team members may not overlap entirely with group goals. A gap between team goals and individual goals sometimes occurs within a cross-functional team. The team wants to achieve

SKILL BUILDING EXERCISE 13–1

The Trust Fall

The class organizes itself into teams. In each team each willing member stands on a chair and falls backward into the arms of teammates. A less fearful alternative to falling off a chair is to simply fall backward standing up. Those team members who, for whatever physical or mental reason, would prefer not to fall back into others or participate in catching others are unconditionally excluded. However, they can serve as observers. After the trust falls have been completed, a team leader gathers answers to the following questions, and then shares the answers with the rest of the class.

QUESTIONS

1. How does this exercise develop teamwork?
2. What did the participants learn about themselves?

a multidisciplinary purpose, such as developing a new product or reducing costs. The individual may have a few personal goals. One goal might be to influence the output of the group so the individual's department prospers. If, for example, the product development team develops a product with a heavy engineering component, the engineering representative on the team will be satisfied. At times, the team member will also have a career goal. He or she is serving on the team primarily as a way of gaining recognition.

The strong team player will commit to team goals even if his or her personal goals cannot be achieved for now. The engineering representative on the cross-functional team will commit to producing a new product even if it will have a small engineering component. The team member seeking visibility will be enthusiastic about pursuing team goals even if not much visibility will be gained.

Help Coworkers Do Their Jobs Better. Your stature as a team player will increase if you take the initiative to help coworkers make needed work improvements. Make the suggestions in a constructive spirit, rather than displaying an air of superiority.

> Liz, a software engineer, suggested to the group that they make their overview charts more exciting. She suggested that they add a logo, produce the charts in color, and be more creative. The change dramatically improved the presentation to user groups. People stayed more alert and interested during briefings. Liz received many words of appreciation for her dedication to the group cause.

Share Credit. An effective team player is willing to sacrifice personal acclaim for the good of the team. It is therefore important to share credit for good deeds with other team members. Instead of focusing on yourself as the person responsible for a work achievement, you point out that the achievement was indeed the product of a team effort.

> Jerry, a production manager, was recognized at a company meeting for reducing the production cost of a critical component by 32 percent. Although Jerry originated the productivity-improvement idea, he immediately mentioned several manufacturing technicians who assisted him. By acknowledging the contribution of other workers, Jerry improved his status as a team player. Later that day a senior manufacturing technician gave Jerry a handshake of appreciation.

Provide Emotional Support to Coworkers. Good team players offer each other emotional support. Such support can take the form of offering verbal encouragement for ideas expressed, listening to a group member's concerns, or complimenting achievements. An emotionally supportive comment to a coworker who appears overstressed might be, "This doesn't look like one of your better days. What can I do to help?" Another form of providing emotional support is to reach out to a group member who is friendless and perhaps lonely. If you engage such individuals in social interaction, your contribution as a team player will be enhanced. However, if the isolated person resists your attempts at friendship, it is best to back off.

Engage in Shared Laughter. Laughter is a natural team builder that enhances understanding and empathy—essential ingredients for team play. Having a sense of humor is also an effective leadership characteristic. The individual can trigger laughter by making humorous comments related to the situation at hand or making in-group jokes. Too much emphasis on humor, however, will detract from the professionalism of the team member. It is important to have a sense of humor, yet being perceived as the office clown can backfire.

Minimize Cynicism. Cynicism is widespread in organizations today about such issues as top-level managers striving to cut costs yet voting themselves huge compensation packages, and insincere attempts at improving quality. In this context, cynicism is a negative attitude toward the organization that leads to disparaging and critical behaviors toward the organization.[24] The popularity of the comic strip Dilbert reflects such cynicism. Scott Adams, the creator of Dilbert, contends that all the material for his cartoons and books comes from e-mail from upset employees.

To be an effective team player, minimize the expression of cynicism. Even if cynicism has merit, its overt expression tends to demoralize other team members and detracts from achieving team goals. To illustrate, assume that you are part of a team whose task is to find ways to improve the quality of your company's automobile leasing service. You tell the group, "Who cares what we do? It will just lead to another way of fleecing the public on buying insurance they don't need." Your sentiments will more likely detract from than add to the team's focus on its goals.

SUMMARY OF KEY POINTS

- Adapting to the organization refers to many things that you have to do in order to get along on the job. Several of these major adjustments or adaptations are described in this chapter. Adjusting to formal rules is often easier than adjusting to informal rules that stem from the informal organization. The latter includes the customs and traditions that develop in the firm, which are learned primarily through socialization. A major by-product of socialization is judging how hard to work.
- Adapting to the organization includes practicing the type of etiquette considered acceptable to the organization. Both manners and etiquette refer to behaving in a polite and kind way. Business etiquette is presented by highlighting appropriate behavior in nine different categories or situations: (1) general office etiquette, (2) relationships between men and women and between people of different ages, (3) introducing people, (4) dressing, (5) dining, (6) travel, (7) using electronic devices, (8) international relations, and (9) interacting with people with physical disabilities. The most general principle is to treat others with consideration.
- Fitting in with the organizational culture is a major way of adapting to the organization. Key dimensions of culture include concern for the customer, concern for employee welfare, innovation and risk taking, degree of organizational stability, and a sense of ownership. Finding a good person–organization fit (a culture that fits your personality) facilitates adapting to the organization.
- Balancing the demands of work and personal life is a major challenge facing the work force, especially in two-wage-earner families. Being unable to resolve

GUIDELINES FOR PERSONAL EFFECTIVENESS

1. A major contributor to career success is to work in an organization in which your style fits the culture. Assuming that you have the opportunity to choose among employers, it is best to work for a firm (or a division within the firm) where you find a good person–organization fit. To achieve this fit you will have to understand your own style, and be able to size up the organization. Speaking to people familiar with your target organization, or division thereof, will often provide valid information about the company's culture.
2. An important strategy of adapting to the organization is to be aware of the informal expectations made of you in such areas as dress codes, socializing on the job, and appropriate business etiquette. To learn of these expectations, make observations and delicately ask questions.
3. If you are a family person, it is important to establish a workable plan for balancing career and family demands. If home matters are poorly attended to, it is difficult to concentrate properly on your job.
4. It is important in general to be a good team player if you want to work for an organization. However, do not carry this approach so far that you lose your personal identity or become "one of the gang." Such behavior could decrease your chances for promotion.

work–family conflict lowers both job satisfaction and life satisfaction, and it can damage relationships. Steps individuals can take to balance work and personal life demands include: (1) plan ahead for family events, (2) discuss work commitments with your partner or prospective partner, (3) become a downshifter, (4) maintain a buffer time between work and home, (5) become a telecommuter, and (6) make use of work/life programs.

- Another part of adapting to the organization is to be a good team player. First, it is important to be aware of the types of skills, knowledge, and attitudes expected of team members, such as acting to create and promote team cohesiveness. Major tactics for becoming a team player include the following: (1) trust your teammates, (2) engage in organizational citizenship behavior, (3) commit willingly to team goals, (4) help coworkers do their jobs better, (5) share credit, (6) provide emotional support to coworkers, (7) engage in shared laughter, and (8) minimize cynicism.

DISCUSSION QUESTIONS AND ACTIVITIES

1. What form of loafing on the job have you observed to be fairly frequent?
2. Describe an organizational culture that you think would fit your personality and personal style.
3. Why should a person take seriously the advice of a handful of etiquette experts like "Miss Manners"?
4. Identify two specific business-related jobs in which good etiquette would be particularly important.
5. An article in *Fortune* magazine (March 17, 1997, pp. 70–90) presented data showing that having a full-time homemaker for a spouse was associated with better career advancement for corporate executives. Why might this be true?

6. Assume that a friend of yours is keenly interested in moving ahead in his or her career. What would you advise this person about making extensive use of work/life programs?
7. Explain how a work/life program can actually improve productivity.
8. To what extent do you believe that being a member of an athletic team is good training for becoming a team player on the job?
9. Which of the tactics for being a good team player presented in this chapter might create ethical problems for you? Explain your reasoning.
10. Search the Internet for a new tip on being a good team player. Be ready to share your findings in class.

REFERENCES

1. Randall P. Settoon and Cheryl Adkins, "Newcomer Socialization: The Role of Supervisor, Coworkers, Friends and Family Members," *Journal of Business and Psychology,* Summer 1997, pp. 507–508.
2. Cited in Jim Rucker and Jean Anna Sellers, "Changes in Business Etiquette," *Business Education Forum,* February 1998, p. 43.
3. Rucker and Sellers, "Changes in Business Etiquette," p. 43.
4. Rucker and Sellers, "Changes in Business Etiquette," p. 43. "Business Etiquette: Teaching Students the Unwritten Rules," *Keying In,* January 1996, pp. 1–7; Dot Yandle, "Do Manners Still Matter?" *Success Workshop Folio* (a supplement to the Pryor Report Management Newsletter), August 1994, pp. 1–4; Letitia Baldrige, *The Executive Advantage* (Washington, DC: Georgetown Publishing House, 1999); Lisa Lee Freeman, "Re-Finishing School," *Working Woman,* February 1999, pp. 84–85.
5. "Disability Etiquette," *Human Resources Forum* (a supplement to *Management Review*) June 1997, p. 3.
6. John Kamp and Paul Brooks, "Perceived Organizational Climate and Employee Counterproductivity," *Journal of Business and Psychology,* Summer 1991, p. 455.
7. Scott Hays, "Ownership Cultures Create Unity," *Workforce,* February 1999, pp. 60–64.
8. Edgar H. Schein, *The Corporate Culture Survival Guide* (San Francisco: Jossey-Bass, 1999).
9. Carol Lavin Bernick, "When Your Culture Needs a Makeover," *Harvard Business Review,* June 2001, p. 54.
10. Daniel M. Cable and Timothy A. Judge, "Interviewers' Perceptions of Person–Organization Fit and Organizational Selection Decisions," *Journal of Applied Psychology,* August 1997, pp. 546–561.
11. Annelies E. M. Van Vianen, "Person–Organization Fit: The Match between Newcomers' and Recruiters' Preferences for Organization Culture," *Personnel Psychology,* Spring 2000, pp. 113–149.
12. Ellen Ernst Kossek and Cynthia Ozeki, "Work–Family Conflict, Policies, and the Job–Life Satisfaction Relationship: A Review and Directions for Organizational Behavior–Human Resources Research," *Journal of Applied Psychology,* April 1998, p. 213.
13. Douglas T. Hall and Judith Richter, "Balancing Work Life and Home Life: What Can Organizations Do to Help?" *Academy of Management Executive,* August 1988, p. 213.
14. John D. Drake, *How to Work Less and Enjoy Life More* (San Francisco: Berrett-Koehler, 2001).
15. Hall and Richter, "Balancing Work and Home Life," p. 218.

AN APPLIED PSYCHOLOGY CASE PROBLEM

"I'm Being Squeezed in Two Directions"

Chad Van Kemp, age 26, works as a technical support specialist for a consultancy firm that installs and maintains large software systems for clients. Among the firm's clients are state governments looking to upgrade their tax systems, and manufacturing firms attempting to improve their inventory-control systems and customer-service systems. The consultants train the clients and help them install the systems. When a technical problem arises that the consultant or the client cannot readily solve, Chad or one of the other technical support specialists are asked to assist.

When Chad accepted the position two years ago, he was told that many of the problems clients faced could be handled over the telephone or through e-mail, thereby minimizing on-site visits. Furthermore, Chad was told that the firm had so many large clients in its own region, that overnight travel would be limited. Chad was also told that although the job of a technical support specialist is demanding, his typical workweek would be between 45 and 50 hours, overtime work included.

During the first year, Chad worked about 43 hours per week, and spent only four nights away from home on business travel. The work arrangement fit Chad's lifestyle well. Married, with a preschool-age daughter, Chad wanted to spend ample time with his wife Melissa and his daughter Angie. Melissa had a demanding job of her own as an executive assistant. Chad and Melissa took turns bringing Angie to the day-care center and picking her up on the way home from work.

After his first full year of employment, Chad received a very favorable performance evaluation. He was told that he was acquiring the right technical knowledge rapidly, and that he had good interpersonal skills in dealing with the consultants and clients. He could therefore anticipate being assigned to more challenging client problems, whatever geographic location that might be.

Having established the reputation of a highly competent technical support specialist, Chad quickly began to receive more calls for his services. One week he worked 60 hours because of a systems crash in a client's tax collection system. Three weeks later he stayed over three nights at another client's site. Soon his long hours led to conflict at home. In recent months Chad has been working about 55 hours per week, and stays at client locations about six nights per month.

Melissa complained that her job was demanding also, yet she was saddled with too much of the responsibility for getting Angie to and from the day-care center. Melissa also noted that several times she had to refuse to work late because Chad was not available to pick up Angie from the day-care center. Also, Chad missed two of Angie's violin concerts.

Chad explained to Melissa, "I don't like these new long hours and heavy travel any more than you do. I miss being away from you and Angie. But that's the nature of my work. If I do a good job, that means I have to spend more time with clients. Also, I hate flying ever since the terrorist attacks on the World Trade Center and the Pentagon.

"I want to be a success at work. It's been hinted that if I keep up the good work, I will have a good shot at being the next tech support team leader. If I refuse to work long hours, or travel, I will be much less valuable to the company. Yet I also want to be a good husband and father. I'm being squeezed in two directions, and I don't like it."

Melissa replied, "I don't doubt your sincerity. But my career counts too. As you travel more, I'm more limited in being able to work longer hours when necessary. Maybe you should speak to your boss."

QUESTIONS

1. What, if anything, should Chad do to resolve his work–family conflict?
2. How might Chad's employer help him resolve his conflict?
3. What is your opinion of the validity of Melissa's complaints?

AN APPLIED PSYCHOLOGY CASE PROBLEM

The Unbalanced Team

Mercury Printing is one of the largest commercial printing companies in San Diego, California, with annual sales of $30 million. Two years ago, Alvera Velasquez, the vice president of marketing, reorganized the sales force. Previously the sales force consisted of inside sales representatives, who took care of phone-in orders, and outside sales representatives, who called on accounts. The reorganization divided the outside sales force into two groups: direct sales and major accounts. The direct sales representatives were made responsible for small- and medium-size customer accounts. As before, they would service existing customers and prospect for new accounts.

Four of the direct sales representatives were promoted to major account executives. The account executives were supposed to work together on strategy for acquiring new accounts. If a particular account executive did not have the expertise to handle his or her customers' problems, another account executive was supposed to offer help. For example, Darcy Wentworth was the resident expert on printing packages and inserts for packages. If invited, Darcy would join another account executive to call on a customer with a complex request for package printing.

After the new sales organization had been in place for 18 months, Ann Osaka, an account executive, was having lunch with Garth Lewis, a production superintendent at Mercury Printing. "I've about had it," said Ann. "I'm tired of single-handedly carrying the team."

"What do you mean you are single-handedly carrying the team?" asked Garth.

"You're a trusted friend, Garth. So let me lay out the facts. Each month the group is supposed to bring in 16 new sales. If we don't average those 16 sales per month, we don't get our semiannual bonus. That represents about 25 percent of my salary. So a big chunk of my money comes from group effort.

"My average number of new accounts brought in for the last 12 months has been 9. And we are averaging about 14 new sales per month. This translates into the other three account execs averaging five sales among them. I'm carrying the group, but overall sales are still below quota. This means I didn't get my bonus last month.

"The other account execs are friendly and helpful in writing up proposals. But they just don't bring in their share of accounts."

Garth asked, "What does your boss say about this?"

"I've had several conversations with him about the problem. He tells me to be patient and to remember the development of a fully functioning team requires time. He also tells me that I should develop a stronger team spirit. My problem is that I can't pay my bills with team spirit."

QUESTIONS

1. What does this case illustrate about effective teamwork?
2. What steps should Alvera Velasquez take, if any, to remedy the situation of unequal contribution of account representatives?
3. To what extent are Ann Osaka's complaints justifiable?

16. "Job-Sharing," *Flexible Workplace Management,* sample issue, 2001, p. 3.

17. "What is the Future of Telework?" *HRfocus,* March 2001, p. 5; Jenny C. McCune, "Telecommuting Revisited," *Management Review,* February 1998, p. 12.

18. Keith H. Hammonds, "Balancing Work and Family," *Business Week,* September 16, 1996, pp. 74–80.

19. Dayton Fandray, "What is Work/Life Worth?" *Workforce,* May 2000, p. 64.

20. Study cited in "The Success of Work/Family Programs Depends on Individual Managers," *Positive Leadership,* bonus issue, 1998, p. 5.

21. Survey conducted by Challenger, Gray & Christmas (Chicago, IL), 1997.
22. Kurt T. Dirks, "The Effects of Interpersonal Trust on Work Group Performance," *Journal of Applied Psychology,* June 1999, pp. 445–455.
23. Philip M. Podaskoff, Michael Ahearne, and Scott B. MacKenzie, "Organizational Citizenship Behavior and the Quantity and Quality of Work Group Performance," *Journal of Applied Psychology,* April 1997, pp. 262–270.
24. James W. Dean, Jr., Pamela Brandes, and Ravi Dharwadkar, "Organizational Cynicism," *Academy of Management Review,* April 1998, pp. 341–352.

SUGGESTED READING

Barker, James R. *The Discipline of Teamwork: Participation and Concertive Control.* Thousand Oaks, CA: Sage, 1999.

Fandray, Dayton. "What is Work/Life Worth?" *Workforce,* May 2000, pp. 64–71.

Flynn, Gillian. "The Legalities of Flextime." *Workforce,* October 2001, pp. 62–66.

Gale, Fister Sarah. "Formalized Flextime: The Perk That Brings Productivity." *Workforce,* February 2001, pp. 38–42.

Ghosn, Carlos. "Saving the Business Without Losing the Company." *Harvard Business Review,* January 2002, pp. 37–45.

Katz, Nancy. "Sports Teams as a Model for Workplace Teams: Lessons and Liabilities." *Academy of Management Executive,* August 2001, pp. 56–67.

Robbins, Harvey, and Finley, Michael. *The New Why Teams Don't Work: What Goes Wrong and How to Make it Right.* San Francisco: Berrett-Koehler, 2000.

Salas, Eduardo, Bowers, Clint A., and Edens, Eleana. *Improving Teamwork in Organizations.* Mahwah, NJ: Lawrence Erlbaum Associates, 2001.

Selinski, Debbie. "The Coach K Difference." *Success,* February–March 2001, pp. 28–33.

WEB CORNER

www.catalystwomen.org (Research on work/family issues.)

www.Homeworking.com (Resources for the teleworker.)

www.workinamerica.org/ (Information about improving productivity and quality of work/life balance presented by the Work in America Institute.)

www.YouCanWorkFromAnywhere.com (Suggestions for improving the productivity of telecommuters.)

CHAPTER 14

LEADING AND INFLUENCING OTHERS

Learning Objectives

After reading and studying this chapter and doing the exercises, you should be able to

1. Describe how leaders use power and influence to achieve goals.
2. Identify important traits, motives, and characteristics of leaders.
3. Identify important behaviors and skills of leaders.
4. Describe participative leadership style.
5. Present an overview of charismatic and transformational leadership.
6. Describe the basics of servant leadership.
7. Explain the basics of 360-degree feedback for improving leadership effectiveness.

Leadership has always been a central topic of applied psychology. Of greater significance, effective leadership is considered the most important ingredient for moving organizations forward in a complex and competitive world. To achieve such ends, effective leadership is needed at all levels, from supervisors and team leaders to top-level executives. Furthermore, professional and technical people are expected to exert leadership in many temporary assignments during their careers. These include such roles as chairing a committee or taking a turn at being the team leader.

An underlying theme of this chapter is that leadership does make a difference—it has an impact on organizational performance and business results. Our study of leadership encompasses the difference between leadership and management, how leaders use power and influence, the qualities and behaviors of leaders, and the participative leadership style. We also study charismatic and transformational leadership, the servant leader, and a systematic method of obtaining feedback on leadership effectiveness.

 LEADERSHIP VERSUS MANAGEMENT

The reason leadership is so important is revealed in its definition: **Leadership** is the process of influencing others to achieve certain objectives. Leadership involves influencing the activities of an individual or a group in efforts toward reaching a goal in a given situation. However, unduly coercive tactics such as gun threats are not part of leadership. If influence is not exerted, leadership, strictly speaking, has not been performed. An employee who performs satisfactorily with almost no supervisor contact is not being led.

To understand leadership, it is important to know the differences among the terms leadership, management, and supervision. Leadership is but one component of *management,* working with and through individuals and groups to accomplish organizational goals. Management includes the major activities of planning, organizing, controlling, and leading. The nonleadership aspects of a manager's job are sometimes referred to as administrative work, while the interpersonal aspects involve leadership.

Leadership is regarded as a force that inspires and energizes people and brings about change.[1] The other aspects of management deal more with the status quo. Among the leadership aspects of a manager's job described in this text are motivation, communication, and conflict resolution. Both good management and effective leadership are important for an organization to run well.

Supervision is first-level management. Supervisors plan, organize, control, and lead, as do other managers. However, supervisors spend more time in face-to-face leadership activities than do higher-level managers. The latter group is more involved with developing business strategy and influencing others from a distance.

HOW LEADERS USE POWER AND INFLUENCE TO ACHIEVE GOALS

A major purpose of leadership is to help people achieve important goals such as earning a profit, improving quality, or doing social good. Power and influence are two basic processes for achieving such goals or purposes. Let's avoid getting involved in a philosophical debate about the difference between power and influence. Think of power as the battery under the hood of a car. The power contained in the battery is waiting to be released. Turning on the ignition is the influence tactic you apply to release the pent-up power in the battery. Here we first look at sources of power, followed by influence tactics.

Sources of Leadership Power

Leaders influence others to achieve goals through the use of **power**—the ability to get others to do things and to influence decisions. When power stems from the formal position you occupy, it is referred to as **position power.** When it stems from your personal characteristics and skills, it is referred to as **personal power.** Here we will examine subtypes of power in detail and point out some guidelines for their proper use.[2] The message for your career is that if you want to be an effective leader, you must be able to use power in an intelligent and sensitive manner.

Position Power. Position power can be divided into three subtypes: legitimate, reward, and coercive. **Legitimate power** is the ability to influence others that stems directly from the leader's position. It is the easiest type of power to understand and accept. People at higher levels in an organization have more power than the people below them. However, the culture of an organization helps decide the limits to anybody's power. A store manager in Los Angeles, for example, does not have the right to demand that a sales associate converse with customers only in Spanish (or English).

Although employees generally accept their supervisor's right to make requests, they do not like to be given orders in a way that implies they are not as good as the leader. Effective leaders therefore exercise authority by making polite requests, rather than arrogant demands.[3]

Reward power refers to the leader's control over rewards valued by the group member. For example, if a sales manager can directly reward sales representatives with cash bonuses for good performance, that manager will exert considerable power. Effective leaders do not use rewards as bribes for getting employees to do what they want. Instead, rewards are used to reinforce desirable behavior after it has already taken place.

Coercive power refers to the leader's control over punishments. It is based on fear and thus may create anxiety and defensiveness. Effective leaders generally avoid the use of coercive power except when absolutely necessary, because coercion is likely to create resentment and undermine their personal power. Yet, if skillfully used, coercion can get some people to comply with rules, regulations, and orders.

Personal Power. Personal power has two subtypes: expert power and referent power. **Expert power** is the ability to control others through knowledge relevant to the job as perceived by subordinates. You can also exercise expert power when you do not have a formal leadership position. An example is the engineering technician who is talented at getting industrial robots to work properly. The company becomes dependent on that individual, giving him or her some power with respect to receiving special privileges. To accumulate expert power, a leader should cultivate an image of experience and competence. Credibility must be preserved by avoiding careless statements and rash decisions. It is also important to remain cool. A leader who appears confused, vacillates, or is obviously panicked will quickly lose expert power.

Referent power refers to the ability to control based on loyalty to the leader and the group members' desire to please that person. A research study suggests that having referent power contributes to being perceived as charismatic, but that expert power also makes a contribution.[4] Some of the loyalty to the leader is based on identification with the leader's personality traits and personal characteristics. Referent power and charisma are both based on the subjective perception of the leader's traits and characteristics. Although both position and personal power are important, effective leaders rely more heavily on personal power to get work accomplished through others.

Influence Tactics Used by Leaders

Having power is the starting point in influencing others. Leaders also use a variety of specific influence tactics to get others to accomplish goals. Several of these influence tactics are described next.[5]

Leading by example is a simple but effective way of influencing group members. This type of leader-manager shows consistency between actions and words. Also, actions and words confirm, support, and often clarify each other. For example, if the firm has a dress code and the supervisor explains the code and dresses accordingly, a role model has been provided that is consistent in words and actions. The action of following the dress code provides an example that supports and clarifies the words used to describe the dress code.[6] Matthew Szulik, the top executive at the software company Red Hat, makes a point of leading by example. He ensures that everyone in the company knows that he works as hard or harder than anyone else in the company, and he expects Red Hat employees to follow his lead.[7]

Assertiveness refers to being forthright with your demands, expressing both the specifics of what you want done and the feelings surrounding the demands. An assertive leader might say, "I'm worried about the backlog of customer inquiries on our Web site. I want the inquiries answered by Thursday at 4:30." A leader might also be assertive by checking frequently on group members.

Ingratiation refers to getting somebody else to like you, often using political behaviors. Two specific ingratiating behaviors reported by workers were "Acted in a friendly manner prior to asking for what I wanted" and "Praised the subordinate just before asking for what I wanted." Strong leaders tend not to rely heavily on ingratiating tactics.

Rationality is appealing to reason and logic. It is an influence tactic used frequently by effective leaders. Pointing out the facts of a situation to a group member in order to prompt that person to act is an example of rationality. One manager convinced an employee to take on a field assignment by informing the employee that every member of top-level management had field experience. The group member in question was ambitious, which made her receptive to a course of action that could help her achieve her goals.

Exchange is the use of reciprocal favors to influence others. Leaders with limited personal and position power tend to emphasize exchanging favors with group members. An example of exchange would be promising to endorse an employee's request for a two-week leave of absence if the employee takes on an unpleasant short-term assignment. As a management newsletter advises, exchange is a two-way street. If a group member goes out of his or her way to help you, you owe that person a favor.[8]

Upward appeal means asking for help from a higher authority. Here the leader exerts influence by getting a more powerful person to carry out the influence act. A specific example: "I sent the guy to my superior when he wouldn't listen to me. That fixed him." More than occasional use of upward appeal weakens the manager's stature in the eyes of employees and superiors and erodes effectiveness as a leader.

Consultation with others before making a decision is a standard leadership influence tactic. The influence target becomes more motivated to follow the leader's request because the target is involved in making the decision. Consultation is the most effective as an influence tactic when the objectives of the person being influenced are consistent with those of the leader.

Joking and kidding, in the form of good-natured ribbing, is effective as an influence tactic when a straightforward statement might be interpreted as harsh criticism. People will often perceive the message within the joking and kidding without taking offense. A business owner was strolling through the office and noticed that one of the office assistants had her shoes off. The owner perceived being shoeless as unprofessional, yet he did not want to criticize her directly. Instead, he said, "Hmm, nice feet!" The assistant laughed and put her shoes back on.

TRAITS, MOTIVES, AND CHARACTERISTICS OF EFFECTIVE LEADERS

Early attempts at studying leadership focused on the traits, motives, and characteristics of leaders themselves. For many years, the trait approach to understanding leadership was downplayed. Substantial research has shown that leadership is best understood when the leader, the group members, and the situation in which they are placed are analyzed. In recent years, new emphasis has been placed on understanding leaders themselves. The study of charismatic and transformational leaders is but one example. The leader also has to possess key skills and take certain actions, as described in the following section. The traits and motives described in this section illustrate ways in which leaders differ from group members (or followers). Figure 14–1 summarizes these differences. Our choice of these particular traits, motives, and characteristics does not imply that others are unimportant.

Power Motive. Effective executive leaders have a strong need to control resources. Leaders with high power drives have three dominant characteristics:

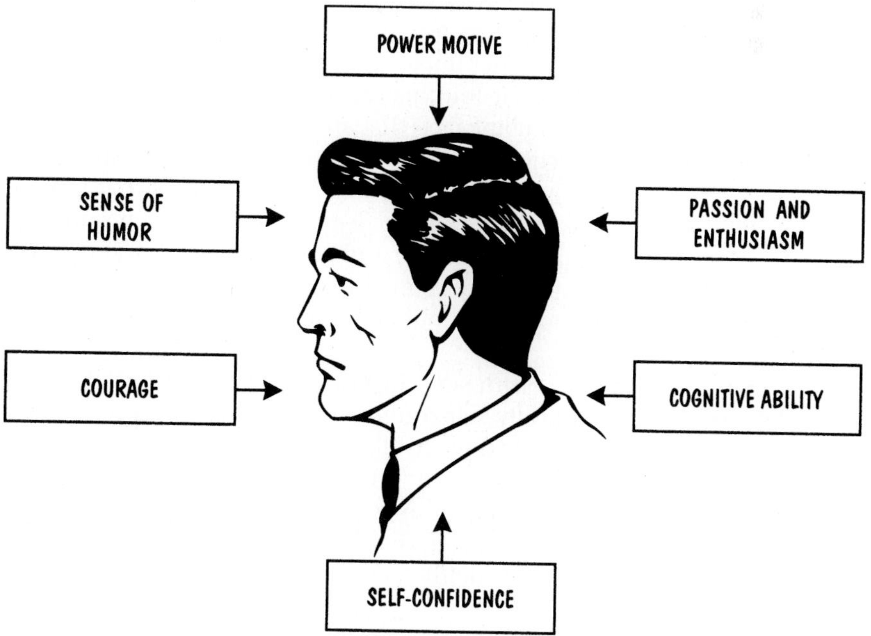

FIGURE 14–1 Portrait of a Leader

(1) they act with vigor and determination to exert their power, (2) they invest much time in thinking about ways to alter the behavior and thinking of others, and (3) they care about their personal standing with those around them.[9] The strong need for power is important because it means that the leader is interested in influencing others. The power needed to satisfy the power motive can be obtained through acquiring the right position or through developing personal power. Donald Trump is an executive with an extraordinary power motive. A tip-off is his penchant for naming buildings, a yacht, and an airline after himself.

Passion and Enthusiasm. A prominent characteristic of effective leaders is the passion and enthusiasm they have for their work, much like the same quality in creative people. The passion reflects itself in such ways as an intense liking for the business, the customers, and employees. Passion is also reflected in a relentless drive to get work accomplished, and an obsession for achieving company goals. Passion for their work is especially evident in entrepreneurial leaders and small-business owners who are preoccupied with growing their businesses. The accompanying box describes a well-known corporate business leader whose passion for his work is described as love.

Cognitive Ability. Effective leaders have good problem-solving ability. To inspire people, bring about constructive change, and solve problems creatively, leaders need to be mentally sharp. Another mental requirement for leaders is the ability to sort out essential information for the less essential, and then store the most important in memory. Two cognitive attributes described in earlier chapters—openness to experience and creativity—are also relevant for leaders. *Knowledge of the business* is another important cognitive attribute because an effective leader has to be technically competent in some area, particularly when leading a group of specialists. It is difficult for the leader to establish rapport with group members when he or she does not know what they are doing and when the group does not respect the leader's technical skills.

Another important cognitive trait of effective leaders is **insight,** an ability to know what information is relevant, find connections between the old and the new, combine facts that are unrelated, and see the "big picture." Insight is also part of practical intelligence. Insight into people and situations helps a leader hire the right people and make work assignments that fit people's talents. Farsightedness is a cognitive skill needed particularly by executive leaders because they have to visualize the future, and guide the company toward coping with the future. For example, a marketing executive often needs to predict what products and services the company should offer in the future.

Self-confidence. In virtually every setting, it is important for the leader to be realistically self-confident. A leader who is self-assured without being bombastic or overbearing instills confidence within group members. Aside from being a psychological trait, self-confidence or self-assurance refers to the behavior exhibited by a person in a number of situations. It is like being cool under pressure. We can conclude that a given leader is self-confident if the leader exhibits such behavior as deftly handling an unrealistic demand by a key employee.

Courage. A study of 200 U.S. and Japanese managers indicates that courage is an important leadership attribute for revitalizing an organization. Managerial

AN APPLIED PSYCHOLOGY CONCEPT IN ACTION

Passion for the Task and People Helps a Leader Succeed

High above Tennessee, the leaders of Tricon Global Restaurants Inc., the largest restaurant chain in the world, are having a casual but strategic conference in one of their corporate jets. Andy Pearson may be sitting in front—but you would never know he is one of the two men who run this company. Like all the others, he wears a golf shirt that bears the logos of their three restaurants: KFC, Pizza Hut, and Taco Bell. The group is talking about partnering with another chain, such as putting a Baskin-Robbins inside Taco Bell. At 30,000 feet, all ideas are good: Pearson isn't about to bring anyone down to earth from up here.

And that in itself is a huge change in Pearson's leadership style. This is the new Andy Pearson, a 76-year-old man who has transformed himself into a new kind of boss. The old Andy Pearson ran PepsiCo Inc., for nearly 15 years. Back then he was known for his skills at bringing people down to earth, from any altitude. His chief weapons at the time were fear, and a fanatical devotion to the numbers. In 1980, *Fortune* named him one of the 10 toughest bosses in the United States.

Every year, without hesitation, he fired the least productive 10% to 20% of his workforce—and he still thinks it's a good idea to let go of a certain layer of the company's lowest performers. But now he's learned to demand high standards in a different way. "There's a human yearning for a certain amount of toughness," Pearson says. "But it can't be unmitigated toughness."

These days, Pearson is focused on a different, more positive emotional agenda. "You say to yourself, If I could only unleash the power of everybody in the organization, instead of just a few people, what could we accomplish? We'd be a much better company."

You can see this new attitude in the way he speaks and listens, even up in the airplane. Someone suggests opening an all-night restaurant. Pearson doesn't think it would work, but he doesn't say so, at least not directly. He finds some nugget of intelligence, and offers what he sees as a challenge. If people want to tackle the challenge, he won't stop them. But they have been warned.

David Novak, another key executive at Tricon, established a culture that elevates the common worker in a way that brings out the emotional drive and commitment that is the heart of good work. As a result, Pearson has seen employees weep with gratitude in reaction to nothing more than a few simple words of praise. Where before he might have dismissed that kind of display as sentimentality, he now recognizes emotion for what it is: the secret to a company's competitive edge.

By watching Novak, Pearson saw how the human heart drive's a company's success—one person at a time—and how this success can't be imposed from the top but must be kindled through attention, awareness, recognition, and reward. Pearson says that great leaders find a balance between getting results and how they get them. "A lot of people make the mistake of thinking that getting results is all there is to the job. They go after results without building a team or without building an organization that has the capacity to change. Your real job is to get results and do it in a way that makes your organization a great place to work—a place where people enjoy coming to work, instead of just taking orders and hitting the month's numbers." Tricon's leaders credit the restaurant chain's improved results directly to their new culture of employee recognition.

In commenting about his changed approach to leadership, Pearson says that he proved he was smart by finding fault with other people's ideas. "I remember bringing one of our market-research women to tears because I told her that the information she was gathering wasn't producing anything. I could just see the breath come out of her. I realized that in today's world, you can't treat people that way. First, people have many more options than they used to. They can leave—and you can't find more talent just by turning over the next log. Second, that kind of treatment demoralizes people. I don't think that woman was ever the same. If you're not careful, you might discard a very good person. There are a lot of ways to ask tough questions without killing somebody."

Source: David Dorsey, "Andy Pearson Finds Love," *Fast Company*, August 2001, pp. 78–86.

courage involves a manager's giving voice to ideas that deviate from current thinking because the manager believes they will produce improved benefits for the organization. Sometimes the ideas recommend change; at other times the ideas advocate maintaining the status quo.[10]

Sense of Humor. Some see a sense of humor as a trait, and some as a behavior. However you classify it, the effective use of humor is an important part of a leader's role. Humor serves such functions in the workplace as relieving tension and boredom and defusing hostility. Humor also builds teamwork, because people who can laugh together well usually can work together well. Because humor helps the leader dissolve tension and defuse conflict, it helps him or her exert power. Self-effacing humor is the choice of comedians and organizational leaders alike. By being self-effacing, the leader makes a point without insulting or slighting anybody. A vice president of human resources at CISCO Systems said a few years ago, "I want you people to design an employee self-service system for inquiring about benefits so uncomplicated that I could learn to use it."

BEHAVIORS AND SKILLS OF EFFECTIVE LEADERS

Leadership effectiveness includes the inner qualities of a leader combined with the right behaviors, or actions, and skills. Next we describe an illustrative group of behaviors and skills associated with effective managerial leadership. Scanning this list will enable you to see the link between traits and behaviors. For example, a self-confident and courageous leader will usually be stable under pressure.

Direction Setting. Given that leaders are supposed to bring about change, they must point people in the right direction. Setting a direction includes the idea of establishing a **vision,** or lofty image of the future of the organization or smaller group. An example of direction setting by a top-level manager would be for the CEO of a toy company to decide that the company should now diversify into the bicycle business. Direction setting by a team leader would include encouraging the group to strive toward error-free work from this point forward.

A powerful term to signify direction setting is the *northbound train.* Karl Albrecht contends that executives should tell their leadership team, "This is our northbound train. This is the direction we have chosen. If you don't feel you want to go north, there are other trains you can ride. But this particular train is going north, and I expect anyone who rides on it to commit his or her energy fully to the journey."[11]

Being Trustworthy. Group members consistently believe that leaders must display honesty, integrity, and credibility, thereby engendering trust. Leaders themselves believe that honesty makes a difference in their effectiveness. Group members, however, measure honesty by the deeds of leaders. Constituents consider their leaders to be honest when the leaders follow through on promises. One study revealed that of all behaviors describing leadership, the most essential was the leader's display of trust to others.[12] In summary, an effective leader is trusted and trusts others. (Note that the trait of honesty leads to acting in a trustworthy manner.)

Asking Tough Questions. We have emphasized that the leader should be knowledgeable. Yet there are many times when leaders can be effective by asking tough questions rather than providing answers. A tough question is one that makes a person or group stop and think about why they are doing or not doing something. In this way group members are forced to think about the effectiveness of their activities. The beauty of a tough question is that it encourages people to ask themselves, "Why didn't I think of that? It seems so obvious." Asking questions is important because quite often group members may have the solutions to difficult problems facing the organization.[13] Here is an example of a tough question:

> The division general manager says to the manufacturing manager, "The delivery date you promised assumes that the one supplier you have for the main components will deliver as promised. Suppose they don't? Why do you depend so heavily on one supplier? What can you do to prevent a crisis?"

Maintaining High Standards. Effective leaders consistently hold group members to high standards of performance, which raises productivity. Setting high expectations for others becomes a self-fulfilling prophecy. Workers tend to live up to the expectations set for them by managers (the Pygmalion effect). The effect works in a subtle, almost unconscious way. When a leader believes that a group member will succeed, that manager communicates the belief to the person without realizing that the belief is being transmitted. By setting high standards, the group members will often gain in self-confidence, leading to higher self-efficacy when performing a task. Setting high expectations might take the form of encouraging team members to establish difficult goals.

Stability under Pressure. Effective leaders are steady performers, even under heavy workloads and uncertain conditions. Such behavior reflects a high standing on the trait of emotional stability. Remaining steady under conditions of uncertainty contributes to effectiveness because it helps group members cope with the situation. When the leader remains calm, group members are reassured that things will work out satisfactorily.

Accessibility to Group Members. Leaders who interact face-to-face with group members frequently are much better liked than leaders who avoid personal interaction. Furthermore, leaders who are more accessible to group members are likely to achieve high group productivity and morale. A potential problem is that managers have so much analytical work to perform, and have to spend so much time at the computer that face-to-face interaction will often receive low priority. Robert A. Eckert, the CEO of toy maker Mattell, provides an example of the importance of the leader being accessible. When Eckert left Kraft Foods to join Mattel, the new company was in deep financial trouble, and morale had plummeted. An important component of Eckert's turnaround strategy was to have meals every workday in the company cafeteria with employees. During these meals with Mattel workers, Eckert strived for honest dialogue, and emphasized asking employees questions about their specialties. The new CEO's accessibility contributed to the company turnaround.[14]

A Positive Attitude, Including Supportiveness. Similar to passion and enthusiasm, expressing a positive attitude in most situations is an effective leadership behavior. As part of research on emotional intelligence, Daniel Goleman and his associates found that the leader's mood and his or her accompanying behaviors have substantial effects on performance. Moods are usually contagious. A cranky and ruthless manager creates a toxic organization that leads to people underperforming. In contrast, an upbeat and inspirational leader helps group members rise to difficult challenges.[15]

Another aspect of a leader being upbeat is to be supportive of group members. A **supportive leader,** one who gives praise and encouragement to group members, usually increases morale and productivity. Supportive supervisors also make an important contribution to preventing burnout among group members, as revealed by a study of working adults in a variety of organizations.[16]

Willingness to Accept Blame. Effective leaders are willing to accept blame for what went wrong, even when the group is mostly at fault. Accepting blame is part of being gracious and sensitive to the needs of others. Joe Montana, the legendary professional football quarterback, says he owes part of his success to being able to say, "I dropped the ball," even if he didn't. In the words of Montana, "When you're a leader, you've got to be willing to take the blame. People appreciate when you're not pointing fingers at them, because that just adds to their pressure. If you get past that, you can talk about fixing what went wrong."[17]

THE PARTICIPATIVE LEADERSHIP STYLE

So far we have described the traits, motives, characteristics, behaviors, and skills of leaders. Another way of understanding leaders is to draw some stereotypes of their behavior called **leadership style.** A leadership style is a leader's characteristic way of behaving in most situations. For the last 20 years, the participative leadership style has received the most attention because this style enables the leader to share decisions with the group and capitalize on the talents of the group. By definition, a **participative leader** shares decision-making authority with the group. At his or her best, the participative leader motivates group members to work as a team toward high-level goals. Encouraging employees to participate in making decisions is the major approach to empowerment. Participative leadership is often favored because workers are more willing to implement decisions when they were involved in formulating the decisions.

Participative leadership encompasses so many different behaviors that it is useful to divide it into three subtypes: consultative, consensus, and democratic.

Consultative Leaders. A **consultative leader** solicits opinions from the group before making a decision, yet does not feel obliged to accept the group's thinking. Leaders of this type make it clear that they alone have authority to make the final decisions. A standard way to practice consultative leadership would be to call a group meeting and discuss an issue before making a decision.

Consensus Leaders. A **consensus leader** encourages group discussion about an issue and then makes a decision that reflects the consensus of the group members. Consensus-style leaders thus turn over more authority to the group than do consultative leaders. The consensus style results in long delays in decision making, because every party involved has to agree.

Democratic Leaders. A **democratic leader** confers final authority on the group. He or she functions as a collector of opinion and takes a vote before making a decision. Democratic leaders turn over so much authority to the group that they are sometimes referred to as free-rein leaders. The group usually achieves its goals when working under a democratic leader. Democratic leadership has more relevance for community activities than for most work settings.

Participative leadership is also referred to as *trickle-up* leadership because suggestions flow from workers to management. Part of trickle-up leadership is for group members to step in when they perceive that the leader is having difficulty. According to Michael Useem, as technology evolves and organizations decentralize, front-line workers have more independence and responsibility. They are more aware of customer demands and how to manufacture a product or provide a service. These same workers can often see what the leaders are missing, and can therefore step in to help a faltering leader. In the Marines, when a superior issues a flawed order, officers are expected to point out the flaws before the order is implemented. For example, four-star general Peter Pace ends his meetings by asking subordinates to tell him what they each think. By encouraging the group members to challenge him, Pace reinforces a culture of trickle-up leadership.[18]

In contrast to the participative leader is the leader-manager who makes decisions more independently. An **autocratic leader** attempts to retain most of the authority granted to the group. Autocratic leaders make all the major decisions and assume subordinates will comply without question. Leaders who use this style give minimum consideration to what group members are likely to think about an order or decision. Group members sometimes see an autocrat as rigid and demanding.

Although the autocratic leadership style is not in vogue, many successful leaders are autocratic. Among them are *crisis managers*—those who specialize in turning around failing organizations or rescuing them from crisis. Other situations calling for crisis management include earthquakes, product recalls, and workplace violence. The autocratic style generally works best in situations where decisions have to be made rapidly or when group opinion is not needed. One situation calling for autocratic leadership would be extinguishing an oil rig fire at sea. Another would be when a company is undergoing liquidation and bankruptcy.

Evaluation of the Participative Style. Although participative management in the form of empowerment is widespread today, the results of participation have been mixed. The three participative styles are suited to managing competent and well-motivated people who want to get involved in making decisions and giving feedback to the leader. A participative style is also useful when the leader wants the group members to commit to a course of action. A supervisor might ask a group, "What should we do with group members who stay outside the building too long during their smoking breaks?" If the group agreed on a fitting punishment, they would tend to accept the punishment if it were administered.

Participative management and leadership often fail when trust is low between workers and upper-level management. Employees lack faith in participative management because they do not believe top management has their best interests in mind. If procedures or alternative solutions to a problem have already been agreed on, participative management is superfluous. For instance, in highly repetitive, machine-paced operations, little room is left for employee problem solving. Likewise, very few bank employees are asked to participate in making decisions about setting interest rates on loans; such decisions are made in the executive suite.

A positive application of participative leadership and management took place at Royal/Dutch Shell—one of the world's largest business firms. To help revitalize the company, top-level management embarked on a program of grassroots leadership involving employees in all lines of businesses, including automobile service stations and dozens of other product lines. The basic approach to participative leadership was to bring six- to eight-person teams from a half-dozen operating companies worldwide to an intense "retailing boot camp." Team members would be introduced to the participative leadership model so they could bring it to employees back home. Participants were also taught a model for improving business that they used as a framework for solving problems locally.

The results were better than the top-level management had anticipated. Cross-functional teams in dozens of locations throughout the world came up with ways to improve their local business. Producing a video proved to be the best training exercise for getting teams to participate in decisions about business improvement. Teams were told: "Here's a video camera. In the next 90 minutes, make a 5- or 6-minute video that illustrates the old Shell and the new Shell."[19]

Gender Differences in Leadership Style

Controversy exists as to whether men and women have different leadership styles. Several researchers and writers argue that women have certain acquired traits and behaviors that suit them for a people-oriented leadership style. Consequently, women leaders frequently exhibit a cooperative, empowering style that includes nurturing team members. According to this same perspective, men are inclined toward a command-and-control, somewhat militaristic leadership style. Women find participative management more natural than do men because they feel more comfortable interacting with people. Furthermore, it is argued that women's natural sensitivity to people gives them an edge over men in encouraging group members to participate in decision making.

Adding to the controversy about gender differences in leadership style is a five-year study comparing how well group members perceive men and women managers. Lawrence A. Plaff, a human resources consultant, found that female managers scored higher than their male counterparts in 20 skill areas. Included in the study were 2,482 managers at all levels from more than 400 organizations across 19 states. Ratings and written comments from group members, peers, and superiors were used to evaluate the managers (360-degree feedback, to be described later here). The sex differences extended beyond the softer skills such as communication, feedback, and empowering other employees to such hard areas as decisiveness, planning, and setting standards.

Plaff believes that women have acquired nontraditional strengths in recent years, but that men have not broadened their strengths in the same way. His study also suggests that male managers still rely on a more autocratic style, emphasizing individual accomplishment and competition. Women place more emphasis on facilitating group processes, using positive motivation, and developing group members' abilities.[20]

The study just cited paints a positive picture of the leadership skills of women, yet anecdotal evidence exists that not all women leaders are warm, supportive, and effective. For example, 200 out of 266 letters sent to a *Fortune* magazine columnist said that many women managers are mean and ineffective. Some women wrote that they became so fed up with trying to avoid bad female bosses that they left the corporate world and started their own businesses.[21]

Assume that these differences in the preferred leadership style between men and women were generally true. Women managers would therefore be better suited for organizations that have shifted to participation and empowerment. It

SKILL-BUILDING EXERCISE 14–1

Contrasting Leadership Styles

In each of the two following role-plays, a group member is given the assignment of estimating the cost of insulating a basement of an old factory. The subordinate later informs the supervisor that he or she doesn't have enough experience to make the right estimate. One person plays the role of the subordinate asking for help from the boss in making the estimate. Two pairs of people are thus required. In situation A, the subordinate makes the request to an autocratic boss. In situation B, the request is made to a participative boss. If you are playing the role of the boss, think through how each style of leader would react to the request.

may be true that more women than men gravitate naturally toward the consultative, consensus, and democratic leadership styles, and men toward the autocratic. Nevertheless, there are many male leaders who find the participative style to be a good fit, and many women who are autocratic.

To better understand leadership styles, do Skill-Building Exercise 14–1.

CHARISMATIC AND TRANSFORMATIONAL LEADERSHIP

In recent years considerable attention has been paid to leaders who are charming, engaging, and inspirational and who move organizations forward in a positive direction. Such leaders have been placed in two overlapping categories: charismatic and transformational. Both approaches to understanding leadership emphasize personal characteristics and behaviors.

Charismatic Leadership

As already hinted, **charisma** is the ability to lead or influence others based on personal charm, magnetism, inspiration, and emotion. Charisma is based on others perceiving you in a very positive way. Charismatic leadership results from a group of behaviors and traits that result in the attribution of being charismatic.[22] A key characteristic of charismatic leaders is their vision. They offer a vision (or lofty goal) of where the organization is headed and how to get there (a plan). A sense of vision inspires employees to perform well. For example, CEO Andrea Jung of Avon Products wants the company to become the "ultimate relationship marketer of products and services for women, and the source for anything and everything a woman wants to buy."[23]

Charismatic leaders are masterful communicators. They formulate believable dreams and portray their vision of the future as the only path to follow. Leaders who are charismatic also use metaphors to inspire people. An example is a favorite of Richard Marcus, president of Neiman-Marcus stores: "If you follow in someone else's footsteps, you never get ahead." An underlying reason charismatic leaders communicate so well is that they are emotionally expressive. They readily express how they feel, which also enables them to form close ties with people.

Charismatic leaders at their best inspire trust. Quite often their constituents are willing to gamble with their careers to follow the chief's vision. Another behavior of charismatic leaders is helping group members feel capable. One technique they use is letting their people achieve success on relatively easy projects. They praise their people and then give them more demanding assignments. Charismatic leaders are energetic and use an action-oriented leadership style. They exude energy, serving as a model for getting things done well and on time. An extreme example is Richard Branson of the Virgin Group, including Virgin Atlantic Airways and about 100 other businesses. Branson spreads himself thin with some personal involvement in all these businesses. He also leads a daredevil lifestyle with such stunts as riding hot air balloons and sliding down a large pole in Times Square, New York, to promote a new store.

Branson's flamboyant behavior illustrates another key characteristic of charismatic leaders: They purposely manage their impressions and promote themselves. They package information about themselves to look good, and they pay careful attention to their appearance. A charismatic person often drops hints about the influential people he or she knows and brings personal accomplishments to the attention of others.[24]

Some aspects of charisma are related to basic personality factors such as extraversion. Nevertheless, it is possible for most people to enhance their charisma. Skill-Building Exercise 14–2 gives suggestions for developing your charisma.

Transformational Leadership

The focus of transformational leadership is on what the leader accomplishes, rather than on the leader's personal characteristics and his or her relationships with group members. The **transformational leader** is one who helps organizations and people make positive changes in the way they conduct their activities. Such a leader stands in contrast to the transactional leader, who is involved mainly in routine transactions with group members such as giving them contingent rewards and punishments. Evidence supporting the difference between transformational and transactional leaders has been gathered so far from all continents except Antarctica, according to Bernard M. Bass.[25]

Transformational leadership is seen as the key to revitalizing large business corporations. Part of revitalizing an organization is energizing people. A transformational leader can develop new visions for a firm and mobilize employees to accept and work toward attaining these visions. Here we look at the qualities and behaviors of transformational leaders and how transformations take place. In addition, we look at the potential downside of charismatic and transformational leadership.

Seven Key Characteristics and Behaviors of Transformational Leaders. Transformational leaders possess the personal characteristics of other effective leaders. Several studies have pointed toward a combination of seven characteristics and behaviors typical of transformational leaders. Several of these qualities have already been described in our study of leadership and creativity.[26]

1. *Vision.* Transformational leaders develop an image of the future of their organization and communicate this vision to their constituents, often by making frequent statements of the vision.

SKILL-BUILDING EXERCISE 14–2

Developing Your Charisma

Establishing the goal of becoming more charismatic is the starting point for developing charisma. You then discipline yourself to develop some of the traits and characteristics described in the text. Here are 11 specific suggestions for skill development.[27]

1. **Use visioning.** If you are the leader of an organizational unit, a club, or a team, develop a dream about its future. Discuss your vision with others in your group or with your immediate superior.
2. **Make frequent use of metaphors.** Develop metaphors to inspire people around you. A commonly used one after a group has suffered a setback is, "Like the phoenix, we will rise from the ashes of defeat."
3. **Inspire trust and confidence.** Make your deeds consistent with your promises. Get people to believe in your competence by making your accomplishments known in a polite, tactful way.
4. **Be highly energetic and goal oriented.** Impress others with your energy and resourcefulness. To increase your energy supply, exercise frequently, eat well, and get ample rest.
5. **Express your emotions frequently.** Freely express warmth, joy, happiness, and enthusiasm.
6. **Focus on the positive.** Charismatic people are optimists who minimize complaints and emphasize what positive steps can be taken to overcome a problem.
7. **Smile frequently, even if you are not in a happy mood.** A warm smile seems to indicate a confident, caring person, which contributes to a perception of charisma.
8. **Be candid.** Practice saying directly what you want, rather than being indirect and evasive. If you want someone to help you don't ask, "Are you busy?" Instead, ask, "Can you help me with a problem I'm having right now?"
9. **Make everybody you meet feel that he or she is quite important.** For example, at a company social gathering, shake the hand of every person you meet. Also, thank people frequently both orally and by written notes.
10. **Multiply the effectiveness of your handshake.** Shake firmly without creating pain, and make enough eye contact to notice the color of the other person's eyes. When you take that much trouble, you project care and concern.
11. **Stand up straight and use other nonverbal signals of self-confidence.** Practice having good posture. Minimize fidgeting, scratching, and speaking in a monotone. Walk at a rapid pace without appearing to be panicked. Dress fashionably without going to the extreme that people notice your clothes more than they notice you.

2. *Staff development.* The transformational leader diagnoses the needs and abilities of each staff member and advises and encourages individual development, usually on a one-to-one basis.
3. *Supportive leadership.* Key supportive behaviors include giving positive feedback to staff members and recognizing individual achievement. It is especially important for the transformational leader to be supportive when the group faces a challenging goal, such as finding a way to become profitable.
4. *Empowerment.* Transformational leaders do not attempt to make all the big decisions themselves. They share power and information with the staff and encourage independent work.

5. *Innovative thinking.* Transformational leaders think of unconventional strategies to achieve their goals. Similarly, they encourage their staffs to search for many alternatives to problems (the essence of creativity).
6. *Lead by example.* Transformational leaders show a consistency between the views they express and their behavior. As such they are good role models.
7. *Charisma.* Above all, transformational leaders are charismatic, which helps them inspire their constituents to high levels of motivation and performance.

The description just given represents the ideal transformational leader. Even the best-known transformational leaders, such as Steven Jobs of Apple Computer Corporation and Pixar, are not equally strong on all seven qualities. For example, Jobs can be quite rude toward people he dislikes or does not agree with.

How Transformations Take Place. The characteristics and behaviors described above facilitate bringing about the transformations. In addition, to accomplish the lofty purpose of making substantial improvements the transformational leader attempts to *overhaul the organizational culture.* The leader also *raises people's level of consciousness about the importance and value of designated rewards and ways to achieve them.* The transformational leader also gets people to *transcend their self-interests for the sake of the work group and the firm.* For example, a support worker might be inspired to work all day Saturday without extra pay so the company can meet a deadline.

The transformational leader helps workers *adopt a long-range, broad perspective and focus less on day-to-day concerns.* It is also essential to help people *understand the need for change both emotionally and intellectually.* A transformational leader recognizes this emotional component to resisting change and deals with it openly. Finally, the transformational leader *commits to greatness.* Greatness encompasses striving for business effectiveness, such as profits and high stock value, as well as impeccable ethics.[28]

The Downside of Charismatic and Transformational Leadership

Charismatic and transformational business leaders are seen as corporate heroes because of their great deeds. Among these contributions are turning around failing businesses, launching new enterprises, revitalizing organizations, and inspiring employees toward peak performance. Nevertheless, there is also a dark side. Some charismatic leaders are unethical and lead their organizations toward illegal and immoral ends. People are willing to follow the charismatic leader down a quasi-legal path because of his or her personal power. For example, several financial deal makers who were found guilty of illegal financial transactions inspired hundreds of people.

An in-depth study of 25 charismatic business leaders concluded that the constructive and destructive leaders among them can be differentiated in terms of their ethics. For example, an ethical charismatic leader uses power to serve others, whereas an unethical one will use power mostly for personal gain or impact. Also, an ethical charismatic leader coaches, develops, and supports group mem-

SKILL-BUILDING EXERCISE 14–3

Formulating a Vision

Along with your teammates, assume the role of the top-level management group of an organization or organizational unit in need of revitalization (or reenergizing). Your revitalization method is to create a vision for the organization. Express the vision in about 25 words. Come to agreement quickly on the organization, or large organizational unit, that needs a vision. An alternative is to choose one of the following:

- The Jeep Division of DaimlerChrysler Corporation
- A sausage manufacturer
- An industrial janitorial service
- The pet food division of a large food company
- A chain of budget motels

After you have prepared your vision statement, the team leader might present it to the rest of the class.

bers and shares recognition. The unethical counterpart is insensitive to the needs of group members and hogs the glory.[29] Given that developing a vision is important for charismatic and transformational leadership, and for other types of effective leaders, do Skill-Building Exercise 14–3.

SERVANT LEADERSHIP

An approach to leadership receiving recent attention is an emphasis on serving the needs of the group. A **servant leader** believes that his or her primary mission is to serve the needs of constituents. Instead of seeking individual recognition, servant leaders see themselves as working for group members. The servant leader uses his or her talents to help group members. For example, if the leader happens to be a good planner, he or she engages in planning because it will help the group achieve its goals.

The idea behind servant leadership, as formulated by Robert K. Greenleaf, is that leadership stems naturally from a commitment to service. Serving others, including employees, customer, and community, is the primary motivation for the servant leader. A servant leader is therefore a moral leader. Servant leadership is accomplished when group members become wiser, healthier, and more autonomous.[30]

A key attitude of the servant leader is to place service before self-interest. A servant leader is more concerned about helping others than acquiring power, prestige, financial reward, and status. The servant leader wants to do what is morally right, even if it is not financially rewarding. For example, a pharmaceutical firm might concentrate on marketing a drug that was less profitable than a comparable drug because the first drug had a higher cure rate. Another key behavior of the servant leader is to inspire trust by being trustworthy. Being trustworthy is a foundation behavior of the servant leader, so he or she is scrupulously honest with others. He or she gives up control, and focuses on the well-being of others.

Servant leadership will show itself in small everyday actions, such as lending a hand to staff members. A servant leader might help an employee jump-start her car in the parking lot or donate money to her charity walkathon.[31]

THE 360-DEGREE FEEDBACK SYSTEM FOR IMPROVING LEADERSHIP EFFECTIVENESS

In many organizations leaders receive feedback that gives them insight into the effectiveness of their characteristics, attitudes, and behaviors. The feedback is systematically derived from a full sampling of parties who interact with the leader. The **360-degree feedback system** is a formal evaluation of superiors by people who work for and with them, sometimes including customers and suppliers. Often, 360-degree feedback includes an optional self-evaluation. When self-evaluation is used, the individual completes the same structured evaluations that all others use to evaluate his or her performance. The feedback is communicated to the leader (as well as to others being evaluated by the same technique) with assistance from a company human resources professional or an outside psychologist. The feedback is supposed to help the leader overcome problem areas.

One frequently used approach to 360-degree feedback is for the leader and a good sample of work associates to rate the leader on a list of specific behaviors. Table 14–1 is a representative example of the behaviors evaluated. Self-ratings are then compared with ratings by others. Assume that a manager rates himself a 10 on "considerate of people." If others rate him a 1 on this behavior, the manager might be counseled on how to be more considerate of others. This example hints at the importance of involving professionally trained counselors in 360-degree feedback. Some people feel emotionally crushed when they find a wide discrepancy between their self-rating on an interpersonal skill dimension and the ratings by others. Upon receiving the feedback just cited, the manager went into a rage (proving the feedback true!), followed by despondency. Professional counseling can sometimes help a person benefit from critical feedback and place it in perspective.

For best results, it is extremely important that 360-degree feedback surveys reflect those behaviors and attitudes that the organization values most highly.

TABLE 14–1
A 360-Degree Feedback Chart

	Manager Evaluated: Bob Germane		
Behavior or Attitude (10 is highest)	***Self-Rating***	***Average Group Rating***	***Gap***
1. Gives right amount of structure	9	7.5	− 1.5
2. Is considerate of people	10	6.2	− 3.8
3. Sets a direction	9	3.9	− 5.1
4. Sets high standards	7	9.0	+ 2.0
5. Gives frequent feedback	10	6.3	− 3.7
6. Gets people pulling together	9	5.1	− 3.9
7. Inspires people	10	2.8	− 7.2
8. Gives emotional support	8	3.7	− 4.3
9. Is a helpful coach	10	4.5	− 5.5
10. Encourages people to be self-reliant	6	9.4	+ 3.4

Note: A negative gap means you rate yourself higher on the behavior or attitude than does your group. A positive gap means the group rates you higher than you rate yourself.

Care should also be taken that the dimensions measured reflect important aspects of leadership functioning.[32]

SUMMARY OF KEY POINTS

- Leadership is the process of influencing others to achieve certain objectives. Management includes leadership, but leadership is regarded as a force that inspires and energizes people and brings about change.
- Leaders influence people through the use of power. The three subtypes of position power are legitimate power (formal authority), reward power (the ability to control rewards), and coercive power (the ability to control punishments). The two types of personal power are expert power and referent power (loyalty stemming from an identification with the leader).
- Influence tactics of leaders include leading by example, assertiveness, ingratiation, rationality, exchange, upward appeal, consultation with group members, and joking and kidding.
- Certain traits, motives, and personal characteristics contribute to leadership effectiveness in a wide variety of situations. Among them are the power motive, passion and enthusiasm, cognitive ability, self-confidence, courage, and a sense of humor. The behaviors and skills of effective leaders include direction setting, being trustworthy, asking tough questions, maintaining high standards, stability under pressure, accessibility to group members, a positive attitude including supportiveness, and a willingness to accept blame.
- A leadership style is a leader's characteristic way of behaving in most situations. The participative leadership style enables the leader to share decision making with the group, and capitalize on the talents of the group. Participative leaders are divided into three types: consultative, consensus-style, and democratic. The participative style works best with people who are competent and well motivated. In contrast to the participative leader, the autocratic leader makes decisions more independently of the group.
- Gender differences in leadership style have been observed. Women tend toward a cooperative, empowering style that includes nurturing team members. It is argued that men lean toward a command-and-control autocratic style. Some evidence is reviewed in this chapter that women outperform men as leaders, and other evidence is presented that many women bosses are ineffective.
- Key characteristics of charismatic leaders include their vision, masterful communication style, ability to inspire trust, helping group members to succeed, and an energy and action orientation. Charismatic leaders also promote themselves and manage their impressions. Some aspects of charisma can be developed, as outlined in Skill-Building Exercise 14–2.
- Transformational leaders bring about major changes, in contrast with transactional leaders, who emphasize routine transactions with group members. Seven key characteristics and behaviors of transformational leaders are vision, staff development, supportive leadership, empowerment, innovative thinking, leading by example, and charisma. Transformations take place by such means as the leader overhauling the organizational culture, and getting people to transcend their self-interests for the sake of the work group and the firm. Transformational leaders bring about transformations in seven ways, among them getting

people to transcend their self-interest, helping people understand the need for change, and committing to greatness.

- The downside of charismatic and transformational leadership is that charisma is sometimes used for unethical purposes. For example, an unethical charismatic leader might use power mostly for personal gain or impact.
- Servant leaders see themselves as working for group members instead of seeking individual recognition. Servant leadership stems naturally from a commitment to service. Such leadership is accomplished when group members become wiser, healthier, and more autonomous.
- Many leaders receive input about the effectiveness of their characteristics, attitudes, and behaviors through 360-degree feedback. Counseling based on the feedback is supposed to help the leader make necessary improvements. A specialist in human behavior should provide the feedback. It is important for 360-degree feedback surveys to reflect behaviors and attitudes that the organization values most highly.

DISCUSSION QUESTIONS AND ACTIVITIES

1. What might go wrong in an organization that had a great leader who was a poor manager?
2. What might go wrong in an organization that had a competent manager who was a poor leader?
3. What steps might you take to increase your personal power?
4. Make up a "tough question" for the executives at McDonald's.
5. Are leaders who hug group members more likely to be perceived as charismatic? Explain your reasoning.
6. How can becoming more charismatic help a person other than being an effective leader?
7. Why is it that most leadership positions in organizations do not really call for a transformational leader?

GUIDELINES FOR PERSONAL EFFECTIVENESS

1. Many of the traits, motives, characteristics, and behaviors associated with effective leadership can be improved with education, training, or experience. Thus, you do not have to be a "born leader" to improve your leadership potential or skill. For example, if your self-confidence is moderate, you might be able to increase it by following the suggestions in Chapter 4.
2. In the present leadership environment, expert power is more important at every level of responsibility. In addition to having good managerial and leadership skills, you also should possess a thorough knowledge of the business, or technical competence.
3. Almost all leadership experience is helpful in developing your long-range leadership potential. A difficult leadership assignment can prove to be valuable experience because it requires more leadership skill to lead poorly motivated, rather than highly motivated, people.

8. How well suited is a highly charismatic person for being a servant leader?

9. How might a person apply the 360-degree feedback technique to become a more effective family member or friend?

10. Use your favorite search engine or engines on the Internet to identify two current methods companies are using to develop leaders.

REFERENCES

1. John P. Kotter, *A Force for Change: How Leadership Differs from Management* (New York: The Free Press, 1990).
2. John R. P. French, Jr., and Bertram Raven, "The Bases of Social Power," in Dorwin Cartwright and Alvin Zander (eds.), *Group Dynamics: Research and Theory* (New York: Harper & Row, 1960), pp. 607–623; Timothy R. Hinkin and Chester A. Schriescheim, "Power and Influence: The Vision from Below," *Personnel,* May 1988, pp. 47–50.
3. The suggestions for using each of the five types of power are based on Gary Yukl and Tom Taber, "The Effective Use of Managerial Power," *Personnel,* March–April 1983, pp. 37–44; Yukl, *Leadership in Organizations,* 3rd ed. (Upper Saddle River, NJ: Prentice Hall, 1994), pp. 197–207; Yukl, *Leadership in Organizations,* 4th ed., p. 149.
4. Jeffrey D. Kudisch, Mark L. Poteet, Gregory H. Dobbins, Michael C. Rush, and Joyce E. A. Russell, "Expert Power, Referent Power, and Charisma: Toward the Resolution of a Theoretical Debate," *Journal of Business and Psychology,* Winter 1995, p. 189.
5. David Kipnis, Stuart M. Schmidt, and Ian Wilkinson, "Intraorganizational Influence Tactics: Exploration in Getting One's Way," *Journal of Applied Psychology,* August 1980, pp. 440–452; Chester A. Schriesheim and Timothy R. Hinkin, "Influence Tactics Used by Subordinates: A Theoretical and Empirical Analysis and Refinement of the Kipnis, Schmidt, and Wilkinson Subscales," *Journal of Applied Psychology,* June 1990, pp. 246–257; Andrew J. DuBrin, "Sex and Gender Differences in Tactics of Influence," *Psychological Reports,* 1991, 68, pp. 635–646.
6. R. Bruce McAfee and Betty J. Ricks, "Leadership by Example: Do as I Do!" *Management Solutions,* August 1986, p. 10.
7. Paul Gallagher, "Be Red-y for Anything," *Success,* April 2001, p. 35.
8. "You Scratch My Back . . . Tips on Winning Your Colleague's Cooperation," *WorkingSMART,* October 1999, p. 1.
9. David C. McClelland and Richard Boyatzis, "Leadership Motive Pattern and Long-term Success in Management," *Journal of Applied Psychology,* December 1982, p. 737.
10. Harvey A. Hornstein, "Managerial Courage: Individual Initiative and Organizational Innovation," *Personnel,* July 1986, p. 16.
11. Karl Albrecht, *The Northbound Train: Finding the Purpose, Setting the Direction, Shaping the Destiny of Your Organization* (New York: AMACOM, 1994), p. 20.
12. James M. Kouzes and Barry Z. Posner, "The Credibility Factor: What Followers Expect from Their Leaders," *Management Review,* January 1990, p. 30. See also Julie Cohen Mason, "Leading the Way Into the 21st Century," *Management Review,* October 1998, p. 19.
13. Ronald A. Heifetz and Donald L. Laurie, "The Work of Leaders," *Harvard Business Review,* January–February 1997, pp. 124–134.
14. Robert A. Eckert, "Where Leadership Starts," *Harvard Business Review,* November 2001, pp. 53–61.

A BUSINESS PSYCHOLOGY CASE PROBLEM

Big Changes at State Bank of India, California

State Bank of India (SBI) is the oldest and largest bank in India and also has offices throughout the world. Brejein Kumar, a manager who had been with the bank for 31 years, had developed a reputation as a troubleshooter who could turn around problem situations. In 1992, he was sent on a four-year assignment as manager of SBI Washington. Two years later, however, he was appointed as the president and CEO of SBI California, located in Los Angeles. The change in assignment came about because the California division was experiencing numerous problems.

SBI California is composed of the downtown Los Angeles branch, the Los Angeles agency, and the Artesia branch. When Kumar arrived in Los Angeles, he was shocked to discover the poor visibility and reputation of SBI California. The bank was virtually unknown to the large Indian community in California. Many new customers closed their accounts shortly because of what they perceived to be poor service and lack of caring for customer welfare. Regulatory agencies had given the bank a poor rating because of its sloppy policies and procedures.

Kumar said, "SBI California was the greatest challenge of my life. I needed to change the bank by improving its performance, and building good relations with customers and regulators. It was also necessary to make the Indian community aware of the bank."

Kumar focused first on improving relations with the regulators, with the hope of improving SBI California's ratings. He dug into paperwork, reviewing as many details as possible of the previous years to understand why the bank was not performing well. After three weeks of analysis, Kumar devised a strategy for improving the bank's performance. He personally interviewed 25 employees to obtain their suggestions for improving the bank's reputation and performance. He added policies and procedures, all of which complied with government regulations. As a result, SBI California received an above-average rating by the regulators.

Next, Kumar focused on strengthening customer relations. He arranged for customer-contact workers to take training courses in management and customer relations. Employees deficient in computer skills were given appropriate training. Soon the entire work environment was computerized, allowing for faster customer service. Unlike previous bank management, Kumar met personally with customers. He organized several meetings to which he invited prominent Indian businesspeople to see the improved SBI California.

Another Kumar initiative was to sponsor programs such as Youth Awards, events for India's Independence and Republic Days, and Indian classical music concerts. He redesigned many of SBI's brochures and promoted the bank through advertisements telecast on the International Channel during Indian programming. Another change Kumar implemented was to assemble an impressive panel of the board of directors comprised of corporate executives and industrialists, as well as the former ambassador to India.

SBI made front-page news in the Indian newspapers distributed in California. New business started pouring into the bank, and profits increased substantially. In the summer of 1996, SBI's chairman came from India to visit the California operation and was greatly impressed by the bank's outstanding performance. The regulators, along with the board of directors, persuaded the chairman to extend Kumar's stay in California one more year.

Company officers requested that Kumar open a branch in San José based on both the booming Silicon Valley and the substantial Indian population in the area. Kumar played a major role in all aspects of launching the San José branch, choosing the site, overseeing the setup, hiring employees, and developing an information technology environment. He also developed a branch slogan that caught on quickly: "An American Bank with an Indian Heritage." The branch became an immediate success.

Kumar's U.S. assignment ended in September 1997. He received several awards for his enormous efforts and for his contribution to the Indian community as a whole. Upon his departure, several bank employees said there would never be another leader as dynamic as Brejein Kumar.

Questions

1. How would you characterize Kumar's leadership style?
2. What suggestions do you have for improving Kumar's approach to leadership and management?
3. To what extent does Kumar qualify as a transformational leader?

Source: Case researched by Kamini Kumar, Rochester Institute of Technology, 1998.

AN APPLIED PSYCHOLOGY CASE PROBLEM

Charismatically Challenged Colleen

Twenty-seven-year-old Colleen McFerguson worked as a merchandising specialist for ValuMart, one of the largest international retail chains. Based in the United States, ValuMart also has a strong presence in Canada, Europe, Japan, and Hong Kong. Colleen began her employment with ValuMart as a cashier, and two years later was invited into the training program for merchandising specialists.

Colleen performed well as a merchandising trainee in the soft-goods line. Her specialty areas included men's, women's, and children's clothing, linens and bedding, men's and women's jewelry, and home decorations. For several years in a row, Colleen received performance evaluation ratings of above average or outstanding. Among the write-in comments made by her supervisors were "diligent worker," "knows the tricks of merchandising," "good flair for buying the right products at the right price," and "fits right into the team."

Despite the positive performance appraisals supported with positive comments, Colleen had a gnawing discontent about her career at ValuMart. Despite five years of good performance, she was still not invited to become a member of the group called "ValuTrackers." The ValuTrackers are a group of merchandising and operations specialists who are regarded as being on the fast track to becoming future ValuMart leaders. The leaders hold high-level positions such as head merchandiser, regional vice president, and store manager.

Several times when Colleen inquired as to why she was not invited to join the ValuTrackers, she was told something to the effect that she was not quite ready to be included in this elite group. She was also told not to be discouraged, because the company still valued her contribution.

One day Colleen thought to herself, "I'm headed toward age 30, and I want a great future in the retail business now." So she convinced her boss, the merchandising supervisor (Evan Tyler), to set up a career conference with three people: Colleen, the boss, and her boss's boss (Heather Bridges), the area merchandising manager. She let Evan know in advance that she wanted to talk about her potential for promotion.

Evan started the meeting by saying, "Colleen, perhaps you can tell Heather and me again why you requested this meeting."

Colleen responded, "Thanks for asking Evan. As I mentioned before, I'm wondering what you think is wrong with me. I receive a lot of positive feedback about my performance, but I'm not a ValuTracker. Also, you seem to change the subject when I talk about wanting to become a merchandising supervisor, and eventually a merchandising executive. What am I doing wrong?"

Heather responded, "Evan and I frequently talk about the performance and potential of all our merchandising specialists. You're a good performer, Colleen, but you lack that little spark that makes a person a leader. You go about your job efficiently and quietly, but that's not enough. We want future leaders of ValuMart to make an impact."

Evan added, "I go along with Heather's comments. Another point, Colleen, is that you rarely take the initiative to suggest ideas. I was a little shocked by your request for a three-way career interview because it's one of the few initiatives you have taken. You're generally pretty laid back."

"Then what do I have to do to convince you both that I should be a ValuTracker?" asked Colleen.

Heather replied, "Start acting more like a leader. Be more charismatic." Evan nodded in agreement.

QUESTIONS

1. What career advice can you offer Colleen McFerguson?
2. What might Colleen do to develop more charisma?
3. What is your opinion of the fairness of the ValuTracker program?

15. Daniel Goleman, Richard Boyatzis, and Annie McKee, "Primal Leadership: The Hidden Driver of Great Performance," *Harvard Business Review,* December 2001, pp. 42–51.

16. Joseph Seltzer and Rita E. Numerof, "Supervisory Leadership and Subordinate Burnout," *Academy of Management Journal,* June 1988, pp. 439–446.

17. Jeffrey Zaslow, "Joe Montana," *USA Weekend,* January 30–February 1, 1998, p. 15.

18. Cited in Bill Breen, "Trickle-Up Leadership," *Fast Company,* November 2001, p. 90.

19. Richard Pascale, "Change How You Define Leadership, and You Change How You Run a Company," *Fast Company,* April–May 1998, pp. 114–120.

20. Research reported in S. Kass, "Employees Perceive Women as Better Managers than Men, Finds Five-Year Study," *APA Monitor,* September 1999, p. 6.

21. Anne Fisher, "Readers Sound Off: Women Bosses Really Can Be a Nightmare," *Fortune,* June 23, 1997, p. 163.

22. Jay A. Conger and Rabindra N. Kanugo, *Charismatic Leadership in Organizations* (Thousand Oaks, CA: Sage, 1998).

23. Nanette Byrnes, "Avon: The New Calling," *Business Week,* September 18, 2000, p. 139.

24. William L. Gardner and Bruce J. Avolio, "The Charismatic Relationship: A Dramaturgical Perspective," *Academy of Management Review,* January 1998, pp. 32–58.

25. Bernard M. Bass, "Does the Transactional–Transformational Leadership Paradigm Transcend Organizational and National Boundaries?" *American Psychologist,* February 1997, p. 130.

26. Sally A. Carless, Alexander J. Wearing, and Leon Mann, "A Short Measure of Transformational Leadership," *Journal of Business and Psychology,* Spring 2000, pp. 389–405.

27. Andrew J. DuBrin, *Personal Magnetism: Discover Your Own Charisma and Learn to Charm, Inspire, and Influence Others* (New York: AMACOM, 1997), pp. 93–111; Roger Dawson, *Secrets of Power Persuasion: Everything You'll Need to Get Anything You'll Ever Want* (Upper Saddle River, NJ: Prentice Hall, 1992), pp. 179–194; "Secrets of Charismatic Leadership," *WorkingSMART,* February 1998, p. 1.

28. John J. Hater and Bernard M. Bass, "Supervisors' Evaluations and Subordinates' Perception of Transformational and Transactional Leadership," *Journal of Applied Psychology,* Spring 1995, pp. 316–318; Bass, "Does the Transactional–Transformational Leadership Paradigm?" pp. 130–139.

29. Jane M. Howell and Bruce Avolio, "The Ethics of Charismatic Leadership: Submission or Liberation," *Academy of Management Executive,* May 1992, p. 45.

30. Robert K. Greenleaf, *The Power of Servant Leadership* (San Francisco: Berrett-Koehler Publishers Inc., 1998).

31. "Blueprint for a Servant Leader," *Executive Strategies,* March 2000, p. 7.

32. David A. Waldman, Leanne E. Atwater, and David Antonioni, "Has 360-Degree Feedback Gone Amok?" *Academy of Management Executive,* May 1998, p. 91.

SUGGESTED READING

Collins, Jim. "Level 5 Leadership: The Triumph of Humility and Fierce Resolve." *Harvard Business Review,* January 2001, pp. 66–76.

Daft, Richard L., and Lengel, Robert H. *Fusion Leadership: Unlocking the Subtle Forces that Change People and Organizations.* San Francisco: Berrett-Koehler, 2000.

Fairholm, Gilbert W. *Mastering Inner Leadership.* Westport, CT: Quorum/Greenwood, 2001.

Goleman, Daniel, Boyatzis, Richard, and McKee, Annie. *Primal Leadership: Realizing the Power of Emotional Intelligence.* Boston: Harvard Business School Publishing, 2002.

Littman, Margaret. "Best Bosses Tell All." *Working Woman,* October 2000, pp. 48–56.

Mans, Charles C., and Sims, Henry P., Jr. *The New SuperLeadership: Leading Others to Lead Themselves.* San Francisco: Berrett-Koehler, 2001.

Teerlink, Rich. "Harley's Leadership U-Turn." *Harvard Business Review,* July–August 2000, pp. 43–48.

Useem, Michael. "The Leadership Lessons of Mount Everest." *Harvard Business Review,* October 2001, pp. 51–58.

Vengel, Alan A. *The Influence Edge: How to Persuade Others to Help You Achieve Your Goals.* San Francisco: Berrett-Koehler, 2000.

WEB CORNER

www.bockinfo.com/docs/5p.htm (The Five Ps of Leadership.)

www.ccl.org (Center for Creative Leadership.)

www.coxegroup.com/articles/leader.html (Journeyman Leadership.)

www.leadershipchallenge.net (Online leadership test.)

proquest.umi.com (Charisma, and How to Grow It.)

CHAPTER 15

ACHIEVING PERSONAL PRODUCTIVITY

Learning Objectives After reading and studying this chapter and doing the exercises, you should be able to

1. Explain why people procrastinate and how the problem can be lessened.
2. Identify attitudes and values that contribute to personal productivity.
3. Identify skills and practices that could improve your personal productivity.
4. Pinpoint common time wasters and how they can be overcome.
5. Explain how individual differences influence the development of good work habits and time management.

Assume that the instructor for this course announced that a term project is due December 31, 2007, at the absolute latest. Close to that date a handful of people would ask for an extension into the year 2008. Among the excuses offered would be: "I just didn't have time to do the paper with all those celebrations going on." "I would have been ready, but my word processor broke down December 30." "Just my luck. My brother-in-law is getting married the same day that the project is due."

One reason for improving your work habits and time management is to avoid the trap faced by people who are always late with projects, even if the lead time is four years! Several other reasons are also important. People who use good work habits and manage time well eliminate a major potential stressor—a feeling of being out of control of one's job. Well-organized people also tend to be more successful in their careers than poorly organized people. Another reason for having good work habits is that it allows you more time to spend on personal life. In addition, personal life is more enjoyable when you are not preoccupied with unfinished job assignments.

Personal productivity refers to your level of efficiency and effectiveness. Efficiency means that you accomplish tasks with a minimum of wasted time, material, and fanfare. If you are a collection agent and it costs you $900 to collect $950 in past due accounts, you are not being very efficient. Effectiveness refers to accomplishing important results while at the same time maintaining high quality. Efficiency and effectiveness are related. Being efficient often clears the way for being effective. If you are on top of your job, it gives you the time to work on important tasks and to strive for quality.

Achieving personal productivity is more in vogue than ever. Companies strive to operate with smaller staffs than in the past by pushing workers to achieve higher productivity. At the same time, there is a movement toward simplifying personal life by reducing clutter and cutting back on tasks that do not add much to the quality of life.

We have organized information about becoming more productive into four categories that show some overlap. One is overcoming procrastination. The second is developing the attitudes and values that foster efficiency and effectiveness. The third category is developing the proper skills and techniques that lead to productivity and quality. The fourth is overcoming time wasters. We also describe individual differences that can influence a person's ability to develop good work habits and time management.

DEALING WITH PROCRASTINATION

Procrastination is delaying action for no good reason. Unproductive people waste considerable time, but even productive people are not immune from procrastination. If these people did not procrastinate, they would be even more productive. Many people regard procrastination as a laughable weakness, particularly because many procrastinators themselves joke about their problem. Yet procrastination has been evaluated as a profound, debilitating problem.[1] The enormity of the problem makes it worthwhile to examine causes of procrastination and how it can be brought under control. Do Self-Assessment Exercise 15–1 to think through your own tendencies toward procrastination—and don't wait until tomorrow.

Why People Procrastinate

People procrastinate for many different reasons. One major reason is fear of failure, including a negative evaluation of one's work. For example, if you delay preparing a report for your boss, he or she cannot criticize its quality. The fear of bad news is another contributor to procrastination. If you think the brake system on your car needs overhauling, delaying a trip to the service station will postpone the diagnosis: "You're right. Your brake system is unsafe. We can fix it for $750." Another major reason for procrastination is to avoid a task that is overwhelming, unpleasant, or both.

Fear of success is another reason for procrastination. People who fear success share the conviction that success will bring with it some unwelcome outcomes, such as isolation or abandonment. Some people procrastinate because they fear independence. These people put things off so long that they bring on a real crisis and hope or arrange for someone to rescue them. Or some may simply prefer to avoid the responsibility that success will bring. And a quick way to avoid success is to procrastinate over something important, such as completing a key assignment.

SELF-ASSESSMENT EXERCISE 15-1

Procrastination Tendencies

Circle yes or no for each item:

1. I usually do my best work under pressure. Yes No
2. Before starting a project I go through such rituals as sharpening every pencil, straightening up my desk more than once, and discarding bent paper clips. Yes No
3. I crave the excitement of the "last minute rush." Yes No
4. I often think that if I delay something, it will go away, or the person who asked for it will forget about it. Yes No
5. I extensively research something before taking action, such as obtaining three different estimates before getting the brakes repaired on my car. Yes No
6. I have a great deal of difficulty getting started on most projects, even those I enjoy. Yes No
7. I keep waiting for the right time to do something, such as getting started on an important project. Yes No
8. I often underestimate the time needed to do a project, and say to myself, "I can do this quickly, so I'll wait until next week." Yes No
9. It is difficult for me to finish most projects or activities. Yes No
10. I have several favorite diversions or distractions that I use to keep me from doing something unpleasant. Yes No

Total yes responses ________

The greater the number of yes responses, the more likely it is that you have a serious procrastination problem. A score of 8, 9, or 10 strongly suggests that your procrastination is lowering your productivity.

A deep-rooted reason for procrastination is **self-defeating behavior,** a conscious or unconscious attempt to bring about personal failure. For example, a person might be recommended for an almost ideal job opportunity. Yet the person delays sending a résumé for so long that the potential employer loses interest. Self-defeating behavior and fear of success are closely related: the person who fears success may often engage in self-defeating behavior.

Procrastination may also stem from a desire to avoid uncomfortable, overwhelming, or tedious tasks. A business owner might delay preparing an employee pension report for the government for all these reasons. Perfectionism can also lead to procrastination. Because the worker does not want to consider a project complete until it is perfect, the project is seriously delayed or is never completed.

People frequently put off tasks that do not appear to offer a meaningful reward. Suppose you decided that your computer files, including inactive files, need a thorough updating. You also have a huge accumulation of temporary Internet files. Even if you know it should be done, the accomplishment of updating active files and purging temporary files might not be a particularly meaningful reward.

A curious reason for procrastination is to achieve the stimulation and excitement that stems from rushing to meet a deadline.[2] Some people, for example, enjoy fighting their way through traffic or running through an airline terminal so they can make an appointment or airplane flight barely on time. They appear to enjoy the rush of adrenaline, endorphins, and other hormones associated with hurrying.

Finally, people procrastinate as a way of rebelling at being controlled. Procrastination, used this way, is a means of defying unwanted authority. Rather than submit to authority and control, the person may say silently, "Nobody is going to tell me when I should get a report done. I'll do it when I'm ready."

Ways of Reducing Procrastination

A general method of coping with procrastination is to raise your level of awareness about the problem. When you are not accomplishing enough to meet your schoolwork, job, or personal goals, ask yourself if the problem could be procrastination. Then, through self-discipline, try to overcome that incident of inaction. You might also consider trying one or more of the seven techniques described next.

1. *Calculate the cost of procrastination.* You can reduce procrastination by calculating its cost. One example is that you might lose out on obtaining a high-paying job you really want by not having your résumé and cover letter ready on time. Your cost of procrastination would include the difference in salary between the job you do find and the one you really wanted. Another cost would be the loss of potential job satisfaction.
2. *Create some momentum to get you moving.* One way to get momentum going on an unpleasant or overwhelming task is to set aside a specific time to work on it. Another way to create some momentum is to find a leading task to perform. A **leading task** is an easy warm-up activity. If you were procrastinating about concluding an audit, you might begin by starting a file for the project. Sometimes just allocating five minutes for working on an uncomfortable task is enough to get you started.
3. *Apply behavior modification to yourself.* Give yourself a pleasant reward soon after accomplishing an unpleasant task, rather than having procrastinated. The second part of the tactic is to punish yourself with something you despise immediately after you procrastinate.
4. *Make a commitment to other people.* Try to make it imperative that you get something done on time by making it a commitment to one or more other people. You might announce to coworkers that you are going to get something accomplished by a certain date. If you fail to meet this date, you are likely to feel embarrassed.
5. *Break the task into manageable chunks.* To reduce procrastination, cut down a project that seems overwhelming into smaller projects that seem less formidable. If your job calls for inspecting 20 locations within 30 days, begin by making dates to inspect the two closest to home. Planning the job before executing it also helps ease the pain. In this situation, you would plan an itinerary before starting the inspection. The planning would probably be less painful than actually getting started at making all the arrangements.
6. *Follow the WIFO principle.* Personal effectiveness coach Shale Paul recommends the technique of *worst in, first out* for dealing with unpleasant tasks you would prefer to avoid. Paul says, "Chances are, you'll find that you

spent nearly as much time worrying and rescheduling it as you did actually doing it. If the task fits high enough on your priorities, simply get it done and out of the way."[3] A related motivational principle is that after completing the unpleasant task, moving on to a more pleasant (or less unpleasant) task functions as a reward.

7. *Satisfy your stimulation quota in constructive ways.* If you procrastinate because you enjoy the rush of scrambling to make deadlines, find a more constructive way of using busyness to keep you humming. If you need a high level of stimulation, enrich your life with extra projects and learning new skills. The fullness of your schedule will provide you the stimulation you had been receiving from squeezing yourself to make deadlines and reach appointments on time.[4]

DEVELOPING THE PROPER ATTITUDES AND VALUES

Developing good work habits and time-management practices is often a matter of developing the right attitudes toward your work and toward time. If, for example, you think that your schoolwork or job is important and that time is a precious resource, you will be on your way toward developing good work habits. In this section we describe a group of attitudes, values, and beliefs that can help a person become more productive through better use of time and improved work habits.

Develop a Mission, Goals, and a Strong Work Ethic. A mission, or general purpose, in life propels you toward being productive. Assume that a person says, "My mission is to be an outstanding professional in my career and a loving, constructive parent." The mission serves as a compass to direct your activities, such as being well organized, in order to attain a good performance appraisal. Goals are more specific than mission statements; they support the mission statement, but the effect is the same. Being committed to a goal also propels you toward good use of time. Imagine how efficient most employees would be if they were told, "Here is five days of work facing you. If you get it finished in less than five days without sacrificing quality, you can have all that saved time to yourself." If the saved time fit your mission, such as having more quality time with family members, the impact would be even stronger.

Closely related to establishing goals is developing a strong **work ethic**—a firm belief in the dignity and value of work. Developing a strong work ethic may lead to even higher productivity than goal setting alone. For example, one might set the goal of earning a high income. It would lead to some good work habits, but not necessarily a high commitment to quality. A person with a strong work ethic believes in quality, is highly motivated, and minimizes time-wasting activities.

Play the Inner Game of Work. Psychologist and tennis coach Timothy Gallwey, developed the *inner game of tennis* to help tennis players focus better on their game. Over time the inner game spread to skiing, other sports, life in general, and work. The key concept is that by removing inner obstacles such as self-criticism, you can dramatically improve your ability to focus, learn, and perform. According to Gallwey, two selves exist inside each person. Self 1 is the critical, fearful, self-doubting voice that sends out messages like, "You have almost solved this tough problem for the customer. Don't blow it now." Intimidating comments like these hinder Self 2 from getting the job done. Self 2 encompasses all the inner resources—both actual and potential—of the individual.

Self 1 must be suppressed so Self 2 can accomplish its task and learn effectively without being lectured. The process required to move Self 1 aside is to focus your attention on a critical variable related to performance rather than on the performance you are attempting to achieve. An example would be for a customer service representative to focus on the amount of tension in a caller's voice.[5] Or, you might focus on the facial expressions of your manager as you attempt to sell him or her on an idea for improving productivity.

WORK SMARTER, NOT HARDER. People caught up in trying to accomplish a job often wind up working hard, but not in an imaginative way that leads to good results. Much time and energy are therefore wasted. An example of working smarter, not harder, is to invest a few minutes of critical thinking before launching an Internet search. Think through carefully what might be the key words that will lead you to the information you need. In this way you will minimize conducting your search with words and phrases that will lead to irrelevant information. For example, suppose you want to conduct research on backstabbing as negative office politics. If you simply use the term "back stabbing," the search engine will direct you to such topics as street crime and medical treatment for wounds. Working smarter is to try "backstabbing in the office."

VALUE YOUR TIME. People who place a high value on their time are propelled into making good use of time. If a person believes that his or her time is valuable, it will be difficult to engage that person in idle conversation during working hours. Valuing your time can also apply to personal life. The yield from clipping grocery coupons is an average of $9 per hour. Would a busy professional person therefore be better off clipping coupons or engaging in self-development for the same amount of time? Being committed to a goal, as described previously, is an automatic way of making good use of time.

AVOID ATTEMPTING TOO MUCH. Many workers become disorganized and fall behind schedule because they assume more responsibility than they can handle. Especially significant is when the stressed-out person has voluntarily attempted too much. A worker already overloaded with responsibility, for example, might accept an invitation to join yet another community activity. His or her work schedule becomes all the more cramped, and the list of unfinished tasks mounts.

To avoid attempting too much, you must learn to say no to additional demands on your time. You cannot take care of your own priorities unless you learn to tactfully decline requests from other people that interfere with your work. If your manager interrupts you with an added assignment, point out how the new tasks will conflict with higher-priority ones and suggest alternatives. However, do not turn down your manager too frequently. Much discretion and tact are needed to use this approach to increasing personal productivity. Knowing when to say no is also important.

APPRECIATE THE IMPORTANCE OF REST AND RELAXATION AND AVOID WORKAHOLISM. A productive attitude to maintain is that overwork can lead to negative stress and burnout. Proper physical rest and relaxation contribute to mental alertness and improved ability to cope with frustration. Neglecting the normal need for rest and relaxation can lead to **workaholism,** a dependence on work in which not working is an uncomfortable experience. Some types of workaholics are perfectionists who are never satisfied with their work and therefore find it difficult to leave work behind. In addition, the perfectionistic workaholic may become heavily focused on control, leading to rigid behavior. However, some people who work long and hard are classified as achievement-oriented workaholics who thrive on hard work and are usually highly productive.[6]

To help achieve rest and relaxation, some businesspeople take naps, as described in Chapter 8. You can train yourself to take these 15-minute naps to give you short bursts of energy and stretch your stamina over a long day. A few minutes' nap in the late afternoon can keep you going for an overtime assignment.

Value Cleanliness and Orderliness. An orderly desk, work area, briefcase, or hard drive does not inevitably indicate an orderly mind. Yet it does help most people become more productive because they can better focus their mind. Also, less time is wasted and less energy is expended if you do not have to hunt for information that you thought you had on hand. Many people label computer files with such general terms that they cannot readily identify the specific file they need. Knowing where information is and what information you have available is a way of being in control of your job. When your job gets out of control, you are probably working at less than peak efficiency. Valuing cleanliness helps in two other ways. According to the Japanese system, cleanliness is the bedrock of quality. Also, after you have thoroughly cleaned your work area, you will usually attain a fresh outlook.

The core attitude here is to perceive clutter negatively. One reason that clutter is counterproductive is that managers spend an estimated five weeks each year hunting for things they have lost. Other workers spend about 10 weeks per year hunting down information and things. Having less clutter reduces the time spent searching for misplaced items.[7]

Reducing clutter is also part of simplifying your life and controlling stress. Andrew Weill, the natural health guru, recommends that you downsize your life. He believes that significant stress stems from the complexity of our lives, a major contributor being our material possessions. Many people have too many physical objects that require attention and maintenance. Weill recommends that you get rid of what you can spare.[8] You will gain greater control of your life situation by having less clutter. At the same time you will be able to concentrate better on your work. A note of caution is that an oversimplified life can also be an impoverished life, creating stress of its own.

Value Good Attendance and Punctuality. Good attendance and punctuality are expected of both experienced and inexperienced employees. You cannot be productive if you are not physically present in your work area. The same principle applies whether you work on company premises or at home. One exception is that some people can work through solutions to job problems while engaged in recreation. Keep in mind, too, that being late for or absent from meetings sends out the silent message that you do not regard the meeting as important.

The relationship of lateness to absenteeism and work performance has been researched. Based on 30 studies and over 9,000 workers it was found that employees who were late also tended to have high absenteeism records. In addition, employees who were late tended to have poorer work performance than workers who were more prompt, but the relationship was not strong.[9] Despite this weak association, being late must still be regarded as a productivity drain.

DEVELOPING PROPER TIME-MANAGEMENT SKILLS AND TECHNIQUES

So far we have discussed two important strategies for improving productivity and quality. One is to minimize procrastination, while the other is to develop the appropriate values and beliefs. You also need the right time-management skills and techniques to become productive and achieve high quality. Later we devote separate attention to a subset of skills and techniques—minimizing time wasting. Next we summarize well-known skills and techniques of good time management, along with a few new ones.

Make Good Use of Office Technology. Only in recent years have companies begun to derive productivity increases from office automation. One reason that office automation was not as successful as hoped is that many office workers did not make productive use of the technology available. Used properly, most high-tech devices in the office can improve productivity and quality. Among the most productivity-enhancing devices are word processors, spreadsheets, computer graphics, the Internet including e-mail and instant messaging, fax machines, and voice mail. How you use these devices is the key to increased productivity.

A major consideration is that the time saved using office technology must be invested in productive activity to attain a true productivity advantage. Assume that you save two hours by ordering office equipment over the Internet. If you invest those two hours in activity such as finding ways to save the company money, you are more productive. Also, if extensive use of office technology translates into fewer workers necessary for the company, the equipment results in a true productivity gain.

Clarify Your Own Objectives. A basic starting point in improving work habits and time management is to define what it is you are supposed to accomplish. A careful review of your job description and objectives with your boss is fundamental. Some people are accused of being ineffective simply because they do not know what is really expected of them. Unsure of what to do, they waste time on projects of limited value to the organization. Your mission statement will clarify what you want to accomplish on a grander scale, such as building a successful career.

Prepare a To-Do List and Set Priorities. At the heart of every time-management system is list making. Almost every successful person in any field composes a list of important and less important tasks that need to be done. Before you can compose a useful list, you need to set aside a few minutes of quiet time every day to sort out the tasks at hand. This is the most basic aspect of planning. Many people find it helpful to set up to-do lists for both work and personal life.

Where Do You Put Your Lists? A to-do list will enhance productivity only if referred to regularly, so the list must be visible and consulted frequently. Some people dislike having small to-do lists stuck in different places. One reason is that these lists are readily lost among other papers. Instead you use a notebook, either loose-leaf or spiral bound, that is small enough to carry around with you. The notebook becomes your master list to keep track of errands, things to do or buy, and general notes to yourself about anything requiring action. A desk calendar or planner can serve the same purpose, as shown in

Figure 15–1. Palm-held computers are also worthy of consideration as a place to record lists. Keeping your to-do list on your office computer is productive primarily for people who do not leave their work area frequently.

Setting Priorities. Not everything on a person's to-do list is of equal importance; therefore, priorities should be attached to each item on the list. A typical system is to use A to signify critical or essential items, B to signify important items, and C for the least-important ones. Although an item might be regarded as a C (for example, refilling the cellophane-tape dispenser), it still has a contribution to make to your management of time and sense of well-being. Many people report that they obtain a sense of satisfaction from crossing off an item on their list, however trivial. Second, if you are at all conscientious, small undone items will come back to interfere with your concentration.

Carefully Schedule Activities. The use of a to-do list and a desk planner enables a person to schedule activities in a productive manner. Five other important scheduling suggestions are described next:

Allow Time for Emergencies. Because many managerial and professional jobs require handling emergencies, enough slack has to be built into the schedule for handling unpredictable problems. In essence, the careful scheduler creates room for unscheduled events. Similarly, a household budget must allow enough room for the inevitable "miscellaneous" category.

Minimize Unscheduled Interruptions. Although legitimate emergencies must be handled quickly, most other types of unscheduled interruptions should be minimized in order to maintain productivity. With brain-powered work, a major challenge is getting into the appropriate flow of thought. When interrupted, we lose momentum and have to launch ourselves all over again.[10] One solution to the problem of interruptions is for you to schedule a period of time during the day in which you have uninterrupted work time. You give coworkers a definite time during which you want to be disturbed with emergencies only. It is also helpful to inform coworkers of the nature of the important work you ordinarily conduct during your quiet period. You might say, for example, "I have to tally the sales figures every Friday afternoon."

Schedule Your Most Demanding Tasks for When Your Energy Is Highest. Tasks that require the most energy, such as creative decision making and confrontations with difficult people, are best performed during energy peaks. Most people have their highest energy at the start of their workday, but others gain energy as the day progresses. The most routine items should be handled during energy lows.

Cluster Similar Tasks. An efficient method of accomplishing small tasks is to cluster (group them together) and perform them in one block of time. To illustrate, you might make most of your telephone calls in relation to your job from 11:00 to 11:30 A.M. each workday morning. Or you might reserve the last hour of every workday for e-mail and other correspondence. By using this method you develop the necessary pace and mental set to knock off chores in short order. In contrast, when you flit from one type of task to another, your efficiency may suffer.

Schedule Yourself by Computer. Software is available that can turn your personal computer into an electronic calendar to help you keep track of appointments

17 WEDNESDAY
NOVEMBER, 1999

44 Days Left

OCTOBER 1999

S	M	T	W	T	F	S
					1	2
3	4	5	6	7	8	9
10	11	12	13	14	15	16
17	18	19	20	21	22	23
24/31	25	26	27	28	29	30

NOVEMBER 1999

S	M	T	W	T	F	S
	1	2	3	4	5	6
7	8	9	10	11	12	13
14	15	16	17	18	19	20
21	22	23	24	25	26	27
28	29	30				

DECEMBER 1999

S	M	T	W	T	F	S
			1	2	3	4
5	6	7	8	9	10	11
12	13	14	15	16	17	18
19	20	21	22	23	24	25
26	27	28	29	30	31	

TO BE DONE TODAY (ACTION LIST)

APPOINTMENTS & SCHEDULED EVENTS

HOURS	NAME • PLACE • SUBJECT
7 0700	
8 0800	
9 0900	
10 1000	
11 1100	
12 1200	
1 1300	
2 1400	
3 1500	
4 1600	
5 1700	
6 1800	
7 1900	
8 2000	
9 2100	
10 2200	

PHONE CALLS

EXPENSE & REIMBURSEMENT RECORD

FIGURE 15–1 A Combined Activity Calendar and "TO DO" List

Source: Reprinted by permission of DAY-TIMERS, INC.

and lists of chores. The first step, of course, would be to enter into your computer your appointments, tasks, and errands. For instance, a person might enter the following:

3/1 Meet with Sherri Godwin to discuss term project.

3/6 Get inventory audit started.

3/7 Lunch with Liz to discuss St. Patrick's Day party.

3/10 Start shopping for gift for parents' Silver Anniversary.

From this point forward, the computer's information-processing capabilities could be tapped. Suppose you couldn't remember the date of your upcoming luncheon with Liz. You would command the computer to "Find lunch date with Liz." Or, if you were an extremely busy person, you might have reason to ask the computer to tell you when you had the next opening for lunch. Another use of this type of software is to command the computer to flag key appointments and chores.

Finally, schedule the next day's activities at the finish of your workday. In this way, you start tomorrow with a plan in mind and a fresh perspective.

Concentrate on One Key Task at a Time. Effective executives have a well-developed capacity to concentrate on the problem or person facing them, no matter how surrounded they are with other obligations. The best results from concentration are achieved when you are so absorbed in your work that you achieve the flow experience (see Chapter 5). Intense concentration leads to crisper judgment and analysis and also minimizes major errors. Another useful by-product of concentration is that it helps reduce absentmindedness. If you really concentrate on what you are doing, the chances diminish that you will forget what you intended to do.

Although attention should be directed to one key task at a time, an effective time-management technique is to perform two or more routine tasks simultaneously, referred to as *multitasking*. While exercising on a stationary bike, you might read work-related information; while commuting, listen to the radio for information of potential relevance to your job. While reading e-mail you might clean the outside of your computer; while waiting for a file to download, you might arrange your work area or read a brief report.

Despite searching for productivity gains through multitasking, it is important to avoid rude and/or dangerous acts. It would be rude to do paperwork or read e-mail while on the telephone. It would be dangerous to engage in intense conversation over the cellular telephone while driving, and checking out e-mail on a laptop or onboard computer would be even more dangerous because you are forced to lose full eye contact with the road.

Streamline Your Work and Emphasize Important Tasks. As companies continue to operate with fewer workers than in the past even during good economic times, more unproductive work must be eliminated. Getting rid of unproductive work is part of *reengineering*, in which work processes are radically redesigned and simplified. Every employee is expected to get rid of work that does not contribute to productivity or help customers. Another intent of work streamlining is to eliminate work that does not add value for customers. Here are some examples of work that typically does not add value:

- Sending e-mail or paper messages that almost nobody reads.
- Sending receipts and acknowledgments to people who do not need them.
- Writing and mailing reports that nobody reads or needs.
- Scheduling meetings that do not accomplish work, exchange important information, or improve team spirit.
- Frequently checking up on the work of competent people.

In general, to streamline or reengineer your work look for duplication of effort and waste. An example of duplication of effort would be to routinely send people e-mail and fax messages covering the same topic. An example of waste would be to call a meeting for disseminating information that could easily be communicated by e-mail.

In following the A-B-C system, you should devote ample time to the essential tasks. You should not pay more attention than absolutely necessary to the C (least important) items. However, if you find that working on C items is tension reducing, then do so, but recognize that you must return to A items as soon as you feel relaxed. When the suggestion of working on high-output items is offered, many people respond, "I don't think concentrating on important tasks applies to me. My job is so filled with routine I have no chance to work on breakthrough ideas." True, most jobs are filled with routine requirements. What a person can do is spend some time, perhaps just one hour per week, concentrating on tasks that may prove to have high output.

In sorting out important tasks, keep in mind the difference between an urgent task and an important one. Some tasks are urgent, but not important, such as resetting a clock for daylight savings time. Other tasks are important, but not urgent, such as developing team goals for the next year. As Steven Covey says in his seminar, "at the very core of *First Things First* is dealing with what's really important rather than responding to what's merely urgent."[11]

WORK AT A STEADY PACE. In most jobs and programs of study, working at a steady pace pays dividends in efficiency. The spurt worker creates many problems for management, while the spurt student is in turmoil at exam time or when papers are due. Some employees take pride in working rapidly, even when the result is a high error rate. An important advantage of the steady-pace approach is that you accomplish much more than someone who puts out extra effort just once in a while.

The completely steady worker would accomplish just as much the day before a holiday as on a given Monday. That extra hour or so of productivity adds up substantially by the end of the year. Despite the advantages of maintaining a steady pace, some peaks and valleys in your work may be inevitable. The seasonal demands placed on public accountants and related workers are a prime example.

STAY IN CONTROL OF PAPERWORK AND ELECTRONIC WORK. Although it is fashionable to complain about paperwork, the effective career person does not neglect paperwork. (Paperwork includes electronic work such as electronic mail and voice mail.) Paperwork involves taking care of administrative details such as correspondence, human resource reports, and inventory forms. Unless paperwork and electronic work are attended to, a person's job may get out of control. An out-of-control job leads to lowered productivity and employee stress. A small amount of time should be invested in paperwork every day. Nonprime time (when you are at less than your peak of efficiency, but not overfatigued) is the best time to take care of paperwork.

A simple system for categorizing the inflow of papers follows this format:

- Action (A): for immediate follow-up.
- File (F): required for doing business.
- Information (I): useful, worth reading or scanning.
- Discard (D): obviously dispensable.

OVERCOMING TIME WASTERS

Another basic thrust to improved personal productivity is to minimize wasting time. Many of the techniques already described in this chapter help to save time. The tactics and strategies described next, however, are directly aimed at overcoming the problem of wasted time.

Make Use of Peripheral Time. **Peripheral time** refers to the scattered minutes people normally waste while waiting for a meeting to start, being stuck in traffic, or waiting on the phone to speak to a customer service representative.[12] These bits of time can add up to a substantial amount at the end of a month. A truly productive person makes use of miscellaneous bits of time both on and off the job. While waiting in line at the post office, you might be able to update your to-do list; while waiting for an elevator, you might be able to read a brief report; and if you have finished your day's work 10 minutes before quitting time, you can use that time to clear out a file.

If you are in the process of learning a foreign language, make comments about what is happening around you to yourself in your target language. Also, always carry something written in that language. You can thereby practice your foreign language every day in time that would otherwise be lost.

Minimize Daydreaming. "Taking a field trip" while on the job is a major productivity drain. Daydreaming is triggered when the individual perceives the task at hand to be boring, such as reviewing another person's work for errors. Brain research suggests that younger people are more predisposed to daydreaming than older people. Apparently, older people use neurons better to focus on tasks. In one study, people aged 24 to 71 were asked questions about their tendency to daydream when working at some task. The researchers asked the same people the same questions six to eight years later. According to the self-reports of the subjects, mind wandering decreased. The conclusion reached was that minds wander less as people get older.[13]

Unresolved personal problems are an important source of daydreaming, thus blocking your productivity. This is especially true because effective time utilization requires good concentration. When you are preoccupied with a personal or business problem, it is difficult to give your full efforts to the task at hand. The solution is to do something constructive about whatever problem is sapping your ability to concentrate (as discussed in Chapter 7 under the section on managing stress). Sometimes a relatively minor problem, such as driving with an expired operator's license, can impair your work concentration. At other times, a major problem, such as how to best take care of a parent who has suffered a stroke, interferes with work. In either situation, your concentration will suffer until you take appropriate action.

Another approach to preventing personal problems from interfering with productivity is to set aside a few minutes a day to worry about a problem you are facing. List your anxieties, numbering them in order of importance. The listing exercise will help you clear your mind, and perhaps prioritize what actions you have to take. When your worry time is completed, you will often be able to concentrate more carefully.[14]

Taking care of personal problems to improve productivity illustrates that becoming more productive involves emotions and feelings as well as mechanical procedures. Psychological factors are important for becoming productive.

Bounce Quickly from Task to Task. Much time is lost when a person takes a break between tasks. After one task is completed, you might pause for 10 minutes to clear your work area and adjust your to-do list. After the brief pause, dive into your next important task. A compliance (with government regulations) officer at a mutual fund says that he turns over an hourglass when he needs to decompress after handling an urgent situation. When the sand runs out, he moves to the next priority.[15]

Avoid Being a Computer "Goof-Off." A major time waster in the workplace is using the computer for unproductive purposes such as surfing the Internet out of curiosity—assuming that poking around for work ideas is not your intent. Surfing the Internet for recreation beyond what is needed for a "stress break" is also unproductive. Online addictions, as described in Chapter 1, represent time wasting to the point of a mental health problem. Other approaches to being a computer goof-off include preparing exquisite graphics far beyond what is needed for a report, downloading software from the Internet you have no intention of using, and playing computer games. Responding to e-mail messages that require no response, passing along jokes, and sending personal messages are other leading productivity drains.

E-mail creates many temptations for wasting time. If your job requires constant attention to e-mail, such as responding to customer inquiries or requests for assistance from other employees, all time invested in processing e-mail is productive. The problem arises when an individual decides to respond to and create e-mail messages rather than move forward with key job responsibilities. Taking care of e-mail often requires less mental energy than performing the more analytical part of your job.

Keep Track of Important Names, Places, and Things. How much time have you wasted lately searching for such items as a telephone number you jotted down somewhere, your keys, or an appointment book? A manager suddenly realized he had forgotten to show up for a luncheon appointment. He wanted to call and apologize but was unable to locate the person's name and phone number! Standard solutions to overcoming these problems are to keep a wheel file (such as a Rolodex) of people's names and companies. It is difficult to misplace such a file. Many other managers and professionals store such information in a database or even in a word processing file. Such files are more difficult to misplace than a pocket directory.

Two steps are recommended for remembering where you put things. First, have a parking place for everything. This would include putting your keys and appointment book back in the same place after each use. Second, make visual associations. In order to have something register in your mind at the moment you are doing it, make up a visual association about that act. Thus you might say, "Here I am putting my résumé in the back section of my laptop computer case."

Set a Time Limit for Certain Tasks. Spending too much time on a task or project wastes time. As a person becomes experienced with certain projects, he or she is able to make accurate estimates of how long a project will take to complete. A paralegal might say, for example, "Getting this will drawn up for the lawyer's approval should take two hours." A good work habit to develop is to estimate how long a job should take and then proceed with a strong determination to get that job completed within the estimated period of time.

A productive variation of this technique is to decide that some low- and medium-priority items are worth only so much of your time. Invest that much time in the project, but no more. Preparing a file on advertisements that cross your desk is one example.

Be Decisive and Finish Things. An often overlooked way of improving your personal productivity is to be decisive. Move quickly, but not impulsively, through the problem-solving and decision-making steps outlined in Chapter 5 when you are faced with a nonroutine decision. Once you have evaluated the alternatives to the problem, choose and implement one of them. By acting quickly, you save time.

Superintelligent and highly educated people are sometimes poor decision makers because they keep on collecting facts. The result is that they procrastinate instead of acting. Some people of more modest intelligence waste time when faced with a decision, not because they want more facts, but because they are fearful of committing themselves. In short, if you agonize too long over too many decisions, your personal productivity will suffer.

A specific productivity drain stemming from not finishing things is the **Ziegarnik effect**—the phenomenon of uncompleted tasks creating a disturbing level of tension. Not finishing a task can thus be a distraction that interferes with productivity on future tasks.

For the teleworker, all the temptations to waste time are a particular challenge. Working without face-to-face supervision, or even being watched by coworkers, lends itself to wasting time. Other aspects of personal productivity are also important for the teleworker, because working alone requires high self-discipline. In recognition of this fact, the financial giant Merrill Lynch trains employees in work habits and time management before granting the opportunity to work at home.

INDIVIDUAL DIFFERENCES RELATED TO WORK HABITS AND TIME MANAGEMENT

Individual differences influence a person's ability to make use of the suggestions for personal productivity improvement described in this chapter. Of particular significance are diagnostic skill, motivation, other personal characteristics, and personal style.

Diagnostic Skill. Many people are unable to identify the reasons behind their poor work habits, including the cause of their procrastination. Often it is necessary to identify the true problem before much progress can be made. For example, some people want to remain disorganized because they are self-defeating. Yet they deny having self-defeating tendencies.

Motivation. As you would suspect, people who are motivated to improve their productivity are more likely to benefit from suggestions for enhancing work habits and time management than those who are not. This painful truth was documented in a study with 102 car salespeople at 60 dealerships across Canada. The general managers of the dealerships were asked to identify their top salesperson and one average salesperson, making sure that each had at least one year of car sales experience. Achievement striving (motivation) and work habits were measured by questionnaire. A major result of the study was that short-range planning combined with high achievement striving to predict good sales performance. In other words, having good time-management practices in the form of short-range planning is likely to lead to high sales performance if the person is well motivated.[16]

Other Personal Characteristics. In addition to motivation, a person needs the right talents and personality characteristics to make the best use of methods for improving personal productivity. A key talent is planning ability. At the top of the list of personality traits is **compulsivity,** a tendency to pay careful attention to detail and to be meticulous. An individual with a compulsive personality takes naturally to being well organized and neat. If you are less concerned about detail and meticulousness by nature, it will be more difficult for you to develop exceptional work habits. Compulsivity is closely tied in with perfectionism, which can lead a person to delay finishing tasks because the task is never done well enough—in his or her opinion.

People who are highly spontaneous and emotional also tend to be naturally inclined toward casual work habits. However, being overly compulsive can also be a detriment to personal productivity. The compulsive person may have a difficult time concentrating on important tasks. He or she may tend to get hung up on details and become the unproductive type of workaholic. The truly productive person finds an optimum balance between concern for detail and time, on the one hand, and being able to look at the "big picture" on the other.

Personal Style. People vary somewhat in which set of time-management principles and work habits are best suited to their personal style. Some people work best when their activities are preplanned and tightly scheduled. They would benefit from a rigid adherence to lists and calendars. In contrast, John Kotter has observed that the best executives do not necessarily map out their daily schedules in advance. Instead, they respond to important situations as they crop up.[17] In essence, these successful executives allow considerable slack time in their schedule within the framework of pursuing a major goal.

Differences in personal style with regard to organizing work are partially traced to brain dominance. Left-brain-dominant people (preference for logical and analytical thinking) take readily to to-do lists and scheduling by a daily planner. Right-brain-dominant workers (preference for creative and intuitive thinking) manage their time best by paying little attention to the clock, schedules, and constraints. What works best for right-brain-dominant workers is knowing how to spend their time most productively.[18] For example, right-brain-dominant workers might develop imaginative solutions to a work problem while stalled in traffic. Or they might choose to jog around the office building instead of taking a coffee break.

SUMMARY OF KEY POINTS

- By improving your work habits and time management, you can improve your job productivity and quality and enhance your personal life. Personal productivity refers to your level of efficiency and effectiveness and thus includes performing high-quality work.
- Procrastination is the major time waster for most employees and students. People procrastinate for many reasons, including their perception that the task is either unpleasant or overwhelming and a fear of the consequences of their actions. The feared consequences can be positive or negative. Awareness of procrastination may lead to its control. Seven other techniques recommended for reducing procrastination are: (1) calculate the cost of procrastination, (2) create some momentum to get you going, (3) apply behavior modification to yourself, (4) make a commitment to other people, (5) break the task down into manageable chunks, (6) follow the WIFO principle, and (7) satisfy your stimulation quota in constructive ways.
- Developing good work habits and time-management practices is often a matter of developing the right attitudes toward your work and toward time. Eight such values, attitudes, and beliefs are as follows:
  1. Develop a mission, goals, and a strong work ethic.
  2. Work smarter, not harder.
  3. Play the inner game of work.
  4. Value your time.
  5. Avoid attempting too much.
  6. Appreciate the importance of rest and relaxation and avoid workaholism.
  7. Value cleanliness and orderliness.
  8. Value good attendance and punctuality.
- Eight skills and techniques to help you become more productive including producing high-quality work are as follows:
  1. Make good use of office technology.
  2. Clarify your own objectives.
  3. Prepare a to-do list and set priorities.
  4. Carefully schedule activities. (This includes allowing time for emergencies, minimizing unscheduled interruptions, making best use of energy peaks, clustering similar tasks, and computerized scheduling.)
  5. Concentrate on one key task at a time.
  6. Streamline your work and emphasize important tasks.
  7. Work at a steady pace.
  8. Stay in control of paperwork and electronic work.
- Another way of achieving high productivity is to minimize time wasting. Seven such techniques are as follows:
  1. Make use of peripheral (bits of) time.
  2. Minimize daydreaming.
  3. Bounce quickly from task to task

GUIDELINES FOR PERSONAL EFFECTIVENESS

Reading about these methods of improving your work habits alone will not lead to permanent changes in behavior. You must select one or two areas in which you are particularly weak and then begin to implement a remedial plan of action. Suppose that you recognize that your day is filled with time leaks because you rarely accomplish what you set out to. Try these steps:

1. Identify the two most obvious time leaks. Perhaps (a) time wasted in gathering your friends for lunch and (b) stopping work 15 minutes before quitting time.
2. For the next five workdays force yourself to plug these time leaks. You might have to say to your friends, "I'm only taking 30 minutes for lunch today. I want to avoid bringing work home tonight. So I'll meet you in the cafeteria at 11:45 sharp."
3. If this approach works, move on to subtle and difficult leaks, such as a tendency to daydream when work pressures lessen.
4. Now try another time-management method of improving your work habits that you think applies to one of your areas for needed improvement.

4. Avoid being a computer "goof-off."
5. Keep track of important names, places, and things.
6. Set a time limit for certain tasks.
7. Be decisive and finish things.

- Individual differences influence a person's ability to use the suggestions for improving personal productivity described in this chapter. Of particular significance are skill in diagnosing the reasons for poor productivity, motivation, other personal characteristics such as compulsiveness, and personal style such as a preference for reacting immediately to demands.

DISCUSSION QUESTIONS AND ACTIVITIES

1. Procrastination is thought to be the leading cause of self-defeating behavior on the job. Why might this be true?
2. If it is true that procrastination is really a psychological disorder, do you think people who procrastinate should be given more time to complete projects in school, similar to people with learning disabilities?
3. How true is it that people get a rush from finishing projects at the last moment? Or from fighting their way through traffic to make it just in time for an event like a sports match or concert?
4. When you meet a stranger, how can you tell if he or she is well organized?
5. How can preparing a personal mission statement help a person become better organized?
6. If you wanted to streamline your work as a student, what low-value activities could you eliminate?
7. Identify two high-output tasks for an office manager.
8. Identify two ways in which using the Internet might improve the productivity of a small-business owner.

9. Identify two ways in which using a computer has increased your personal productivity.

10. Ask an experienced high-level worker for his or her most effective method of time management. Be prepared to report your findings to the class.

REFERENCES

1. Robert Boice, *Procrastination and Blocking: A Novel, Practical Approach* (Westport, CT: Greenwood Publishing Group, 1996).
2. "When to Procrastinate and When to Get Going," *Working Smart,* March 1992, pp. 1–2.
3. Cited and quoted in "Get With It: Nip Your Procrastination Right in the Bud," *Entrepreneur,* September 1998, p. 94.
4. Dru Scott, *How to Put More Time in Your Life* (New York: New American Library, 1980), p. 113.
5. Mark Hendricks, "The Voices in Your Head," *Entrepreneur,* July 2000, pp. 105–107.
6. Mildred L. Culp, "Working Productively with Workaholics while Minimizing Legal Risks," syndicated column, Passage Media, 1997.
7. Culp, "Looking for Harmony? Swat the Clutter Bug for Greater Efficiency," syndicated column, Passage Media, 1998.
8. Andrew Weill, "Beating Stress," *USA Weekend,* December 26–28, 1997, p. 4.
9. Meni Koslowsky and Abraham Sagie, "Correlates of Employee Lateness: Some Theoretical Considerations," *Journal of Applied Psychology,* February 1997, pp. 79–88.
10. Robert E. Kelley, *How to Be a Star at Work: Nine Breakthrough Strategies You Need to Succeed* (New York: Times Business, 2000).
11. *First Things First*™, SkillPath® Seminars, 1995.
12. Joseph T. Straub, "Your Time: Manage It to the Max," *Getting Results,* July 1996, p. 7.
13. Paul Chance, "The Wondering Mind of Youth," *Psychology Today,* December 1988, p. 22.
14. "Produce to the Max: Replace Time-Wasting Talk with Orchestrated Action," *WorkingSMART,* September 1999, p. 7.
15. "Beating the Clock: Time Management When You Are Under the Gun," *WorkingSMART,* March 1999, p. 1.
16. Julian Barling, E. Kevin Kelloway, and Dominic Cheung, "Time Management and Achievement Striving Interact to Predict Car Sales Performance," *Journal of Applied Psychology,* December 1996, pp. 821–826.
17. Cited in "Time Management Techniques—A Rundown," *Personal Report for the Executive,* August 1, 1987, p. 4.
18. "From the Right," *Executive Strategies,* November 1991, p. 10.

SUGGESTED READING

Burke, Michelle. *The Valuable Office Professional.* New York: AMACOM, 1997.

Fletcher, Jerry L. *Patterns of High Performance: Discovering the Ways People Work Best.* San Francisco: Berrett-Koehler Publishers, 1995.

Hemphill, Barbara. *Taming the Office Tiger: The Complete Guide to Getting Organized at Work.* Washington, DC: The Kiplinger Washington Editors, Inc., 1996.

Kanar, Lisa. *Everything's Organized.* Hawthorne, NJ: Career Press, 1997.

AN APPLIED PSYCHOLOGY CASE PROBLEM

The Meridian Workers Go Surfing

Charlie Yang is the director of logistics at Richardson Furnishings, a furniture manufacturer based in Durham, North Carolina. Logistics plays a major role in company operations because virtually all the furniture Richardson manufactures is packed and shipped to customers. Late deliveries are a chronic problem in the furniture industry, so Richardson management attempts to gain a competitive edge by making shipments as promised. At times the logistics group has to make particularly rapid deliveries to compensate for manufacturing delays.

All employees in the logistics division work at computers for such varied tasks as keeping track of deliveries and the location of trucks, e-mail, word processing, and budget preparation. In addition, logistics workers search the Internet for information such as road conditions, shipping rates for truckers and the railroad, and changes in government regulations about shipping.

In recent months, Yang has become concerned that many logistics workers at Richardson are slipping into a pattern of sometimes using the Internet for recreational purposes. For example, while walking around the office, Yang has seen several instances of travel agency and sports Web sites on computer monitors. Richardson has a written policy that is explicit about Internet use. Web access and e-mail are company resources that are to be used for business purposes only. The policy also stipulates that violators could be subject to disciplinary action. The Internet policy, however, has almost never been discussed after it was originally established.

Before bringing the potential problem of Internet misuse to the attention of employees, Yang decided to obtain more information. To help determine the extent of the problem, he hired a consultant who specializes in monitoring employee use of the Internet. The consultant, Carolyn Stein, studies server logs. The logs record all the Internet activity on a network, indicating who visited what Web site, how long they stayed, what they looked at, what they searched for, and which Web site they visited next. Stein also helps the company retrieve old e-mail messages so they can be audited.

Stein dug into the server logs and also sampled e-mail messages. Her findings indicated some Internet and e-mail misuse, but not an alarming pattern of substantial neglect of work. One of the activities revealed by the report was that on average, employees were spending about 30 minutes per day surfing the Web for purposes not directly related to Richardson business. The diversionary visits to Web sites included reading the news, making travel arrangements, visiting job search sites, company recruitment ads, playing video games, and the occasional visit to pornographic sites. About 10 percent of e-mail messages were nonwork related, including sending messages to friends, and forwarding jokes to other Richardson employees.

Although not stunned by the evidence, Yang decided to confront employees about the problem. First, he held a meeting with his four supervisors to review the consultant's findings. Stein attended the meeting to present the findings in detail and answer questions. The supervisors had varied reactions to the findings. One supervisor thought the company should begin to impose strong sanctions on any employee violating the Internet policy. Another thought the recreational use of the Internet was not substantial enough to bother bringing to the attention of employees. A third supervisor thought that the company should monitor Web use regularly, and punish only the severe violators. The fourth supervisor suggested that the company should hold an information-gathering session with employees to go beyond the statistical report.

Yang was impressed with the idea of an information-gathering session, so he scheduled a town hall meeting with all interested employees for 4 P.M. the following Friday. Every eligible employee attended the meeting, and most contributed input to the situation of nonwork-related use of the Internet. Several employees explained why the recreational use of Web sites probably *helps* the company.

A logistics technician said, "I spend much less time on my surfing breaks than the time the smokers eat up on their smoking breaks outside the building. Since I'm not a caffeine addict either, I don't take breaks to feed my habit. Besides that,

continued on next page

AN APPLIED PSYCHOLOGY CASE PROBLEM (cont'd)

the few moments I spend surfing the net or reading an e-mail joke give me the energy I need to dig back into work."

An office assistant contributed this input: "With all due respect to company policy, the so-called nonwork use of the Web and e-mail is a low-cost stress reducer. When I'm having a stressful day, I browse one of my favorite online stores. Five minutes of walking down the virtual isles of Abercrombie and Fitch lowers my stress level like magic. In some of those high-tech companies, you get a back rub at your desk with a real massage therapist if you're stressed out. That would cost Richardson a lot more, and take much more time than a few minutes of surfing the Web. (Laughter.)

The most senior supervisor said, "Employees always find a way to spend a few minutes not working. It could be a trip to the water cooler, a chat at the copy machine, or watching birds outside the window. So now it's surfing. Except for a few workaholics nobody puts in 100 percent effort on the job. Even top execs have been known to take an afternoon off for golf." (More laughter.)

Yang ended the meeting with these words: "Thank you so much for your candor and your useful input. We're going to study our Internet policy a little further and then get back to you." As he left the meeting Yang pondered whether some of his employees were making excuses for surfing, or actually using the Internet to enhance productivity.

Questions

1. What is your opinion of the effectiveness of using Web surfing to enhance productivity?
2. What is your opinion of the effectiveness of using Web surfing to relieve stress?
3. What policy recommendations can you make to the logistics division of Meridian about the nonwork use of Web surfing and e-mail?

Source: Several of the facts in this case are from Alan Cohen, "No Web for You," *Fortune Small Biz,* October 2000, pp. 44–56.

Kanigel, Robert. *The One Best Way: Frederick Winslow Taylor and the Enigma of Efficiency.* New York: Viking, 1997.

Katzenbach, Jon R. *Peak Performance: Aligning the Hearts and Minds of Your Employees.* Boston, MA: Harvard Business School Publishing, 2000.

Oncken, William Jr., and Wass, Donald L. "Management Time: Who's Got the Monkey? with Commentary by Stephen R. Covey." *Harvard Business Review Classic,* reprinted, November–December 1999, pp. 178–186.

Wild, Russell. "Think Fast." *Working Woman,* September 2000, pp. 89–90.

WEB CORNER

www.theinnergame.com (The inner game of work, sports, and team building.)

www.kasper.com (Streamlining your schedule.)

www.napo.net (National Association of Professional Organizers)

AN APPLIED PSYCHOLOGY CASE PROBLEM

The Busy Office Manager

Mike Powers looked at the kitchen clock and said to Ruth, his wife: "Oh no, it's 7:25. It's my turn to drop off Jason and Gloria at the child-care center. Jason hasn't finished breakfast and Gloria is still in her pajamas. Can you get Gloria dressed for me?"

Ruth responded, "OK, I'll help Gloria. But today is your turn to take care of the children. And I have a client presentation at 8:30 this morning. I need to prepare for a few more minutes."

"Forget I asked," said Mike. "I'll take care of it. Once again I'll start my day in a frenzy, late for child care, and just barely making it to work on time."

"Why didn't you get up when the alarm rang the first time?" asked Ruth.

"Don't you remember, we talked until one this morning? It seems like we never get to talk to each other until midnight."

After getting Jason and Gloria settled at the child-care center, Mike dashed off to the public accounting firm where he worked as the office manager. After greeting several staff members, Mike turned on his computer to check his e-mail. Ann Gabrielli, one of the partners in the law firm, left the following message: "See you today at 11:30 for the review of overhead expenses. Two other partners will be attending."

Mike quickly looked at his desk calendar. According to his calendar, the meeting was one week from today. Mike called Gabrielli immediately and said, "Ann, my apologies. My schedule says that the meeting is one week from today at 11:30, not today. I'm just not ready with the figures for today's meeting."

"My calendar says the meeting is today," said Gabrielli harshly. "I'm ready for the meeting, and so are Craig and Gunther (the other partners). This isn't the first time you've gotten your weeks mixed up. The meeting will go on, however poorly you have to perform."

"I'll be there," said Mike. "It's just a question of reviewing some figures that I've already collected."

After putting down the phone, Mike calculated that he had about 2 hours and 40 minutes in which to prepare a preliminary report on reducing overhead. He then glanced at his desk calendar to see what else he had scheduled this morning. The time looked clear except for one entry: "PA/LC."

"What is 'PA/LC'?" thought Mike. "I can't imagine what these initials stand for. Wait a minute, now I know. The initials stand for performance appraisal with Lucy Cruthers, our head bookkeeper. I'm not ready for that session. And I can't do it this morning. Mike then sent Cruthers an e-mail message suggesting that they meet the following week at the same time.

Cruthers answered back immediately. She wrote that she would not be able to meet the following week because that was the first day of her vacation. Mike sent her another note: "I'll get back to you later with another date. I don't have time now to make plans." Next, Mike informed the department assistant, Lois Wang, that he had to hurriedly prepare for the 11:30 meeting. Mike asked for her cooperation in keeping visitors away the rest of the morning.

He then retrieved his computer directory to look for the file on overhead expenses he began last week. As he scanned the directory, he found only three files that might be related to the topic: COST, EXPENSES, and TRIM. Mike reasoned that the file must be one of these three.

Mike retrieved the file COST. It proved to be a summary of furniture expenses for the firm. Upon bringing EXPENSES up on the screen, Mike found that it was his expense account report for a business trip he took seven months ago. TRIM was found to be a list of cost estimates for lawn care services.

Agitated and beginning to sweat profusely, Mike asked Lois Wang to help him. "I'm stuck," he pleaded. "I need to find my file for the overhead expense analysis I was doing for the partners. Do you recall what I named the file? Did I give it to you on disk?"

"Let me see if I can help," said Wang. "We'll search your directory together." Wang scanned about 100 files. "What a clutter," she sighed. "You ought to clean out your files sometime soon. Here's a possibility, PTR."

"I doubt it," said Mike. "'PTR' stands for partner. I'm looking for a file about overhead expenses."

"But you are preparing the file for the partners, aren't you?"

continued on next page

A BUSINESS PSYCHOLOGY CASE PROBLEM (cont'd)

Lois proved to be right. The PTR file contained the information Mike sought. Within 30 minutes he completed the spreadsheet analysis he needed. He then prepared a brief memo on the word processor, explaining his findings. With 20 minutes left before the presentation, Mike asked Lucy if she could run off three copies in a hurry. Lucy explained that the department's photocopying machine was not operating. She said she would ask to use the photocopier in another department.

"Bring them into my meeting with the partners as soon as you can," said Mike. "I've run out of time."

On the way to the meeting, Mike exhaled a few times and consciously relaxed his muscles to overcome the tension accumulated from preparing the report under so much pressure. Mike performed reasonably well during the meeting. The partners accepted his analysis of overhead expenses and said they would study his findings further. As the meeting broke up at 12:30, the senior partner commented to Mike, "If you had gotten your weeks straight, I think you would have presented your analysis in more depth. Your report was useful, but I know you are capable of doing a more sophisticated analysis."

After returning from lunch, Mike revised his daily planner again. He noticed a Post-it note attached to the light on his desk. The entry on the slip of paper said, "Racquetball, Monday night with Ziggy."

"Not again," Mike said to himself in a groan of agony. "Tonight I've got to get Jason and Gloria to bed. Ruth has a makeup class scheduled for her course in Japanese. I'll have to call Ziggy now. I hope he's in his office."

Mike left an URGENT message on Ziggy's e-mail, offering his apologies. He thought to himself, "I hope Ziggy won't be too annoyed. This is the second time this year I've had to reschedule a match at the last moment."

Mike returned from lunch at 2:00 P.M. He decided to finish the report on overhead he had prepared for the partners. By 4:00 P.M. Mike was ready to begin the tasks outlined on his daily planner. At that point Lois Wang walked into Mike's office and announced: "There's a representative here from Account Temps. She said she was in the building so she decided to drop in and talk about their temporary employment services."

"Might as well let her in," said Mike. "We will be hiring some temporary bookkeepers soon. Account Temps has a good reputation. It's getting too late to do much today anyway."

Mike made it to the child-care center by 5:45 and packed Jason and Gloria into the family minivan. Gloria, the eldest child, asked if the family could eat at a fast-food restaurant this evening. Mike said, "OK, but I'll have to stop at an ATM first. I don't have enough cash on hand to eat out. We'll stop at the ATM, then stop by the house and see if Mom wants to eat out tonight before class."

Mike and the children arrived home at 6:15 and asked Ruth if she would like to eat out this evening.

"I have about one hour to spare before class," said Ruth. "Why not? By the way, how was your day?"

"My day?" asked Mike with a sigh. "I just fell one day further behind schedule. I'll have to do some paperwork after the children are asleep. Maybe we can watch the late news together this evening. We should both be free by then."

Questions

1. What time-management mistakes does Mike appear to be making?
2. What does Mike appear to be doing right from the standpoint of managing time?
3. What suggestions can you offer Mike to help him get his schedule more under control?

SKILL-BUILDING EXERCISE 15–1

Helping a Busy Office Manager

The preceding case presents background information for this role-play. One person plays the role of Mike Powers, who has decided to meet with a time-management counselor to discuss his problems. Mike believes that if he doesn't get help soon, he will be doing serious damage to his career and perhaps his marriage.

Another person plays the role of a time-management counselor who will listen to Mike and attempt to understand the root of his problem. The counselor will then make some recommendations. This particular counselor has a reputation for being a good listener, yet is known to give dogmatic recommendations.

AN APPLIED PSYCHOLOGY EXERCISE

Improving Your Personal Productivity

Studying this chapter alone will rarely lead to improvements in productivity. You need to back up these ideas with a specific plan of action for improvement as described in "Guidelines for Personal Effectiveness." A useful mechanical aid toward achieving this end is to study the checklist presented next, which covers the techniques mentioned in this chapter. Pick out the five or six items on the checklist in which you need the most help. For each item you select, write a one- or two-sentence action plan. Suppose you checked the item "Be Decisive and Finish Things." Your action plan might take this form:

- Next time I'm faced with an important decision, I'll make up my mind within two days instead of the usual entire week.
- I'll make note of the date on which the problem occurred, and the date on which I finally made up my mind.

The Personal Productivity Checklist

PROCRASTINATION

1. Calculate the cost of procrastination.
2. Create some momentum to get you going.
3. Apply behavior modification to yourself.
4. Make a commitment to other people.
5. Break the task down into manageable chunks.
6. Follow the WIFO principle.
7. Satisfy your stimulation quota in constructive ways.

ATTITUDE, VALUE, OR BELIEF

1. Develop a mission, goals, and a strong work ethic.
2. Play the inner game of work.
3. Work smarter, not harder.
4. Value your time.
5. Avoid attempting too much.
6. Appreciate the importance of rest and relaxation and avoid workaholism.
7. Value cleanliness and orderliness.
8. Value good attendance and punctuality.

TIME-MANAGEMENT SKILLS AND TECHNIQUES

1. Make good use of office technology.
2. Clarify your own objectives.
3. Prepare a to-do list and set priorities.
4. Carefully schedule activities.
   a. Allow time for emergencies.
   b. Minimize unscheduled interruptions.
   c. Make best use of energy peaks.
   d. Cluster similar tasks.
   e. Schedule yourself by computer.

continued on next page

AN APPLIED PSYCHOLOGY EXERCISE (cont'd)

5. Concentrate on one key task at a time.
6. Streamline your work and emphasize important tasks.
7. Work at a steady pace.
8. Stay in control of paperwork and electronic work.

Time Wasting

1. Make use of peripheral (bits of) time.
2. Minimize daydreaming.
3. Avoid being a computer "goof-off."
4. Bounce quickly from task to task.
5. Keep track of important names, places, and things.
6. Set a time limit for certain tasks.
7. Be decisive and finish things.

CHAPTER 16

ACHIEVING A REWARDING AND SATISFYING CAREER

Learning Objectives

After reading and studying this chapter and doing the exercises, you should be able to

1. Understand the meaning of career success.
2. Describe how people choose a career and the difference between a vertical and a horizontal career path.
3. Give a thorough rundown on how to conduct a job campaign, including the use of the Internet.
4. Describe at least 10 career-advancement strategies and tactics.
5. Explain the essential points of developing a portfolio career and career switching.

Although many companies have career-development programs, you must still assume major responsibility for managing your career. One reason is that employers freely continue to adjust the number of employees necessary to maintain high profits. Even during periods of high prosperity and low unemployment, layoffs and early retirements are standard business practice. When one company merges with another, for example, a large number of layoffs are almost inevitable to reduce job duplication. Many baby boomers are still in the workforce competing for high-level positions. Even when there is a shortage of workers to fill entry-level positions, promotions are still scarce because there are fewer managerial positions available. Quite often teams assume many managerial responsibilities. In short, managing your career is important for moving beyond entry-level positions.

The major purpose of this chapter is to present information that will help you manage, or develop, your own career. A **career** is a lifelong series of experiences that form some kind of coherent pattern. We ordinarily think of a career as involving progressive achievement over most of its course. A useful perspective is that you are a career capitalist because you invest time, energy, and money into your career.[1] You expect to receive a healthy return on your investments in terms of such outcomes as income, status, and personal satisfaction. With these goals in mind, you do your best to manage your career effectively.

The information in this chapter is organized according to the logical flow of events a person faces in building a career: arriving at a personal definition of career success → finding a field → finding a job → selecting relevant career-advancement strategies and tactics → diversifying your approach to earning a living or switching careers.

THE MEANING OF CAREER SUCCESS

A major part of achieving a rewarding and satisfying career is achieving career success. The traditional approach to defining career success emphasizes vertical mobility (promotions) and high earnings. Many people still measure success by rank and income. Another approach to measuring career success is to emphasize psychological factors. Douglas T. Hall contends that the ultimate goal of a career is **psychological success.** Success of this type is the feeling of pride and personal accomplishment that comes from achieving your most important goals in life, whether they are work achievement, family happiness, or something else.[2] To achieve psychological success, you would have to specify your most important goals in life and work toward achieving them both on and off the job.

Psychological success does not exclude traditional success. Your important goals in life might include attaining a high-level position and earning a high income. To be inclusive, **career success** means attaining the twin goals of organizational rewards and personal satisfaction. (As described above, you want a good return on your investment.) Organizational rewards include such experiences as a high-ranking position, more money, challenging assignments, and the opportunity for new learning. Personal satisfaction refers to enjoying what you are doing. If your employer highly values your contribution and your job satisfaction is high, you are experiencing career success. Achieving a successful career is an important contributor to self-realization or self-fulfillment.

FINDING A FIELD AND AN OCCUPATION

A starting point in establishing a rewarding and satisfying—and therefore successful—career is to find a field compatible with one's interests. Many readers of this book may have already identified a field they wish to enter or are already working in that field. But many other readers are probably still in the process of identifying a field of work and an occupation within that field to their liking. And even if you have identified an occupation or a profession, you still need to refine your choices. For example, an accountant might work for a CPA firm, a private company, the government, or an educational institution. Here we identify eight of the most likely ways of identifying a field and occupation to pursue.

1. *Influence of parent, relative, or friend.* "My uncle owned a supermarket, so I became interested in retailing at an early age."
2. *Reading and study.* "While in high school I read about investments, so I decided I wanted to work somewhere in the securities business."

3. *Natural opportunity.* "I was born into the business. Who would give up a chance to be a vice president by the time I was 25? Our family has always been in the retail business."
4. *Forced opportunity.* "I had never heard about electronics until I joined the army. They told me I had aptitude for the field. I enjoyed working as an electronics technician. After the army I applied for a job with IBM as a field service engineer. It has worked out well."
5. *Discovery through counseling and/or testing.* "I took an interest test in high school. My guidance counselor told me that I had interests similar to those of a social worker. Not knowing what else to do, I decided to become a social worker."
6. *Matching yourself with a role model.* An indirect way of finding a field and occupation within that field is first to locate a person with whom you have similar interests. You then choose that person's field of work for yourself, using this reasoning, "I seem to like what that person likes in most things. All things being equal, I would probably like the kind of work that person does."
7. *Making use of occupational information.* Acquiring valid information about career fields can often lead to sensible career choices. Such information can be found in reference books about careers such as the *Occupational Outlook Handbook,* computer-assisted career guidance (available in most counseling centers), newspapers and trade periodicals, and by speaking to people working in fields of interest to you. When speaking directly to career people, it is helpful to get the perspective of people at different stages in their field.
8. *Surfing the Internet.* Closely related to exploring occupational information is surfing the Internet to find out about a potential career for yourself. You might go directly to a site such as *America's Job Bank* to see information about a potentially appealing occupation. Or you might be looking for one type of information, such as buying car insurance. You focus the search engine on "insurance" and then happen to hit upon information about "insurance claims examiner." The work sounds interesting, so you explore the career possibility further.

THE VERTICAL AND HORIZONTAL CAREER PATHS

Planning and developing your career involves some form of goal setting. If your goals are laid out systematically to lead to your ultimate career goal, you have established a **career path,** a sequence of positions necessary to achieve a goal. Here we look at the more traditional career path, with an emphasis on moving upward, along with the more contemporary path, which emphasizes acquiring new skills and knowledge.

The Vertical (Traditional) Career Path

The vertical, or traditional, career path is based on the idea that a person continues to grow in responsibility with the aim of reaching a target position, such as becoming a top-level manager. The vertical career path is synonymous with "climbing the corporate ladder." The same path is based somewhat on the unwritten contract that a good performer will have the opportunity to work for a long time for one firm and receive many promotions in the process. However, a vertical career path can be spread out over several employers. Many employers still emphasize the old-fashioned idea of cultivating corporate loyalty by emphasizing promotions for good performers. And many employees strive to have a high-level position that will justify having a private office.

A career path should be related to the present and future demands of one firm or the industry. If you aspire to a high-level manufacturing position, it would be vital to know the future of manufacturing in that firm and in the industry. Many U.S. firms, for example, plan to conduct more of their manufacturing in the Pacific Rim and Mexico. If you were really determined, you might study the appropriate language and ready yourself for a foreign position.

While laying out a career path, it is also helpful to list your personal goals. They should mesh with your work plans to avoid major conflicts in your life. Some lifestyles, for example, are incompatible with some career paths. It would be difficult to develop a stable home life (spouse, children, friends, community activities, garden) if a person aspired toward holding field positions in international marketing. Contingency ("what-if") plans should also be incorporated into a well-designed career path. For instance, "If I don't become an agency supervisor by age 35, I will seek employment in the private sector." Or, "If I am not promoted within two years, I will enroll in an advanced degree program."

Lisa Irving, an ambitious 20-year-old, formulated the career path shown in Figure 16–1 prior to receiving an associate degree in business administration. Lisa's career goals are high, but she has established contingency plans.

A career path laid out in chart form gives a person a clear perception of climbing steps toward his or her target position. As each position is attained, the corresponding steps can be shaded in color or crosshatched. The steps, or goals, include a time element, which is helpful for sound career management even in work environments that are less predictable than they were in the past. Your long-range goal might be clearly established in your mind (such as regional manager of a hotel chain). At the same time, you must establish short-range (get any kind of job in a hotel) and intermediate-range (manager of a hotel by age 27) goals. Goals set too far in the future that are not supported with more immediate goals may lose their motivational value.

The Horizontal Career Path

A significant feature of the horizontal career path is that people are more likely to advance by moving sideways than by moving up. Or at least, people who get ahead will spend a considerable part of their career working in different positions at or nearly at the same level. In addition, they may occasionally move to a lower-level position in order to gain valuable experience. With a horizontal career path, the major reward is no longer promotion, but the opportunity to gain more experience and increase job skills.

The horizontal career path is closely linked to the new employment contract that offers shared responsibility for career growth. The old employment contract was lifetime employment in exchange for corporate loyalty. Instead, today's employees get a chance to develop new technical and professional skills. Instead of being offered job security, they become more employable because of the diversity

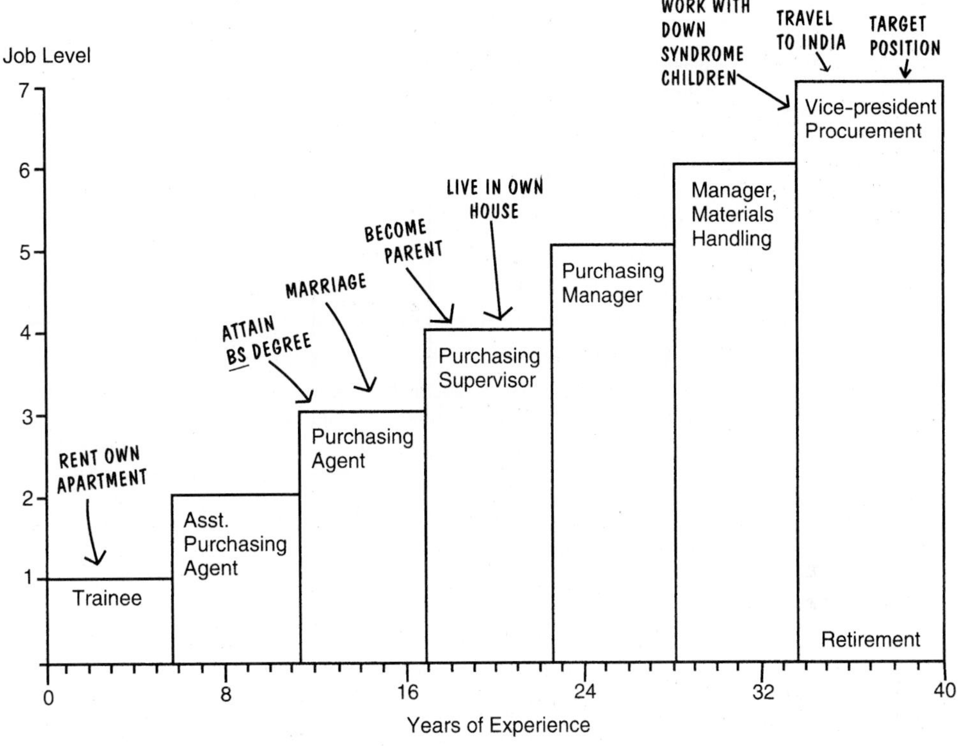

FIGURE 16–1 A Vertical (or Traditional) Career Path

of skills they acquire. The company provides the environment for learning, and employees are responsible for developing their skills.[3]

A horizontal career path, as well as a traditional (or vertical) career path, does not necessarily mean the person stays with the same firm. For example, a worker might spend three years in one company as an electronics technician, three years in another as a sales representative, and then three years in a third company as a customer service specialist. All three positions would be approximately at the same level. The third company would then promote the individual to a much-deserved position as the marketing team leader. Figure 16–2 illustrates a horizontal career path for Michael Wang, a career school graduate who did attempt to make long-range predictions about his career. Notice that all the positions through year 17 are at the first level, and the positions for years 22 and beyond are at the second level. Wang's career contingency plans are as follows:

> (1) If cannot obtain experience as a market research analyst, customer service rep, or sales rep, will continue to develop as electronics technician. (2) If cannot find employment as a sales manager, will attempt to become supervisor of electronic technicians. (3) If do not raise sufficient funds for starting own business, will continue in corporate job until retirement.

For both the horizontal and vertical career paths, contingency plans are helpful for dealing with the possibility of being demoted. Many people who are downsized have to accept a lower-status position.[4] Although being assigned to a lower-ranking position with lesser pay may hurt a person's pride, the new position can be a constructive learning experience. For example, the team leader who

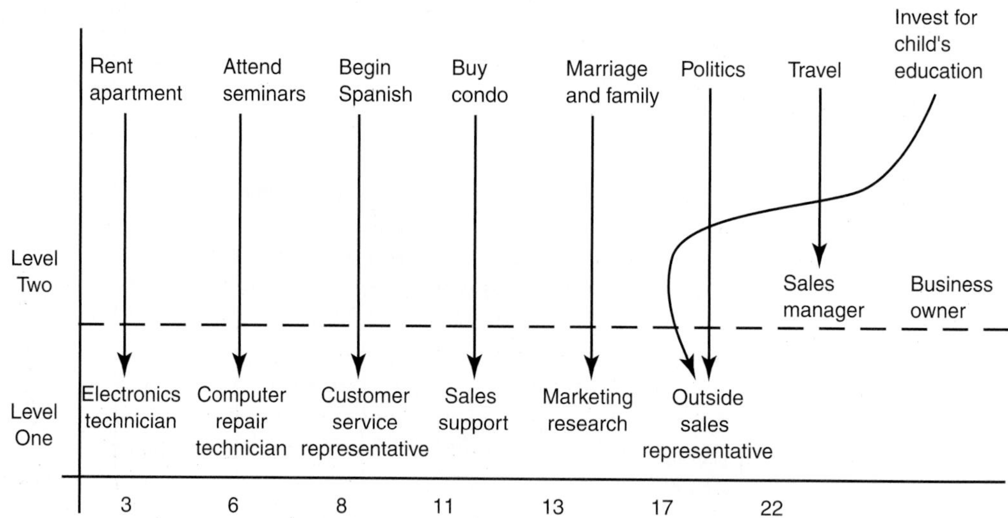

FIGURE 16–2 A Horizontal Career Path

is demoted to a full-time technical position can now concentrate on updating his or her technical skills. Another factor easing the sting of demotion is that people are less obsessed with job titles today. The contribution you make is more important to the company and many coworkers than your position title.

CONDUCTING THE JOB CAMPAIGN

Some people who have identified a career field never have to look for a job. Some of them enter into family businesses. Others are in such high-demand occupations that employers come looking for them. And some people capitalize on chance opportunity, with small effort on their part, such as being offered a job by a neighbor. Most other people have to conduct a **job campaign** to find employment at various times in their career. Employees in large organizations sometimes have to conduct a job campaign within their company, such as looking for a position in another division. Included in the job campaign are job-hunting tactics and preparing a job résumé and cover letter.

Job-Hunting Tactics

Some of the ideas about job hunting discussed next will be familiar to you; some will be unfamiliar. We recommend using this list of tactics and methods as a checklist to ensure that you have not neglected something important. It is easy to overlook the obvious when job hunting because your emotions may cloud your sense of logic.

IDENTIFY YOUR JOB OBJECTIVES. An effective job search begins with a clear perception of what kind of position you want. If you express indecision about the type of work you seek, the prospective employer will typically ask in a critical tone, "What kind of work are you looking for?" Your chances of finding suitable employment increase when several different types of positions will satisfy your job objectives. Assume that one person who majored in management is only willing to accept a position as a management trainee in a corporation. Another person with the same major is seeking a position as (1) a management trainee in a corporation; (2) an assistant manager in a retail store, restaurant, or hotel; (3) a management analyst; (4) a sales representative; or (5) an assistant purchasing agent. The second person has a better chance of finding a suitable position.

Be Aware of Qualifications Sought by Employers. What you are looking for in an employer must be matched against what an employer is looking for in an employee. If you are aware of what employers are seeking, you can emphasize those aspects about yourself when applying for a position. For example, applicants for almost any type of position in business should emphasize their information-technology skills. Job interviewers do not all agree on the qualifications they seek in employees. Nevertheless, a number of traits, characteristics, skills, and accomplishments are important to many employers.[5] Self-Assessment Exercise 16–1 summarizes these qualifications in a way that you can apply to yourself as you think about your job.

Identify Your Skills and Potential Contribution. Today's job market is skill based. Employers typically seek out job candidates with tangible skills that can be put to immediate use in accomplishing work. Skills as an important source of individual differences were described in Chapter 3. Job-relevant skills you might identify include information technology skills, bookkeeping skills, written communication skills, oral communication skills, foreign language skills, sales skills, problem-solving skills, math skills, and listening skills. A successful job candidate for a customer representative position told the interviewer at NYSEG (a gas and electric utility), "I know I can help you resolve customer complaints. In college I worked as a dorm counselor and had to listen to problems as part of my job. Give me a chance to listen to your customers."

Develop a Comprehensive Marketing Strategy. A vital job-finding strategy is to use multiple approaches to reach the right prospective employer because employers use several different sources for recruiting job candidates. Classified ads in newspapers are still the number one job search tool, but the Internet ranks second, ahead of employment agencies, referrals from friends, and word of mouth.[6] A job seeker whose specialty is not strongly in demand will have to use more recruiting sources and generate more contacts than a person whose specialty is in demand. For example, some business majors seek a position as a "sports administrator" for a professional athletic team. These people have to engage in more marketing and be more persistent than would a computer programmer.

Use Networking to Reach the Internal Job Market. By far the most effective method of finding a job is through personal contacts. In regard to job hunting, **networking** is contacting friends and acquaintances and building systematically on these relationships to create a still wider set of contacts that might lead to employment. A key advantage of networking is that it taps you into the **internal job market.** This is the large array of jobs that have not been advertised and that are usually filled by word of mouth or through friends and acquaintances of employees.

SELF-ASSESSMENT EXERCISE 16–1

Qualifications Sought by Employers

Following is a list of qualifications widely sought by prospective employers. After reading each qualification, rate yourself on a 1-to-5 scale on the particular dimension. For scoring, 1 = very low; 2 = low; 3 = average; 4 = high; and 5 = very high.

1. Appropriate education for the position under consideration, and satisfactory grades	1 2 3 4 5
2. Relevant work experience	1 2 3 4 5
3. Communication and other interpersonal skills	1 2 3 4 5
4. Motivation, tenacity, and energy	1 2 3 4 5
5. Problem-solving ability (intelligence) and creativity	1 2 3 4 5
6. Judgment and common sense	1 2 3 4 5
7. Adaptability to change	1 2 3 4 5
8. Emotional maturity (acting professionally and responsibly)	1 2 3 4 5
9. Teamwork (ability and interest in working in a team effort)	1 2 3 4 5
10. Positive attitude (enthusiasm about work and initiative)	1 2 3 4 5
11. Customer service orientation (wanting to meet customer needs)	1 2 3 4 5
12. Information technology (computer) skills	1 2 3 4 5
13. Internet research skills	1 2 3 4 5
14. Willingness to continue to study and learn about job, company, and industry	1 2 3 4 5
15. Likableness and sense of humor	1 2 3 4 5
16. Dependability, responsibility, and conscientiousness (including good work habits and time management)	1 2 3 4 5
17. Willing and able to work well with coworkers and customers from different cultures.	1 2 3 4 5
18. Leadership skills (displays initiative and influences others)	1 2 3 4 5

Interpretation: Consider engaging in some serious self-development, training, and education for items on which you rated yourself low or very low. If you accurately rated yourself as 4 or 5 on all the dimensions, you are an exceptional job candidate.

To use networking effectively, it may be necessary to create contacts aside from those you already have. Potential sources of contacts include almost anybody you know, as summarized in Table 16–1. The networking technique is so well known today that it suffers from overuse. It is therefore important to use a tactful, low-key approach with a contact. For example, instead of asking a person in your network to furnish you a job lead, ask that individual how a person with qualifications similar to yours might find a job. Another way of reaching the internal job market is to write dozens of letters to potential employers. A surprisingly large number of people find jobs by contacting employers directly. Prepare a prospective employer list, including the names of executives to contact in

TABLE 16–1
POTENTIAL SOURCES OF NETWORK CONTACTS

Coworkers and previous employers
Friends and neighbors
Faculty and staff
Graduates of any school you have attended
Former employers
Present employers (assuming you hold a temporary position)
Professionals such as bankers, brokers, and clergy
Political leaders at the local level
Members of your club or athletic team
Community groups, churches, temples, and mosques
Trade and professional associations
Student professional associations
Career fairs
People met in airports and on airplanes
People met at aerobics classes and health clubs
People you get to know through Internet chat rooms
People you get to know in bars and nightclubs (a long shot!)

each firm. The people who receive your letters or e-mail messages become part of your network. A variation of this approach is to develop a 30-second telephone presentation of your background. After you have researched organizations that may have opportunities for you, call them and make your pitch. However, the widespread use of voice mail has made the telephone tactic much less effective.

USE THE INTERNET AND RÉSUMÉ DATABASE SERVICES. The Internet is a standard part of job hunting. For little or no cost, the job seeker can post a résumé or scroll through hundreds of job opportunities. Many position announcements on the Internet require the job seeker to send an electronic résumé (described later in this chapter), while others request one by attaching a document to the e-mail message, fax, or paper mail. Technical positions such as computer programmer, engineering technician, or accountant are more likely to be found on the Internet than general positions. Although, thousands of nontechnical positions are also listed on the Internet. Job hunting on the Internet is menu driven, as you will discover if you visit the Web sites listed in Table 16–2.

Job hunting on the Internet can lead to a false sense of security. Using the Internet, a résumé is cast over such a wide net, and hundreds of job postings can be explored. As a consequence, the job seeker may think that he or she can sit back and wait for a job offer to come through e-mail. In reality, the Internet is just one source of leads that should be used in conjunction with other job-finding methods. Remember also that thousands of other job seekers can access the same job opening, and many of the positions listed have already been filled. Although you conduct a job search on the Internet, the final step is usually a face-to-face interview. The Internet alone does not find you a job.

TABLE 16–2
POPULAR JOB SEARCH WEB SITES

INTERNET JOB POSTINGS	
America's Job Bank	http://www.ajb.dni.us
Best Jobs in the USA Today	http://www.bestjobsusa.com
CareerMosaic	http://www.service.com:80/cm
CareerBuilder	http://www.careerbuilder.com
CareerPath	http://www.careerpath.com
HispanData	http://www.hispandata.com/hd/default.asp (for employers searching for Hispanic workers, and workers looking to fill such positions)
Job World	http://www.jobworld.com
Monster Board	http://www.monster.com
ONLINE RÉSUMÉ-POSTING SITES	
Career Web	http://www.cweb.com
E-Span Résumé Bank	http://www.espan.com
Intellimatch	http://www.intellimatch.com
Job Center	http://www.jobcenter.com
Online Career Center	http://www.occ.com
JOB HUNTING ADVICE	
First Magnitude	www.firstmagnitude.com/career/plan.htm
Job Hunter's Bible	http://www.jobhuntersbible.com

SMILE AT NETWORK MEMBERS AND INTERVIEWERS. Smile during your job search, because happy people get jobs. A statement by James Challenger still stands, "People would rather work with people who have pleasant dispositions. If you have been looking for a job for three months with no success, it may be hard to smile, but make yourself do it. It works."[7]

The Job Résumé and Cover Letter

No matter what method of job hunting you choose, inevitably somebody will ask you for a résumé. Sometimes you will be asked to complete a job application form instead of, or in addition to, a résumé. Résumés are also important for job hunting within your own firm. You may need one to be considered for a transfer with a large firm. Another use for a résumé is to present it to your manager to help evaluate your career progress.

RÉSUMÉ PURPOSE. Regard your résumé as a marketing tool for selling your skills and potential to handle new responsibilities. The most specific purpose of a résumé is to help you obtain an interview that can lead to a job. Your résumé must therefore attract enough attention for an employer to invite you for an interview. A hiring manager or employment official on average gives a résumé an initial scan of somewhere between 10 and 15 seconds.[8] If your document looks favorable, it will then be studied more carefully. Recognize that you are competing against many carefully prepared résumés. However, if the demand for your skills is high enough, it is conceivable that you will be hired without an interview.

Résumé Length and Format. For a recent graduate with limited work experience, a one-page résumé may be acceptable. For more experienced people, it would seem too short. Employers today demand considerable detail in résumés, particularly about the candidate's skills, accomplishments, and leadership experience. Nevertheless, a four-page or longer résumé may irritate an impatient reader. Two pages are therefore recommended for early stages in your career. Hiring managers and human resource professionals have widely different perceptions of what constitutes an effective length and format for a résumé. A general-purpose hard-copy résumé that fits many preferences is presented in Figure 16–3.

A current development in résumé construction is to prepare one primarily for electronic databases. Many companies store résumés electronically, making it important to prepare one that is suitable for this purpose. If you prepare an electronic résumé, remember to create a file for your hard drive and a disk. If a job search Web site calls for an electronic résumé, it can be entered into the right place on the Web page. At other times an electronic résumé is printed and mailed to the employer, who in turn uses an optical scanner to enter the résumé into the company database. A distinguishing feature of an electronic résumé is that it contains key words that fit the requirements of a keyword search. The job-seeker should isolate key words (nouns and adjectives) by placing them right under the individual's name, address, and telephone numbers. Zane K. Quible recommends that key words be selected from among the following:[9]

- Titles of jobs held by applicant
- Names of job-related tasks performed by the applicant
- Industry jargon such as "zero defects," "customer delight," or "just-in-time inventory management." Also use acronyms such as JIT for "just in time."
- Special skills or knowledge possessed by the applicant
- Degrees earned
- High school program or college major. (For college graduates, information about the high school program can be deleted.)
- High schools or colleges attended
- Special awards or honors received
- Nature of interpersonal skills the applicant possesses

Most of this information, of course, should also be included in a conventional printed résumé. Figure 16–4 illustrates an electronic résumé.

In preparing either a hard-copy or an electronic résumé, keep in mind that certain key words or references attract the attention of managers and specialists who scan résumés. In today's market these are as follows: languages, computer, experience, achievement, hardworking, overseas experience, flexible, and task-oriented.[10] A sensible tactic would be to mention the words that apply to you. Except for languages and overseas experience, these terms are widely applicable.

A recent study conducted with 64 business professionals provides some useful information about which résumé characteristics are perceived positively enough to invite a job candidate for an interview. The following résumé characteristics were more likely to lead to first choices for an interview: one page in contrast to two pages; a specific objective statement in comparison to a general objective statement; relevant course work better than no course work listed; GPA of 3.0 in contrast to no GPA listed; and accomplishment statement in contrast to no accomplishment statement.[11]

Scott Wayland
170 Glenview Drive
Dallas, Texas 75243
Phone/Fax (312) 555-3986
swayland@frontiernet.net

Qualification Summary	Experience in selling industrial machinery. Education in business administration, combined with apprenticeship in tool and die making. In one year sold $400,000 worth of excess machine inventory. Received letter of commendation from company president.
Job Objective	Industrial sales, handling large, complex machinery. Willing to work largely on commission basis.
Job Experience	
2001–present	Industrial account representative, Bainbridge Corporation, Dallas, Texas. Sell line of tool and die equipment to companies in Southwest. Responsibilities include servicing established accounts and canvassing new ones.
1999–2001	Inside sales representative, Bainbridge Corporation. Answered customer inquiries through e-mail and telephone. Filled orders for replacement parts. Trained for outside sales position. Served as sales team representative on company quality-improvement team.
1995–1999	Tool and die maker apprentice, Texas Metals, Inc., Dallas. Assisted senior tool and die makers during four-year training program. Worked on milling machines, jigs, punch presses, computer-assisted manufacturing, computer-assisted design (CAD/CAM).
Formal Education	
1995–2001	Madagascar College, Dallas. Associate Degree in Business Administration; graduated with 3.16 grade point average. Courses in marketing, sales techniques, consumer behavior, accounting, and statistics. President of Commuter's Club.
1991–1995	Big Horn High, Dallas. Honors student; academic major with vocational elective. Played varsity football and basketball. Earned part of living by selling magazine subscriptions.
Job-related Skills	Professional sales representative. Able to size up customer manufacturing problem and make recommendations for appropriate machinery. Precise in preparing call reports and expense accounts. Good skill in gathering input from the field for market research purposes.
Personal Interests and Hobbies	Information technology enthusiast (developed and installed own Web site), scuba diving, recreational golf player, read trade and business magazines. Auto enthusiast, including restoring a 1976 Corvette.
References	On file with placement office at Madagascar College.

FIGURE 16–3 A General-Purpose Résumé

The Cover Letter. A résumé should be accompanied by a cover letter explaining who you are and why you are applying for this particular job. The cover letter customizes your approach to a particular employer, while the résumé is a more general approach. Most job applicants use the conventional approach of writing a letter attempting to impress the prospective employer with their background. An alternate approach is to capture the reader's attention with a punchy

Sara L. Adams
123 Elmwood Terrace
Framingham, MA 01701
(617) 555-1485 FAX (617) 555-4587
SLAdams@hmp.aol

Key words: Accountant. Bookkeeper. Accounts receivable ledger. Accounts payable ledger. Financial reports. Business Administration. Lotus 1-2-3. Excel. Windows 98. Windows Professional. French. Supervision. President's Honor Roll. Superior oral communication skills. Superior written communication skills. Self-starter. Quick learner. Conscientious. Detail oriented. Reliable. Top 5 percent of class. IBM-compatible computers. Lakeville College, Framingham, MA.

Job objective:	To work as accountant or bookkeeper for private or public business, with eventual goal of becoming supervisor of bookkeeping or accounting, or office manager.
Education:	Lakeville College, Framingham, MA, 2000–2002. Accounting major. Associate's degree in Business Administration with High Honors. East Framingham High School, National Honor Society, 1992.
Experience:	London's Department Store, Framingham, MA, 1996–present. Full-time for four years, part-time while attending college. Performed bookkeeping and cashier activities. Maintained accounts receivable and accounts payable ledgers. Prepared variety of financial reports.
Key Accomplishment:	Developed a system of prompt payments that saved employer approximately $60,000 per year.
College Activities and Honors:	President of Accounting Club for two years. Team Leader of Student Misconduct Committee. President's Honor Roll each semester, 2000–2002. Delta Phi Kappa Honorary, 2000–2002.

FIGURE 16–4 Electronic Résumé

statement of what you might be able to do for them. Later in the letter you might present a one-paragraph summary of your education and the highlights of your job and educational experience. Here are two examples of opening lines geared to two different types of jobs:

1. Person seeking employment as customer service manager in a large automobile dealership: "Do you want your old customers to return to your dealership when it's time to purchase a new car? Then give me the chance to help you operate a smooth-running, 'service with a smile' customer service department."
2. Person looking for position as administrative assistant in hospital where vacancy may or may not exist: "Is your hospital drowning in paperwork? Let me jump in with both feet and clear up some of the confusion. Then you can go back to taking care of patients."

The second opening line may come across as a little brash to suit some tastes. It is important to use an opening line that suits your personality.

Richard H. Beatty recommends a slightly different version of the attention-getting cover letter. He explains that an effective cover letter has five parts: an attention-grabbing introduction, a paragraph selling your value to the employer, a background summary paragraph, a compelling follow-up action statement, and an appreciative close. Beatty recommends mentioning a personal contact as part of the attention-grabber.[12] An example: "John Kowolski, your computer operations manager, mentioned that you are looking for a talented person to manage your Web site. I would very much like to talk to you about this position."

Performing Well in a Job Interview

After a prospective employer has reacted favorably to your cover letter and résumé, the next step is a telephone screening interview or a job interview. The purpose of the telephone screening interview is generally to obtain some indication of the candidate's oral communication skills. Such an interview is most likely when one applies for a customer service position or one that requires knowledge of a second language. Having passed the screening interview, the candidate is invited for an in-person job interview. Another type of screening interview is to respond to computerized questions, including a sample job problem. Your answers are printed for the interviewer to review. Candidates who get through the computer-assisted interview get to be interviewed by a company representative.[13]

Typically one person at a time interviews the applicant, yet team interviews are becoming more commonplace. In this format, members of the team or department with whom you would be working take turns asking you questions. One justification for team interviews is to observe how the candidate fits in with the team.

A general guide for performing well in the job interview is to present a positive but accurate picture of yourself. Your chances of performing well in a job increase if you are suited for the job. Therefore, "tricking" a prospective employer into hiring you when you are not qualified is self-defeating in terms of your career. Outright deception, such as falsifying one's educational or employment record, is widely practiced during the interview and on résumés and cover letters. If the person is hired and the deception is discovered later, he or she is subject to dismissal. Here we list some key points to keep in mind when being interviewed for a job you want.

1. *Be prepared, look relaxed, and make the interviewer feel comfortable.* Coming to the interview fully prepared to discuss yourself and your background and knowing key facts about the prospective employer will help you look relaxed. Many people today use company Web sites to gather background information about the prospective employer.
2. *Establish a link between you and the prospective employer.* A good rapport builder with the prospective employer is to mention some plausible link between you and that firm. To illustrate, if being interviewed for a position at a Wal-Mart, one might say, "It's fun to visit the office part of Wal-Mart. Our family has been shopping here for years. In fact, I bought a CD player here last month. It works great."
3. *Ask perceptive questions.* The best questions are sincere ones that reflect an interest in the content of the job (intrinsic motivators) and job performance, rather than benefits and social activities. A good question to ask is "What would you consider to be outstanding performance in this job?" If the issue of compensation is not introduced by the interviewer, ask about such matters after first discussing the job and your qualifications.

TABLE 16–3
QUESTIONS FREQUENTLY ASKED OF JOB CANDIDATES

An important way of preparing for job interviews is to rehearse answers to the types of questions you will most likely be asked by the interviewer. The following questions are some of the same types found in most employment interviews. Rehearse answers to these questions prior to going out on job interviews. One good rehearsal method is to role-play the employment interview with a friend who asks these typical questions, or videotape yourself.

1. Why did you apply for this job?
2. What are your career goals?
3. What do you expect to be doing five years from now?
4. What salary are you worth?
5. What new job skills would you like to acquire in the next few years?
6. What are your strengths (or good points)?
7. What are your weaknesses (or areas of needed improvement)?
8. Tell me about a time when you resolved a difficult problem with a customer.
9. How would you describe yourself?
10. How would other people describe you?
11. Why should we hire you instead of other candidates for the same job?
12. How well do you work under pressure?
13. What makes you think you will be successful in business?
14. What do you know about our firm?
15. Here is a sample job problem. How would you handle it?

4. *Be prepared to discuss your strengths and developmental opportunities.* Most interviewers will ask you to discuss your strengths and developmental opportunities. (These and other frequently asked questions are presented in Table 16–3.) Knowledge of strengths hints at your potential job performance. To deny having areas for improvement is to appear imperceptive or defensive. Some candidates describe developmental opportunities that could be interpreted as strengths. A case in point: "I have been criticized for expecting too much from myself and others." Do you think this approach is unethical?
5. *Be prepared to respond to behavioral interview questions.* A **behavioral interview** asks questions directly about the candidate's behavior in relation to an important job activity. The job candidate is expected to give samples of job behaviors that the company has found are related to good performance.[14] The behavioral interview is therefore more applicable to candidates with substantial work experience. Two behavioral inquires are "Tell me about a time in which your ability to work well on a team contributed to the success of a project" and "Give me an example of a creative suggestion you made that was actually implemented. In what way did it help the company?" To prepare for such questions, think of some examples of how you handled a few difficult job challenges. The idea is to document specific actions you took or behaviors you engaged in that contributed to a favorable outcome. Question 8 in Table 16–3 is a behavioral interview question.
6. *Show how you can help the employer.* A prospective employer wants to know whether you will be able to perform the job well. Direct much of your conversation toward how you intend to help the company solve problems and

get important work accomplished. Whatever the question, think about what details of your skills and experiences will be useful to the employer.

7. *Send a follow-up letter.* Mail a courteous follow-up letter several days after the interview, particularly if you want the job. A follow-up letter is a tip-off that you are truly interested in the position. You should state your attitudes toward the position, the team, and the company and summarize any conclusions reached about your discussion. Now do Skill-Building Exercise 16–1 to practice an important phase of job hunting.

In case you doubt that the job search activities described here actually work, an analysis of 36 studies involving 11,010 job seekers provides positive evidence. The researchers concluded that individuals who engaged in higher levels of job search behavior were more likely to obtain employment than those who reported lower levels of such behavior. The relationship between job search behavior and finding a job was stronger among laid-off workers than among new entrants or among employed people who were looking for a new position.[15]

CAREER-ADVANCEMENT STRATEGIES AND TACTICS

The approaches to improving personal relationships on the job described in Chapter 6 through 10 of this book can be regarded as ways of advancing your career. People who enhance their relationships with higher-ranking individuals and coworkers are in essence making plans for career advancement. Here we will describe a number of other strategies and tactics for career advancement divided into two groups. The methods in the first group relate to taking control over your own behavior, whereas those in the second group relate to controlling the external environment.

Indiscriminate use of any method of career advancement may backfire. For example, if you overdo networking, you may spend so much time relating to people in your network that you will be neglecting your job. It is also important to choose methods of getting ahead that fit your circumstances and personal style. A case in point is the advice given later about taking risks. An adventuresome person without dependents would find this tactic to be ideal. A cautious person with dependents might find this tactic to be anxiety provoking.

SKILL-BUILDING EXERCISE 16–1

The Job Interview

As described in Table 16–3, a good way to prepare for a job interview is to rehearse answers to frequently asked questions. In this role-play, one student will be the interviewer and one the interviewee (job applicant). The job in question is that of property manager for a large apartment complex in Fort Lauderdale, Florida. Assume that the applicant really wants the job. The interviewer, having taken a course in applied psychology, will ask many of the questions listed in Table 16–3. The interviewer, however, will also have other specific questions such as "Why do you want to work in Fort Lauderdale?"

Before proceeding with the role-play, both people should review the information in this chapter about the job interview and in Chapter 11 about listening.

Advancement through Taking Control of Yourself

The unifying theme for the strategies, tactics, and attitudes described in this section is that you attempt to control your own behavior.

Develop a Code of Professional Ethics. A good starting point in developing a career is to establish a personal ethical code. An ethical code determines what behavior is right or wrong, good or bad, based on values. The values may stem from cultural upbringing, religious teachings, and professional or industry standards. A code of professional ethics helps a person deal with such issues as accepting bribes, backstabbing a coworker, or sexually harassing a subordinate, coworker, vendor, or customer.

Make an Accurate Self-appraisal. A critical tactic for career advancement is to obtain an accurate picture of your strengths, areas for improvement, and preferences. Introspection is a good starting point in self-appraisal. The Self-Knowledge Questionnaire presented in Chapter 4 is a useful vehicle for introspection and self-analysis. In review, information for self-appraisal can also be obtained from self-assessment devices, feedback from people on and off the job, and from counselors.

> A sales representative constructed a brief form asking questions about him, such as "What have I done this year that displeased you?" He gave the form to customers, his manager, and the office staff. The information he received helped him become more effective with others. In this regard, he learned that he was standing too close to people when he talked to them.

Develop Expertise and Passion, and Build a Career around It. A starting point in getting ahead is to develop a useful job skill. This tactic is obvious if you are working as a specialist, such as a paralegal assistant. Being skilled at the task performed by the group is also a requirement for being promoted to a supervisory position. After being promoted to a supervisory or other managerial job, expertise is still important for further advancement. It helps a manager's reputation to be skilled at such things as memo writing, computer applications, preparing a budget, or developing a marketing plan.

The surest path to career success is to identify your area or areas of expertise and then build a career around it or them. The executives most in demand today have general experience, but at least one area of expertise, such as launching a new product. Becoming wealthy and achieving recognition are by-products of making effective use of your talents. Part of developing expertise is being passionate about your work. Expertise is unlikely to be sustained unless a person has passion for his or her field. Even if passion does not lead directly to career advancement, it has other benefits. In the words of Randy Komisar, a silicon valley entrepreneur: "Don't let a career drive you, let passion drive your life. That may not get you up any ladder, but it will make your trip down a long and winding road more interesting."[16]

Combining expertise, passion, and a code of positive ethics leads to a positive reputation. The better your reputation, the higher the return on your investment of time, energy, and money in your career.

Attain High Job Performance. Consistently good performance is the foundation on which you build your career. Job competence is still the major success ingredient in all but the most political firms (those where favoritism outweighs merit). Before anybody is promoted in virtually every organization, the prospective new manager asks, "How well did that person perform for you?"

Keep Growing through Continuous Learning and Self-development. Given that continuous learning is part of the new employment contract, engaging in regular learning will help a person advance. Continuous learning can take many forms, including formal schooling, attending training programs and seminars, and self-study. It is particularly important to engage in new learning in areas of interest to the company, such as developing proficiency in a second language if the company has customers and employees in other countries. Many companies support continuous learning, making it easier for you to implement the tactic of growth through continuous learning. Self-development can include any type of learning, but it often emphasizes personal improvement and skill development. Improving your work habits or team leadership skills would be job-relevant examples of self-development.

A key output of continuous learning and self-development is that it leads to enhanced skills. Skill development not only enhances job performance but it is the basis of job security. Table 16–4 will help you understand the type of skills and behaviors that are required of professionals in organizations.

Document Your Accomplishments. Keeping an accurate record of what you have accomplished in your career can be valuable when being considered for reassignment or promotion. The same log of accomplishments is useful for

TABLE 16–4

Core Behaviors for Individual Employees at MetLife

At MetLife, individual employees are rated on a 1-to-5 scale based on the following competency model of core behaviors.

- **Adapts to and implements change.** Embraces change with innovation, courage, and resiliency.
- **Promotes key values.** Consistently demonstrates company values. Conducts business endeavors with truth, sincerity, and fairness.
- **Communicates effectively.** Shares information and engages in candid and open dialogue.
- **Focuses on customers.** Works to exceed customer expectations.
- **Produces results.** Directs action toward achieving goals that are critical to the company's success.
- **Completes work without close supervision.** Accepts direction but does not require continuous monitoring of work.
- **Manages own performance effectively.** Organizes time and priorities to achieve business results.
- **Uses sound business judgment.** Applies knowledge of the business and the industry, and common sense, to make the best decisions.
- **Demonstrates technical and functional expertise.** Has thorough knowledge of the job and continues to expand knowledge.

Source: Expanded from MetLife company document as reported in Janet Wiscombe, "Can Pay for Performance Really Work?" *Workforce,* August 2001, p. 30.

résumé preparation. It is preferable to point to tangible, quantifiable accomplishments than to another person's subjective impression of your performance. Let's assume that a retail store manager reduced inventory shrinkage by 30 percent one year. It would be better to state that fact than to record a statement from her manager saying, "Kelly shows outstanding ability to reduce inventory shrinkage."

Documenting your accomplishments enables you to promote yourself in a dignified, tactful way. When discussing work with key people in the company, let them know of your good deeds without taking too much credit for team accomplishments. If you distinguish yourself in the community, for example, by fund-raising for a shelter for the homeless, let your manager know of your activities. The rationale is that most companies want their workers to be responsible community members.

Project a Professional Image. Your clothing, desk and work area, speech, and general knowledge should project the image of a professional, responsible person. Good grammar and sentence structure can give you the edge because so many people use highly informal patterns of speech. Being a knowledgeable person is important because today's professional businessperson is supposed to be aware of the external environment. Projecting a professional image is also useful because it hastens the development of trust and rapport in business relationships.

Minimize Career Self-sabotage. Procrastination was described in Chapter 15 as a leading form of self-defeating behavior that can damage one's career. Many other behaviors can also defeat your own purposes and result in career self-sabotage. A way to overcome these behaviors is to solicit feedback from others on any aspect of your behavior under your control that could be harming your career. You would then attempt to overcome these behaviors on your own or get help through reading, attending seminars, or seeking professional assistance. Table 16–5 lists self-defeating behaviors that can result in career self-sabotage, thereby blocking career advancement.

Advancement through Exerting Control over the Environment

In this section we emphasize strategies and tactics requiring you to exert some control over the outside environment. If you do not fully control it, you can try to juggle it to your advantage.

Identify Growth Fields and Growth Companies. A sound strategy for career advancement is to seek jobs where possibilities for growth exist. Generally, this means seeking out growth industries, but it can also mean seeking out growth firms or areas of the country with plentiful job opportunities. Information about growth opportunities can be found in government publications such as the *Occupational Outlook Handbook,* newspapers, and Internet sources such as *America's Job Bank.* The local chamber of commerce can be a valid source of information about growth firms in your area. A summary of good job opportunities for the start of the 21st century is presented in Table 16–6.

Obtain Broad Experience. A leading strategy for career advancement into high-level positions is to strengthen your credentials by broadening your experience. Broad experience is particularly important for attaining a high-level management

TABLE 16–5
COMMON FORMS OF CAREER SELF-SABOTAGE

- Procrastination (carried out to the point that the person develops the reputation of being unreliable).
- Self-sabotaging life script (repeated pattern of messing up just when things are going well).
- Narcissism (wanting so hard to be liked that the person avoids necessary confrontations).
- Emotional immaturity (the person shows poor judgment and plays the role of office clown).
- Self-defeating beliefs (the person makes many negative self-statements).
- Unrealistic expectations (the person has such high goals that disappointment and discouragement are inevitable).
- Revenge (the person attempts to get even with the employer for reasons such as low salary increase or performance review).
- Attention seeking (the person will do almost anything to get attention, including being overcritical of management).
- Thrill seeking (just for kicks, the person might even make unauthorized use of company equipment).
- Excessive absenteeism and lateness (the person develops the reputation of being unprofessional and uninterested in career).
- Crossing swords with powerful people (the person argues too often with people who can damage his or her career).
- A negative attitude so strong that it cuts the person off from the constructive criticism needed to perform the job better. If a person develops a reputation for not listening to what people tell him or her, the person will soon receive no useful feedback.

Source: Gathered from information throughout Andrew J. DuBrin, *Your Own Worst Enemy: How to Prevent Career Self-Sabotage* (New York: AMACOM, 1992); "No More Excuses! Overcome Self-Imposed Obstacles for Career Gain," *Executive Strategies,* February 1998, p. 1; Julie Connelly, "Career Survival Guide," *Working Woman,* April 1999, pp. 58–62.

position. For example, a person who held positions in sales and manufacturing would have broad experience. Breadth could come about also by experience in different industries such as retailing and manufacturing, or by holding positions in different companies. A study of 69 female executives and 69 male executives indicated that career success in terms of job level and compensation was positively related to breadth of experience.[17] The broadening strategy also works to some extent for technical positions. A computer specialist who has worked with both Microsoft and Linus operating systems might be considered more valuable than a counterpart with experience in only one system.

An excellent vehicle for obtaining broad experience is to become part of a management trainee program, after which you are permanently assigned to one department. Being assigned to different teams, projects, and committees is another natural broadening experience. Another approach to broadening is to self-study different aspects of business.

TAKE SENSIBLE RISKS. People who make it big in their careers usually take several sensible risks on their journey to success. Among these risks would be to work for a fledgling company that offers big promises but a modest starting salary, or to take an overseas assignment with no promise of a good job when you return. Industrial relations manager Michael Oliver offers this advice:

TABLE 16–6

FASTEST-GROWING OCCUPATIONS AND OCCUPATIONS PROJECTED TO HAVE THE LARGEST NUMERICAL INCREASES IN EMPLOYMENT THROUGH 2010

Fastest-Growing Occupation	Largest Numerical Increases in Employment
ASSOCIATE'S DEGREE	
Computer support specialists	Registered nurses
Medical records and health information technicians	Computer support specialists
Physical therapist assistants	Medical records and health information technicians
Occupational therapist assistants	Paralegals and legal assistants
Veterinary technologists and technicians	Dental hygienists
Hotline handyperson (visits the home to repair electronic equipment)	
BACHELOR'S DEGREE	
Computer software engineers, applications	Computer software engineers, applications
Computer software engineers, systems software	Computer software engineers, systems software
Network and computer systems administrators	Elementary schoolteachers, except special education
Computer systems analysts	Network and computer systems administrators
Network systems and data communications analysts	
Database administrators	

Source: www.bls.gov/oco/ocotjtl.htm; Julie Rowe "What Will Be the Ten Hottest Jobs?" *Time,* May 22, 2000, p. 72.

> If you want to achieve something really creative, thus enhancing your profession, then try a little risk taking. That doesn't mean you should pick up a lance and seek out a windmill. Balance your risk taking with good sense so you will be able to reach a new comfort level somewhere between the role of a bureaucratic follower and leaper of tall buildings. The goal should be to develop credibility without perpetrating a maverick reputation.[18]

FIND A MENTOR. Most successful career people have had one or more mentors during their career. A **mentor** is a more experienced person who guides, teaches, and coaches another individual. Today mentors can be peers and even lower-ranking individuals. A lower-ranking individual, for example, can educate you on how other parts of the organization work—something you may need to know in advance. In the traditional approach, finding a mentor takes place spontaneously, just like finding a friend. Many companies, however, have formal mentoring programs in which the newcomer is assigned a mentor. Many mentees stay in contact with their mentors through e-mail, thereby decreasing the number of face-to-face meetings and telephone calls. Staying in contact over the Net is particularly useful when the mentor lives and works far away.

Mentorship is an important development process in many occupations: master–apprentice, physician–intern, teacher–student, and executive–manager of lower rank. A new twist on mentoring is that your mentor can be from a different skill area, such as a computer analyst being paired with a mentor from marketing. Another new form of mentoring is to be mentored by a person of lower rank than oneself, if the other person has important expertise you might lack. At Intel Corp., for example, one senior administrative assistant has so many valuable contacts, and so much knowledge of how the company operates that she has taught her skills to a manager who outranks her.[19]

The cross-skill mentor coaches the less-experienced person in nontechnical areas. An emotional tie exists between the less-experienced person, the mentee, and the mentor. (*Mentee* is the generally accepted new term for *protégé.*) The emotional tie is more likely when mentors are chosen spontaneously. Mentors help mentees in many ways, yet not every mentor can provide all of these services:

- Act as a positive role model and trusted friend.
- Share their knowledge and experience.
- Guide mentees into understanding the consequences of their own behavior.
- Encourage mentees to solve problems for themselves, rather than handing them solutions.
- Share information about opportunities within the organization.
- Look beyond the company to guide the mentee toward good career decisions such as joining another firm.
- Keep the mentee informed about his or her progress.
- Listen to problems without passing on confidential information.[20]

To understand the impact of mentoring on a more personal level, we quote Joellyn Willis. She is the youngest employee ever to be appointed as vice president of operations at an electrical distribution and control company in Chicago:

> Mentoring has played an important role in helping me accomplish my business and career goals as well as my personal goals. The vice presidents of human resources and finances both assumed advisory roles early in my career and helped me choose the most appropriate and efficient plans. They also helped me identify training and job opportunities. I started in the financial area but it was my human resources mentor who helped me realize that to advance to the position of a general manager or a CEO, I'd have to broaden my experiences.[21]

Receiving good mentoring is a major career-advancement strategy for all, yet is particularly important for minorities. Most minority group members who advance high in the organization, or who are successful business owners, acknowledge the contribution of receiving good mentoring. Based on three years of research in three major U.S. corporations, David A. Thomas concluded that minorities who advance the farthest share one characteristic: a strong network of mentors and higher-ranking managers who recommend them for good assignments and promotions.[22]

Use Your Network of Contacts. Networking has already been described as a major assist to finding a job. Members of your network can also help you by assisting with difficult job problems, providing emotional support, buying your product or services, and offering you good prices on their products and services. A recommended approach to networking is to keep a list of at least 25 people whom you contact at least once a month. The contact can be as extensive as a luncheon meeting or as brief as an e-mail message. The starting point in networking is to obtain an ample supply of business cards. You then give a card to any person you meet who might be able to help you now or in the future. While first developing your network, be inclusive. Later, as your network develops, you can strive to include a greater number of influential and successful people.

People in your network can include relatives, people you meet while traveling, vacationing, or attending trade shows, and classmates. A substantial amount of social networking also takes place over computer networks, specifically in the form of community groups (such as astrology buffs) on the Internet. The people in these groups can become valuable business contacts. Community activities and religious organizations can also be a source of contacts. Golf is still considered the number one sport for networking because of the high-level contacts the sport generates. In recent years, the number of businesswomen who have learned golf for networking purposes has increased substantially.

Recent research has supported the widely accepted belief that networks contribute to job performance and career success. Network and general work attitudes surveys were administered to 269 culturally diverse individuals from five organizations. A major finding was that being part of an advice network was positively related to job performance, including performing beyond the requirements of the job description. Furthermore, being part of a negative network (such as being part of a network of chronic complainers) lowered performance.[23]

Develop a Proactive Personality. If you are an active agent in taking control of the forces around you, you stand a better chance of capitalizing on opportunities. Also, you will seek out opportunities such as seeing problems that need fixing. A **proactive personality** is a person relatively unconstrained by forces in the situation and who brings about environmental change. Although developing a proactive personality might be classified as taking charge of oneself, the focus is on learning to take charge of the outside world. Highly proactive people identify opportunities and act on them, show initiative, and keep trying until they bring about meaningful change. A health and safety specialist with a proactive personality, for example, might identify a health hazard others had missed. He or she would identify the nature of the problem and urge management for funding to control the problem. Ultimately that individual's efforts in preventing major health problems would be recognized.

Managers prefer workers with a proactive personality because these workers become proactive employees, or those who take the initiative to take care of problems. The modern employee is supposed to be enterprising. Instead of relying solely on the manager to figure out what work needs to be accomplished, he or she looks for projects to undertake.[24] The proactive employee, however, may clash with an old-fashioned manager who believes that an employee's job is strictly to follow orders.

A study conducted with close to 500 men and women workers in diverse occupations examined the relationship between career success and a proactive personality. Proactive personality, as measured by a test, was related to salary, promotions, and career satisfaction.[25] A similar study with 180 employees indicated that proactive personality was positively related to being innovative on the job, developing knowledge about organizational politics, and taking initiative to advance one's career. Innovation, political knowledge, and career initiative in turn showed a positive relationship to salary growth and number of promotions.[26]

It may not be easy to develop a proactive personality, but a person can get started by taking more initiative to fix problems and attempting to be more self-starting. A major advantage of being a proactive personality is that it helps you capitalize on luck. Unless you are prepared to take advantage of an opportunity, it is difficult to capitalize on luck. Luck, in fact, is often defined as what happens when preparation meets opportunity.

DEVELOPING A PORTFOLIO CAREER AND CAREER SWITCHING

It is becoming increasingly common for people to either switch the emphasis of activities in their work or switch careers entirely. A Career Education Corporation survey found that nearly half of all workers would consider changing careers, and 25 percent plan to do so within one year.[27] An example of switching the emphasis of activities would be for a computer salesperson to shift to a new field in which he or she worked primarily with computers and did no selling. People modify their careers for a variety of reasons, all centering around the idea that something is missing in their present one. Here we look at two closely related approaches to changing direction in a career: developing a portfolio career and career switching.

Developing a Portfolio Career

Many people would like to change careers yet not be confined to focusing on one major type of job activity. To accomplish this, a growing number of people are developing a **portfolio career,** in which they use a variety of skills and earn money in several different ways. In addition to fulfilling their desire to diversify, a portfolio career helps many people cope with the trend toward fewer full-time positions available. According to the Bureau of Labor Statistics, 20 percent of the U.S. workforce works part-time (35 hours or less per week). To earn the equivalent of a full-time salary, many people are piecing together more than one part-time position. Because more part-time positions pay benefits, working for several employers becomes more feasible.

Having a portfolio (or collection) of income-generating possibilities makes you more resistant to the effects of losing one job. You spread your risk by earning money in several ways. The career portfolio minimizes risks by accumulating groups of skills that can provide income. If one skill is not in demand, another might be. For example, a human resources specialist who also sold real estate might shift to full-time real estate sales if his or her company decided to outsource human resources. A common example of a skill portfolio is a person with a full-time position who has a part-time position requiring different skills. A department manager within a retail store might install satellite dishes as a part-time activity.

An important part of developing a portfolio career is to keep your occupational skills current. Suppose a person is able to translate documents from Japanese to English and English to Japanese but is currently not working as a translator. Translation skills fade rapidly, so the person should continue to practice this bilingual skill at home.

Career Switching

Whether in pursuit of psychological success or traditional success, many people find it necessary to switch careers. Negative factors as well as the search for more excitement, challenge, and money can trigger a career change. Among the negative trigger events are traumatic experiences such as the terrorist attacks of September 2001, job loss, severe illness, divorce, or the death of a loved one.[28] A major principle of career switching is to *be thorough*. Go through the same kind of thinking and planning that is recommended for finding a first career. Everything said in this chapter about choosing a first career is also relevant for choosing a later career. The advantage for the career switcher, however, is that the experienced person often has a better understanding of the type of work he or she does not want to do. *Explore the options* through such means as scanning career information and brainstorming with knowledgeable people.

A new career should be *built gradually.* Few people are able to leave one career abruptly and step into another. For most people who switch careers successfully, the switch is more of a transition than an abrupt change. A constructive approach would be to take on a few minor assignments in the proposed new field, and then search for full-time work in that field after building skill. An electronics technician, for example, might ask to visit customers with sales representatives to facilitate a switch to industrial selling.

A major reason that many employees consider a new career is that they crave more independence. As a consequence, an increasingly popular path for the career switcher is to move from salaried employment to self-employment. Many people making the move to self-employment are chronologically young. According to the Small Business Administration, 20 percent of all small business owners are between the ages of 25 and 34. Furthermore, people in this age bracket have three times as high a start-up rate for new businesses as any other age group.[29]

The prospective self-employed person needs to decide upon which particular business to enter. For many people, self-employment means continuing to perform similar work, such as a company cafeteria manager entering the food catering business. Other formerly employed workers go into competition with their former employers, such as a print shop manager opening a print shop of his or her own. For those who lack specific plans of their own, prepackaged plans can be purchased. Examples of these are listed in Table 16–7.

Another self-employment possibility is to purchase a franchise, thus lowering the risk of a start-up business. Currently, franchises account for about one-third of retail sales in the United States and Canada. Yet franchises require a substantial financial investment, ranging from about $6,000 to $500,000. Another caution is that some franchise operators may work around 70 hours per week to earn about $13,000 per year.

Whether a person starts a new business or becomes a franchisee, he or she needs substantial cash on hand, a good credit rating, and usually some business experience. The chances of succeeding in a new venture increase substantially if you have an established network of people who might become your customers.

TABLE 16–7
EXAMPLES OF OPPORTUNITIES FOR SELF-EMPLOYMENT

COMPUTER-BASED BUSINESSES	**PERSONAL SERVICES**
Computer consulting	Private investigator
Computer repair service	Event-planning service
Electronic bulletin board service	Image consulting
Laser printer recharging and repair	Operating a 900 number
FINANCIAL SERVICES	**FOODSERVICE BUSINESSES**
Check-cashing service	Coffeehouse
Financial aid services	Food court restaurants
Financial broker	Mobile frozen yogurt
Property tax consultant	Mobile restaurant/sandwich truck
Real estate investment	No-alcohol bar
CLEANING/MAINTENANCE BUSINESSES	**WHOLESALE BUSINESSES**
Apartment preparation service	Import/export business
Damage restoration service	Liquidated goods broker
Garage detailing service	Wholesale distribution business
Parking lot striping and maintenance	Marketing a family recipe
SERVICES TO BUSINESS	**RETAIL BUSINESSES**
Collection agency	Antique sales and restoration
Event-planning service (such as a party)	Body care boutique
Language translation service	Coin-operated vending
Medical billing	Gift basket service
Mobile bookkeeping	Pet hotel and grooming service
Temporary help agency	Self-storage center

Source: Gathered from information at various places in Entrepreneur Magazine *Buyers Guide to Franchise and Business Opportunities,* 1997 edition; *Home-based Businesses from Entrepreneur Magazine,* undated.

SUMMARY OF KEY POINTS

- You must accept the major responsibility for developing your career despite help offered by your employer. One reason is that you are likely to change employers either voluntarily or involuntarily.
- A field and an occupation can be found through a variety of formal and informal methods. Informal methods include natural opportunity and following a role model. Formal methods include counseling and/or testing and making systematic use of occupational information.
- The vertical, or traditional, career path is based on the idea that a person continues to grow in responsibility with the aim of reaching a target position, such as becoming a top-level manager. A vertical path is based on the traditional employment contract. A vertical career path should be related to the present and future demands of one firm or the industry. The horizontal career path is less predictable; it emphasizes lateral moves with an opportunity to gain more experience and increase job skills. A horizontal path is closely linked to the new

employment contract that offers shared responsibility for career growth. Career paths should have contingency plans.

- Recommended job-hunting tactics include the following: (1) identify your job objectives, (2) be aware of qualifications sought by employers, (3) identify your skills and potential contribution, (4) develop a comprehensive marketing strategy, (5) use networking to reach the internal job market, (6) use the Internet and résumé database services, and (7) smile at network members and interviewers.
- Job hunting almost always requires a résumé, with two pages recommended. Constructing a résumé for an electronic database is sometimes necessary. Résumés should emphasize skills and accomplishments. A résumé should almost always be accompanied by a cover letter explaining how you can help the organization and why you are applying for this particular job.
- Screening interviews, including computer-assisted ones, precede a full job interview. A general guide for performing well in the job interview is to present a positive but accurate picture of yourself. More specific suggestions include: (1) be prepared, look relaxed, and make the interviewer feel comfortable, (2) establish a link between yourself and the prospective employer, (3) ask perceptive questions, (4) be prepared to respond to behavioral interview questions, and (5) show how you can help the employer.
- One set of strategies and tactics for career advancement relate to taking control of your own behavior. These include: (1) develop a code of professional ethics, (2) make an accurate self-appraisal, (3) develop expertise and passion and build a career around it, (4) attain high job performance, (5) keep growing through continuous learning and self-development, (6) document your accomplishments, (7) project a professional image, and (8) minimize career self-sabotage.
- Another set of strategies and tactics for getting ahead center around taking control of your environment, or at least adapting it to your advantage. Included here are the following guidelines: (1) identify growth fields and growth companies, (2) obtain broad experience, (3) take sensible risks, (4) find a mentor, (5) use your network of contacts, and (6) develop a proactive personality so that you can capitalize on opportunities.

GUIDELINES FOR PERSONAL EFFECTIVENESS

1. Some people achieve career success (including both rewards and satisfaction) without a deliberate, planned effort. For the vast majority of people, attaining these ends requires careful planning. Planning is particularly helpful when you are getting started in your career and during its early stages. Planning includes choosing a field, finding a job, and using career-advancement tactics and strategies.
2. Should you be confronted with the task of finding a job, do not be overly apprehensive. Much useful information has been collected to aid you in the job-finding process. Following this information carefully will increase your chances of finding suitable employment.
3. Any of the strategies and tactics described in this chapter must be used with selectivity. A helpful approach is to select those suggestions that seem to fit your personality and preferences. Avoid those tactics and strategies that you think are in conflict with your values.

- It is becoming increasingly common for people to either switch the emphasis of activities in their work or switch careers entirely. A portfolio career is one in which a person has a variety of skills that can be used to earn money in different ways. The skill portfolio is particularly useful when a person holds two or more part-time positions. Switching careers follows many of the same principles as choosing a first career. A new career should be built gradually, often by phasing into it part-time. To satisfy a desire for independence, many young people switch careers from being an employee to self-employment.

DISCUSSION QUESTIONS AND ACTIVITIES

1. How much of your identity is tied up in your career or contemplated career?
2. Do most people have satisfying and rewarding careers? What evidence do you have to support your opinion?
3. Why should employers be concerned whether or not their employees do an effective job of career management?
4. How does a newcomer to the job market know which skills he or she possesses?
5. Use computer graphics to prepare your own career path, however tentative. Compare your path to those of several classmates and look for major similarities and differences.
6. How well do the qualifications sought by employers listed in Self-Assessment Exercise 16–1 fit the type of education and training you have received so far?
7. Give an example of a value that you might incorporate into your code of professional ethics.
8. What have you done in the last 30 days to build or maintain your network?
9. What do you perceive to be a couple of disadvantages of having a portfolio career?
10. Check through your network of contacts to find a business owner. Ask the person's opinion about what it takes to be successful as a business owner, and share your findings with your classmates.

A BUSINESS PSYCHOLOGY CASE PROBLEM

Why Isn't My Résumé Getting Results?

Billy Joe Wentworth was working in the family business as a manufacturing technician while he attended career school. Although he got along well with his family members, Billy Joe wanted to find employment elsewhere so that he could build a career on his own. Billy Joe's job objective was a position in industrial sales. He compiled a long list of prospective employers. He developed the list from personal contacts, classified ads in newspapers, and job openings on the Internet. Billy Joe clipped a business card with a brief handwritten note to each résumé. The note usually said something to the effect, "Job sounds great. Let's schedule an interview at your convenience." The résumé is shown in the accompanying box.

EXHIBIT 1. Résumé of Billy Joe Wentworth

BILLY JOE WENTWORTH
275 Birdwhistle Lane
Cleveland, Ohio 44131
(216) 614-7512 (Please call after 7 P.M. weekday nights)
Billyjoe@wentworth.com

OBJECTIVE

Long-range goal is Vice President of marketing for major corporation. For now, industrial sales representative paid by salary and commission. Want the right experience to help me achieve my goals.

JOB EXPERIENCE

- Five years experience in Wentworth industries as manufacturing technician, tool crib attendant, shipper, and floor sweeper. Voted as "employee of the month" twice.
- Two years experience in newspaper delivery business. Distributed newspapers door to door, responsible for accounts receivable and development of new business in my territory.

EDUCATION

- Justin Peabody Career College, business administration major with manufacturing technology minor. Expect degree in June 2004. 2.65 GPA. Took courses in sales management and selling. Received a B+ in professional selling course.
- Cleveland Heights High School, business and technology major, 1992–1996. Graduated 45th in class of 125. 82% average.

SKILLS AND TALENTS

Good knowledge of manufacturing equipment; friends say I'm a born leader; have been offered supervisory position in Wentworth Industries; real go-getter.

REFERENCES

Okay to contact present employer except for my immediate supervisor, Jill Baxter, with whom I have a personality clash.

After mailing out 200 résumés, Billy Joe still did not have an interview. He asked his uncle and mentor, the owner of the family business, "Why isn't my résumé getting results?"

QUESTIONS

1. What suggestions can you make to Billy Joe for improving his résumé? Or does it require improvement?
2. What is your evaluation of Billy Joe's approach to creating a cover letter?

REFERENCES

1. Kerr Inkson and Michael B. Arthur, "How to Be a Successful Career Capitalist," *Organizational Dynamics,* Summer 2001, p. 48.
2. Douglas T. Hall, "Protean Careers of the 21st Century," *Academy of Management Executive,* November 1996, p. 8.
3. Jennifer J. Laabs, "Embrace Today's New Deal," *Personnel Journal,* August 1996, pp. 60–66; Aaron Bernstein, "We Really Want You to Stay," *Business Week,* June 22, 1998, p. 68.

AN APPLIED PSYCHOLOGY CASE PROBLEM

"I Know I Can Make a Contribution Somewhere"

Brad Martinez, age 43, is a senior account manager for Western Office Supply, a company that sells a wide range of products to business firms, hospitals, and schools. Western does not manufacture any products of its own, but resells the products of several hundred manufacturers, much like being a department store for other firms. His company typically sells supplies in much larger quantities than sold by giant office-supply stores like Staples and OfficeMax. Western also sells office furniture and decorations such as lamps and wall hangings.

Although Brad's job title is account manager, he is essentially an outside sales representative who reports to the sales manager of Western Office Supply. Brad personally calls on about 50 established accounts and also solicits new business regularly. After Brad opens an account, replacement sales for smaller items are usually made by e-mail or telephone. However, he periodically makes in-person visits and telephone solicitations to sell office equipment such as small photocopiers, desktop computers, printers, fax machines, and office telephones.

After graduating from a career school with a major in business administration with a marketing concentration, Brad thought he would explore the world before settling on a career. He joined the United States Army, and worked in the medical service field as a medic in several army hospitals. Since Brad was not in service during armed combat, he assisted in training injuries and injuries to dependents of army personnel. Brad served admirably in the army, and worked his way up to the rank of sergeant.

In Brad's words, "I left the army proud of my service, but looking for a more promising career. No matter how much the army liked me, they weren't going to make me the Surgeon General. I thought it was time to get started in the business field."

After the army, Brad worked six years in the purchasing department at a machine-tool company, working his way up to a position as purchasing supervisor. After that he joined Western as a sales trainee and progressed to his present position.

During the last several years, Brad's sales commissions have begun to decline. One problem he has faced is that many of his customers are now purchasing their supplies directly from distributors and manufacturers over the Internet. Another problem is Western's own e-commerce initiative. Brad and the other sales representatives receive a very small commission when a new customer makes an Internet purchase, or an established customer orders more supplies.

Brad has recently become discouraged with the diminishing direct people contact in his work. As he explains, "Three times during the last month I have been turned down by purchasing agents or business owners when I asked them out to lunch. Up until a few years ago, I made some of my largest sales over lunch. I'm hearing more now that my customers just want to buy over the Internet. I guess they would rather sit at the keyboard and eat yogurt for lunch rather than talk over business in a restaurant.

"The phone has become a major headache for me also. Instead of talking to a manager or a purchasing agent, I have to conduct my business with a voice-mail message. A woman flat out told me the other day that when she wanted to order something from Western, she would use our Web site. She told me that phone conversations take up too much of her time."

During the last six-month period, Brad's commissions declined 45 percent from the previous six months. For Brad, this was the last straw. He has decided to change careers, as soon as he can figure out what else he could do to earn the same kind of living he did previously. For three consecutive years, Brad had earned a six-figure income.

One Saturday morning Brad was looking at the job search site, Monsterboard. He murmured to himself, "Let's see Brad, the world no longer needs a good sales rep with a personal touch. You have no more talent with the computer than most 19-year-olds. Being an astronaut is out because I get motion sickness. The NFL doesn't want any 43-year-old quarterbacks without experience. My few years as an army medic don't qualify me to be the chief of surgery at the Mayo Clinic.

"Oops, here's an opening for a Chief Financial Officer for a $50 million company, but they want experience as a controller. Here's another one I like, an international marketing specialist. Except that the successful candidate must speak English, Spanish, and Italian. All I have is English and about 20 words of Spanish I know from listening to Salsa music.

"Maybe I should start by updating my résumé. I know I can make a contribution somewhere, but I'm not sure where to start."

Questions

1. To what extent do you think Brad Martinez really needs a career switch?
2. What approach should Brad take to finding a new career?
3. What improvements do you think Brad needs to take in his attitude before he gets down to the serious business of finding a new career?
4. What criticisms do you have of Brad's career direction so far?

4. Matthew Boyle, "Going Down," *Fortune,* September 3, 2001, pp. 233–234.
5. "CEOs Speak Out: What Is Needed to Work in Today's Ever-changing Business World," *Keying In,* November 1996, pp. 1–2; Brien N. Smith, Carolee Jones, and Judy Lane, "Employers' Perceptions of Work Skills," *Business Education Forum,* April 1997, pp. 11–17; "Hot Commodities: How to Be the Job Candidate Everyone Wants," *Working Woman,* February 2000, pp. 40–45.
6. "Online Recruiting: What Works, What Doesn't," *HRfocus,* March 2000, p. 11.
7. Quoted in "Job Hunt," *Business Week Careers,* February 1987, p. 77.
8. Advice from See Solutions cited in "Tips for Those Seeking Jobs," *Democrat and Chronicle,* Rochester, New York, December 30, 2001, p. 1G.
9. Zane K. Quible, "Job Seeking Process," in *The Changing Dimensions of Business Education* (Reston, VA: National Business Education Association, 1997), p. 176.
10. Carol Kleiman, "Key Words Bosses Seek When Scanning Résumés," *Chicago Tribune* syndicated story, October 27, 1997.
11. Peg Thomas, et al., "Resume Characteristics as Predictors of an Invitation to Interview," *Journal of Business and Psychology,* Spring 1999, pp. 339–356.
12. Richard H. Beatty, *The Perfect Cover Letter* (New York: Wiley, 1997).
13. Linda Thornburg, "Computer-Assisted Interviewing Shortens Hiring Cycle," *HR Magazine,* February 1998, pp. 73–79.
14. "Preparing Students for the Job Search Process," *Keying In,* November 2001, p. 5.
15. Ruth Kanfer, Connie R. Wanberg, and Tracy M. Kantrowitz, "Job Search and Employment: A Personality-Motivational Analysis and Meta-Analytic Review," *Journal of Applied Psychology,* October 2001, pp. 837–855.
16. Randy Komisar, "Goodbye Career, Hello Success," *Harvard Business Review,* March–April 2000, p. 174.
17. Karen S. Lyness and Donna E. Thompson, "Climbing the Corporate Ladder: Do Female and Male Executives Follow the Same Route?" *Journal of Applied Psychology,* February 2000, pp. 86–101.
18. Michael Oliver, "Taking Risks Will Get Your Career Moving," *Personnel Journal,* April 1983, p. 319.
19. Fara Warner, "Inside Intel's Mentoring Movement," *Fast Company,* April 2002, p. 118.
20. "What Mentors Do to Help Others Attain Potential," *Getting Results,* Special Report, 1997, pp. 1–2.

21. Shimon-Craig Van Collie, "Moving Up through Mentoring," *Workforce,* March 1998, p. 36.
22. David A. Thomas, "The Truth About Mentoring: Race Matters," *Harvard Business Review,* April 2001, pp. 98–107.
23. Raymond T. Sparrowe, et al., "Social Networks and the Performance of Individuals and Groups," *Academy of Management Journal,* April 2000, pp. 316–325.
24. Donald J. Campbell, "The Proactive Employee: Measuring Workplace Initiative," *Academy of Management Executive,* August 2000, pp. 52–66.
25. Scott E. Seibert, J. Michael Crant, and Maria L. Kraimer, "Proactive Personality and Career Success," *Journal of Applied Psychology,* June 1999, pp. 416–427.
26. Scott E. Seibert, Maria L. Kraimer, and J. Michael Crant, "What Do Proactive People Do? A Longitudinal Model Linking Proactive Personality and Career Success," *Personnel Psychology,* Winter 2001, pp. 845–874.
27. Lisa Belkin, "Re-invent Yourself," *Working Woman,* February 2001, p. 46.
28. Carole Kanchier, "Life-Changing Tips from a Psychologist," *USA Weekend,* January 11–13, 2002, p. 18.
29. "Generation X: The New Entrepreneurs," *Keying In,* March 1998, p. 6.

SUGGESTED READING

Austin, Linda. *What's Holding You Back? 8 Critical Choices for Women's Success.* Boulder, CO: Basic Books/Perseus Books Group, 2000.

Brown, Eryn. "The Humbled Generation." *Fortune,* April 2, 2001, pp. 92–97.

Graves, Earl G. *How to Succeed in Business Without Being White.* New York: HarperBusiness, 1997.

Meyerson, Debra E., and Fletcher, Joyce K. "A Modest Manifesto for Shattering the Glass Ceiling." *Harvard Business Review,* January–February 2000, pp. 126–136.

Wells, Susan J. "A Female Executive Is Hard to Find." *HR Magazine,* June 2001, pp. 40–49.

Wild, Russell. "The Best Career Advice I Ever Got." *Working Woman,* December–January 2001, pp. 77–80.

WEB CORNER

www.aboutwork.com/ (Job search.)

www.fortune.com/fortune/careers (Advice about job finding and job keeping, as well as a résumé-posting service and job listings.)

www.vault.com (Career advice about a wide variety of subjects.)

GLOSSARY

Active listener One who listens intently with the goal of empathizing with the speaker.

Addictive behavior A compulsion to use substances or engage in activities that lead to psychological dependence and withdrawal symptoms when use is discontinued.

Anger A feeling of extreme hostility, indignation, or exasperation.

Assertiveness Being forthright with one's demands, expressing both the specifics of what one wants done, and the feelings surrounding the demands.

Attribution theory The process by which people ascribe causes to the behavior they perceive.

A-type conflict Affective; disagreement that focuses on personalized, individually-oriented issues (like personality clashes).

Autocratic leader One who attempts to retain most of the authority granted to the group.

Behavior modification Changing behavior by rewarding the right responses and/or punishing or ignoring the wrong responses.

Behavioral interview A job interview that asks questions directly about the candidate's behavior in relation to an important job activity.

Behaviorism A school of thought in psychology based on the assumption that psychologists should study overt behavior rather than mental states or other unobservable aspects of living things.

Brainstorm A clever idea.

Brainstorming A conference technique of solving specific problems, amassing information, and stimulating creative thinking. The basic technique is to encourage unrestrained and spontaneous participation by group members.

Brainwriting (or solo brainstorming) Arriving at creative ideas by jotting them down yourself.

Burnout A state of exhaustion stemming from long-term stress.

Business etiquette A special code of behavior required in work situations.

Business psychology The application of organized knowledge about human behavior to improve personal satisfaction and job productivity.

Career A lifelong series of experiences that form some kind of coherent pattern.

Career path A sequence of positions necessary to achieve a career goal.

Career success Attaining the twin goals of organizational rewards and personal satisfaction.

Carpal tunnel syndrome A condition that occurs when repetitive flexing and extension of the wrist causes the tendons to swell, thus trapping and pinching the median nerve.

Cause-and-effect diagram A decision-making technique widely used by quality-improvement teams.

Charisma The ability to lead or influence others based on personal charm, magnetism, inspiration, and emotion.

Classical conditioning A basic form of learning in which a stimulus that usually brings forth a given response is repeatedly paired with a neutral stimulus. Eventually the neutral stimulus will bring forth the response when presented by itself.

Coercive power The leader's control over punishments.

Cognitive Referring to the intellectual aspects of human behavior.

Cognitive psychology The study of mental processes such as thinking, feeling, learning, remembering, and making decisions and judgments.

Cognitive restructuring A method of conflict resolution whereby you mentally convert negative aspects into positive ones by looking for the positive elements in a situation.

Cognitive style The characteristic mode of functioning individuals show in their perceptual and intellectual activities.

Common sense Natural wisdom not requiring formal knowledge.

Communication The sending, receiving, and understanding of messages.

Communication (or information) overload A condition in which the individual is confronted with so much information to process that he or she becomes overwhelmed and therefore does a poor job of processing information.

Compulsivity A tendency to pay careful attention to detail and to be meticulous.

Conflict Simultaneous arousal of two or more incompatible motives, or demands.

Confrontation and problem solving A method of identifying the true source of conflict and resolving it systematically.

Consensus leader One who encourages group discussion about an issue and then makes a decision that reflects the consensus of group members.

Consultation Leadership influence tactic whereby the leader motivates the target of the influence by involving him or her in making the decision.

Consultative leader One who solicits opinions from the group before making a decision yet does not feel obliged to accept the group's thinking.

Counterproductive (or difficult) person One whose actions lead him or her away from achieving work goals, often because of a personality quirk.

Creativity The ability to produce work that is novel and useful.

C-type conflict Cognitive; the type of disagreement that focuses on substantive (having substance), issue-related differences.

Cultural sensitivity Awareness of and willingness to investigate the reasons why people of another culture act as they do.

Decision A choice between two or more alternatives.

Defensive communication The tendency to receive messages in such a way that one's self-esteem is protected.

Democratic leader A person in charge who turns over virtually all the authority to the group.

Denial The process of excluding from awareness an important aspect of reality.

Dependent-care option Any company-sponsored program that helps an employee take care of a family member.

Dependent variable A variable in an experiment that is measured to see how it is changed by the manipulation of the major variable under study.

Developmental opportunity A specific area in which a person needs to improve.

Disarm the opposition A technique of conflict resolution in which one person disarms the other by agreeing with his or her criticism.

Dopamine A chemical substance in the brain and a neurotransmitter that is associated with pleasure and elation.

Downshifting Investing more time in family and less in career.

Dysfunctional conflict A condition that occurs when a dispute or disagreement harms the organization.

Electronic brainstorming A problem-solving method in which group members simultaneously enter their suggestions into a computer, and their ideas are distributed to the monitors of other group members.

Emotional intelligence A group of qualities such as understanding one's own feelings, empathy for others, and the regulation of emotion to enhance living.

Emotional labor The process of regulating both feelings and expression to meet organizational goals.

Empathy Understanding another person's point of view.

Employee network group A group composed of employees throughout the company who affiliate on the basis of a group characteristic such as race, ethnicity, sex, sexual orientation, or physical ability status.

Empowerment Giving workers more power by granting them more authority to make decisions.

Ethics The study of moral obligations or separating right from wrong.

Exchange The use of reciprocal favors to influence others.

Exercise and sport psychology The field of psychology that develops concepts and provides direct assistance to enhance the performance of athletes.

Expectancy The probability assigned by the individual that effort will lead to performing the task correctly.

Expectancy theory An explanation of human motivation that centers around the idea that people will expend effort if they believe the effort will lead to a desired outcome.

Experience of flow The phenomenon of total absorption in one's work.

Expert power The ability to control others through knowledge relevant to the job as perceived by subordinates.

External locus of control A belief that external forces control one's fate.

Extinction The weakening or decreasing of the frequency of undesirable behavior by removing the reward for such behavior.

Fear of success A conviction that success will bring with it some unwelcome outcomes, such as isolation or abandonment.

Field experiment An attempt to apply experimental methods to real-life situations.

Fight-or-flight response The body's physiological and chemical battle against the stressor in which the person tries to cope with the adversity head-on or tries to flee the scene.

Five-factor model of personality A model indicating that personality can be described by the five factors of neuroticism, extraversion, openness, agreeableness, and conscientiousness.

Flow experience (See **experience of flow**) The phenomenon of total absorption in one's work.

Formal communication pathway The official path over which messages are supposed to travel in an organization.

Formal group A collection of people deliberately formed by the organization to accomplish specific tasks and achieve objectives.

Formal organization The job descriptions, organization charts, procedures, and other written documents that specify how individuals should work with each other.

Frame of reference A perspective or vantage point for receiving information.

Frustration A blocking of a need or motive satisfaction by some kind of obstacle.

Functional conflict A condition that occurs when the interests of the organization are served as a result of a dispute or disagreement.

Functionalism An early school of psychological thought emphasizing the functions of the mind.

(general) factor A person's ability to perform complex mental work, such as abstract reasoning and making analogies.

Galatea effect Improving your performance through raising your own expectations.

Game A repeated series of exchanges between people that appears different on the surface from its true underlying motive.

General adaptation syndrome The body's response to stress that occurs in three stages: alarm, resistance, and exhaustion.

Goal What a person is trying to accomplish.

Gossip Idle talk or tidbits of information about people that are passed along informal communication channels.

Grapevine The major informal communication channel or pathway in an organization.

Group A collection of individuals who regularly interact with each other, who are psychologically aware of each other, and who perceive themselves to be a group.

Group norms The unwritten set of expectations or standards of conduct telling group members what each person should do within the group.

Group polarization A situation in which postdiscussion attitudes tend to be more extreme than prediscussion attitudes.

Groupthink A deterioration of mental efficiency, reality testing, and moral judgment in the interest of group solidarity.

Halo effect A tendency to color everything that we know about a person because of one recognizable favorable or unfavorable trait.

Hawthorne effect The tendency for people to behave differently when they receive attention because they respond to the expectations of the situation.

Health psychology The study and practice of how human behavior can be modified to prevent and treat illness.

Human relations The art and practice of using systematic knowledge about human behavior to achieve organizational and/or personal objectives.

Human relations movement A concentrated effort by managers and their advisors to become more sensitive to the needs of employees or to treat them in a more humanistic manner.

Humanistic psychology An approach to psychology that emphasizes the dignity and worth of people, along with their many other positive but intangible or "soft" attributes.

Implicit learning Learning that takes place unconsciously or without an intention to learn.

Independent variable The variable in an experiment that is manipulated to test its effects on the dependent variable.

Individual differences Variations in response to the same situation based on personal characteristics.

Individual dominance A problem in group decision making that occurs when one individual dominates the group, thus negating the potential benefit of group input.

Industrial and organizational psychology The field of psychology that studies human behavior in a work environment.

Informal communication pathway An unofficial network of communications used to supplement a formal pathway.

Informal group A natural grouping of people in a work situation that evolves to take care of people's desires for friendship and companionship, and sometimes to accomplish work.

Informal learning Planned or unplanned learning that occurs without a formal classroom, lesson plan, instructor, or examination.

Informal organization A pattern of work relationships that develops to satisfy people's social needs and to get work accomplished.

Ingratiation Getting someone else to like you, often using political behaviors.

Insight An ability to know what information is relevant, find connections between the old and the new, combine facts that are unrelated, and see the "big picture."

Instrumentality The probability assigned by the individual that performance will lead to certain outcomes or rewards.

Intelligence The capacity to acquire and apply knowledge, including solving problems; the mental abilities necessary for adapting to and modifying one's environment.

Internal job market The large array of jobs that have not been advertised and that are usually filled by word of mouth or through friends and acquaintances of employees.

Internal locus of control The belief that fate is pretty much under one's control.

Intrinsic motivation Motivation stemming from a person's beliefs about the extent to which an activity can satisfy his or her needs for competence and self-determination.

Intuition An experience-based way of knowing or reasoning in which weighing and balancing evidence are done automatically.

Job campaign All the activities included in finding a job.

Job enrichment Making a job more motivating and satisfying by adding variety and responsibility.

Job sharing An arrangement in which two people share one job by each working half-time.

Joking and kidding As an influence tactic, good-natured ribbing is used when a straightforward statement might be interpreted as harsh criticism.

Law of effect In behavior modification, rewarded behavior tends to be repeated, whereas behavior that is ignored or punished tends not to be repeated.

Leadership The process of influencing other people to achieve certain objectives.

Leadership style A leader's characteristic way of directing people in most situations.

Leading by example Influencing group members by serving as a positive model.

Leading task In time management, an easy warm-up activity.

Learning A lasting change in behavior based on practice or experience.

Learning style The fact that people learn best in different ways.

Legitimate power The ability to influence others that stems directly from the leader's position.

Maslow's need hierarchy A widely quoted theory of human motivation that arranges needs into a pyramid-shaped model with basic physiological needs at the bottom and self-actualization needs at the top.

Mentor A more experienced person who guides, teaches, and coaches another individual.

Meta-analysis A study of many studies combining quantitative information from them all.

Meta-communicate Communicating about your communication to help overcome barriers or resolve a problem.

Mirroring (or posturing) A form of nonverbal communication used to establish rapport with another individual by imitating that person's physical behavior.

Mixed signals Sending different messages about the same topic to different audiences. Also, sending one message to an individual about desired behavior, yet behaving in another way yourself.

Modeling A form of learning in which a person learns a complex skill by watching another person perform that skill. Also called *learning by imitation.*

Motivation An energizing force that stimulates arousal, direction, and persistence of behavior.

Motivational state An inner state of arousal directed toward a goal that could include any active needs and interest at the time.

Multiple intelligences The theory stating that people know and understand the world in distinctly different ways, or look at it through different lenses.

Need An internal striving or urge to do something.

Negative affectivity A tendency to experience aversive emotional states.

Negative reinforcement Receiving a reward by being relieved of discomfort.

Negotiating and bargaining Conferring with another person in order to resolve a problem.

Networking Contacting friends and acquaintances and systematically building on these relationships to create a still wider set of contacts that might lead to employment.

Nominal group technique (NGT) A group problem-solving method that calls people together in a structured meeting with limited interaction.

Nonverbal communication The transmission of messages through means other than words.

Nurturing person One who promotes the growth of others.

Open-door policy A policy whereby any employee can bring a gripe to higher-level management's attention without checking with his or her immediate manager.

Operant conditioning Learning that takes place as a consequence of behavior.

Organizational citizenship behavior Working for the good of the organization even without the promise of a specific reward.

Organizational culture A system of shared values and beliefs that influence worker behavior.

Paraphrase Repeating in your own words what the sender says, feels, and means.

Participative leader A person in charge who shares decision-making authority with the group.

Passive-aggressive personality A person who expresses anger and hostility by not performing expected tasks.

Peer evaluation A system in which coworkers contribute to an evaluation of a worker's job performance.

Perceived control The belief that an individual has at his or her disposal a response that can control the aversiveness of an event.

Perception The various ways in which people interpret things in the external world and how they act on the basis of these perceptions.

Perceptual congruence The degree to which people perceive things the same way.

Peripheral time The scattered minutes people normally waste while waiting for a meeting to start, being stuck in traffic, or waiting on the phone to speak to a customer service representative.

Personality An individual's characteristic way of behaving, feeling, and thinking.

Personality clash An antagonistic relationship between two people based on differences in personal attributes, preferences, interests, values, and styles.

Personality quirk A persistent peculiarity of behavior that annoys or irritates other people.

Personal power The ability to influence others based on personal characteristics and skills.

Personal productivity An individual's level of efficiency and effectiveness.

Person–organization fit The compatibility of the individual and the organization.

Person–role conflict The conflict that occurs when a person wants to obey orders but does not want to perform an act that seems inconsistent with his or her values.

Persuasiveness Ability to convince the receiver to accept one's message.

Portfolio career A career in which the individual uses a variety of skills to earn money in several different ways.

Position power Power stemming from the formal position you occupy.

Positive mental attitude Expecting to succeed in a given undertaking.

Positive reinforcement Receiving a reward for making a desired response.

Positive self-talk Saying positive things about oneself to oneself.

Positive visual imagery Imagining yourself doing well in an upcoming situation that represents a challenge.

Post-traumatic disorder A battlefield-like stress reaction with symptoms that include recurring anxiety, difficulties in concentration, and withdrawing from people.

Power The ability to control resources, to influence important decisions, and to get other people to do things.

Primary reinforcer A reinforcer that is rewarding by itself without association with other reinforcers, such as food.

Proactive personality A person relatively unconstrained by forces in the situation and who brings about environmental change.

Problem A gap between an existing and a desired situation.

Procrastination Delaying action for no good reason.

Projection A shortcut in the perceptual process in which we project our own faults onto others instead of making an objective appraisal of the situation.

Psychiatry A medical specialty that deals with the diagnosis and treatment of emotional problems and mental illness.

Psychoanalysis A specialized type of psychotherapy in which the patient may spend up to three or four years, several times a week, working on personal problems.

Psychological success The feeling of pride and personal accomplishment that comes from achieving your most important goals in life, whether they are work achievement, family happiness, or something else.

Psychology The study of behavior and mental processes.

Psychotherapist Any mental health professional who helps people with their emotional problems through conversation with them.

Punishment The introduction of an unpleasant stimulus as a consequence of the person having done something wrong.

Quality-improvement team A group of workers who use problem-solving techniques to enhance customer satisfaction.

Rationality Appealing to reason and logic.

Recognition need The desire to be acknowledged for one's contributions and efforts and to feel important.

Referent power The ability to control based on loyalty to the leader and the group members' desire to please that person.

Reflectivity–impulsivity The tempo a person uses in approaching a problem.

Relaxation response (RR) A bodily reaction in which you experience a slower respiration rate and heart rate and lower blood pressure and metabolism.

Resilience The ability to withstand pressure and emerge stronger for it.

Reward power The leader's control over rewards valued by group members.

Role A set of behaviors a person is supposed to engage in because of his or her job situation or position within a group.

Role ambiguity A condition in which the jobholder receives confusing or poorly defined expectations.

Role conflict Having to choose between competing demands or expectations.

Role confusion Being uncertain about what role you are carrying out.

Role overload Having too much work to do.

Role underload Having too little work to do.

Rumor A message transmitted over the grapevine, although not based on official word.

(special) factor Primary mental abilities, including numerical and verbal.

Script A program in the brain that orients a person in a particular direction toward solving a problem.

Secondary reinforcer A reinforcer whose value must be learned through association with other reinforcers, such as money.

Selective attention Giving exclusive attention to something at the expense of other aspects of the environment.

Self The total being of the individual or the person.

Self-actualization Making maximum use of the potential in oneself; like self-fulfillment.

Self-concept What you think of you and who you think you are.

Self-confidence A basic belief in one's ability to achieve the outcome you want in many situations or in a specific situation.

Self-defeating behavior A conscious or unconscious attempt to bring about personal failure.

Self-disclosure The process of revealing your inner self to others.

Self-efficacy A component of self-esteem; confidence in your ability to carry out a specific task in contrast to generalized self-confidence.

Self-esteem Appreciating self-worth and importance, being accountable for your behaviors, and acting responsibly toward others.

Self-monitoring The process of observing and controlling how we appear to others.

Self-respect A component of self-esteem; how you think and feel about yourself.

Servant leader A leader who believes that his or her primary mission is to serve the needs of constituents.

Sexual harassment Unwanted sexually oriented behavior in the workplace that results in discomfort and/or interference with the job.

Shaping The process of learning through approximations until the total skill is learned.

Socialization The process of coming to understand the values, norms, and customs essential to the organization.

Social loafing Shirking individual responsibility in a group setting.

Stereotyping A common method of simplifying perception by evaluating an individual or thing based on our perception of the group or class to which the person or object belongs.

Stress The mental and physical condition that results from a perceived threat or demand that cannot be dealt with readily.

Stressor The external or internal force that brings about the stress.

Structuralism The school of psychology that emphasized the basic units of experience, and the combinations in which they take place.

Style A person's typical way of doing things.

Success cycle A situation in which each little success builds self-confidence, leading to more success and self-confidence.

Supportive leader One who gives praise and encouragement to group members, usually increasing morale and productivity.

Support network A group of people who can listen to your problems and provide emotional support.

Synergy A phenomenon of group effort whereby the whole is greater than the sum of the parts.

Team A special type of group in which members have complementary skills and are committed to a common purpose, a set of performance goals, and a specific approach to a task.

Teamwork An understanding and commitment to group goals on the part of all team members.

Telecommuter An employee who performs regular job responsibilities from home or another location.

Theory of multiple intelligences Gardner's theory that people possess eight different intelligences in varying degrees: linguistic, logical-mathematical, musical, spatial, bodily/kinesthetic, intrapersonal, interpersonal, and naturalist.

Theory X Douglas McGregor's famous statement of the traditional management view that considers people as usually lazy and needing to be prodded by external rewards. A rigid and task-oriented approach to management.

Theory Y Douglas McGregor's famous statement of an alternative to traditional management thinking. It emphasizes that people seek to fulfill higher-level needs on the job and that management must be flexible and human relations oriented.

360-degree feedback system A formal evaluation of superiors by people who work for and with them.

Toxic person One who dwells on the negative.

Transformational leader One who helps organizations and people make positive changes in the way they conduct their activities.

Triarchic theory of intelligence The theory that holds that intelligence is composed of three different types: analytical, creative, and practical.

Type A behavior A demanding, impatient, and over-striving pattern of behavior also characterized by free-floating hostility.

Upward appeal Asking for help from a higher authority to resolve a dispute or conflict.

Valence The attractiveness of an outcome.

Value The importance a person attaches to something such as education, religion, or sports.

Variable pay An incentive plan that intentionally pays good performers more money than poor performers.

Virtual team A small group of people who conduct almost all of their collaboration by electronic communication rather than face-to-face meetings.

Vision A lofty image of the future of the organization or group.

Wellness A state of mental and physical well-being that makes it possible to function at one's highest potential.

Wellness program A formal organization-sponsored activity to help employees stay well and avoid illness.

Win–win The belief that after the conflict has been resolved, both sides should gain something of value.

Workaholism A dependence on work in which not working is an uncomfortable experience.

Work ethic A firm belief in the value and dignity of work.

Work–family conflict A situation that occurs when an individual has to perform multiple roles: worker, spouse, and, often, parent.

Work team A small group of workers with total responsibility for a task that manages itself to a large extent.

Ziegarnik effect The phenomenon of uncompleted tasks creating a disturbing level of tension.

INDEX